THE DIARY OF SEREPTA JORDAN

The Diary of Serepta Jordan

A SOUTHERN WOMAN'S STRUGGLE WITH WAR AND FAMILY, 1857–1864

EDITED BY

Minoa D. Uffelman, Ellen Kanervo,
Phyllis Smith, and Eleanor Williams

VOICES OF THE CIVIL WAR
Michael P. Gray, series editor

THE UNIVERSITY OF TENNESSEE PRESS, KNOXVILLE

The Voices of the Civil War series makes available a variety of primary source materials that illuminate issues on the battlefield, the home front, and the western front, as well as other aspects of this historic era. The series contextualizes the personal accounts within the framework of the latest scholarship and expands established knowledge by offering new perspectives, new materials, and new voices.

Library of Congress Cataloging-in-Publication Data

Names: Jordan, Serepta M., 1839–1894, author. | Uffelman, Minoa D., editor. | Kanervo, Ellen, editor. | Smith, Phyllis (Historian), editor. | Williams, Eleanor S., editor.

Title: The diary of Serepta Jordan : a Southern woman's struggle with war and family, 1857–1864 / edited by Minoa D. Uffelman, Ellen Kanervo, Phyllis Smith, and Eleanor Williams.

Other titles: Voices of the Civil War series.

Description: First edition. | Knoxville : University of Tennessee Press, 2020. | Series: Voices of the Civil War | Includes bibliographical references and index. | Summary: "Serepta Jordan . . . kept her diary from 1857 to 1864. She is a lively writer whose insights into New Providence and Clarksville, Tennessee, in the years before and during the Civil War provide a fine-grained feel for Middle Tennessee daily life and culture. Wartime and the fall of Fort Donelson meant an early end of Confederate rule in her area, and she relates the hardships suffered by citizens cut off from what they considered their country. Not particularly given to romanticism, Jordan provides generally clear-eyed observations about the failures of the Confederate army, and her extreme hatred for upper-class people in Clarksville makes her voice unique indeed."— Provided by publisher.

Identifiers: LCCN 2019049561 (print) | LCCN 2019049562 (ebook) | ISBN 9781621905455 (paperback) | ISBN 9781621905882 (pdf)

Subjects: LCSH: Jordan, Serepta M., 1839–1894—Diaries. | Women—Tennessee—Clarksville—Diaries. | Clarksville (Tenn.)—Biography. | New Providence (Clarksville, Tenn.)—Biography.

Classification: LCC F444.C6 J665 2020 (print) | LCC F444.C6 (ebook) | DDC 976.8/45—dc23

LC record available at https://lccn.loc.gov/2019049561

LC ebook record available at https://lccn.loc.gov/2019049562

Serepta Jordan's diary is dedicated to
Evelyn Hunter and Ann Alley.

CONTENTS

ILLUSTRATIONS

FOREWORD

THE VOICES OF THE CIVIL WAR SERIES is dedicated to its readership in bringing out journals, diaries, and letters from women and showing the vital roles they played before, during, and after the conflict. Recent scholarship on the long Civil War demonstrates such contributions, especially in the burgeoning literature on our understanding of the home front, both North and South. Class, region, religion, and social customs tell a complicated story in dealing with occupied locales, relationships with neighbors (before, during, and after the war), how women would handle intimidation from the enemy, whether soldiers or neighbors, and how they attempted to support their cause. The women featured in volumes in the series can be found fending off guerillas, attempting the management of their homes and businesses in the absence of fathers and sons, dealing with complicated family situations, and suffering from disease and loneliness. Undeniably, these women were not passive but rather engaged in activism, providing stability, solace, and relief as they tried to persist on the home-front.

Just two years after the inception of this series in 1994, under inaugural editor Frank L. Byrne, *A Very Violent Rebel: The Civil War Diary of Ellen Renshaw House* was published. Daniel E. Sutherland splendidly brought Ellen Renshaw House in East Tennessee to life, intertwining editorial comments within the carefully kept journal. The drama unfolded with nineteen-year-old Ellen supporting the Confederacy in Yankee-occupied Knoxville. Ellen's parents instilled Southern nationalism in her as a young woman, as the family moved from Savannah to Knoxville, leading to her admission of being "a very violent rebel." She was middle class, and held deep Confederate convictions with a ferocious devoutness to the cause, demonstrated in deeds she carried out. House's stance demonstrated one side of the volatile nature of the region, as divided loyalties on the edge of Appalachia ran deep. Ellen witnessed neighbors being arrested, inhospitable Yankees taking advantage of their situation, and the deprivations of Southern soldiers and citizens. When the city fell in the fall of 1863, Renshaw's violence particularly played out in her language toward the enemy. As General James Longstreet tried to take back Knoxville, unsuccessfully, prisoners piled up in local jails. Ellen attempted to alleviate their deprivations by donating provisions, but these and other acts, coupled with Union leaders suspicions that she was a spy, earned her excommunication back to Georgia.

As the series moved into the twenty-first century, it underwent a change in editorship. Under the skillful eye of Peter S. Carmichael, two excellent volumes appeared and addressed different women's roles in order to further diversify as well as contextualize the series. In 2004, *Sanctified Trial: The Diary of Eliza Rhea Anderson Fain, A Confederate Woman in East Tennessee* featured an editor who was employed as a professor of molecular science but took up the historical editor's pen. Professor John N. Fain painstakingly edited his distant relative's diary, and such motivation brought a superb addition to our collection. Living in Rogersville, between Bristol and Morristown, Eliza's husband and five of her six boys left their farm for the Confederate army—and she was left with the management of the household as well overseeing their nine enslaved persons. Eliza was an ardent supporter of slavery, secession, the Confederacy, and the Bible. A devout Presbyterian, her faith supported a characteristically Southern nationalist position that a major cause of the war was Northern "misunderstanding" of what she read as Biblical support for slavery. She would have to defend that stance, as well as her home, as she graphically describes atrocities of "bushwhackers" and "looters." As her cause came to a crushing end, she had the integrity to consider that the Southern nation may have been doomed by its own sin of miscegenation.

In 2010 the series ventured beyond Tennessee, with a female voice that came from the Eastern theater. *In the Shadow of the Enemy: The Civil War Journal of Ida Powell Delaney,* edited by Mary L. Mackall, Stevan F. Meserve, and Anne Mackall Sasscer, chronicled the intriguing private life of their subject. When Ida Powell Delaney's male family members left for the Confederate army, she was left alone, isolated as the lone proprietor of a plantation in piedmont Virginia, along border state Maryland. In this area, fears over harassment from both sides placed Ida in a precarious setting near Yankee forces on the edge of government borders. Fortunately for her, she had a unique husband, considering the era, Hal Grafton Dulany felt she was equal to the task in being the decision maker in his absence at the front. Ida's independence was definitely needed, and she demonstrated steady business skills in overseeing a plantation while literally standing up to Union soldiers. Her faith in God, her demonization of Yankees, and support for the exploits of partisan ranger John S. Mosby, are all brought to light while living in the enemy's shadow.

In 2014, the press was extremely fortunate in acquiring a project edited by

Minoa Uffelman, Ellen Kanervo, Phyllis Smith, and Eleanor Williams, which focused on a young, elite woman living in middle Tennessee. Their subject's birth name was Martha Ann Haskins, but she was better-known simply as "Nannie." Nannie was anything but simple, and her witty, precocious writings reflect her sparkling personality, age fourteen at the outbreak of war. Her complete story has never been told before: only short portions of Nannie's diary were known by historians, and when utilized, her words, most notably, in Ken Burns's PBS series *The Civil War*, were just used in piecemeal fashion in another story. However, Uffelman, Kanervo, Smith, and Williams's laborious work brought much of Nannie's life to light, unifying her divided writings by combining Nannie's accounts at the Tennessee State Archives with her post-war writings housed at the University of North Carolina. And the result was an award-winning book, *The Diary of Nannie Haskins Williams: A Southern Woman's Story of Rebellion and Reconstruction, 1863–1890*. Nannie lived in Clarksville on the Cumberland River, where this privileged young lady received a private school education as she honed her writing skills. For all intents and purposes, she became a local historian, recording names and stories of people throughout her community who had sacrificed in war, detailing those killed, wounded, or taken captive. Indeed, the latter category hit close to home, as both of her brothers were incarcerated, one succumbing at the enlisted men's prison at Camp Douglas in Chicago, while the other survived at Johnson's Island, Ohio, an officer's prison. Nannie's work reveals a budding, sophisticated woman in the slave-holding South, but her station in life was disrupted by war. Details about societal pressures, family discord and enmity, disdain for the Lincoln administration, and an enemy within her backyard abound in her entries. Her post-war account is just as informative, sketching a war-torn South as Reconstruction brought financial challenges, while the Gilded Age embraced industrial growth and diversification in a labor force that included women, but in so doing wrought new dangers.

   Clarksville was established at the confluence of the Cumberland and Red Rivers. In the distance of Clarksville rested New Providence to the northwest, separated only by the Red River in the 1860s. In the 1960s, New Providence was absorbed into Clarksville proper, but back in the nineteenth century, there was more than separation by the flowing river and competition for railroad links—there was division in class rank, pitting working-class New Providence against professional Clarksvillians. There is also congruence, and division, between *The Diary of Nannie Haskins Williams* and this present volume. Some forty years ago, a modestly water-damaged ledger book was discovered in a smokehouse in Clarksville, but the inside managed to remain intact. Its discolored pages revealed a carefully kept diary divided into "morning," "midday." and "evening" during the antebellum and Civil War years. The ledger book's author, named Serepta Jordan (known as "Rep" by family and friends), came from across the river, in New Providence. And Nannie Haskins lived just five miles from Serepta Jordan. Yet similarities in proximity, lively pens, and those that edited both volumes more than a century later were about all both women held in common. Serepta Jordan despised elite women, and it showed in her sometimes tart diary. The reader can even find an entry about Nannie's mother, as Rep scoffed at those that exuded pretentiousness.

Orphaned at a young age, Serepta was raised with the help of other family members. She began writing her diary at age eighteen, tabulating her thoughts from 1857 to 1864. But Serepta's story is not an analog to Nannie, but rather a much different voice that fits into the fabric of women during the war. Jordan's antebellum information is enlightening as she especially details Montgomery County's first agricultural fair. She writes about a professor who led students from a nearby college into war, ultimately coming into the ranks of the 14th Tennessee, that suffered terrible casualty rates. Serepta tells how she helped a Confederate prisoner escape and writes about Fort Defiance for the training of African American soldiers. Her entries also record the messy and sometimes violent end of slavery. Her domestic chores included sewing, gardening, fishing, and making preserves, and faithfully attending church. She tells chilling stories, including describing a hanging and a steamboat accident, as well as assessing accurately the strategic value of the region. The dual communities of New Providence and Clarksville held an important position on rivers, and their war production included iron foundries, slaughter houses, and agriculture—the area was very sought-after by both the Confederacy and Union.

Another contribution of *The Diary of Serepta Jordan* is it highlights a story of collaboration in putting this long-awaited volume together so Serepta's voice might be heard. As women's roles in the long Civil War are finally getting the attention they deserve, it still took a group effort for this volume to move forward; its discovery in a smokehouse launched a nearly fantastic series of events that make this book available to its readers. Scholars, public historians, family descendants, and politicians were all involved as this community effort required many helping hands. Coming to the forefront were Professors Minoa D. Uffelman and Ellen Kanervo of Austin Peay University, as well as Mount Olive Cemetery historian Phyllis Smith and Montgomery County historian Eleanor Williams. Grants were obtained for funding the diary's

restoration, and other preservation efforts were supported by private donations as well as organizations. This abridged publication allows for Serepta's
story to be told to a larger audience, but the original has been returned to the
Clarksville Customs House Museum and Cultural Center after being fully
restored. Hopefully Serepta would have found it a good landing spot, even if
her home was on the other side of the Red River.

Michael P. Gray
East Stroudsburg University of PA

ACKNOWLEDGMENTS

IT HAS BEEN FOUR DECADES since this diary was discovered in an out-building near Clarksville, Tennessee. Serepta's descendent, Evelyn Hunter, dedicated the rest of her days to having this book transcribed and published. She dedicated years to educating people to the historical significance of her ancestor's story. She, along with a committed group of friends, transcribed Serepta's handwritten tome. An early proponent of publication was the late Charles Holt, an English professor at Austin Peay State University. Evelyn Hunter's children, Millie Armstrong, Sallie Armstrong, Liz Ledbetter, and Ben Hunter, kept Serepta's memory alive and preserved her artifacts including clothing and books, which they donated to the Customs House Museum and Cultural Center.

Ann Alley spent fifteen years of her retirement from the Tennessee State Library and Archives improving the diary with annotations, research-ing local and family histories. She entrusted her work with us so that we could continue the last stage of annotating and editing. Thank you to Jill Hastings-Johnson, Montgomery County Archives, for her helpful research. Genealogist Irene Griffey contributed significantly to understanding the complicated family histories. Dr. Dewey Browder, APSU professor emeritus of history, gave helpful advice in tracking down historical references. Kali Mason, while curator of collections at the Customs House and Museum, se-cured grants to preserve the diary. Melissa Miller assisted with photographs from the Customs House Collection. William Bailey Allen and Amelia Allen Hartz, experts in local history, shared their knowledge. We appreciate the insightful comments by the University of Tennessee Press anonymous read-ers, who eventually were not anonymous, Aaron Astor of Maryville College and Antoinette van Zelm, Middle Tennessee State University.

EDITORIAL DECISIONS

SEREPTA JORDAN HOMER was an educated, well-read, thoughtful woman. She wrote diligently every day about her daily life and made insightful statements about politics, religion, and human nature. Because she was so dutiful in writing every day in addition to her busy schedule of cooking, sewing, visiting, and reading, one can imagine she was getting her thoughts on paper as fast as she could, not worrying about punctuation, spelling, or proofing for omitted or repeated words. Her diary, as with all diaries, was private and not intended for anyone else to read. It contains grammatical mistakes that Serepta would have corrected upon revision for publication. As with all editors, we had to decide how much to clean up her mistakes to make her amazing diary more accessible to twenty-first-century readers but still maintain the feel of this particular nineteenth-century writer.

The diary contains entries for every day from 1857 through 1864. To print the entire journal would be cost prohibitive. We believe the entries before the War years give a nice picture of antebellum life in a Middle Tennessee town. Therefore, we selected highlights from 1857 to 1859 entries. Next, we cut about 150 pages from the 1860 to 1864 years. The journal contained many comments about visiting family and friends, cooking, attending church, redundancies in expressing thoughts. We deleted many of these comments. Sometimes we took out entire entries; sometimes we cut sections of entries. We tried to keep the tenor of her writing and reports of her daily life, but by cutting more mundane entries, we probably overemphasized sections on the War. The uncut, unedited transcription of the diary is available at the Customs House Museum and Cultural Center in Clarksville, Tennessee.

Some of the changes we made were to make words easier to recognize for twenty-first-century readers. We now write as one word many words that nineteenth-century writers wrote separately: *to day* and *to morrow, any one, any where, every body*. We adopted the modern spellings for these words. Serepta was irregular with spelling some words. We have most often corrected misspelled words and friends' names that she wrote with different spellings. Her writing is difficult to decipher at times. Simple words such as *morn* and *noon* looked very similar and, on many occasions, we stared long and hard, having lengthy discussions about which it was. In unclear cases we used context to decide which word she meant.

Serepta was inconsistent with her use of apostrophes, sometimes employing them to indicate an abbreviation and other times not. Often, she left out apostrophes to indicate possessiveness. We added those apostrophes to aid in understanding. She regularly spelled contractions as do'nt, is'nt, have'nt, won't, ca'nt; we moved the apostrophes. Frequently, she used a double *l* when today we use one: allmost, allready, alltogether, allthough, Willson; we deleted the second *l*. She was more likely to use lowercase letters than capitals: mr, mrs, miss, cousin as a title, days of the week, religious denominations. We capitalized and added periods when we thought changes would ease reading. We left some words lowercased when we thought it would not affect readability and would keep authenticity.

We corrected her plurals of *ladys, buggys, familys* to *ladies, buggies, families*. We corrected and standardized her spelling with the exception of *hicrenuts* for *hickory nuts*, because we thought that misspelling might have been intentional. She spelled names haphazardly. Even her husband's name was as often spelled *Homar* as *Homer*. Her beloved Aunt Tabitha was spelled Tabbie 29 times and Tabby 13 in the entries we included. We changed all to Tabbie. Miss Fannie Pettus, who married Uncle Trice after Tabitha died, was Fannie 78 times and Fanny 10 times. We changed all to Fannie. We standardized the dates of the entries, keeping all of the details she included.

While Serepta's thoughts were generally recorded in complete sentences, she did not use punctuation to indicate standard sentences. She rarely began sentences with capitals or ended them with periods. Instead, she used extra spaces or sometimes commas between thoughts. Items in a series were never separated by commas. We most often standardized her punctuation for ease of reading. When she repeated words, we omitted the extra. "After supper Mr. Homer came up after supper" became "Mr. Homer came up after supper."

In compiling notes for the diary entries, we searched for names in as many sources as we could find. Even then, we were not able to identify every person mentioned. If the individual does not have an identifying note, we were unable to find information on him or her.

In addition to the Montgomery County 1850 and 1860 censuses, we searched other census records, listed in the bibliography. Before the days of recorded birth certificates, exact, legal names are difficult to determine. Nicknames appeared in marriage records, obituaries, and even on tombstones; names were spelled differently on legal documents; and census and military records often listed initials only. The names and spellings in footnotes represent those found most often in the documents we searched. Therefore, spellings in notes may differ from diary spellings. When we could not find individuals through traditional sources like censuses; marriage, birth, or death records; newspaper accounts; city directories; cemetery lists; or published local histories, we turned to unofficial sources like the various Family Tree pages constructed by descendants on ancestry.com. We acknowledge these untraditional sources may include errors, but they contain useful information that helped us piece together family connections we would not have discovered through other sources.

When we decided a first-name-only reference, or an initial, such as C for Clarksville, needed clarification, we included the extra information in brackets, [ ]. We also used these brackets to supply a word we thought Serepta had inadvertently omitted. When we could not figure out what an entry said, we indicated that in one of two ways: we either put the closest approximation we could determine in italics in brackets, { }, or we noted the word was {*indecipherable*}.

The names of newspapers cited in references changed throughout the years with mergers, new owners, and current trends. Citations reflect the name of the newspaper at the time of the event.

INTRODUCTION

Minoa D. Uffelman

THE CIVIL WAR WAS a traumatic and violent experience for all those who lived through it. Diaries and journals offer us insights into firsthand accounts, reactions to events as they occurred. There is not one "women in the Civil War" narrative, there are as many stories as there were women, each one determined by the region of the state they lived in, their race, their class and which side they supported. Catherine Clinton, who studied the Civil War for five decades, summarizes current scholarship in *Stepdaughters of History* and issues a clarion call to add more women's voices to Civil War history.[1] Of all Civil War diaries, Mary Boykin Chesnut's massive diary is the most famous and is often used to describe the female war experience.[2] Yet, Chesnut was as an elite slave-owning aristocrat in upper echelons of South Carolina. Her life bore little-to-no resemblance to women in other regions and classes.

As each additional diary is published, we gain more clarity to the myriad of ways women experienced the war. Within four hours of Clarksville, Tennessee, two different women's diaries tell of extremely different experiences and world views. Both describe communities of divided loyalties but each chose different sides. In Union occupied East Tennessee, passionate secessionist Ellen Renshaw House called herself "a very violent Rebel" and wrote of her hatred of Yankees and hope the Confederacy would prevail.[3] Another woman, Josie Underwood of Bowling Green, Kentucky, was from a slave owning Unionist family with friends and relatives that fought for the Confederacy.[4] Two women in Clarksville left diaries. Nannie Haskins Williams[5] and Serepta Jordan lived a mere five miles apart but experienced the war years in vastly different ways. Nannie was from the professional class of Clarksville and had a large nurturing family. Serepta Jordan was orphaned, living with her aunt and merchant uncle in bustling New Providence. Jordan was a woman in personal crisis during national crisis with events outside of her control limiting her options for the future.

Serepta Mildred Jordan (1839–1894), known as Rep to her family and friends, kept a voluminous diary from 1857 to 1864.[6] The name Serepta is a biblical name meaning a goldsmith's shop. Nothing in Serepta's life was golden. Her life was filled with tragic loss, separation, and sadness. Much of her life story is shrouded in mystery. Her mother was Damaris Trice Jordan Bennett but identity of her father eluded family genealogists and archivists until recently. William Jordan's name is listed as husband of Darmaris in her father's will probated in Robertson County, Tennessee, in 1836.[7] Early in Serepta's life her father died and in 1844 her mother remarried a widower, John Bennett, who had a daughter about Serepta's age. Together they had three more children. Serepta would have been the only child in the house not related to Bennett. When she was twelve, her mother died and young Rep went to live with her maternal aunt Tabitha Trice in New Providence, Tennessee. Ironically, Serepta was listed in two censuses in 1850, Calloway County, Kentucky, with Bennett and Montgomery County with Trice.[8]

Serepta received a good education and had a lifelong love of reading. She often referred to her current reading, which included heavy tomes about religion and history. Her mother's estate included guardian documents that chronicled payments to a teacher in New Providence.[9] Her journal entries are insightful, revealing daily life of a young woman who suffered great losses through death to those closest to her. She had an active social life of church, visiting, suppers, and lectures and recorded numerous and varied work activities. Serepta described food preparation, giving insights into everyday diets of ordinary people living in upper Middle Tennessee. She avidly followed the political conflicts that led to secession and wrote of war preparations as she watched her friends enlist in the Confederate Army. When Serepta began her diary in 1857, she was living with her maternal aunt Tabitha and husband, Elsey Trice, whom she called Uncle T, in New Providence near Trice's Landing. Today, New Providence is part of Clarksville but in the mid-nineteenth century the two communities were distinct rival towns on either side of the Red River, a tributary of the Cumberland. Elsey Trice was involved in several enterprises; he ran a cooper shop, stored and shipped tobacco and other products such as lumber, and traded horses. Serepta had a loving relationship with her Aunt Tabbie and her entries show deep mutual affection.

Provenance of the Diary and Decades of Editing

The diary was discovered in a smokehouse in Clarksville in the mid-1980s and donated to the Customs House Museum and Cultural Center in Clarksville. It is a well-constructed large store ledger with thick sturdy covers. Serepta was not a long forgotten ancestor to her descendants but remembered as a revered matriarch. An amazing amount of her possessions were passed down through the generations of primarily female descendants. A treasured family chest contained her clothing including a beautiful dress, a shawl, three hats, and handbag. The young girls in the family played dress-up in these nineteenth century garments well into the twentieth century. Serepta's love of reading and learning also was passed to subsequent generations as a box of her beloved books still exists.[10] Indeed, the actual books Serepta recorded reading in the diary have been on display at Fort Defiance in New Providence, some with her handwritten notes in them. Upon the discovery of the diary, the family knew they wanted it published and began transcription. For three decades a cobbled together, uncoordinated group of interested people worked on it, sometimes working together, at other times independently.

Initially Serepta's great-granddaughter, Evelyn Glenn Hunter, worked relentlessly to have the diary transcribed, recruiting her friends to help. She asked retired Austin Peay State University English professor, Dr. Charles Holt, to begin editing and to pursue publication. The editing was a monumental task given the length of the diary and the scores of family, friends, neighbors, enslaved people, and acquaintances she wrote of. Additionally, Jordan maximized writing space by sometimes writing crossways and in the margins. Holt improved the transcript but eventually dropped the project. For the next fifteen years, Ann Alley, a retired archivist from Tennessee State Library and Archives (TSLA), spent countless hours continuing to research people and places, trying to build a family tree. Alley generously entrusted the current editors with her massively improved manuscript in hopes that we could get it published. The same four editors of Nannie Haskins Williams' diary grabbed the academic baton and have spent four years working on it as we could. Jill Hastings-Johnson, Montgomery County archivist, researched family trees and was the researcher who finally found the elusive father, William Jordan.

At some point along the editorial process someone decided the published diary should start when Serepta first used the word "disunion," September 7, 1860. The assumption being that the only parts of interest were during the Civil War. This decision excluded the first three years of the diary. The current editors could not disagree with this decision more. We believe including the years leading up to the war gives invaluable insight into what Southerners experienced as the sectional crisis inched closer to armed conflict. The complete diary contained 500 typed pages, without any additional footnotes, appendixes, photos, or introduction, much too long for an affordable book. The editors spent months cutting over 100 pages and adding excerpts from the earlier years, determined to keep the integrity of the diary, maintaining the same balance of local news, descriptions of her labor, and descriptions about Serepta's busy network of friends and neighbors. Our editorial process is explained in Editorial Decisions.

In 2017 Customs House curator of collections, Kali Mason, received a TSLA grant to conserve the diary. Along with donations she secured, the diary was sent to the Northeast Document Conservation Center in Boston for preservation. Experts cleaned the delicate pages and put them in covers. The thick journal covers that protected Serepta's entries from the elements while in the outbuilding were beyond repair. The binding served its purpose. Because of the sturdiness of the journal, today we can read about Serepta's mid-nineteenth-century world.

Daily Life

The diary offers wonderful insights into daily life in New Providence and Clarksville during the build-up to war, the secession crisis, war preparations, conflict and occupation. Serepta was never idle and described a dizzying array of activities. Entries are filled with different types of labor Serepta performed, courtship, her regular church attendance, often recording scriptures and commentary on the quality of different ministers' sermons, and her complex community network of friends and neighbors. She mentioned slaves and their personal interactions as she inadvertently described the breakdown of the peculiar institution. She was a one-woman sewing factory, listing scores of items she made with wonderful descriptions of details of fabric, trim, and sewing techniques. She was conscious of styles and asked people who had traveled north to describe the latest trends. She pored over any fashion books she could obtain. She made nets for women's hair and pocket watch holders. One item she liked was decidedly sectional, a "Jeff Davis hat."[11]

Serepta lived in the hub of a bustling trading and market community of New Providence and would have had entree to the advantages of the urban community such as easy access to retail stores, a variety of churches to choose to attend, closeness to telegraph, and public transportation, repair shops, undertakers and professional services. She kept up with the daily news because of her access to local newspapers. Barges and boats brought people from all parts of the South sharing news, newspapers and gossip. Yet, despite her urban setting the labor she performed would not have been different from the chores of rural women. Town and country people ate the same foods based on the seasons, not just vegetables and fruits but also oyster season. She complained her uncle could not kill hogs because the weather turned too warm. Like her country sisters she made wreaths of hair to remember someone and created flowerbeds for beauty. She raised a garden, baked cakes, pies and breads. Meat for supper might be squirrel, groundhog or partridge. Food preservation included making wine and drying fruit. As with most Southerners, oranges were a treat at Christmas. She mentioned some canned products such as peaches.

A couple of entries describe her bitter class resentment toward the elite ladies of Clarksville. New Providence, a community of Montgomery County, was across the Red River from Clarksville and is today considered part of Clarksville. The two areas experienced class rivalries between old monied Clarksvillians and the merchant class in New Providence. You might say it was akin to living on the wrong side of the tracks but in this case the wrong side of the river. Interestingly for this editor, she saved particular invective for a certain Mrs. Haskins, Nannie's mother, who deigned to cross the river to deal with her social inferiors in New Providence to solicit war aid.[12] This is the only reference Jordan made about Mrs. Haskins and she revealed deep anger and bitterness.

First Agricultural Fair

In the months leading toward secession, Montgomery Countians eagerly followed events in the newspapers. At the same time as the regional tensions worsened, Montgomery County civic and business leaders organized the first Agricultural Fair, to promote agricultural products and livestock and publicize Clarksville and Montgomery County as an important progressive city ready to market its products across the state and country using railroads and rivers. Serepta's diary records her impressions of the first Agricultural Fair in Montgomery County, which was an impressive and large event the city leaders planned with considerable organization that required coordination from an astonishing number and kinds of people, both public, private and governmental. What the city thought would be the first grand fair in a long tradition of fairs was not to be because of the war. Indeed, everyone that attended would have their lives profoundly changed and certainly some who attended would perish during the war.

Agricultural Fairs had a long tradition in the United States and Clarksville leaders and boosters certainly understood the significance of promoting local agriculture, livestock, and crafts.[13] The venue of the fair was forty-three acres, three miles northeast of Clarksville between the rail line and Russellville Pike, a main road to Kentucky. An amphitheater had nine tiers of seats with a seating capacity of 4000 and the potential for 3000 more. The show ring was 200 feet in diameter and the judges' stand was three stories high with a flag staff in the middle. A Nashville band was hired to entertain attendees. Two 600-barrel cisterns were dug to provide water. One hundred large stalls, eight feet wide, eleven feet high, nine feet deep held the livestock.

M C & L Railroad established a convenient schedule from Clarksville for ten cents. The toll turnpike reduced its rates to half and an omnibus service transported people from the downtown main depot. The heavy promotion paid off. Attendance ranged from 3,500 to 8,500 each day. Organizers were proud that the *Bowling Green Gazette* was part of the visiting press. Serepta's October 23, 1860, entry indicates the great multigenerational interest of the first fair, "A day long to be remembered not only by the youth and children of our county but by the old too. For among the many that have passed today on their way to the first agricultural fair of Montgomery Co. were a great many whose heads were frosted over and form bent with age. They will tell their grandchildren of the great sight they saw while the younger are left to reflect on the progress of the age, vast improvements and fast trotting horses. . . . Embroidery, quilts, cakes &c &c, lady's work generally and a few horse were all that were exhibited."[14]

The next day, Serepta seemed less impressed than other attendees with the exhibitions." She did, however, enjoy seeing "several old acquaintances while promenading."[15] She wrote, ". . . by tomorrow or the next day the last McAdotion and Dover Rodin will have seen the Elephant."[16] This was a clever way of saying all the residents of McAdoo community and those on Dover Road, communities from opposite ends of the county will have attended and apparently all those who attended were attractive. A local paper wrote, "We venture to say that as large an assemblage of fine looking men and women were never seen in Tennessee. There were more pretty women and handsome men, and they were elegantly dressed, than we have ever seen before."[17]

By Friday Serepta had become more impressed. She wrote, "Hogs, sheep farming, utensils, specimens of portrait painting, marble work, carpenters' work, leather and various other things were on exhibit. Several rings this evening. A youth of 12 or 13 years of age excelled in horsemanship. Several rode in the tournament." The "world and his wife" were in attendance and watched premium stock horse competition. She estimated the crowd was "6 or 7 thousand." Serepta's favorite event was the Tournament of Knight, a popular nineteenth-century version of medieval jousting.[18] She wrote a Mr. Gill of Russellville won $50 and the privilege of crowning the Queen of Love and Beauty, choosing his cousin. The large prize money indicates the significance organizers placed on the tournaments. The largest prize was $75 for best stallion, then decreasing amounts of $40 for best brood mare, $15 for best jack and mule, $10 for best ewe. Needlework included best suit jeans (cashmere) $5, homemade sewing silk $1. Other prizes, best glass painting $2, homemade candles $2, hair work $2 and penmanship by a girl $1.[19]

By Monday the excitement of the fair was over and Serepta wrote, "Commenced work this morning in the old fashioned style." The community's break from regular labor was over. However, a controversial decision by the judge ensured that people were debating. She felt a Mr. Field had been robbed of a victory in one of the competitions and apparently there was a talk of a do over. "Mr. Field's friends want to see that he has justice done him. If I were in his place and they had the impudence to ask me over, I wouldn't go a single step."[20] It may be impossible to know the details of this particular controversy but it does suggest that people felt an injustice had occurred and the judges awarded a prize to the wrong person.

Daily life returned to normal rhythms. National news, however, would be anything but ordinary. On November 6, 1860, Serepta's entry was long and newsy about people visiting, someone being ill, a death, pondering the punishment his soul might receive and ends with this single sentence. "Today is the Presidential election and I never knew less excitement, notwithstanding the number of candidates, Bell, Lincoln, Breckenridge and Douglass." She ends the day's entry with "Tomorrow cousins Jennie and Alley leave for Williamstown if the babe is well enough."[21] The next Montgomery County Fair would not be until 1869.

Civil War

In late 1860, Clarksville had a population of about 5,000 and was overwhelmingly Unionist but after Fort Sumter, attitudes swung toward secession. In June 1861, in a statewide referendum, Montgomery County favored secession, 2,632 to 32 and Clarksville 561 to 1. In preparation for war, citizens raising local units established four recruiting and training camps often on their private property. By the time Fort Donelson fell in February 1862, the soldiers trained at these camps had moved to other battle sites. Young men and Stewart College students joined the Confederate Army. A professor commanded a unit of students which was later incorporated into the 14th Tennessee Infantry. They were sent to the Army of Northern Virginia, and fought in virtually every major battle in the Eastern Theater. Of the twenty-nine seniors, sixteen were killed and seven died of disease or wounds.[22]

Clarksville and its sister town of New Providence, located at the conflu-ence of the Red and Cumberland rivers were strategically important. They were thriving market towns that were heavily dependent on processing and shipping tobacco. Pig iron was an important industry and hundreds of work-ers, including slaves, refined ore in vast quantities in the area's seven iron furnaces. Foundries in Montgomery and the adjacent counties were among the nation's leading iron producers. There were also numerous slaughter-ing houses. Consequently, the goods produced in Clarksville and New Providence were vital to the war effort. The Confederacy planned to use these war resources; however, after February 1862, the USA would benefit from Clarksville's iron works, not the CSA.[23]

Women in communities across the county formed organizations to sup-port the war effort. The women of New Providence formed the Volunteer's Friends Association in April of 1861 and Serepta was elected secretary. She wrote a letter to the paper to announce the formation of the organization and state the goals:

> The object of the Association, as the name indicates, is to render such aid, comfort, and protection to our Volunteer friends as circum-stances will justify, and to act in concert with all similar organizations throughout the county and State.
> All communications must be addressed to the undersigned.
>
> S. M. Jordan, Sec'y, V. F. A.
> New Providence, Tenn.[24]

The loss of Fort Donelson in February 1862 was the beginning of the end for the Confederacy because it opened the entire Cumberland Valley to US Forces. The Union controlled both the Tennessee and Cumberland rivers. On February 19, a Federal gunboat and steamer approached Fort Defiance at New Providence, and despite the name of the fort, Montgomery County authorities surrendered without a shot being fired. Former US Postmaster General Cave Johnson, Clarksville Mayor C. G. Smith and Judge Thomas Wisdom informed naval officer A. H. Foote that Rebel forces had left the city and fled to Nashville after attempting to burn a nearby bridge.[25] Foote issued a proclamation that residents could expect safety but also outlawed Confederate flags and demanded the surrender of military stores.[26] Nashville became the first Confederate capitol to fall to the Union by the end of the month.

Entries during this period included stories of chaos and violence. Both thievery and legitimate appropriating of livestock and produce were devastating to local farmers and merchants. Serepta wrote of pickets, having to carry passes, the required, but hated, loyalty oath, and of ministers being arrested. Locals sold goods to the military, to the Confederacy before the fall of Fort Donelson, and after occupation, some sold goods to the Union. Like all Montgomery Countians, she was desperate to obtain reliable news of the war and was skeptical of Union newspapers. In the early months of occupation she reported the rumors of troop movements and was knowledgeable of commanders and strategies. As news of deaths and casualties reached New Providence she recorded the names of dead and injured from the local regiments, the 14th, 49th and 50th.

Jordan wrote, "Latest news from Clarksville and Nashville both have raised white flags. Clarksville is almost depopulated. All the escaped soldiers have been ordered to the main army via Clarksville before the Yankees get in. I ripped the stripes off a young man's coat over at Uncle W'm's this evening that he might not be detected on his journey. Once I enjoyed sewing them on, but now I take them off as willingly."[27]

The entries now told of Union gunboats and the effect of rain on the river. Clarksvillians attempted to burn a railroad bridge to prevent the Union from using it. Locals began to learn what occupation meant. Colonel Sanders Bruce euphemistically announced that property would be respected, "so long as no secessionist feelings were exhibited. . . ." She noted the change of flags, "The old stars and stripes now wave over our forts from some of the public buildings of the city." She then bemoaned that Confederate soldiers were ordered to Murfreesboro leaving Montgomery County unprotected. "What a move! And what may we poor Rebels in this part of Lincolndom expect? Now that we are left entirely to the mercy of the vandals." People were leaving for places they felt safer, she called it "running from the Lincolnites." "Such long faces as they did wear; the thought of leaving home was enough to sadden their hearts but I rather guess the thought of losing 50 or 100 negroes was the most maddening of all."[28]

Clarksville and New Providence were nominally behind Union lines at this point. A large garrison was left at Donelson but most Union soldiers headed south toward Shiloh to capture the railroad junction at Corinth, Mississippi. Montgomery County underwent sporadic occupation and patrol. On February 23 she wrote, "Mr. H says two Regiments are stationed at the Fort and one or more are in Clarksville; our streets are seldom clear of the rowdies, and splendidly dressed officers prancing round on their fine horses are sights not uncommon; the wounded from Fort D continue to come in." She recorded that, "Forrest and his brave company had possession of our town in place of the Lincoln negro worshippers."[29] The Confederates did not hold the town long and a permanent Union garrison was established. Still the situation was chaotic and dangerous with the area changing control several times. Most people stayed home to avoid trouble. In March 1862 Federal troops vandalized Stewart College, stripping it bare of books and scientific equipment. Soldiers arrested preachers, commandeered horses and wagons, and required oaths of allegiance from worshipers. Business men had to take the oath to conduct business.[30]

Union authorities realized quickly that Southern women aided the Confederacy.[31] Indeed, Serepta had already removed CSA rank from a soldier's jacket to aid his escape. Women throughout the South were performing countless acts of resistance and sabotage. Therefore, females had to take the loyalty oath as well as men. Serepta rightly observed that "Tennessee is now considered a conquered province." Travel required passes and Serepta chafed when pickets demanded compliance, complained that it made her realize that she was "a citizen of Yankeedom." She hated the sounds of different accents and languages spoken by Union soldiers. "If a couple of ladies wish to make a call just without the guard line they must be halted and rudely questioned by a set of ignoramuses using a greater variety of languages than was known at the building of the Tower of Babel." She hated the "demon abolitionist" and called Andrew Johnson a "dark hearted and treacherous Arnold" who was in "a negro stealing, liberty displacing party." Serepta even worried trains from the North would bring small pox to her community.[32] By April of 1862 Clarksville and New Providence experienced an uneasy truce. Serepta wrote "us poor semi Lincolnites. Here we are just exactly situated on the line that separates Lincolndom from Dixie, we neither share to greatest extent the disgrace of one nor enjoy the privileges of the other but after all we are tolerably quiet. . . ."[33]

Jordan's world was devastated on July 2, 1861, when her aunt died suddenly at a huge community party to honor the newly enlisted local soldiers held at one of the hastily constructed camps. The celebration of Southern patriotism was in full swing as friends and neighbors came to bid the soldiers farewell. At the party Aunt Tabby collapsed and the local physician was too drunk to properly attend her. The local paper reported her death but neglected to print her name: "Sudden Death: The wife of Elsey Trice of New Providence fell dead at Camp Quarles on Tuesday Last, while on a visit to the Camp from a stroke of apoplexy. Up to the time of the attack she appeared to be enjoying usual good health and at the time was removing some articles of provisions, which she had taken out for some of the boys from a basket."[34]

Serepta's only source of love and familial support had died. Within weeks, the widowed uncle began to cast his eye on a single neighbor and his attitude toward Serepta turned cold. She recorded her immense grief in contrast to his lack of sorrow and her disgust at him sprucing up the house as he began to court his next wife. Five months later she wrote, "Oh! is it possible that in so short a time he has forgotten one of Earth's best and brightest ornaments." Then she wrote that if he had died instead, her aunt would still be grieving.[35] The new mistress of the house was hostile to Serepta and made her feel unwelcome in the only home she had.

While visiting her aunt's grave, she noted the cemetery allowed her to "enjoy the quiet beauty; that calm peaceful stillness no where else to be found. . . . The stillness of the place seems in striking contrast with the stir and confusion of the outer world." Still the death of the war could not be escaped. Nearby she observed, "The Soldiers' graves we found more numerous than we had anticipated; among them almost every Southern state was represented; how sad to think of a soldier's dying from home and filling a strangers grave with no pitying eye of kindred dear or loved friend to shed over him the tear of sorrow and regret."[36]

By December of 1863, the fort near Serepta's home, known at the time as Fort Bruce, became a recruiting and training camp for African Americans, members of the United States Colored Troops. Approximately 3,000 African Americans from Clarksville and surrounding counties joined the Union Army. Serepta recorded disgust of seeing black men in Union uniforms. Most African American troops went to Nashville to build and garrison Fort Negley.[37] Later USCT units transferred for garrison duty in Chattanooga. Ironically, given the changing fortune of the war, B. B. and Serepta Jordan Homer rented a room to the white USCT officer, Adjutant Bishop Perkins, in order to makes ends meet.

Throughout the war years, Jordan recorded news of battles as she learned from newspapers she could acquire, legitimate news and sometimes rumor. Rarely was news good for the Confederacy and as the months passed her

Confederate patriotism faded and her bitterness increased as the Union victory became more likely. The diary ends before Lee's surrender so we do not know her reaction.

Marriage

Jordan's personality was at times caustic and her observations harsh. She was particularly cynical about weddings and marriages. When she recorded the death of a neighbor's third wife, she predicted he would be remarried "in less than 4 months. He's been preparing for the 4th one ever since Mrs. B has been low, sodding his yard and setting out shrubbery &c and she lying there slowly dying." [38] She is silent on her father and did not write often of her dead mother. She was maddeningly vague when discussing intimate issues and did not record conversations she had with two young men, Tom Trabue[39] and John Mallory,[40] both enlisted in the Confederacy. After they left Clarksville, Rep corresponded with both. Trabue died during the war and afterwards Serepta communicated with his mother. Almost nightly she was visited by a widower twenty years her senior who hoped to obtain her hand in marriage. B. B. Homer,[41] whom she referred to as Mr. Homer and who was in the mercantile business, visited the home and pressed Serepta to marry him. Her entries were ambivalent about him at best. She often criticized him, recounting their quarrels and complained about him annoying her or drinking too much. Yet, she recorded several occasions of combing his hair, which seemed to indicate an intimacy. He was persistent though and never gave up despite her friendship with other young men.

The three Christmas entries chronicled Jordan's changing fate. Christmas 1861, after her aunt's death Serepta continued her aunt's tradition of purchasing presents for, as she called them, the servants. She baked a cake and tried to put on a brave face. She, however, wrote with longing of past happier Yuletides, "thoughts . . . continually carried me back to Christmas Eve' in years past; when my young heart would leap at the bright anticipation of what I would receive on Christmas morning, and my impatience made the night seem a week in passing." She continued to remember her aunt's generosity and love as she passed gifts of stockings and baskets, noting the new woman was very happy in her uncle's presence but only looked at Serepta once the entire night. The neighborhood ritual of masquerading continued despite Serepta's heartache.[42] Christmas 1862 found Jordan preparing for the holiday by baking a cake "which turned out admirably" and crocheting watch cases for gifts. The evening was spent with Mr. Homer, "*slightly*

touching on the subject of matrimony."[43] In July 1863, she married him and
recorded no sentiment of love and happiness.

December 1863 was her first as Mrs. Homer and she was in dispute with
her uncle about what possessions she could take to her new home. She listed
a bed, the few items he allowed her to take, "such bed clothing as he thought
fit" which refers to pillows, bolster, slips sheets, blankets and also a bookcase
and her school books.[44]

She rose Christmas morning and woke her young slave Inez to see what
"Old Kristkringle brought." "It did me good to see how she enjoyed the
presents simple though they were." She described her gift to Homer, "I
made him a very pretty & neat little watch case, hoping in return he would
at least, make me a present of some little something similar to what Aunt T
was always in the habit of giving me." He, however, gave her nothing and
instead told her that she, "must be a woman now and put away 'childish
things,' and to bring about this change he seems absolved," She continued
writing of her dearly departed aunt, "[A]t her death I lost the last friend that
ever cared or felt to humor in the least on of my childish notions. . . . The
name of husband, seems with some to hold the dearest of affections, but with
me her name before all others, from her have I received the *kindest* words."
She noted she was twenty years younger than her husband and he should
take that into consideration. She was so disappointed she declined visiting
a neighbor and pretended to sew. Later a cousin sent some pickled apples
but she "was in no frame of mind to even enjoy them."[45] Thus, was her first
Christmas as Mrs. Homer.

B. B. Homer gave his wife silver spoons which she had engraved. She
was quite pleased with them but wanted to make sure that if she died before
him that a potential new wife would not enjoy them without thinking of
her. She wrote, "They are really very fine — so heavy & stout. According
to my request there are no initials engraved, but simply "Rep" in large legible letters. I tell Mr. H his next wife, if she ever uses them, shall certainly
know whose they were."[46] The plan proved unnecessary because B. B. died
before Serepta. Still she was determined if there was another Mrs. Homer
succeeding her that she would eat with a utensil engraved with Rep's name.
Generations of her descendants have passed these spoons to the next.[47]

On May 1, 1864, Serepta's entry began by describing how fatigued she was
and how she felt worse and worse through the night. She sent for a doctor
"whose presence was *considered indispensable.*" She continued, "I grew *sadly
worse* until about 11, when to make short of a long matter, I gave birth to a
little "wee bit' of a girl babe which after including clothes & all weighed

5 lbs." "Mr. H with the rest seemed disappointed that it was not a boy, however, just *for the time*, I was well pleased."[48] Serepta found joy in her baby, "A thousand things I could write about this little treasure, but the want of time and her immediate presence forbids. To write with her in my lap and this great book too is quite a serious undertaking."[49] "She grows sweeter every day."[50] Serepta's life in other ways remained similar to her pre-baby time. She mentioned the battles, sewing, large numbers of contraband coming to Clarksville, and Mr. Homer working on his tobacco patch.[51]

The last entry June 2, 1864, "Little Tabbie is growing prettier every day, she's getting so fat that it tires me smartly to carry her over to Cousin Jane's; she laughs frequently now and is—in a word, *remarkably sprightly* for one of her age, only 7 weeks old." Serepta and B. B. Homer would have four children. Perhaps the demands of children prevented her from continuing her journal. Perhaps she continued to write but the diary is lost to history. This diary was lost to history for over 120 years and it now offers incredible insight into one woman's struggles in a world with few options for poor women. Serepta's choices were even more limited given the death of so many young men. Even at the time people worried that a generation of women would be destined to a life of spinsterhood. Demographers have crunched the numbers and now know this generation of women married in the same percentages that you would expect but that because of the dearth of young men they married outside of their class or age. Nannie Haskins married Henry Williams, twenty years her senior. Serepta had rejected her young suitors who went to war, then married Mr. Homer, perhaps only because she felt she had no option. In 1863 she found herself with no home, and no extended family to provide financial support. She married a persistent older widower.

Slavery and Freedom

Jordan's entries on slaves, both general and specific, constitute a small percentage of the diary. Her recordings about enslaved people and the institution of slavery are simply a part of her everyday world. Nevertheless, one of the most fascinating aspects of the diary is that Serepta described the break-down of slavery under Union occupation as enslaved people struggled to obtain freedom. The diary offers insight into particular enslaved people's lives but also gives a general sense of slavery in an upper Middle Tennessee town.

When modern Americans think of the end of slavery it is usually in the following way: the South fought to maintain slavery, the North fought to end slavery, the North won, and slavery ended. However, gaining freedom was messy, bitter and hard fought. The stakes could not have been higher, freedom for some, loss of valuable property for others. As the Union gained control of Southern territory, slavery ended as one enslaved person at a time made decisions about how to secure freedom. Each person, couple, and family chose actions based on what they decided was best for them. These decisions were influenced by their owners' behavior and attitudes, the availability of a safe place to go, their network of family and friends, opportunities for employment, or proximity to contraband camps and Union troops for protection.

The fierce struggle of one of Elsey Trice's former enslaved women to gain and maintain custody of her baby is heart wrenching. The tenacity with which Winnie fought her enslaver and Union soldiers intent on keeping her child enslaved is epic. The entries show that white Southerners tried desperately to continue to deny African Americans freedom and keep children from mothers. Serepta's outraged attitude toward African Americans reveals deep-seated racism despite her affection for her particular slave, Inez.

In 1857 when she began the diary, slavery was firmly entrenched. White supremacy was the law of the land. She noted slave marriages, deaths, and births in the entries along with other news. For the most part, entries are matter-of-fact references to "servants." However, Serepta related the harrowing story of a murder of a business owner. His enslaved man was suspected and the crowd decided that non-judicial justice would be imposed, a lynching. As the man was hanging, but not dead, he indicated he wanted to say something. They took him down. He said he killed his owner because of the horrible, repeated beatings and torturous treatment. If expecting leniency because of mitigating circumstance, he was wrong. The crowd now satisfied with a confession of guilt, strung him up and left his dead body hanging for hours. Serepta watched the whole event and expressed excessive grief and sorrow for the white man. She offered not one word of compassion for the enslaved man, who was beaten by his master, perhaps beaten and executed by a mob, a mob of her friends and neighbors.[52]

In the prewar years Serepta wrote of shared labor with Inez and routinely mentioned the specific tasks they performed to keep the house running. On August 24, 1858, Serepta recorded, "Made Inez an apron this morning, a little negro girl that Uncle Trice gave me soon after her birth, she is now 5 or 6 years old and a more spritely child black or white is scarcely to be found." The 1860 Slave Schedule lists Inez as seven years old. Her Uncle

Trice owned nine people, the oldest a 45-year-old man, the youngest a six-year-old girl. These were the enslaved people with whom Serepta would have had the closest interactions. If Serepta had not recorded Inez's age, the reader would assume she was much older given the labor Serepta mentioned her performing, sometimes alone and sometimes assisting her owner. Jordan showed concern about Inez's physical well-being. Once when Inez was sick she brought in a doctor and also saw that she and the other enslaved children were vaccinated.[53] Her entry on February 28, 1861, exhibits the complicated attitude of Serepta toward Inez, whom she owns.

"Inez, the only piece of property to which I've the least claim and the only servant for whom I've much love, is now in bed and very ill. Her death will give me much pain should it occur and yet, I can scarcely hope for her recovery. The attack from the first has been so violent. Dr. H, I fear, is not sufficiently acquainted the disease to afford much relief. Yesterday was the first of her complaining though she has been looking badly for some time. Her limbs all seem to be very sore and her body generally swollen, though to a slight extent. Her fever is not high, she perspires very freely, and yet talks like one entirely crazy with a most violent fever. How could I give her up?"[54]

The last sentence is ambiguous. Was Serepta contemplating the loss of a child she loves or the loss of her only financial asset, or both? She made clothes for Inez and took time to make Christmas gifts for her and recorded pleasure from seeing Inez's happiness at opening the gifts. One Christmas morning, Serepta woke Inez to see what "Old Kristkringle brought," adding, "It did me good to see how she enjoyed the presents, simple though they were."[55]

After the fall of Fort Donelson life was chaotic and lawless as Montgomery Countians suffered looting and robberies. Serepta and her family hid their valuables up the chimney. Her entries reveal that in her view, not just physical property but human property was being stolen as well. In February 26, 1862, Serepta wanted to see the changes occupation had wrought, "I'll take a peep at the negro stealing, housebreaking, thieving, &."[56] The next month she wrote about blacks leaving by river with the assistance of the Union military. White New Providence residents were not happy. "Col. Wright protected and succored all who went to him for assistance. . . . Several from this place and surrounding neighborhoods went off with them. He also took several hundred barrels of Mr. Pettus' flour but gave him a receipt both for the flour and Frank and his negro. Because some of the citizens interfered, the old wretch threatened to burn our town."[57] Appropriating human property resulted in a receipt just as appropriating wheat did.

Serepta was angry with troops "pressing" blacks for labor and aiding in their emancipation and was disgusted with the Union soldiers' attitude toward African Americans. "They converse as freely with the servant as though they were old friends. Indeed they seem at home only with the negroes, and the negroes in return seem to be perfectly at home with them. A great many of them have been running off and going to the camp. Some have succeeded in making their escape on boats going downstream. Some of the officers — the real Lincolnites or abolitionists — encourage and aid them in getting away."[58] However, not all Union soldiers assisted enslaved people to gain freedom. She wrote, "while others — those who are honest enough to think they are fighting for the Union and Constitution and 'the negro' — seriously object to having one enter within the guard lines and in many instances assist the owner in recovering them."[59] Serepta held the Southern understanding that the Constitution protected slavery, and the Union should not assist in helping people obtain freedom.

By February of 1862, Serepta learned of a contraband camp in Nashville and hoped that local freed people will be sent there, commenting, "How glad I will be. Every hole and corner is stuck so full of them and filth is accumulating so fast as a result that disease will undoubtedly break out soon, and then the suffering that will come none of us can depict."[60]

As New Providence adjusted to Union occupation, cracks developed in the foundation of white supremacy. Whites no longer were in control and felt threatened. One woman turned to an unlikely source for protection, African Americans. On October 9, 1862, Serepta wrote, "Miss Fannie is looking to the negroes for protection — a pretty pass we Americans have come to. To one she has given her blankets, to another something else; just here and there where she finds one she can trust, she gives them up something, thinking out of all she may save a little."[61]

By summer of 1863 the loss of enslaved people's labor caused farmers' hardships. "Ike was out on the farm at work. Out of 6 or 8 negro men, he has one remaining — Everywhere the farms seems miserably neglected." She added that the bad weather was contributing to crop failure. "The wheat crop will prove almost an entire failure on account of the long continued rains; it sprouts standing in the field."[62] It was a double whammy loss for white landowners.

White women also found the loss of slaves forced them to perform unaccustomed chores. This is a typical entry that listed war news, lack of access to news and the escape of two enslaved women. "Rosecrans, rumor says, is being heavily reinforced and another crash is expected soon between he and Bragg. The cars have been pressed and we get no more papers for some time. The negroes are flocking into the Yanks here at the Fort by droves. It is thought this will be made a recruiting post for them. Old Mrs. Trice's two maids, her dependence almost for cooking and homework, left last week, and Mr. Homer has been lecturing Cousin Jane and I ever since we heard of it, for rejoicing over the old lady's downfall."[63] Despite her belief in slavery, Serepta wrote of her schadenfreude at hearing that Old Mrs. Trice was having to cook and clean.

A few days later it seems that the two newly free women returned to challenge Trice for custody of their mother and two children. "Jack told me while over there, that Jane and Paralee had sent up for their mother & Jane's two children, so old Mrs. Trice and Mary are left without a single maid. Tom, they say, does their cooking and as for washing that has to be done from home just whoever will, may. One thing certain Mary won't put her hands to the tub nor pot either if there can be found a preventative. I heard they called in a neighbor to turn a hoecake for them."[64] While white Montgomery Countians' primary concern was maintaining their human property for labor, for black Montgomery Countians the primary concern was gaining freedom for their intact families.

Fort Defiance served as a recruiting and training camp for US Colored Troops. As soon as white troops entered Clarksville they pressed African American men to perform manual labor for the army. Serepta had heard news the Union would enlist black troops and one day she saw black soldiers in blue uniforms drilling and acting as pickets. "Went over to Cousin Jane's this evening. She didn't get much news up town yesterday. The negro pickets were stationed just across the street from us today—and a more contemptible sight I didn't care to see. I thought a view of the Regiment at a distance was bad enough. They were practicing this evening for tonight I suppose, trying to mimic the Yankees. "Halt," they would say with the Yankee brogue, and then "who comes there?"[65]

In May she wrote that "all the negroes round were flocking in to the abolition negro thieves down here at the Fort and that Winnie, one of Uncle T's women, had gone among the rest—She left a good home and will, I hope, have cause to regret it."[66] Trice successfully appealed to the Union commander to obtain Winnie's child. She wrote, "Uncle Trice has at last succeeded in getting Ida, Winnie's baby, and Col. Bruce has given him an order for Winnie herself, though I think his getting her is rather improbable, as the abolition Yankees have sworn vengeance against him for taking the child. It would not surprise me to hear at any time that they had attempted to take his life, or burn him out. During his sprees of dissipation he says and does so much to excite their hatred that I live in constant dread."[67]

In September Winnie returned to take possession of her child. Two Union soldiers accompanied her but Trice refused to recognize their authority over his property. "Winnie, escorted by two Yankee soldiers, walked up to the gate and demanded her child. Uncle Trice came up in the meantime, took possession of Winnie." However, the soldiers fought Trice and "the Yankees have succeeded in getting her off somewhere — the place is yet unknown to me. She called him a liar and almost cursed him. Such independence, I suppose, never escaped a Negro's lips. I expect he was almost, if not quite, killed."[68] Even with soldiers, Winnie not only failed to secure her child but was almost re-enslaved. Serepta was disgusted by Winnie's rebellion against her uncle and expressed concern for his physical health in the struggle over his human property with US soldiers.

The next day, Trice heard that Winnie was in Hopkinsville and asked Mr. Homer to go with him to investigate and bring her back. The final time Winnie was mentioned was four months later. "Cousin Jane was telling me yesterday that Winnie had gotten back to camp. What will Uncle T and Miss F do now? They are leaving Christian Co., Ky., almost by the hundred."[69] Winnie and her child's fates are unknown.

Serepta was so angry with African Americans that she wrote she would prefer her assets to be non-human. "What love some people have for a negro. I'm glad my cow and calf, wardrobe, and bed didn't consist of wolly headed negroes."[70] However, she did own one negro and young Inez proved to be instrumental in helping fill the family coffers. In early 1864 Serepta and Inez worked together to sell produce to the military camp earning essential income for the household. Apparently Homer did not like Inez's attitude or perhaps was suspicious that she planned to leave. He beat her more than once. It seems that Inez pretended to be contrite as if the beatings worked as she bided her time to leave. "It was after 3 this evening before Inez had time to go to camp. She sold 49 cts worth of milk for me — doing quite well for a little thing like her. The whipping Mr. H gave her this morning had a very agreeable effect. The children are popping corn; I must stop anyway to eat some."[71] This was a rare acknowledgment that Inez was a child. It is unclear if Inez was allowed to enjoy popcorn along with Serepta's young cousins.

The next day Homer beat Inez again. Serepta wrote, "Have been busy all day making Inez's dress. Finished it late this evening. She has been unusually sweet since the whipping this morning. Went to camp and made for me

95 cts. This week my milk & butter has brought me in over 6.00. Soon I will have made 50.00 and where has it all gone to?"[72] Inez was instrumental in earning money for the household.

On February 19, 1864, Inez left. "This morning at the first tap of the drum over at camp awakened Inez, and as usual she dressed, made the fire, and had the room half swept before going out. I waited, of course, thinking she would be in directly, but to my surprise she kept staying and after 15 or 20 minutes, I remarked to Mr. Homer that she had gone to the Yankees. He went down to the cabin and came back in the same notion." When Serepta checked, she "found everything helter skelter, and knew from the very appearance of things, that she intended going last night. At dinner Margaret came to let me know that Inez had gone up to her house and that she had gone with great tales in regard to my treatment. She couldn't please me and I couldn't tell what all. I simply remarked that Inez had left without any good excuse whatever, agreeably to my notion, and that she should never again set foot on the place when I could prevent it. At this she seemed to take offense and not very pleasantly asked for her clothes. I readily gave them to her. She left mad, went up home, told Uncle Trice a great tale, and tonight I suppose I have the name worse than ever of being "sharped nose for nothing."[73]

Serepta could not believe that Inez would have negative things to say about how she was treated. Her worldview simply did not allow her to entertain the thought that she had mistreated Inez. The last entry of the diary is June 2, 1864. Slavery was over in New Providence. Contraband camps were crowded and locals hired freed people. Quite a change, having to pay African Americans for labor performed. "Here the contraband negroes are overrunning the place and still coming in averaging 50 a day. Every hole and corner seems to be alive with the filthy things and disease in every form almost has taken hold of them. Many of the older ones have died and are dying from the smallpox while the children suffer dreadfully from measles, whooping cough, and similar diseases. The citizens are hiring them now to a great extent, both men & women. Mr. H had as many as 5 today in his tobacco patch. Uncle Trice was down this evening and said Gilbert had 15 in the same employment."[74]

When Serepta began this diary she could never have anticipated that Southern society predicated on white supremacy and slavery would end. Still the legacy of slavery determined how this story of liberation was told. White, educated Serepta had a large journal with thick covers to record her daily life. Inez did not. Serepta received an excellent education. Inez did not attend school; instead she labored. At her death Serepta left books, clothes, photos to her daughters, and her descendants lovingly saved and preserved them. Perhaps Inez left books, clothes and photos to her descendants. We will never know. We do not even know Inez's last name. Inez is lost to recorded history. When she became free she was young and had her whole life ahead of her. We can only hope she had a happy, healthy life.

Epilogue

Perhaps Serepta Jordan Homer continued writing the account of her life after the pages of this volume were filled. She managed to find time to write copious amounts despite her busy days of tasks and responsibilities. Perhaps the responsibility of motherhood prevented further diary keeping. If she did continue writing in diaries, they did not survive. After the birth of Tabitha (1864–1926) she bore three more children. Evaline, "Eva," was born in 1867 and died in 1934. Her one son, Bailey, was born in 1869 and died at age two. Her youngest daughter, Janie, arrived in 1870 and died in 1937. Serepta was widowed in 1873 with the death of Bladen Beverly Homer, whom she referred to as Mr. Homer throughout the diary. Serepta Mildred "Rep" Jordan Homer died in 1894 at age fifty-five. Some of her descendants live in Clarksville.

CHAPTER ONE

November 1857– June 1860

SEREPTA JORDAN'S PRE-WAR ENTRIES painted a portrait of a vibrant New Providence community as she recorded the news of her neighbors, weddings, deaths, church services. She described mundane and dramatic events. She was living with her beloved aunt but had an emotional visit with her step-father and half siblings after several years' separation. The visit was fraught with tensions and resentment as well as happiness. Her days were filled with visiting, shopping, and labor. She recorded friends' and neighbors' illnesses both minor, such as head and tooth aches, and serious, consumption and typhoid. She recounted deaths, unexpected and expected, baby and elderly, even accidental. There was a drowning as well as a near drowning. A man was murdered and the accused, his enslaved man, was lynched by a mob. She witnessed the lynching.

Serepta saw the brilliant Donati Comet and wrote of the completion of a trans-Atlantic cable. Upon the completion of the L&N Railroad, she took her first trip "on the cars" to Nashville. She wrote of businesses being sold and another opening. Serepta read histories and serious tomes.

Slavery was woven into everyday life and she recorded the births, deaths, and a wedding of enslaved people. Her uncle had given Rep a young girl named Inez and during this period she wrote of her fondly. That fondness would change by 1863 as white Clarksvillians could no longer maintain mastery over the enslaved.

New Providence, Tennessee, November 17, 1857

Tonight, I have commenced copying the portion of my journal that was written before the reception of this book.

New Providence, Tennessee. Thursday night, January 1, 1857

[Blanks in this entry due to water damage]

Rose early before the sun. The ground as yesterday was carpeted over with snow, very cold. The morning passed very pleasantly. My Auntie[1] was in a talking mood. Several friends to dine with us, three young gentlemen from the country together with an old acquaintance from Ky. Everything passed off very well excepting the dinner, and that did very well as far as it went, after which it didn't do quite so well. They were most too late to have their names handed over to the cook; however, I made the best of it. They left soon after dinner very well contented with their hospitable reception and fine repast. A friend sent for me to spend the afternoon with her. I reluctantly consented; walking was very unpleasant. I enjoyed the visit of course, but no conversation occurred worth notice. Her daughter Mattie Riggs[2] came home with me. We had fine fun snow balling until a few moments prior to supper during which time we prepared ourselves for the table. Nothing more usual was set before us though we enjoyed our biscuit and coffee very much [Mattie and] I are always contented in each other's society, (at least generally so) we read awhile — no conversation of interest taking place. An old box of magazines were brought out as much for {*indecipherable*} as amusement of my friend [before we] had examined the contents they were replaced in the box. A chapter is read and we are ready for bed, or resting {*indecipherable*}. Nature sweet restorer brings sleep.

Went to school to Mrs. Hendrick's[3] (at Clarksville) in the spring of 1853.

New Providence, Tennessee, Wednesday night, January 7, 1857

Breakfast was usual. Made an engagement with Miss Lou Peterson[4] to go down to Mrs. Howard's this morning. From some cause she was detained until it was late. Left about 10, there in time for dinner. Disagreeable ride, cold and very muddy. Found Jane (Mr. H's daughter) much better. Her cough almost entirely cured. Pigeon pie for dinner. Mrs. Meacham[5] supped with us, more cheerful than usual. Her brother came about 3 o'clock to spend a few hours with us. The negro insurrection[6] and Miss Milly Beaumant[7] were the two topics of conversation.

New Providence, Tennessee, Sunday night, January 11, 1857

Ready for prayers. Breakfast rather early for Sunday morning. John sat awhile at breakfast. I enjoyed his company very much. After he left I prepared for church. Afterwards, I was alone for a while. Aunt T to sleep and Uncle T to the Fairfaxes.[8] I read awhile and talked to Inez[9] awhile & combed my hair. After supper Uncle Trice went with me over to see Mrs. Jackson (at Fairfaxes). Spent but a few minutes when I was sent for. Mr. G. Trice[10] & Dr. Alsup[11] had called to see me. They made themselves as interesting as might be expected. Gregory gave a description of his trip from Trice's Landing[12] to Linwood.[13]

New Providence, Tennessee, January 21, 1857

Nothing of interest has occurred. Cousin left soon after breakfast. Jo took her in the buggy, the snow being too deep to walk and still falling very fast. Mr. Buck Neblet[14] and Miss Randolph are married. Wife been dead about 3 months. Sewing all the evening. News came about dark that Uncle Sam, an old negro man of ours, was dead. He was staying at Mrs. Crabtree's.[15] He has been complaining for a long while, has been a faithful servant here and I hope he has gone to a land of rest. Commenced a cap for grandmother.[16]

New Providence, Tennessee, Sunday night, February 1, 1857

Commenced snowing early & continued until about 10, when the sun shone out and soon all the snow disappeared. Read until dinner. 3 visitors considerable fun, with Tam & Emma (servants)—married them by making them jump the broomstick. They left late. Cousin Mollie[17] stayed all night. Mrs. Riggs and the children sit a good while after supper. The children were quite rude.

New Providence, Tennessee, Wednesday night, February 2, 1857

We have again been favored with clear sunshiny day. Mr. Noel[18] left this morning, after selling his negroes, for home. Dinner better than usual. A fine rool[19] made of some peaches presented by Cousin Jane.

New Providence, Tennessee, Thursday night, February 26, 1857

Rose late. Cousin Mildred[20] left soon after breakfast. Aunt T presented me a nice bridle and being anxious to use it, L and I took a ride. Went out to Mrs. Gordon's. Read a letter from Cousin Mat.[21]

At Mr. Yancy's[22] Saturday night, March 14, 1857

Succeeded at last in going to the country. Teased Mr. Hodge until he thought like some of the girls he would send me to get rid of me. He came over early yesterday morning. Told me that my stepfather had heard of my arrival at this place, that he cared nothing about my visiting him and would really prefer my staying away. This he told me with a great deal more, all of which I've since had reason to doubt. After finding that I was determined on going but to see their children I was just as much determined on as I had the opportunity. Very true I've been separated from them for years but the love that was cherished for them years ago when they were prattlers on my mother's knee seemed to revive and grow stronger as the distance between us grew less. For her sake alone if for no other I would have regretted to the day of my death not seeing them. I went and never in my life did I meet with a more cordial reception and never have I seen anyone express more joy in meeting with an old friend.

She[23] is what I've thought she would be from her childhood, symmetrical in form, handsome in the face but more lovely and beautiful in disposition than in form or feature. She is what is called a truly noble and sweet tempered woman. After the meeting a while, Mr. Brashears[24] stepped out and we had a great time in which to talk over old times. She has a gentlemanly and worthy husband (seemingly) to whom she seems devoted except she is a little foolish about him. A lovely little cherub of a babe, the perfect facsimile of herself. She looks to be at home with plenty sense and better than all contented; happiness is hers at least for a while.

The first thing after making Mr. Groves' acquaintance was an inquiry from him whether or not he should send for the children. It was then late and he sent for them to come early in the morning which they did before we were through with breakfast. Pa came with his wife.[25] On account of not having a special invitation, refused to eat. The children seemed delighted to think they had once more seen me. Every countenance expressed joy even to the old smiled and kissed. The father who had been separated for years from an only and idol daughter could not have met her with more affection than he did. The meeting with him however was over in short time. I turned without adding words as quickly as possible knowing his aversion in former years of crying children, but under the circumstances who could have refrained from weeping. How often had I met him before and under what circumstances with mother at this side ever ready to greet me with pleasure? Let him frown with contempt or give a sarcastic smile and fond embrace. Yes that recurring smile and warm embrace which no other than a mother can give. My eyes of course were fast filling with tears as I turned to my seat disappointed and feeling more sensibly than ever that the she was gone never more to meet with daughter or friends in this world of troubles. I however overcame my feelings to some extent in a few moments and entered into the conversation. His conversation was mostly to my appearance in what respect I had changed &c. The children were exceedingly talkative especially the youngest, Ann & Sue. Judson is more quiet but when he does speak it is apt to be to the point, from what I could see he has quite a strength of mind. It does no good to think they are so much attached to me and really know so little about me. They fondled on me and seemed to love me as though we had been reared under the same roof. Pa seemed disappointed that I was not going to visit him and I had almost concluded to go when Mr. Brashears came and said that Mollie intended leaving on the first boat, frightened again about the small pox. I felt disappointed in not going but was gratified and satisfied to think the rants of Mr. H's incorrect. I could scarcely make him believe that I was coming away & not going to see him. I parted with them in all my visiting having passed like a dream in which everything had taken place in a few moments. My tears flowed freely as I felt privileged to weep as much as my feelings called, for never had I seen Pa's when he seemed to be affected. He wept aloud as we shook hands and said Rep, "I want you to come to see me. You do remind me so much of your mother." In referring to her it seemed almost heart rending. Never had I expected to see a tear drop roll down the cheek of such a stern man as John Bennett on my account. May we meet again is my desire. I returned and found the girls gone, left on the Mide about 2. Went over to see Cousin W, found him dying. Been dying since 3 o'clock this morning. When on earth was so sad.

New Providence, Tennessee, Monday night, March 23, 1857

Rose early. Aunt T has been quite ill all day. Uncle Trice went down to grandmother's. Mrs. Gordon & mother spent the day with us. Uncle T returned about dark. As expected brought the sad intelligence of grandmother's death. She breathed her last about dark yesterday evening. It seems wrong to grieve when we think of her sufferings here and of the happiness which we have every reason to hope she is enjoying in the world of the spirits. She reared a large family of children all of whom have gone before her, excepting three, among the dead my mother. Among the living Aunt Tabbie. Oh should she be the next called what would, what could I do? Where find another home? Was there ever a place on earth which could be called home without a mother (that is to a child)? Aunt T be spared to teach and prepare me to face the storms and tempest of life is my greatest desire.

New Providence, Tennessee, Sunday night, June 7, 1857

Unusually warm; no preaching in town. Mattie, the negroes and I went over to the orchard where [we] spent most of the morning. Found some tolerable nice apples. Mrs. Riggs spent the evening with us. John came down and supped and Mr. Harris for the first time since our return. Dr. Alsup sit until bed time.

New Providence, Tennessee, Sunday night, June 14, 1857

Services at both churches. Mr. Nixon[26] at the Baptist; Mr. Fagan[27] at the Methodist. Of course attended my own church. Mr. Nixon's sermon was good but dry text: If any will follow me let him take up his cross &c.[28] Mr. Day[29] preached at the Methodist church at 3. Mr. Nixon baptized some negroes, Horace among the rest. Dick called this evening on his way from Springfield.[30] Went down late to see Inez down at Dr. Herring's.[31] Returned, found Mrs. Gordon and her mother here.[32] She, Mrs. Gordon, being very ill returned home. Mrs. Ogburn remained to attend church. Mr. McDaniel[33] went with us down, Mr. Fagan preached from 1st Chron 28th chap[34]— a good sermon by which he influenced Mrs. Neely[35] at the close to come up and be prayed for.

New Providence, Tennessee, Sunday night, June 28, 1857

Jennie[36] and I went out to Mrs. Gordon's early this morning and from there we all went down to Liberty. Heard Mr. Nichols[37] preach, after which we received several invitations to dinner. We concluded to go down with Sarah. It is useless to say the dinner was excellent. Met with Harriet and Mr. McDaniel. Their difficulty was adjusted. Attended church at Mt. Pleasant[38] at 3. Mr. West [39] preached. About the close a rain came up, but in spite of new bonnets and dresses we all came home. Found John Mallory[40] & Mrs. Herring here! They supped with us (I wish . . . had never been heard of).

New Providence, Tennessee, Saturday night, July 25, 1857

Still very warm, little hope of rain. No company tonight but Mattie. Miss Mary left this evening at 5—rather lonely. We went down this evening to see Mrs. Riggs and her cousin Miss Mockeby[41] from the neighborhood of Antioch.[42] We were treated with some nice lemonade and cakes. Still a prosperous meeting at West Fork[43] but as it seems impossible to get ministerial aid the meeting will close tomorrow. Miss Mary and I went down to see Mrs. Pollard[44] and Miss Speaker this morning. Miss Jennie gave us some fine music. We also went up to the store this morning.

New Providence, Tennessee, Wednesday night, August 12, 1857

Very warm all day, no rain, not much company. Florence Crabtree[45] spent the night with us, Dr. Lindsey[46] spent an hour or two with us this morning, quick as ever, Mrs. Morrison called this evening, very enjoyable indeed. An accident this morning—Mr. Fairfax's horse ran away with the buggy with Miss Dicks[47] and Miss Dirett [sic],[48] slightly injured, the buggy broken and the horse badly crippled. Dawse Ogburn[49] is with us tonight; his health is no better—slight cough, two chills a day, and looks worse than usual. All well at home. Mrs. Atkinson[50] is worse again.

New Providence, Tennessee, Saturday night, August 22, 1857

Rose tolerably early. Went up town for Cousin Julia, soon after breakfast. We were ready as soon as possible to go down to the landing. Cousin Julia has been waiting for a boat a good while but is with us tonight. We spent the day with Mr. Homer. Not even a boat passed up or down. I guess she will leave on the stage for Nashville in the morning. Rather warm again. Mrs. Riggs was up this evening and told Aunt Tabbie about Mrs. Hart and Mr. Hart. They came to see us while we were in Ky. I never regretted anything so much in my life scarcely as I did not being at home. Probably I may never see them again—more than probable. How glad I would have been to have seen little Jo, but alas it seems that I am doomed to disappointment. It would seem to others that I might become hardened, but really I sometimes think I can deal with disappointment, with less patience than ever. News: Dr. Drane[51] bought Mr. John K Smith's[52] residence and factory today. His lots and houses were all put up to the highest bidder this morning.

New Providence, Tennessee, Wednesday night, September 16, 1857

Still very warm, as warm as any day we have had this season. At home all day except a few minutes that passed while I was up at the store. Mr. McDaniel came down to sit a while and I went with him up to purchase a silk. Aunt Tabbie had her teeth worked on this morning, and tonight congratulates herself that she is done with the toothache.[53] Mr. Watts[54] came up awhile tonight. His subject as usual was on religion. Been busy all day sewing, preparing for an anticipated trip to Nashville, not gone yet.

Left home about 4 o'clock in the morning after a very pleasant ride considering the distance. Arrived there about ½ 3 o'clock and found Mr. Noel's family well, Mrs. Sawyer tolerably well. Her youngest son George[55] had been and was at that time very ill, with the fever all over excepting in the face.

Nashville, Tennessee, Monday night, September 21, 1857

Still very cool. The forenoon passed very pleasantly reading and occasionally joining in conversation with Mrs. Noel, Mrs. Sawyer and Mrs. Skipwith,[56] a visitor. The afternoon passed in the same manner until about 5 o'clock when I dressed myself to go with Mrs. Noel and Aunt Tabbie out to the cemetery. Saw a great many fine monuments—marble so exquisitely wrought and finely polished that it was astonishing to think for a moment of once rough and coarse exterior. Mrs. Noel's uncle supped with us, Uncle Trice[57] left for home about 1.

Nashville, Tennessee, Tuesday night, September 22, 1857

Today has been cool, cloudy, dark and generally unpleasant, real gloomy, a slight shower about noon. Mrs. Noel has been sick all day with the headache, so had the weather been pleasant we would not have gone out. George is no better; his disease is typhoid fever,[58] sleepy.

Nashville, Tennessee, Wednesday night, September 23, 1857

Clear but yet cool. Have been out nowhere during the day and consequently nothing of importance to record. Aunt T and Mrs. Noel went out this evening spending. Mrs. Mullins and son[59] called to see [us] after supper, a while found them very pleasant, the Dr. especially. Aunt Tabbie had retired just like her, she was rather flat.

Nashville, Tennessee, Thursday, September 24, 1857

I have spent the day riding round and visiting the public buildings, generally, and of course time has passed more pleasantly than on yesterday and day before. In the first place Mr. Noel took us out to the lunatic asylum about 7 miles from town.[60] Mrs. N, Aunt T and myself saw Dr. Minor, an old acquaintance, who has now been there more than a year. He was tolerably well mentally; physically he was as well as I ever saw him. He was more than delighted to see us, gave us a kiss and almost a hug. We saw a great many lunatics though didn't think to enquire the number. The building is certainly very fine, the situation good and a great variety of rare flowers in the yard and garden. They also have a great many more flowers in the green house which is not yet completed. We were at home by dinner and at the stable by 2 where met with Mr. Noel and made him promise to take us to the penitentiary and capitol.[61] We went out shopping and were back at the stable before he was ready to go with us. We spent an hour at the stables and left for the penitentiary about 4. Went all over the building, saw all the trades going on, and were perfectly willing to leave in about ½ an hour. They have 200 and 92 convicts. A more magnificent building I have never seen than the capitol. I believe it is now the finest house in the United States. From there we rode all over town and were at home by dark. Headache and very much fatigued.

Nashville, Tennessee, Friday, September 25, 1857

Again we have spent the day trotting round. Went over this morning to Edgefield[62] to see Mrs. Carbet, an old acquaintance of Aunt T. She was delighted to see us. Mrs. Noel and I rode all over the village. Saw Dr. Shelby's residence, one of the most splendid I ever saw. Called to see Mrs. Carneal[63] and Mary Harrelson,[64] old acquaintances also; Mary was at school. At home for dinner. In the afternoon went out to the blind asylum.[65] Had a young lady read, perform on the piano, saw her work a sum also. She is perfectly blind, never did see. George is improving.

Nashville, Tennessee, Saturday night, September 26, 1857

Out nowhere during the day. Aunt Tabbie spent the day with Mrs. Johnston;[66] her eldest daughter is to be married Thursday. Mrs. Carneal and Mary Harrelson called to see us this evening. Mrs. Noel was absent. Mary has changed very little. Drs. Mullins and Haskins[67] called tonight, also the Misses Story.[68] They were very affable, agreeable, and entertaining. They remained until about 11 and of course dull and sleepy.

Nashville, Tennessee, Sunday night, September 27, 1857

Indoors all day, Mrs. Noel being very unwell. Uncle Trice and George came about 2. Mrs. Skipwith called, no news.

Nashville, Tennessee, Monday, September 29, 1857

Left Mr. Noel's about 8; arrived here about 11. Today has been very cool. At home all day. Aunt Tabbie went out calling this evening. Mr. McDaniel called tonight. Mr. Whitefield from Memphis also called this evening. Very late, all asleep.

New Providence Tennessee, Saturday night, December 5, 1857

What changes have taken place since this night 1 year ago? About this hour (9 o'clock) exactly 12 months ago I was standing by the death bed of one of my best friends. Since that time how many have passed away just as he did? Doubtless thousands perhaps that were then in all the enjoyment of health and prosperity have paid the last debt and now lie unthought of and uncared for with the dead though it has not been my lot to witness but one or two similar scenes since the one referred to above. Really I have not seen anyone in their last moments though death was so near the door that hope was banished.

One of those was my aged grandmother, and though she was a friend true and steadfast, a parent that studied my interest and my happiness, I could not for a moment when looking on her face and marking "each furrow that had been made by the plowshare of time" think she would be here to counsel, encourage and assist much longer a rising generation. Such a thought was not to be nourished, for a single glance on that aged and care worn face was enough to satisfy the observer that her days were about numbered. Though her last birthday if remembered correctly was in [her] 60th, she had out lived most of her children there being 8 and only 3 living. Three of them died about the same time my mother, who married the second time to John Bennett of Ky. and was living in that state at the time of her death. Aunt Sue, and Mrs. Dycus, died here. Aunt Nancy, Mrs. Anderson, was living in this place, at the time of her death; 2 others died several years ago: Aunt Milly, Mrs. Chisenhall, and Aunt Harriet,[69] never married.

Again according to nature we could give this aged parent up more willingly than a youthful noble and imagined friend. For really an equal was scarcely to be found just commencing in the world with prospects before him bright and unvarying, mental qualities superior in almost every respect, friends on every side, beloved by all who knew him. How could it be possible I say to give up one of this character as the one that has {*endured*} the ill of life and feels that death alone can release them from trouble almost unendurable, that of dependence on the young and careless for assistance, but it is God's will that the young should be taken as well as the old and it is right and though it grieves his friends to give him up we can only think that we too must even go the same way. To use his own language, he only going before us; we will soon follow on. This is indeed a subject that would keep me writing no short length of time but knowing my disposition as I do, I close, expecting soon to have the painful task of recording the deaths of his two younger brothers[70] that are both at this time very near the door of death with the same fatal disease, consumption.[71]

Rainy all day. Cousin Lou[72] is still with us, we have in our imaginations taken several trips tonight. We have enjoyed ourselves finely since supper, taking trips and joking generally. She has, however, granted herself long enough to write a good long letter to her absent brother.[73]

New Providence, Tennessee, Monday night, December 21, 1857

Cloudy but little rain. Lucy Helm[74] spent the day with me and will stay all night. Assisted her about a dress. Mr. Smith from Memphis called this evening, looking better than usual. Miss Lou dined with us, all excitement about the wedding which will be tomorrow night. John Mallory just from Hopkinsville[75] called tonight and made one of his long visits, rather talkative. He has come down to wait on Mr. McDaniel. I will try my first time in the capacity of brides-maid.

New Providence, Tennessee, Thursday morning, December 24, 1857

Tuesday 22nd spent the forenoon at home. Mr. J. McDaniel[76] and lady, Miss McDaniel, and Mr. Smith called and dined with Aunt Tabbie on their way to the wedding. Mr. Leigh[77] according to request accompanied me out to Mr. Barbee's.[78] There by 2 o'clock. All excitement as might be expected. The bridesmaids together with several others were more than elated [a little intoxicated] with the prospect of so much enjoyment with their "sweetness" as he would say. The crowd had collected by 4 o'clock by which time the groom and groomsmen were there. Mr. McDaniel and Miss Sue Barbee were certainly and without doubt married Tuesday evening ½ 4. **December 22nd** by the Rev. S. A. Holland.[79] The ceremony was brief but appropriate. A crowded room of friends and acquaintances were ready to congratulate and wish them unparalleled happiness. In ½ hour supper was commenced, not an unwelcome sound by any means. Mr. McDaniel and lady were in front, Cousin Will Trice and I next, the remaining three couples following. My first attempt in the capacity of bridesmaid. The company was as much composed, bride and groom not excepted, as if seated round the old fireside with only the old folks present.

Wednesday 23rd spent the day at Mr. Barbee's. The groomsmen and most of the company left early after breakfast; however, enough were left to make themselves pleasant. Mr. Hewitt[80] made himself remarkably interesting, introduced a conversation that lasted about 2 hours. The topic was quite different from those that we generally introduced on such occasions, the history of the Israelites. He is a man indeed of fine conversational powers. A short nap after dinner. The groomsmen were there by 5 o'clock. The bridal company consisted of the bride and groom of course, Mr. Will Trice[81] and myself, Mr. John Mallory and Miss Mollie Barbee,[82] Miss Bell Jenkins[83] and Mr. Wilson. The couple remaining could not conveniently attend, Miss {indecipherable} Trice and Will Henry Leigh. Found no one here but Miss Lou Peterson and Miss Lucy Helm. Several came in before supper, really had quite a nice time of it, just enough to be pleasant. Unexpectedly had the pleasure of Hewitt's company again for a few hours. He with most of the gentlemen left rather early. This morning we are entirely alone with the exception of Miss Lou and the bride. Mr. Osborne and Lynes[84] called a few moments Christmas eve, and I'm so glad old Santa Claus is going to bring me so many nice things.

New Providence, Tennessee, Saturday night, January 2, 1858

Agreeable to the request of Lucie Helm and the other young ladies I went down last night and stayed with them, enjoyed ourselves very much, George made himself unusually interesting. Owing to the inclemency of the weather and of streets Aunt T sent down for me. No company during the morning. This evening Dr. Alsup and brother[85] gave us another call, through Aunt T's persuasion they remained until after supper. Really the Dr. made himself more agreeable and pleasant than he has ever done since my acquaintance with him. He left about ½ 9; his brother will remain with us until May. Went to worship tonight, read the 10th Psalm, a very good prayer. Miss Susan A. Boatwright[86] died last night of consumption, rather unexpected though she has been very ill for some time.

New Providence, Tennessee, Tuesday night, February 9, 1858

Rainy and cool, Aunt T and I spent most of the morning at Mrs. Staton's.[87] Met with Mrs. Davis.[88] Time passed pleasantly, not much news. Mrs. Hargrove's babe died on yesterday.[89] A new drug store in town. Mr. Thomas[90] from Clarksville has commenced business at Porter's old stand. Prospects rather unfavorable for Smith & Brother. John Ogburn[91] called a few moments this evening on his way home from school. The scarlet fever[92] having attacked several of the students, Mr. Ross[93] dismissed school for a month.

New Providence, Tennessee, February 10, 1858

Very cold but no ice. George Trice[94] came down this morning quite sick to spend the day. Found such attention that he has concluded to spend the night. Uncle Berry Dycus very unexpectedly called this evening with the two little girls on their way to Nashville. The good lady called but remained in the hack[95] being speechless from excitement and of course not prepared to see a Trice. He is going to Nashville for the purpose of purchasing a boat. From there he expects to return to Texas, his home. The first visit he has given us since the "fracas" when he married last Elsey, the older, is very near grown, favors Aunt Sue considerably. Cassus,[96] the younger, is very pretty—dark hair & still darker eyes, & might almost be considered a brunette.He promised to let them call as they came down from Nashville. Really the children have changed but little until now, they have now been from here about 4 years, that is in personal appearance but who knows the changes that have taken place in their once childlike and sweet dispositions. That unladylike—the word in its full meaning—stepmother has taught them to "frown indifferently" on those who should mention one of this family's names—the ones that had previous to that time been all that father or mother could be—but they have left us. We know but little about them & we will wish them happiness and say no evil, may they [be] prosperous, fortunate & happy through a long life is my desire.

New Providence, Tennessee, Wednesday night, February 17, 1858

Rather pleasant. Great many persons in today attending tobacco. Some excitement, prices considerably raised, over $10. Mrs. Colbashen spent the day up Meacham town.[97] Returned this evening to go to church & from there, home. Mr. Slaughter[98] left the sales, about 1, this evening. Mrs. Atkinson for the first time in several months, Mrs. Lynes and Mollie Crabtree, Mr. Benton from Springfield, an old boarder, greatly improved, very fleshy & fine looking generally, & Mr. William Mallory Junior[99] [came for] a business call. At preaching again tonight, not of any difference, as good a sermon as last night, 10th chap of Acts, so tied with other miracles in olden times.

New Providence, Tennessee, Friday night, February 19, 1858

Very cold, slight snow this morning and invitation from Lucie Helm to stay all night. Declined going as it was so cold. Sad and awful news. Mr. Jo Harris[100] is certainly dead. A negro about ½ 7 o'clock called for Uncle Trice saying that the office in which Mr. H sleeps was seen smoking though not blazing about supper time, and his brother with several of his hands commenced trying to extinguish the flames that had commenced rising within, supposing Mr. Harris, who was lying before the fire, was asleep, but on examining him found his clothes burning and him almost dead, and the only words uttered "boys take me out of here or I shall strangle to death." Uncle Trice, who was at the store, was sent for and left immediately. Since, a negro, one of the hands, has come up and says without a doubt the office had been set on fire in three places and a large hole found in his skull with the brains lying on the floor and from his statement though a negro he was evidently murdered and that in the most barbarous manner. However, Uncle Trice will bring us the particulars.

Oh, how sad. How unfortunate. Young, just commencing a prosperous and flattering life in the business world. The future spread out before him this morning doubtless seemed to him almost unlimited, calculating perhaps the vast amount received for some large quantity of tobacco to be cultivated and brought to Trice Landing many years hence, but alas how sad and how different are the result of such anticipations. Man born of woman is a few days and full of trouble.[101] Mr. Harris came from Virginia last fall a year ago, with the intentions of commencing the tobacco business for a large firm in his native state. Succeeded in preparing a house and everything necessary by this winter, when he {indecipherable} business. Has been ever since prospering finely. Left at home a proud father, devoted mother, several brothers and sisters. He returned last summer to his native state and brought out with him a younger brother as an assistant in business. He was attentive to his business, kind, kind towards humanity generally and generally a boy to be loved and admired. Prior to this sad and memorable night he had found in the West a home of happiness, many true friends to cheer him on his way, but tonight, who can estimate his wretchedness, no mother, no brother, no sister, no nothing but his friends to warm and reconcile his troubled heart. May he prove to be a lesson ere he will be called to pay the last great debt that his brother has who has only gone before for a short while.

New Providence, Tennessee, Saturday night, February 20, 1858

Providence with its few inhabitants has from time to time met with seasons of uproar and excitement. Politics has apparently robbed every citizen of reason while excitement of entirely a different character has found the same result. For instance grand celebration of the different orders Masonic Temperance, etc. But never since my recollection, which has been from the infancy of the village, has the citizens been drawn so near insanity from any excitement whatever the cause. Surely the day just closed is one to be wondered by the aged, to be remembered with sorrow and heartfelt grief by the middle-aged, a day to find a place in the memory of every youth that witnessed the awful scene, a scene that will surpass any of the bold and daring deeds perpetrated by the highway robbers and fearless a demon John A Murrel.[102]

Uncle Trice returned last night giving us the particulars of the murder and death of the noble and unfortunate man. Mr. Harris (Vol)[103] was in the stemmery[104] attending to some business, being about sundown and as usual Mr. Harris had taken his account in the office. He had noticed, Vol had, that William, the negro they brought from Virginia and the villain that murdered the poor man, was missing though thought but little about it. He had missed about ½ an hour when he returned and remained in the stemmery about 10 minutes which brought around supper time and as usual Vol called round at the office for his brother and found to his astonishment the office full of smoke and the bedclothes burning and Mr. Harris before the fire with his face and shoulder almost in the chimney. He, supposing had a fit or something, ran immediately for assistance. The hands, several of them, came and succeeded in taking him to Drane's, the nearest house, while others ran in every direction to spread the news. But it is said that Vol knew nothing of the wound in his head until they had succeeded in laying him down at Drane's. But so soon as the wounds were found and the last hope extinguished, Vol commenced sobbing and mourning most distressingly and had no sooner commenced than this villain much in the same manner if anything worse. He was [being] watch[ed] [by] more than one [because of] the circumstance of Mr. Harris having whipped him the day before and also of keeping him handcuffed and in the office at night the three nights previous. The two wounds were very deep having penetrated the skull up to the eye of the ax. One in the back and one on the left side.

He was immediately arrested on suspicion and taken by the constable to jail, about (9 o'clock), pled innocence of course, but guilt was his countenance. This morning early the citizens being so enraged concluded to go over and take him by force independent of the law and the results of such an undertaking, and bring him as near as possible to the place where he had murdered a just master, and end his life by hanging. Persons from every quarter flocked to see the result. A jury was held which gave in the decision of guilty. He still pleading innocence. Sent for Vol and entreated but all to no use. (I and Aunt T spent most of the day at Mr. Helms' where we could see everything as it happened.) They let him swing for a few minutes when he said he would make a confession. He accordingly did so acknowledging that he gave him two or three licks. He didn't remember exactly how many and that he had hid the ax under the house where George Helm had found it and when questioned as to the sense. It is sad he said because Mas Jo whipped me so much and treated me so badly, told where he was setting and what he was doing, reading I believe, but that after he had done this threw some coals on the bed and made an attempt to set fire in two places the blaze which caused it to gape considerably. So as soon as the confession was made (however, they inquired if any other was engaged when he immediately exclaimed yes naming a certain negro belonging to the Davis estate, but the fact of his not bringing in this negro's name though he was absent at the same time of himself convinced the people there was not truth in it) but no sooner than the confession was made the whole crowd together with those who had previously advocated the sense of letting the law take its course, cried out hang him hang him. Lucie, the smaller children, and I were sufficiently near to see him swing both the first and last time. A sight horrible in the extreme. He died about 12, hung until about 3. The Drs. will dissect him tonight.

The crowd dispersed and Lucie, Aunt T, Mr. Helm & myself on our way home went as near as the factory to see him. Aunt Tabbie went down this morning to see Vol and as expected found him grieved almost to insanity. He has little doubt the shock will end the life of his doting parents. He will be buried in Clarksville for a while. His funeral preached at the Episcopal church tomorrow at ½ 2 o'clock by Dr. Ridley.[105] The excitement has subsided with the mess but who knows the feeling of that brother and those aged parents? Have they heard? A telegraphic dispatch was sent immediately. O had that poor man prepared for such a sudden change: But Alas we have no hope of his exchange being for the better though a fine citizen, a worthy man in every other respect. He was a sinner. Religion was his last thought, respect for the house of God ever his limit. Had we the least hope how much better would it be to give him up?

New Providence, Tennessee, Thursday night, February 25, 1858

Much warmer & clear. Mrs. Riggs sent for us early this morning to attend the wedding of a runaway couple from Christian Co., Ky.[106] Names forgotten. Owing to the dampness of the streets Aunt T declined going, found the bride dressed and looking like a snow flake ready to jump into that most awful and untried state of existence, hurriedly worked up the white brilliantine[107] and substituted a calico and left for old Ky. Through much persuasion concluded to dine with Mrs. R when she and Mattie came up home with me to see William's lungs, Dr. Alsup having sent them previous to my going down. They remained but a few moments. After this visit, I went over to see Mrs. Staton, first visit since her removal. Delighted with housekeeping as a matter of course. Called also to see Mrs. Pollard a while, alone eating bread and cheese. Supper as usual, after which, Drs. Smith[108] and Alsup inflated those lungs and gave us a brief but adequate explanation of the different cells, ventricles of the heart with which they were connected, etc. Considerably edified. After they left, spent several hours reading the Post. Considerable excitement to the atrocious attempt on the life of the Emperor and Empress, by some villains on the 14th of Jan found to be Italians,[109] also some relative to the recent royal marriage Prince of Russia & Victoria's[110] daughter, a notice of the calculating machines, invented by Babbage of England[111] and improved recently by Thomas,[112] until it seems to have arrived at that state of perfection that none of the other various inventors can claim.

New Providence, Tennessee, Wednesday night, March 3, 1858

Another sad death — Esq. Nace Trice.[113] We were awakened last night about 10 by one of the servants who informed us that a negro was in the kitchen who had brought the news that Uncle Nace was certainly dead, Uncle Trice & Aunt T went over immediately, leaving Lucie and I alone, not a little uneasy. He has been having chills for several months. Some friend advised him to take silk weed bitters,[114] which he did immediately but instead of proving beneficial in the least they made him very ill, the spell lasting several days. He, having recovered from that spell, but continued to have the chills and through mistake he swallowed another very large dose, the bottle carelessly having been placed near another bottle of bitters on the same mantle. It was thought until late yesterday evening that he was improving, the only change then being an unpleasant feeling of the stomach, but although he seemed to be more restless than usual, none thought him dangerous. Consequently his death was very sudden. His wife had raised up for some purpose and without the least warning [he] fell dead in the floor. Assistance was called and he breathed but few minutes after adjusting him on the bed. He has left a large and deeply grieving family, a wife, 2 boys, 5 girls, 3 of whom are widows. Lucie and I spent the day there. Funeral to be preached tomorrow, buried by the masons. Cousin Willie Trice[115] from Hopkinsville & Mr. Slaughter called this evening.

New Providence, Tennessee, Wednesday night, March 10, 1858

Still very warm. Spent the forenoon at Mr. Helm's. Met with two ladies late from Hopkinsville, Mrs. {*Colmise*} & Coalman [*sic*]. Considerable excitement relative to Esq. Trice's will, the partiality exhibited in favor of his last wife and children. After having received almost all of his property, both real estate & servants, by his former wives, only left Mrs. Crabtree 100, Mrs. Lynes 100, Mrs. Osborne 500, & Bettie Homer,[116] his granddaughter, 500, the most of this having been left them by their grandfather. It was certainly very unjust from beginning to end.[117] We went up town with Harriet again this evening. Dick called a few moments. Made some very nice candy tonight. Considerable fun with Harriet.

New Providence, Tennessee, Tuesday night, March 16, 1858

Went according to promise to have my teeth extracted, succeeded in the first two attempts but failed in the third. He left town this morning but will return in a week or two and complete the job. Sarah has come at last and [the] mean thing now only to spend a day or two, but this short visit then none at all, which will soon be my lot. Oh how sad to think of. I wish she'd never seen him. Mr. Slaughter & Mr. Bennett came this evening. Went over to town and brought Mr. Duncan,[118] the pastor of the Clarksville church, back with them. Mr. Bennett preached tonight, and a most excellent sermon it was, they say, though Sarah and I have no right to judge, text 1st Chap of Matthew 21st verse.[119]

New Providence, Tennessee, Friday night, March 19, 1858

Raining slowly all day, but clear & pleasant tonight. No company. Borrowed of Dr. Alsup Abbots' history of Bonaparte.[120] Commenced reading it this evening. The citizens had a meeting tonight for the purpose of electing officers for the city. No other news.

New Providence, Tennessee, Wednesday night, March 24, 1858

Considerable excitement down at the tobacco sales. Prices still favorable. As many [as] 100 and 25 hhds.[121] sold today. Mr. Slaughter & Uncle John Mallory[122] called this evening. Went up to Porters and Riggins this evening & purchased for myself quite a nice bonnet. Mrs. Stevens called a few moments on her way to the "sunny South."

New Providence, Tennessee, Wednesday night, April 7, 1858

Mr. Griffey, lady, & Miss Georgia left about ½ 12. Mrs. Herring & sisters spent the day with us. If anything, more interesting than at first—Mrs. Crabtree & Lynes were here this morning. An effort was made yesterday for breaking Esq. Trice's will. It is thought extremely doubtful about the older children receiving their portion.

New Providence, Tennessee, Friday night, April 9, 1858

Warm enough to be pleasant. Can almost see the buds unfolding, vegetation is growing so rapidly. A letter from Cousin Mat today. Miss Eliza Trice[123] called this morning. Mrs. Staton spent the day and of course, the carpet is ready for tacking down; needles for once have been busier than tongues. Idleness seems to have taken her flight from Aspen Cottage[124] during the day, and Industry for once taken her place. Her visits are fun and for that reason we hope she will remain until the Spring season is over at any rate. V. W. Smith[125] supped with us and seems to be rather "down [in] the mouth."

New Providence, Tennessee, Thursday night, April 22, 1858

Clear and exceedingly pleasant at last. Miss Annis Buck[126] and Lucie passed most of the evening, with me yesterday evening. Went down to the pond late to spend a few hours fishing. Poor success. Dr. Alsup being the only one & he's to be married, Madame Rumor, says the 4th of next month.[127] Miss Mildred Ray[128] and Mrs. Staton called a few moments yesterday morning. A nice present yesterday morning of some nice books by Aunt Tabbie, Plutarch's Lives,[129] McCauley's History of England,[130] Rollin's Ancient History.[131] Stayed all night with the young ladies, an interesting time as usual playing command concert, wig wag,[132] etc. etc. Spent most of the forenoon with Mrs. Pollard, dined at home, went up town, selected me a new gingham dress. Dr. Alsup left for home this morning, will be absent for some time. Uncle Trice is also absent, will return however in a day or two.

New Providence, Tennessee, Monday night, May 3, 1858

Cloudy & considerable rain during the day. No company. Mended one or two old dresses in the morning & read Bonaparte in the evening. Aunt Tabbie went down to see Mrs. Rogers & Pirtle.[133] Uncle Trice purchased a new buggy today. Not at home yet

New Providence, Tennessee, Tuesday night, May 4, 1858

Mrs. Kelly, an old school teacher of mine, on her way to New York called at the hotel and sent for me to go down & see her this morning. Went of course, spent most of the day. Found a Mrs. Dirret there who will accompany her as far as Cincinnati on her way to Virginia. She seems to be sweet, amiable & very agreeable though a little reserved in her manners. Fell very much in love with her. Left for the hotel late with the promise that we should go down to the landing & sit with her a while tonight. We went all very busy. Mr. Homer, quarreling as usual. Left the company there & very much discouraged as the prospects for a boat before morning were rather dull. Mrs. Kelly seemed to be herself entirely but very little change excepting a new ruche in her bonnet. Attended her school in '54 if I remember correctly.

New Providence, Tennessee, Monday night, May 10, 1858

Several heavy showers and a wind storm during the day. No company. The excitement relative Dr. Alsup's & Mr. Scudder's fight Saturday morning seems to have (to some extent) at least subsided. The Dr's face is considerably scratched though not as badly as Mr. Scudder's. The fight if I mistake not was caused by Scudder's repeating some remarks relative to Eliza Trice, that were made while the Dr. & he were on terms of friendship. Several of his friends have deserted him while a few have adhered if possible the more firmly. There has been considerable uneasiness manifested on Miss Eliza's part, so much so that some have gone so far as to think she will probably discard him. General opinion is that he'll be the first to withdraw affections at least.

New Providence, Tennessee, Friday night, May 14, 1858

Tuesday 11th—Spent most of the day at home. Went fishing with Janie & Gertie Helm[134] late in the evening. They supped with us, after which went with them down home & stayed until next day. **Wednesday 12th**—Lucie, Mr. Helm & I went down to Red River fishing. Only one fish caught. Lucie spent most of the evening with me. Mrs. Riggs came up after supper. Sit an hour or two & took me home with her. **Thursday 13th**—She and I went out to the Dennis farm of which Mr. Riggs has the management. Spent the morning there until after dinner which was very nice, having some fried chicken for the first time & some nice potato custards. From there over to old Mr. Len Johnston's to see his daughters Bettie & Jane. My first visit. Met an exceedingly kind & hospitable family. Made a very narrow escape of our lives, the creek being very high & muddy. Both traces broke, besides being almost washed in a deep hole that the driver knew nothing of. We were all very much frightened & not without a cause. But a few steps farther down the stream and our lives probably would have been lost. When I think of the many hairbreadth escapes that I made during short but eventful life, I feel indeed astonished to think of the preserving care the All Wise has continued to exert over me not withstanding my many wicked & sinful ways. Spent the night with Dr. Pirtle's family, our first visit since their removal to the country. Found them all well & cheerful, the children sweet as ever and the old folks better than ever if possible. **Friday 14th**—Spent most of the day over at the farm, at least down on the creek. Bennie and I did fishing, caught some very nice little silver sides & perch. Aunt Prissy gave us another nice dinner. Returned by Mrs. Pirtle. Spent but a few moments during which time we enjoyed some excellent strawberries & cake. Left for home about 5. Made time & no more. All well. Sad accident happened. Sarah [Mrs. Spence],[135] she & her father-in-law left Nashville Tuesday for Palmyra[136] on the steamer Huntsville.[137] She sank that night a short distance above the said place. Destroyed some lives, injured others & lost a considerable amount of baggage, freight, etc. Sarah by a miracle almost was saved from what I learned of Aunt G who received her news from her husband. She was endeavoring to go ashore by a stage plank that was thrown out and, losing her hold or being pushed off by the hurrying crowd, she fell & sank two or three times, and had it not been for Mr. Spence who swam in for her, but a few moments more, her existence would have been ended. He caught by her clothes, swam some distance before reaching the shore, and in the attempt her dressing caught in some brush. The only way he could extract her was by clinching a limb with his teeth. I shudder to think of my escape but what must be her feelings as she thinks of being thrown out in the broad Cumberland with no idea of swimming dark as ebony (11 o'clock) and no one to look to for assistance but an aged father-in-law. In attempting to save Sarah's life he made a very narrow escape of his own, a trial of his affections in the environment. How sweet to think of him as a future father.

New Providence, Tennessee, Thursday night, May 27, 1858

Aunt Tabbie & Sarah spent the morning in Clarksville. Sarah purchased a very pretty $12 bonnet with several other nice articles of dress. She left for home about 3 o'clock. Mr. Slaughter came this evening, will remain with us until tomorrow. Mrs. Herring & sister called a few moments this evening. Mrs. William Young[138] died on yesterday evening, an acquaintance of mine left two little children and husband to mourn her death. Mr. Clark, a gentleman who was expected to lecture tonight on music, failed to come. Some misunderstanding relative to the churches in which he was to lecture. A large crowd was assembled consisting of all the beauty and intelligence of our fast growing town. Dr. Morrison,[139] the Misses Donaldson[140] & one or two others gave us some excellent voice music with which Mr. Slaughter was delighted. Wishes me to go home with him tomorrow but it is doubtful as my dresses are yet unmade.

New Providence, Tennessee, Saturday night, June 12, 1858

Left home Friday 4th for Trenton, Ky.[141] Arrived at Mr. Waller's[142] by 10 o'clock. Found all well and glad to see us. **Saturday 5th** — Very busy assisting Cousin Alley about her dress though a visit from Cousin Sarah Smith called for our time a few hours. Dined with her. **Sunday 6th** — Slept most of the morning. Early dinner and all of us (Cousin Alley and Baily,) were at Mr. Slaughter's, Pembroke,[143] by 4 o'clock. Met with Miss Rollins. Cousin Ann[144] very ill with a headache. Mr. Bennett called to see us. **Monday 7th** — Read a little in the morning. Dined heartily, and unexpectedly in the evening visited, in company with Mollie Slaughter, Mr. Slaughter, and Mr. Williams, Downer's garden,[145] a flower garden of some notoriety about 5 miles from Pembroke, and one that I have been very anxious to visit for several years. As usual a little disappointed, expected too much. Mr. Williams, good fellow, purchased Mollie and I a very fine bouquet each, selected the flowers for Hellen (Mr. Slaughter's 2nd daughter) wreath to graduate in. **Tuesday 8th** — Left rather early for Hopkinsville. Our company consisted of Mr. Slaughter's family, Cousin Alley and Mr. Bennett. The object for visiting the city was to see Aunt Zelpha Trice[146] and attend Mr. Buster's examination. Aunt Zelpha was apparently happy to see us notwithstanding the number of our crowd. Dined with her. Went up to the academy about 2. Spent most of the evening. Heard one or two Chaps examined and met with several old schoolmates and acquaintances which afforded me much pleasure. **Wednesday 9th** — Spent the morning in the schoolroom, dined with Cousin Steve Trice,[147] and a better dinner I never ate at Mrs. Riggs'. Supped again with Aunt Zelpha. Shower late in the evening. Mollie, a gentleman, Dr. Drake,[148] Mr. Slaughter and myself went out to the lunatic asylum[149] about 2 miles from town. After supper went up to the church to see the diplomas given. The graduates were 6 in number, Miss Usher, two Misses Boatwright, Miss Bibb, Miss Hellen Slaughter, and Miss Fannie Holland. Heard some fine music and saw more pretty girls than was necessary. House was crowded. Hellen read the valedictory and did with the other young la-dies exceedingly well. **Thursday 10th**—Dr. Winstone[150] of Nashville de-livered at the Baptist church an address to the pupils of the school to those particularly who graduated the night before. The address was very fine. Left for home early after dinner, or rather Pembroke. Called by the asylum through the request of Cousin Ann, Aunt T, and one or two others. Through many showers and difficulties, we arrived safely in Pembroke about 8 o'clock leaving Cousin Ann behind as she returned to her mother's from the bridge on account of a severe attack of neuralgia.[151] Dr. Drake was our guide. **Friday 11th**—Mr. S and I at home early. Dr. Drake spent the day and night again, giving his whole attention to Miss Mollie, [a wedding before long].[152] Quite sick all night. **Saturday 12th**—Left Pembroke for Trenton about 8. Met Uncle Trice coming for us. Dined with Cousin Alley and through the many dangers that accompany a bad road arrived safely at home about dark.

New Providence, Tennessee, Thursday night, June 17, 1858

The last of the wedding left early this morning. None of the groomsmen & maids accompanied them excepting his brother, and his brother I think, un-like his last departure, left with all of his possessions. His {*indecipherable*} were not left this time wandering about "as if in search of something, some-thing they knew not what." He's so funny. A new visitor arrived this morning just about 8, a young lady by the name of Riggins. Mr. McDaniel, a boarder of Mr. Riggins, left home on the strength of it and both breakfasted and dined at his old home, i.e., that is here. There must be something very pe-culiar in her person debut or appearance that boarders should have to leave. The first baby, what joy, what fears, what excitement. Aunt T gave her a call this evening. She thinks her rather pretty having more favor of Alice than Cousin Tom,[153] very small round face, large eyes of a beautiful blue, and dark hair. Cousin Jane Crabtree & Marion Osborne[154] spent the day with us. The wedding of course was the principal topic. Our trip to Dycusburg[155] the next.

Mrs. Pat Riggins and her stepmother Mrs. Cherry called this evening. Made Uncle Trice two bosoms today and sauce for dinner, but very little was said about it. A fashionable lady, for 58, commenced at her head, hair pasted as tight as bees-wax close to her forehead, large braids on each side, bonnet a "rich profusion" of lace and flowers large enough only to cover the twist and a comb with teeth at both ends to hold it on with. Drapes, five points, 2 before 1 on each hip and 1 behind with neck low and cape, skirt very full, and long, hoops very extensive and expensive and expansive just as you please large or small, from 10 to 30 or 40 feet in circumference, shoes slipper style with heels sufficient to elevate you about well from 1 to 3 inches and above that considerably should one be so fortunate as to have a right nice little foot and some right nice flesh-colored hose.

New Providence, Wednesday night, June 23, 1858

Still very warm, no company excepting Mattie Riggs few moments this evening. Quite busy all day preparing some presents, for my half brothers and sisters living in Livingston Co., Ky. Went down home with Mattie. Passed only an hour or two. Mr. Gemmie Rogers[156] seems to be giving Mattie particular attention about this time. Dr. Cabiness[157] supped with us. Intend leaving for Dycusburg tomorrow if nothing prevents—Cousin Jane Crabtree, Mr. Homer, Aunt Tabbie and myself.

New Providence, Tennessee, Friday evening, July 2, 1858

Another trip to the city of Dycusburg, & Fredonia[158] has once more been made. We left Trice's Landing about 10 o'clock **Thursday 24**—Arrived at Cousin Julia's about ½ 11. **Friday 25**—Mr. Homer made himself quite useful as well as ornamental. Found him better suited for a traveling companion than a visitor at home. Cousin Jane, Aunt Tabbie, and Bettie Homer seemed to enjoy themselves finely. The Minatonce[159] though small offered every accommodation & comfort that could be expected in warm weather and on low water. Saw the wreck of the Huntsville as we passed Palmyra. Found Cousin Julia not so well as when she left here last winter. The children not as bad, but worse than ever, but what else could be expected? Dycusburg being situated immediately on the bank of the river and surrounded on all sides by hills that resemble the rocky mountains more than ordinary hills making it at once about as warm as any of Mississippi's or Louisiana's pent-up hot little villages. While the children are greater in number and worse in every respect than any other town of the same size that I have ever visited. Mr. Homer and Bettie returned that night on board the same steamer. **Saturday 26**—Indoors all day with the exception of an hour or two late in the evening we all went downtown. Dr. Gordon called. **Sunday 27**—Intended going. Cousin Julia and I out to Fredonia. Was disappointed on getting a buggy. Went to Sunday school and was disappointed there. Several pupils but few teachers and no books. **Monday 28th**—Succeeded in getting a buggy and with the good company of Mr. Brashears left for Fredonia about 9. Dined with Mrs. Blue,[160] an old acquaintance of Cousin Julia. Went over to see my old home a few moments. Mr. Donrough is at present residing there. His wife was an old acquaintance & friend. She recognized me immediately although 7 or 8 years have elapsed since we last saw each other. My mother was buried in the garden there but having that little or no attention had been given it within the last year or two I thought perhaps I would feel better to leave and not visit it at all although I know that her spirit is now dwelling in another world, perhaps a world of happiness and joy. It deeply grieves me to think that her remains are there. Her dust at least and not a soul to visit it and drop a tear of sorrow over her solitary grave. Mr. Bennett had her placed there with the promise of bringing her up at some future time and burying her in the family grave yard. He has married since.[161] Separated and with his wife has moved some miles from here and now leaves her grave to the cold and careless negligence of strangers, unmarked I suppose by a single stone. From Mrs. Blue's we went out to Fredonia (the town in which I resided for several years after my mother's second marriage). Conie Byrd and I while there drove out to another place where we lived nearer the town than the one last mentioned. Mrs. Byrd seemed delighted to see me, but Conie more so, we being while at school particular favorites of each other. My sisters were in two miles of where I was, but we hadn't possibly time to stay longer and consequently [were] compelled to return without seeing them at all. Met with but few acquaintances—Mrs. Byrd's family, Mrs. Donrough and Emily being the only ones. I regretted very much that I couldn't remain longer, and would had it not been for the low water. The scenes connected with childhood are always interesting. I could have passed a month or two there without being the least wearied. **Tuesday 29th**—Mrs. Blue according to promise spent the day with us. Dr. Gordon called again. Went up town again. **Wednesday 30**—Had a very hard rain. Looked over all Cousin Julia's old letters and left for home about ½ 11 aboard the same boat. Arrived at Trice's Landing ½ 2. **Thursday 1st July**—Slept until 8. Prepared to quit with George Trice. Out to Mr. Hewitt's examination and Barbecue. Enjoyed myself finely. Heard most of the classes examined and had a very nice dinner. Remained until about 12 o'clock last night, taking supper at Mr. Barbee's and returning to the school room. We had some first rate speeches and dialogues. They all acquitted themselves finely. Mr. Hewitt's speech is not to be overpassed. His subject was science [?] in a closing address to his pupils. **Friday 2nd** Rose very late, John Mallory came about 11 and remained until after dinner on his way from Murfreesboro[162] home. No further news, excepting the death of 2 esteemed members of the Baptist church, Mr. N. B. Whitefield[163] living near this place and Mr. John Pendleton of Christian Co., Ky. They both died during our absence.

New Providence, Tennessee, Wednesday night, July 21, 1858

Spent the morning at Mrs. Smith's & Mrs. Lawton's. Called at the hotel for Mrs. Porter. Met at Mrs. Smith's her mother & sister Nannie. Conversations entertaining & (fast). Topics: Mr. Porter's northern tour curiosities — artificial & natural — the submarine, telegraph, Dion [*sic*], balloons, the perennial crises, etc. So much information. Conversational powers so superior. How fortunate to associate with ladies of such extraordinary mental qualities. John Mallory spent several hours with us. Mrs. Porter supped & sit until ½ 9. Mr. Homer quite ill. Sent him some cordial[164] & {*indecipherable*} & such a nice message in return. Next time he wishes me to send him a piece of my gizzard and a nice little note.

New Providence, Tennessee, Tuesday night, August 24, 1858

For the last three days the weather has been very cool, cool enough for October, some warmer this evening. Made Inez an apron this morning, a little negro girl that Uncle Trice gave me soon after her birth, she is now 5 or 6 years old and a more sprightly child black or white is scarcely to be found. There are but few business houses in private residences within this place but what she is perfectly familiar with and ready at any time to carry a verbal message of most any length. There are but few who though they meet with her daily running up and down the pike that can refrain from expressing wonder at her almost unnatural sprightliness. Her greatest fault is bigotry, having been spoiled by every member of the family. Her wonderful abilities are altogether natural not that she has received any very superior training or attention. Do I speak of her in the above terms but that she merits them and deserves them independent of anything I have said or taught? Spent most of the evening putting up peaches. Went up to see Sue and Alice a while. Alice is quite ill. Called a few moments after supper to see Miss Bell Trabue[165] from Keysburg,[166] Mr. Atkinson's granddaughter.

New Providence, Tennessee, Friday night, September 3, 1858

Aunt Tabbie quite unwell in bed most all day. Dr. Herring came this evening and succeeded in cleansing the boil on her face. Mrs. Herring called a few moments and also Cousin Jane. Once more a letter from my old Sarah. Commenced a novel tonight in The Prize, the hero of the story being Benedict Arnold. His history is all that induces me to read it. Having been out of the practice of novel reading so long I feel at quite a loss to get my imagination to work in the right track.

New Providence, Tennessee, Thursday night, September 9, 1858

Sue McDaniel[167] and I went out to her father's yesterday morning where we spent the morning. Dined. Spending the evening with Mrs. Thos. Barbee. Lucie, Louise, and Mrs. Helm came up last night. I stayed with Lucie. Returned this morning after having made 2 calls, Dr. Herring and Mrs. Riggs. Made a cake this evening in anticipation of some company tomorrow or next day. Went up town with Lucie & looked at Riggins' new goods. Nothing of interest going excepting the Atlantic telegraph celebrations.[168] The bible is at present the subject of the writer, the theme of the orator, and the delight of the poet. As far South as this no celebrations have been given, no eulogies passed through the press excepting speeches from northern papers. Surely it is the wonder of the 19th century and an achievement that will reflect honor and glory on the names of those engaged in its execution.

New Providence, Tennessee, Saturday night, September 18, 1858

As expected Mr. Duncan came over this morning for the purpose of going out to West Fork.[169] Aunt T being still unwell I was compelled to fill her place. Starting rather early we were the first at church. I went down to see a while. Thinking I would remain until service commenced and finding the company very agreeable and the apples still more so, I missed the text entirely and part of the sermon. After repeated solicitations we dined with Mrs. Killebrew, At home in time for Mr. Duncan to walk over to town and a long visit to Mrs. Riggs, Mrs. Comagys, and Miss Lizzie, who has been quite ill for several days. Saw for the first time in my life a comet[170] tonight. Walked almost to Meacham town and the trail was hardly visible then owing I suppose to the "Italian clearness of the sky" and the brilliant moonlight.[171]

New Providence, Tennessee, Monday night, September 20, 1858

First thing this morning Aunt T and I went up to see Fairfax's new goods. His stock is much improved, the hoop skirts particularly. 2 dresses for myself, calico and poplin, and hoop skirt was the extent of our purchases. Peeled peaches until dinner to fill up the remainder of our jars. Afterwards went to Cousin Mat Meacham. Just as I was closing Sue and Alice came, spending 2 or 3 hours. I went home with Alice; Sue with Aunt T to take a ride. I took supper with A and was at home by 8 o'clock. Riggins sold his lots of dry goods today to Ezekiel Wilson & brother (Robert).[172]

New Providence, Tennessee, Monday night, September 27, 1858

Finished first thing this morning Goodrich's history of England.[173] Commenced tonight McCauley's. So far find it rather dull & uninteresting. Cousin Alley and I according to promise went over this morning to spend the day with Cousin Jane but were disappointed as Mrs. Wilson came soon after we left to pay Cousin Alley a visit. We remained with Cousin Jane until after dinner (and an excellent one it was). When we all came over only to spend a few moments with our friend as she left soon after we came. Cousin Jane and I went up late to the store. The extent of my purchases was two pair of shoes, one pair 1 story heels and one pair without any at all. Met with Mr. Homer so completely under the influence of liquor that he couldn't talk as straight as he walked. I never have, as he says, seen him out on such a "bust" before. He almost staggered. Cousin A is quite ill with a chill.

New Providence, Tennessee, Tuesday night, October 5, 1858

Commenced my new calico yesterday. Aunt T and I together very nearly finished this evening. Sit up last night with Lizzie Riggs. She is still very low. Miss Ellen Pettus[174] & Mrs. Staton sit with me. Miss P was "well"-ing and using a number of other bywords altogether characteristic of the company she is most frequently seen with. She even expressed surprise last night by calling the name of Jehovah. What can a young lady's object & what her expectation when, after making use of bywords after bywords, she goes so far as even to take the name of the Lord in vain? Surely self-respect & a proper regard for the refined and intelligent of this {*indecipherable*} time have forsaken them. Efe [175]came tonight and paid me one of his long & most annoying visits. "The Comet now blazing through the heavens and visible in the north-west for two hours after sundown, begins to look vicious. It increases its size and brilliancy nightly, and is evidently swelling with indignation over our article about him last week. It presents a beautiful appearance and is observed nightly by multitudes of both the curious and the timid." (copied from the Jeffersonian[176]) This is the first comet I have ever seen though several have appeared within my recollection. I have brought over my old astronomy tonight to learn something more of their nature and disposition. Almost forgotten, Mr. Wilson & I attended another of those very interesting weddings last night, a runaway match from Ky. There were several at Mr. Jenkins' about 7 o'clock. A droller set is rarely to be seen. The bride was anxious to return home last night although she had bid all the night previous. She wanted to avoid the sun & hot lanes. Some of our, I'm sorry to say, citizens charivaried[177] them last night. They did, I think, exceedingly wrong not only treating the couple disrespectfully but the family.

New Providence, Tennessee, Sunday night, October 31, 1858

After an absence of 2 weeks, which seems more like two months to me, I find myself again seated around the ever pleasant fireside of home and I'm happy to say in the full enjoyment of all its charms. Time has not dragged heavily for even a moment without some enjoyment.

Verbatim: That my visit seemed long but the unusual length of which compared with any visits for the last 5 or 6 years. The first visit that I have made of any length since my trip to Memphis last Spring a year ago. Well Aunt Tabbie keeps talking so I scarcely know what I'm writing. Such a short wedding that she's attended, another runaway match. Uncle Trice and I left Trenton about 1 o'clock and were home by sunset. Met with Lucie. Aunt Tabbie and all the boarders in fine spirits and apparently glad to see us. How I do like to find that they were all anxious to see me. More fun. My visit the first week was bustle and excitement all the time. As expected Cousin Alley and I attended the fair. Our first trip not as much into {indecipherable} as I expected though very well planned. Went to see the two-headed girls which have created so much excitement recently. They have 2 heads, 4 limbs, but body all in one. They seem to create more interest than the Siamese twins.[178] They are now only {indecipherable} years old, quite handsome, very sprightly and will doubtless make their names in future equal to any men's in this state before close of another year. The last week of my visit I spent with Cousin Alley and being alone much of the time enjoyed myself finely. Solitude I almost conclude sometimes is preferable to excitement. I think I'd better stop writing until I know what I'm about. I've been almost giddy for an hour talking and listening to their talk. Lucie left about 3 hours ago. George came and would have her go. Dr. Trice (John) from Mo.[179] has arrived and spent most of the afternoon with Aunt T yesterday. Mr. Riggs has gone. Staton has moved. Boatwrights have moved. A letter from Cousin Julia and the arrival of D. T. Porter[180] & Dave Smith is about all the news. I permitted Cousin Alley to copy my journal at the close of the week and send to her but I've come to the conclusion that a blank check enveloped and sent {c/o}[181]would benefit and interest her about as much as what I've written tonight. I will stop anyway.

New Providence, Tennessee, Thursday night, December 2, 1858

Efe has just left. His visit it is true was short, but unusually annoying especially with Aunt T as she is very much complaining and anxious to retire. The weather is considerably warmer much to the annoyance of the hog killers.[182] I don't remember of ever seeing more hogs pass during a day than have today. Mr. Holland brought his down this morning. He gave us a short call.

New Providence, Tennessee, Saturday night, December 4, 1858

The rain and warm weather still continue. At work all day. Dr. Pirtle dined
with us. Being a preacher makes but little change with him. He is the same
plain unassuming and good Dr. Pirtle. Aunt T is sick from a chill today. The
family consequently is in an uproar. Who knows what yet may be my end? I
wish Aunt T would never be sick.

New Providence, Tennessee, Wednesday night, December 15, 1858

The weather is much cooler. Never was so fatigued from sewing in my life
than tonight. Commenced Aunt Tabbie's dress this morning. And have
given myself no rest excepting a few moments that Mrs. Herring, Miss Sallie
& Johnnie were here. They had been uptown to purchase their Christmas
presents. They are the only ones I know of who seem to be making any to
do whatever about Christmas. Among the articles they called for uptown
this evening (so Jo says) was an elongated perforated convex comb. Visitors
frequently tease our clerks. The Misses Wilson seem to take a great delight
in it. They went up to the Drug store not long since and enquired of Mr.
Smith[183] for some stationery. He rather hesitatingly told them he thought it
doubtful about finding any in the city. Will Trice says he told them 3 or 4
times this evening before they had finished the comb question that he hadn't
the article in the house.

New Providence, Tennessee, Wednesday night, December 22, 1858

I have been so interested for the last three or four hours in Irving's sketches[184]
that in looking round I find myself without company, without fire, and with
but very [little] inclination to retire. For certainly if anything would tempt
me to pass a night without sleep it would be a production of this far famed
author. His ideas seem to be purer, his language more beautiful, and his
illustrations more applicable than those of any other American author. His
style altogether pleases me [more] than anything I have met with since reading Abbott's history of Napoleon.[185] How many would laugh at this the idea
of Abbot surpassing W. Irving in style of writing. I acknowledge it may be
ignorance or want of taste in me but I will say that nothing I have ever read
has so completely withdrawn my attention from everything else as this history of Abbott's. Abbott's style of writing is truly simple and even childlike
at times, but I find that one gains more real, useful, and important historical
information from one of his biographies than is sometimes gained from a
complete history of a nation or people.

I neglected yesterday to notice the marriages of two old widowers or rather a young and an old one. Messrs. Bones & Smith. By referring to the time of Mrs. Smith's death, I found that she will have been dead exactly three months on Christmas day. What can he be thinking of? He married the Widow Hopkins of Ky. yesterday. The day before Mr. Bones without a doubt was married to the Widow Moore of the same state. Sammie Ogburn,[186] Lucie Helm and the Misses Wilson have been to see us today. How late it's getting and I'm here writing away as if tomorrow was a week off.

New Providence, Tennessee, Friday night, December 24, 1858

Christmas Eve. I have just returned from the parlor where I had quite a pleasant meeting with old Santa Claus. He has made great preparations for the children or rather every servant on the place, both old and young, even to Horace, a negro man 25 or 30 years old hung up his basket. I left soon after hanging mine fearing my company would be considered an intrusion. I'm so afraid my presents will be on the funny order. Sam sit a good while with us this morning and called again this evening long enough to take one or two good smokes and divide some nice oranges which he had brought the children. Went down this morning to see Mrs. Comagys. Found her quite ill, suffering intensely with the headache. The society met here again tonight. Irving's sketches of Christmas holidays, the old customs kept up by the English during these days, the way of passing Christmas was of what each repast consisted of, if certain rules were to be observed, & was read. A ticket through the kindness of Mr. Hewitt was presented me this evening to a party to be given at Mr. Allen's.

New Providence, Tennessee, Saturday night, December 25, 1858

Christmas night. Lucie and I have had such a nice time for the last three or four hours. We have kept up an uninterrupted conversation just by ourselves ever since supper. I dined with her and spent the afternoon with Misses Sallie & Johnnie and Miss Brim, a niece of Mrs. Morrison, who will spend the winter in our town. We were highly entertained with some music on the melodeon.[187] Christmas began in the right spirit last night we had one of the finest serenades (I ever saw). So fine that Aunt T had to awaken me. The boys seem to have wasted all the turpentine in the country in making balls.[188] Kris Kringle disappointed me somewhat this morning though agreeably. His presents were nicer and the number greater than I expected. The work box was exceedingly nice, the soap dish just what I needed, and the toy tumblers very acceptable. Old Kris seems to anticipate in every instance my wishes. During the day we have received some very handsome presents indeed. Ogburn sent us some excellent cakes and Miss Sallie & Johnnie some "sposations" [sic] hicrenuts [sic] dressed with eyes and mouths painted so as to represent the human form. Some of them were very expressive. Mrs. Riggins presented us with some very nice little tricks too. Oh, I could write for a week about things that have occurred today, but I know Lucie's getting impatient. I hope she's gotten my place right warm.

New Providence, Tennessee, Friday night, January 21, 1859

Finished this evening my slippers. Like them very much. Mr. Holland left for home about 2. Jo Staton called this morning. Leaves for Nashville Sunday. Clarksville's too small a place for him. Mr. Pardue, Mr. Mc{*Lerdand*}, & Sam are with us tonight. Sam and I went down to hear Pro Palmer lecture on Threnology.[189] His subject tonight was the different temperaments, Lymphatic, Nervous, Bilious, Sanguine. He will, if nothing prevents, give a series of lectures.

New Providence, Tennessee, Saturday night, January 29, 1859

The weather continues beautiful. Mrs. Comagys called about the same time as on yesterday morning. She had us up to the Ambrotype[190] gallery. Left home about 3 for the purpose of returning Sallie Cowherd's[191] visit. On my way down stepped in a few minutes to see Mrs. Staton & Comagys. From thence to Mr. Pettus'. Ellen and Sallie both absent. From thence I went to Mr. Helm's for the purpose of getting Lucie'[s] company & calling on Misses Sallie and Johnnie. Lucie & Mrs. Helm were both absent and heard that Misses S and J were from home. So Bettie and I went up to Mr. Bise's, where we found Lucie. My first call on Mrs. Bise. Like her tolerably.

New Providence, Tennessee, Tuesday night, February 1, 1859

Not a letter or even a paper from the office today up town this morning. By times didn't know but I might have the pleasure of awakening some of the clerks from a sweet slumber. Succeeded in getting up a check to send for Godey's Lady's Book.[192] Gave Sue & Alice a passing call. Sue looks—not exactly symmetrical. Misses Wilson called again only for a few minutes. Mrs. Alsup passed several hours with us this afternoon, nothing new or interesting. Strange that I should forget to say something of the oyster supper given us by Uncle Trice tonight. I enjoyed, as Mr. W would say, much.

New Providence, Tennessee, Saturday night, February 5, 1859

Jennie left early yesterday morning. Went with her up as far as the gallery. No company until late when Mrs. Helm & Lucie called in. Bettie Homer came home with me and remained until late this evening. Aunt T and Bud Trice[193] went down to Mr. Bingham Trice[194] poor fellow his sickness as expected for some time [*missing word*] in death, he was buried about 3 this evening. The boys both John & George came in time to spend several days with him. But news of a different character. Sam Ogburn called this evening, and to think, I can scarcely realize it, in a few weeks more he will have paid us his last visit without being hurried and in a (fidget) to get home. He tells me that on the 24th of this month he leads forth a lovely & timid bride[195] to the hymenal altar.[196] The whole secret was revealed. He seemed I thought to be all and all as though it would to some extent afford relief to say the truth. Sam looks a little like (I wish it wasn't so near at hand). Poor fellow. I'm sorry for him. Cousin Lou and Jane Howard called in a few moments this evening on their way to St Louis. Jane has heard that Dr. Vansant thinks he can cure her.

New Providence, Tennessee, Wednesday night, February 9, 1859

I have been copying off my old journal until my hand is almost frozen. The rain last night resulted in a snow of some depth. The heaviest decidedly we've had this winter. It has been thawing very fast all day and of course no company. And if no company not much news. A little too. Uncle Trice brought us a box of sardines this morning and a can of oysters tonight.

New Providence, Tennessee, Friday night, March 11, 1859

Sit up last night to administer medicine last night until 12 o'clock. Horace is still very ill. Dr. Herring and all who have seen him think his case is a very serious one. The pneumonia this winter and spring seems to be more fatal than it has for years. Went up town this evening and the wind blew so hard it almost took my breath to say nothing of my dress and petticoats. But business before modesty always. I was compelled to have some linens to finish my work. Something new. A corn Dr. is in town. He can extract corns without pain but with a good chance of money.[197] Aunt T had two taken out and if she finds entire relief with them she will have the rest extracted.

New Providence, Tennessee, Sunday night, March 13, 1859

Mr. Duncan opened school this morning with 22 scholars 4 or 5 spectators and 2 regular teachers. Drs. Herring & Morrison and Miss Johnnie were both absent. By request of Miss Sally I took charge of Miss Johnnie's class and such a set of young ones I never had to manage before. Jennie Whitefield came down early to attend church. Mr. D preached from the 9th Chap 15th and 16th verses of Acts.[198] We had a disagreeable time returning in the rain and mud. Found Aunt T quite sick with a chill. Horace continues to grow worse. Dr. Haskins came over this evening to consult with Dr. Herring. Mr. Pollard, Mrs. Pollard, Mrs. Herring, and Mr. Alsup all paid us a visit this evening, rather calls on the sick. Mr. A's being a visit, for I was bored with his company nearly all the evening. He preached by request of Mr. Duncan[199] tonight from the 10th Chap 29th verse of Numbers.[200] He doesn't come down very often and I'm glad he doesn't if all his sermons are the same length as the one he preached tonight. Mr. Homer came up this evening. Took supper with us and escorted me down to church tonight.

New Providence, Tennessee, ½ 10 o'clock Monday night, March 14, 1859
Dr. Herring has just left much to Uncle Trice's satisfaction. Though I would have been pleased for him to have remained several hours longer as Uncle T sit up last night, and tonight is my turn in course. He (Dr. H) made himself more interesting than usual telling us of his mischief and real badness while he was studying medicine in Trenton. Dr. Haskins came over again this evening, and though he spoke encouragingly of Horace's case, yet I think he has but little hope of his recovery. Dick Ogburn[201] called to see us a few minutes this evening for the first time in a great while, the 2nd time since he bought out Waller & Co.[202] Death in town today, an old negro of Mr. Burgess.[203]

New Providence, Tennessee, Tuesday night, March 15, 1859
Rather cool clear and windy. Prospects fine for a heavy frost "and then" the fruit is gone. Sewing all day. Took time to make a potato pie for dinner which the boys said was very nice. Mrs. Gold[204] spent several hours with us this evening. Went up home with her and sit until dark getting monstrous thick. Dr. Johnson[205] came in Dr. Haskins' place to see Horace. He is some better than he was yesterday. Mrs. Helm, George, Lucie, and Walt sit with us until 9 tonight. They all seem to be in fine spirits.

New Providence, Tennessee, Wednesday night, March 23, 1859
The weather is warm and spring-like. At home yesterday with the exception of a few minutes up town. Spent most the evening assisting Mrs. Pollard about a braid. Lucie came in but didn't offer a helping hand. Very busy until

supper and then didn't finish it. Messrs. Slaughter and Jameson[206] passed the night with us. Mr. Homer sit a while. Suffering with the toothache too much to write. Mrs. Herring, Uncle William Mallory,[207] and Dr. Pirtle called to see us today. Uncle William seemed a little dissatisfied about his tobacco, the highest price being 7.25 while others brought 9.40. Went up after finishing Mrs. Staton's tatting[208] to see Mrs. Gold a few minutes. Went down to the pond fishing. Bites were numerous but no fish.

New Providence, Tennessee, Monday night, March 28, 1859

Spent most of the day in Clarksville not shopping but looking over the new goods. Left the shopping for Mrs. Riggs and Mattie. Together they made a considerable account at Mr. Moore's, but the handsomest purchase of all was a nice set of jewelry was presented by Mrs. Riggs to Mattie. But little improvement has been made in the style of goods. To be candid no real improvement according to my judgment has taken place. For the dress goods are large figured and broad striped while the bonnets are smaller and worn farther back than ever. But the best of all is heel shoes and hoop skirts continue to be worn, and while they last, grace and beauty as well as health will be promoted. We carried Mattie down to school and had the honor of making Dr. Hamilton's[209] acquaintance as well as the pleasure of meeting with several old acquaintances among the girls. Dr. H doesn't seem to spare any trouble or expense in advancing the education of his pupils. The faculty is composed of the best informed & the most accomplished of teachers while the institution is fitted up in the most elegant style offering every inducement that could be desired by any of a good boarding school.[210] All fatigued and ready for a good night's rest. Mrs. R made me a present of such a nice collar.

New Providence, Tennessee, Tuesday night, March 29, 1859

My books have come at last and I'm no longer in suspense at least about the fashions. Mr. H is a clever fellow. Mrs. Riggs received news this morning of Mr. Riggs' sickness and left soon afterwards although Toby was quite sick from an attack of croup last night produced by exposure yesterday. Went with Cousin Jane up town this evening shopping and paid Mrs. McDaniel a good long visit. Mr. Homer has been to see us tonight and in a greater notion of marrying than ever. I don't know when I saw him in such a way. Showed me a letter of Mrs. Ellen Pettus although I've no doubt he gave his word to breathe it to no one.

New Providence, Tennessee, Friday night, April 1, 1859

Slight mistake about the birth of Sarah's boy. Since reviewing her letter I have found that it was Saturday week in place of last Saturday that it was born.[211] To say the least of it the little curly headed fellow she used to dream of is really in existence. Cousin Lou, Blanche and Mrs. Pollard spent the day with us. Went down to the pond fishing. Met with usual success. Went down late to see Miss Sallie and Johnie. Called on my return home to see Mrs. Comagys. Wasn't caught exactly in the same trap that Aunt T was yesterday morning. Met with the madame at the gate. Mrs. Comagys seems to have improved greatly in spirits from her visit but looks badly in the face. Mr. Blakeney[212] is with us tonight. Uncle Trice has just had a real round with Margaret.[213] I sometimes think slavery is almost a curse. Wrote one April fool and received one. I know Cousin Will will wonder.

New Providence, Tennessee, Friday night, April 8, 1859

Finished my slippers, and ready to commence on my quilt again. Mrs. Ogburn and Sam called this morning on their way to Clarksville. Aunt T went over with them. Spent most of the day. Brought me such a nice basket for my quilt pieces. Carried the girls down home. Vacation for some time. George Barbee[214] called this evening with an invitation to attend a fishing party tomorrow. Went down to Mr. Helm's few minutes late. Read a little in Plutarch's lives and but thought more thing else [*sic*] during the day. I love to study and think sometimes, but this didn't chance to be one of the times.

New Providence, Tennessee, Saturday night, April 23, 1859

Well as expected Mrs. Riggs sent for me last Monday and I have been rusticating ever since until this morning I really had on the bank of the gurgling stream. Drank in the sweet music of the forest warblers, and I expect had something of the Poet's feelings when looking over the broad forest and seeing as it were the tiny green leaves just peeping from their snug retreat. Enough of the kind. I wish I was a poetess or even had the language with which to clothe my few simple ideas. Suffice it to say my visit was enjoyed to the fullest extent. No pains seemed to be spared either by Mrs. Riggs or the children to render it agreeable and pleasant. Riding horseback and fishing were the principal amusements. Went over and spent the evening with Mrs. Cowherd and West, stayed all night with Dr. Pirtle's family where I met with Mrs. James Ogburn[215] and Sam Johnson. Mrs. O had on hand her usual supply of wit. Found all at home well and apparently glad to see me. Dr.

Pirtle and Will Leigh dined with us. Mrs. Pollard and I made two calls first on Mrs. and the Misses Fauntleroy,[216] our new citizens, and then on Mrs. Comagys, who made herself quite agreeable but not so cheerful as usual.

New Providence, Tennessee, Tuesday night, April 26, 1859

Still more rain. Cloudy and showery all day and at this time thundering and lightning severely. Commenced Inez a dress this morning. Uncle John Mallory dined with us. Mrs. Enice spent the evening.

New Providence, Tennessee, Wednesday night, May 4, 1859

Commenced this morning my blue gingham. Aunt T went down to see Mrs. Rice about 10. Georgia Smith[217] came; she is on her way to Canton[218] and will remain with us for a day or two. Fannie Nesbit paid us a visit this evening. Mrs. Gold also came down few moments. The hearse with a long procession passed this evening and an enquiry found that a Miss Carter, niece of Dr. Thomas,[219] was drowned yesterday evening by attempting to ride across a mill dam.[220] The horse, becoming frightened, backed into the pond and, having no company but a small boy, was drowned in a few moments. Her hoops [*kept her*] near the surface until assistance was present. A more distressing circumstance I have not known since the death of Mr. Harris.

New Providence, Tennessee, Wednesday night, May 18, 1859

The recent rains have given Aspen Cottage a more charming appearance if possible than ever. The foliage of the trees seems to have grown darker and more beautiful while the undergrowth is so dense that only one curtain need be lowered to make the room sufficiently dark for an invalid; or an ordinary parlor; and as the poet would say we can almost drink in the liquid fragrance of the honeysuckle & {*indecipherable*}. Wrote to Sarah according to Mrs. Ogburn's request.[221] Jennie[222] and Cousin Lou went over to Clarksville this morning to return this evening and have not been heard of since. Mrs. Howell spent the morning with us. Went up town with Lucie. Mr. Holland came down to the sales and gave us a call of some 10 or 15 minutes' length.

New Providence, Tennessee, Friday night, May 20, 1859

The weather is pleasant and [for] once seems settled. Read a while in Plutarch this morning. Finished my buff bonnet and spent the rest of the day lounging and visiting. Went down to see the Misses Fauntleroy and after so long a time called on Mrs. Harrelson. Cousin Lou and Jennie are both with us yet. News: received a letter today from Mr. Trabue, a gentleman I never saw but once and I think only spoke to him once.[223] No company excepting Cousin Jane a while.

New Providence, Tennessee, Sunday night, May 29, 1859

Aunt Tabbie's birthday, 46 years old; 50 is almost in sight, and then if she is spared, I will be compelled to look on her as rather an old woman. Though now the thought makes me sad; but what if her head is gray and the wrinkles more numerous; her heart I know is unchanging. We spent the morning down at Mr. Howard's. Jane[224] is, if possible, looking worse. Spent the evening at home with the exception of [a] few minutes up at Mr. Atkinson's. Sam Ogburn gave us a short call.

New Providence, Tennessee, Thursday night, June 2, 1859

Finished my dress this evening about 4 and had spare time enough to take a nap or two. Aunt T spent the morning up at Mrs. Davis's. Went down since supper to see Mrs. Herring. The nights are cool and more pleasant for visiting than the days but there are other advantages: we can go without changing our dress, with only one skirt over our hoops, a hole in the toe of each shoe; in few words like we go every day and not have the gentlemen at Hoover's, Boatwright's,[225] and the hotel staring at us[226] as though they were trying to count the threads in our unmentionables that we wouldn't have them see for a fortune.

New Providence, Tennessee, Thursday night, June 9, 1859

The wedding day of Dr. Swift and Mrs. Martin[227] this morning at 9. They launched their boat on the——"uncertain sea of matrimony." Passed most of the morning trotting round with Cousin Mollie;[228] she left about 2 for home. Slept from ½ 2 until 4. We then went down to see Cousin Jane and Marion.[229] Found no one at home but Cousin Bet, the rest having gone to Mr. Leonard's to spend the day. Called a while at Mr. Blakney's; found them all complaining. Sit until 2 with Mr. Staton's family. Called particularly on Miss Mary Duff.[230] A gentleman by the name of Grubbs has opened a music school or designs opening one in our town for the benefit of those who may wish to take lessons without leaving home.

New Providence, Tennessee, Thursday night, June 16, 1859

Received yesterday from Aunt Tabbie a present of 6 biographies and Webster's unabridged dictionary. Spent the day reading. Finished by 5 the history of Josephine. Mrs. Riggs came in late and prevailed on us to go with her over to Mrs. McDaniel's concert. We went and such a squeeze.[231] Notwithstanding the girls performed admirably and looked beautifully. All did very well with one exception. I wish old Mrs. R and her son T——had have been in ——Bowling Green.[232] Cousin Alley spent the day with Mrs. Howell,[233] Laura [234]with me. Mrs. Ogburn called this morning for me to go over to the {indecipherable} auction with her but as usual I was compelled to disappoint her. Laura and I went over after supper for Cousin Alley. On our return we met with Mr. Blakney, wife,[235] and Gibby all together (Mr. Wilson and Trice included). We had quite a large party and considerable fun; oh, I want to be talking so bad I don't know what I'm writing.

New Providence, Tennessee, Wednesday, June 29, 1859

The excessive warm weather has deprived me for the last day or two of memory and almost every other faculty. I retired last night and the night before forgetting there ever was a journal. However, Aunt T has made several visits during the time, and Cousin Lou and I have had fine times eating baked potatoes and blackberry cobbler. Aunt T has made the long-talked-of visit to Mrs. Ogburn; she also went to Aunt Susan O and Mrs. Smith's. Mr. Smith and Mr. Elliot gave us a call on Monday with an invitation to a picnic on Friday; 3 invitations within a week to dances. Mrs. Pirtle and the Dr. are with us tonight; they have been to consult some physicians about their little boy, his mouth has been bleeding from a fall for 2 weeks or more.

New Providence, Tennessee, Sunday night, August 14, 1859

Read until most time for church. Mr. Homer came and for once asked me politely for my company. I consented provided no better came in (disappointed). Mr. D preached about as usual, sermon about as usual, subject "the judgment." Mrs. Pollard & daughter came home with us. Mr. Homer spent most of the evening with us and Mrs. Rise, Mr. and Mrs. Baptist, Mr. Hopson, and Col. White, Bettie Helm and George all gave us a call of two or three hours' length. Baptist has another joke on Hopson. They'll run the poor fellow to death, but certainly such a mistake never was made before, {Macedo} the woman and the goats. Mr. Caskey preached at the Methodist church. Preached from the text, But God forbid that I should glory & etc. He spares none but the pedobaptist;[236] old Mr. Rough is with us tonight with his usual supply of questions on hand.

New Providence, Tennessee, Saturday night, August 20, 1859

Spent the days yesterday & today sewing on my quilt; made considerable progress. Mrs. Trabue from Keysburg and Mrs. Atkinson[237] spent several hours with us. Cousin Lou came to spend a day or two (Aunt T's teasing her now). Mr. Noel stayed with us last night; he's more mischievous if possible than ever. Aunt T and Cousin L went out to West Fork today leaving me to take care of the preserves and house, but the quilt was the thing hard and of course received most of my attention. I can't for my life give two or three things proper attention at the same time. Mrs. Trabue took tea with us tonight. Also, Sy Trice.[238] They sit but short time afterward. Mr. Homer paid another accidental call and for once left without lecturing an hour or two on matrimony.

New Providence, Tennessee, Sunday night, September 25, 1859

Bright and early this morning Cousin Alley, Willie, and I were ready to go down to Mt Pleasant to church. Mr. Rise called and was kind enough to accompany us down. Politeness of course was carried to an extreme. Were there just in time to get a seat where hoops stood but little chance. Thought we were doing well to get seats for ourselves. Mr. Hanah not himself, subject the distinction of earth & Heaven, text in 3rd chap. 2nd Peter. Dined with the preachers at Mrs. Ogburn's. The dinner was too good to eat enough. Found here this evening Cousin Jane and her children, Cousins Marion and Johny, and the children. I can't hear myself what—even think, positively don't know what I'm writing. Mr. Homer and Cousin Will have been with us tonight and what jabbering by them as well as the children. Mr. H is just about as tipsy as I ever saw him. My opinion's settled and that forever he won't do and that's certain. By the way a new neighbor, Mrs. Gold has a (don't know whether fine or not) daughter; grieved, I know, because it's not a boy.[239] The children are teasing me to leave so they can play. Heard something today both sad and pleasing. Millie informed me that a piece written by poor Jo previous to his death had recently appeared in the Chronicle in which a very affectionate allusion was made to me.

New Providence, Tennessee, Monday night, October 3, 1859

Much warmer and very pleasant. Aunt T went up town this morning and brought me down that black silk wished for some time since I've been busy with it all day with the exception of an hour or two spent running around with Mrs. Baptist. But few calls—Mrs. Atkinson, old Mrs. Colashaw[240] [*sic*] this evening, and T. Riggins from Hopkinsville since supper. Not much news. The Rutland case[241] has the third time now been decided: the first time he was sent to the penitentiary for 3 years, the next 9, and this time 3 again. He's now going to carry the case to the Supreme Court and I guess will have his last trial. Quite a to-do made over the ill treatment of one man to his wife. Aunt T thinks if they are going to try all that are guilty of so common a thing as that is they had better commence nearer at home as they are so numerous round here. She's not the one to spare man in any of his meanness.

New Providence, Tennessee, Sunday night, October 9, 1859

Breakfast rather late. Sit few minutes. Swept my room. Sit again for ½ hour. Then read as many as 8 chapters in the book of Jeremiah. Rested a while and then read most of the important items in the Tennessee Baptist. Laid that down to chat awhile with Mr. Rise, who as usual paid his Sunday morning call. He left rather late. Played with my hands until dinner when they were again {*indecipherable*} not so much for the fun of it. After that took up again a paper. Read myself to sleep. Slept but few minutes when I combed my hair, changed my dress, heard the servants' lessons, and awakened Aunt T up to go down to Cousin Jane's where we remained until sunset. Found Mr. C T and George Trice[242] waiting for us. G acted and talked until 8 when Uncle and Aunt T went to bed and I at what I'm now doing. No preaching in town.

New Providence, Tennessee, Monday night, Oct 24, 1859

The weather is again clear, warm and beautiful; a more lovely day we've not had for months. Cousin J and the children left about 9. No company during the morning excepting a short call from Dr. Acree[243] He brought me a note from Harriet and enclosed within it the piece of poetry written by poor Jo a few months previous to his death. The allusion to myself was touching & affectionate. In reading it memories were awakened that were better never to have been aroused; but as he once said in a letter to me, "such is life," a few moments sunshine and then a cloud which chases everything like happiness from our view. Uncle Steven[244] dined with us. Cousin Ann and Mr. February after dinner went over to C'sville. For a while we were alone which time was consumed in cutting Aunt T's new dress. Had quite a pleasant time since supper chatting with Mr. S; the conversation being turned to my prospects for getting a husband.

New Providence, Tennessee, Thursday night, October 27, 1859

Commenced my new dress this evening Lucie went up this morning and bought one just like it to travel to Texas in I expect. She and Sallie Cowherd were to see me this morning. Sallie's has all of the {*indecipherable*} on and a little more. "I ask" and "I can't" &c seem to come perfectly natural with her. If I were to try my very best I don't think I could ever put on like some. I went down to Mr. Helm's after dinner. Remained until about 3 when I went over and spent the remainder of the evening with Mrs. Herring. She just as funny as ever and laughs as heartily as ever. Received a letter from Mr. Whitefield today and I am in a hurry to answer it.

New Providence, Tennessee, Thursday night, November 3, 1859

Spent Tuesday until late writing letters when agreeable to previously made arrangements. Will Leigh came by for me to go down to the wedding. Were there by sunset. Found Cousin Lou in one of her real lively moods. The girls upstairs looking as if they were sent for. Mr. and Mrs. Leigh of course looking a little sad. The guests were all assembled by 7 and by 8 Tine and Mary had bidden farewell to a life of single blessedness and plunged into the turbulent sea of matrimony.[245] Mr. Neely[246] tied the knot. I unexpectedly stood as bride's maid, having an uneven number. Will Henry and I were just in place, my dress as it happened exactly suitable. The bride was dressed very plainly but becomingly as well as comfortably. Her dress was of solid {*indecipherable*} blue silk with double skirt, high necked with plain collar and no under sleeves, head dress a simple wreath of white flowers with one end drooping gracefully on her shoulders. She was indeed a timid, unassuming, and lovely looking bride. She was a youthful and loving bride and as such acted. The bride's maids were Bell Jenkins, Tom [*sic*] Long, Mary Smith, and myself were all dressed in collared silks; the groomsmen Bug Cowherd, George Trice, Bob Wilson,[247] and Will Leigh. I believe I've nothing to say for them. Mr. W disappeared about ½ 8 or 9 and was not seen again for several hours. I afterwards learned he was upstairs taking a game of euchre[248] with some gentlemen. The table was set in taste, but not stylish, with everything plenty. The cake was all prepared by Cousin Lou and of course excellent. The evening passed in conversation, no other amusement being introduced. I will except, however, card playing which only a few engaged in.

I met with Mr. H for the first time since his return from Va. He was unusually interesting and agreeable; his trip having afforded him so much food for conversation he doesn't seem to be at a loss at all to interest any with whom he may come in contact. We all retired that night about 1 but not to sleep. We were so crowded and the girls kept such a noise about room that none of us slept much. Left there next day about 10 for Mr. Smith's where a nice dinner was given us and where we remained until four in the evening when the bride and groom, Bell Jenkins, Mary Smith, and their beaus came up home with me. Aunt T had a nice supper awaiting us. Cousin Jane, Dr. and Mrs. Herring, and Mr. Homer also supped with us. We retired about 9, a dull and lifeless crowd, not however without having my temper a little roused with some of G T's bigoted and disgusting ways. The girls left early. Tine and Mary will board with us a while; they went over tonight to Mr. Peterson's. I find myself at home in time to act as bridesmaid for one of my friends. Lucie has acknowledged all and wishes me to have my white dress in order by next Tuesday night. Mr. {*indecipherable*} spent the evening with us and is with us tonight.

New Providence, Tennessee, Wednesday night, November 16, 1859

Not much time to write now nearly 9 and I've several chapters yet to read in Josephus;[249] Mollie and I have done a good day's work everything considered. Mrs. Comagys and her son, who is visiting her, paid us a good long visit this morning. This evening we passed down at Mr. Howard's and tonight finished off two garments cut out this evening. We enjoyed our visit finely; a nice luncheon was given us and some nice presents to bring home, among them some hops and pieces for my quilt, some ribbons of Jane's which I prize very highly.

New Providence, Tennessee, Sunday night, December 11, 1859

The day has been fine above, but the roads are in a dreadful condition; nevertheless, Mr. H came up and went with me down to Sunday school and after that went back to church. The congregation was small, doubtless owing to the mud.[250] Mr. D preached the funeral sermon of a Mr. Waters—text in Amos 4th chap 12th verse.[251] I was surprised on returning from school to find John Trice here from Mo; he brought up some negroes to sell. This being the healthy season down at Birdsville[252] he's spending time to the best advantage. Uncle John Mallory came in to hear Mr. D this morning, dined with us and preached to the negroes this evening. Mollie and Mr. Smith spent the day at Mr. Howard's company until since supper and now it isn't more than 9 and I feel as if we'd been sitting here for hours. A good piece of company is more missed I'm certain than a piece of furniture however useful or ornamental it may be about a room; nothing leaves such a vacuum, nothing more to be regretted than the absence of such a piece.

New Providence, Tennessee, Saturday night, December 24, 1859

Harriet left early. Dr. Neblett[253] took her down and returned about 4. Although I've missed her greatly during the day, tonight her place will be completely filled at least in one sense of the word; Cousin Lou is with us and with her arrival commenced Christmas. Aunt T has Mary employed now in writing a card to put in her stocking purporting to be from Dr. Neblett enjoying her company for church tomorrow. Nothing very new; our number of visitors has been as usual during the day. All are in a state of excitement about hanging up——their baskets, myself of course included. Mr. Smith is going to bring us down some sky rockets[254] tonight so we'll have a little fun in advance of Christmas.

New Providence, Tennessee, Sunday night, December 25, 1859

Dr. N has just left the room. Mr. Homer came before supper and sit until after 10, and by this time I'm so sleepy I can scarcely collect an idea but for the effort. My basket this morning with the rest was completely filled. The one I had [in] the parlor may be excepted though in reality it contained more than the other, the gift being more condensed or ({*indecipherable*}). Well, it wasn't exactly a "sure enough" something in——in a bag! but something very near akin to it. Besides other presents I received a valuable book, Miss Sophie's behavior book, and a traveling satchel; and also a nice pair of net {*indecipherable*}. Cousin L left in right good humor for Mr. Howard's about 9, owing possibly to the eggnog drank before breakfast. The rest of us have been at home all day, talking nonsense. Sarah and Mr. Spence called on their way down home.

New Providence, Tennessee, Friday night, January 27, 1860

Today I'm 21, and although I've had a few sober thoughts about my birthdays coming so much oftener than they used [to] I feel somewhat reconciled when [I] think of each of them bringing me a nice present. And though it is sad to think of growing old so young I must confess than I look forward to all my birthdays with some degree of pleasure, as one never comes without something coming with it to cause me to wish almost they were oftener. I've received but one present today and that was from the fountain head; on my bureau I found this morning a handsome set of coral jewelry from my

Auntie. My dinner was very good—Mrs. Rise spent the day with us. She and I went up to town this evening. No news of interest. Ervy Staton is worse and the scarlet fever[255] is prevailing to a great extent.

New Providence, Tennessee, Tuesday night, February 14, 1860

Not yet 9 o'clock and I have read the complete history almost of Matilda of Flanders, William the Conqueror's wife. She was certainly one among the greatest, if not the greatest, queens that ever "shared the throne of England." Generous and warmhearted toward her subjects, respectful to her equals, devotedly attached to her children, ever exhibiting true affection for her husband, she was all with a few exceptions that could be asked of a queen—of a woman. I say few exceptions remembering that exceptions in these enlightened times are numerous. Matilda's faults at least were few, and among them might be classed her indulgence to her eldest-born, Robert, a son—remarkable for recklessness and foolish extravagance. Her greatest fault however was the intense hatred she ever manifested for an enemy; her enmity once aroused knew no bounds. Revenge she would seek at the peril of all she held most dear. Indeed she went so far on one occasion as to cause her husband to endanger his position as King by carrying out a vow, made previous to their marriage. That was the destroying of the lord of Gloucester for his inconstancy while paying his attention to her as duchess of Flanders.[256] An enemy knew no limit to her cruelty; a friend no bound to her mercy. After all, taking the condition of affairs into consideration, the darkness of the 11th century, the neglect of proper training &c, &c, Matilda was no less a superior woman than a model queen. She certainly possessed a mind of no ordinary cast, and had her son (William Rufus) partaken more of her mind and disposition about things, he might have enjoyed and governed more satisfactorily the country only gained by the hardships of his father, his countrymen, and the prayers of a mother.[257] Raining all day. Aunt T still quite sick. Made some teacakes this evening. Mr. Case called. No other company. Advanced rapidly on my skirt.

New Providence, Tennessee, Saturday night, March 17, 1860

Spent yesterday and half of today down at the hotel taking plaiting lessons of Mrs. Johnson. Miss Fannie Pettus was engaged making the hair flowers while I was plaiting. We had rare fun, at the expense of Mrs. Johnson and her mother old Mrs. Batsford; they snapped at each other every other word. I made some beautiful plaits, both handsome for jewelry and useful for fob chains; went out home with Miss F and spent the evening. Bud Trice made me a plaiting machine today and about Tuesday I'll be ready for work again. An omnibus line has been established between Clarksville & our town, a progressive age this.[258]

New Providence, Tennessee, Monday night, March 19, 1860

Prepared my head this morning with some assistance and succeeded in making quite a pretty braid; my machine works admirably. After dinner Aunt T and I went up to see the new goods. Jo Staton brought me a most beautiful organdy robe, also a handsome veil, a pair of heel slippers, with several other nice little tricks. Went up this evening to see Mrs. Atkinson for a change; Dick Ogburn took tea with us. Dr. N and I went down tonight to hear Dr. Lawton lecture on Spiritualism, the first time I ever listened to anything of the kind on the subject. I was agreeably disappointed though not converted.

New Providence, Tennessee, Wednesday night, March 21, 1860

Cousin Jane and I went uptown this morning and were so interested in the new goods that we could scarcely believe after returning that we had spent at least more than half the morning. Saw some of the Wilsons' new bonnets. They certainly have taken a change for the worst, great heavy fussy buggy-top looking affairs. I imagine they will give some [of] the best looking of us a most ridiculous appearance. His organdies are rich and handsome. Indeed, "Bob's" selection is not to be laughed at, in anything; the shape of bonnets, he can't control. Tus Lawton was brought up this evening on the Minetonka.[259] Though yet breathing they think he is dying or will die soon. Dr. N is almost broken down; however, we talked "old Mrs. Barksdale" out of the room tonight.

New Providence, Tennessee, Friday night, March 30, 1860

Spent the morning making tape trimming and listening to John Trice's yarns. The evening I spent fooling over some horsehair.[260] Succeeded in making Cousin John a fob chain such a one as it was. After supper went up with Aunt T to see Mary Smith; she's looking confused as usual.

New Providence, Tennessee, May 18, 1860

As expected we left early Wednesday morning for Nashville, our company consisting of Mr. McDaniel, Mr. Barbee, Uncle Trice, and myself. We had quite a nice time going up although the most felt some little uneasiness it being our first trip in the cars.[261] We left at 6 and were in Nashville at 11. Went out, stayed all night with Mr. Gordon where I had lots [of] good things to eat, but above everything else was the green house of Acklen's.[262] Certainly if heaven could be on earth it would be found at a place like that; he certainly has the prettiest and the greatest variety of flowers I ever saw. The next morning we spent sleeping. Dined with Mrs. Noel and left for home at ½ 2. By dark we were at home. Found all well in body but little weary in mind.

New Providence, Tennessee, Tuesday night, May 29, 1860

Aunt T's birthday today; she's 47 years old. Cousin Jane prepared her an excellent dinner, but visitors prevented our partaking [of] it with her. Old Mrs. Blakney,[263] Mrs. Ed Ogburn, Ann,[264] Mrs. Heart and the children all came this morning and left late this evening. We were up at the gallery after dinner, and while there, Uncle Steven, Aunt Eliza, and Mr. Billy Mallory called. The day has passed very pleasantly indeed. An hour since supper though is worth all the rest. The nearer the time approaches for Dr. N and Mr. H to leave the less I feel like giving them up; indeed, all the fun and life of the family will leave with them, Mr. H especially. Dick and Mr. McCauley[265] are so dry & say nothing. Mr. H daily makes himself more agreeable and proves himself such a true friend of mine. He gives me such nice oranges. I love him for that if nothing else.

New Providence, Tennessee, Wednesday night, June 27, 1860

Monday and yesterday I spent out at Mrs. Pettus's[266] learning to make the hair flowers. Yesterday evening I finished Mrs. Ogburn off a very pretty bouquet. They live finely out there, no gentlemen about and so retired, and then they keep such a nice table. Mrs. Grinstead, Tommy, Mary, and Jo Hatcher[267] all came to see them yesterday. Monday night Mr. McCauley and I went over to Mr. Herblin's concert.[268] Dr. Hamilton has just finished his hall, and a more spacious and elegantly finished room I have never seen, so much taste displayed, and so well suited for the entertainment of vast crowds. The young ladies all acted their parts admirably, but none so well as {*indecipherable*} "old maid"; never did I enjoy anything of the kind more and Mr. McC no less than myself. Last night we went to one of the Providence — I scarcely know what to call it — Mrs. Engle's varieties, however, would be a very suitable name as the entertainment consists of music, vocal and instrumental; dialogues; and examinations on different studies. The crowd was very large and the heat so very oppressive that I declined going again tonight. The examination will continue until tomorrow night. Mr. Monroe and Miss Everett[269] were married this evening at ½ 1 and left for Nashville immediately. Mr. McCauley stood as groomsman and went up with them. Tom Riggins and family have been with us three days, at least here most of the time; and two as bad little brats as ever were.

CHAPTER TWO

September 1860 – May 1861

SEREPTA COMMENTED ON ordinary local activities, her numerous visits with friends and neighbors. Several people married and she wrote pessimistically about their unions. She perceived a lack of compatibility or age difference in the brides and grooms. Her negativity may have been tempered by her attitude toward Mr. Homer, who visited often, pressing for her hand in marriage. Montgomery County hosted two large regional events, the Tennessee Conference of the Methodist Church and the first Agricultural Fair. Serepta knew some ministers that attended and commented about them and their sermons. Government, civic organizations, and businesses coordinated to hold the first massive agricultural fair attended by thousands from the surrounding area. Nationally, she wrote about the 1860 election, the turmoil of politics, potential secession and the possibility of war. She used the terms disunion and Civil War for the first time.

She indicated that her uncle's financial situation was precarious. They were distressed at the loss of her aunt's chickens. Throughout she sewed, embroidered and quilted. She described women's fashions and what people wore to weddings. The seasons determined foods she prepared and preserved. The entries during this period display melancholy. B. B. Homer visited regularly.

New Providence, Tennessee, Friday night, September 7, 1860

In peaches all day last Friday and Saturday until dinner, drying and cooking them up. After dinner John Mallory came and although I felt that my work wouldn't admit of my leaving it at all, he and Aunt T together prevailed on me to go up and spend a week in Williamstown.[1] After a long though pleasant ride I found myself comfortably seated in Uncle William Mallory's[2] porch enjoying the prospect of a warm supper. Aunt Brit[3] is such a nice old lady and Uncle William is so fatherly and good to all the "young folks." The next night I spent with Cousin Mollie.[4] John and Hugh sat with us until bedtime. The next day Jennie Mallory[5] came over and that night we went over to Uncle William Donaldson's,[6] the place for fun. An old, old woman subject to the hysterics could surely remain there an hour without laughing herself well. With the fun, considerable excitement prevailed in regard to politics. Disunion is threatened strongly, and the Bell and Everett[7] men seem to be scared that the fears of the people are well grounded.

The next day "all hands" went over and spent the day with Cousin Mollie Frank.[8] There we ate and drank so imprudently and Cousin M treated us so kindly that it is a wonder any of the company escaped without the sick headache. Fortunately, I was the only sufferer though it seemed mine ached badly enough for the whole company. Alley,[9] that day as usual, tried herself, though once or twice the jokes turned against her and in my favor. To see her teased was the wish of the company generally. Whether to gratify us or not I won't say, but once in the course of a lifetime, she at least assumed a little confusion or embarrassment. That night I stayed with Aunt Eliza and Uncle Steven. Times were more quiet, enjoyed the calm very much after so much excitement. Aunt T came to Uncle William's the next day and sent for me. We stayed with Cousin Mary[10] that night and again spent the day at Uncle Steven's. Two Misses Collins[11] and Mrs. Weaver[12] were here. With our company the house was about full. The day passed very pleasantly. John gave me some damsons[13] to bring home with me; Uncle Steven, some hair to make him a bouquet.[14] That night, which was the last night, we went over to Uncle William Donaldson's. There we had our last fun. The boys[15] serenaded us. We threw them a doll, drew up one of their hats, talked until 12 and told yarns on each other. Alley spared none of us. At home by 11 o'clock today. Found a sick negro. Went down and called on the Misses Fauntleroy and Mary Harrelson,[16] an old friend and schoolmate. She is visiting Mrs. McGowan[17] tonight. Mr. and Mrs. Vaughan are with us from Ky. Uncle Trice is hurrying me off to bed.

New Providence, Tennessee, Saturday, September 8, 1860

Dressed in time to receive a short call from the groom, Mr. Tom Ogburn.[18] He's been married now since Tuesday night. He's himself, composed and dignified, rather melancholy looking. Invited us to see his wife. What changes are continually going on — 5 years ago and who could have made Mrs. Jones[19] or Tom Ogburn believe that in so short a time they would be man and wife? He's 60 years old, she 32. She's six small children, he four grown ones, though how long he can claim so many none of us can say. Hockett is at present very low with consumption, sharing the fate of three other brothers that have gone before him. [20] Mrs. Staton and Wilson[21] were to see us this evening. John Mallory supped with us. He and Uncle Trice have gone over to hear Quarles'[22] speech tonight. He didn't come, Billy Archy[23] said at four o'clock this eve.

New Providence, Tennessee, Monday night, September 10, 1860

Strained up my wine soon after breakfast and from that time until now felt undecided about what to commence with; concluded at length to commence tucking a skirt.[24] Dr. Minor dined with us; his mind is about as usual. This evening Mollie Harrelson, Kate Fauntleroy, Mr. and Mrs. Col. Rogers have been to see us. Mollie is looking handsomer than ever. She's certainly very childish to be a wife. Her dress was elegant. Jennie[25] made her a present today of a 60 dollar cloak, silk velvet with Honiton[26] lace. She may regret not being more economical. A new firm Jo Staton has sold out to George Trice.

New Providence, Tennessee, Tuesday night, September 11, 1860

Spent the morning making cake, the evening, sleeping, reading, and sewing a little. The Talisman I'm so pleased with. I'm so well pleased with as Ivanhoe.[27] Had no company.

New Providence, Tennessee, Saturday night, September 15, 1860

Aunt T sometimes very sick. I greatly fear a spell of the fever. Mrs. Howell and Alley Donaldson called to see her this morning. George Trice's boy[28] died with typhoid fever today. Finished tucking my skirt today with Jennie's assistance. She now sits by me vainly endeavoring to read each word as I write. She takes an interest and engages, if convenient, in all that I do, so unlike most children. A child she is in years, but in many things old and intelligent. She has a way of suiting herself to the company she is in. If with children, gay and frolicsome, if with older persons, quiet and ready to assist. Cousin Will Trice supped with us.

New Providence, Tennessee, September 17, 1860

Awakened early this morning by Uncle getting off to Clarksville. He, George, and Will Trice[29] have gone to Meachamville. Jennie and I have been making hair flowers today; she's so much company for me. Aunt T is some better. Several have called to see her. With the rest, Mr. McCauley, Jennie, and Cousin Jane went over to Clarksville this evening.

New Providence, Tennessee, Wednesday night, September 19, 1860

Have scarcely pretended to anything today in the way of employment excepting to wait on Aunt T. She remains very ill and Dr. Herring has at length decided she has fever, and I greatly fear it will terminate in typhoid. The bridal train came in this evening, and by this time I guess the fairy-like bride and attendants are whirling around in the giddy dance as though health and sunshine would continue through ages. Poor fragile flower, beautiful as she appears no doubt tonight, a year hence it would not surprise me to know that she was the victim of disease, a complete wreck of her former self. She with thousands of other girls now before the mirror, doubtless primping for the ballroom or some other gay place, will find an early grave, and all on account of imprudence in dress and the dissipation now so generally engaged in.

New Providence, Tennessee, Thursday night, September 20, 1860

Another marriage, scarce times seem to have but little terror for the "Young folks." Billie Burgess[30] and Miss Settle[31] were married this evening. Billie is so young. I can scarcely realize that he is a man, much less a married man. Aunt T is some better; several have called to see her. Mr. Gold sent me some of the nice things of last night. Aunt T is grunting so I must attend to her.

New Providence, Tennessee, Friday night, September 21, 1860

Indeed, I'm well attended; Jennie's right at my knee, Inez is holding the candle, Emma[32] the ink bottle, all as attentive to the motion of my pen as if I were writing them a deed of gift or something of great importance to them. Uncle Trice is on one bed and Aunt T on the trundle[33] groaning. She has a nervous spell about this time every night. Finished at last the bouquet—it is rather pretty, too much crowded. Jennie and I went up town this evening to see the new goods and came back with but little to talk about.

New Providence, Tennessee, Monday night, September 24, 1860

Yesterday morning went to Sunday school. Returned and went over to Clarksville to hear Mr. Duncan preach. Spent the evening at home with the exception of a short ride, Mrs. Comagys and I. (Aunt T rode out today; she's improving.) Went to bed last night with pains, and Miss Annie B would say, all under my apron.[34] Wrote to Cousin Mat this morning. Embroidered two pockets for a silk apron. This evening assisted in putting up some cider. Uncle Steven Mallory called on us. Seemed very much pleased with his bouquet. Gave me hair enough to add one or two more flowers.

New Providence, Tennessee, Tuesday night, September 25, 1860

The happy day has at length arrived. After seven long years waiting—& disappointments occurring frequently during the time sufficient to test the patience of a Job and almost cause him to curse his creator—Bunk Boatwright[35] and Gibbie Donaldson are married. I said the happy day; that seems, however, a one-sided business. The happiness seems confined only to one of the two and that to her, who has proven so faithful and devoted through all these years of bitterness and anxiety (so report says). He, I have heard, has declared that he'd no love for her and that it was only certain circumstances that forced him to a marriage. To my certain knowledge within the last two or three years he has addressed several other young ladies, while at the same time he was engaged and holding out false pretensions to her. No longer than a week since, one of the young ladies to whom he has been engaged left town a mere skeleton, it is said, from disappointment and misplaced affection. Gibbie herself is now and has been for some time almost a wreck of her former self, just wasting gradually from grief at hearing of his attachment for others and his inconstancy to her. To think of a sensible girl being duped by such a specimen as he is it seems unreasonable. Five years ago, she ought to have known him and forever afterwards frowned at every effort to renew his acquaintance, but instead, tonight she is happy as she thinks in gaining his love and affection and feels that trouble and she are strangers, while he is perhaps miserable and will regret only more the steps taken today and finally, perhaps, bring her and a family to suffer the evil consequences attending a union so unsuitable. She will soon discover his coldness. He will grow more distant as other cares increase and from that she will sink probably into a premature grave—the victim of a broken heart, the ill-treated of a brutal man. But why hadn't she more independence, why so much of the weakness characteristic as some say of our sex? Who will be her sympathizers when this mountain of trouble presents itself? Only a few perhaps and those unacquainted with her early history. Weakness will be her only excuse in asking the sympathy of anyone. Mr. Duncan married them at 4 this evening. He dined with us today. We've lots of brides now in our town; as many as three were on the street this evening.

New Providence, Tennessee, Friday night, September 28, 1860

Finished my fancy apron this morning. Mr. Homer was present when I tried it on and eulogized my taste considerably. He's a man of taste himself and, of course, I should be pleased with it. He drank some of my wine and praised that too, which greatly encouraged me as it is my first attempt and I have feared all the time that it prove a failure. He's still all interest on the subject of matrimony and takes particular pains to introduce it the first opportunity. Commenced Uncle Trice's shirts today and how I dread the task.

New Providence, Tennessee, Wednesday night, October 3, 1860

The rain today has had but little effect on the atmosphere; the weather is still warm. Finished Uncle Trice's shirts. Aunt T has been up to her eyes in trouble all day about her horse. She lent him to one of the Godsey[36] tribe for two hours and he kept him all day.

New Providence, Tennessee, Saturday night, October 6, 1860

For the last two days I've been quite unwell, though sewing busily all the time. The Methodist Conference[37] commences in Clarksville next week and soon after that the fair, so that if I don't make use of time now, I'll not be prepared to honor them with my presence. Mr. Duncan preached tonight and held a meeting for the purpose of electing messengers for the association,[38] which comes off in Russellville[39] next Saturday and Sunday. My back aches too much to write any more.

New Providence, Tennessee, Monday night, October 8, 1860

Spent the morning in Clarksville shopping and, as Aunt T says, I'd as live been in the penitentiary[40] for the same length of time, only though as a spectator. Wore my new bell-shaped hoops[41] and I'll declare they look ridiculously small after wearing such large ones. Sewed all the evening, notwithstanding the compliment Aunt T heard passed on me this morning. Uncle Billy Mallory called. Tonight we went down to see Mrs. Knox.[42] What strange and unaccountable things are daily occurring even in our midst? Tomorrow two weeks ago, Gibbie Donaldson was the gay and innocently happy bride of Bunk Boatwright. Today he boldly and unblushingly left on the 12 o'clock train beside a woman of defame, the lowest of the low. A few days since she visited him at his shop, cussed him to his face and in the presence of the workmen told him of his promises of marriage to her, and dared him to deny it, declaring if he did she would "draw the papers out on him." This with other things she told him, I suppose, with the most savage look and uttering at the close of each sentence a most bitter oath. What may his wife expect? What may the girls expect—the mothers of future generations classed with the young men of the present day? What must be the character of the offspring and, in a word, what will be the fate of our nation? What has sustained it these long years but the strict morality and the true piety of our forefathers? Do away with these and we do away with the freedom, the prosperity, and even the laws of our great republic.

New Providence, Tennessee, Wednesday night, October 10, 1860

Sewing busily yesterday and today. Mrs. Ricks[43] and Helm[44] spent the day with us today. Mr. Homer called tonight. Mr. Boatwright's trip is the topic generally introduced. His return is thought doubtful by some. Aunt T made me a present of a nice 35 dollar silk velvet cloak yesterday. Bless her old soul. My breast and back are paining me from constant sitting.

New Providence, Tennessee, Thursday night, October 11, 1860

Commenced a new calico after sunset yesterday evening and almost finished it today. Uncle Trice and Mr. Homer and others left for Hopkinsville fair this morning before day. Cousin Jane spent the day with us. Uncle Trice said conference would send some of "the strikers"[45] over here and sure enough old Mr. Escue[46] came over and preached for us tonight from the "fust" Psalm. Such preachers are so tiresome.

New Providence, Tennessee, Saturday night, October 13, 1860

Dressed early, put on my new cloak and went over to conference this morning. The house was crowded, the weather very cold, and I was compelled to occupy a seat near the door so that I heard but little of the conference. Though had the pleasure of meeting with several of my old acquaintances among the preachers, among whom were Mr. Davis and Mr. Henderson.[47] Mr. H came over with me and remained until about ½ 3. He reminded me so much of old times, of Mr. and Mrs. Hart and poor Jo, through whom I first made his acquaintance. Though a husband and a father now, he's as funny and mischievous as ever. Mr. Carneal took supper with us.

New Providence, Tennessee, Sunday night, October 14, 1860

For three mornings past we've had frost, and this morning a very heavy one. The weather still remains very cold. Jo Staton and I went over to Clarksville this morning and heard the great Bishop Pierce.[48] In size he is small though well-proportioned and with a large and very fine head, a noble forehead, and eye that speaks when language fails. His sermon was excellent, his delivery good, his style easy and calculated to attract the attention of a congregation. His text 1st Epistle of Peter, 20th and 21st verses.[49] This evening again we went over to hear the celebrated Cross,[50] at least the husband of the celebrated Mrs. Jane T. Cross. With him I believe I was as much pleased as with Bishop Pierce. His voice and manner of addressing the people was so much like Mr. Mouton that I fell in love with him on that account. He is, however, a minister superior in many respects and well deserving the position given him by the conference. He preached today from the 142nd Psalm, latter part of the 4th verse.[51]

Met with preacher Hart today and I was sadly glad to see him. Many recollections rushed my mind and some of so melancholy a cast that my voice trembled and tears were with difficulty kept back. Some inquiries, one in particular, was kept back for fear of betraying emotion. Whether he observed it or not I am unable to say. Though if he knew all, no doubt, his sympathy would be offered and I made to feel that outside of home one friend is still left me. He and his wife are associated with many pleasant recollections of the past and have been instrumental no doubt in giving me many a moment's enjoyment. I feel {perhaps} to thank them for their kind intentions, and yet tonight perhaps I had been happier had things been otherwise. The past would that I could recall it, the changes of a few are scarcely credible. 6 years ago, and who could have made me believe what now I know and sadly feel. Life is too short for me to indulge in thoughts so melancholy and I will stop right here. Aunt T and Uncle Trice have gone down to hear a Mr. Cherry.[52] Their absence with the meeting with Mr. Hart today has given rise to the pregoing thoughts and if it were right, I could continue in just such a strain for hours. Past pleasures are all that I enjoy. For me the future is gilded with no bright hopes, not a dream of happiness to come is ever permitted me.

New Providence, Tennessee, Tuesday night, October 16, 1860

Busy sewing all day. Uncles Steven, William, and John Mallory dined with us today. All I believe were delighted with their ride on the cars.[53] Uncle Steven gave me a nice present for making his bouquet. The congregation was disappointed tonight in hearing Baldwin.[54] Mayhew[55] preached in his place and succeeded in getting considerable excitement. As many as 5 or 6 went up to be prayed for. Dick Ogburn is with us tonight. He says they are taking the young preachers "through" over at conference. Had a young gentleman up yesterday for kissing a girl, a very slight offense indeed, one at least that most of themselves are guilty of. I'd no idea they were so rigid in their rules. The preacher's text tonight was 2nd Cor. 9th Chap 8th verse.[56] Mr. Erwin's funeral was preached in Clarksville today at the Methodist Church.

New Providence, Tennessee, Wednesday night, October 17, 1860

Went to church tonight. How delighted I was to see Mr. Hart walk in and enter the pulpit. Just that was worth all the preaching and conference that I've heard. 6 years have elapsed since we met last in that house and notwithstanding all the changes that have occurred during that time, I find in him as ever the same genuine and sincere friend that he was the year he preached for us.

New Providence, Tennessee, Thursday night, October 18, 1860

Conference closed today. Mr. Hart and Dr. Pirtle were off by 8 o'clock this morning. We have great hope of Mr. Hart's coming to live by us. He is on the Montgomery circuit[57] and I'm so pleased with the idea of having Mrs. H for a neighbor. Mrs. Pirtle, I think, is not a little vexed with Dr. P's appointment.[58] They left late this evening for home. Too tired to stop any longer. Almost forgotten, received a letter from Tom Trabue.[59] His reply in regard to what I said about writing ½ sheet of paper was quite amusing.[60]

New Providence, Tennessee, Sunday night, October 21, 1860

Spent most of the day at Cousin Jane's yesterday. Today Aunt T and I went out to West Fork. Uncle Steven preached a sermon about as usual from the text, "But God forbid that I should glory &." We dined for a rarity at Mrs. John Wilson's.[61] She's as funny as ever. Mr. Homer and Sylus[62] sit until bed time with us.

New Providence, Tennessee, October 22, 1860

The first thing I did after breakfast was to go down to the tinners and buy for myself two cake molds, and for Aunt T two pie pans. I intended making cakes in each of the molds this morning, but Aunt T's arrangements prevented me. Mrs. Ogburn came in about 12 and remained with us until 3.

I made the cakes this evening and made other arrangements for the fair, which commences tomorrow.[63] Dr. Herring gave us a call tonight, no news particularly.

New Providence, Tennessee, Tuesday, October 23, 1860

A day long to be remembered not only by the youth and children of our county but by the old too. For among the many that have passed today on their way to the first agricultural fair of Montgomery Co.[64] were a great many whose heads were frosted over and forms bent from age. They will have to tell the grandchildren of the great sights they saw while the younger are left to reflect on the progress of the age, vast improvements and fast trotting horses. They all, no doubt, went with the expectation of seeing the elephant[65] in all of its huge proportions, and tonight not one can say they saw anything that they had never seen before. Embroidery, quilts, cakes &c &c, lady's work generally, and a few horses were all that was exhibited. Uncle Trice and George say there were a great many in attendance. Received a letter from Mr. Hart saying he would be unable to make our town his home next year.

New Providence, Tennessee, Wednesday night, October 24, 1860

Sure enough Mr. Homer and I went over to see the monkey[66] today. The attendance was ordinary and the exhibition very, very poor, saw nothing worth riding from here to the bridge and back; that is, nothing within the ring. I had the pleasure of meeting with several old acquaintants while promenading. Among them was Mr. McCauley—, friend whose company I enjoyed very much. He partly engaged my company for Saturday. No company still.

New Providence, Tennessee, Thursday night, October 25, 1860

Something strange and new, Aunt T and Uncle Trice went to the fair today and I stayed at home. I can't say whether or not I deserve any credit for it after taking all things into consideration. Mr. Griffy's[67] family on their way home called and spent several hours with me. With that exception I've been alone, though not lonely much. I almost finished The Betrothed[68] today. Aunt T was late getting home. The exhibition was good she says, was good of the kind but uninteresting to her. The crowd has increased greatly, by tomorrow or next day the last McAdotion and Dover Rodin[69] will have seen the elephant. Mr. Homer came up after supper.

New Providence, Tennessee, Friday night, October 26, 1860

Uncle Trice and I went over to the fair today and had quite a pleasant time with the exception of the ride home this evening. Uncle Trice would pass every vehicle and just kept me frightened out of my wits most all the time. Hogs, sheep, farming utensils, specimens of portrait paintings, marble work, carpenters' work, leather and various other things were on exhibition. Several rings this evening. A youth 12 or 13 years of age excelled in horsemanship. Several rode in tournament.[70] The judges hadn't decided when we left. Among other old acquaintances, met with Mr. Billie Lowry and James Foster.[71] Mrs. Brunty[72] and I were together most of the time. John Mallory took tea with us.

New Providence, Tennessee, Saturday night, October 27, 1860

"The world and his wife" were at the fair today notwithstanding the inclemency of the weather, which has until today been very pretty indeed, and today the showers were only light enough to lay the dust. The rings this morning were mostly of the premium stock. This evening there were several rings of match horses and among them a very large and a very small one together. The tournament ring was the most interesting of any. Mr. Gill[73] of Russellville received the $50 wreath and crowned his cousin[74] though everyone most thought Mr. Fields[75] of this place deserved it. He only liked[76] 3 rings of getting them all. His time, they say, wasn't correct, though some that timed him say he made the round in less than 25 seconds, the specified time for each ring lot. The crowd was immense, such a concourse of people never were assembled in Clarksville before. The estimate I believe was 6 or 7 thousand. I'm really glad it is all over with. I'm so tired.

New Providence, Tennessee, Sunday night, October 28, 1860

The morning was so gloomy that neither of us went out anywhere. Took a nap after dinner and walked down to see Mrs. Ricks awhile. Found Mrs. Herring crying over a letter from "Sis Stermin" and Mrs. Ricks absent. Everything presented such a gloomy aspect. Mrs. R and Mrs. Fauntleroy came in afterwards and we a little relieved. Since supper George gave me a dollar to go with him over to Mr. Wilson's to see Missouri Madole.[77] We remained until after seven. The conversation and excitement everywhere is about the injustice of the judges yesterday in not giving Clark Fields the wreath. He richly deserved it in the opinion of all that I've heard speak of it.

New Providence, Tennessee, Monday night, October 29, 1860

Commenced work this morning in old fashion style. Aunt T and I together have almost made Horace[78] a coat today. Took a long walk with Mo Madole, and since supper we all went down to see Laura Helm.[79] She has been quite ill for a week, but at present seems to be improving. There is some talk of having the fair over. Mr. Field's friends want to see that he has justice done him. If I were in his place and they had the impudence to ask me over, I wouldn't go a single step. He'll certainly do away with all the independence he's hitherto manifested by going. Uncle Steven and Uncle Trice swapped horses today.

New Providence, Tennessee, Tuesday night, October 30, 1860

Emma placed my book and ink on the stand before I noticed her, and I suppose something ought to be written to save the trouble of bringing and carrying it back; but what to write I don't know, more than I have made Marshal[80] a coat today, took a long walk with Miss Madole, and tonight we sit a while with Mrs. Bit. Persons outside of and in Providence are still interested in Clark Field's failure or rather in the injustice of those rascally judges. Dr. Drane[81] thinks it the most absurd thing ever conceived of, the idea of missing his time a ½ second.

New Providence, Tennessee, Friday night, November 2, 1860

Cut out Hellen[82] a dress this morning. Entertained Mr. Homer an hour, and then Mrs. Ricks and I went down to Mrs. Howard's to spend the day, which was passed in sewing, talking, eating, and gathering apples. The last employment was principally engaged in by self. I brought home a lot of very nice apples. Mrs. Ricks is going to stay all night with me and I'm so glad, for my feet get most awfully cold these nights.

New Providence, Tennessee, Tuesday night, November 6, 1860

Yesterday morning Cousins Jennie, Alley, and myself went down to see Mrs. Blakeney[83] and family. Found him abed slowly spitting blood. He, I think, will finally go into consumption. In the afternoon we all "bundled up" and went over to Mr. Dudley's.[84] We were received by Mr. and Mrs. D very cordially and should have had quite a nice visit had it not been for Cousin Alley's babe, which was quite ill all night. We left for home about 10 and were here by 12. Found Mrs. Wilson[85] and Miss Nancy Jones[86] here. A few moments after we came, Aunt T told us certainly of Dr. Neblett's death.[87] Since then I've felt unusually depressed, not so much to think that I have lost another of my few friends, but on account of permitting so many precious opportunities to pass without even a reference to that most important of all subjects. I regret, and deeply regret, that our conversations generally have been of the most trivial character. We were intimately associated for months and if, as some say, the influence of an associate is felt through eternity, what will that poor boy have to attribute to mine, an eternity of happiness, or a still greater degree of punishment in that world of woe. Today is the Presidential election and I never knew less excitement, notwithstanding the number of candidates, Bell, Lincoln, Breckenridge, and Douglas.[88] Tomorrow Cousins Jennie and Alley leave for Williamstown if the babe is well enough.

New Providence, Tennessee, Wednesday morning, November 10, 1860

The negroes had a great piece of news for us, "Miss Mary Smith"[89] had a fine boy born yesterday. Will Ogburn[90] supped with us tonight and gave us more information in regard to Dr. Neblett's death. Poor boy, he died as I have been fearing all the time, in a strange land without friends and without the proper attention, if indeed he received any. Will says the young man who attended him wrote that he was in his room about 10 o'clock and that Dr. Neblett told him he was getting on very comfortably, and that he entered his room no more until about 2 o'clock when he found that he was dying, only breathed a few moments after he entered. Perhaps if the truth were known, he suffered alone, struggled alone, and drew his last breath without a single eye to witness the sad sight or one hand to administer a drop of cold water. Had there been one present to watch the changes of the disease, offered a remedy at the proper time and given him necessary attention, tonight he might have been well and enjoying life. But when shall I cease to reproach myself for passing so carelessly by his last letters in which were expressed with so much warmth and kindness his esteem, his love for our family, and particularly for myself. How strange that I with so few sincere friends should even pass by one word with indifference spoken in my favor, much less sheet after sheet filled with declarations of regard and affection. Never again do I want to cultivate the acquaintance of a person as intimately as I did Dr. N's and give one unkind look or word when it is in my power to give one pleasing thought or a second's happiness. At too late an hour I have found that indifference toward a friend gives pain in the place of pleasure, sorrow in the place of joy. A lesson so severely learned will surely be long remembered.

New Providence, Tennessee, Sunday night, November 11, 1860

Went to school this morning and found only one of my class present. None of the other teachers being in attendance, I included all that were present in my class and heard a short lesson. The infant portion were better posted than some of the grown young ladies and gentlemen. Went with Florence home to get a good dinner and the good part of it was I was not disappointed. Spare ribs and chine[91] were in abundance. After dinner Aunt T and Cousin Bet[92] went to negro meeting.[93] Cousin Jane and I, after a pressing invitation, went up and paid Mr. Homer a visit. He spared no pains in trying to make our visit agreeable and gave us some of the sweetest apples I've seen lately. They all, even Bell and Mr. Duncan,[94] came home with us and took tea, remained afterwards until 9, and Cousin Bet stayed with me and I'm so glad; for I still am reminded of many things that have occurred which the presence of another would drive away.

New Providence, Tennessee, Monday night, November 12, 1860

Finished off my blue delarue bonnet[95] this morning. Received three calls, Mrs. Ricks and McFerrin[96] and Mrs. Gold. Mrs. Gold told us that Mr. James Oldham,[97] they thought, was dying. He has lingered for a long time, and at a late hour found that religion is the only comforter in the hour of death. Truly in the midst of life, we are in death. Some excitement prevails in regard to Lincoln's election. The South intends holding a convention to decide whether or not they shall secede.[98] What will come next to deprive us of a moment's happiness? Received Dr. Neblett's obituary today and hope soon to see his brother.[99] Mrs. Ricks is with me tonight.

New Providence, Tennessee, Wednesday night, November 14, 1860

Sewing constantly all day on my quilt. I am joining it with an old dress I wore at 10 and 12 years of age—raw silk plaid. Aunt T went out to see the babies. I a few moments over to see Mrs. Wilson. Ann and Mary Ogburn[100] called a while on their way from Clarksville. Considerable excitement is prevailing in regard to the Civil War.[101] Many are wearing long faces on account of it. Mr. Homer sit with us tonight until 9. Matrimony is still his theme, notwithstanding the perilous times. He's come to the conclusion since conversing with Mrs. Toler[102] today that education is unnecessary and the mind unpolished passes through life a great deal better than when cultivated and stored with information from books.

New Providence, Tennessee, Sunday night, November 18, 1860

Aunt T and I went down yesterday morning and spent the day with Ann Ogburn. We enjoyed ourselves talking and eating hickrenuts[103] until late bed time.

New Providence, Tennessee, Monday night, November 19, 1860

Well, whoever heard of a like? While we were down at Mrs. {blank}[104] she told us that Sam said a stranger had recently been introduced into his school with "not a" shirt on its back and could not speak a word of English. And what was our surprise on coming home to find two of a similar character in our town, and among the number a young Mr. Gold. At least 50 of these singular specimens will have been introduced in our town by Christmas. Finished joining my quilt, at last. Aunt T spent the day running round to see the babies. Mr Homer called this morning. Tonight, Cousin Lou and Mary Jane[105] are with us. Cousin Lou's prospects for a husband rich with land and negroes are rather flattering, and as a matter of course, she's an unusually fine flow of spirits.[106]

New Providence, Tennessee, Thursday, November 22, 1860

Tuesday, Mary Jane and I were plaiting all day, Cousin Lou trotting round generally. Aunt T had a chill with her cold and was in bed of course most of the time. That night Mr. Bob Wilson and Eliza Barbee[107] bade farewell to the "state of single blessedness." Wednesday, Aunt T was some better. Mary Jane and Cousin Lou left about dinner. Mrs. Kirby[108] came in and spent the day with us. She and Miss Fannie Pettus assisted Aunt T about putting her rug in. Miss Fannie returned home early on account of having company that night (last night). I went with Mr. Jack Wilson out to his father's to a party given to "Bob" and his bride. But few were present excepting the bridal company consisting of Miss Mollie Barbee,[109] Mollie Trice,[110] Miss Mollie McDaniel,[111] and Miss Sue Smith as bridal maids, and George Trice, Will Leigh, and John Mallory as groomsmen. They came late, dressed in dark colors, and, of course, I thought by the time they decked themselves in all their bridal attire, the hour for supper would be unusually late. So after giving them sufficient time to warm, I acquainted them with all the circumstances, reminded them of hour &c. And what was my surprise to find that "they were afraid of taking cold" and that they stood before me just as they expected to appear in the parlor. Missouri Madole and I had gone with the expectation of wearing our tarletons.[112] She'd none but a calico besides and to appear without the wedding garment was all that we could do. So after a few moments' consideration we dressed and down we went, for the sole purpose of making an impression — if we could. How we succeeded, at least how I succeeded, is yet veiled in I should say what. Missouri I'm sure succeeded admirably. The gentlemen clustered round to the great annoyance and chagrin of other young ladies present.

New Providence, Tennessee, Monday night, November 26, 1860

To my great annoyance, the weather has grown warmer and the rain has been falling constantly all day. "Tell me, ye winged winds, is there no place where beef is not found and spare ribs and back bones can be found in plenty."[113] Uncle Trice would have killed hogs today if the weather had been suitable. For once Cousin Lou has spent a day within doors. I assisted Aunt T a little on her rug and made a few hair flowers. Mr. Homer gave us a short call, and nothing could be heard but "Miss Nannie," "Miss Nannie."[114] Some things I like to hear repeated; others again I'm pleased to let pass after the first hearing. Read the whole of Dora Dean by Mrs. Holmes[115] tonight with the exception of a few pages.

New Providence, Tennessee, Tuesday night, November 27, 1860

"The happy day has at length arrived." Uncle Trice killed hogs today, and I'm so glad. Soon after breakfast, wet and rainy as it was, Cousin Lou and I went over to Clarksville, she for her new brocade silk, I to have a new bonnet made. Our dresses certainly very elegant looking and better than all, fits beautifully. The body is perfectly plain, the sleeves tight with two puffs at the top. I'm so sorry tight sleeves are becoming so fashionable. Homely wrists and strong arms will suffer and, if hoops are entirely abandoned, what will we do? All that has added so much to our appearance for the last few years seems to be giving place to some of the most abominable fashions. What a figure some of us will display, with gored dress sleeves tighter than the skin, if possible, and boots minus heels slipping about like the spirits of those who departed long before the reign of heels and crinoline. Made several hair flowers today and intended to read Maggie Miller[116] almost through tonight, but Mr. Homer came and remained until late bed time.

New Providence, Tennessee, Wednesday night, November 28, 1860

Not a fashion will I write or think about tonight, but of "hard times," failure in business, and the introduction of so many weighty responsibilities.[117] New born babes are heard crying on all sides, banks are suspending, and business is almost on a complete stand still, while the news of some friend's failure is almost of daily occurrence. The business world generally is recessing and has received a shock that I fear will not be recovered from soon. Mr. Knox, one of our best citizens, was deprived yesterday of the last servant that he owns. He's left with no visible means of support and with a wife and two helpless little children.[118] Many other cases, no less serious than his, are anticipated by the close of the year.

The crisis of 1860 will long be remembered by many, no doubt, with anything but feelings of pleasure and satisfaction. The political world for some time past has been greatly agitated, the business world greatly shocked. Even the domestic has partaken somewhat of the disturbance. Our homes, some of them, are less quiet than usual — Mrs. Harrelson's and Davis's particularly. On Sunday, Mrs. Davis admitted a young lady into her house hoping to receive from her some comfort or consolation in regard to the troubled times, and on Saturday night, Mrs. Harrelson admitted a young gentleman on the same account. How the two succeeded I'm unable to say. But one thing I do know Mr. Homer called this evening and left us some very nice partridges, and tonight George treated us to some very fine oysters, with the promise of a handsome present if I would make for him a flower of Missouri's hair.

Thursday, Mr. Garrett[119] came down and Cousin Lou and I threw all our other engagements aside and went up home with him. After four hours' travel we found ourselves seated round this comfortable fireside of one of Ky.'s wealthiest planters. We had a fire large enough for "all out-doors," as many as eight covers on our bed, and fresh meats in abundance, but anything now before fresh turnpikes[120] if we didn't have the roughest ride up there "perhaps." Inez[121] is still very low. The rest of the family were in tolerable health and all seem to join in making our visit agreeable. Little Ella Riggins[122] was, however, the principal source of amusement. She is without a doubt an oddity. We left for home early this morning. Here in time to hear sad news, the Hopkinsville Asylum was burned a day or two since and with it several of the inmates consumed.[123] The scene must have been horrifying. Dr. Shaw[124] was also burnt out yesterday. This evening went over to Clarksville and brought myself home quite a nice bonnet, blue velvet trimmed with black, a plume of rich color and in front handsome velvet flowers with gilt ones interspersed. I think it rather small.

New Providence, Tennessee, Tuesday night, December 4, 1860

Still cold, indoors all day until late when I went over to see Mrs. Wilson a while. Met with my — not friend but the opposite, Mary Trice.[125] Since supper Mr. Homer paid us a visit; he's rented his home to the preacher though is still in the notion to marry of late. He's not very choice.[126] Miss Fannie, Miss Nannie and I, he says, may throw up straws for him.

New Providence, Tennessee, Saturday morning, December 22, 1860

Two weeks ago today I left home for Hopkinsville, my object being to visit the families of cousins Steve Trice and Louis Waller.[127] The first Sunday I went to hear Mr. Sears[128] preach and the next to hear Mr. Trimble[129] lecture on the condition of Africa. He exhibited several curiosities & specimens of work made by the native Africans. His lecture was in the highest degree entertaining and instructive.

New Providence, Tennessee, Sunday night, December 23, 1860

After writing yesterday Archy Ferguson[130] and Mr. Osborne[131] called to see us. Mr. Homer came up after supper and was seemingly glad to see me. He says he wrote to me while at Hopkinsville;[132] but I scarcely believe it, never would a letter have been more acceptable, for I was exceedingly anxious to hear from home. Matrimony is yet his favorite theme. This morning I joined the bible class. Mr. Malone has reorganized the school. He preached at 11 o'clock. After dinner went with Cousin Lou to Mrs. Pollard's. She and Mary Britton[133] are both considerably disappointed about their Nashville trip. After waiting 3 days for the Rover, she packed up last night and left them. Tonight Mr. Homer, Bettie, and Jo Wray[134] and myself went to church. Mr. M's text was 48th chap & 8th verse.

Political matters are growing worse and worse. South Carolina we've heard has already seceded, and it is thought the cotton states will follow, and more than probable Tenn. and Ky.[135] A disunion, it is thought, will bring about civil war, and then what desolation and ruin will be spread over the country. In view of such a state of things, old men are already beginning to carry sad faces, and the young ones to think seriously of leaving home and friends for the battlefield. A cloud seems to be hovering over this beautiful land of ours which I greatly fear will soon burst forth in such fury as to tear asunder all that has hitherto given to it such charm and attraction.

New Providence, Tennessee, Tuesday night, December 25, 1860

Spent yesterday morning baking cake. Cousin Jane and Uncle William Mallory dined with us. Sylus Trice called and made arrangement for going out to Mr. Barbee's to a party. We went, but few were there. The amusements were various — card playing, thimble playing, &c. The most agreeable with me, however, was the oyster game. Mr. Hewitt and I ate against each other, and strange to say Mr. H quit almost a saucer ahead of me. He never made himself more agreeable. Miss Mollie B's[136] face all the while reminded me of an April day, sometimes sunshiny and sometimes — not showery, but quite cloudy. The performance closed last night with a "big" egg nog about 1 o'clock. I was the first to retire and the first to appear in the parlor this morning; so, for once I have something to brag of. Breakfasted at 9 at home; by ½ 10 found Mrs. Wilson, Mo Madole, and Cousin Lou here. Old "Santa Claus," I soon found, had been sparing with his gifts. Of course, my stocking was the first thing looked for. Found in it nothing but a book, some apples, oranges, nuts, &c. Nothing of interest has occurred during the day. Tonight, at a late hour, several distinguished gentlemen honored me with a call; among them was the celebrated Garibaldi, the Chinese ambassador, and others whose names I disremember.[137] Mr. Garrigues[138] introduced them and made himself enough more agreeable than the renowned visitors. They were all in disguise so completely masqued that I recognized none but Jo Staton. I'm glad the young gentlemen have thought of something to make us laugh a little. Received a letter today from TT[139]—8 pages long. He's improving.

New Providence, Tennessee, Friday night, December 28, 1860

Mrs. Helm spent the day with us yesterday. In the morning Cousin Lou left for New Orleans. Where she is now I'm unable to see. In the evening I went down to see Mr. Ward's[140] family off on the Rover. They are going to Ark. to live. Met with Mr. and Mrs. Malone and Mr. and Mrs. Smith down there. We were compelled to leave before the boat came. The young gentlemen of the place gave a party at the hotel last night. I unexpectedly went, accompanied by Sylus, Jo Wray, and Charlie Tandy.[141] Returned with Charlie alone, the others having selected each a more agreeable companion. The parlor was filled with all the youth and beauty of our town. Conversation was the principal source of amusement, though a play called trip was introduced several times during the evening in which most all of the ladies and gentlemen engaged. I drank, ate, laughed at Garriques, and enjoyed to a great degree the company of one or two. Unexpectedly met with John Mallory there. He dined with us today and spent several hours. Assisted Aunt T about her rug today and paid Mrs. Wilson a short visit. Mrs. Bridgewater[142] and Mrs. Gold called. The last dispatch says Mr. Buchanan[143] has resigned. What will the next news be?

New Providence, Tennessee, Saturday night, December 29, 1860

We had our Christmas dinner today. Cousin Jane, the children, Bettie Homer, and Bell Dunn[144] partook of it with us. The turkey was nicely cooked but some [how] I was not in the humor for enjoying it. Bettie Helm and Mr. Homer paid us a visit after dinner.

New Providence, Tennessee, January 1, 1861

The outdoor world has been calm, clear, and beautiful all day. The little world within Aunt T's room has also been calm and peaceful enough, until just as "old Sol" was making his exit. About that time a cloud gathered suddenly, and the day that had opened so beautifully closed, leaving a gloom which spread over our entire household. Mrs. Ogburn came at the time referred to. She is on her way to Miss. where the next four years of her life will be passed if not the remainder of it. In giving her up we give up one of our best friends. We sever a tie that has been binding us more and more closely ever since the first acquaintance. Her house for years past has been to me a second home. Will and Ann[145] will take possession of the old place and now I will bid farewell to it and all connected with it in person, for my visits henceforth will be few and far between. Made myself a pair of indispensables.[146]

New Providence Tennessee, Wednesday night, January 2, 1861

Read until 10. Then made another pair of indispensables before night. Mrs. Ogburn is still with us. She doesn't know whether or not the boat has left Nashville. She spent the day writing; Jennie trotting round, rainy and muddy as it was. Tonight we've been engaged in some very childish plays. Dick all the while looking on too old, too dignified, hardly to give an approving smile. Miss Dora Broadie[147] was probably occupying his thoughts; if so, of course he was excusable.

New Providence, Tennessee, Thursday night, January 3, 1861

Jennie and I spent the morning making Sarah's hair bouquet. Had a long conversation with Mrs. Ogburn about old times. This evening we went down to pay Mrs. Fauntleroy's family[148] a farewell visit. They were all compelled at last to take a Paducah[149] packet. After supper Uncle T and Aunt T and myself went down with them to the river. The whole of Prov. most was down there to see the last of the F's. The young gentlemen portion of the crowd, each and all wore sad faces, more particularly Sylus, Billie Watts,[150] and Harry Garrigues. The distress indeed seemed mutual. The girls assumed a cheerful air but assumed was all; when off their guard their faces were unusually long. Really, I felt sorry for them all, though it has been so long since I had any experience of the kind that my sympathy didn't extend as far as it would otherwise. The brass band gave them or honored them at least with a few farewell tunes. Mrs. Ogburn left looking very sad and crying. As Aunt T says, we've parted with one of our best friends and perhaps forever. Jennie, the rude romping careless girl of 12, left to return in four years the educated and accomplished Miss Ogburn. But who knows what four years may bring round?

New Providence, Tennessee, Friday night, January 4, 1861

When shall I write 60 without first placing a 0 in the place of the 1? This has been the day appointed by the chief magistrate as a day of fasting and prayer, and shameful to say, not a member of our family has kept it as such.[151] Aunt T I believe did refrain from eating any breakfast. We attended Mr. Malone's prayer meeting at ½ 10. Few were present, though the doors of all the business houses were closed. In the afternoon I went up and presented my Auntie to Mrs. Smith. Mr. Smith came in while we were there and our visit was not regretted. For three hours I have been reading Goodrich's Reflections of a Lifetime,[152] and for the same length of time almost Aunt T and Uncle Trice have been snoring.

New Providence, Tennessee, Monday night, January 7, 1861

Early after breakfast Aunt T and I went down to see Mrs. Ricks for the last time perhaps. We were just in time to pass a few words with her and bid her farewell. I drove her down to the river. She with all her negroes left for Va. about 10 o'clock on the Gen. Anderson. At Nashville she will take the cars through. We gave her freely, thinking it would be to her interest to leave. Yet all were sad, and she the most so of all. She has been in the midst of affliction almost ever since the day she came to make this her home, and it seems on this account we are doubly attached to her. I shall long cherish her memory as her friendship for me has been manifested under more than one circumstance. Dined with Mrs. Staton. Aunt T came home, though afterwards returned and we all went over to pay Mrs. Malone a call and Cousin Jane a visit. Found Mrs. Herring at Cousin Jane's and she in the midst of her cooking utensils, busy getting dinner. Mrs. Herring had a great deal to say about the anticipated war. South Car. has seceded and war is now going on there[153] or is expected to commence there soon. The cloud is gathering fast, and "what will we do?" is the question almost hourly asked. There is no breeze that brings with it good tidings; each dispatch increases the gloom and despondency of the people. Billie Henry[154] and a Mr. Richardson[155] supped with us. Since supper Mr. Homer came up and altogether we've had quite a nice time of it. Mr. R makes himself very agreeable, and Mr. Homer more so than he did on Saturday night. He regrets now some things that slipped from his tongue that night—I expect.

New Providence, Tennessee, Wednesday night, January 9, 1861

Since supper George, Will Trice, and myself went down to hear a lecture from some man I can't say who. I've heard his name was Bell. His subject was Physiology and the ills arising from leading a fashionable life; he reads tolerably well, but lectures badly.

New Providence, Tennessee, Thursday night, January 10, 1861

Read a while after breakfast. Then went to work on a braid and it yet remains unfinished. Mr. Holland[156] and Mr. Carneal both called about dinner and some time was spent in conversation with them. And after they [left], which was about 3, no more work was done—a new arrival and one unexpected prevented. I was called for and went into the parlor afraid almost to guess who it was, so afraid of disappointment. To my surprise I found Mr. Trabue from Memphis. After hearing Mrs. Atkinson say what she did, I was indeed surprised. He's looking better than usual (his personal appearance). He wears a sedate meditative air not atal [at all] like himself; otherwise he looks some little like himself, I think. He talks less—misfortune and disappointment no doubt have had a share in changing his manners, disposition, and indeed his very countenance. He sit [sic] with us in Aunt T's room until late; then left & returned since, and only left a few minutes since it now being nearly 12. The conversation that we've had I don't suppose would interest our most imminent lawyers. My pen is so bad I will not attempt another line.

New Providence, Tennessee, Friday night, January 11, 1861

Finished this morning the braid commenced yesterday. Read a while and talked to Aunt T a while. About 10 o'clock Mr. Trabue came. The remainder of the day was passed in trying to entertain him. Whether or not my lecture to him in regard to old habits proved agreeable I've yet to learn. I didn't spare him in a single instance, "The round unvarnished tale was delivered." We made a partial engagement, not of a political character—a ring was given as a pledge but ha how common this is. Conversation turned on various subjects. The advantages of Mem. over other cities for business &c was the principal topic while Uncle Trice was in the room. The waiter of hickrenuts came at a very acceptable time. Not that interest was dying out, but words; a little time was required to find words with which to express a few ideas. In few words, to sum up the whole of the conversations that have taken place today and write legibly here on one of these blank pages, I doubt whether Johnson[157] would feel improved from reading them or not. He left for Memphis about 4. At 7 Mr. Homer came in and at 8 the bell rang, and a servant entered with a farewell note written at Trice's Landing. The curiosity of all present seemed greater than mine. I alone was disinterested and to me it was addressed. After giving Aunt T permission to read it and her refusal, I read it myself, and not to his credit will it be said that note was as long as if it had been written from home and we had not been together three hours previous. After all it was a simple request. A picture was drawn today, and when that is no longer a picture but a reality, then perhaps the request will be granted.[158]

New Providence, Tennessee, Sunday night, January 13, 1861

I did very well while engaged in Sunday school and church this morning but must acknowledge that my spirits this evening have almost as much depressed as Aunt T's. After dinner all went to sleep but myself. I took up Josephus and had read but few chapters when Mr. Homer came in. Of course my book was laid aside and for a while we chatted away as usual, but soon he began to complain of the effects of a hearty dinner and without even asking permission fell into a heavy sleep. However, intended with me and was not objectionable and I soon found myself as deeply engaged as ever in the history of the Jews. A chunk rolled down and was the first to disturb his quiet slumbers. Then Aunt T came in and, of course, all reading was at an end.

The remainder of the evening was passed in conversation, the principal topic of which was some noted characters in Nashville and the adventure of his and poor Mr. Jo Harris'[159] was related, which today if he were here would be referred to with more regret than pleasure. The deep, deep depravity of the human race. How much to be regretted and how much to be feared? Why need we wonder at our present condition as a nation? What have we not done to bring down the wrath and curses of God? Even in our midst in our daily walks we see enough to call forth his displeasure continually. Still we go heedlessly on, never considering for once what will be the awful result of the present political strife. The latest papers say that the Southern states have gone to fighting among themselves[160] and if this be true what may we yet expect? Who can tell what will be the sad state of things a year hence? Prosperity has done the most of this. Success has made men unmindful of the laws of his God or his country, and nothing but humility and submission will ever bring to him again the happiness so long enjoyed by us as a people.

News: Fannie Holland[161] and Bennie Bradshaw[162] are to be married on next Wednesday. Received an invitation to the wedding today but the present rain and weather I think will prevent my attendance.

New Providence, Tennessee, Tuesday night, January 15, 1861

At the close of a rainy day what has one to write, particularly one who never saw the sublimity of a thunderstorm or felt the music of the raindrops pattering against the window? Mr. Crittenden of Ky.[163] has presented some resolution which if adopted will I hope bring once more peace and quiet to our country.

New Providence, Tennessee, Friday night, January 18, 1861

I was in the bed most of the morning suffering with, Miss Annie would say, pain under the apron. This evening made several stars for my quilt, read several pages in Milton and some in Shakespeare. Tonight Mr. Homer came up and brought with him bad news — Crittenden's resolutions were rejected and the {*indecipherable*} received, dissolution is now at hand.[164]

New Providence, Tennessee, Saturday night, January 19, 1861

Cousin Lou has come and brought me a nice pineapple, some oranges, and a pair of slippers all the way from Canal St, New Orleans. She's got so much to tell us; the excitement in the city on the 9th of Jan.[165] she says can scarcely be imagined. We know nothing up here about excitement and etc. compared with the people down there.

New Providence, Tennessee, Tuesday night, January 22, 1861

Received a letter from Tom while at the dinner table. Such a letter, one not familiar with us both would readily infer from reading it that we were actually engaged and that a consummation of the matter was not far in the future. What reply shall I make is now the question.

New Providence, Tennessee, Friday night, January 25, 1861

Finished joining my calico[166] quilt today and Milton's works,[167] two very important items. At last we've some prospect of an ice spell. Today has been very cool. An old drunken man, Mr. Ross, froze to death last night. Mr. Andrew Long[168] also died this morning. His disease I think was consumption. Mr. Homer gave us [a] few moments' call this evening. Mr. Edlin[169] called to see if Aunt T could hire him Emma.[170] Went up and took tea with

Mrs. Smith this evening. George is with us tonight, looking quite dull from the effects of last night's dissipation (a party at Sol Barbee).

New Providence, Tennessee, Monday night, Jan 28, 1861

Unexpectedly Uncle Trice came tonight. He brought with him nothing but news. The political excitement there is still at the highest pitch. All are for disunion or the most of them.

New Providence, Tennessee, Tuesday night, January 29, 1861

Mr. Homer was up tonight. Uncle Trice gave him me with the Stanley house. The "consent of other parties" was not taken into consideration at all. He with others seems more serious about political affairs than ever, but this is not Uncle Trice's greatest trouble. He is security for B. Pollard[171] to the amount of seventeen hundred dollars. And news has recently come that he's owing as much as $10,000 in New Orleans and that the men have sent for it and that with other debts he's compelled to pay now in a very short time. If he fails what will the rest of us do? Uncle Trice says that within less than a year Aunt T and I will be doing the work of servants unless a change for the better takes place soon.[172] Were such times ever known before? And yet I fear the worst has not come. Uncle Trice certainly occupies a very precarious situation and the prospects for extricating himself are very slim.

New Providence, Tennessee, Saturday night, February 9, 1861

Finished my band this morning, read an interesting letter to Cousin Jane, and after dinner read a chap. in Judson's life.[173] Then went into the kitchen to make some cabbage pickle and just as I was up to "the elbows of my feet" in work, Mr. Hewitt came. And what was I to do? Aunt T had gone up town. Inez went to invite him in and couldn't unlock the parlor door, so I found myself in a "fire" and the only way of extricating myself was to make my appearance as soon as possible and relate the circumstances. When was I so surprised? Uncle Trice today while Cousin Jane was here, came in with the most beautifully finished broom in his hand I ever saw. He handed it to me and remarked that it was [a] present. From whom or from whence such a present could have come I couldn't imagine. (Mr. Homer's return I had not then heard of) The secret was soon told, "that was all he saw in Cairo[174] worth bringing home." Tonight he came up at 8 o'clock and gave us the details of his trip and corn speculation. The Methodist quarterly meeting commenced today.

New Providence, Tennessee, Tuesday night, February 12, 1861

The world yet stands and Cousin Lou is as large as ever. She is with us tonight and has been all day. Cousin Will and I went to church tonight, heard that Mr. Gooch would preach, but in his absence, Mr. Malone occupied the stand. Previous to opening the exercises, he gave a reproof to some of "the fast" young ladies about town—the most severe, the most cutting I ever listened to. He referred them to their standing as citizens of Tennessee, the mortification given to parents, the want of self-respect displayed by so doing, but all to no effect. The second and most cutting of all had to be given before even the whispering ceased. Mr. H and Cousin Lou had fine times in my absence.

New Providence, Tennessee, Wednesday night, February 13, 1861

Mr. Homer was on his return home tonight. He called at my door, and after compliments were passed, I rose to offer him a seat. After refusing what most agreeable to me, he drew from his pocket a bundle and in a moment more I was in possession of some of the nicest maple sugar and some of the finest oranges I have seen anywhere. These he said were sent me by my sweetheart. "It must be a very nice sweetheart to present such nice things."

New Providence, Tennessee, Friday night, February 15, 1861

Mr. Homer called this morning and according to promise brought Aunt T's pipe stems.[175] Tonight he sent me up ½ bush. of the nicest apples I've seen lately.

New Providence, Tennessee, Saturday night, February 16, 1861

Uncle Trice's birthday, 50 years old today. The winter of his age is coming on, and the winter of '61 too if I should be allowed to say, and it is almost freezing cold and the snow has been falling most all day. Disagreeable as it seems, Tom went up town and spent the evening. Mr. Homer called long enough to interrupt me while writing a letter to Memphis. I had to finish it after tea and my —— aches dreadfully from bending over this old book.

New Providence, Tennessee, Monday night, February 18, 1861

Mrs. Gordon was up and ready to leave this morning at 4. At 5 Uncle T saw her comfortably situated on the cars. Sewing all day until late when I went up to Mary Smith's a while. Nothing but secession and disunion could be talked of. The general opinion is that war will commence at the capitol within a few days. The 4th of March[176] is near at hand and then the decision will come. I'm almost glad of it, for we've been in suspense so long. That day will perhaps be the bloodiest America ever knew and then we had wished it farther off.

New Providence, Tennessee, Thursday night, February 28, 1861

Inez, the only piece of property to which I've the least claim and the only servant for whom I've much love, is now in bed and very ill. Her death will give me much pain should it occur and yet, I can scarcely hope for her recovery. The attack from the first has been so violent. Dr. H, I fear, is not sufficiently acquainted the disease to afford much relief. Yesterday was the first of her complaining though she has been looking badly for some time. Her limbs all seem to be very sore and her body generally swollen, though to a slight extent. Her fever is not high, she perspires very freely, and yet talks like one entirely crazy with a most violent fever. How could I give her up? [This sentence is written at the top of the page in Rep's hand:] "These lines were not intended for your peepers."

New Providence, Tennessee, Saturday night, March 2, 1861

Today has been equal to yesterday in beauty, though not quite as pleasant, for it has been uncomfortably warm ever since dinner. And this morning while I was up at the pond fishing with Ann Amelia & Laura Helm, [177] the sun for a while before we left was really oppressive. After dinner I tried to take a nap, but the intrusion of an idle thought, just as the gate of "dreamland" was being opened, drove from my eyes each time "quiet nature's sweet restorer,"[178] and failing in this I lazily went about making some cakes, and as might be expected the result was anything but a dishful of nice cakes. About 12 I received a letter from Tom in which was written distress, more than once. It seems my letters are about to prove thorns rather than flowers. At least my last seemed to give very little satisfaction and altogether was the source of many unpleasant thoughts. I'm left to infer that my letters like myself are "hard to understand." Not a sentence in my last was intended to give a moment's uneasiness; yet my letters are not commenced correctly, not closed correctly, too many blanks are referred to, and in a word, they are all wrong, Let it go. Time and studel [sic] may improve me. The news from Washington is anything but favorable.[179]

New Providence, Tennessee, March 4, 1861

A day long to be remembered by the American people, more particularly by Abe Lincoln and W Upton Hoover.[180] This is the day for Lincoln to take to his seat as president of a few United States, and Mr. Hoover to take his as the—not president.—but subject of Miss Nannie Smith.[181] Whoever heard of a similar case? They were married by Dr. McMullen[182] today at 11 and tomorrow at 1 he leaves for the eastern cities. She is to remain in the country until just before he returns. Then she will come down and be ready to receive him. Mrs. Pollard was here later this evening and says he's not even going to stay out there tonight. Certainly it is the strangest way of doing I have ever heard of. To say the least of it they were put to it to introduce something novel. What is it though a Yankee wouldn't think of? How Lincoln's case will result is just about as hard to determine as Hoover's. It has been said that he went the greater part of the route to Washington in disguise,[183] and it has been prophesied for months that the Southern people would not allow him to take his seat today. Rumor has already reached here that they are fighting up there. We've no reason to believe this however.[184] Indeed, when I hear anything I never know whether to believe it or not. So many dispatches have been sent and so many things published that were entirely false.

New Providence, Tennessee, Tuesday night, March 5, 1861

How changeable the weather is. This morning the ground was covered with snow; this evening scarcely a trace of it is to be seen. Still it is very cold. Went down after breakfast to see Mr. Hoover about having a hair breastpin tipped.[185] He actually left Nannie yesterday evening, actually left this evening at 1 for New York. Sewed busily until dinner. Mr. Keezee,[186] Mr. Garrett, and Tom Riggins dined with us. Bettie Helm spent the evening. Late she and I went down to see Miss Nannie Davidson & Maggie. Lincoln, the dispatches say, is making preparations to force the South into {*secession*} and is thought war will commence now very soon. The gentlemen scarcely talk of anything else, and all seem to be excited. What will we do?

New Providence, Tennessee, Wednesday night, March 6, 1861

Spent the morning answering letters. Cousins Bet and Jane called. After dinner went up to spend some time with Mrs. Gold. Mrs. Malone came and Aunt T soon sent for me. She remained an hour or two, long enough to take two long smokes. I sewed until late, went up town, brought some white-lined envelopes, and some yellow ones. Tonight, I read for two hours and a half an old history of Rome.[187] No company, not even Uncle Trice, was here to interrupt me. The last papers contain the most important parts of Lincoln's speech. He says he's going to take all the public property recently levied on by the South by force unless given up peaceably.[188] That the South will never do, so we are expecting each day to bring the news that war has commenced.

New Providence, Tennessee, Saturday night, March 9, 1861

Commenced a shirt at 8 and finished it at 1. Had the remainder of the evening to play in. Paid Mrs. Wilson a good long visit. Read Lincoln inaugural address; he intends retaking the forts and collecting the revenue. The papers, as far as I've seen, consider it a declaration of war.

New Providence, Tennessee, Sunday night, March 10, 1861

Our school is still increasing. Left before school closed, on account of going over to Clarksville to hear Mr. Duncan. Emma and I went over. His congregations are improving, not in appearance but numbers. The sermon was excellent; the congregation unusually good. After dinner read about 40 pages in Josephus.[189] Dr. Herring called in to see Inez.

New Providence, Tennessee, Friday night, March 15, 1861

Uncle Steven paid us a short visit too, and last but not least, John. His business was to get a tight sleeve pattern for the girls. His conversation was mostly about Lincoln and his inaugural speech. We've been listening to the band from the porch and the music is indeed splendid. We didn't attend "Pro Johnson's" complimentary benefit[190] for reasons best known to ourselves.

New Providence, Tennessee, Saturday night, March 16, 1861

Rose in time this morning to hear the result of "Pro Johnson's" concert at the table. Vocal & instrumental music lasted until 9; then dancing commenced and that lasted until about 12 at which time the whole affair was broken up with a row between Coalman, the watch, and a negro. One or two members of the church danced; still I'm accused of selfishness and my course unapproved by a great many just because I refrain from attending such places and from mingling with such people as we might naturally expect to meet with. Bad news—one [of] Aunt T's setting hens was taken suddenly ill today, and her recovery is very doubtful. We've been "counting chickens" that I fear will "never hatch." Mrs. Staton, Mrs. Howard, and other ladies that have called this evening say that it is nothing unusual for French's[191] to die on their nest in that way.

New Providence, Tennessee, Wednesday night March 20, 1861

I paid Mrs. Hoover a call. She was dressed up—to the neck in a pink morning wrapper with velourens[192] collar and undersleeves. She showed us several handsome presents Mr. H brought her from "the East." Among them was a handsome bonnet, a lace mantle, and a beautiful ring made of his hair. The last was exquisitely beautiful; the design was so pretty. He brought my hair breastpin nicely finished off. I like it very much. Mrs. Hart and Mattie Carneal[193] would scarcely recognize their own hair.

New Providence, Tennessee, Thursday night, March 21, 1861

Mr. Homer was up tonight with one of Campbell's[194] books. He's no longer a believer in infant baptism, but an immersionist[195] throughout. It doesn't take a tornado to change his mind, for that like his body is rather diminutive and liable of being turned by the slightest zephyr. His want of stability is one of his greatest deficiencies.

New Providence, Tennessee, Wednesday night, March 27, 1861

Mr. Slaughter and Mr. Garrett were off early for the tobacco sales. I went up town for several little articles and returned to make preparations for going home with Mr. Slaughter. We rather expected to leave this evening, but Mr. S's business would not admit of it. Mrs. Pendleton[196] from Ky. called a while today. We've not seen her in so long; still she looks perfectly natural. Mary & May Trice and Mrs. Wilson called this evening. I was put to it for something to talk about. For an hour I did my best and failed after all no doubt to interest them. When I'm forced to entertain a certain class, "soap gives out" about the time the weather is dispensed with. One of John Helm's children paid Aunt T a visit today. She did manage to leave her chickens long enough to talk to him about ½ hour. She has 13 of the prettiest & sweetest little chickens I ever saw. We pet them almost as much as if they were infants.

New Providence, Tennessee, Wednesday evening, April 10, 1861

How strange to think I've been away from home the whole of two weeks; at least tomorrow will have been two weeks. I went up with Mr. Slaughter to Pembroke. Found Cousin Ann, Hellen, & Donie[197] at home; and all pleased with idea of having me pay them so long a visit.

New Providence, Tennessee, Friday night, April 12, 1861

Mattie Rogers called a while this morning. Volunteers are going south in large numbers and country is on the eve of being totally ruined.[198] What will we do? I had hoped the excitement was all over with.

New Providence, Tennessee, Sunday night, April 14, 1861

The morning was clear and beautiful. Hellen and I spent an hour or two in Sunday school. Returned and went over to Clarksville to hear Mr. Lowrie,[199] the Methodist minister. His congregation was large, subject special and general Providences. In few moments we were enjoying to the fullest extent the luxury [of] a good nap and continued to do so until about 4 o'clock when a card came saying that Messrs. Glenn and Barker from Clarksville wished to call. The card was soon answered, and with all our hurrying we were not ready to make an appearance for some time after they came. Mr. B I was very much pleased with; for Mr. G I have no use: "this is only the suburbs of Clarksville," "you must visit the city before you leave." [200] I wish the heart of their great city could boast of a few things now in possession of "the suburbs." The conversation of the evening turned on various subjects, the principal of which was Miss Carrie Williams,[201] and the neighborhood of Pembroke, the pleasure in visiting it &c &c. They left after sunset.

New Providence, Tennessee, Monday night, April 15, 1861

Never have I seen rain fall more steadily than it has today. Hellen and I've not been permitted even to venture to the front gate, and so many calls we'd laid off for day. We've knit almost a stocking apiece however on the strength of it. Such sad news the last dispatch tonight. Lincoln has called for 75,000 men and today probably they were fighting in Charleston.[202] The Mexicans too are trying to retake Texas.[203] Oh what times! What bloody times we are yet to have!

New Providence, Tennessee, Tuesday night, April 16, 1861

There is a call for volunteers from all the states, and it is thought an attempt will be made to take Washington City. A company is being made up in Clarksville[204] and it is said so much excitement never was known there before. Gray headed ministers of the gospel have enlisted in the cause.[205]

New Providence, Tennessee, Wednesday night, April 18, 1861

Mr. Homer was up tonight. The political news grows worse. A company was formed here this evening; 30,000 Northerners are on their way to Harpers

Ferry,[206] they say, to take it, and the Virginians are weak enough to suppose they can defend it.

New Providence, Tennessee, Thursday night, April 19, 1861

After considerable confusion this morning Mr. Layne & family[207] left for home about 9. They heard through the driver that one of the servants at home had been shot. It gave them great uneasiness; indeed, the whole family have [been] dreading something of the kind for a good while. Before dinner, made Inez and Hellen a bonnet and about 12, Cousin Marion Osborne came. She and I spent most of the evening with Cousin Jane. Mr. Homer went with us down and was just tipsy enough to make himself ridiculous. He's so provoking when in one of his ways. He was up tonight and notwithstanding the presence of Cousin Lou and Mrs. Trabue, he carried on to the greatest extent about sweethearts marrying &c, his favorite themes. He laughed very singularly when Mrs. T wanted to know when I heard from Memphis.[208] I didn't know exactly how to account for it. I hope however that all is dark to him as yet. Great many of the rumors of yesterday and those most distressing have been contradicted today. So, I scarcely know what to believe and yet dare not hope for the better while I see so much preparation being made for the defense and protection of us weaker vessels. The excitement is still very high. Political with that in regard to the great sirens has brought as many persons in town today, as might be expected if war had commenced as near as Nashville. All wore sad faces and speak mournfully of the future. Mrs. T really cries while talking on the subject. Her brother is up from Memphis and brought such discouraging news that she feels worse no doubt than she would.

New Providence, Tennessee, Saturday night, April 20, 1861

Mrs. Gold gave me a pet squirrel yesterday and that has added greatly to my amusement. My idle moments are not passed so much in grieving over the sad condition of our country. Took a long nap after dinner. Went over to see Mrs. Wilson afterwards. I shouldn't be surprised if the thought of her "darlings" having to go to war had such an effect on her as to render her unfit for discharging duty at home or making herself agreeable abroad. Really, I believe it will take but little more to cause a derangement of the mind. She declares if "Darling" goes, she is going too. Bettie Helm came up to read this evening, but a call from Mary Britton prevented our making much progress. Indeed there was so much excitement and passing on the street that we were not very much interested in our book before she came. Late Mrs. Smith, her sister, sister-in-law and brother, Bettie H, and myself went down to see them parade. The company was small—and their officers smaller.

New Providence, Tennessee, Sunday night, April 21, 1861

The cool spell which has lasted for the last few days has given place to a warm spring-like time. Much uneasiness has been felt on account of the wheat crop, and the heavy frosts a few mornings back may have injured it slightly. Our school is still flourishing. Dr. Mc offers new inducements each Sunday morning to the children; the blue rosette[209] may be seen on almost every hat and beneath the same is generally worn a face over which a cloud has passed, leaving few traces of its former cheerfulness. News came today that Jeff Davis,[210] the Southern president, was marching with 75,000 men to take Washington city, but like many other of the reports I can scarcely credit it.[211] Cousin Jane spent the evening with Aunt Tabbie, Mr. Homer with me. We took a short ride, and I have my doubts whether or not I did right in doing so. Sunday evenings, I think, might be better employed.

New Providence, Tennessee, Tuesday night, April 23, 1861

Read and sewed all the morning. After dinner Dick and Archy Ferguson spent an hour or two with us. Arch has joined the Minute Company.[212] Ross Donaldson[213] supped with us tonight; he joined a minute company today with several other school boys and he's looking miserably over it. Their school is entirely broken up and Mr. Hewitt, the teacher, is Capt. of the company.[214] John Mallory and Efe Manson[215] joined the same company, and all of them they say are wearing faces 5 inches longer than usual. Had a letter from Tom today. It was so thoughtful in him. Though he hadn't received my last letter, he sit down and wrote me not a long but a satisfactory letter in regard to his future course. He plainly told me that he had joined a minute company called the "Memphis Southern Guards"[216] and he had only done "what any man with spirit, pride, or love for his country, would do," He's ready he says for any emergency and feels that he would be acting cowardly and "not worthy a citizenship or sweetheart," to act otherwise. While I approve of his course and honor him for his bravery, I deeply regret that circumstances are such as to leave no other alternative.

He's enlisted, it is true, in a good cause but one in which danger is to be contended with on all sides and from which I fear he will not be released until by death. Though each volunteer and indeed every Southerner seems so confidant of success, I greatly fear that death and not victory will be their fate. There is so little on which we can ground the least hope. Nevertheless, history abounds with instances in which a courageous few have been successful over thousands and may this be another ever memorable instance added to the list. May history yet record the heroic deeds of a Southern Themistocles[217] and the downfall of a northern Xerxes.[218] Mr. Homer was up tonight and is curious to know whether or not I am going to cry about my "sweetheart is having to go to war."

New Providence, Tennessee, Wednesday night, April 24, 1861

Sick, sick, both in body and mind. Mrs. Wilson spent most of the morning with us and it was nothing but the war — war. Her friends that have enlisted to go off and the negroes at home is all she can talk of. She's enough to sicken the heart of the most resolute and to madden the brain of the strongest mind. Mrs. Gold was down this evening and she's as nervous almost as Mrs. W. She fears more from a negro insurrection than anything.[219] And indeed the fears of a great many of the gentlemen seems to be on this account. Still not a word can be gathered from them, as to their intentions. Their conduct, during the whole of the excitement, has been such as to excite suspicion. They seem too attentive to every conversation, and so perfectly ignorant when questioned.[220] How gratifying it would be to know that it was the African and not the Indian race so near extinct. We were up at Mr. Atkinson's tonight, and his funny jokes for a while took the place of sad thoughts & bad feelings.

New Providence, Tennessee, Thursday night, April 25, 1861

Went out with Mr. Smith and his scholars to the burial of Ann Eliza Brittain[221] this morning. Her disease was diphtheria,[222] and many think she would have finally revived if she remained at Mrs. Pollard's, though the attack was very severe from the first. She was a sweet child and will be greatly missed both in the schoolroom and at home. After dinner Mrs. Gold and I went up to see Mrs. Smith. Mr. Smith made himself very agreeable indeed. He took such interest in showing me some geological specimens and a variety of pretty shells. ½ 4 went down to attend a meeting of the Ladies of New Providence,[223] for the purpose of forming themselves in an association to assist the volunteers. The Volunteer's Friend Society was the name selected. I was elected secretary and have about as much business with the office as Inez would have. News was received today that Ft. Pickens[224] had been taken after a great struggle by the Southerners. The loss on both sides very great. Before breakfast perhaps we will hear the same contradicted.

New Providence, Tennessee, Friday night, April 26, 1861

There was considerable excitement and distress this morning, in our village. News came that Gov. Harris[225] had called for the company of volunteers at Clarksville and to which belong several of our young men over here, but the order was recalled, and we had the melancholy pleasure of mingling with them again tonight at a party given complimentary to them. Most of them look very sad indeed, though an effort is being made all the while to assume an air of cheerfulness. Mr. Garrigues and his letters from home seem to be attracting general attention. He's a native of Philadelphia. He's been with us but a few months and in spite of a mother's entreaties and a father's advice, he's joined Mr. Forbes'[226] company of minute men, dressed in the complete uniform, and is ready at a moment warning to engage in the service of the South. Strange but true are the above facts, and yet — and yet, as Mr. Lowrie says. Mr. Hewitt spent several hours with us today, and tonight I had the exquisite pleasure of his company to the party. He's Capt. of a company of young men among whom are many of my — acquaintances. To see him leave and they too would surely bring the tears. The Ladies Volunteer's Friend Society met this morning but no business of importance was transacted.

New Providence, Tennessee, Saturday night, April 27, 1861

Read, knit, and thought all the morning. After dinner did nothing particular but answer Tom's last letter (received by today's mail). He's camping with a large company in Memphis, "gone into regular recruit camp" and all of them he says are growing impatient, eager for something more exciting than the regular soldier life they are now leading. He says I "would laugh to see him cooking." There is little I think connected with a soldiers' camp to make one laugh. The Northern troops at Cairo seized the Hillman yesterday and by threats and force took powder, munitions, &c to the amount of 12,000 belonging to this county.[227] The gloom seems to hang heavier than ever over our citizens since the news came. Many of them are very desponding while some have yet great hope. Mr. Homer was up tonight and he brought such discouraging facts that we all are feeling considerably depressed.

New Providence, Tennessee, Sunday night, April 28, 1861

Read Josephus until church hour this morning; then went to hear Mr. West preach. I suppose he preached a good sermon as, generally, my thoughts were wandering for some cause. I know the sermon was good tonight; his text was "As for me I will be satisfied when I rise in the image of the Lord."[228] Took a short nap and a long ride with Mr. Manson this evening. Mr. Burgess[229] called to see me about 4 o'clock. He thinks, 'he'll be off to the war" soon. To give up such a brilliant intellect will be quite sad. He dislikes sentimental poetry so much, I wonder if he ever composed any other kind.

New Providence, Tennessee, Monday night, April 29, 1861

My mind is much more composed than it has been for some time. I read a good long while after breakfast this morning without giving a single thought to war, Cairo &c &c. At least my mind was sufficiently under control to prevent my thoughts wandering too far off. Mr. Homer though came in and put an end to my composure, with his bible stories, Yankee tales, &c.

New Providence, Tennessee, Tuesday night, April 30, 1861

Cousin Jane and Alley left early after breakfast. I then knit steadily until 9 o'clock, when Aunt T came in from Mrs. Atkinson's, and who did she bring with her? I will only say a grandson of Mr. A's (his name I can remember without writing it). We talked until 12. The prospect of war, life in camp, the march of the company from Memphis to Randolph, &c, &c were the subjects of conversation. Tom came again and remained until 6. Before he left, Cousin Lou and Mrs. Gold came. A subject for 12 months known only to a chosen few will now, I suppose, be heralded forth.[230]

New Providence, Tennessee, Wednesday night, May 1, 1861

Mr. Hewitt and John Mallory took supper with us. John is still with us. Mr. H left about 8 o'clock. Both are looking sad but J the more so of the two. He scarcely makes himself agreeable; he's so serious and sad looking all the time. He says but little excepting about the affairs of the country, and about that he presents the dark side of the picture entirely. He, with the rest of Mr. Hewitt's company, are going into camp tomorrow.

New Providence, Tennessee, Thursday night, May 2, 1861

The weather is so cool again. John and I sit out in the porch this morning a good while and as a consequence I've suffered with a severe headache most ever since. The subject of conversation while we were out there was the war, the dangers associated with it, the soldier's life as a general thing, and other things relating to the subject, that it were useless to mention here. The piece written on the blank leaf of an old chemistry, however, was the most interesting thing that claimed my attention and I'm sure many bloody battles will have to take place in this beautiful land of ours before the sentiments so beautifully expressed in that impromptu piece will be erased from my mind. Memory will cherish them long as a precious memento of this day, and should they finally be given up to oblivion it will be when all the pleasures of Earth are lost in the same. John seems to take a right view of the case and is prompted no doubt from the right motives, yet he looks sad, very sad when he talks of leaving. Capt. Hewitt's company all went over this morning to the camp. Aunt T and Mollie Barbee did crying enough both for Cousin Lou and myself.

Aunt T went down to see old Mrs. Helm[231] just from Va. She's very old, 86 years old, born the year the Revolutionary War commenced. Remembers perfectly the gratitude and thanksgiving of the people when peace was declared and yet has her mind almost as sound as ever and seems wide awake to all that is now going on in these times of war and famine. She has lived to see the stars & stripes wave over our land in triumph, has heard the sweet song of "many in one" and sad to say she has seen those stars united by the precious blood of our forefathers, torn asunder, and perhaps has heard for the last time the songs that have ever called to mind so many soul stirring remembrances. The star that was so long obscured beneath a dark horizon she has seen rise, bidding defiance to the most threatening clouds and pursuing a steady course till reaching the zenith of its glory. She has followed it through the entire course, and now finds that with her own decline that too has taken the downward path. And strangest of all is, that star has run its course more swiftly than the human life. Scarcely a generation will have passed away before our country is in ruins. Even now it is a wreck compared with its former greatness. May god avert the awful calamity that is about to sink us beneath the wave of oblivion. And bless us again as a nation, undeserving as we are.

Mrs. Helm says extensive preparations are being made throughout the state of Va. for the battle at Washington City. Jeff Davis and Beauregard both are there busily, though secretly, engaged the whole time. The RR bridges are guarded everywhere, and seats are being added to all the cars for transporting the soldiers from the Southern states. Mr. Homer was up tonight; came to see how I "was taking about my sweethearts leaving." He brought me some such nice beef, (dried). This reminds me — Aunt T had broiled chickens for supper, and they were right good size.

New Providence, Tennessee, Friday night, May 3, 1861

Missouri Madole came over early this morning to spend the day with me. Aunt T left us to ourselves the greater part of the morning. After dinner the

Association met, and we spent the evening altering and making jackets for the Home Guards.[232] Tonight Mr. Slaughter is with us. He and Uncle Trice are now on a high string about the North & the South; no other subject claims the attention of any two more than a moment at a time. The excitement just here seems to be subsiding. Ky. at last seems "to be up and doing." Mr. Manson came over from the Barracks this evening and supped with us.

New Providence Tennessee, Saturday night, May 4, 1861

Mr. Slaughter left soon after breakfast and soon afterwards I left for the church. About 15 of us finished the jackets by 12 o'clock. Mrs. Wilson, Mr. John Mallory, and Ross Donaldson came. John and Mo, Ross and I chatted nonsense for about two hours. They seem to be finely pleased with the soldiers' life. After they left, Mrs. W, M, and I went down to see the home Guards drill. They look quite nice with their new jackets and red stripes. Took tea with Mrs. W; the fish was cooked so nicely. Found Mr. Homer here at 8 o' busy reading the Chronicle.[233] Quint Atkinson[234] spent the morning with Aunt T. How much I missed by being absent.

New Providence, Tennessee, Monday night, May 6, 1861

We had a long rain that continued from 8 until 12 this morning, I read until about 10 when I was interrupted by Mr. Homer. He came to bring me some radishes sent him by his sweetheart. After dinner I reduced my hoops slightly; they were most too extensive for the times. Ross Donaldson came in before I finished & brought me ribbon to make him a cockade.[235] I made it; carried it to him about sunset. We hear so little to comfort us. The latest papers say that all the eastern countries are about to engage in war with each other. Garibaldi is again in the field.[236] England and France are the only ones at present disengaged and it is thought that they will soon declare themselves in favor of certain countries and of course unite their efforts to assist them.[237] Surely such times were never known before.

New Providence, Tennessee, Tuesday night, May 7, 1861

Paid Mrs. Gold and Mrs. Wilson a short visit. Mrs. G is quite sick. Mrs. Wilson and I went out and spent the evening with her and Missouri. We almost made ourselves sick eating green apples, dried peaches, drinking wine cordial &c. Bad news meets us on all occasions. No sooner had we returned than Aunt T told us of a very sad circumstance that occurred today out at the campground. Two young men belonging to Mr. Forbes' company by the names of Brown and Anderson attacked each other this evening after passing a few short words. And although Anderson was the stronger man of the two and for some time had the advantage, Brown succeeded in getting his knife and in a few moments {*indecipherable*} cutting him four times and each time near the heart. Indeed the knife pierced him quite through the heart once. I regret seriously that anything so sad should occur but more so that it took place out at the camp.[238] Mr. Homer was up tonight and brought with him some pecans for bunny. He's so thoughtful, and yet for all his kindness I was compelled to ask him to leave. The fear of my throat's growing worse I hope was a sufficient excuse. There is great danger in sitting so long on the porch these cool evenings. Received two letters from Tom today, one written before and one since I saw him, my "letter gratifying." It seems strange that one should write so, for indeed they seem to me anything else.

New Providence, Tennessee, Wednesday night, May 8, 1861

Employed myself in various ways this morning. For one thing I assisted Mr. Homer in making a horse cover. I managed this time so as not to sew up the pockets. As an evidence that my assistance was appreciated, he sent me up such a nice basket of apples. With all of his faults, he's some good traits (his apples are good at least). I would like for all who make me presents, particularly of nice things to eat, to be of unexceptionable character; for, were they ever so undeserving, my decision would always be in their favor. Made a cake and some custards for the volunteers this evening. Went over to Mrs. Wilson's few moments with Mary Smith late. Met with the Saint, there, but had little to say to her. The Legislature at last has sent Tenn. to the right place, Southern Confederacy, and has also ordered 25,000 men and left it with the Gov. to order more if necessary.[239]

New Providence, Tennessee, Thursday night, May 9, 1861

Did little of nothing this morning. This evening Mr. and Mrs. Wilson, Missouri, her brother George, and myself went over to the Barracks.[240] We remained until very late. Our acquaintances were so glad to see us. They all look so cheerful and happy that we almost forget the sad circumstances that have called them together. The first company perform finely, but the Irish Tigers are the ones for service.[241] They will all be marched into regular service Monday—at least they expect to be received by the governor at that time. The boys are so sunburnt now I don't know what they'll look like before the summer is ended. They are more Indian like than American like now. Mr. McCauley has undergone less change than any of them; that, however, is easily accounted for. John Mallory's hands are the color of an old hickory bark tooth brush, one that has been used for some time. They appreciated so much the cake, custards &c, &c that I felt shamed of not carrying more.

New Providence Tennessee, Saturday night, May 11, 1861

John Mallory also called a few moments. For some time nothing but the privations, horrors, &c attending a soldier's life were allowed to occupy our thoughts. John looks so sad while he talks of it, yet he seems as determined as anyone I ever saw. He seems to have such a horror of the battlefield that I wonder sometimes he doesn't resign and wait to be drafted. And again, I think of the motive that prompts him. Nothing but the love of country, the love of home, and the love of friends would ever induce him to engage in so perilous an undertaking. He thinks to go will only be to sacrifice himself, to stay would to sacrifice his country. And of the two he thinks the latter of much the most importance. To die in defending his country, he says, will be a glorious death, and who does not admire the spirit?

New Providence, Tennessee, Monday night, May 13, 1861

Read until 9. Spent the remainder of the day making hair flowers for Aunt T. Went up late to see Mrs. Atkinson few moments. Since supper walked with Mrs. Smith down to see Mrs. Staton. Nothing particularly talked of but the row at St Louis. About 20 persons were killed, several wounded, and a complete surrender made by the Northern troops.[242]

New Providence, Tennessee, Tuesday night, May 14, 1861

I scarcely know how to employ myself these days. I can't feel like confining myself to any steady work and fancy work.

New Providence Tennessee, Wednesday night, May 15, 1861

The bell rang early this morning for the meeting of the Society. I went down and found that the volunteers had sent over 10 coats & 10 pairs of pants to be made. So many were present that two were employed to make a suit or a pair of pants together. Fortunately for me Mary Smith and I had only a pair of pants between us. We were kept busy until 5 o'clock to finish them. We had such a nice dinner today. Among the many good things were fried chicken and strawberries, the first I've eaten this season. George Helm[243] called this morning. He came up from Miss. Yesterday. He says there as well as everywhere else there's nothing but excitement. Another row occurred in St Louis yesterday or day before it was too. Mr. Forbes' company took the oath of allegiance today. Mr. Hewitt was over this evening & regrets exceedingly that his company is not prepared to do the same.

New Providence, Tennessee, Thursday night, May 16, 1861

Spent the morning with the Society sewing, and after all our haste, we couldn't finish in time for the young men to have their suits by 3 o'clock. After dinner Mr. Homer and I went over to the Barracks. Found a good many spectators assembled to witness the presentation of a flag to Capt. Hewitt and company by Miss Poore.[244] Her speech for the occasion was short but expressive, and beautifully spoken. She was herself completely, not the slightest embarrassment was observed and the beauty of all was she spoke loudly, distinctly and clearly.[245] John Mallory replied. What he said was to the point, but a want of time to prepare prevented the finish that might have been added; and of course made it the more interesting. But a want of experience, brass, and other requisites were a sufficient excuse for what was lacking in him as an orator. The life of a soldier preparatory to going into real service must be very monotonous — nothing but the same steps to be practiced over and over again, the same pieces of meat and bread to be dispensed with at each meal, and between times nothing but the sad prospects for the future employ their minds.

New Providence, Tennessee, Friday night, May 17, 1861

First thing after breakfast this morning I commenced sewing the stripes on George's pants. They were not half done when he came in and, as I expected, objected to the way they were put on. A murmuring soon commenced and he without further words offered me a half dollar to take them off and place them as he wished. The quarrel was over with and soon the pants were just as he wished them. About 8 Aunt T went over to Mrs. Wilson's. She spent several hours, met with Mary Trice[246] over there. A subject of conversation was introduced and while under discussion Mary took exception to something that was said. She remarked that John Mallory had been preparing for the last few weeks the speech he made yesterday in reply to Miss Poore's. Aunt T, not in reply to her but to Mrs. Wilson, said that it was entirely unexpected to him, and that a day or two only had been given him in which to prepare himself. She waited until ready to start home and all of sudden, she jumped up and says, "Well Aunt T, I wanted to know whether you thought I told a lie or not." Aunt T says if I haven't said it. I will say it. With that she made a regular speech to which Aunt T replied in very few words but those

very sarcastic. Nothing but a guilty conscience ever made her take exception in the first place, for Aunt T had not spoken to her or alluded to her.
Bettie Helm, Missouri Madole, and I went out fishing this evening. We had
anything else but success. We walked about four miles over the most rugged,
wild looking country I ever saw. The first thing we knew we were in a dark
forest so dense and surrounded by such high hills that we began to think of
Lincoln, the Yankees, and everything else horrible.

New Providence, Tennessee, Saturday night, May 18, 1861

Mr. Homer was up tonight, but I gave him such a lecture about drinking
whiskey I don't know when I shall see him again.

New Providence, Tennessee, Monday night, May 20, 1861

Heavy rains continue to fall. The army worms[247] continue to increase in the
corn and wheat fields and the Northern troops continue to attack the boats
at Cairo.

New Providence, Tennessee, Tuesday night, May 21, 1861

Today has been really cool. Fire has been agreeable from sunrise to sunset,
for several days past. The spring up to this time has been unusually cool; as
a consequence the cut worms are daily proving to us that their name was not
wrongfully given. They cut down cabbage and lettuce that have headed up
besides other vegetables supported with stalks almost as large. The farmers
have been compelled to plow up fields containing many ears and plant over
their corn.

New Providence, Tennessee, Wednesday night, May 22, 1861

Mr. Charles Peterson[248] and Cousin Lou came. We had a long social chat
with "old Charlie" about these Lincoln times, and not a little was said about
the past. Cousin Lou is still with us. Before sunset awhile a note came accompanied with a nice basket of strawberries. The note, however, was not so
nice as I have seen, "Well, Miss S M Jordan, please have the berries served
for supper" "for a friend"———. Mr. McClennon and Mr. Homer took
tea with us. Mr. H called for his hat about 3 minutes after leaving the table,
and I think he really wished it handed over to him. Whether he called for it
just for the effect or otherwise I'm unable to say. One thing I do know—he
seemed surprised that the hat was found so readily and left without further
ceremony.

New Providence, Tennessee, Thursday night, May 23, 1861

Received a letter from Ft. Wright[249] today, and still I'm requested to grant a "simple favor" — "the favor" that's been talked of for almost a year, and why it is after so many refusals the request is still made I can't see. Ft. Wright was completed a few days since and the Memphis S Guards are now in possession of it.

New Providence, Tennessee, Friday night, May 24, 1861

Mr. Garrett dined with us today; he says he's ashamed to own that he lives in Ky. now that she has acted so cowardly about separating from the Northern States.[250] Governor Magoffin[251] is a strong secessionist, & yet with all he can say, the people are immovable without knowing if they are now making the rope that is to hang them. The latest news says the Federal troops are preparing to take Paducah, and really, it may be for the best. Then perhaps the Kentuckians will open their eyes. We all went down to Mr. Howard's this evening. Mr. Homer came up tonight and sit until after the 9 o'clock bell rang. His subject as usual — war, love, courting a lady the second time, &c. He's a case if ever there was one.

New Providence, Tennessee, Monday night, May 27, 1861

Finished this morning the pants commenced Saturday. Carried them to the church. Found 10 or 12 ladies engaged in making the two coats that were left untouched Saturday. At least most of the ladies were at work. Some of the younger ladies were more agreeably employed, blowing grass between their hands, laughing at old Mrs. Collishaw,[252] &c. Cousin Mary and Mr. Mills called a while this evening. Cousin Jane, the children, Aunt Pollie Campbell,[253] Bettie Homer, Bud Campbell,[254] and Mrs. Collishaw [came also]. After tea, Mr. and Mrs. Pollard, Mrs. Dunn, and Mr. Homer were added to the list. For the first time lately, the war news was dispensed with and other topics as interesting were introduced, such as the cultures of strawberries (or the crating of strawberries), visiting the Barracks, &c. Uncle Steven brought Aunt T such a nice present this evening from John — a pair of pipe tongs.[255]

New Providence, Tennessee, Tuesday night, May 28, 1861

The crocheting of a little braid has been my day's work, making pies for dinner excepted. The last dispatches say that the Federal and Confederate troops fought at Hampton Roads[256] and that only 50 of our men were killed

while 600 of the Northerners were slain. This is too good to be true. I can
scarcely hope for anything so favorable.

New Providence, Tennessee, Wednesday night, May 29, 1861

Cousin Mary and Uncle William left early for Clarksville. Cousin Lou was
in by times preparing to go over to the Barracks (Camp Duncan).[257] We, together with Mary and Fannie Britton,[258] went over in Mrs. B's carriage about
9 o'clock. Found the companies, at least parts of all the companies, on drill. I
don't think any one company was complete by 25 or 30. As many as 300 have
been added to those already in camp since my last visit, and several more
companies are daily expected. They have now nearly enough for a regiment,
and by next week many think there will be in all a thousand men.[259] Tenn.
has never flinched yet and may this test give her beyond a doubt the noble
position she so well deserves the first and foremost of all the sister states for
bravery and celerity of action. A visit to Camp Duncan is enough to make
any Tennessean feel proud of his birth place and kindle afresh within his
bosom the love for his country and his people.

Among the young men engaged in this great and noble work are many
of the brightest stars of which society can boast. Social circles have given
up their greatest ornaments; family groups have been deprived of all "that
made their joys complete." While men of talent have not thought it improper
to fall in rank with the common private and learn with him the first lesson
generally given in the preparatory department of our military schools. These
with the rougher, hardier youth of our country are the kind of men collected
at Camp Duncan, and these are the men who are to fight for our rights and
our liberty. And all in opposition to the iron will of a black republican[260] who,
were it in his power, would see annihilated the last drop of Southern blood
that his sway might be unlimited. He, with his fiendish class, are the ones
depriving us of those we most love and esteem, while distress and confusion
have taken their place in our once quiet homes. May the defeat at Hampton
Roads prove a timely lesson for them, and should another attempt be made
to invade Southern soil, may the result be even more disastrous than that.

Camp life, associated as it [is] with so many things sad and gloomy while
seated round our firesides, is disconnected with everything of the kind when
in the midst of it. It is like trying to recall the features or last words of some
dying friend in the midst of a bridal party to think of such a thing. We see
no sad faces, we hear no sad expressions but rather something to amuse,
something to make us laugh all the while. Here we see a fellow turning sum-
mersaults so fast we can scarcely distinguish his head from his feet. There

we can see a group of 56 or more all clustered round a fiddler while dancing, joking, jumping, and singing are all carried out at once. Again, we see a game of marbles and ball going on at the same time, and those engaged so masked up that is difficult to determine who belongs to one game and who the other. Indeed, they all seem to be as busy during rest hours as when drilling. Their amusements all require so much walking and stirring about.

The cooks, however, call forth more hearty laughs than any others. One man builds his fire and sits himself flat down on the ground until his meal is finished, while another jumps about so much that one thing isn't finished before he commences another. Some slice the bakers' bread and fry it, while others prefer theirs made from the beginning by themselves. They pour the flour into a vessel of some kind, take an old sardine can in which they keep their salt, and pour into the flour until it seems to be pretty well emptied, and then the water is added. And after that their hands are introduced up as far as the sleeves of their shirts will admit. If any lard was added to the above ingredients, I did not see it. This they knead and work over for some time and then make into cakes and I suppose fry it. That part of it was gone through with after I left.[261] Their coffee is made in a pot containing about 2 gallons water and so much coffee is added that I expect it will sometimes almost support an egg. All this they are accustomed to now and will soon enjoy a meal cooked by themselves no doubt as much as some of us would one cooked at a first class hotel. Mr. Hewitt, John Mallory, Robert Brown, and Mr. Thompson—none of them were cooks today and not one of our company, I'll venture to say, was sorry of it. They dined with us, and though no luxury, no delicacy, was offered them, they ate heartily and enjoyed I believe what to them at home would be a common meal. Some of the gentlemen were neither on duty or compelled to remain silent. This was very agreeable with some of us.

New Providence, Tennessee, Friday night, May 31, 1861

Today has been cloudy and gloomy. Cousin Lou and I late called on Sue McDaniel and Mary Smith. Mr. Barnes is with us tonight. He says Mr. Hewitt's company was sworn in this evening. He also says a supposed spy has been taken up belonging to his company and that he is now under guard. More than 75,000 men have offered themselves to Harris, and still new companies are forming.[262] The Volunteer State will support to the last her name.

CHAPTER THREE

June 1861 – December 1861

B. B. HOMER CONTINUED to court Serepta. She also had a friendship with Tom Trabue and though she was vague, she hinted that he wanted to become engaged. She wrote of receiving his letters and commented disapprovingly when Homer overindulged with alcohol. John Mallory also offered an engagement, but she declared herself undeserving of his attention. Political news of secession was of primary concern to Serepta. She recounted the formation of local units and national war news. Serepta was pro-Confederate and used pejorative terms such as "black republicans" and "vandals" to describe Northern politicians and Union men. She commented frequently that Kentucky should see the error of its decision not to leave the Union. At the same time, she recognized that the men who enlisted in the local regiment were sad and a bit frightened of what awaited them. She noted they believed they owed service to their country. The lack of accurate information and inability to know what to believe led her to record rumors. She was actively involved in a local women's war aid society. Her bitter condemnations of elite women across the river reveal local class conflict. She recorded the sudden death of her aunt and wrote at length with heart wrenching sorrow. The loss of her familial protector removed the certainty of a secure home.

Local war preparations continued.

New Providence, Tennessee, Saturday night, June 1, 1861

Cousin Lou took Inez and walked over to Clarksville and back by ½ 9 o'clock this morning. About 10, John Garrard[1] came along and, of course, that was the last we saw of her. John Mallory came about 11 and remained with us until 3 when he went over to hear Jesse Ferguson[2] speak on the present disastrous state of affairs. Mr. Ross Pollard dined with us and soon afterward Mr. Homer came up and he with Mr. Pollard almost made Kit Jones conclude to vote an open ticket the 8th of Jun.[3] Bud Jenkins[4] called this evening late and says that Mr. Forbes ordered 40 of the ablest new men belonging to his and Golson's companies to be ready to march tonight at 6 o'clock. Where he wanted them to go is unknown and for what purpose. 7 of the men ordered are citizens of our town. Mr. Homer was up tonight and brought with him an Extra, informing us of the intended blockade of the Louisville and Memphis RR by Col. Anderson.[5] He also attempted to swear in some of the home guard companies of Louisville to support the government of the U States.

New Providence, Tennessee, Monday night, June 3, 1861

Went down to the church soon after breakfast; found 4 suits to be made and about 15 ladies to make them. I brought a pair of pants home to finish by sunset, but a call from Mr. Hewitt, a visit from Efe Manson, and indisposition on my part have prevented their completion. If Aunt T would let politics and the newspapers alone, she might assist me greatly. The last Courier says that Governor Letcher[6] of Va. will send soon to Alexandria for the family of James W Jackson, recently murdered for refusing to let a lot of ruffians take down at his house a secession flag.[7] He intends supporting them at the expense of the government. He also intends erecting as soon as possible a monument to the memory of Jackson. While we regret the loss of so noble a man, we rejoice over the death of the tyrant Ellsworth. It is a remarkable fact that the first man who attempted to take down a flag of the Southern Confederacy was shot, and that the first man who attempted to rear one of the US fell and broke his neck.

New Providence, Tennessee, Wednesday night, June 5, 1861

Since the withdrawal of Uncle and Aunt T into their own room we've had undisturbed possession of the front porch, a place almost sacred to me on account of the many pleasant associations with which it is connected, and which will hereafter no doubt have double attraction. Friends I now meet with there and with whom I engage for hours "in sweet converse," will, perhaps before this fratricidal war shall have closed, be numbered with the slain on some bloody field of battle. And when all save a remembrance of the past fails to give me comfort, how pleasant it will be for me to refer to these times and place of meeting and again through the kindness of memory live over again hours of enjoyment and pleasure. Among the most happily spent of those hours will probably be those that have just passed. For years rumor with her busy tongue has been unceasing in her endeavors to convince the news loving people of our little village that an engagement actually existed between John Mallory and myself and tonight for the first time the subject was introduced by John himself. He made an open declaration as unexpected to me as it seemed to be unpleasant to him. Indeed, a disinterested person might have thought the conversation unpleasant to us both. Yet a deep sense of my unworthiness will account for silence on my part. While astonishment on his part may account for the same. Truly he may be astonished when he thinks of offering his heart to one so undeserving, so unworthy the noble gift. Not that I feel myself inferior to him in every respect is this remark made, yet I candidly acknowledge his piety, amiability, sweetness of disposition, &c. far surpasses mine. While in a woman all these traits are looked for and expected, whether a gentleman has even a civil way of treating people or not. However, I shall ever feel honored, undeserving as I am, and refer with pleasure to the time, place, and circumstances connected with our meeting tonight.

New Providence, Tennessee, Friday night, June 7, 1861

The weather is very warm. Wheat crops fine and corn promising, while garden vegetables were never known to grow more rapidly or come into market earlier. If old Abe did but know the productiveness of our soil, the industry of our people, and the contempt they feel for him and all who talk of "Starving us out" here in this land of corn and cotton, certainly he would crouch into a smaller space than he did even while passing through Baltimore.[8] Tonight we went to hear Mr. James Quarles[9] speak. His subject, of course, was the present crisis; his object to influence Union men to vote tomorrow the secession ticket. If he failed in his object, he did not in presenting his subject and that in its true colors, a more telling speech I never listened to. (I never heard many.) The past glory of our country he alluded to briefly, while the dark cloud that now hovers over and threatens to deluge the State in blood he described as being now very near at hand and that the decision of the people tomorrow would only decide her fate. At the close of his remarks he was very complimentary to the ladies and says that the only appropriate place of the head of beauty is on the breast of valor.

New Providence, Tennessee, Saturday night, June 8, 1861

The long looked for day has come at last. Today the fate of Tenn. is decided, and tonight no doubt she belongs to the Confederate States of America. Already she has proven herself worthy, an exalted position among the sister states of the South, and may she long sustain it. Our town voted almost to a vote the secession ticket today.[10] One man alone voted the union ticket and that can scarcely be considered a disgrace as he is even more insignificant than Lincoln himself. Read Woodstock,[11] slept, and did nothing today, all favorite employments. Late we drove down to see Nannie Hoover and Mrs. Harrelson. A threatened storm hurried us home. Mr. Homer was up tonight; still discusses his favorite theme. Received a long letter from Tom—no particular news; the same subject is continued.

New Providence, Tennessee, Monday night, June 10, 1861

Did nothing of consequence this morning, and this evening the Society sent up a pair of pants and Uncle Billie brought in from the country a bushel of cherries for me to put up. With assistance I seeded the most of them and will have them ready for drying. Went up this morning and bought for myself an English bergh[12] which I think will make up very prettily. Mrs. Pirtle and the Dr. were over this evening; as usual both were very agreeable. Some of the companies from Camp Duncan are moving up to Hampton's Spring[13] today. Everything since about sunset has assumed a more gloomy appearance. Why is it, I wonder? Dare I breathe to even my journal what I suspect to be the cause?

New Providence, Tennessee, Tuesday night, June 11, 1861

After so long a time this morning Cousins Marion and Jane, Bettie, Florence, and myself got started over to Camp Duncan. We were there by 11 o'clock. The most of our friends were ready to give us a hearty reception, though several had left for Camp Quarles. About 500 men are still there. 6 of the companies have left. Our acquaintances did everything in their power to make our stay agreeable and succeeded so far that our visit was prolonged greatly beyond our expectation when we went over. Mr. Hewitt (Capt. I should say), John, and one or two others were particularly attentive. Dr. Broadie, an acquaintance of Cousin Marion's, was introduced into our circle. When we left late this evening our only regret was that we had not met with him earlier. He is very agreeable—most too familiar on short acquaintance is my only objection.

Mr. Homer is up tonight and a few minutes after he came in I withdrew abruptly, not to return until he left and some[one] else came in less quarrelsome and "gabby." For one hour he quarreled about the trip over to the Barracks today just as though [we] had deprived him of horses, buggies, money, &c for a day that we might make a useless visit. He didn't see me after I left the porch except to call at my door [a] few minutes as he passed out, and then received in reply to his questions nothing but frowns mixed with sarcasm. To think of the abuse so often heaped on innocent women I sometimes want to step into Fannie Fern's[14] slippers just long enough to tell the abominable bipeds what I think of them. After so long a time John Mallory has gotten a furlough. He left the Barracks soon after we did though it was 9 o'clock or near it when he came up to see us. The clock has just struck 1 while he, I hope, is sweetly dreaming out in the hall lounge and I enjoying the sweets of an empty stomach. Cousin Marion will whip me for disturbing her at such a late hour.

New Providence, Tennessee, Wednesday night, June 12, 1861

After Cousin Marion and John[15] left this morning, I went agreeable to promise to work on Dr. Broadie's calico shirt. I have worked faithfully on it most all day, and tonight I'm so tired a walk down to Cousin Jane's late and up to Mr. McDaniel's since has relieved me considerably. The Oak Grove cavalry company[16] passed through today. And for the first time we prevailed on Aunt T to go over to the Barracks. She went over with the hope of seeing them received by the company over there but was disappointed. They design returning tomorrow. She met with several old acquaintances, among them Uncle Steven, Aunt Eliza, Jennie, & others. Heard of a very sad affair today. Miss Rollins,[17] a young lady out in the country who for years has been badly treated not to say abused by a step mother, concluded yesterday to put an end to her miserable existence by drowning herself. She was not found until today. Poor girl, for a long time, she has been the subject of deep interest and sympathy. For years her friends have looked with saddened heart on her sad condition but felt that only death would give her that peace and freedom for which she sighed.

New Providence, Tennessee, Friday night, June 14, 1861

Yesterday, the 13th of June, was the day appointed by Jeff Davis to be observed as a day of fasting and prayer by the people of the Southern Confederacy.[18] In the morning early Mrs. Clark, Mrs. Atkinson, and Bettie Helm called. Soon after they left, Aunt T and I went out to West Fork. A prayer meeting was held there which lasted until near the middle of the afternoon, but few were present. After some persuasion Aunt T consented that I might go home with Cousin Mollie Mills. We spent the remainder of the evening with Uncle Billie, and the night with Cousin M. Jennie Mallory stayed with me. We had such a cozy chat down on the bluff about sunset. The scenery all around was beautiful and the subject discussed no less pleasing. Cousin Mary and Mr. Mills came with me home. The morning she spent at Dr. Castney's[19] having her teeth repaired. Mr. Hewitt called just before we came and said that his company (Company E) left for Camp Quarles today.[20] I regret that necessity forces them so far from home. Governor Jackson of Missouri has called for 50,000 volunteers and says he's determined to repel any invasion of the Federal troops.[21] She's on the road to secession I hope. They continue to have small battles in Virginia, none of much importance. A very heavy one is expected at Newsoms Gap soon.[22] The seat of government has been moved to Richmond, Va.[23] on account of being more convenient to Davis and those with whom he is most intimately connected.

New Providence, Tennessee, Saturday night, June 15, 1861

Assisted Aunt T this morning on Uncle Trice's pants. Mrs. Howard came about 1 just as I had finished writing to Tom and will remain with us until tomorrow. Sue and Mollie McDaniel[24] called and spent an hour just before tea. Tonight Mr. Homer has been up, and for two hours he has been trying to smooth over the Camp Duncan scrape but every effort made the matter worse. Not soon will he make it up with me. What if I should go to Camp D and spend a week? What is it to him? The last accounts say that the battle fought at Bethany, Va., resulted very favorably for the South; only 10 or 15 were killed while several hundreds of the Northerners were killed.[25]

New Providence, Tennessee, Tuesday night, June 18, 1861

Went down to church early. Found 9 suits to be made. Brought home a pair of pants and had them ready for use by 2 o'clock excepting buttons and straps. Aunt T did that much for me and I went cherry gathering. Brought home several gallons, but oh how dearly bought were they, such tiresome work and so tedious. Nannie Hoover and Aunt T helped themselves pretty freely when I came back, and all the time I was wishing they only knew the drops of sweat shed over them. They would have appreciated them more. In today's Courier is a speech of Ex Gov. Morehead[26] and in it I think is {*indecipherable*} all that could be said relative to the present crisis. If he fails to exert any influence over the Kentuckians, they are lost, lost forever, and no longer need claim any right or privilege with a free and independent people. Received full accounts from the election today. Tenn. left the Old Union with a majority of 57,848 so the Courier says. Dick Ogburn just from Miss. and Charley Tandy just from Memphis called today.

New Providence, Tennessee, Wednesday night, June 19, 1861

Spent the whole morning working over my cherries. After dinner slept, read, and did nothing until about 4 when some company came in and I of course brought out my work. Quintin Atkinson called this evening and such egotism so nicely blended with modesty and diffidence. Mr. Homer has given me a round since supper. I wonder now what Gov. McGoffin[27] and the Union men of Ky. will do. He in his proclamation said that his state should remain strictly neutral and that her soil should neither be invaded by North or South. And the Unionists forced him to say that. Now they find that her soil has been invaded and that by those outrageous scamps at Cairo.[28] A company of them have actually torn down the flag at Columbus and threatened the whole place unarmed as the citizens are with an attack very soon.[29] A company of Hunt's men were also attacked and captured as far as I know. These outrages they will bear with and still cry for union, when union these days means Lincoln and his cabinet composed of the grandest set of rascals now unhung if I may be permitted to use an expression so rough.

New Providence, Tennessee, Thursday night, June 20, 1861

Spent the whole day with Nannie Hoover. Almost made myself an English bereghe bonnet.[30] Mr. Homer was up tonight and seems delighted with the last reports. He says Lyon[31] is certainly captured.

New Providence, Tennessee, Friday, June 21, 1861

The consequences of "war"—warm weather, drought, etc. are dreadful in the extreme. Jimmie Howard[32] and Mr. Manson supped with us this evening. They were just from Camp Quarles—brought the first news we've had since the companies left. I was grateful to hear that all were in usual spirits and health, and that some of them designed coming town next week.

New Providence, Tennessee, Monday night, June 24, 1861

This morning was spent in constant expectation of seeing the cavalry company come in. Bettie and Laura Helm, Bettie Homer, and Anne Staton remained until after dinner to see the sight; but we were all disappointed— not any more so I presume than the company of ladies that went out to meet them. They cut a figure to use a common expression.[33] But two gentlemen were in company and they were scarcely visible. It is no uncommon sight these days to see young ladies unusual in stature with boys for escorts, who standing by their side would like more than a foot of reaching their head. The striking contrast between some of the ladies and their gallants calls for many a rude laugh and funny remark. Notwithstanding the excitement, this morning a letter was prepared for Camp Quarles and safely in Jo Wray's care by 11 o'clock. This evening I paid five calls, Mrs. Helm's, Mrs. Magaren's,[34] Mrs. Herring's, Mrs. Cook's, Mrs. Davis'. Mrs. Helm is looking wretchedly. She is so much reduced that she doesn't favor herself. Mr. Homer was up tonight "grunting" terribly. He ate, "ahem," "ahem," he ate too many green apples yesterday.

New Providence, Tennessee, Tuesday night, June 25, 1861

Cousin Lou came in early and spent the day with us. This evening the hall and front porch has been filled with girls, impatiently waiting the arrival of the cavalry company. But finally went home without seeing the sight, at least they hadn't a view from Aspen cottage. The Co. came in so late that most of us despaired of seeing them. When they did come, however, they were well worth looking at, a finer looking Co I never saw. The band preceded them with some excellent music. I must try and fix up Florence a Sunday school speech and haven't time to write further.

New Providence, Tennessee, Wednesday night, June 26, 1861

George Trice breakfasted with us this morning for the last time perhaps for a good while. He and Dick Ogburn joined the cavalry Co a few days ago and they all went into camp this evening. Cousin Lou and I have worked busily all day and yet my dress is unfinished. The weather is so warm and I'm lazy. Dr. Cabiness and Mr. Homer were up tonight.

New Providence, Tennessee, Thursday night, June 27, 1861

Finished my dress at last. Cousin Lou almost made a finish of Aunt T's white muslin. Had slight rain this morning or this evening it was. Jimmy Howard was with us during the shower. I thought he was just from Camp Quarles. He came in so dryly and soberly and says first thing—Did you know the 1st Lieutenant in Hewitt's Co[35] was very ill. For a moment I believed it, but a dry laugh soon relieved me. Mr. Garrett is with us tonight and no other conversation but the war has been continued five minutes. Daily attacks in

Va. are expected from the Federal troops. Hoops have been some advantage at last; a lady succeeded in bringing over to the Confederacy a great many pistols and a good quantity of ammunition etc. The pistols she attached to her hoops; the caps, etc. she brought in carpet bags, companions, and little unsuspicious looking baggage.[36] Several trips of the kind brought over a good many useful articles.

New Providence, Tennessee, Friday night, June 28, 1861

Cousin Lou came in early and brought some news not at all of a disagreeable character. We went to work but Mrs. Pollard & Susy came in and for a "while operations were suspended." Before she left, John Mallory (Lieutenant Mallory I should say) came in. His new cap trimmed off with so much gold was so becoming; his boots too almost reflected the images of things around. Altogether he was looking better than I've seen him for a long time. Though Billie Donaldson's[37] sickness was the source of sad feelings &c, it afforded me pleasure to know that he was placed under the care of such a good nurse to be brought down. Cousin Lou and I went down to Mr. Howard's this evening and brought home some such fine apples and plums. On our return heard that 4 of the companies had been ordered from Camp Quarles to East Tennessee. I hope the report is false. And Mr. Homer gives such poor consolation. He took it on himself to come up tonight through the rain to tell me "that after all I might be glad to accept an old widower." Frank Smith[38] is with us tonight, quite sick with measles. Came down from Camp Quarles this evening.

New Providence, Tennessee, Saturday night, June 29, 1861

The weather is so warm. Mrs. Smith came in early spent the day and took Frank home with her this evening. So many of Mr. Hewitt's company are coming home sick, some of them very sick—Louis Gold, George Barbee, and Herndon[39] among the number. They don't {indecipherable} Mr. Hewitt at all; they almost abuse him for his negligence. John Mallory is getting all the praise for his attention and kindness to the sick.[40] Many of them seem anxious to have a reelection that he may be elected Capt.[41] If goodness is all that's necessary to prepare a man for the office, he's well deserving it. Aunt T though persists in excusing Mr. H; she knows "it isn't negligence." Mrs. Magaren and Mrs. Cockerall, her sister from Nashville, was to see us this morning. Some apples and plums are coming in abundance now, and I've eaten enough today for them to go out in abundance.

New Providence, Tennessee, Monday night, July 1, 1861

Commenced altering an old dress this morning, but company prevented me making much progress. Mrs. Staton, Emmie,[42] and Miss Fannie called. This evening Cousin Lou and I prepared a dinner to take to Camp Quarles tomorrow. Today Mr. Homer and Charley Peterson; both promised to go with us. Tonight, they both met here and thinking I had agreed positively to go with them and just such another quarrel and such a misunderstanding was never heard of. Cousin Lou let herself out; "She wouldn't go with Homer."

New Providence, Tennessee, Tuesday night, July 9, 1861

This morning one week since according to arrangements made the day before, Aunt Tabbie, Cousin Lou, Mr. Charley Peterson, and myself left home for Camp Quarles. Never a gayer party left home on an excursion of pleasure with faces more bright and cheerful. The day was pleasant and beautiful; and during the whole ride not an obstacle presented itself that seemed in the least, calculated to rob our trip of that pleasure so long anticipated by all of the company. But, oh! the sad history of that day. The sun that rose so beautifully that morning to gladden the hearts of those already buoyant with life closed on a world that evening that seemed to me filled with nothing but darkness and gloom. But oh! when we think of Heaven's gaining another bright star how sad this thought that we must pass through the remainder of life without her smiles of encouragement, her words of comfort, and above all her kind counsel and instruction in the hour of temptation. None ever went to her either for advice or consolation that left feeling no relief. The afflicted and distressed no difference their position in life, the aristocrat and the pauper at his door received equal attention at her hands. She was so kind, so good, so unselfish, so unlike anyone I may ever expect to meet again in this cold dark world. To me she was everything that friend, that a mother could be, and yet oh! yet, I must give her society and her influence up—all that has heretofore kept me in the path of duty or even drawn forth one good trait in my character. With all my faults, with every imperfection, the little good that is remaining I owe to her. Left to myself and today perhaps without money or friends. I would have been adrift on the sea of time, not knowing, not caring the final result.

As before remarked, we left home on Tuesday, 2nd day of July. The ride up there was very pleasant. Indeed, Aunt Tabbie as she had been for several days past seemed unusually cheerful. The morning passed away and nothing seemed to interrupt her unusual flow of spirits. All of our acquaintances at

the camp came up one by one seeming very happy to see us and time passed
swiftly in lively conversation with them. The dinner we had prepared before
leaving home was brought out about 12, and she was slightly stooping over
the bench on which the basket was sitting, taking out the dishes, when suddenly she raised her eyes to me with her hands pressed to her forehead, said
"Oh, Rep, my head, my head." John Mallory was standing near me talking. We were both with her almost instantly, but too late, too late. Death it
seemed to me was present by the time I had touched her, and as I had feared
from the moment almost that she was attacked, apoplexy[43] in a few hours had
done its work. So often has she told me that death would visit her in that way.
But oh how could I believe it, and even now how can I realize it? She suffered
but few hours perhaps not more than 3, but during that time no mortal could
suffer more intensely.

All was done for her that friends could do; she was surrounded by them,
but as for medical assistance she had none. A youth about 20 years of age
calling himself a physician came up soon after the first attack but a blanker
looking face I never wish to see. He seemed completely stunned and as a
natural consequence did nothing. Afterwards they told me the regular physician of the Regiment[44] came up and he, it was thought, was so completely
under the influence of whiskey that he neither knew or did anything. And
such is the dependence of that whole regiment for medical aid and be it ever
so necessary that health and life should be cared for. I shall never cease to
regret that no abler physicians were present, and none near enough to come
in time for relief.

She died in camp surrounded by friends that were untiring in their attention and was afterwards removed to Mr. Hampton's,[45] the nearest residence,
where we remained until about twilight when the cars came and with a great
number of acquaintances and friends left for home. So ended a day that
at the beginning seemed to bring with it nothing but sunshine and happiness. At 3 o'clock the day after her death Mr. Duncan preached her funeral
sermon from the text "But the righteous hath hope in his death," the latter
clause of the 32nd verse and 14th chap of Proverbs. She was interred the
same evening at the city cemetery of Clarksville, she having long since requested that that should be her last resting place.

The neighbors have been exceedingly kind to me, offering sympathy and
everything else that could in the least comfort me. Cousin Lou, Cousin Jane,
and the young men at the camp with a great many others will hereafter
hold a much dearer place in my affections. Uncle Trice too seems doubly
attached to me and were it not for these facts to comfort me what would life

be? Human nature is the same the world over and should the worst be yet in store for me, which I sometimes fear is the case, oh! who will know the depth of my sorrow? Who will there be to speak one word of comfort, to soothe one pain of an aching heart? Yet none may say, "should coming days be cold and dark" that "poor thing she little suspected this." My lot in life, be it ever so hard, will not find me wholly unprepared to bear even the worst. What right have I to expect that my path will ever again be strewn with flowers? But one alone is under the least obligation, and years have elapsed since he first disowned me, and when a mother proves neglectful and leaves an orphan in a world like this unprovided for, what may she expect at the hands of strangers and disinterested persons?

[In margin, in Rep's hand] Boast not thyself of tomorrow; thou knowest not what a day may bring forth.[46]

New Providence, Tennessee, Thursday night, July 11, 1861

Rose this morning before even the table was prepared for breakfast. Uncle Trice doesn't require or request me to rise earlier than I've been in the habit of rising. Yet I know too well what his feelings and thoughts would be to come in to breakfast and find the house not in order, the table not ready, etc. These are things he's been too long accustomed to to give up just at this time otherwise than reluctantly. To give up my morning nap is anything but pleasant at present, yet the future will no doubt convince me that it is all for the best. Received a letter from "Pillow Battery"[47] today and the firm belief "of a certain young man" there is that the fighting is over with, and that in a few days he will be "free." But oh, how sad, a number of the young men from Camp Quarles were over today and brought the sad intelligence that a heavy battle had just been fought in Virginia,[48] and that they all without an exception were to march tomorrow, to what place none of them knew. But one of them called to see me, Ross Donaldson, and, poor fellow, he was weeping so all the time that his visit gave but little satisfaction.

New Providence, Tennessee, Friday night, July 12, 1861

Uncle Steven Mallory and Mrs. Smith called to see me. Uncle S was on his return from Camp Quarles. The boys left this evening but for where no one seems to know. A very large number of troops came in from Memphis this evening, neither have I heard their point of destination. Uncle Trice seems so much distressed again. Sad news and his distress together unfits me for almost anything.

New Providence, Tennessee, Saturday night, July 13, 1861

Elsey[49] and I have been working with blackberries the whole day. She's so kind about assisting me and does everything so willingly. Emma went with Cousin Jane gathering berries, and Winnie[50] was left to tease me. She's so slow and has so little judgment, my patience I sometimes think is taxed beyond endurance. But ha! with all my trials and sad feelings, I've something left to cheer me. A long letter filled with affection, words of comfort, and kindness came today. And in each line was more plainly written than anything else truth sincerity. This is the most pleasing thought of all. Yet to know that I occupy the thoughts, much less the affections, of one so noble hearted, so worthy, is pleasing too. Will it be presuming to place confidence in what he says? Dare I breathe to my journal that I think him sincere? Oh, yes, one so free from all the rest of sins so common among young gentlemen of the present day must be free from the greatest and most unpardonable one of all. He would not deceive; he would not make false pretension. Deception is a word unknown to him and one that I dislike to associate with his name. But yet—but yet—why do I encourage such thoughts? Why not stifle them and make an effort rather to grow indifferent and callous to all such feelings? Will it not be my sad lot to spend the future as I have the past, to let hope take possession of the present and disappointment the future? I fear that to indulge even in one fond hope will be to prepare the ground in which are to spring up weeds of sorrow and disappointment.

New Providence, Tennessee, Wednesday night, July 17, 1861

Sent Winnie down to Mrs. Adkins this morning thinking her assistance would not be needed here and just when I was least prepared for them a "houseful" of company came in, Mr. and Mrs. Layne from the country among the number. I resolved to enjoy Cousin Nannie's company and gave up the dinner to Emma and Florence. And was agreeably surprised when dinner came in perfect order at the right hour, as the gentlemen all went down to hear Jesse Ferguson. He's candidate for some office in the Southern Congress. Mr. Layne left late. I disliked to give up Cousin Nannie's company. She's so good, so near what she pretends to. A sister would scarcely grieve more over the death of Aunt T than she did. After she left Cousins Marion and Jane came in a such a long—long conversation Cousin Marion and I did have relative to her last visit up to Camp Quarles. And every word of it was full of interest to me. Mr. Homer was up tonight and oh how discouragingly he talks. He says "the boys" are in East Tenn. and I may bid farewell to all them. He does not presume for a moment that any of my friends will return, but Uncle Trice says as if to console me "oh yes he will come back Rep."

New Providence, Tennessee, Thursday night, July 18, 1861

According to arrangements made yesterday, Elsey, Mr. Forbes, and I went over to Clarksville this morning. We first went shopping, and after getting through spent an hour or two in at Johnsons waiting very impatiently the return of Mr. McCormac,[51] the artist from the country. He finally came and the remainder of the morning was spent in having pictures taken. They had one of themselves taken for me, and I had one of myself taken for them. Also another one for whom it is unnecessary to say, as memory will retain perhaps a circumstance so unimportant. Elsey had one of Aunt Tabbie transferred. Dined at 1 o'clock. Elsey and Mr. Forbes[52] then packed their trunks after which we drove down to see Cousin Jane. Came home, supped early, Mrs. Davis with us. And just after sunset, they left for home, will remain in Clarksville tonight, and [in] the morning take the train for Nashville and from there on to Florida. Mr. Forbes, I believe a gentleman. He's very pleasant but quiet, retiring while E is all life and gaiety. Oh, I shall miss her so much. She was such good company, so cheerful, so girlish, such a romping wild puss. One couldn't be low spirited or down cast in her presence. Were it not for Cousin Jane and the children what would I do tonight? We're having a splendid rain and Mr. Homer is afraid to venture out. Wonder if he would sleep on a bed of ours?

New Providence, Tennessee, Saturday night, July 20, 1861

Wrote a little, sewed a little, and did a good deal of nothing today. Had no other company than Florence until tonight. She went home this evening and Bettie Helm is staying with me. She and Mr. Homer are now in the front porch talking about the sad state of affairs. News from Missouri (from Jackson and McCullock[53]) is cheering indeed but from Virginia very gloomy indeed. The Federals are making rapid progress into the state and one or two little battles have been fought in which they were successful.[54]

New Providence, Tennessee, Monday night, July 22, 1861

Dispatch after dispatch continues to arrive. The last one Mr. Homer read me and oh! what news for us. Beauregard has used up almost completely the Ellsworth Zouaves.[55] The dead, dying, and wounded are being carried into Washington by wagons full and these are the men that they thought to frighten the Southern people into subjection simply with their hideous appearance.

New Providence, Tennessee, Tuesday night, July 23, 1861

The weather is really chilly; fire has been pleasant most of the day. Went up town this morning to buy some books for Florence. She commenced a regular course of study today. Cousin Lou came about 10 o'clock to spend a day or two with me. We rode out this evening and returned in time to hear the joyful news of yesterday confirmed. "Our boys" they say have left for Va. This report I hope is false.

New Providence, Tennessee, Wednesday night, July 24, 1861

Cousin Lou has been with me all day this evening. We went down to Mr. Howard's and nothing but the first fight at Manassas[56] can be heard. The details came in yesterday's Courier but we hadn't an opportunity of getting the paper until this morning. The first great battle fought in the second struggle for independence commenced last Sunday morning, 3 o'clock, the 22nd of July 61, and continued 11 hours. Jeff Davis made his appearance on the field about noon, and not until then was the fortune of the day decided. Already Beauregard had command of the right wing, Johnson the left, of course leaving the center column for Davis. His only command "was onward, my brave column, onward."[57] That was sufficient. But a few hours and the tale was told. The Confederates had possession of the field; the battle was won, while Scott, Patterson and McDowell[58] were left to make their escape to Washington as best they could. Out of 1300 of the Fire Zouaves only 200 the dispatches say had made their appearance the day after the battle. Sad news again. Our regiment was ordered to Virginia this evening at 7 o'clock they say.[59] The part they are to act in this great struggle I fear is near at hand. No longer can we look forward to their approach into the regular field as something that may be but not probable. Tonight it may be they are within a short distance of the seat of war.

New Providence, Tennessee, Sunday night, July 28, 1861

Our school is still flourishing. We have everything to encourage us in pushing forward the great and good work. Our class is composed almost wholly of young ladies now. Mr. Homer has "been promoted." He has a class of young men; Dr. Kelly also has a class. Dr. Cabiness and one or two others just left us. Dr. McMullin preached at 11 from a text taken from 1st chap Timothy. His subject related mostly to the great battle fought on last Sunday. Today was appointed—at least an act in the Confederate Congress was passed last week—requesting every church in the S Confederacy to observe this as a day of thanksgiving for the brilliant achievement of our troops at Manassas. (The children are so noisy I scarcely know what I'm about) Cousins Marion and Jane were here today when I came home from church. In consequence of a heavy rain this evening they are still with me.

New Providence, Tennessee, Monday night, July 29, 1861

At supper Uncle T handed me two letters and how hastily were both seals broken. News from two very important points is greatly desired, and a glance at both those letters told me they were from the very places. But what was my surprise to find that both were written some time back? The one from John was the first he wrote after leaving Camp Quarles. The other from Fort Pillow[60] was dated way back the first of the month some time. It may be that each of the poor boys are at present hourly expecting an engagement and how little did either think of such a thing when writing.

New Providence, Tennessee, Tuesday night, July 30, 1861

Spent the morning finishing off John's and Ross's letters.

New Providence, Tennessee, Wednesday night, July 31, 1861

Made some cordial and baked a cake today. The last treat was given to the boys tonight. Several of them have called in, among the number Mr. Garriques and Billie Donaldson. Mr. G seems determined to return with old Lincoln's scalp. The boys all seem to have recovered fully, and all seem delighted with the idea of rejoining the regiment. Billie discourses quite differently from Ross. He was thinking of everything else but crying. Oh, I'm so vexed I can't write.

New Providence, Tennessee, Thursday night, August 1, 1861

I feel but little more like writing than I did last night. The weather is too warm to almost to do anything. The morning, however, I spent over the fire—making apple jam. If our tax is increased as the tax of the North has, this will be a trouble dispensed with in a short time. Uncle Trice would soon spend a fortune buying sugar. The House of Representatives has passed a law, "A direct tax law" as they call it, imposing on the people of the United States a tax almost unendurable, an additional 2 ½ cts for every lb of brown sugar they get will have to be given. On coffee 5 cts will be added, on salt 18 cts per 100 lbs, and everything else in proportion.[61] Now I presume, if not before, the Kentuckians begin to see where they stand. And how much more may they expect, while they remain under the despotic sway of "Old Abe the Rail splitter."

New Providence, Tennessee, Friday night, August 2, 1861

Tonight Mr. Homer has been up doing all in his power to discourage me. Says that not 50 out of Forbes' regiment will ever return.[62] George leaves tomorrow for Camp Trousdale.[63]

New Providence, Tennessee, Monday night, August 5, 1861

Oh, me! I'm so sleepy — too sleepy to scarcely remember what has occurred during the past day, much less to embellish with imagination the sober facts that have presented themselves. Early after breakfast, I set in to do a good day's work, and before I had stitched round the wristbands of Uncle T's sleeve, Mrs. Smith came in. And before she left, about 10 o'clock the bell rang and a stranger was announced. My old wrapper was disposed of soon as possible and what was my surprise on entering the parlor to find Tom Trabue seated there. He's was late from New Madrid, the last camp of the Memphis Southern Guard, but one never would have supposed so from his dress. His black cloth suit, his nicely blackened boots, smoothly combed hair, &c, &c gave him the appearance of the "city gentleman," rather than a volunteer of the S Confederacy. He spent the remainder of the day and returned since tea to spend nearly the same length of time. Really, it is too late to say anything of the subjects introduced today.

New Providence, Tennessee, Tuesday night, August 6, 1861

Mrs. Edwards, Mrs. Smith, and Mary Britton came in this morning, and spent the greater part of the day with me. Mrs. E is such an amiable creature. I know I shall love her more as our acquaintance extends. Mary B leaves for Winchester tomorrow. Tom Trabue returned from Keysburg this evening, and unexpectedly paid me another visit. He presented me such a handsome bible tonight. It's so late.

New Providence, Tennessee, Wednesday night, August 7, 1861

Although I retired so late last night and this morning had nothing to force me up early, still I rose before the last bell rang at the hotel and by 8 was ready for work. Mr. Homer called about that time and an hour or two passed chatting with him. His absence for the last two evenings I presume was the cause [of] his prolonging his visit this morning. So many inquiries were to be made, "who he was," "where he came from," the bible to be examined and many other things were referred to, though they mostly related to the same object. Tom passed this morning, and scarcely gave Aspen Cottage a look. Strange he didn't call, though he said last night he would not see me again. I had my thoughts however when he told me. And tonight, I have some more, but they are of a different character. Uncle T left for Nashville this morning early and has not yet returned. Cousin Lou, Cousin Bet, and Florence are with me tonight. I feel so badly, and have, since a conversation with Uncle T last night soon after tea. Oh, if my worst fears should be realized so soon.

New Providence, Tennessee, Thursday night, Aug 8, 1861

Went up to see Mrs. Atkinson about 8, sit an hour or two, met with Mrs. Trabue. Tom left last night, she says. Sewed until after rain ceased. Drove down to Cousin Jane's. Brought Cousin B up with me, and our present intention is to go to the country tomorrow.

New Providence, Tennessee, Sunday night, August 11, 1861

Early after breakfast Friday Cousin Bet and I left home for Williams'town. We were at Uncle Wm. Donaldson's by 9 and seated for the day. That night we stayed with Cousin Mollie Mills. She's is looking badly from a late attack of measles. It left her very deaf. She fears her hearing is injured for life.[64] We left for home about 3 by way of Uncle Billie's. Met with Mr. Homer there. Had the pleasure of a seat in his buggy. Oh, how lonely Uncle T looked as we drove up this evening; how sad, how sad, he feels no doubt tonight.

New Providence, Tennessee, Tuesday night, August 13, 1861

After a long conversation with Uncle Trice this morning on a subject that afforded me anything else but pleasure, I with Florence went up to see Mrs. Riggins and Mrs. McDaniel. The morning passed—at 11 I was home busy preparing some pears for preserving. Before making much progress, Dr. McMullin and Mr. Hirst[65] came in. They remained until near dinner. Mr. H is so agreeable, so pleasant I should delight to cultivate his acquaintance. "Went on to my preserving" after dinner, but not until I had read a letter from T. E. Trabue. He wrote between Memphis and New Madrid. In it he gave me particular gop[66] about owing him a favor that was granted some time since to another volunteer. He is certainly good at stratagem or else spares no opportunity in making inquiries. How he finds out so much is a mystery to me.

New Providence, Tennessee, Wednesday night, August 14, 1861

Time moves so slowly, the days are so long, they seem like weeks, and the weeks like months. And yet the approach of winter is dreaded, more dreaded perhaps (by me) than was the approach of Bonaparte's men to Moscow. How greatly do I fear that with first frosts the Northern vandals will recommence, and with renewed energy, their work of devastation and slaughter. Already the news has come that 5 of our regiment have been killed in a skirmish.[67] This I hope with the thousand and one other rumors that we hear is false. I should be glad to get a letter tomorrow. At home all day until about 5 o'clock busily engaged with my preserves and tatting inserting. Mr. Homer was up tonight but brought with [him] no news or papers.

New Providence, Tennessee, Thursday night, August 15, 1861

Florence and I have spent another day visiting and oh how relieved we feel at the close of a day to think that such a job is through with.[68] I wish people were not expected to visit except when they feel like it. We spent the morning with Mrs. Kirby; this evening with Mrs. Kelly's family, Cousin Jane, and Mrs. Dunn. On our return home we passed a cannon, the first I ever saw. Mr. Homer was with us and through his kindness we were permitted to examine it closely. Tonight, few moments went up to see Mrs. Atkinson and as "Uncle" leaves tomorrow I must have a letter to send by him. News from Missouri is very flattering. Indeed the latest dispatches confirm the news of Lyon's death[69] and the complete rout of Federal forces generally.

New Providence, Tennessee, Friday night, August 16, 1861

Tonight, Uncle Trice brought us up today's paper and oh! what good news: peace meetings are being held in several of the northern States[70] while success is given us in every battle. The news is confirmed both in yesterday's and today's papers relative to the death of Lyon. McCulloch as his antagonist is henceforth one of our first generals. His name will pass on down to history blended with his many achievements in Missouri; and none but the vandals of the North will ever deny the justice of his cause.

New Providence, Tennessee, Saturday night, August 17, 1861

Oh, so much good time in visiting is consumed that might be passed so much more pleasantly, in conversation with Mattie. But I must say something about that a good, good letter I received this evening. Were it not for the warm, affectionate letters that sometimes I've the pleasure of reading, what would I do? There is at this time nothing, to use a quotation from the one received this evening, "that gives me more solid pleasure." Dr. Cabaniss[71] came up this evening to extract some teeth for me and I was such a coward that I declined letting him operate on them at all. Really, I've felt ashamed of myself ever since. Mattie and I drove out to Mrs. Pettus this evening. Met with Cousin Marion, since I'm very anxious to see her privately.

New Providence, Tennessee, Tuesday night, August 20, 1861

Went to work at my peaches early. Commenced drying today. Mattie's beau came in this morning (Mr. Newell[72]), and oh such a nice present he did send us after leaving—some of the most delightful peaches I ever tasted. He with Tommie Grinstead[73] [and] Jo Hatcher[74] leave tomorrow for Va. They will join the 14th regiment. They came with us up from church tonight, and so sad we've been feeling since, though they seem to leave cheerfully. Cousins Jane and Bet dined with us. Emma Jackson[75]spent the evening. She plaited a beautiful plait, on my machine and with my assistance. Dr. M preached tonight a revival sermon from the text—"many will seek to enter that will not be able." The congregations are large, but little interest seems to be felt. Sent John's letter with a large package of paper and envelopes by Tommie. I hope he'll be needing them just as they get there.

New Providence, Tennessee, Thursday night, August 22, 1861
(written in someone else's handwriting)[76]

Mr. Donaldson, one of the recruits of Forbes Regiment, came, stayed a few hours. He expects to go on to his calling soon. Rep pulled off her hoops and went to gather cucumbers and after supper we were sitting around the pleasant fireside when Mr. Homer came and made Rep run. We enjoyed a nice and social chat. He likes to talk on the subject of matrimony, which generally pleases young persons. But Alas! there is not much pleasure in it now since all of the gallant young gents have left their homes and friends and are realizing the horrors of a soldier's life. Tomorrow I expect to go home, and Rep is going with me. I anticipate a glorious time!

New Providence, Tennessee, Saturday night, August 24, 1861

Tonight Mr. Homer came up and went with us down to hear Mr. Wardlaw.[77] He's an able preacher but, oh, he preaches so long. Text 1st Chap 21st verse of Matthew. One thing recently developed has destroyed to a great extent my enjoyment in the meeting. Oh! can it be that I am to realize so soon what I have so much feared.

New Providence, Tennessee, Sunday night, August 25, 1861

My tooth commenced aching this morning about school hour this morning so that I was both absent from school and church. Mattie and Uncle Trice went to church. This evening Mr. Homer spent with us.

New Providence, Tennessee, Friday night, August 30, 1861

Monday, just as I was under head-way making jelly and jam, Mr. Carneal came for Mattie and I. Hurriedly the jam was put up, the jelly left to the care of Winnie, and at ½ 2 o'clock we with Bettie Helm were on our way to "Neutrality" or to one of the United States at least. The rain, bad roads, &c made the ride rather unpleasant. Mattie lost her bonnet, and that detained us some longer on the way. Everything was done after getting there to make our stay agreeable—that could be done taking rainy weather, the toothache, &c into consideration. We left for home soon after dinner and, oh, how relieved I felt after getting here. "Not that I love my friends less but home more." Truly it is not the home that it has been, but still, no other place has the same attraction. Oh, if my return could have been the same that it was from the same place about this time last year. But oh! how different, how changed is everything. "What is home without a mother" are words that so often force themselves on my mind, but never do I feel the loss more sensibly than just as I enter the door of "home" after a long visit and find none but the lonely looking house dog or some other pet wearing the same deserted appearance to meet me. Oh, who can realize the sad truth? I wonder sometimes that I ever smile or seek pleasure of any kind. Were it not for a few that are left and the kind, affectionate, and encouraging letters that I sometimes receive what would life be?

Uncle Trice soon after I came this evening handed me two from his drawer and never did anything come in better time. Just when I was feeling worst, the only antidote that could possibly have had any effect was offered. One was from Virginia, the other from Mo. Tom wrote rather despondingly, as he had orders that day to march next morning farther out into Mo., and of course that much nearer danger. He closed by saying, "Rep, if we never meet again, remember I died in defense of my country and loving you. Farewell." Truly the horrors of war are becoming more and more familiar to us every day. John wrote rather more cheeringly. Indeed, he seems to be in right good spirits, and how pleasant it is to receive such letters. The boys too were all well (mostly at least) and the prospect for a battle soon not very favorable. Such letters are flowers along the wayside, strewn by hands more than willing to remove each thorn and make all pleasant.

New Providence, Tennessee, Saturday night, August 31, 1861

Since dinner Cousin Lou has been with us most of the time and is still with us. She's all excitement about sending "the boys" socks—pin cushions, paper, ink, &c, &c. Several members of the 14th Reg. leave Tuesday and she's preparing by the time. Unexpectedly another letter came today from John. He's still in good spirits and health, the prospect for a fight soon very favorable. The Reg. was under marching orders when he wrote and perhaps by this time, they have made an attack on Rosecrans's troops.[78] Oh, how much would I give to know for the next 9 months the true history of that noble band of Tenn. volunteers? This last, like all the letters from his hand, was filled with cheering words and kind wishes for his friends. I'm so glad he was thoughtful enough to send it by a friend and not through the office. The paper I sent him some time since will doubtless prove very acceptable as he says paper in Western Va. is "more precious than much fine gold" and sells readily for 1.50 quire.[79] His letters all are so interesting. I learn that one of our most useful citizens since I left has died—Uncle Randle,[80] an old negro long and well known in this place and a consistent and worthy member of the Baptist church.

New Providence, Tennessee, Sunday night, September 1, 1861

This evening just as we were most interested in reading the last letters from the Reg. Mr. Homer came in and only left in time to sup at home. We stole time, however, to converse a while on a subject that has for some time given me so much trouble. And as a natural consequence I was unfit tonight to even listen to Dr. McMullin's sermon, much less feel interested in it. I dare not breathe my thoughts even here. My cheek no doubt would color with shame to look over them in coming years for one who seems to be without shame for himself.

New Providence, Tennessee, Monday night, September 2, 1861

True, I've been in a buzz the day throughout and truly the day has been unusually beautiful without. Those coming in and going out have all been in a most lovely mood; many things have seemed to combine in the attempt to drive away sad thoughts. But all to no effect. Tonight I feel very sad, very sad indeed. I look around, but nothing wears a cheerful or pleasing aspect; the world within and without alike presents a dismal and gloomy appearance. Time, that cure for most troubles, only seems to increase mine and causes me to feel more deeply the great and irreparable loss I at first too deeply felt.

The morning I spent or attempted to in writing to John, and after all my hurry I shall have to send it by mail, as Mr. Barnes arrived yesterday and says "our boys" must not leave before the 16th. He left the Reg. the 26th and says all are well with a few exceptions. Mrs. Griffey, Nannie, Mrs. Pollard, and Mrs. Herring, with many others, have called to see me today. Cousin Lou has been in and out nearly 20 times I'm sure, and at last her running around was useless as she will have [to] lay her little bundles "on the shelf." Until the boys leave I can't feel like writing.

New Providence, Tennessee, Thursday night, September 5, 1861

Mr. Barnes called yesterday fresh from Western Va. just from the 14th Regiment. He seemed unusually communicative and with what interest I listened to every word. The hardships, privations, &c with which "our boys" have had to encounter and under which they have stood up so bravely, seems scarcely credible. Through mud, rain, over mountains, and through streams 4 feet deep with water, they continued a march of some 75 or 100 miles, and without a murmur or scarcely a complaint until at Big Spring they found a suitable place for erecting their tents. There many of them from fatigue, colds, and other causes sunk under disease, and sad to say among the number are some of our own loved citizens. There without proper food, without a pillow perhaps on which to rest their heads, without the smiles and kindly spoken words that none but an invalid knows how to appreciate, many, perhaps many, will breathe their last. How sad the thought.

New Providence, Tennessee, Friday night, September 6, 1861

Have been knitting busily all day. No company excepting an old lady, who called to get conveyance down [to] the country [a] few miles, and Ross Donaldson. Tonight [Mr.] Homer was up and sit until late. He came in while Uncle Trice and I were engaged in a conversation that afforded me anything else but pleasure. Shakespeare had better said "Frailty, thy name is man."[81] Surely the composition of man is something strangely different from everything else. Today he's one thing, tomorrow something else, and the third day he's so entirely changed that you scarcely felt to own him as an acquaintance. The subject of our conversation this evening I would like to bury with many other things of the past, but memory too true to her office will I fear bring up many things in the future that have and will continue to darken my lonely path through life. Bettie and I spent most of the evening with Mrs. Pollard.

New Providence, Tennessee, Sunday night, September 8, 1861

Cousin Marion, Mr. Cobb, and Miss Quick came in to church today and arrived just as we had gotten home. They all seemed disappointed and surprised that they were so late. Cousin Marion was all anxiety to hear from the 14th Reg. She has several correspondents in the Reg. and would want a great many more, but the idea of having to pay on each letter sent addressed 10 cts[82] is rather discouraging. We both correspond with the same gentleman and sometime since he favored me rather more than he did her in the way of letter writing &c. and such a joke as I did have on her. Yesterday's Courier says positively that Lincoln's troops have taken possession of Paducah and that the Confederates have taken Columbus and Hickman.[83] Farewell to Kentucky's "neutrality."

New Providence, Tennessee, Monday night, September 9, 1861

Commenced this morning a job long dreaded—the servants' winter clothes. Made one pair of pants and part of another today—Mr. Homer was up this evening and assisted me a little but bragged on me less. Really, I thought I'd been unusually smart but woman, poor woman, her "work is never done." She may stitch and stitch until eyes and back have both given out, and she's nothing left but her thumbs and fingers. Still she must ply the needle more briskly [with] her fingers or be pointed out as the personification of laziness. We heard Mr. Gooch tonight from Lafayette preach. His subject was Pilot's decision at the trial of Christ.[84] He "handled it well" to say the least of it. Many, beautiful and favorable, were the ideas he advanced, and all seemed to feel their power. 5 professed to be renewed in heart, and many more presented themselves as mourners. I'm so tired.

New Providence, Tennessee, Sunday night, September 15, 1861

After so long a time yesterday morning we all were on our way to Williamstown; The ride was very fatiguing and seemed much longer than usual. Dined and spent the evening with Uncle William and family. Last night I stayed with Cousin Mollie, leaving cousins Ann and Alley to finish their visit with Uncle W'm. Left early this morning for home. Parted with cousins Ann and Alley perhaps for the last time. Times are so uncertain now none [of] us know and their State is in such a precarious and perilous situation. They themselves scarcely know what to expect. Found no one at home but the servants.

Uncle Trice had gone to church and straightway I sit me down to write to John as tomorrow the boys leave for Virginia. The morning passed and the letter remained unfinished, but late this evening it was closed and safely placed within the hands of Ross Donaldson, he and Mrs. Howell coming in just as I was closing. About sunset I received two letters, one from John and one from Tom. In Va. they are getting on finely; with Tom's Reg. not quite so well. Pillow has withdrawn his troops from Missouri[85] and has stationed them in Columbus, Ky. T writes rather discouragingly. As the Lincolnites are already in possession of Paducah and Smithland[86] he, of course, will not be surprised if called into an engagement soon. Tonight Florence, Uncle T, and I went down to hear Dr. McMullin. He preached from Jeremiah 29th chap, 12 and 13th verses.[87] Congregation small as Mr. Malone preached his farewell sermon tonight. All were, at least many were, anxious to hear him. Since commencing this, Ross has called to take a final leave. Poor fellow, he looks so sad. I'm so sorry for him.

New Providence, Tennessee, Monday night, September 16, 1861

Went to work early on the negroes' shirts but with all the assistance given me (Emma and Florence) but little progress has been made. The wedding this evening interfered considerably. Just before dinner Florence and I noticed as many as three couples passing, and judging from the peculiar appearance of their dress, &c, &c, that a runaway match had made their escape to the Southern Confederacy for the sole object of expressing their Union sentiments.[88] We dined hurriedly and soon were on our way to the hotel, where Florence for the first time witnessed the union of two at the bridal altar. Mr. Malone performed the ceremony in the presence of only a few, the news going out so late that many who would have been delighted with the place were not permitted to attend. To say the least of them they were a bald, unembarrassed, rude set, not in the least acquainted with refinement and gentility.

New Providence, Tennessee, Tuesday night, September 17, 1861

Mr. H was up tonight but I guess he half regrets coming. The lecture on drinking whiskey, so often heard before, was repeated tonight, with a few additional remarks, for him to say that John Mallory ever 'Drank like a fish.'

New Providence, Tennessee, Friday night, September 20, 1861

Early Wednesday morning Cousin Jane, the two children, Sylus Trice, and I were off for old Mr. Osborne's.[89] After a rough ride over a hilly rough country we were housed safely beneath the roof of the old but inviting mansion. As expected, found Cousin Marion absent. She had gone to see the soldiers leave Camp Boone for Mullins Hill. She came about 5 o'clock and shortly afterwards two young ladies of the neighborhood came in to spend the night with her. Not the least important personage in our midst after tea was Dr. Johnson. His call, however, was a professional one, not by any means— He left about 9, but before 1 o'clock the horn was blowing, and a regret now and then expressed that he hadn't spent the night. They blew him up, however, about 2 o'clock and by 3 quiet was restored. At least everything in one of the cabins seemed more quiet. Cousin says its name shall be Serepta Jane Mary Inez in honor of her guests that night.[90] The girls were off early yesterday morning; the day was given in which to talk confidentially and read each other's letters. Mr. O had a nice pig killed and at dinner we feasted on that and other good things. Late took a walk far as Mr. Whitefield's.[91]

Today spent as yesterday until after dinner when we left for home. We came a different route and a much better one accompanied by Cousin M as far as Cobb's Mill. Met with Uncle T at the toll gate and an allusion was made to his frequent visits out there, which called forth a reply from him that made my heart ache, and the recollection of which will make me sad to my latest hour.[92] How, how, can he forget so soon? Can Earth forget the genial rays and warmth of the sun; can the mariner forget the heavens light that has so often brought him in to the port of safety? Yes, yes, they may forget, but it seems to me that erring man should not forget the earthly angel (if such there be) that has for years and years administered to his wants and sought only his happiness. Mr. Homer was up tonight but brought with him little news as the cars between Louisville and Clarksville have been taken by the Tennesseans and no news can be brought. At least the *Couriers* will not in future be brought from Louisville by RR. He says the report that Rosecrans has whipped our Reg. in Va. has been corrected and that the victory is on our side. How glad I will be to hear this confirmed.

New Providence, Tennessee, Saturday night, September 21, 1861

The rain last night cooled the atmosphere so much that fire and winter clothing have been comfortable all day. I involuntarily look round for one who in other days was ever present on such occasions, and with the tenderness and loving kindness of a mother, was ready to remove each tear-drop, check the rising sigh, bid bright anticipation take the place of despondency. The conversation with Uncle T since tea has added no little to the gloom that has for a few hours past seemed to envelope my very soul. Had I the pen of Shakespeare the abominable character set forth in "Hamlet," would be of the other sex, and "no draw on the imagination," would be necessary to give a darker shade of coloring to that by nature too dark to appear natural.[93] But woman is the target when man has the writing of plays, prose, or anything else in which someone is to figure as the heartless, the forgetful, the inconstant, and everything else that's objectionable to the fastidious tastes of the constant loving ones who style themselves "lords of creation."

New Providence, Tennessee, Sunday, September 22, 1861

The weather remains very cool; a merino[94] dress would have been comfortable all day. With the exception of Dr. Mc's and his wife's, this morning school opened as usual. With another exception, I had almost forgotten, important as it was, Mr. Malone, last Wednesday night before leaving for conference, gave his members their orders: they were not to send their children to our school to be taught Calvinism. He told them plainly they had better be taught by their own parents. The consequence was a large school opened at the Methodist church this morning. The children were ordered to return their books to Mr. Hirst, and with renewed energy to set in with the determination of building up a Methodist school. As yet they have not been defeated in their purpose. Envy — jealousy, back biting, &c will take the place, or rather be encouraged more than a love of truth, wisdom, and knowledge, and of course the result will be anything but favorable to a prosperous continuance of the school. In sadness I will predict a speedy downfall of the establishment but hope to be disappointed. Taught the servants, read, and lounged until late after dinner when Mrs. Magaren and Mat Harrelson[95] came up and remained with me until after tea.

New Providence, Tennessee, Tuesday night, September 24, 1861

Another mail day and no letter. Isn't it too bad? A paper from Memphis containing the news of Capt. Hamilton's death was all (the Capt. of the "Memphis Southern guards").[96] His loss will be deeply felt. Sick all day with headache. Several calls, Mr. Garrett and Mr. Duncan among the number. Mr. D is still with us. Florence and Bettie have a little party on hand. Mr. Homer interfered, however, as usual. I felt really sorry for B when he ordered her to keep out of the parlor.

New Providence, Tennessee, Wednesday night, September 25, 1861

The party closed last night at an early hour about 9. They were invited in to worship and that closed the performance. After getting the company out on the back gallery and in the yard, Bettie appeared quite cheerful. At least she seemed oblivious to all that had taken place at my room door. Made today the last catsup of the season. Indeed, I'm done preserving or doing anything of the kind and I'm so glad. Mrs. Staton called this evening. Since tea we went over to see Mrs. Wilson; she's improving. The street for two weeks past has been almost crowded with travelers, persons seeking places of safety from Louisville and other places in Ky.[97] Hacks heavily laden with baggage and freight of a more precious character are almost hourly passing. Wagons loaded with goods both dry and groceries are also coming in frequently. Some of them are brought from Evansville, Ind., mostly from Louisville. So much for Ky.'s neutrality. Already her citizens are about to be convinced of the fact that her soil is again to be "the dark and bloody ground," and none are to be blamed for her fortunes but the advocates of "armed neutrality," and the Lincolnites, who style themselves "Union men."

New Providence, Tennessee, Saturday night, September 28, 1861

Attempted several things today but finished only the potato custards.[98] George Trice breakfasted and dined with us. Since his company has been encamped near Bowling Green, he and Greenhill together have succeeded nobly in killing one Yankee or rather first cousin to a Yankee a "Ky. Union man." While out scouting on last Sunday morning they came across a man of genteel appearance and one who made himself very agreeable for a while after they met. He soon had occasion however to leave them but returned in a few moments and on approaching near enough as he thought to let a stone do its work with Greenhill's head, he threw and the object was not missed. Of course G, after so friendly a conversation, wasn't suspecting anything of the kind. No sooner had he fallen than another stone was aimed at George, but he, taking warning from the blow given his companion, was thoughtful enough to dodge and in a moment his gun was at his command and so soon as he succeeded in getting Greenhill from between himself and the villain he fired. The first fire would have accomplished all, but to be certain, George gave him the second load. The first load entered his breast. After receiving that, he says that will do, but George thought differently and so told him, firing at the same time the second load into his brain. After finding that G had him in his power and the gun raised, the man says, "oh save me," and those words no doubt will ring in George's ear until deafened by the roar of artillery on the battle field, and only the present has command of his thoughts. He denies feeling badly about it but he evidently does. I know from his appearance. He acknowledges feeling badly for the wife and little children. He saw them running from home as he mounted his horse. The man he left lying in the road. Cousin Jane spent a few moments with me this evening.

But for Cousin Marion she would have stayed longer. Our "Home Guards" have at last had a call. They were ordered all the way to Long View[99] this evening. Some of the Union men they say intend taking their cannon away from them up there.

New Providence, Tennessee, Tuesday night, October 1, 1861

Finished one and commenced another dress today. Cousin Jane and Cousin Lou have been in to see me few minutes. Mr. Homer sit tonight until late, Uncle T being absent his company was very acceptable. Since the Courier was stopped some weeks ago, we get but little news.[100] Through Mr. H I learned tonight that another great battle had been fought in Lexington, Mo., between Price and Milligan.[101] The slaughter was greater than at Manassas we are told. How dreadful it must have been. The "Hopkinsville battle"[102] is all the excitement with "our boys." The Home G were called on to join a company last Friday to go up and take the guns from the Unionists of that place. Several of them went and such wonderful tales they have to tell us since their return, so many "hair breadth" escapes, such a perilous rout they had to undergo, such a rough country. Oh, so many dangers, I shall not attempt to enumerate them. Like a warrior of old they went, they saw, they conquered.[103] Some 15 or 20 Lincolnites were captured, their guns taken, they sworn to protect the Southern Confederacy, and released — a sweet way of doing up things, just as though everyone served so wouldn't redouble his energy in attempting to tear down the Southern flag. Afterwards Mr. Homer gave me another rub about my ugly walk tonight. I wish he was compelled to look at Miss Davidson and Beck Wiggins until an awkwardly walking girl would be a relief to his eyes. I wish too he knew what someone said about his "tobacco stick legs." I know I'm no graceful walker and I know that ridicule will do but little towards improving me.

New Providence, Tennessee, Wednesday night, October 2, 1861

Sewed all morning, slept most all the evening. I've felt badly all day. No company until since tea. Mr. H came up. We walked down to see Mrs. Pollard [a] few moments. Met with a cousin, Miss Jennie Pollard. The Secessionists have possession of Hopkinsville, and it is said 18,000 are marching on to take Paducah. Johnston[104] I expect has command of the forces.

New Providence, Tennessee, Friday night, October 4, 1861

Made some cakes this evening. Read several pages in Lafayette's life.[105] Tonight we went up to see Mrs. Smith.[106] Her babe was very fretful; she's been sick for some time. A large company of Miss. soldiers[107] passed today on their way to Hopkinsville. The place is now entirely in possession of the Secessionists. Wonder what the union loving citizens are doing with their armed neutrality?

New Providence, Tennessee, Sunday night, October 6, 1861

The weather is undecided, gloomy cloudy and occasionally sunshiny. School opened with comparatively few scholars this morning, my class with several others having dwindled down to two or three. Dr. Mc and Mr. Hirst, however, seem untiring in their efforts. Dr. M preached at 11 from 42nd Psalm 11th verse.[108] He preached a real strengthening sermon to the christians. This evening I had set apart to read, but as usual Mr. H interfered. He came up soon after dinner. Uncle T came in with him and brought a letter from John. Notwithstanding my attempt to read it while Mr. H was here, my efforts proved fruitless, and not until late was the precious privilege given me of reading it alone and undisturbed. Just after Uncle T handed it to me Mr. H boasted of having made some very important discoveries: he "never knew before how much I did think of John." Through his persuasion, we walked down to Cousin Jane's this evening. Found all gone. Went in to see poor Mr. Blakney [a] few moments. Dr. Drane returned last night with James, his son, a corpse[109] from the 14th Reg., and with Hugh, another son, quite ill. Poor family. How much distressed they must be.

New Providence, Tennessee, Monday night, October 7, 1861

Went to work soon after breakfast, determined to do a good day's work, but how little do we know what a day will bring forth. About 9 o'clock Cousin Billie Mallory came in and though I feared his errand was a sad one from the melancholy expression of his face, I little dreamed that he had brought the sorrowful news of little Willie Mills"[110] death. He said Cousin Mollie told him to call and tell me that Willie was dead. The second time I inquired if it were true and even then, I could scarcely realize that he was certainly dead.

Immediately I sent for Cousin Jane and about 12 we left for Mr. Mills'. We were there in time to see the little treasure placed in his coffin and hear the farewell words of two loving parents to the priceless jewel, at least the casket in which the jewel was held. That the spirit that had for so short a time given life and beauty to that lovely form had taken its flight to realms of bliss, they never seemed to doubt. But, oh, how heart rending, how impossible it was for them to give up their all, their only darling. His remains were carried to the family burial ground and there with the sympathetic tears of many friends, the stricken mourners shed their most bitter tears. Uncle T went to Nashville today; came [a] few moments since, with a large package of letters from the Reg. How eagerly they were all glomed over until the well known, familiar hand met my gaze. Then my curiosity was satisfied. I had seen enough of the Regiment letters. I am so anxious to see the contents I must close.

New Providence, Tennessee, Wednesday night, October 9, 1861

Such a nice possum we had for supper tonight; Mrs. Gold was present to help us enjoy it.

New Providence, Tennessee, Saturday night, October 12, 1861

At last my gowns are finished, but not until half of the day passed today. Laura Helm has been with me most of the day plaiting hair. Jennie Howard[111] and Brown Cherry[112] paid me a visit this evening, for a "rarity." Late I called on Inez Davis.[113] Met with her cousins, a Miss and Mr. Herring, cousins of Dr. Herring. Mrs. Herring seems to fear very much that Elmore[114] will take hydrophobia[115] from "the dog bite" he received from Johny Baker the other day. How blinded most mothers are to the faults of their children. Now E. was as much to blame the other day for getting into that fight as Johny B was. And yet Mrs. Herring approves of Elmore's course and tells him always to resent an injury or insult under like circumstances. Probably if she knew to what result such advice will finally lead to, her instruction would be different. But it may be too late when she sees her error to be of much advantage to her son. News came today that the trunks of Lieuts. Brown[116] and Mallory had been burnt, to prevent the Yankees from getting them. I should like to know the contents of each.

New Providence, Tennessee, Monday night, October 14, 1861

Through Uncle Trice's persuasion together with a painful recollection of last night's suffering I consented this morning to have a tooth extracted. Dr. Cabaniss was up early, and but a few moments after his arrival elapsed before the long dreaded operation had been performed, and I as contented as though his visit had been made through friendship and not with the intention of giving me for a few moments the most intense pain. After so long a time I summed up courage to have the second one drawn, but my nerves were terribly out of order long before the first was out. Making tatting insertion and cooking preserves over all day. Uncle T seems very much out of humor with servants tonight; such language as he used tonight I hope never to hear fall from his lips again. The cord that for years has kept him at least near the right path seems now to be weakening, and at a most rapid rate. What will be the result of such recklessness, none can tell, but if I could only do or say one thing before he is beyond recovery, how gladly would I do it—Soon I fear there will be but little hope.

New Providence, Tennessee, Friday night, October 18, 1861

According to arrangements made some time since, Cousin Jane and I left early Tuesday morning for Uncle Billie Mallory's. We were there in good time for our dinner, but my gums were so sore than I didn't enjoy it much. Met with Cousin Mollie and Mr. Mills. That night we went with her home, and there I remained until today. My object was to visit Cousin Mollie, knowing that she felt badly, while Cousin Jane's was to visit the neighborhood. Cousin Mollie is yet very sad on account of Willie's death. She talks and cries about him most all the time. Through the kindness of Mr. Mills, I was permitted to read a letter from John (written to his father). In it was an allusion or two to my letters; but my name was not called. I wonder if they suspected who it was? Found all well at home and a nice bouquet, not from Tom but his "Mommy."

New Providence, Tennessee, Saturday night, October 19, 1861

In looking over the lines above, I find that I closed last evening by saying 'found all well at home." But tonight I will be denied that pleasure. Uncle Trice seems to be in a dreadful state of mind. He is anything else but well, and the true cause of his derangement what would I not give to know? Were he well in every sense of the word, how different would life appear. True, many things have occurred to detract from its brightness, yet all would not be so dark if he would only confine himself to that narrow track that would finally lead to joys eternal. What am I to do? is a question that often comes up, particularly when Uncle T is in one of his melancholy spells. And as often as it comes up, so often do I fail to fall on any plan that encourages me in the belief that all in a short time will be well. Provided I'm spared until this day year, what changes will have taken place to make life more {*indecipherable*}?

New Providence, Tennessee, Sunday night, October 20, 1861

Mr. Homer sit so late that time is scarcely given me to undress, much less to write much. I'm too sleepy to concentrate my mind my eyes on this page in such a manner as to make it more interesting than while it was in its blank state. An attempt, however, may not prove entirely useless. School rather dry this morning. The decrease in the number of scholars has a very sad effect. Dr. McMullin preached at 11 from 1st epistle of John, 3rd verse 1st and 2nd verses.[117] Cousin Jane and the children dined with me and spent the evening. Mr. H likewise. Late we drove Cousin Jane down home. Afterward Mr. Homer and I drove over to the cemetery. There I visited the last resting place of my dear aunt. A few months since and that spot was looked forward to as something belonging to the future, as being too far off for me ever to behold it with eyes undimmed by age or {indecipherable} by time. But from infancy to childhood, from childhood to womanhood, she was kindly spared to direct me in the path of duty, and from that time until death, be it long or short, the all wise saw fit for me to walk alone through life—at least, without her careful guidance and protection. Mr. Homer told us tonight that one of the bridges between here and Tenn. River had been burned by the Lincolnites. If so communication between Clarksville and Memphis will be cut off and we may expect the wretches in our very midst soon. The river is rising rapidly, and the appearance of one of their gunboats need not surprise us.

New Providence, Tennessee, Tuesday night, October 22, 1861

At last we've a slight prospect of frost; the fall has been the latest I ever knew. At home all day until late. Cousin Jane came up, and Florence and I walked with her as far as the store. She told us that poor Mr. Blakney, she thought, was dying. Uncle John Mallory paid us a short visit this evening. Tonight Mr. H paid a long one—several subjects were introduced, but none that drew me out fully until whiskey drinking was brought. On that subject I took particular pains to give my views in plain decided terms. Well I ventured as far as prudence would permit without being too personal or too rigid. Uncle T guessed right when he said it was only an indirect lecture for he and Mr. Homer. I——intended every word I said to have its full force, and that it may have some effect is my humble wish. Mr. Homer predicts for me a drunken, disagreeable husband, and it may be my fate to have one, but, oh, how bitter will be the pill. Already I've seen too much.

New Providence, Tennessee, Sunday night, October 27, 1861

The anniversary of Aunt T's and Uncle Trice's marriage. Today 21 years ago they were united. Tonight they are separated. She, I trust, is in Heaven, while he is still here—but a changed man, different in many respects from what he was on that day. Could I but think him even the same man that he was this day one year since, how relieved my heart would be. How much lighter. But oh! the change that has come over his feelings within a short time past! How is it possible for man to be so unlike man? How can he do and act like he does? I have thought myself prepared for the worst, but this trial, second only to any I have yet endured, it seems unfits me for anything. I think sometimes how am I to bear up under it? School and church as usual. Cousin Marion dined with me. After dinner she and Uncle T had a long conversation, which she repeated to me. About ½ 2 we drove down to Cousin Jane's. There I passed two or three hours. Not agreeably, for not an agreeable moment has passed with me since I left church this morning. After leaving there, we drove up street a short distance. To my surprise met with Uncle T in a stable buggy. Seeing old Mrs. Kirby at the gate with bonnet and shawl on and a bouquet, I readily guessed where he had been. He went to church tonight, fretted I know because I wouldn't go. But how could I go feeling as I did?

New Providence, Tennessee, Monday night, October 28, 1861

What a lovely day I have passed. The absence of company is not all that produces this feeling. No, the giddy and the gay might have surrounded me today by thousands and still my heart would have felt lonely. Too keenly do I feel the sad truth. This evening I sought my best earthly comforter, Cousin Jane. Found her at home and alone. Spent the whole evening with her and then wished it were longer, that my visit might be prolonged. Home is anything else but home with me now. Reluctantly, sometimes I return to it, particularly after making such a visit as the one this evening. There is so little here to cheer me and nothing to console. No difference, what may be the case. If Uncle T could to the slightest extent take Aunt T's place, how much sweeter would home be, but no, the wish is vain. Never will he in a single instance fill her place as a comforter. Mr. Duncan was over this morning, but I was not in a humor for entertaining him and he left after spending a short time. Mr. Leonard's residence and granary were burned last night and nothing of consequence was saved. It is supposed his own servants were the ones that set it on fire.

New Providence, Tennessee, Thursday night, October 31, 1861

The weather is clear and pleasant. Concluded to make the best of it and by 10 this morning every bed-quilt-blanket and most everything else was outdoors, and the house upside down. Not until late was Aspen Cottage "itself again." Received a letter from John about 4 and of course a better state of feeling has been existing ever since on my part. So taking everything into consideration we are doing better tonight than we ought to expect or deserve.

New Providence, Tennessee, Friday night, November 1, 1861

The first day of Nov. and still we [are] having vegetables from the garden such as tomatoes, butter beans, &c. Surely, we've not been favored with so late a fall for many years, but the picture begins to fade. The rain has been falling slowly all day and tonight it continues with considerable change in the atmosphere. Since tea we almost shiver even near the fire. Poor boys in Va., now we'll begin to feel sad for you. Our own hearts must be touched before we can truly sympathize with others. News came today that a large no. of Lincolnites were approaching Hopkinsville and that the commander then had orders from Buckner to retreat. If such be the case, we may look for them here soon with all the horrors that follow in their train. The great no. of flouring mills immediately in this Co. will, I fear, be the great attraction for drawing them hither. Should they get possession of them, the S Confederacy will have to give up all hope of future supplies. The consequences would be ruinous, distressing.

New Providence, Tennessee, Saturday night, November 2, 1861

Cold and gloomy, oh so gloomy. My feelings are exactly in keeping with the dull aspect of things without. Mrs. Wilson came over this morning, but I could find but little to talk to her about. She was over again this evening with Mary Smith. I tried to do better. Mr. Spence from Paris and Dick Ogburn have both called in during the day for short whiles. This evening I interested myself for an hour or two ransacking the presses and safe,[118] cleaned them all out and brought the safe into Uncle Trice's room. The move displeased him. His "room already was crowded with boxes of peas, beans, &c." Soon after tea, the safe was removed to the old place, the boxes all set away in the region of mice and rats, and even the jug of vinegar was hid and the jar of eggs brought into my room.[119] No more I'm sure will his room be crowded, unless by the orders of one who has power to exert more authority than myself. He's so different from what he used to be. Such things he never seemed to notice before, and as to being particular about his room, that is nothing compared with the attention he gives to his person. A year since and it was through persuasion and begging that he changed his dress on Sunday morning. Now "the negroes have but little to do anyway" "and they'd as

well be washing." 700 Texan Soldiers[120] passed through today on their way
to meet Tilghman[121] from Hopkinsville. Some of the Co.'s were composed
of splendid looking men.

New Providence, Tennessee, Sunday night, November 3, 1861

Still dull and gloomy. Florence was quite sick during the night last night;
went to Sunday school, however, this morning. Dr. Mc preached a stirring
sermon from the text, "In as much as ye did it unto the least of these little
ones, ye did it unto me."[122] He also solicited a little help for the hospital in
Clarksville. A great many of the Texas Soldiers are over there very sick. The
college with other buildings has been vacated for them. Read from dinner
until near sunset, Josephus mostly, though I sent down to Mr. Homer for the
Chronicle and read over that. Mr. H, I guess, is done bringing me papers. He
has not been up since last night a week ago. Truly I miss his visits greatly. It
has been so long since he failed to come up every night or two anyway. It may
be what I said to him down at Cousin Jane's last Sunday evening in reference
to teaching the servants offended him. I was no little provoked that evening,
and only a few words from him disapproving my course was sufficient to call
forth anything but pleasant words from me. It may be that I said too much,
but he never gives me an encouraging word. Let me do what I will, he has
some objection to find. And he ought to know that any one's patience would
wear out after a while. Some "change has come over the spirit of his dreams"
I'm sure, but Cousin Marion may have given him a few hints. I know not.
Late walked down to Mr. Helm's and Dr. Herring's. Laura came home with
me. Florence is complaining so much. She went home.

New Providence, Tennessee, Monday night, November 4, 1861

At home alone until after dinner, Went down and spent some time with Mrs.
Pollard. Met with Nannie Hoover. Mr. Hoover has sold out to Mr. Pettus
and will leave with his family in a short time for Iowa. Interested myself during the morning sewing on a new brilliant gown.

New Providence, Tennessee, Thursday night, November 7, 1861

Commenced work early, determined to finish my gown. But soon George
Helm came in just from the seat of war, and, of course, all was laid aside to
talk over for a while the news of the day. He says he left the troops preparing
to make a forward move but knew not how far they would go. Large companies continue to pass here on their way to Hopkinsville. Recently the wagons
have all been pressed into service, Wilson's among the rest. Before G left,

Mary Britton came in and stayed with me until late this evening. We both did a good day's work besides doing our share of talking.

New Providence, Tennessee, Friday night, November 8, 1861

The weather remains warm and pleasant. Finished at last my brilliant gown. Uncle Trice gave me an agreeable surprise this morning; brought up from the office two letters, one from the 14th Reg. "Corp. Jo E Wray," and one from "Private T E Trabue" Columbus, Ky. Poor Tom, he may tonight be a lifeless corpse on the bloody battlefield or a wounded soldier groaning with pain and suffering from hunger and thirst—all that mortal man can suffer and still live. News came today that the troops at Columbus have been engaged with the Enemy on the opposite shore (on the Mo side), and that though we were the successful ones, yet the loss on both sides was heavy.[123] Tom little dreamed while writing that the battle ground was so near him. He anticipated a fight at Paducah. Spent most of the evening pasting pieces in my scrap book. Uncle T went over with Ellie and Uncle Billie to fill up dear Aunt T's grave.[124] I wish while he is interested, the tomb stone could be erected and the paling fixed round. His last resting place I'm sure never would have been neglected so long. He seemed a little provoked today that I didn't talk more to him. If I could tell him why I felt so little inclined, he would not wonder perhaps at my silence. Hearing as much as I do about the subject that mostly engages him out of my presence, it unfits me to talk with him when he comes in, feeling assured that not a word I could add on his favorite theme would please him.

New Providence, Tennessee, Saturday night, November 9, 1861

Spent the morning writing to Jo and to John. At dinner Uncle Trice brought in an extra, confirming the news of the Columbus battle. But worst of all, the Enemy have gained their first victory and that at one of our most important points. Savanah, the last dispatches say, is completely in their possession.[125] Lincoln's fleet has done its work, and our cotton, our support gone.

New Providence, Tennessee, Monday night, November 11, 1861

Made the body of a gown today and a potato pie for dinner. Tonight Mr. Steeger, a member of George's company, supped with us. He was on the battle ground at Columbus at 4 o'clock in the afternoon of the day on which was fought the great battle. He brought with him some buttons he cut off the Yankees' coats, also a cannon ball that we did not see. He represents the fight as terrible indeed for some hours. During the retreat the Yankees were compelled to cross a fence and there, he says after all was over, might be seen the vandals strewn for a long distance, most of them having been shot in the back. Soon after the first attack, the ammunition of General Pillow's men gave out, and as they fell back to replenish, the wretches entered the hospitals and brutally murdered a great many of our sick soldiers. Such cruelty may almost be classed with that practiced by Nero[126] or Demetrius.[127]

New Providence, Tennessee, Tuesday night, November 12, 1861

Sewed busily all the morning. Uncle Trice sent me in the "Union and American,"[128] but not until dinner did I take time to read. George brought over the "Memphis Argus." In it was contained a complete history of the Columbus fight. "Hamilton's M S Guards," said one of the correspondents, "fought bravely and stood to their guns like veterans." Tom's fate is to me yet unknown. Mollie Smith[129] spent the evening with us. Tonight, Efe came and for a while I enjoyed his idiotic manner, conversation, &c, &c, but soon an end was put to everything akin to enjoyment. Tears took the place of smiles while Uncle T was plaguing him about marrying & he retaliated by enumerating his [Uncle T's] sweethearts. And no less than three were brought up, all of whom Efe said was out Sunday and "one looked mighty pretty at" Uncle T. How can Uncle T endure such conversations, much less encourage them? And he must, else others would [not] dare to do as they do in my presence. No longer than today he wept bitterly and I suppose he intended me to think it was all about Aunt T. But from what continually meets my ears, his conduct from home and his grief at home don't agree at all. The one is too inconsistent for the other, and how am I to obey under the circumstances the commandment that says weep with those that weep? Never are my tears farther back than when he calls me to him (as he does every few days) and with face all bathed in tears, and a heart apparently crushed with grief, asks me what he is to do. The first thought that comes up is about how he jests and talks up town about ladies of his acquaintance that it is useless just here for me to mention.

New Providence, Tennessee, Wednesday night, November 13, 1861

The middle of Nov., or near it, and not a spark of fire is to be seen on the hearth; while a seat on the porch even at this late hour of the night is pleasant indeed. The weather is mild and pleasant enough for spring—How grateful we are on the soldiers' acct. Cousin Jane and Mrs. Wilson have been to see us this evening. Cousin J is really 'low down.' She finished Ellie's and Uncle

Billie's coats today. She only charged 75 cts, but Uncle T had given me two dollars with which to pay her, and the whole of it was given her cheerfully. Better she enjoy and feel the benefit of it than some others.

Another long letter from John today. What would I do surrounded as is so often the case with despondency and gloom, with nothing to give me one moment's relief, were it not for his frequent and cheering letters? They come as the gentle shower after our earth has for weeks been scorched and parched beneath the burning rays of our August sun, as dew to the thirsty plants, as an oasis to the weary traveler are his letters to me. They never come too often, nor have I ever read one that seemed too long. May Our Father continue his health and permit him to return safely to home and friends. "The Soldiers Aid Society" was renewed again. A meeting was held today with a few of the ladies, so Mrs. Staton and Morrison told me, and arrangements were made for creating this side the river a hospital for the soldiers. Mrs. Herring, it seems, was at the head of the move, and her object was nothing more nor less than to let us all know we had best to keep our donations until all have an opportunity of waiting on the sick as in our own homes.

New Providence, Tennessee, Friday night, November 15, 1861

Today was the one appointed by Pres. Davis as a day of fasting and prayer. It has been generally recognized I believe by our citizens and I hope by the Southern Confederacy. As we had no service at the Baptist church, I went down to hear Mr. Taylor. His discourse was not so interesting to me as the one on last Sunday. His text was in Rev. and of course mysterious. I fasted until near 2 o'clock today and thought only one meal was missed. I must say that tonight I know more of what is meant by the term than ever before. Went up to see Mrs. Gold this evening. She had but little [to] say except in reference to Mr. Hoover's disappointment. He and wife left early this morning for Iowa "via Elkton, Ky." Georgina, her two brothers, and old Mrs. Smith[130] were to accompany them that far, but before getting scarcely without the limits of Clarksville, they were ordered to "halt" and then to return to the city. Mr. H readily consented as the command was from one of high military authority. He was gallanted in to the presence of the military board and there examined with his baggage, but not alone was he in passing through this ordeal. Nannie would go with him and says she's going with him tomorrow to Hopkinsville where Gen. Tilghman will take him generally through. Met with Georgina up at Mrs. G's this evening and she was so mad while relating the adventure that she was really nervous.

New Providence, Tennessee, Saturday night, November 16, 1861

The rain night before last left us in quite a different climate; the weather has been really wintry for the last two days. Made three night caps today and a cake, besides going to Cousin Jane's and reading a long letter from Tom. Poor fellow, he says he sometimes "fears to write," thinking I will probably "claim the letter under a different name." He then adds, you know the finality. He with his co. were engaged at the Columbus battle but not one of them were killed. Met with Cousin Marion at Cousin Jane's. She came down to hear Mr. Ford tonight, but he came in so late that we had given him out, and of course the church was not prepared for him. Mr. Homer was up tonight and soon after getting in he took his text. True it was divided into two or three different heads, but marriage was the principal one and "the duty of a wife" the next. "Yes, now I contend that the woman had as well make some advances as the man." This is the way he always commences and in about the same way he ends. It seems to me that after so long a time the subject might fail to interest me, but he always seems fresh in the cause.

New Providence, Tennessee, Monday night, November 18, 1861

Commenced work early. Finished about 3 this evening a dress commenced last Dec. Really, I'm pleased at the idea of wearing it; it has been on hand so long. Necessity was not so nearby at its commencement as at its conclusion. Now a calico costs me almost as much as that did a nice piece of DeBege quality very good and only 40 cts per yard. Calico is sold now very nearly the same price. Cousin Jane was up this evening. Walked with her as far as Mrs. Pollard's; found Nannie Hoover wearing quite a long face. Georgina had just left for Ark., and her ma for Elkton. Uncle Trice went up to Nashville tonight (at least started). Mr. H is with us, and for once he dispensed with his favorite theme and interested us with one of Dr. Campbell's works. He read, it seems to me, without stopping a minute for two or three hours. His apples, however, at the close of the exercises more than repaid us for our attention — and long silence.

New Providence, Tennessee, Tuesday night, November 19, 1861

Florence and I prepared early this morning to go out to West Fork. Our horse being lame, we were compelled to go very slowly. Mr. Hodge preached from Rev., 3rd Chap. and 20th verse. He dwells too long on his words to be an agreeable speaker, and then his ideas are nothing more than we might expect of one of his years. Two presented themselves as seekers, and the church seemed somewhat revived. Mrs. Gold was down this evening almost by the time I was in. She's all interest, not to say curiosity, in what is going on. Before she left, Mrs. Haskins[131] from Clarksville came in on a begging errand. She with Mrs. Henry[132] is out collecting blankets, socks, &c for the soldiers. "Oh! Yes, you must give. They are needing everything" and "We've deprived ourselves of so and so." Now it is strange that Providence is never thought of until "assistance" is wanted, but let there be a call on their purse, time, &c and we are the first ones thought of. And then, "Oh, dear me, how glad I'd be for you to visit me" "Do come over to the meeting of our Society soon, won't you"? "I'll be delighted to see you." Now but few of our town, unimportant as it is, can say they have not [done] a good part by the soldiers, and the Clarksville ladies had as well keep their invitations, solicitations, &c to themselves. As for what they will accomplish, for my impression is, the Providence ladies will act when and where they think it necessary and not be gulled into what will finally redound to the great honor and glory of the Cl'sville ladies. We may give and give, but so soon as the bird is in their hand they cease to praise its plumage. And so we may aid, influenced by their flattery and compliments, but that will be the last of it. After they've gotten our blankets, we may go to Guinea.[133] Let a fort be commenced,[134] as they did on yesterday, and rather than include Providence under its protection they will commence it in a flat just without the suburbs of their city, a place liable to inundation at any time and where it will protect them about as little as it will us. They permit their selfishness to so blind them that their main interest is overlooked. Mr. H has come in and I will cease for a while my abuse on Clarksville and its citizens.

New Providence, Tennessee, Saturday night, November 23, 1861

Thursday morning almost by "the break of day" as old Mrs. Ray[135] [says], I was up and making preparations for spending a day or two in the country. But first one thing and another prevented me and it was 10 o'clock before I left. Mrs. Trabue, for one thing, hindered my movements. She came down "to hear something from Tom" as you said. Strange, a mother would go to a disinterested person to hear from a son. I cheerfully gave her all the information and satisfaction within my reach. In her pocket she had an epistle or something on that order, which she supposed would not be wholly uninteresting to me. And rather reluctantly I glanced over its pages, for my time was limited. At 11 I was at West Fork. Mr. Hodges preached from the text, "But the wicked are driven away in their wickedness." Only two presented themselves as seekers. In the afternoon the subject was continued, but his appeals were more urgent and solemn, and more feeling was manifested by all the congregation. 6 or 7 came forward and all seemed deeply convicted. Mr. Homer has just stepped in and I must quiz him a little about going into camp. The Militia will know their destiny Monday.

New Providence, Tennessee, Sunday night, November 24, 1861

Uncle T for a while after dinner (not according to habit) kept his own room, after which he came in and took a seat with us. For an hour or more but few words were passed between any of us. Finally, the silence was broken by Uncle T saying he believed he "would go up on the hill to see Fannie."[136] I said not a word, but he continued the subject and at last attempted, as was his object at the first no doubt, to draw from me a reply. With tears and a heart almost bursting with grief at the recollection of my dear aunt's utter aversion to such conduct, I asked him if he had forgotten Aunt Tabbie. No, he says, "I haven't forgotten her. I think more of her than you do." These I firmly believe were remarks intended as an introduction to what he was going to say, for with them he entered fully into the subject, telling me that he had been to see Miss F four times, the particulars of each visit, that they were practically engaged, her attachment for me and for cousin Jane, her unwillingness to take the place of one so much beloved as Aunt T, and that she commended him for saying that, if she made this her home, she must share it now and hereafter agreeably with me. She said his befriending me and giving me the privileges of a child was just and right and she admired him for it. Told him to make me a deed of gift to the lot joining this, that she had no objection [to] it, and among other things. She said, that, I regret to say, has been acted out by few. If legal fathers and mothers reject and disown their children, what may we expect of uncles-in-law and their wives? Truly not so much as of an own parent.

Uncle T may prove faithful to what he now says, and she may prove a mother in kindness, love, &c; but this remains yet to be tried. And not until then will I acknowledge that I know her. She says, and I heard her when she said it, that she believed if there ever was a curse sent on Earth it was sent in stepmothers and this to a certain extent will be the relationship that she will bear to me. So if her belief is carried out in practice, she will prove anything else but an agreeable companion for me.

But all this is nothing—Aunt T's memory I want respected and cherished as she was while living, and certainly it seems that Uncle Trice has forgotten her when he tells us that on such a day he went and called at old Mrs. Pettus' especially to see Miss F, that on such a day he took her riding, &c. Now if he loved Aunt T, why is it that he permits another to take her place so soon? But still this isn't the worst. With young gentlemen and ladies, they tell me, he's all life, all gaiety, that a boy 18 is more sedate and less talkative on the subject of matrimony than he is. (I thank him for respecting my feelings; he seldom does it in my presence.) Now if he would visit Miss F as becomes one of his age, talk the matter seriously over with her, and be quiet and act as an old gentleman should with in and out of presence, the matter would be different. But, oh, how sad it is.

Of Aunt T he never seems to have a thought while love, matrimony, the ladies, &c engages his whole attention. Could she have followed his footsteps into the future for a while before her death, how deep, how keen would have been her mortification. Much rather would I that Uncle T had married three weeks after her death than to have pursued the course he has, for I'm certain Miss F has been the subject of his thoughts, ever since the third day after that sad, saddest of all days to me. He would have shown more respect to Aunt T in so doing, for I'm certain it was not more than a week or two before he told Cousin Jane his intentions, and also, in a very disinterested manner, inquired of me about her disposition, but I so unsuspecting. Did I dream of his true thoughts? No, and had another accused him of such I would have been tempted to have given in return a most positive insult. But human nature: When [did] I learn even the first lessons? While the subject was under discussion, Mr. H came in to take me riding. But I didn't make my appearance. How could I? With eyes all swollen and heart too full to speak. Tonight, he was up again and as Uncle T had gone to church, a suitable time presented itself for explaining to him the "fuss in camp," as he called it. He received a hint from Florence and says he knew the sense directly. He would have said a good deal of the subject but for the intrusion of Uncle T as on today. The report in circulation of Mary Harrelson we talked over, but not satisfactorily. We differed as usual. My head aches and it is so late; my feet are very cold too.

New Providence, Tennessee, Monday night, November 25, 1861

The weather remains very cold, so cold that Mr. Fairfax killed hogs today and Uncle T borrowed one from him. The spare ribs for supper were so delicious as to make us almost forget the whitleather[137] that has been for so long supplied us at the market house. Commenced a gown this morning. Mr. H came in soon after breakfast to show me a dog, which he says is for me as soon as he is trained. Late drove down to Cousin Jane's. Mr. H was in but gave us an opportunity for a short "tete-a-tete." Called at the post office on my return. Mr. Helm handed me a letter from Mrs. Becks and a paper from TT—at least I think I recognize his name in the superscription. Poor Mrs., she sent much love to Aunt T and says she often thinks about how happily we all get on (i.e. our family) but little she thought, while penning those lines, that Aunt T's body had been reposing for the last four months in a lonely cemetery and that the husband, so loving and attentive when she left us, only remembered her now as one that was, one that had lived. Almost forgotten, Miss F called this morning. Her visit was short, but I tried to make it agreeable. She is a deserving woman no doubt, but singular in some respects. How she could receive Uncle T's addresses so soon—so soon—is strange to me and will be until I cease to live. Read a few chapts. in Rollin tonight.[138] I will be pleased with it I think.

New Providence, Tennessee, Tuesday night, November 26, 1861

Sewing busily all day, finished my gown—assisted in making a bone pie[139] for dinner, which I think was very good; Mr. H was up again this morning with my is-to-be pet.

New Providence, Tennessee, Monday morning, December 2, 1861

Well, another unexpected visit has been made and one that I feel truly thankful is done with. I sometimes wonder what I leave home for at all; there is so little enjoyment in company for me. Thursday about 12, Mr. Holland and Mr. Garrett came in and nothing would do Mr. G but I must go home with him. Feeling that the sooner the trip was over with the better for me, I soon consented to go, and by 2 o'clock was on my way to "Armed Neutrality." After one of the roughest imaginable rides over "muddy road" and new turnpike, we arrived as Dr. N used to say "right side up with care" at the homestead of one of Christian Co.'s most wealthy farmers. Our arrival it seems was unobserved until we were at the threshold; and then all was so quiet that a deaf person would only have known a meeting was going on from the motion of our hands. They are not the people to make a great noise; neither am I. Miss Babe Trahern[140] and a Miss Thomashad come over to spend the night with them. Miss B only added to the solemnity of the occasion; for there, as she used to be here, she occupied with dignity the place of a walking mummy. Miss T was a little more talkative, but the huge fire, the constant expectation of supper, and the continual prattle of Alice R's children,[141] all did but little in driving away thoughts of home and a foolish desire to be back again. So often I said to myself what did I come for? That day the Surgeon of Hopkinsville[142] had orders to move the sick to Clarksville. And soon after supper a clatter and noise was set up on the pike and calls from the soldiers commenced which it seemed to me continued nearly all night.

The next day was more gloomy if possible than the day before. The steady rain kept the young ladies with us until late in the evening. And the monotony of things was only broken by an occasional call from some of the passing soldiers, who continued to pass that day and the day following. As many as 800, so Surgeon Lyle and his matron told us, were on the sick list. He and his matron dined with [us] and we did have some little excitement at their expense. We all united in the conclusion that she was something more than a matron (at least to him). The rain seemed to fall on her dress at a very peculiar place and that afforded old Mrs. G fun for a day or two. When the ladies left that evening, their pistol was brought out just as though they were in an enemy country and they were soldiers starting out to hunt them. It seems so strange to me to think of ladies carrying weapons, but up there they tell me the ladies most all arm themselves whenever they leave home. Saturday my ruffles employed my time. I never hemmed as many ruffles in one day before in all my life. Late in the evening Mr. G and Alice Riggins came; she had been on a visit to her sister. Time from then passed very well until yesterday at 1 when George came for me. I was so glad to see him. Surely if they knew how unpleasant it was for me to stay up there they would cease to tease me so about going. My ride home was almost as unpleasant as it was going up. The roads were a great deal worse, and then after a visit of that kind the thought of not meeting with Aunt T when I get here adds no little to a melancholy state of feelings.

New Providence, Tennessee, Tuesday night, December 3, 1861

Before closing yesterday morning, Mary Britton came in. She will spend a day or two with me. Yesterday she commenced a plait, which was finished this evening about sunset. Mr. H was up last night. He brought up right sad news in regard to the cannonading heard today. The gunboats are expected at Clarksville hourly almost. (I wish Mr. H could find his hat.) He stays so late, and nothing but Campbell or matrimony can interest him. A long letter from John today. He says fate has decreed that the 14th Reg. is to remain the winter out in W Va. and near Huntersville,[143] that name so repulsive to every soldier. Really, I regret to hear of their disappointment. Two visitors this morning cold as it was—Mrs. Pollard and Sue McDaniel. Slight fall of snow yesterday and today. Oh! pshaw! These girls (Florence and May) won't let me write.

New Providence, Tennessee, Wednesday night, December 4, 1861

Hard at work most all day on my double wrapper. Mr. H came in something less than a dozen times to trouble me with his old coat, a pocket handkerchief, some bread and meat to catch bait with, and I can't say how many other things. To take us down to see the fort was another thing.[144] Mary progressed slowly with her plait. We walked up town late. Billie Leigh[145] came home with us. Really, I feel sorry for him; he looks wretchedly. Under the late call for the militia he was included, and rather than be drafted, he has volunteered. So forlorn, so forsaken a look I never saw man wear. Mary and I have laughed no little tonight at his quaint expressions. Death seems to be his greatest fear, but the horrors of war generally seems to be fully appreciated by him. Mr. H's conjectures in regard to the gunboats, I'm happy to say, were untrue.

New Providence Tennessee, Thursday night, December 5, 1861

This evening late my wrapper was laid aside, and just as I had given the finishing touch toward improving my brown face and frizzly head, Mrs. Trabue called at the fence. She's just from Ky. and says that one of the bridges between here and Russellville has been burned by the Unionists. Great excitement prevails. Only part of the letter received from Tom this evening was read to her; she'd one of the same date. He closed by telling me to "kiss Ma when I saw her" but the fence prevented. He said tho that after the great Battle at Columbus, Pillow's brigade would be removed to Clarksville for winter quarters, and "then I'll be at home." If he knew all, Columbus would probably have more attraction.

[The following entry was not written in Rep's hand.]

New Providence, Tennessee, Friday, December 6, 1861

Mr. Wilson called today, to request the meeting of the Society, for making overcoats for Bailey's Company.[146] I went down, but finding no one there, called in at Mrs. Howell's a few minutes. Mary plaited while I was gone, and Mrs. Zeke Wilson stopped as she returned from the store. Mr. Homer took us to the fort tonight and from there to the Landing to see a Company of Volunteers leave for Fort Donelson. But getting cold and tired before the boat came, we left. Mary seemed very much disappointed because she did not get to see her darling Walker.

New Providence, Tennessee, Saturday night, December 7, 1861

Well, well, Mary used the first person in the case above but without my permission. True I requested her to write but not in my name; and I told her not to speak of B's Co as a set of volunteers while writing. She knows well enough they are nothing more or less than a Co of drafted men. The draft came in at the front door and they run out at the back door and volunteered. What else can we make of it? They deserve but little credit for volunteering, to say the least of it. If "pretty little Walker" is among the number after all, Capt. Bailey has a right fine looking co. Many of them are men of families of influence and of wealth. Mr. Gold, contrary to the expectation of all, enlisted, and tonight Mrs. G's widowhood commences. She's to be pitied. Mary and I boiled us some candy soon after breakfast this morning, but before we had time to pull it, news came that "the boys" were still at the landing and so everything was forgotten in the hurry of getting off to see them. The "Gen. Anderson" came down soon after we got there. Quite a motley crowd were assembled on the dock to see the last of father, son, brother, sweetheart. Not as many tears were shed as the occasion required according to my opinion. The band accompanied them down. Several very pretty pieces were played in our hearing. Mary's disappointment was great at not seeing "pretty little Walker." Dined about 10 and nothing would do but I must take her out home. I went and returned in the rain; every step of the way the rain just poured.

Mrs. Wilson came in soon after my return—and more excuses for Mr. W's not volunteering than can be written on—this—line. George Barbee[147] took supper with us. Mr. H has been with us for the last two or three hours and through Uncle T's persuasion stayed all night. Dr. Pirtle[148] called today, the first glimpse I've had of him since his return from W Va. He speaks so highly of—I can remember without writing his name just here.[149]

New Providence, Tennessee, Monday night, December 9, 1861

Late walked down to Cousin Jane's. From there Mr. Homer took she and I down to the fort. The work is progressing rapidly and will yet no doubt prove a strong defense for our town and country. He sat with me last night until about 7 when Mrs. Smith sent for me to come up and sit up with the corpse of her little girl Ida. As we were alone, conversation turned on a subject that has been confined strictly between Cousin Jane and myself. His opinion in regard to the course pursued by Uncle T and mine are so different, but he is a man and of course to some extent allowances are to be made. I suppose another ride was taken by him and Miss F yesterday evening. The buggy was out early and his person in primp soon after dinner. Ed Pettus seems to be the confederate and that is evidence enough of his derangement on the subject: he 51, she merely 40, and E about 10.[150] How strange! How strange! Nearly made a gown today. Mr. Spence and Dick Ogburn called [a] few moments this morning. D insisted that I should go down home with him. Miss Dora's marriage to old Archibald Fletcher[151] has had some effect. Mrs. Gold has sent for me to stay with her. I must close.

New Providence, Tennessee, Tuesday night, December 10, 1861

I never set apart a day in which I expect to do a great deal of work but I'm certain to be disappointed. After coming home from Mrs. Gold's this morning, my sewing was brought out and in imagination I had gone through with the day and accomplished wonders. But Cousin Lou came in and for a while my time was taken up with her in trying to get her to laugh, &c. She's so low spirited. I never saw her more so. John Garrard expects to go into camp soon and of course we can account for it.[152] Soon after she left Cousin Maude Davis sent for me to go down to her house. Billie Donaldson came last night from W. Va. and she knew how much delighted I would be at seeing him so she sent for me, and to my surprise the additional pleasure of two letters were added to that of seeing him, one from John and one from Ross. Before I had scarcely time to realize that it was B I was looking at (he has fattened up astonishingly) or ask him a question about the boys, Emma came for me and said that Miss Mary Britton wanted to see me. She and Fannie had called for me to go over to Clarksville with them. We went, F had a picture taken, went to Rice and Moore's,[153] did our shopping, called at Cook's[154] out of curiosity, and went to Coulter's[155] and called for muslins and they wanted to know if it was domestic wanted, and I can't say how many other things. At home about 2. Sent to the office and got a letter from Jo Wray, so I've been fortunate indeed — 3 long, long letters from the Regiment. Uncle T had one of his spells this evening. I scarcely know what to think of him. He says he's crazy and there are times when he acts so much like it as he does when he grieves so about Aunt T, indeed more so. Tonight we supped alone. None were present but Florence, Uncle T, and I. Sylus left about 4 for Western Va. He goes to take George Burgess' place. So, we are without a boarder. (Mr. H was up tonight and says Cousin Jane and I have ruined ourselves with Miss F and I should like to know who's keeping her posted).

New Providence, Tennessee, Monday night, December 16, 1861

Determined to make a visit after my disappointment Friday and knowing that Cousin Bet was anxious to go out to Cousin Mary Mills, in the afternoon of Saturday I went down and proposed taking the trip with her. She readily consented and by sunset or before we were at Cousin Mollie's, one among the most agreeable of my visiting places. She and Mr. Mills both seemed glad that we had come and we in return seemed glad that we had gotten there. Yesterday each of us framed excuses for not going to church and so set ourselves down for the day. About 11 Mr. Homer, for once according to promise, came and soon afterwards Billie Donaldson. We chatted on various subjects, confining ourselves mostly to W. Va. until dinner. As usual Cousin M had spread before us a most bountiful repast, among other good things some of the best canned peaches. Oh! me, so good. About 3 Mr. H proposed a walk over to Uncle Wm. Donaldson's. We all went excepting Cousin Mollie. Found the house full of company—Billie Steven,[156] Jennie,[157] John Collins,[158] and others. We left early, took supper with Cousin M, and "all hands" went over to see Billie Steven, perhaps for the last time. He and Mr. Jo Gold have volunteered[159] and left this morning for Fort Donelson.

The whole neighborhood it seemed to me were present; but none less talkative or so long faced as Cousin Mollie or Mrs. Gold. Uncle Steven prayed a long prayer and their sobs were distinctly heard over the room. How glad I am that the young men of our acquaintances were the first to volunteer, for twelve long months. Cousin M has to endure such dreadful suspense. Stayed all night at Uncle Wm.'s. This morning Cousin Bet had to go over and console Cousin Mollie Frank. Mr. H and I were alone for a while and by request I trimmed his hair while he told me of what had happened at home during my absence. The ride to the fort after I left Saturday evening engaged us mostly. Uncle T hired the "old grey" and took Miss F down and from there out home, but on the way called at his gate and asked "if she would go in." She of course declined for a more suitable time. Now isn't this nice carryings on for such as they are? Dined with at Uncle Wm.'s. Left for home about 2. Went down for F, came back and found Mary Britton here. She, Mrs. Vaughn, Mr. Homer, and Uncle T have had a time tonight.

New Providence, Tennessee, Wednesday night, December 18, 1861

Cut out a dress soon after Mary left this morning. (She spends the days with "Sis Nannie" and the nights with me) and have almost finished it. According to promise Mr. H took us over the camp again this evening and though we were present some earlier than on yesterday we were not in time to see the whole performances. What we did see however was highly pleasurable. The dress parade was gone through with admirably. Uncle T was untiring in his attentions to Miss F. After leaving the camp Mr. H drove us down to the fort. The work is going on rapidly. And a most splendid promenade is already completed. But sad feeling passes over me when I see that beautiful cedar grove giving place to the workman and his ax and think of the cause, the circumstances associated with it, &c. "Oh, war, what horrors follow in thy train?"[160] (I believe I've quoted it correctly.) Since supper Mary, Mr. H, and I have taken a long walk. It extended as far as Cousin Jane's. She and the children were frightened at first thinking perhaps some of the soldiers were paying them a call.

New Providence, Tennessee, Saturday night, December 21, 1861

Yesterday the weather changed considerably and all for the worst. Really, we are cold by the fire. But a jaunt was proposed yesterday evening and weather, with other things, were left out of the question. We went and met with the whole neighborhood nearly, all the young ladies particularly, with one or two Tarts thrown in (brothers-in-law of Mr. Peterson). Ike[161] is looking much better since his return from W Va. At first he scarcely resembled himself, so reduced in flesh. (Our Reg., the 14th, the last papers say have been ordered to Winchester, Va.) How dissatisfied I know some of the boys are at the move. Came home this morning in company with Ike, Jimmie, and Cousin Lou. Jimmie left tonight for Ft. Donelson. We had considerable work to get Mary to kiss him. She and Cousin Lou are both with us tonight. Mr. Homer has paid us a long visit; says that the general belief is that he is very much in love with "Miss Mary."

New Providence, Tennessee, Sunday night, December 22, 1861

Such a rainy day as we have had, had if not been for the nice basket of oranges and apples sent us by Mr. Homer this morning what would we have done? Mary would have read her novel more, and Cousin Lou the bible I suppose, and all of us would have joined in pitying the soldiers more. Incessant as the rain has been, they have been passing to and fro the live long day. Poor fellows, how I pitied them. A great number of them belonging to Quarles' Reg.[162] are very sick and scattered around in private homes. If they remain much longer with us, a hospital will have to be opened. Mr. H and Will Leigh have been with us tonight and such a romp as we did have just before they left.

New Providence, Tennessee, Wednesday night, December 24, 1861

Early this morning Cousin L and I went up town to purchase some little Christmas presents for the servants, a custom that has been kept up by my dear aunt for so many years and one which I by no means wish to discontinue with other things. I bought for Florence a blank book, which I intend her to use as a journal. Came home and made preparation for baking some cake. Thoughts notwithstanding, surrounding circumstances continually carried me back to Christmas eves in years past, when my young heart would leap at the bright anticipation of what I would receive on Christmas morning, and my impatience made the night seem a week in passing. Just one year tonight and perhaps about this hour Aunt Tabbie (that most precious of all names) was preparing for me a present for the following morning. I disremember for now what it was but something I know even if not of much importance was always found "in my basket" on Christmas morning. I well know the "Santa Claus" from whom all my presents came. None were forgotten by her — from the least to the negro man were remembered and each stocking or basket bountifully filled.

But tonight how is it? And in Uncle T's room where he now sleeps I hear the sound of voices. He has a companion while I am more lonely than a few months after Aunt Tabbie's death. I scarcely think he has an unhappy moment nowadays except when Miss F treats him with assumed indifference or tells him that I "don't want her to come here" or something so. The sad truth that another so soon has taken Aunt T's place will be painful of itself enough but added to that will be the indifference that will take the place of affection, kindness, &c once bestowed on me. How will I endure it? My only answer is the fall of the burning tear drop on this page, all around me enjoying the luxury of sound undisturbed sleep. From a hint of Mr. Homer's, we, the trio, have concluded to continue the old custom of bringing up one basket but fear the result will be anything but pleasing. Know his love of mischief and delight in playing off pranks. I suppose Uncle T has presented Miss F with a costly something; I've not heard what as yet.

New Providence, Tennessee, Wednesday night, December 25, 1861

Uncle Trice was the first to awaken us this morning. He with all the servants were before us in catching gifts. Cousin Lou was the first to look into our baskets, but as Mr. Homer prophesied, she found them empty. Such was never the case before. At ½ 9 Mary and I went down to the church to see the children receive their Sunday school premiums.[163] But few spectators were present but most all the children, and in such spirits, they were all highly delighted at the idea of receiving a premium and the most of them were not disappointed. Even to Dr. Mc's class all received premiums. Cousins Marion and Jane and the children came up home with me. Stayed until about 3 and left expecting me to go home with Mary. But Mrs. Britton came in and she left to meet with her at Mrs. Pollard's and I for Cousin Jane's. Once more we had two minutes' conversation alone. What a luxury, but only a moment was given us, for soon Mr. H and Cousin M came by for us to go to the fort.

On our way down, who should [we] come up with but Miss F and Uncle T sitting back with the buggy top and they apparently in the finest spirits immediately. We went over to the other fort from which place the cemetery was in full view. I wonder if Uncle T gave to the dead one sad thought, but from appearances he did not. She seemed so pleased with his company. How am I ever to have confidence in woman again, much less man? During the whole round I caught her eye only once. She must feel badly in my presence if she remembers any of the past. Came by Mrs. P's and brought Mary back with me. Uncle T left soon after tea and Mr. Homer has been our only company. He brought with him the presents expected last night in baskets, excepting the oranges.[164] Candy for Mary and the long wished for toilette set for me; oh, it is so beautiful—white smoked glass with gold mountings. It is so pretty. After all he's a right dear old fellow. The children about town have come in masquerading and we must go and see them.

New Providence, Tennessee, Friday night, December 27, 1861

Cousin Jane intended leaving early after breakfast but Uncle T had a private conversation as usual which lasted until 10 o'clock. She then went down home and I had to wait for the buggy, making it very late before Mr. Homer and I went out to pay our promised visit to Miss Fannie Pettus. Just as I was leaving Dr. McMullin called and presented me a book, Somebody's notes on Mark and Luke; so our premium has come at last. Met with him again at Mrs. P's; he dined with us; left about 2 for home. Soon afterwards Miss F and I took a walk and determined no longer to be tortured with threats and sour looks. I boldly introduced the subject that has recently given rise to so many hard feelings and begged of her if she intended making this her future home to come immediately, as delay I too well know would bring with it no good. She seemed to appreciate my feelings on the subject; and promised to look over in future what might have the appearance of indifference on my part. Yesterday was a day of darkness to me, second only to one I have experienced. When we returned we found Mr. H had come for me, and soon

I was on my way home with a somewhat lighter [heart] than when I left this morning. Went up [a] few moments to see Alice Riggins. She moved into her old home Monday. She and three little ones appeared very happy. Tonight, Uncle has been [in] a rage from where word one of the soldiers sent him. Told him of what had passed between Miss F and I, and he's taking a long nap on the strength of it. Mr. H has just left, and such another lecture he did give me. Really, he must feel some interest in my welfare. Florence and I are alone once more.

Early photograph of Serepta Mildred Jordan Homer. Courtesy of Customs House Museum and Cultural Center Collection, gift of Serepta's great granddaughter Evelyn Hunter.

These miniatures show a young Serepta beside a woman the family believes is her Aunt Tabitha Trice. The January 24, 1862, diary entry contains a reference to Serepta's going to McCormac photography gallery to get a photograph of her aunt. Courtesy of Serepta's great-great granddaughter Millie Armstrong.

Bladen Beverly Homer (ca. 1828–1873) in an undated photograph. Courtesy of Customs House Museum and Cultural Center Collection, gift of Serepta's great-granddaughter Evelyn Hunter.

Serepta's diary indicates she was interested in fashion with frequent mentions of sewing, selecting bonnets, and making jewelry. Her great-great granddaughter Millie Armstrong remembers as a child playing dress-up in Serepta's clothing, including this dress. Courtesy of Customs House Museum and Cultural Center Collection, gift of Serepta's great granddaughter Evelyn Hunter.

This hat is one of several of Serepta's accessories passed down through the family. Courtesy of Customs House Museum and Cultural Center Collection, gift of Serepta's great granddaughter Evelyn Hunter.

Serepta mentioned buying six of these silver-plated spoons for twelve dollars in her January 25, 1864, diary entry. Instead of initials, she had her nickname "Rep" engraved, she told Mr. Homer, so that if his next wife used them, she would know whom they belonged to. Courtesy of Customs House Museum and Cultural Center Collection, gift of Serepta's great granddaughter Evelyn Hunter.

Serepta Homer with her three grown daughters, Tabitha (1864–1926), Janie (1870–1937), and Eva (1867–1934). Courtesy of Customs House Museum and Cultural Center Collection, gift of Serepta's great granddaughter Evelyn Hunter.

After their marriage, Serepta lived with her daughter and son-in-law, Eva and Christopher Smith, in their home in New Providence. Courtesy of Serepta's great-great granddaughter Millie Armstrong.

Serepta spent her final years with her daughter Eva's family at Oak Top, a Greek Revival-style house built in the 1850s in Clarksville, Tennessee. The family bought Oak Top, now listed on the National Register of Historic Places, in 1890.

Serepta Jordan Homer later in life. Courtesy of Customs House Museum and Cultural Center Collection, gift of Serepta's great granddaughter Evelyn Hunter.

The daughters, sons-in-law, and grandson of Serepta and B. B. Homer—Janie and Parker Dibble, Christopher Smith, Tabitha Homer, Homer Smith with his dog Zip, and Eva Homer Smith—in a photograph that was probably taken in the Smith home in Clarksville around 1895, shortly after Serepta's death. Tabitha Homer married Hart Myers in 1901. Courtesy of Serepta's great-great granddaughter Millie Armstrong.

Serepta's Bible, shown here, was an important pillar of her life. Her diary frequently recorded church attendance, sermon synopses and critiques, visits of ministers, Biblical quotes, and Sunday School teaching. Courtesy of Customs House Museum and Cultural Center Collection, gift of Serepta's great granddaughter Evelyn Hunter.

Many of the books Serepta mentioned in her diary, from religious treatises to histories to novels, were gifts from friends and family members with inscriptions dated from 1857 to 1861. They have passed down through the family. Courtesy of Serepta's great-great granddaughter Millie Armstrong.

Serepta Jordan's journal was found in an outbuilding in the New Providence area of Clarksville, Tennessee, in the mid-1980s and donated to the Customs House Museum and Cultural Center. Courtesy of Customs House Museum and Cultural Center Collection, gift of Serepta's great granddaughter Evelyn Hunter.

The 1857–1864 diary of Serepta Jordan Homer is housed in the Customs House Museum and Cultural Center Collection in Clarksville, Tennessee, gift of Serepta's great granddaughter Evelyn Hunter.

Serepta Jordan Homer and Bladen Beverly Homer with daughters- and sons-in-law Eva Homer Smith and Christopher Smith and children, Janie Homer Dibble and Parker Dibble, and Tabitha Homer Myers, are buried in Greenwood Cemetery, Clarksville, Tennessee.

Serepta Mildred Jordan Homer (1839–1894) in the early 1860s, probably just before she married B. B. Homer.

CHAPTER FOUR

January 1862 – August 1862

SEREPTA RECORDED local war preparations and constructing breastworks built with Irish and African American labor. Soon the fall of Fort Henry and Fort Donelson would cause white Montgomery Countians to panic and flee as Confederates retreated and Union occupation began. She clung to the hope that Confederate bravery would prevail in the long run. She wrote despairingly of the Federal troops and their attitude toward the enslaved. Occupation included pickets, passes, oaths of allegiance and prohibition of church services when ministers refused to take the oath. Enslaved people emancipated themselves as Union forces gained control of the area. She recorded prices of goods in Tennessee.

Mr. Homer continued to court Serepta as she also continued corresponding with Tom Trabue. She received letters from other young men that described their experiences as Confederate soldiers. She wrote of the battles the summer of 1862 as she read through the newspapers.

Serepta sewed many items often describing fashion, even wrote of a "yankee bonnet." After her aunt's death, she and Inez cared for the chickens, but several died because of their apparent lack of skill. Her Uncle Trice married a neighbor, Fannie Pettus, in April of 1862 and tensions escalated because the new wife wanted Serepta out of the house.

New Providence, Tennessee, Monday, January 6, 1862

Very cold indeed; have scarcely budged from my room today. Made for myself a black silk apron first thing after breakfast. The green tassels are very becoming. After finishing that had an old dress brought out, and with Emma's assistance have almost made a new one of it today. Old dresses these days answer in the place of new ones. They can be made to look very nice too. Kid shoes with no heels answer a very good purpose in the absence of others — particularly when others cost from 3 to 4 dollars and they only 1.75.

New Providence, Tennessee, Tuesday night, January 7, 1862

Suffering all day with headache; felt too unwell to pay the promised call. Uncle T killed hogs again today. What a luxury! I'm in anticipation. Mr. H brought up some such delightful oranges tonight. What would F and I do were it not for the nice oranges, apples, &c he brings us, and his visits occupy many moments that otherwise would pass slowly and monotonously away. George Trice's wedding night.[1]

New Providence, Tennessee, Thursday night, January 9, 1862

Rainy and damp as it was this morning we all put out for Cousin Jane's about ½ 9. Mr. Homer came up and took Cousin Mary down while Jennie and I went in one buggy. The day passed very pleasantly. Cousin Bet was not quite so gay as usual, but the children made themselves very interesting with their singing, and Mr. H spent the evening with us and would have us go occasionally out to his observatory to see the cars pass the fort &c. &c. This evening late Jennie and I drove round to Mrs. Edwards'; my excuses for not calling before were given in and a promise left to call in the morning to see she and Miss E. Mr. H paid Cousin Mollie a call again tonight, but I'm sure my presence was not altogether objectionable, for he had me to comb his hair for 1 long hour I'm sure. The subject under discussion last night according to his request was not resumed. Really, the joke's on him. Last night were most too cutting, though we knew nothing of them until he himself told us. A letter from Tom this evening, written New Year's day. He seems to have had a jolly Christmas notwithstanding his "disappointment in not seeing ma and "others" about that time." His time he says will have expired the 21st of Apr and then his meeting with friends will be more agreeable on account of its "long continuance."

New Providence, Tennessee, Tuesday night, January 14, 1862

The morning was so intensely cold that Laura and I clung to the bed as long as the looks of the thing would permit. We breakfasted as a matter of course at rather a late hour. She left for home about 10. I went to work and continued in the good cause until 12, about which time Uncle T and Mr. C Peterson came in to dinner. Mr. P had no little to say about his new wife and a word on two in regard to my future prospects. He does love to tease. Sit with old Mr. Atkinson from 1 to 2. Mrs. Trabue[2] is with him. Thinks he improves very little if any. Came home. Went down to see Mrs. Harrelson, her visitors, and boarders (Miss Harrelson, Miss Maynard, and Mrs. Galbreath). I was very agreeably entertained both by them and the children for several hours. Mrs. G had rather a woebegone forsaken languid sort of look but after all is quite pleasant. Went by for Florence. Stayed long enough for Cousin Jane to read two letters received today: one from John and—not exactly a letter either but a card from Tom. He dropped it at the office passing through Clarksville Sunday. The simple words were "on my way to see Ma, will see you on Wednesday" with "T. E. Trabue Memphis" on the opposite side.

John's was of quite a different character; only 6 pages (large ones) were completely filled. He began by telling me of the disappointment of the boys after receiving orders to leave the huts that many had reared with the hope of spending the remainder of their term in them (the camp near Huntersville, W Va.). From there he gave me a minute description of the route leading to Winchester, Va., the country, towns, villages, &c and even the appearance "of the many fair ones that met their eager gaze." Truly the faces of the "fair sex" (as he was pleased to call them,) and the extraordinary beauty of the country must have contrasted greatly with the rough uncultivated appearance of things in W Va. He says that Winchester, the town near to which they are encamped, is under such strict military law "that glittering bayonets in the hands of guards are seen at almost every door & street corner." Even citizens find difficulty in passing. Anderson's Brig.[3] with three others are all encamped within a mile of each other. The place he says is well fortified. How I do hope they will remain there at least until May. If they [leave], however, before that time, we may almost as well despair of their return, for already they are (I think he said) within 20 miles of Harpers Ferry and if once there what hope can we have of their return?

John's letters are such a mixture of the sad and hopeful that I scarcely know how to place them. He gives me not the slightest ground on which to build a castle with wings to bring him home before the time expires and yet he writes cheerfully and hopefully in regard to everything else. Mr. Homer didn't bring us either orange, apple, or an excuse for not doing so tonight and made me comb his head too for about an hour. Well, I should not grumble, I'm sure. He gave me a bill for combing his hair; a 5 ct bill; "shin plasters"[4] I believe he calls them. At all events they are nothing more nor less than 5 and 50 cts done up in paper fashion to use as substitutes for change these hard times. The gold and silver was not to be had and something had to [be] resorted to.

New Providence, Tennessee, Thursday night 1 o'clock, January 16, 1862

Once more we've had a pretty day. Really, I had begun to grow very tired of gloomy weather. Read and sewed today. Sam and Dick Ogburn dined with us, only sit a few moments. And so Miss Emma Staton is Mrs. Jackson no longer.[5] Florence tells me that she was married to Mr. Wray of Springfield this evening at 5 o'clock. The Federals, rumor says, have taken possession of Ft. Henry.[6] If it be true we may expect a call at Clarksville soon. A few moments after tea a card was handed [to] me. "T. E. Trabue. 7 o'clock this evening." The answer was "S. M. Jordan at home." Brevity with us seems is the soul of correspondence as well as wit. He came, I think, a few moments before the time, and since then we've been busy—at what (now 12 o'clock), talking. Yes, talking and talking was all, or rather the motion of our tongues and the noise accompanying it was all, for surely all we've said wouldn't amount to one common sense sentence. To play the agreeable is task enough for me, to "be a flirt" more than I care about undertaking. I wish he knew all, and yet I dread the consequences. His conduct after we parted the night I so positively refused him my picture convinces me more firmly of his reckless disposition. And added to that I've proof in abundance from his own lips. With all he is very candid, and for this I admire him, while the display of certain traits is offensive altogether. His black suit trimmed with red and cap of the same is quite becoming, while the "soldier's overcoat" with great cape give him quite the appearance of a full grown man.

New Providence, Tennessee, Friday night, January 17, 1862

Up this morning as usual. Late hours would might suppose had but little effect but tonight I can say to the contrary. Mr. Trabue according to promise called this evening about 9; he sit [*sic*] until ½ 11, notwithstanding he had an engagement to be in Clarksville at 12. But one topic was introduced that claimed for any length of time our attention and that would have been better left alone. For I'm sure but little satisfaction was given on either side. At least my replies to his many direct questions seemed anything else but satisfactory to him. I know he considers me — not only a Beulah,[7] but a complete bundle of mysteries — and well he may for I'm unknown to myself. A promise was asked and granted just as he left and that was to post him at least three weeks before Mr. H and I were married. So simple a request of course was granted, as I had but little idea of ever being put to the trouble. He is certainly a singular specimen. One moment he argues the innocence of a flirtation and the next pleads his sincerity, his constancy &c. To know that he had been engaged in carrying out the former for the last 18 months would be more agreeable with me, strange as it may seem, than to know that during the same length of time he had been playing the part of the devoted. Flirtations do very well under certain circumstances but never let me even assume the character of one of the actors. Any other character would be preferable (from what I've seen).

New Providence, Tennessee, Saturday night, January 18, 1862

The day has passed swiftly away; notwithstanding the rain has been pouring in torrents most [of] the time. I have been writing most of the time; indeed, the whole of the time would have been so employed but for a visit from Mr. Homer. He dined and spent two or three hours afterwards. We had a long romp which interrupted Cousin Lou considerably. He sees the commencement of a letter to John today which I think puzzled him a little as he was about to conclude that Tom had my undivided affections. Really, he seemed to be thinking today. Report says that Fort Henry has been taken by the Yankees and Fort Donelson is threatened.[8] I hope there is nothing of it.

New Providence, Tennessee, Sunday night, January 19, 1862

If late hours continually injures my hand as it did in the above instance my words in a short while will be illegible. I wrote last night until 11 or 12 o'clock. Taught Cousin Jane's class in connection with my own this morning. Dr. M preached on the subject of death. Read one or two chapters in Genesis. "And he died" was his text. Uncle T rode with Miss Fannie up home again so I dined alone. Read a while and felt so lonely that I drove down to Cousin Jane's where I spent the evening. Mr. H, Dr. Herring, & wife were with us most of the time. Tonight Mr. Homer has been up and for one hour he teased me for permission to read the record of Thursday last. We finally had a scuffle over the book but he was compelled to give it up without gratifying his curiosity. I'm so sleepy.

New Providence, Tennessee, Monday night, January 20, 1862

Finished John's, Jo's, and Ross's letters and wrote to Will Trice this morning. Really, I feel relieved. Writing a letter, much as [I] love receiving them,
is one of my greatest tasks. This evening I went up to see Alice, Mrs. M P
Riggins, and Mollie Smith. Alice was in bed with measles, and one of the
children [had measles also].

New Providence, Tennessee, Tuesday night, January 21, 1862

Commenced and finished Uncle Trice a pair of drawers today. My shoulders are now aching like all the world from constant sitting. Mary Britton
and Fannie gave me a short call this evening—at last Mary has the cloth
for making her cloak. Fannie was all smiles as usual. Late walked up to see
Mrs. Gold. Found her in Jack's room with a long, long face. Her cook is sick.
Mr. G in danger of being in a fight. Her children are fretful and oh so many
things to dishearten her. She is to be pitied. Such constant passing of the
soldiers today. The remainder of Col. Quarles Reg. moving down to the fort.
Mr. H was not up tonight.

New Providence, Tennessee, Wednesday night, January 22, 1862

Florence leaves me every day now and goes down home every day to assist
her ma in making flour bags—bags for garment flour, so that I am alone the
greater part of today. Mr. Noel from Nashville dined with us today and Billie
Donelson[9] also called for a while, but Mr. N's presence suppressed his usual
flow of wit and he left without giving me an opportunity to indulge in that
most healthful of all exercise, laughing. Mr. N is as talkative as ever, can tell
of many wondrous escapes from the Lincolnites while out on speculating
expeditions. About the time of the first blockading arrangement, he came
in one of being captured in Louisville, and but for the watchfulness of the
guards and the blockade, would have made $40,000 on the goods that he had
already bought. Late this evening run up to see Mr. Atkinson; he is still sink-
ing, though his inquisitiveness seems unimpaired. While there he called me
to his bedside and what should his business be but to ask if "Tom and I were
going to marry." Some surprise was manifested on my part; as "I expected
he wanted to ask me something of importance" and "well, it is of importance
and ought to be to you" was his reply.

The innocence of old age truly amounts to the second childhood. Florence
is getting on badly with her love scrapes. She tells me that she and Johny
Baker have had a "blow up" and that today she returned his presents. Books,

and little keepsakes of various kinds were, she says, all sent whirling! Again, we've had the pleasure of reading after tea, the time so frequently misspent or thrown away entirely. Since hearing F's lessons, I've read more than I have for the past week altogether most. Grace Truman[10] is quite interesting. Uncle T was down to see Mr. Homer tonight, says he insisted on his coming up, but he didn't feel well. Was "low down," ate too much supper, several horses were in, and more might come in, the war news was so spirit depressing. Strange that Uncle T would ask him to come up with all those hindrances and knowing as he did [h]is aversion to leaving home after tea. Without jesting the war news is very unfavorable. Mr. J Atkinson (uncle) was telling me this evening that a battle was expected within 12 miles of Hopkinsville and that a large no. of Lincoln troops were within the same distance of a RR bridge somewhere between here and Memphis. I disremember where. Excitement is pretty high everywhere.

New Providence, Tennessee, Thursday night, January 23, 1862

Uncle Trice and Mr. Homer have just come in and still they bring distressing news—a heavy battle is hourly expected at Fort Henry. All of our boys have left Fort Donelson and Zollicoffer[11] is reported to be killed.

New Providence, Tennessee, Friday night, January 24, 1862

Mr. H still persists in carrying out his independence. Although he stayed with Uncle T last night he didn't come in to my room at all, neither had any conversation with me. Wonder if he don't think [he's] somebody. He is a little independent. The beautiful weather of yesterday has been continued today, a lovelier day I never saw. Florence and I were up this morning in time to see the most beautiful sunrise I ever witnessed; true they have been few, but this among the few surpassed by far anything of the kind. Alone all morning. Aunt Milly Ogburn called [a] few moments about noon. This evening Florence, Ed Pettus, and I went over to the gallery—my business was to see about having a photograph of Aunt Tabbie taken. Mr. McCormac says the job will be rather difficult but will finish it off as best he can for 10.00. Florence and I sit for a picture, and she seems to admire it very much. But my case is something similar to Queen Elizabeth, my objection at least. The likeness is too correct (not flattered enough).

Uncle Trice, according to custom, called me into his room tonight for a conversation on his favorite subject. He commenced by saying "Well, Rep, don't you reckon I had best go and bring Fannie along home." Now the idea of his asking me this question when I've been telling him for the last three months to bring her now if he ever intended to. And each time he has told me that he didn't want her to come now. How I'm to understand him I can't tell. No other subject will interest him; no other seems to engage his thoughts. Still three days ago he "didn't [want] her to come now." The fact of the business is as old Mr. Holmes would say, he's crazy just on the subject of matrimony and tonight is a monomaniac fit for the lunatic asylum. Oh, if he had pursued one straight forward course for the last 6 months what would I not give? In many respects he's a fatherly, good man. In some instances—too indulgent, but, oh, how he has erred in consigning to oblivion at such an early day the embodiment of what was so pure, so good, so loving, so self-sacrificing. If her advice would be remembered, her words of counsel be constantly ringing in his ears, perhaps he might be a different man.

New Providence, Tennessee, Saturday night, January 25, 1862

Such delightful weather [we] are having. Not until this evening have I gone out to enjoy it. Brown Cherry, Bettie and Laura Helm came up about 3 for me to take a walk. First we went up to the drug store where I laid in for myself a good supply of letter paper and envelopes. From there we walked down as far as Mr. Helm's (John's) and Cousin Jane's. How great was my surprise to see that beautiful grove just in front of cousin J's leveled to the ground, and hurried preparations going on for rearing in its place a breastwork.[12] A great number of hands were employed from Irish down to negroes. The timber will remain as it is for some time to obstruct if necessary the progress of the Lincoln cavalry. "Oh, war, what horrors follow in thy train."[13] To think just within the last three months of the destruction that has been going on here in our very midst, to say nothing of the bloody battlegrounds and surrounding country in which a few months since peace and quiet smiled. If horrors follow not in the train of the present war, they never followed in those at the head of which were some of the master spirits of the world. How long will sin and wickedness be pushed to such an extent? Now we begin to realize something of the correction due a people too proud and stiff-necked to deserve any longer the rich blessings of an indulgent father.

New Providence, Tennessee, Sunday night, January 26, 1862

At school for once before Dr. Mc and Mr. Hirst, if it was accidentally. He with his wife and Emma Deering got as far on their way over this morning as the bridge where they were not permitted to pass the guard line on account of Mrs. Mc and Emma's not having passes. Notwithstanding the pretty morning, but few were present either at Sunday school or preaching. Owing to Cousin Jane's absence I had an additional member to my class, rather small even with that. Dr. Mc read and explained the 1st chap of Hebrews. Came home. Finding my door locked proceeded to Uncle T's and the first thing that met my gaze was a chair filled with pants, suspenders attached as if just disposed, coat, boots, &c. Soon my eyes were directed to the bed and what was my surprise to find—not Blondel,[14] but something in the shape of Mr. Homer all crouched up with the cover closely packed, hot rocks to his feet, and groaning, grunting, and shivering worse than Lincoln did the night after his miraculous arrival in Washington City. Inquiries were soon made as to his complaints, and in the haste to make a cup of sage tea forgot our quarrels and ill feelings. The tea had great effect. Was up by three, sit until 5, walked down to the stable, and returned with Uncle T. Spent the night [with] him, though he sat with Florence and I until 10. We entertained him with looking over an old scrapbook, commenting on the pieces, referring him to some written by friends and acquaintances. His health I guess will be entirely restored by tomorrow.

New Providence, Tennessee, Monday night, January 27, 1862

My birthday and who would believe it but a few weeks it seems to me has elapsed since the 27th of last Jan. Not a present from any source—Mr. Homer "forgot it" and Cousin Jane "was too blue." Well, well, I don't care about too many things to remind me of the sad truth anyway. Mr. H has been with us all day, still grunting and groaning. His jaw is very much swollen and seems to be very painful. Cousin Jane came up to see him this evening and found him so much complaining that she will remain all night. Old Mr. Howard[15] was buried today, and tomorrow old Mr. Atkinson[16] will be taken to his final resting place. The family sent for Uncle T about 3 last night and about ½ 5 he died.

New Providence, Tennessee, Tuesday night, January 28, 1862

Left Cousin Jane and Mr. Homer last night about ½ 7 to sit up with the corpse of Mr. A. But few were present excepting the family and those few "sit up and slept." It [*descended*] on Quint (Junior) and I to do the waking part. We didn't close our eyes for sleep during the whole night. He is quite agreeable after wearing off the embarrassment occasioned by the introduction of the past few remarks. We parted this morning on friendly terms, to say nothing of a previous exchange of rings &c. He says "Cousin Rep" so nice. Not a few questions were asked me about Tom's recent visit. Slept this morning until ½ 9. At 10 went to the burial, returned, found Mr. Slaughter here. He dined with us; left soon afterwards for home. Took a long nap again after Cousin J and the children left. Mr. H walked down home but soon returned with his jaw paining him very much. Tonight, he insisted that I rub it again as that gives more relief than anything else.

New Providence, Tennessee, Friday night, January 31, 1862

Mr. H is still with us. His jaw and health, however, are greatly improved. Tonight, he has interested us with the recent accounts of the battle of "Fishing Creek" in East Ky., at which Zollicoffer with two of his staff (Baily Peyton, Fogg) and many others were killed.[17]

New Providence, Tennessee, Saturday night, February 1, 1862

The weather is warm enough for April plenty, and by 12 tonight it may be cold enough for Dec. The changes are very sudden & frequent. At home all morning; heard Florence's lessons; made some S Confederacy lace;[18] read a little &c. This evening we drove down to Cousin Jane's. Found that several other beautiful groves in the neighborhood of her cottage had shared the same fate with hers. Really, that part of town doesn't resemble itself. A gloom seems to surround every dwelling while the face of each inmate seems to be in perfect keeping with the scenes without. Cousin J is almost the picture of despair. She seems to think that, if her home is to be robbed of every external charm it possessed, that the Lincolnites had as well take possession at once. The engineer even ordered the small trees in her yard to be cut down today, and already the heavy trees falling round have broken down her fence in several places. As many as 30 or 40 negroes are right in her midst all the while. The building of the fort progresses rapidly. Through the kindness of Mr. H have seen the Courier, Nashville Union, & Chronicle[19] today. The Chronicle says we have but little to comfort us, notwithstanding our many successive victories, "when we remember that upon the banks of Fishing Creek perished one of Tenn.'s noblest sons Felix K Zollicoffer." Yes, we have but little, it may be truly said, for in truth he was one of Tenn.'s idolized sons as well as one of her bravest. With him spared, our first serious reverse could have been more easily recovered from, but that with his death has cast a deep shade of sadness over the heart of every true patriot.

New Providence, Tennessee, Sunday night, February 2, 1862

About 6, received a card from "Q C Atkinson" (Jun). He came at the hour appointed ½ 7 and remained until few moments since (the next time the clock strikes I guess it will be 1). After all he's not the timid, backward young man so often represented by his friends and acquaintances. He's anything but silent in conversation and indeed might be called communicative. His remarks in regard to the four past years of his history were surprising, not to say startling. "The spark not yet vanished" alluded to astonished me still more. In fact, what he said amounted almost to a declaration, and to think of how the four years have passed since our first meeting. One would scarcely believe friendship had been existing during the while.

New Providence, Tennessee, Monday night, February 3, 1862

Mr. Homer left soon after breakfast and started out on his mission of charity. The soldiers' wives and their wants engage most of his time and attention. The task I guess is not as unpleasant as it might be, taking everything into consideration, much as he murmurs and complains. Archy Ferguson paid one of his unexpected calls this morning. He's just from Virginia though he has not been with the Reg. for some time. We supped and Uncle T commenced about Miss F. Not a subject could be introduced, no difference how foreign it might be, but he managed to bring in her name some way. Yes, I believe her name is whispered or spoken with every breath he draws when not forced to think on subjects. The sting of realizing the sad truth of a friend's being forgotten so soon and by those two who should hold her memory as most sacred. Who—who—can feel it so sensibly as the genuine friends of the person while living and the nonforgetting after death?

New Providence, Tennessee, Wednesday about noon, February 7, 1862

Rose in good time. Breakfasted about the same hour, but gaiety and levity were done away with about 11 o'clock when the roar of canon was heard.[20] And sad forebodings with wonders and many conjectures were heard from every lip. The roaring was so loud and so long continued that even the servants were excited, while the children looked anxiously at each older face to know the cause of such alarm. About 12 news came that Ft. Donelson was taken; but that proved to be a mistake as I heard on my way home this evening. After leaving Mrs. B's (about ½ 2 this evening), the first thing that I saw that is on the pike was a train of wagons ¼ of a mile long & the next a small cavalry company—Gen. Clark[21] and his staff I suppose. Mary, under the circumstances, failed to come with me and not a soul for company did I have but Inez. My heart at one time beat pretty fast, but I soon summed up courage and putting the whip to Dick I took a "bee line" for home and not [a word] was passed between I and the soldiers during the time except with Billie Whitefield (an acquaintance). He halted long enough to tell the sad story of our defeat at Fort Henry, of the Yankees taking possession of it yesterday after an hour and 15 minutes engagement, of their burning the RR bridge over Tenn. River, and, in a word, of our total defeat in and around Ft. Henry. For 9 months the Southerners have been fortifying that place and now the Yankees were in possession of it an hour after the first attack. Have we not reason for believing that with Zollicoffer's failure our star has commenced declining? The fact is too sad to dwell on.

An hourly attack is now expected at Ft. Donelson and as much expected is another defeat. We have but little on which to base a single hope. Gen. Pillow sends Gen. Tilghman to stand his ground and in two days he will have 10,000 more troops at his command. But even with so many reinforcements an attack both in rear and front by the gun boats and land force could not be repelled. I see no other chance but for them to take possession of Clarksville, from here to go to Nashville, and from there they can very easily proceed to Memphis and then the S Confederacy is gone—gone! Clark's brigade from Hopkinsville[22] is camped about 4 miles from here tonight and will be in tomorrow to assist if necessary in driving back the gun boats and land force should they make an attack on Clarksville.

All over there as it is here is confusion, excitement, and hurry to get out of the place. Many of the citizens confidently expect the town to be shelled tonight, and many are packed ready to leave with their wives and children at a moment's warning. Cousin Jane was ordered from her home yesterday and is with us tonight. Expects to leave for a home in the country tomorrow. Many of the families of our town will also leave for the country tomorrow. Both our livery stables with the food &c for horses have been prepared and tonight Mr. Homer says his stable is running over. Many of the private houses have been vacated with the belief that the canon would tear them to pieces. Was up at Mrs. Gold's [a] few minutes this evening and she looks as if Ft. D had already been taken. Mr. G left for there this morning.[23]

New Providence, Tennessee, Saturday night, February 8, 1862

The bustle and confusion on the pike today has almost completely drawn our minds from domestic and social affairs. True, Cousin Jane and I have enjoyed one or two quiet chats, but the greater part of the time has been passed on the porch, cold as it was, looking at the continual rush of cavalry men, infantry, and baggage wagons—just one continual rush—going to and fro has been kept up during the whole day. Clark's entire brigade passed with Forrest's Reg. of cavalry. The last had not gotten as far as Clarksville before they were ordered to Fort Donelson, and as they returned, such rushing, such haste was displayed that I feared the Lincolnites were at their heels. But was delighted to find that the excitement and haste manifested was all in consequence of the expected fight at Ft. D—really, I felt encouraged while the Reg. were halted in front of our door today and to some extent elated at the prospect of our success in the next battle. For surely such bravery—such courage—will not submit to the disgrace that attended the defeat of our troops at Ft. Henry. No, it cannot be—Forrest with his brave men will never retreat.

Retreat is a word yet unknown to them; not the first letter of it was written on their countenances; not the first word went to prove that they know anything of it. The infantry have or will go down to Ft. D on boats. To beat them back there is now our only hope. If unsuccessful we are surely gone. Among the many that have passed (3000) during the day we have recognized but few acquaintances. But among the few was Sy Crabtree[24]—he came along late this evening with Capt. Hewie's company and with the Capt.'s permission stayed all night with us. We have enjoyed his company very much since tea, and it is a gratification to me to think that I can assist in making a soldier comfortable. Tonight it is very cold and he speaks so sadly of how his messmates are faring.

New Providence, Tennessee, Sunday night, February 9, 1862

Today has been calm, clear, and beautiful, but little excitement. Only one cavalry company have passed on their way to Fort D. Another bridge has been burned by the Lincolnites, the one near Tuscumbia.[25] All communication is now cut off between our forces in Ky. and in the south. The Yankees have us now almost completely in their power. No further news from Ft. Donelson. Mr. Crabtree left early—no Sunday school or preaching at the Baptist church.

New Providence, Tennessee, Tuesday night, February 11, 1862

Mr. H has spent yesterday and today packing the remnant of Mr. Pettus' stock of goods; how thoughtful in him to think of the two little things that for the present I need above all others. In my opinion worse men have lived and are now in Lincoln camps [than] the noted B. B. Homer. "Q C Atkinson Jr" sent his card down again this evening and we've been talking since ½ 7 until [a] few minutes since almost incessantly. The engagement existing between Tom and I was the subject mostly talked of. I find him right well posted and not at all inclined to believe my version of the story. Though he says it would be an agreeable belief. He gave [me] two such nice pencils tonight, one a card pencil[26] that I appreciate very much. War news more favorable though blended with something sad. Several members of Baily's Reg. down at Fort D have been killed or taken prisoner by the Yankees while our boys have captured two of their Col's and 1 private.

New Providence, Tennessee, Thursday evening, February 13, 1862

Cousin Jane, Mr. H, and I drove down to see the breastworks, forts, &c recently thrown up near her house. That end of Prov. doesn't in the least favor itself. The houses and lots look so bare without a tree anywhere near to relieve the bleak and desolate appearance of things. Some of the houses are occupied by the fort hands, others are without occupants entirely, while some seem to say in their actions that home is the last place they intend to forsake. Sit up with the corpse last night until ½ 1. At home by sunrise, ate breakfast, and sit down to finish a letter to Tom Trabue, but Mr. H called directly for me to go out to the burial. Left about 9. We had gone only a mile or two when a heavy cannonading was commenced, supposed to be at Ft. Donelson[27] which continued until this evening 3 o'clock. Since going home we've heard that General Pillow has dispatched that they are certainly fighting at Ft. D, both on land and water, and that he was determined this time the victory should be ours. The fight commenced either yesterday or last night, but they did not get under headway until about 12 today.

Such booming of canon I never heard; like the roar of distant thunder it lasted for hours and hours, carrying terror to the hearts of many fond mothers, wives, and sisters, who seem to listen with breathless impatience for the 1st item of news, faintly hoping to hear of some favorable turn of the battle and that yet an opportunity may be given them for seeing again loved and idolized faces. But, ah, the disappointment. Many a fond and doting mother has gazed for the last time on the manly form and handsome features of a loving son. Found Cousin Marion here this evening. Cousin Jane & the children went out home with her. Laura, I guess will stay with me tonight. Since commencing this, Uncle T has come in and says that the battle was decided in our favor.[28] The Yankee defeat both on land and water was complete.

Gen. Pillow has ordered all the hospitals cleaned out and all the spring wagons are to be in readiness to convey the wounded up from the river. The news if true is more than glorious. Report also says that we have been equally successful at Manassas and Columbus. If so, how thankful should we all be. I couldn't refrain from weeping tears of gratitude at the news from Donelson, and if the other reports be true, how much more cause have I to feel thankful. Mrs. Gold & Jack[29] called for me to take a walk this evening and they seemed no little surprised that I should weep tears over news so glorious. Mrs. G, although her husband is there, says she can't shed a tear. Another glorious piece of news—Forbes' Reg. has been ordered back, whether to Donelson or Bowling Green I can't say.

New Providence, Tennessee, Saturday night, February 15, 1862

Agreeably to Uncle Trice's orders commenced packing early this morning—bed clothes, wearing clothes, and such things as would be most valuable in case the Lincoln gun boats should pass Fort D and come on up the river, on the way committing every outrage and cruelty imaginable. With Mr. H's assistance several boxes, trunks, &c were soon filled. He's a most splendid hand to pack; seems to understand the business as perfectly as any dry goods merchant. Had it not been for his kindly assistance I surely would have made poor progress. After dinner he and Uncle T went over to Clarksville. Brought with them some good news and some bad. Up to last reports "the day was ours," but the Federals were constantly reinforcing, and the result may yet be against us. The soldiers, however, with Gen. Pillow for their commander were in high spirits and sent word to their friends to only send them a piece of meat and bread, and "all would be right." A good deal has been sent over from this side [of] the river such as boiled hams, baked bread, &c. to be sent down in Dr. Drane's care tonight. The amount sent from here has seemed to disturb very much Uncle T's usually smooth temper. I thought from his directions that the bread was very well proportioned to the meat, but on receiving it he seemed not only surprised but vexed that I had not cooked more bread. Whether or not Miss F didn't talk to please him this evening I can't say. From some cause I do not know however that he's in anything but a good humor. I wish I had known exactly the amount of bread to have cooked.

At Mr. Mills',[30] Monday night, February 17, 1862

And so, my Journal dear for the first time we find ourselves not separated though 7 miles from home. May our first visit prove an agreeable one though we were forced from Aspen Cottage, under circumstances quite the contrary of pleasant.

At Mr. Mills', Tuesday morning, February 18, 1862

Yesterday morning we rose, breakfasted as usual, and had just seated ourselves (Mr. H and I; Uncle T had retired in consequence of headache) with the expectation of spending a quiet and peaceful sabbath. But "who knows what a day may bring forth"? Mr. B K Gold called just as we were talking of getting our bibles and to our great surprise told us that Fort Donelson was surrendered the night before between 12 o'clock and day—the hour was not exactly known. How contrary to the report received the evening before, that we had repulsed them time and again both on land and water. They were fast falling back when reinforcements to the number of 30 or 40,000 came in to their assistance. And, of course, weakened and exhausted as our men were, they were compelled to give way and cease to combat with forces so unequal. Various reports are in circulation as to the number taken as prisoners; from 6 to 10,000 is supposed to be the number while only 2 or 300 are supposed to be killed and as many as 7 or 8000 are reported to have escaped—a bloodier battle has not and I presume will not take place during the continuance of this war or one that will last longer.

The firing from the gun boats was opened on the Fort and since that time up to Sunday morning, the booming of canon and the firing of the musketry has been almost incessant. But while we have much to regret, we have much for which to be thankful. Our boys fought bravely—stood to their guns like soldiers of old. Time after time they repulsed the enemy and, to the very last, many Reg'nts refused to surrender and vowed to fight their way through. Col. Forrest's was among the number.[31] The Mississippians and Tennesseans have won for themselves the most laurels. May the few who have escaped find their way to the main army now stationed near Nashville (Have left Bowling Green, given it over to the Yankees) and there avenge the deaths of those who fell so nobly at Ft. D.—But enough, "the tale is told," the victory not ours; and all that words, tears, and entreaties can do will not restore some of our best friends. After the first few moments of excitement were over yesterday morning, Uncle T concluded that my best place would be to "retreat," fearing the Lincoln cavalry would rush right on to Clarksville. The remainder of my "estate" was soon in boxes and Mr. Homer and I on our way to "Cousin Mollie's," my place of refuge, under all circumstances. Found the road was very muddy but arrived safely without even meeting a Lincolnite in good time.

The bad news had already reached [the] neighborhood and of course our meeting was not attended with many smiles. Uncle Wm Mallory and Esq. Collins[32] had come over to talk over with Mr. Mills the disastrous state of affairs both here and elsewhere but left to all appearances without "feeling much better." Mr. Homer left early this morning; promised to send us the news and come himself every opportunity. Slept an hour or two this morning. This evening went over to Uncle Wm.'s—Cousin Mary, Cousin Bet,

& I. Four of the escaped soldiers from Fort D are staying with him tonight. They are Mississippians and brave as lions if they did run when that was all that could be done. They represent the slaughter as awful. Latest news is that Clarksville and Nashville both have raised white flags. Clarksville is almost depopulated. All the escaped soldiers have been ordered to the main army via Clarksville before the Yankees get in. I ripped the stripes off a young man's coat over at Uncle Wm.'s this evening that he might not be detected on his journey. Once I enjoyed sewing them on, but now I take them off as willingly.

At Mr. Mills, Tuesday night, February 18, 1862

Rose this morning with the prospect of hearing something from home before night. Before retiring last night Mr. Mills gave us some reason to believe that he would go to town today. His business was to see the soldiers at Uncle Wm's that far on their way to Nashville and to get the news from Yankeedom. Not long after he left, Cousin Bet "put out" in the same direction so Cous. Mollie and I have been alone the greater part of the day. Time, however, has passed none the less pleasantly. For in the first place I read an interesting letter from John and one also from Ross. Commenced Mr. H a pair of socks and have almost knit the leg of the first one. Besides, Cous. M and I have enjoyed confidential chats on more than one subject. Mr. Mills came in about sunset, his head full of news, his pockets full of apples — the latter from a good source, the former altogether unreliable.

With other good things was a note from Mr. Homer in which he said Pillow and Floyd were the only Gen's who made their escape from Ft. D. His information came through Mr. Dan Gold,[33] Quartermaster in Baily's Reg. and an actor in the horrible tragedy. The loss he says on both sides is considerable while the no. escaped is not exactly known. Nashville, Clarksville, and N Providence have surrendered and raised the white flag. He adds "I have just raised one on the Ware House." The enemy says they will protect all such property. Providence, he says, is in a state of confusion and bustle — no order, no law, or anything else. The Lincoln Cavalry are still hourly expected. Mr. Mills says that the Government pork, flour, and everything of the kind was forgotten in the panic and left to be packed away by negroes, low Irish, Dutch, &c that have not known what plenty was since the commencement of the war. The whiskey they turned out into the streets, while hoes, spades, shovels, axes, and such implements were packed from the forts by such as had nothing to fear either from Yankees or southerners.

At Mr. Mills', Wednesday night, February 19, 1862

The rain awakened me last night about 2 and I don't think it ceased 10 minutes at a time until 12 today. Such long and heavy showers will certainly, will doubtless, raise the river again and then the gun boats, may make their appearance without fear of meeting the stars and stripes of the S Confederacy. No particular news from town today. As many as 20 of the wounded soldiers were buried at Clarksville yesterday.

Saturday night, February 22, 1862

Thursday [Feb 20th] morning early we all i. e. Cousin Mollie and I "jumped into the wagon" and put out for Uncle Steven's; found the family including Cousin Mollie F quite "blue"; not a word definitely have they heard from Cousin Billie though all join in the opinion that he with the rest of his company are prisoners.[34]

Forest Cottage,[35] Tennessee, Sunday, February 23, 1862

Stayed all night, and next morning Mr. H came up and brought what we were all eager to hear—the latest news. The first thing on docket was the landing of the long talked of gun boats at Trice's and Red River Landing. After giving us a full description both of the boats and the officers who came ashore, he drew from his pocket a document issued the day after their arrival (which was Wednesday) in which Foote,[36] the Flag officer, proclaimed to the citizens that they nor their property would at all be disturbed and that they might rest assured so long as no secessionist feelings were exhibited so long might they claim protection at their hands. Three of the boats came up together. Two of them left Wednesday and the other (Conestoga) is still anchored just opposite Clarksville, her canon all just ready to shell the place at the first sign of rebellion. The old stars and stripes now wave over our forts and from some of the public buildings of the city.

Just before the arrival of the boats the citizens set fire to the RR bridge and so another great amount of money has been spent for nothing—almost millions of government property has been destroyed at the small and insignificant place, Clarksville, within the last few months. (Another piece of news) Our grand Army has passed Nashville, left it exposed to the depredations of the Yankees, and have stationed themselves near Murfreesboro.[37] What a move! And what may we poor Rebels in this part of Lincolndom expect now that we are left entirely to the mercy of the vandals? But enough, We can't mend the matter now; the day of hope it seems to me has entirely flown. Before leaving Uncle S's yesterday Old Mr. and Mrs. Millerson came.

"Running from the Lincolnites" was our first thought and but a few moments were needed to convince us of the fact. Such long faces as they did wear. The thought of leaving home was enough to sadden their hearts, but I rather guess the thought of losing 50 or 100 negroes was the most maddening of all.

Forest Cottage, Sunday night, February 23, 1862

The rain ceased in time for it to clear off last night and so we have it to say another clear sunshiny day has been given us notwithstanding the dull and gloomy prospect in regard to national affairs. Mr. Homer and Cousin Nat[38] took advantage of the pretty morning and rode down home for the news and not until late did they return. Many were the surmises and conjectures as to the cause of their late return; Billie Donelson would have it that they were detained by the Lincolnites to take the oath of allegiance to the Union. Cousin Mollie Frank spent the day with us and waited until very late to hear the news, but after all heard nothing definitely of her husband. Mr. H says two Regiments are stationed at the Fort and one or more are in Clarksville. Our streets are seldom clear of the rowdies, and splendidly dressed officers prancing round on their fine horses are sights not at all uncommon. The wounded from Fort D continue to come in. Uncle T and Miss F were down at the Fort, Mr. H says, looking as pleasing as though Forrest and his brave company had possession of our town in the place of the Lincoln negro worshippers. No particular news from home.

Forest Cottage, Monday night, February 24, 1862

Cousin Nat and Mr. Homer left for town soon after breakfast. Cousin N returned without Mr. H about 4. Brought with him no particular items. Says the Yankees are coming in very rapidly. As many as 6 boats have landed with troops today; they are as "plenty" in Providence as bees round a gum. No communication between the two towns. The water from Cumberland and Red rivers is above the new turnpike higher than it has been for years if ever before. Two of Mr. Mills' boys missing this morning.[39] Some suppose they are in the hands of the Yankees; others that they are water bound. Billie Donaldson sit with us until bed time tonight. Made his W Va. yarns right interesting. Too sleepy to hold my pen.

Forest Cottage, Wednesday evening, February 26, 1862

In the afternoon Mary and Gold Collins[40] came over and remained until near sunset. Nothing but the "Yankees," Old Lincoln, and many of the leading men in his cause was talked. Mary doesn't spare even our own Gen'ls; says that it was through the treachery of Tilghman that Forts Henry and Donelson were surrendered and that he was no doubt paid by the Northerners for so doing. And Sydney Johnston now in command of our troops near Nashville, she is confident, will or has received part of the pay. She ridicules very much the idea of Nashville and Clarksville surrendering so soon and says as for her part she doesn't care for any such "shirt tail protection." Her only hope now is Beauregard[41] and Price.[42] If they fail to deliver us, we are hopelessly ruined as a nation. Cousin Nat came from town about 4; says the Yankees are leaving constantly for Nashville. Buell,[43] I suppose with his command, is now occupying that city. Our Capitol! What a shame that it should be so disgraced. Johnston, report says, has fallen back as far as Huntsville Alabama. That he may draw B farther into the South and by so doing prevent his reinforcing is doubtless his object. We know nothing definitely of his movements or of any of the other Gen's as we are cut off from all communication with the South, and everything in the shape of a paper seems to have taken its everlasting flight. The Yankees won't even let us see their papers. Cousin N says the—(as Mary Collins would say devils) have been visiting all the private houses in Providence and demanding of the ladies something to eat. Many have been badly frightened. Mr. H says he's coming up for me tomorrow and then I'll take a peep at the negro stealing, housebreaking, thieving, &c.

New Providence, Tennessee, Wednesday evening, March 12, 1862

And so, I find myself at Cousin Mary's again after an absence of two weeks at home. Mr. Homer came up for me Thursday 29th according to promise, and early after dinner the same day we "put out" for home. Expecting, of course, to find every street, lane, alley, and good many of the houses filled by the Yankees, my astonishment was no little excited on entering the village to find in their stead perfect peace and quiet. No stir—no bustle, scarcely a citizen could be seen at any of the favorite resorts or on the street. Our ride was extended to the river and there we met with Mr. Pollard who took no little pleasure in describing their appearance and the manner of their exit that morning for Nashville. Some he said were not all depressed at the thought of again engaging in battle, while some were very sad, and others actually shed tears as they passed on to the boat. Many, no doubt, were worn out and so fatigued with what they had gone through with at Ft. Donelson that the thought of so soon going over the same hardships was enough to sadden them.

Only one or two companies were left at the Ft., and not expecting any [of] those who left to return soon, my immediate conclusion was not to return to the country so soon as I had expected. Notwithstanding, my trunks and the greater part of my wardrobe had been left with Cousin Mollie. Peace and quiet were enjoyed from the day I arrived until Saturday, and my chagrin was no less than my surprise to hear Saturday evening late that all three of the Regiments had returned and would probably be stationed at the Fort for some time. (Buell, I suppose, concluded that the future would probably offer a more favorable opportunity for attacking Johnston.) Mr. Homer and I rode out that evening and passed near where they were erecting their tents. Such a motley crew I never saw and their language was as varied as their appearances. If any had the ascendency I think it must have been the Dutch and the very lowest of the Dutch, real sauerkraut Dutch they seem to be.[44] No doubt I saw in them a pretty fair sample of the Lincoln soldiery, generally.

They have rendered themselves very annoying. A chicken dare not make its appearance. Sudden death at all events is the penalty. Our kitchens are preferred by them to the most elegantly furnished parlors. They learn the back ways to our yards and kitchens so readily that we are left to infer that scarcely one of them knew the intention of a front door or door bell. They converse as freely with the servant as though they were old friends. Indeed they seem at home only with the negroes, and the negroes in return seem to be perfectly at home with them. A great many of them have been running off and going to the camp. Some have succeeded in making their escape on boats going downstream. Some of the officers—the real Lincolnites or abolitionists—encourage and aid them in getting away, while others—those who are honest enough to think they are fighting for the Union and Constitution and 'the negro'—seriously object to having one enter within the guard lines and in many instances assist the owner in recovering them.[45] One of the Col's protected a negro the other day whilst he was making [h]is escape on board a boat that was just ready to leave; and one of the Missouri Capts. declared he would stack arms if his men would back him and leave such a negro stealing set as they were. Report says great dissatisfaction is prevailing among most all the border State troops just on this account. They have been made [to] believe until since they have gotten so far into the South that the Union and not "the negro" was what they were fighting for ———
On Tuesday last two of the Regs. left again and so now we have but one to be troubled with, but the Lincoln law is growing so severe that we have worse things to fear than the depredations of the privates. We are nothing more nor less than prisoners of war.

At first private property of every kind was to be protected; quite the contrary has been practiced time and again. Again, citizens were to be allowed former privileges, and in that they have deceived us, for we have not been permitted to leave Clarksville for some time without a passport. And yesterday morning when Mr. Homer and I were coming out, he went down for a pass and not until he had taken the oath to support the Lincoln government would they consent to give him a pass. He excused himself and so we came out the back way. No doubt before we return all the back paths will be guarded. Wagons are pressed, forage taken, vegetables and anything that the rogues may need, and when called on for the money, the reply is, when you take the oath you can have it. And such has been their course. Gradually the reins have been tightening here since their arrival. Mr. Homer left about 9 this morning for Roaring Spring.[46] Will be back tomorrow and next day we'll go home. Rode with him over to Uncle Wm.'s. Met with Cousins Jane and Bet. They spent the day with Uncle Steven's family. Cousin Jane will probably make her home in this neighborhood. As the Yankees are so bent on making Providence their home, she would not be safe or protected there.

New Providence Tennessee, Wednesday evening, March 14, 1862

The roads were very muddy, the creeks rather high, and altogether the ride might have been anything but pleasant, but Mr. H introduced a subject soon after we had started which gave place to bad roads, swollen creeks, or anything else until we were reminded of our near approach to home by the picket guard stationed in the suburbs of our town. Perhaps a history of such conversation could appear to better advantage recorded on "memory's page" than just here. At all events the envious will not be so apt to criticize or intrude comments. Found all well. No particular news. Dr. Pirtle from the 14th Reg. passed through a few days since but was too badly frightened to leave much news in regard to our friends.[47]

New Providence, Tennessee, Saturday night, March 15, 1862

Such long and continued rains I never knew before; five days out of seven almost the rain falls and oftener than otherwise it descends in torrents. Yesterday evening and today no outdoor business could be carried on just on account of frequent and heavy showers. But for Mr. H's presence the day would have passed rather slowly. But with his company and my needle I have succeeded in driving out into Lincolndom the "blues" with their heart sickening attendants. What is there to prevent us dying from ennui and despondency? Here we are penned up within a space not extending far enough to give us room for healthful exercise, with Yankee and Dutch guards at every post ready to say "halt and where's your pass" before you have fully realized that you are a citizen of Yankeedom. If you apply for a pass, the oath of allegiance is placed before you and not until your miniature personal appearance &c is sit down on the blank leaves set apart for the purpose and you have sworn to support Lincoln and his monarchy, can you get one. Wagons even must be stopped for hauling wood not more than ¼ mile from town. If a couple of ladies wish to make a call just without the guard line, they must be halted and rudely questioned by a set of ignoramuses using a greater variety of languages than was known at the building of the Tower of Babel. If a wife in the absence of her husband attempts to defend his property, she is called by names and language used too indecent to soil the page on which I'm now writing. These and many more instances might be given as specimens of the lenient treatment and kindly protection of the abolition demons so loudly proclaimed by Com. Foote on his arrival in Clarksville. But even with this we could content ourselves better were it not that the future promises a great deal worse.

Tenn. is now considered a conquered province by the U States. Andrew Johnson, in whom we scarcely find an equal in the dark hearted and treacherous Arnold, has been appointed Provisional Governor of the State.[48] He with the grand army of Buell at Nashville to back him will not only seek to carry out the designs and purposes of a negro stealing, liberty displacing party but will no doubt at the same time attempt a cruel resentment for what he considers personal injuries both of a private and public nature. With this state of affairs existing what have we to hope for? What have we to expect? Truly we are beginning to realize something of the "horrors of war." And in the train small pox is included. The Yankees have several cases in Clarksville and, report says, it is prevailing among the citizens. Surely the worst is near at hand. The above is partly "hear say"; we Rebels are not permitted to see papers.

New Providence, Tennessee, Sunday night, March 16, 1862

No Sunday school, no preaching, no anything but Yankees and hard times; alone most all day. Mr. H spent the greater part of the morning with me and brought up the Jeffersonian but in it was nothing but the laws, rules, &c by which we Rebels are to be governed. The penalties are also laid down and in neither case are the women forgotten. That no distinction will be made in regard to sex is positively stated, and nothing more remains to convince me that the rascally cowards are actually afraid of the Southern women. The evidence is clear and not to be doubted. "Mas Abe" in his last message lets himself out in regard to the negro question and recommends the "gradual emancipation" [49] of the Slaves. Thinks too sudden a dismissing of them would probably injure too seriously the interest of the country. The Union loving, Constitution abiding men of the border State now see, I hope, for what it is war has been waged and will even at this late day turn from the error of their ways—surely they have been blinded long enough.

New Providence, Tennessee, Monday night, March 17, 1862

We rode down near the Fort this evening. The Yankees were strutting round looking as pompous as if they had assisted in erecting the breastworks on which was floating in rather a downward direction the old stars and stripes. While there three transport boats went up with troops but little cheering was carried on. I imagined the cause, for doubtless they felt as though they were on their way to their own funerals. At least I expect they thought "the day of their destiny" was near at hand.

New Providence, Tennessee, Tuesday night, March 18, 1862

The Yankees went out today and took the last piece of Mr. Lackey's[50] meat. Isn't it too bad?

New Providence, Tennessee, Thursday, March 20, 1862

Today Mrs. Pollard and I went out and spent the day with Mrs. Britton. The picket guards turned us back because of not having a pass—but we were not to be disappointed, so we turned our horse's head but not homeward. Mary, Fannie, Mrs. B, and Cousin Lou turned their tongues loose and of course the Yankees have suffered. Mr. Yarington gets his share with the rest. Since getting home I've learned that the last orders require the guards to shoot a person down that attempts to evade them; so the oath we are compelled to take, else remain at home forever.

New Providence, Tennessee, Friday night, March 21, 1862

Col. Morgan[51] of the S Confederacy with his daring exploits seems to be the topic of the day. He succeed a few days since in capturing a train of cars on the Nashville and Louisville RR on which were several Federal officers with more than a million of dollars for the soldiers in and around Nashville. The money he took possession, also of the officers. Released the common passengers, set fire to the train, and turn[ed] the Locomotive loose to shift for itself.[52] A Federal officer was over this evening and acknowledges him to be one of the most daring men in service, Forrest not excepted.

New Providence, Tennessee, Saturday night, March 22, 1862

Mrs. Davis paid me a short call today. She seems to take the times very quietly. "Rumor says that the Federal troops now in Clarksville will leave soon. The sick have already left." Will Trice proposes that "the citizens make up a pony purse and give them a belly full of nigger before they leave." The negro seems to be their soul, mind, body, and heart's great desire.

New Providence Tennessee, Monday, March 24, 1862

Mr. Homer came about 11, and Mary Smith and Blanche Howard[53] called after dinner a while. Dr. Herring, a while after they left, called and vaccinated the negro children and myself. Mr. Homer brought me up a can of such nice oysters this evening, the first I've seen this season. They were splendid. Report says (our only informant) that the Southerners are slaying the Yankees down at Island no. Ten;[54] "The Memphis S. Guards" have destroyed seven of the gunboats and the fight is still going on, a week today since the first attack. The Yankees all still are committing their depredations with us. They went out today as far as Uncle Wm Donaldson's after government meat sent out there by Mr. Davis.

New Providence, Tennessee, Tuesday night, March 25, 1862

Uncle T and Mr. Homer went over to Clarksville this morning. They had the pleasure of seeing the last of the "Yanks" take their leave but here had the nonpleasure of hearing of the arrival of some more this evening. As one hungry half-starved set leaves, another takes their place. Col. Bane's Reg.[55] sent the negroes off their boat with an oath and a hearty shove, but Col. Wright[56] protected and succored all who went to him for assistance. Several from this place and surrounding neighborhoods went off with them. He also took several hundred barrels of Mr. Pettus' flour but gave him a receipt both for the flour and Frank and his negro.[57] Because some of the citizens interfered, the old wretch threatened to burn our town.

New Providence, Tennessee, Thursday night, March 27, 1862

My book was placed on the table last night as usual, and Mr. H taking advantage of my absence looked over several pages, a privilege denied my bosom friends. Why did he do so, knowing so well my objection is something unmeasurable? I pouted a good while with him this morning for it and not [until] he explained matters and cut out a pair of pants for me did I give him many smiles. Pleasant weather continues. This evening went over to see Alley D and Mrs. Howell. Spent several hours, returned, sit two hours, washed some butter,[58] and paid Jack Gold a call. There I came up with the banner in which is given in full, Johnson's speech (Andrew Johnson, Military Gov. of our State).[59] He is a disgrace to the halls of our capital and I hope will soon be compelled to give way to a more worthy officer. Of Gov. Harris he speaks in the most contemptible terms; at the same time no doubt feels as sensibly as any of us that he is greatly his superior in every respect. Old Mr. Ike Garrett[60] is with us tonight; no doubt left home that his life may be preserved. The Secessionists of his neighborhood are suffering greatly from the continued threats of the so-called Union men.

New Providence, Tennessee, Friday night, March 28, 1862

Jack G was down late this evening and through her kindness I've been permitted to see another paper—Mr. H and I've been reading it since tea and greater pack of stories never were printed. Victory according to Yankee accounts has attended every effort of theirs—but one and that they tried to put a good face on but failed most admirably. No. 10 Island is still occupied by the Confederates after more than a week's hard trying to possess it. Gun boats they find will have gained for themselves when the war is over no distinction above that of a common transport. At least they have done nothing at the Island but make their appearance and exit. To concentrate their forces and make a heavy land attack is now their only hope—and that is expected will soon be done. Another report says Jackson has been in an engagement with Gen's Banks and Shields[61] and that we were totally defeated. No statement to the effect that the 14th Tenn. Reg. was engaged is given though it is one of the Reg.'s composing Jackson's Brigade.

New Providence, Tennessee, Wednesday night, April 2, 1862

After not a very pleasant night's rest we all were able to eat our allowance this morning. Mary suffered all night with neuralgia—both she and Cousin Lou left after breakfast a while—busy making negro pants all day—Mr. H spared me a considerable job by altering Uncle Trice's pants this evening—He will doubtless have a use for them soon as he went out to old Mrs. Pettus' this evening and says that Miss Fannie Pettus has set apart Sunday evening as a suitable time for celebrating their nuptials—Uncle T imagines that I've been rather depressed since hearing the news. Has he not a sufficient cause for so deciding?

New Providence, Tennessee, Thursday night, April 3, 1862

Can't get a paper—and of course have no reliable news.[62] One thing I know because I've ocular proof—Uncle T is having a thorough cleansing carried on. The yard must be swept, the garden must be in perfect order, and a thousand directions given in matters that once I thought he knew nothing about.

New Providence, Tennessee, Friday night, April 4, 1862

[The following entry was written by an unidentified person.]

At the request of Miss Serepta, I have assumed the task to contribute to the pages of her journal. The day has been rather gloomy; the weather cloudy and cool. Uncle Trice has by request of Mrs. Pettus postponed his nuptials until Tuesday next and I am truly glad to find Miss S more cheerful tonight than a few nights ago. We heard yesterday that a considerable battle had taken place at Corinth, Miss., but as yet have not heard the particulars or its confirmation. It was reported that we whipped them badly, killing and taking prisoners to the amount of ten or twelve thousand.[63]

New Providence, Tennessee, Sunday night, April 6, 1862

The corpse of one of our Ft. Donelson prisoners passed through today and shameful as well as sad to say he only had a shirt and pair of socks on, the plight in which he was buried by the Yankees.

New Providence, Tennessee, Monday, April 7, 1862

Mrs. Wilson came in today—has been absent since the surrender of Ft. Donelson and even now seems afraid the Yankees will come in again and take alive herself, Eunice, and "Darling." Mr. Brown and Mr. Shackleford[64] have just come in from Fredericksburg, Virginia, at which place the 14th Reg. is encamped and say that "our boys" are well, have not been in battle as reported, and have not reenlisted. The Corinth battle they also report as false.

New Providence, Tennessee, Tuesday night, April 8, 1862

After breakfast this morning I made preparations for baking a cake. Winnie cooked them for me and they turned out very nicely indeed. The remainder

of the day has been occupied with nothing particularly. The servants gave
the finishing touch to each of the rooms. The bridal bed was being prepared
when Mrs. Staton called, little thinking "the wedding"[65] was so near at hand.
About 4 Mr. Holland came and at 5 he, Mr. Homer, Uncle Trice, and I were
out at old Mrs. Pettus. The ceremony took place soon after our arrival. But
few were present. Cake and wine were handed, after which the buggies were
ordered, and by sunset we, with the future mistress of the house and Cousin
Marion added to our company, were at home. Mr. H sit with us until bed
time, and looked not a little awkward when he had to leave, so long had been
staying with Uncle T. The day has been cloudy and gloomy—rather in
keeping with my spirits. Cousin M insists that I come to bed.

New Providence, Tennessee, Wednesday night, April 9, 1862

The rain poured in torrents for a while after breakfast, and after that ceased,
the snow commenced falling and continued until 2 this evening. From some
mysterious cause Cousin Marion would venture through it all and about 10
with Uncle T and Mr. H's buggy she left for Mr. Cobb's where she expects
to spend a day or two as Mrs. Wilder is hourly expected to die. Mr. Homer
sit with Miss F and I until 2 this evening—after which we were alone until
Uncle T came. I asked Miss F last night rather jestingly to take the head of
the table but she refused. Again tonight I made the same request, and finding her still seemingly unwilling, I pulled her around and so for the first
time since shortly after the death of my dear aunt, I have taken my old seat.
Tomorrow I intend giving up the keys, though I believe her choice would be
for me to keep them. At least if Uncle T be correct I have good reasons for
so thinking.

New Providence, Tennessee, Friday night, April 11, 1862

Yesterday morning a while after breakfast I removed the few remaining
articles of clothing &c from Aunt Tabbie's wardrobe and gave Miss F the
key. At the same time, giving her the others—those belonging to the press
closet &c. A while afterward Winnie came to get our dinner. I took her to
the smoke house, gave her as I thought all necessary explanations, and left
her with the keys and access to every place on the premises excepting my
wardrobe, a large chest bought by Aunt T and containing her clothes, and
the bureau. With difficulty the tears were kept back as I handed her Aunt
T's wardrobe key. My voice I know trembled as the lock to which each of
the keys belonged was pointed out. But to all of them she was more welcome
than to Aunt T's wardrobe key. That for so long was held by her own hand.

None scarcely dared to touch it except with her permission, and to think a stranger is now its possessor and that Aunt T's clothing must be removed to give place for hers. The thought without the reality is enough to bring tears. Mr. Mills came yesterday before dinner with two loads of Cousin Jane's furniture &c. After dinner Mr. Homer and I went up with him and this morning with Cousin Jane and the children and the remaining load of her goods we came home. So tonight she finds herself again in her own little home, with no Yankees near to threaten or disturb. Late war news very favorable on the Southern side.

New Providence, Tennessee, Saturday sunset, April 12, 1862

We have had one continuous gloomy spell the greater part of this week; indeed, heavy rains have fallen most every day. Have kept my own room most of the day. Through Uncle T Miss F inquired this morning if I wouldn't prefer exchanging wardrobes, she supposing I would rather keep Aunt T's. I readily consented and soon her clothing was removed from Aunt T's and it placed in my room while mine was carried into her room. In cleaning out the drawers, some valuable papers were found concealed between the drawer and extreme lower part of the wardrobe; a place only thought of as a fit receptacle for such papers by Aunt Tabbie. The discovery was purely accidental and well may Uncle Trice's "second wife" thank her stars that I, and not she, made the discovery; for among others were papers which Aunt T said years ago should be reserved for the eyes of Uncle T's "second wife." Mr. H has not been up today. Mr. Pettus sent Miss F's paper up this morning and this evening Ed brought up a Memphis paper, the first southern paper we've seen since the surrender of Ft. Donelson. In it was given a most glorious account of the brilliant achievements of our forces at Pittsburg, Tenn.

Without a doubt the southerners have once more been successful, though sad to say it was at the sacrifice of so many valuable lives, among whom was the lamented A. S. Johnston, Commanding General.[66] The battle destined to occupy so important a place on the page of history was fought near Pittsburg Landing[67] on Tenn. River; the attack was made by the Southerners. A S Johnston commanded the right wing of our army; Beauregard the left. The fight continued all day on Sunday last (the 6th of Apr) and five hours on Monday. Three days were requested by the Yankees to bury the dead. Their loss is immense, while ours, though less, is very heavy. Johnston was shot during the heat of the battle in the leg, but fearing the knowledge of the fact would have a bad effect on his men, he kept his horse. And only after finding that death was near from the continual flow [of] blood which had been kept up since the ball struck him did he ride to the rear of his command, and there died a few moments after alighting from his horse. Bravery no doubt had as much to do with his death as the ball, for all agree that his life would have been preserved if timely attention had been given his wound.

New Providence, Tennessee, Thursday night, April 17, 1862

Mr. Blakemore[68] is up from Memphis & says they are fighting at Ft. Pillow[69] and have been for several days. I shouldn't be surprised to know at this moment the Yankees have possession of Memphis. The cotton, sugar, molasses, &c have been hauled out some distance from the city and will be burnt so soon as the citizens find that their entrance cannot be avoided. What a dreadful state of affairs, 50,000 h'heads[70] of sugar to be burnt in one pile.

New Providence, Tennessee, Saturday, April 19, 1862

About 3 Cousin Lou came up again and Mary Britton. Nothing would do Cousin L, but she and I must go out home with Mary; we went through rain and mud and tobacco wagons. This morning bright & early through the same obstacles we returned. Tobacco is coming in so fast that we can scarcely ride with any satisfaction on the pike or any of the public roads. The Northerners are taking advantage of the raised blockade. Raining all day. Such gloomy weather we do have. But for Cousin L's fun the day would have been very long. Mr. H has just stepped in but brought with him no "war news" as Yankee Yarington says.

New Providence, Tennessee, Monday, April 21, 1862

Rainy weather continues. April showers seem to have lengthened into what we may call long rainy spells; the farmers are growing very tired of such weather indeed. Esq. Oldham dined with us today and says it has been raining at his house for two weeks. Cousin Lou left through mud and rain soon after breakfast. Called at the gate long enough this evening to tell me that Ike Howard[71] has returned from St Louis and that Jamie[72] was there under the protection of a rich widow faring like a Prince. She seemed overjoyed at the news, and I think her horror for Lincoln prisons is to some extent done away with. Ike says at least two thirds of the citizens of St Louis are Secessionists.[73] Drove down to Cousin Jane's between two showers this evening and had quite a quiet time with she and the children. The report in regard to my behavior the evening of the marriage is quite ridiculous, just such as generally has its origin with negroes and crack brained old women.

New Providence, Tennessee, Tuesday night, April 22, 1862

At last the clouds have disappeared and we've enjoyed another sunshiny day. Cousin Jane came up about 10 ½ this morning and sit until 11 when I walked with her down as far as Hoover's old stand and for the first time in many months laid my eyes on shelves filled with goods. Mr. Pettus bought out a "Yankee" the other day and with the remnant of his old stock he opened a pretty fair stock considering the circumstances. The calico at 35 cts is quite pretty, the domestic at 50 tolerably good, while the ladies shoes are nothing extraordinary and the cheapest of them sell for 3.00. Glorious news again if it be true: Beauregard has whipped out Buell with his forces.[74] The "Yanks" have re-crossed Tenn. River, fallen back near Nashville, and have commenced fortifying. Several boatloads have passed up today, so Mr. Homer says ("and I reckon he told the truth"). The "Yanks" are reported to have run like deer and Ike Howard says when the wounded were carried into St Louis they were found shot in the back and heels. Just like a Yankee—men will prove themselves cowards in defending such a cause.

New Providence, Tennessee, Wednesday night, April 23, 1862

Well, well, if I'd known Mr. Homer had intended going off in such a doleful strain last night I should have taxed his patience a little more severely before putting up my book. I'm sure the time with me passed far more agreeably while engaging his presence as candle-holder. The subject doleful in its nature as was his countenance in its appearance was continued from the time he first introduced conversation until he left; his exit was quite unusual though he did promise to go with me over to Clarksville this morning. We went; and not a thing that I went for could I find in the whole place: a narrow piece of valencia edging, a doz. pearl buttons, a corset. Nothing scarcely wearable is to [be] found in any of the stores. The streets seem almost deserted, the business houses most all closed, and in what few are open the shelves are almost entirely empty. But for the Yankee soldiers round and near the ct. house, one might consider the place almost depopulated. Not even a set of silver spoons could I buy for Miss Fannie. Was at home by ½ 9. Sewed rest of the day. Very late run over to see Mrs. Wilson. Mr. Homer was up tonight but I managed to keep him on subjects a little more agreeable with myself.

New Providence, Tennessee, Friday night, April 25, 1862

Yesterday morning the rain set in again and not until this evening have we had much prospect of fair weather. Certainly the planters will be very much behind-hand with their crops. Such singular seasons we are having. The second winter has now passed without a freeze sufficient for putting up ice. Yesterday and last night Mr. H sent & brought up some late papers. All Lincoln of course, but even in them we now and then find an acknowledgment of their late defeat at "Shiloh Church."[75] They admit themselves that 4,000 prisoners were captured by the Confederates, Gen. Prentiss[76] among the no., and they in return only captured 7 or 800 of ours. While such facts are freely acknowledged by their leaders we may well claim and boast of the victory, though dearly bought, at Pittsburg Landing.

New Providence, Tennessee, Sunday night, April 27, 1862

Another pretty day. Went to Sunday school this morning for the first time since the fall of Ft. Donelson. Was pleased to find such a general turnout of the children. My class has been divided and subdivided until no one was left for me. Sit with the bible class. The history of Joseph was the subject introduced, and Dr. Mc made it very interesting.

New Providence, Tennessee, Tuesday night, April 29, 1862

For once Mr. Homer didn't disappoint us; he, Cousin Lou, and I went out to Barker's Mill[77] fishing this morning and spent the live long day and only caught two trout and a few perch. Cousin Lou seems to regret that I caught all the trout though she brags smartly on her perch. Mr. H didn't get a bite, "remarkably strange" Cousin Lou thinks. The day has been very favorable for fishing. The banks have been strewn with fishermen — women — children, black and white, old and young, babies and sires. Oh, me, I'm too tired and sleepy to sit up.

New Providence, Tennessee, Wednesday night April 30, 1862

Unexpectedly we took another fish today. Cousin Lou not satisfied with her recent luck has determined to continue her trips to the creek until she catches a trout I tell her. "Oh yes" she says "because you have caught one or two trout you think nobody else can." Today Ed went with us to Davie's pond. With Mr. Hanbough's assistance and altogether we caught 20. All of us feel greatly encouraged, and Cousin L caught the only trout; how proud she is of it. Mr. Homer came up tonight just to rejoice that I didn't catch one. The last report of much interest is that New Orleans has certainly surrendered.[78] If so the Confederacy, to use a soldier's phrase, "has gone up" and the Yankees are swimming in molasses and growing fat on sugar.

New Providence, Tennessee, Thursday night, May 1, 1862

I'm so sleepy, so worn out. I do wish people could learn the meaning of a gape, a yawn, or an invitation to leave. Quint came over tonight and from dark until now have I been in the parlor not trying to entertain him but trying to be entertained. He talks enough, but what does it amount to? Went down home with Florence this morning. Stayed until nearly 4 this evening. Met with Mr. Staton. He is just from Corinth and by some accident met with a letter from "R R Donelson, Co L, 14th Reg. Tenn. Vol" on the way addressed to myself. The superscription was John's and at first I was certain of its being from him. Mr. H was up tonight and says a Dutchman has brought him some more new goods.

New Providence, Tennessee, Monday, May 5, 1862

The rain ceased about 10 this morning, and, although at that time the streets were too muddy for boots or overshoes, by 12 they were in fine order for walking and at 3 I was ready to test them more fully. Went up and spent the evening with the two Mrs. Rigginses. The war at last with its horrors and calamities has given place at least in conversation to hens and chickens, gardens, and new calicoes. This evening the war subject during the whole time didn't engage us more than an hour. Each had to tell of their success at chicken raising, of the backwardness of their gardens, and now and then the baby — what it did. Well, these are old topics it is true but what would not be preferable to a repetition of the thousand and one lies now filling the columns of the Yankee newspapers? And it seems decreed that Southern rumors, much less papers, are nevermore to furnish food for the conversation of us poor semi Lincolnites. Here we are just exactly situated on the line that separates Lincolndom from Dixie. We neither share to greatest extent the disgrace of the one nor enjoy the privileges of the other but after all we are tolerably quiet and I should not like to spare the paper just here in recording to the contrary if it were so. For more paper already has been wasted in recording their lies than the whole of them would be worth (were they sold to a cotton planter). After coming home this evening, went up to the garden and assisted in setting out some plants. Ate supper and commenced reading but Mr. H soon came in, and of course my book was laid aside though the subjects at first introduced were as commonplace as those before referred to. We managed to keep each other's eyes open, and finally the subject in which both were mutually interested was brought up. And though discussed for 2 hours or very near, we separated leaving the matter in no better condition than when first it was introduced and that it seems to me has been a year or very near it. Mr. H's manner of persuading, the inducements he offers with his earnestness on the occasion, and his attempts to force another to think his way are really amusing.

New Providence, Tennessee, Tuesday night, May 6, 1862

Mr. H took me over to the cemetery, and there I enjoyed that quiet beauty, that calm peaceful stillness nowhere else to be found, that loveliness so pure in its nature, so unlike the world as it presents itself daily and hourly to our view. If the grave be dreaded by anyone, let them visit a cemetery at the seasons of the year and just before the setting of the sun. Certainly a scene so inviting, so sadly beautiful in its appearance, would be well calculated to drive away every, every horrifying association. No lovelier place have I ever visited. The stillness of the place seems in striking contrast with the stir and confusion of the outer world. Visited Aunt Tabbie's grave, but sad to say neglect seems written on the space surrounding it. Unprotected save by the high wall encircling the whole grounds, it is there with only head and foot board to mark her resting place. How soon are some of Earth's richest gems forgotten and by those too who should hold their memory as most sacred. But for this my visit this evening would have proven melancholy pleasure. The soldiers' graves we found more numerous than we had anticipated. Among them almost every Southern state was represented. How sad to think of a soldier's dying from home and filling a stranger's grave with no pitying eye of kindred dear or loved friend to shed over him the tear of sorrow or regret. Can we love them too much or spend too much time in contributing to their wants in making them comfortable? Certainly they [are] brave enough and endure enough for us to feel that we can never repay them.

New Providence, Tennessee, Thursday night, May 8, 1862

Mr. H was up tonight and speaks vaguely of a Confederate victory at Corinth. Morgan has had a cavalry fight with the "Yanks" at Lebanon, Tenn.[79]

New Providence, Tennessee, Monday night, May 12, 1862

Tonight Mr. H came up and brought some corsets for me to try. Only two of three fit and they are not as I would like them by any means. Mr. H is so thoughtful. Those corsets I had forgotten and they might have been sold and gone forever before I would have thought of them.

New Providence, Tennessee, Wednesday night, May 14, 1862

Cousin Mollie selected the tomb stones for little Willie's grave. Heard both good and bad news. Morgan, it is said, has captured some train of cars on which was two or three hundred thousand dollars of the Federal money and besides burnt the bridge across Green River so recently finished.[80] Tobacco and wheat agents have been ordered to stop buying for fear of having it remain on hand. While the Lincolnites generally seem "low down," but unfortunately for us the Yorktown or Williamsburg fight resulted very disastrously on our side, if reports be true.[81] While the "Merrimack," it is stated, has been blown completely up.[82] McClellan is said to be within 20 miles of Richmond.[83] They boast that Norfolk, Portsmouth, and the navy yard "are ours." They but little dream of what is going on in the west. Another battle is reported to have come off near Corinth in which Beauregard has sustained his character as the victorious Gen. of the South; 21,000 prisoners were captured by him while the dead and wounded on the Yankee side is immense.[84]

New Providence, Tennessee, Thursday night, May 15, 1862

The weather continues very warm, oppressively warm, and dust I never [saw] the like before. Cousin Jane, Bet, and I walked down to the Fort this evening and were completely covered with it—never in August have I seen the pike dustier. Rain is very much needed. Mrs. Barbee died this evening—the third wife of Isiah Barbee—and I'll venture to say he will be married again in less than 4 months. He's been preparing for the 4th one ever since Mrs. B has been so low—sodding his yard, setting out shrubbery, &c and she lying there slowly dying. I wouldn't have to be forced into his presence and continue in it from this until he marries—not for his residence. The Corinth rumor as usual turned out to be a Yankee lie.

New Providence, Tennessee, Sunday night, May 18, 1862

Bright and early yesterday morning Cousin Lou and I put out for Mr. Peterson's.[85] She spent an hour or two in packing up her "duds" as she calls them and was off again for Clarksville; there she met with several cheap bargains in the way of green, purple, and blue organdies. Florence's present was prettier than becoming—we were at home by 2. She then left for Mr. Whitefield's and I've not seen her since. Late yesterday evening Mr. H, Cousin Marion, and I drove over to town. Mr. H on our return brought a most beautiful bouquet—very beautiful he thinks. Through an invitation from him I remained with Cousin Jane to tea and partook of some of the finest strawberries imaginable. They were excellent if old Mrs. Sisco did have something to do with them. This morning about 9 o'clock I was sent for to come home in haste. What was the matter? Sylus had come "just from Va." "right from the 14th Reg." Cousin M came with me and in the short space of an hour almost a thousand questions were asked. A reorganization of the Reg. has taken place. Many have been thrown out of office while as many have been promoted. John has superseded Capt. Hewitt & henceforth bears that honorable and well deserved title himself.[86] The ex-Capt., they say, is coming home. I went to Church at ½ 10. Dr. M preached on the subject of Heaven. This evening read, slept, talked, and paid a call—Sunday as it is. Only went up to see Jack [a] few minutes. If nothing prevents, will go with Cousin Jane up to Uncle Tom Campbell's[87] tomorrow.

New Providence, Tennessee, Wednesday night, May 21, 1862

And I have made a visit to Uncle Tom Campbell's. How strange it seems that I have in reality made the visit and find myself at home again, for so long a trip to Uncle T's has been classed among many other things as a something impossible. Cousin Jane, Marion,[88] Tommie Barbee,[89] and I left about 8 o'clock Monday morning. The weather was cool enough but dust—I never knew the like for this season. We were riding until about 2 and our appearance after getting there I imagine anything else but what it was when we started. The attire of each had assumed quite a different shade and with our teeth we realized this as well as with our eyes for even our mouths were dusty. We passed through the far-famed city of Lafayette[90] and had the pleasure of viewing most of the public buildings as it is planned somewhat like our own little village: one straight street running through with the buildings both private & public situated on either side. Two handsomely constructed school buildings with the same number of neatly finished churches gave me the character of the citizens without farther inquiry. Churches and schoolrooms are two signposts generally reared in villages & cities and on them may be read in full the character of the inhabitants. Found Uncle T and Aunt Polly looking for anyone else before us. Bettie seemed pleased to see us but more so at the thought of a ride on "Old Gray." Yesterday the rain kept us penned up with the children most all day (only 6 were present trying to see who [could] keep [the] loudest noise and be most annoying. Late in the evening we drove down to the Roaring Spring. Went out far enough to see Dr. Bacon's[91] residence;

he certainly lives at a most beautiful place. I had forgotten almost to say and I regret having it to do that Uncle Tom with his whole family excepting the (Better half) his wife are Unionist, in other words, Lincolnites. I will not dishonor them or myself either by saying I have been paying a visit to a Yankee family—though they almost deserve it. For all followers of Lincoln are nowadays termed Yankees. Once or twice while in the heat of an argument on the war subject my ears began to tingle but with considerable effort my temper was kept down at least to some extent, and we generally wound up with good feeling existing all around. We left there this morning at 7. Were at home by 8. No news excepting a stolen piece—Miss F overheard Sylus telling Uncle T today that two of Morgan's men were in town. He saw them and knew them.

New Providence, Tennessee, Thursday night, May 22, 1862

Before getting out my work this morning went up to see Jack Gold's babe. Found it very ill indeed, suffering greatly with cold and flu. Came home— but I forgot to say that old Mrs. Fairfax was on hand with her usual budget of news. She says "the North intends emancipating the South before they rest." If such is the case the South will find herself "in a dab" as old Mrs. Sisco would say. Came home, went downtown, laid out the whole of 25 cts liking half dime in calico worth from 15 cts in silver to 20 cts in Tenn. money. So much for the uncertainty of Tenn.'s position; her currency is neither passable as U States or as Southern Confederacy.[92] While at the store, a Yankee Cavalry company passed. They seemed to be out merely on a trip of curiosity; returned soon after passing out. I guess they were rather preparing to give Morgan a reception. Sewed all evening. Have taken a walk since tea. Not alone, neither with Uncle T or Miss F—Mr. H is criticizing so severely the above that I guess I had better wait a while.

New Providence, Tennessee, Saturday night, May 24, 1862

As Mr. H was present again last night, I deferred writing though his corrections the night before gave us offense whatever. Nothing had occurred worth taking up this old book, for the same might be said however on many other occasions. This morning Mr. H came up early and we drove over to Clarksville. After so long a time Mr. McCormac has finished the first photograph of Aunt T. We called and got that and ordered two more this morning, one for Cousin Nat and one for Cousin Jane. Uncle Trice says Cousin Ann must also have one as she with the other two were her nearest friends. Brought home with us 40 cts worth of newspapers and in them all but little news was found. The Yankees still are blowing over the loss of the Merrimack and anticipate a most brilliant victory at Corinth. The first we have only to regret while hope is given us in regard to the future. Uncle T has discovered a plot of Winnie's to run off and really, I'm too excited to hold a pen—When mad, he uses such outrageous language that I'm frightened the whole time.

New Providence, Tennessee, Wednesday, May 28, 1862

During the evening I had slight symptoms of the flux[93] and not until yesterday evening did those symptoms entirely disappear. Mr. H had driven him out in an hour or less time, perhaps; judging from his appearance he could have kept pretty good time with the Yanks at Pittsburg—Mr. H carried out a paper last night, the "Louisville Express"[94] in which was recorded another brilliant victory of the Southerners. Banks and Jackson have again come in collision with their forces and the result was most gloriously in favor of the South. Jackson succeeded in cutting most his army to pieces, pursued the remnant until they crossed the Potomac, and then took possession of the whole of Shenandoah valley, which has been in the possession of the Federals only two or three months. This battle will probably be known as the Bull Mountain or Front Royal battle.[95]

New Providence, Tennessee, Friday night, May 30, 1862

Spent yesterday morning with Cousin Jane. Bettie Homer came home with me, stayed until 4, and went down to practice for the concert. This morning early Miss F and I went down to see Mr. Pettus's new goods; found them very pretty and some cheaper. Calico is still at 20 cts Tenn. currency 15 specie in Ky.

New Providence, Tennessee, Saturday night, May 31, 1862

About 8 o'clock this morning Billie Leigh and I left home with the intention of spending the day at Mrs. Britton's. As expected met with considerable company. Several of the "young folks" had met for the purpose of taking a little fishing spree. The sun shone so warmly that the house and other amusements were preferred until after dinner, which by the way was most excellent—such nicely baked shoat[96]and such nice strawberries. After dinner Archy Ferguson, Ike Howard, Frank Broady, Mary and Fannie B, and Jennie Acree all put out for the creek. They were gone only a few hours, and as expected returned with but few fish. Miss Lou and I stayed at home, preferring the corner to such a tramp. About 5 this evening a Mr. Browder from Corinth called. He's a soldier under Morgan's command. He told us the 14th were engaged in the battle at Williamsburg, Va.[97]

New Providence, Tennessee, Sunday night, June 1, 1862

Mr. Homer came up this morning with his pockets full of kiss verses and with them and conversation we interested ourselves until school time. Walked down to the church and found that Mr. Hirst had resurrected my class. Rather reluctantly I again took hold, feeling assured that my little help would scarcely be felt in pushing forward the great work. A sense of my inability alone is the cause of any unwillingness that I have as will manifest in taking charge of a class. The children are turning out finely now. The grand concert will come off Tuesday week and all are looking anxiously forward to the time as one of general enjoyment. Dr. Mc preached this morning from Judges 10th chap 13 and 14th verses.[98] His congregations are very small but still he perseveres. A heavy rain this evening prevented me going down to hear a Campbellite.[99] Mr. H has come up and brought some new papers. I must look them over.

New Providence, Tennessee, Monday night, June 2, 1862

Rose this morning determined to have a coop for my chickens if I had to make it myself. So I went to work and with Tom's assistance soon finished off two. They would have been of great service today if the hens would have gone in them, for the rain nearly drowned several of the little chickens, and Inez smothered seven. So with the one I mashed as many might have been killed. I've spent most of the day in attending to them. Cut out my brilliantine dress but only basted the body. Drove down to Cousin Jane's about sunset. Mr. H came back with me and took tea with us. The strawberries sent by Miss Meda[100] was the inducement.

New Providence, Tennessee, Tuesday night, June 3, 1862

Spent the morning sewing on my dress. This evening Bettie Homer came up for me to go with her out to Miss Mollie Ward's. We drove out expecting to be gone only an hour or two but through Miss H's persuasion we were until near 6 o'clock getting in. I then drove B down home, came back, saw to putting up my chickens, ate supper, and another drenching rain nearly drowned my chickens. A good many were brought in almost dead. Uncle T seems to take it very hard because I didn't order Uncle Billie to place planks under the coops. Says he don't care if they all die. My reason for not doing so was that it was time & trouble for nothing as the rain I thought about

over with. The last papers say the Southerners have evacuated Corinth.[101]
For what purpose none can tell.

New Providence, Tennessee, Wednesday night, June 4, 1862

Have sewn six long widths up in my dress and joined it to the body! What a
day's work. A few more chickens I fear would claim all my attention. Uncle T
brought in a new paper today; McClellan and Johnson have had a very heavy
engagement near Richmond[102] so the Telegraph column says. As many as
50,000 are said to have been engaged on each side. Went over few moments
to see Mrs. Wilson late.

New Providence, Tennessee, Friday night, June 6, 1862

The yesterday's paper says the Yankees are within 5 miles of Richmond.

New Providence, Tennessee, Monday night, June 9, 1862

The Chickahominy battle and the fate of the 14th were the subjects mostly
talked. After getting home this evening walked up town to see if I could find
an arithmetic. Limited as my education is and unpleasant as I anticipate 5
months confinement would prove, I have decided if an opportunity is offered
to take a school and if possible to make for myself at least money enough to
buy a bunch of braid or a pair of gloves—two articles that I have been wanting now for some time. And because Uncle T refused me a hoop skirt some
time since, have not had the resolution to ask him even for a penny's worth.
With what little idea I have of arithmetic and with what little I may learn
during the next month or two, I think I may venture at least to take a class
of the smaller children so plentiful in our town—provided Miss Turbyville
doesn't take another school. If she does, then all my hope of having a whole
dollar to call my own will vanish. If I teach,[103] money will be purely the
inducement. And if I succeed in getting any, the first dime will be spent no
doubt toward filling in Aunt T's grave, for if I have a desire on earth it is
to see that attention and respect given to the memory and last resting place
of one [of] Earth's brightest monuments. Too soon forgotten are the good
always.

New Providence, Tennessee, Wednesday night, June 11, 1862

Bright and early I started out the morning for Marion's dress—with the
tarleton left of my dress and the piece Mr. H gave me. Cousin Bet [and] I
have today made her a very pretty dress. It is composed of two skirts, upper
& under both trimmed with narrow blue ribbon. She will quite eclipse some

of the older girls I'm certain; for with the upper skirt looped up on each side with flowers and those composing the trimming for the neck a finish will be given not surpassed by any of the others. Her singing will be so much admired on account of her age, size, &c that I was anxious for her dress to be in keeping with her musical talent. The entire day I've spent at Cousin Jane's. For dinner she gave me fried chicken and beans. This evening Cousin B came home with me; Miss F is out at her mother's. Old Mrs. P is very ill. The last papers are filled with accounts of the surrender of Memphis to the Federals after the naval engagement of last week between Com. Davis and Jeff Thompson,[104] and Memphis has surrendered! What important point will the Yankees gain next? Only one or two points on the Mississippi River now are in our possession. Vicksburg, I believe is yet held by the Southerners, but daily we are expecting to hear of its surrender.[105] The loss at the battle of Fair Oaks or Chickahominy whatever it may be called on the Federal side increases every hour. From 200 it has gone up to 7,000; the loss on both sides was immense.[106]

New Providence Tennessee, Friday, June 13, 1862

Fearing on Mr. Hirst's account that the turnout to his concert would be rather small I have used my best endeavors in persuading persons to attend. So much interested was I that yesterday morning after Cousin Bet left, I drove out to Mrs. Britton's for Mary. Quint Atkinson came at least an hour too soon (or very near it). I regretted so much that Mary had no company. If Mr. H had have had the politeness that every civilized man ought to possess he would have been "on hand," but no he "didn't intend to be troubled with any woman." Just such might be expected from just such a source. We all managed, however, with the help of our quarters to get a peep at the youth and beauty of our town, and I must say the children together with the young ladies presented a very pretty appearance indeed. Their music also did splendidly considering they practiced so little. Cousin Jane's children to the gratification of us all performed most admirably. Marion looked very sweetly in her tarleton dress and sang beautifully. She excited the admiration of many with the sweetness of her voice. For one so tiny and so young to sing so well is enough to call forth astonishment on any occasion.[107] They all performed their part well, Mr. Hirst not excepted. He sang alone two very pretty pieces, one I remember was "Her bright smile haunts me still."[108] The assembly to our surprise was very large for this place. At least $40.00 was received, a sum that we might have begged for this whole year and then not have succeeded. As it was, not one I guess regretted spending his quarter and our library will be greatly increased too.

New Providence, Tennessee, Saturday night, June 14, 1862

Mr. Homer called by this morning and sit until 8. From that time until 6 this evening I've been hard at work; the hardest work in the world, altering an old dress. My shoulders ache so badly. The Express of yesterday gives an account of another battle near the Chickahominy (which will probably be known as the Cross Pines Battle)[109] in which the surgeon of the 14th Reg. was killed.[110] Others, or perhaps nearly all the rest, were killed but only Martin's name was mentioned in the extract from the Richmond paper. Stonewall Jackson is accomplishing wonders in Va.;[111] his movements are looked forward to with almost as much interest as those of Beauregard.

New Providence, Tennessee, Sunday night, June 15, 1862

Dressed in muslin this morning for the first time this year.[112] Calico seems to have superseded fine dress goods of most every description. Our school this morning was rather slow. Let a picnic be prepared and crowds will flock in again. Dr. Mc preached at ½ 10. Tried to sleep this evening from 12 to 2 but didn't succeed. At 4 Quint came over and sit until near 6 — I didn't give him a definite answer in regard to his ring. What if I did throw it away? The cause justified me. Mr. H came and left while he was here and since tea has been up again but only stayed long enough to get a memorandum of some articles for Miss F and I. He leaves in the morning for Louisville. Uncle T sent for me a bonnet. I know I shall be ashamed to wear the Yankee looking affair except in Hopkinsville.[113]

New Providence, Tennessee, Thursday night, June 19, 1862

Bad news was awaiting us this evening; the last report in regard to the 14th Tenn. Reg. is anything but cheering. During one of the recent engagements on the Chickahominy, their Brigade was called in to action and of the 14th only 11 are said to be alive. The slaughter [it] is said was horrible indeed; how can such an unholy war be protracted? Mr. H has not yet returned, and as his time expired last night, we have reasons to fear the interference of the Lincolnites.

New Providence, Tennessee, Friday, June 20, 1862

Finished my corset covers this morning by 10 o'clock and as Mrs. Pettus had sent a very pressing invitation by Miss F yesterday I concluded to go out and spent the remainder of the day. As expected, met with Mrs. Brunty, her mother, and Miss Angling. The day passed very agreeably. Miss A and I interested ourselves for a good while with the Stereoscope.[114] She is such an agreeable young lady. Came home in time to ride down and see Mrs. Herring [a] few minutes; her babe is quite sick. Tonight, Sylus and I walked down to see Mrs. Pollard or rather Mary B but she had gone out home. Sylus has discovered a very important secret in regard to Mr. "Quint" and I. He thinks he knows it all.

New Providence, Tennessee, Saturday night, June 21, 1862

A conversation between Uncle T and Sylus awakened me rather earlier this morning than usual. As they passed my door something was said about "your sweet heart," "The Yankees didn't get him," &c. Of course my toilette was soon completed and I at the breakfast table anxious to hear "Which one of them" it was creating so much excitement. The story was soon told and not many hours elapsed before Mr. Homer himself was in our midst. Just from Louisville: the man of fashion, he had neglected to notice nothing which would give us an idea of the latest agony. For fear of failing to give us a correct idea of the latest style lady's hat, he brought one along and desires that we start the fashion in Providence straight away. He calls it Dunstable straw,[115] the brim turned down with ribbon and flowers composing the trimming. It is indeed very handsome but can't compare with my bonnet, in which I must say Mr. Homer exercised most splendid taste. Of course he's not responsible for the way it points up to the sky in front, or the acute point it terminates in just under the chin; these Madame Fashion must be held accountable for, while Mr. H's excellent taste must be admired in the blending of the colors, the nice straw flowers, &c composing it. After all it is nothing more nor less than a Yankee bonnet, but when one calculates on paying a visit to Yankeedom, of course they must prepare accordingly. Mr. H bought for himself a very nice watch. With other little presents for myself was a little jewel for my necklace representing a small seashell or something of the kind in which either a picture or hair may be set. The design is very pretty indeed, and as for thanking Mr. H sufficiently for his kindness and attention to me would be almost impossible. He's so like a brother to me. Went up this evening to see the Mrs. Golds. Went with them down town, and for myself with other little things bought a pair of Mr. H's prettiest picnic gloves. They are beautiful according to my notion and taste. Tonight we went down to carry Cousin Jane her present, a pair of lasting gaters.[116] They were too small. For the children he brought a hat apiece.

New Providence, Tennessee, Sunday night, June 22, 1862

Mrs. Brunty and Sallie Angling came in to church and I went out home with them, and came in again at 4 expecting to hear Mr. Taylor but was disappointed. However, my new swiss[117] was brought out. The warm evening was a sufficient excuse and with my new slippers and hat my appearance presented something of the Yankee as well as the half-starved, half- clothed "Secesh." Yesterday's paper says in the Richmond battles the 7th Tenn. Reg. lost 174, the 14th 125, the 1st 89. How sad to think of so many of our best friends meeting with such a hard fate.[118] Several have started for the 14th but it will be many weeks before we can hear anything definitely.

New Providence, Tennessee, Monday night, June 23, 1862

Went to work early to finish off my brilliantine dress this morning; the braid I've so long been waiting for I made myself. Before finishing, however, Jack Gold and Jennie Mallory came in. Jack sit until 10, about which time Jennie and I went down town. She came in for the purpose of laying in a small am't of goods before the expected rise, which will soon no doubt take place as cotton goods of all description continues to advance. Among other things she bought for herself a "Jeff Davis hat,"[119] one very much like mine. We trimmed it this evening in solid pink and really, it proved very becoming indeed. Rode out as far as Mrs. Brunty's this evening — Sylus and I. He was most too blue to enjoy the ride much.

New Providence, Tennessee, Saturday evening, June 28, 1862

After waiting some time Tuesday morning for some decision in the weather, we concluded to risk the consequences. And with Uncle T and Miss F in one buggy, Eugene[120] and I in the other, we all set our faces Lincolndomward, and notwithstanding the prospects for a heavy rain — dark clouds threatening all the way — we arrived safely at Mr. Grinstead's about ½ 11 without being dissolved either from water or heat. Mrs. G soon had prepared for us a most excellent dinner. The baked shoat was splendid while the cherry tarts were so nice to "finish off on." Soon after dinner we were invited to take a lounge, which to myself proved very agreeable and not until 3 was I dressed and down stairs.

That evening I commenced a crochet cap for the back of my hair and with that I employed myself for a day or two. During the time, however, walks were taken when the rain would cease long enough, music was listened to, and on Wednesday evening we paid old Mrs. Evans[121] a call — one of the darkest dyed old Yankees I ever saw. She's too mean and selfish to have company and prefers living alone just with the servants to giving some poor girl a home in her house. Thursday evening Tomy G[122] drove me over to Mr. Carneal's. Again my visit was unlooked for, and Mattie seemed scarcely to realize that I was there for some time after I had made my appearance. She with Mary did everything in their power to make my visit agreeable, at least seemed to. Mary has just returned from Memphis. She took great pains to tell me all about Cousin Mat and the children, Mrs. Galbraith, and other friends down there. What she said of Tom was particularly interesting (how presumptuous he must be). Saw a list of the killed and wounded while gone belonging to the 14th Reg. Among them were none of my acquaintances except Mr. {*indecipherable*}.

New Providence, Tennessee, Wednesday night, July 2, 1862

The 2nd of July. What heart rending recollections come up with those words. That day in all my history to be remembered as the saddest, most heart breaking of all. The 2nd of July, the anniversary of Aunt T's death. Is it possible? Can it be that within one short year Life with its attractions and death with its most solemn effects should both be presented to us in the person of one whom we held as dear almost as existence itself? The lateness of the hour prevents a farther indulgence of my feelings else I might write for hours on the subject so sad and yet most interesting to me of all others.

Quint called after tea and not until near 12 would he leave. Strange to me is the fact that some young men have no mercy whatever for young ladies. A declaration of his — love he would call it — was made to me tonight, but if I were [to] honor it with a name, I should call it boyish fancy. For two hours I tried to convince him of his error, but he persisted in urging the matter and at our next meeting the question is to be decided. I wish without further trouble he knew my feelings. Another great fight has come off before Richmond in which the Southern armies were most glowingly victorious and the Federals completely routed. Their own papers give the statement, and of course it must be true. Beauregard and Stonewall Jackson, it is said, were both present on the occasion. Their gun boats was all that saved them at all.[123]

New Providence, Tennessee, Friday night, July 4, 1862

Nothing of interest occurred yesterday. A little plaiting was done and after supper Mr. Homer came up and teased me for two hours about Quint Atkinson. Today though we've had no papers, the Yankee guns over in

Clarksville have reminded us of the absence of Southern soldiers, notwithstanding our daily expectation of their arrival. Will, a negro just from the
14th Reg., reports 6,000 cavalry on their way to Nashville. He brought with
him a journal from one of the boys in which a detailed account of their movements up to the battle of Fair Oaks is given. The "Yanks" in Clarksville are
paying great honors to their national day; firing of guns over there has been
going on over there all day.[124] Mrs. Harrelson, Mrs. Magaren, and Mollie
Harrelson spent the morning with us. A general ridiculing of our Fleet[125]
took place.

New Providence, Tennessee, Saturday night, July 12, 1862

A while after breakfast last Sunday morning Cousin Lou and Reny Ogburn[126]
left for home concluding that the evening would be entirely too warm for so
long a ride. Rather later than usual I went down to Sunday school, and not
so usual did school and services close that morning. Several things somewhat
unusual occurred before school was dismissed, but not until then was the
secret revealed. At that time Mr. Hirst took occasion to make a few remarks
in regard to several situations that had been offered him as Teacher during
the previous week, one of which he said he had concluded to accept. With
these last words, every countenance was instantly saddened. From the gray
headed father down to the infant almost that sit by his side seemed to feel
the shock. We were so little prepared for anything of the kind that the
dead silence which reigned for several minutes was the only way in which
our surprise was manifested. Certainly never did a teacher accomplish
more or win more hearts than he has during so short a time. Teachers,
children, and all were as much attached to him as could be. As we left the
church, more than one was heard to say our Sunday school is done with
now. If Mr. Hirst leaves, we had as well discontinue the school, prophe-
cies which I fear will too soon be fulfilled.

Mr. Mills and Cousin Mollie dined with us that day. Insisted that
I should go with them out home that evening. I went and at last have
paid the visits so long promised and dreaded. We started early Monday
morning. Spent a day and night at Uncle Steven's. From there we went
to Cousin "Mollie Shaw's." Spent the day between she and Mrs. Gold.
Next day we spent at Esq. Collins' and a very pleasant time we had.
A more interesting set of sisters I never knew, all of them so agreeable
and entertaining.[127] {Sarah} gave me several lessons in hair work which
she seemed to take great delight in, as that, she says, is her favorite employment. Thursday morning we went over and paid Miss Cowherd[128]

a fashionable call. Of course, as we were visiting a lady of fashion, our visit must be somewhat of that character. She with Mrs. Long both made themselves very agreeable. Thursday morning, Mr. Homer came up. We went over, stayed all night with Uncle Wm's family and until after dinner yesterday. Jennie Mallory stayed with us. We went blackberrying yesterday evening late and certainly gathered some of the nicest berries I ever saw. This morning early we left for home; were here by 8 o'clock. Joe Hatcher[129] came in soon afterwards and sit until about 11. Since dinner Mr. Hirst has called; paid us perhaps his last visit. Says he will leave to take charge of his school in Lexington, Ky., Monday if nothing prevents. —— The columns of the last papers have been teeming with accounts of the great battle so long expected and so long dreaded. I allude to the battle before Richmond.[130]

McClellan with his mighty army—than which (agreeable to their own accounts) a grander one never faced an enemy[131]—has at length given the first blow toward possessing himself of Richmond, the Capitol of the Confederate States. For weeks and months he has been busy in making preparation for this great move, but not until the 26th of June did he strike what he had fondly hoped would be the decisive blow. But how intense must have been his disappointment. Instead of mowing down before him as the grass of the field the "few pitiful" "half famished," "half clad" soldiery under the weak and cowardly Generals Lee, Jackson, Johnson, and others, they were themselves forced to flee at the first onset. And not until 7 successive battles were fought, during a retreat of the greatest confusion and disorder, did they reach the protection of that mighty advocate they are themselves pleased to style half God and half man. Their only support in time of need, their only defense in time of danger (the all-powerful Gun boats).[132] But for these (and the James River) scarcely a man of McClellan's grand army would have been left to have recorded the sad fate of his brothers.

Under their protection however a few are left; and those few we hope soon to hear have shared the fate of the others, as in the next papers we expect to hear the 8th, if not the 9th, battle has been added to those already fought. Young Trice[133] from the 14th Reg.[134] came last night and says his Reg. were drawn up in the line of battle the day he left, and that the firing was soon expected to commence, which was about two weeks since. He also reports the health of the Reg. as being very bad; poor John Mallory he says is looking wretchedly. Mr. Hirst was telling me this evening that John Morgan was in Cave City[135] and had reared there the Confederate flag never again to be taken down. From some unknown cause the Louisville papers have failed to come today.

New Providence. Tennessee, Tuesday, July 15, 1862

Have been engaged in nothing particularly either yesterday or today. Went down yesterday evening and bought for myself a calico dress, only one. Asked Uncle Trice for two but he thought one sufficient. The first I've bought since the rise. Gave 25 cts for it, a price I never before gave for calico. Stayed all night out at Mrs. Pettus's last night. Mary Grinstead is down. She and I spent the morning in Clarksville, and between us bought about 3.00 worth. While there heard that Forrest and his men had captured two Regt's stationed at Murfreesboro, with also two Brig Gen'ls.[136] Great excitement prevails in Nashville, and many Union Loving souls are leaving as the Yankees would say, "skedaddling." In the event that the city is evacuated the "Yanks" have placed guns to shell it. Mr. Homer brings up a paper tonight in which he says is a Southern account of the battles before Richmond. The Federals own to have lost near 80,000 men there, and of course it must be greater. Dr. Thomas says we must always multiply their no. by 4.

New Providence, Tennessee, Thursday night, July 17, 1862

Early yesterday morning Mr. Homer, Bettie, and I started out blackberrying. We spent the whole morning. Walked it seemed to me 10 miles and came home with about 2 gal's berries. News came today that Morgan was expected in Lexington[137] and that the city was under military control. Not a man is allowed to appear on the street without his gun. So of course we may expect a frustration of Mr. Hirst's plans and possibly have him with us again Sunday.

New Providence, Tennessee, Saturday evening, July 19, 1862

Sewed steadily all day yesterday and today, the first two days I've been closely confined for two weeks. Just as I was under head-way yesterday evening Tommy Grinstead came and without hoops, collar, or scarcely with my dress on, I was compelled to face him. As he came in at the gate, however, the latch was kind enough to warn me of his approach, and before he could form any very correct conclusion about my size, weight, &c I was before the mirror with comb in one hand, towel in another, and all haste to resume the seat so lately and abruptly deserted. He was all {*indecipherable*} and "agreeableness" while present and left in the same conviction. While at tea a card came from Mr. Atkinson and before it was answered Mr. Homer called. His visit however was not prolonged as usual. So from dark until near 11 the parlor was given up to Quint and I.

The subject introduced some time ago was renewed. But contrary to his request I had given it but little attention and of course was but poorly prepared to present any new ideas or thoughts on the occasion. He urged the case notwithstanding and to my regret it may prove a decided answer was given him without further ceremony—an answer that was positive and unconditional. My decision surprised him I know, for men under all circumstances are so self-connected that to reject them seems a matter next to an impossibility. He tried to assume a friendly appearance on leaving, but chagrin if not disappointment was visibly seen in the background. Late papers give accounts of no new battles; all is quiet before Richmond.

New Providence, Tennessee, Sunday night, July 20, 1862

Dr. McMullin came over this morning and brought the good news of Mr. Hirst's actual return. More than one of us expected him to be present but all were disappointed. School was rather full under the circumstances. Dr. Mc at ½ 10 preached from John 1st chap and 1st verse.[138] I had the hysterics so bad after dinner that a walk down to Cousin Jane's was decided on notwithstanding the [sun] shone warmly enough to melt all soft objects. We came up to the church so late that the bible class were half through with the lesson. Cousin Jane supped with us for a rarity; Mr. H and I drove her down home.

New Providence, Tennessee, Wednesday night, July 23, 1862

Found Nannie Grinstead and Mary Cook[139] here this morning. They remained until about 2 when they went down to spend the remainder of the day with Mrs. P.[140] Mr. Mills called about 9 on his way to the 14th Reg. As no letter can be carried from here to Richmond for fear of the bearer being snatched by the "Yanks," all our messages were done up in a few but expressive words and carefully handed over to some friend to be recorded on memory's page and there kept as some precious treasure until the first meeting with the one for whom they were intended.[141] Capt. Woodward's Ky. Squadron has been disbanded.[142] Jo and Charlie Staton with several others got home yesterday. Charlie was up this evening. He seems to think there is no necessity of his enlisting again and the "Rebels" will soon have accomplished all they started out to do. He also says the Southern Troops from Chattanooga he thinks are marching over to Nashville.

New Providence, Tennessee, Thursday, July 24, 1862

Have been sick for a month but worse off today than ever; my health without a doubt is gradually declining. Hemmed three handkerchiefs this morning and went down the country for some peaches. Did nothing this evening but lounge, sleep, and read a little; life never was less attractive. News came this evening that the "Rebels" were advancing on Clarksville—within 4 miles of the city.[143] The greatest excitement and confusion exists among the Yankees while the citizens doubtless are in the same predicament. For threats have already been made that in case the town was evacuated they would leave it in ashes.[144]

New Providence, Tennessee, Friday night, July 25, 1862

Have been within doors all day, and though apparently everything has moved on quietly, I'm convinced that a domestic struggle has been going on for some time in which I am not wholly disinterested. Today particularly Miss F has spoken but seldom except in reply to some question directly asked. She looks coldly toward me, and the conversation accidently heard yesterday between she and Uncle T is proof still more conclusive that something in some way has gone wrong. And if language is not to be mistaken, I am the offending party. But why need I be surprised occupying the position I do? Prejudice against me I'm firmly of the opinion this long time has only been concealed from me while a secret power has been incessant in its endeavor to keep it up. Sometimes I am almost ready to give up and despair of ever even seeming cheerful again. So many things occur to head my mind back to the past, and the contrast with the present is always so striking that one train of sad thoughts, reflections, &c. follows another in such quick succession that I'm scarcely prepared to appear in society even for a short length of time with any degree of comfort to myself or others. Not like some can "I seem gay when my heart is breaking all the while." A true child of nature acts out nature always, and to be one of the truest has fallen to my lot.

New Providence, Tennessee, Saturday night, July 26, 1862

Plaited hair all morning and read. This evening went out calling, first to Mrs. Davis, from there to Mrs. Magaren's, and from there to Mrs. Herring's. At Mrs. M's my visit was longest, for there time passed most agreeably. She and Mr. M both are very entertaining. Dr. Herring gave me a most beautiful bouquet; he has some so pretty verbenas & geraniums as I ever saw. (I must close. Mr. H will talk about Quint and I can't help but—listen).

CHAPTER FIVE

August 1862–June 1863

SEREPTA EMBARKED ON an extended to trip to Hopkinsville to visit friends and family. Upon her return she wrote of local hostilities including what would be called the Battle of Riggins Hill and locals burning a bridge. Serepta wrote despairingly of Federal troops and of their appropriation of goods and livestock. She wrote of robberies of neighbors and violence perpetuated by both sides as law and order broke down. She hid valuables up the chimney and in secure places. Enslaved people freed themselves by leaving with Union troops. She wrote of war news both national and local, mentioning the loss of local men. She recounted the activities of local Confederates Thomas Woodward and John Hunt Morgan and wrote of Lincoln, the Emancipation Proclamation and the Battle of Stones River. She wrote with anger at the Yankees.

Serepta's profound grief was compounded by the hostile treatment by her uncle and his new wife as she felt unwelcome in the only home she had lived since her mother died.

New Providence, Tennessee, Wednesday morning, August 27, 1862

Four weeks ago yesterday morning[1] I left home for Hopkinsville. After a rather tiresome ride of 23 or 4 miles we found ourselves at half past 11 enjoying that delightful state of feeling known only to friends who have met after months separation. Cousin Louis and the children were very well; Cousin Alley just recovering from a spell of sickness.[2] That day she had dressed for the first time in several weeks, and from that day she improved so rapidly that all fears of an early decline were done away with. Mr. Homer remained with us the next day and the next until the afternoon. After he left Cousin A and I began to talk over the prospect of enjoying ourselves the coming three or four weeks and to arrange affairs so as to allow ourselves time for taking frequent rides, making visits, &c. But soon the gilded prospect vanished and we were left to make the best of home & content ourselves with a visit occasionally to Cousin Steve's or Willie's[3] and even then were liable to be disappointed by being forced to return home by some of the low down Dutch pickets. For three weeks of my visit we were not permitted more than twice to ride through town.

The Federal cavalry kept the town so closely guarded and in their absence the citizens took it on themselves to fill their places. But such a state of affairs we are thankful to say was not allowed to continue. About a week before I left, Col Johnson[4] and his Rebel Regiment came in, demanded a surrender of the place, arms, and of the citizens who had been so actively engaged in using those arms. They were readily handed over to a superior force and they themselves forced to take the oath never again to take up arms in opposition to the S. Confederacy. [5] After the surrender, we felt free to go where and when we pleased. Our first visit was to Mr. Slaughter's. On Sunday during our visit (last Sunday week ago) we had the pleasure of dining with a good many of Col. J's Reg.; they were passing through Pembroke on their way to Clarksville and called for dinner. That night they came on down, joined Woodward, and by 12 the next day Clarksville was again in the possession of the Southerners.[6] A note from Mr. Homer gave us a description of the surrender, the turnout of the citizens, and grand display of banners,[7] &c &c. Such a scene he said "had not been witnessed in Clarksville since '44."[8] They captured property to the amount of 300,000 dollars' worth. The prisoners, Col Mason included, were paroled and sent home. Many of them it is said expressed great delight at the idea of seeing home again;[9] they were heartily tired of Federal service. (Day before yesterday Woodward's company went down to make an attack on Ft. Donelson,[10] but the artillery was brought to bear with so much effect that they will be compelled to return today without much success.)

New Providence, Tennessee, Tuesday night, September 2, 1862

Well, well, what will happen next? (I hope the war will close) Two successive visits I've made with not a whole day spent at home between the two. Uncle Wm Mallory called last Wednesday morning and as a seat was offered and my promise was out anyway to spend a week with Cousin Mary, I decided to protract my visiting until the most of it at least was over with. Found Aunt R and Cousin Mollie both up to their elbows drying fruit. Cousins Lourane and Jennie M[11] soon after my arrival came in to spend the night with Cousin M.[12] Altogether we had rather a gay time. Cousin Nat's vacant chair for a while had but little claim on our attention, with other subjects introduced during the evening. One in regard to myself and not altogether disconnected with Mr. Homer was introduced. I will let it suffice just here to say that from the remarks that were made neither of us have much to boast of as being the subjects of flattery or eulogy. From Cousin Lourane particularly each of us received I'm very certain not an over portion of commendation but allowing myself an opinion a full measure if not a little more of censure. But as Bonnie Rogers says, every tub must stand on its own bottom.[13] So what arrangements Mr. H and I may see proper to make we will be responsible for, not those above referred to. Until Monday evening I stayed with Cousin M— employing myself in various ways, but eating principally. Mr. H came out Sunday morning and in the afternoon we walked with Miss Quarles down to the sulphur spring,[14] a young lady boarding with Uncle Wm. and attending the spring for her health. Since getting home have heard but little news. Woodward after his failure at Donelson left Clarksville and in his place are Col Dortch[15] and his Regiment. Spent this evening with Cousin Jane. She's just the same; good as ever.

New Providence, Tennessee, Wednesday night, September 3, 1862

Of the grapes gathered at Cousin Jane's yesterday evening I decided this morning to make jelly and not wine as there were so few. After finishing that off I went to work on a dish mat. My table set I fear will be a long time on hand, but the beauty of them in the end will fully repay me. War news all in favor of Southern arms. They are represented as being successful on all occasions. The late engagements between Jackson and Pope at Culpepper C H[16] and other places are said to have resulted most gloriously in our favor.[17] The Tenn. Brigade is still crowning themselves with imperishable laurels and proving themselves worthy sons of a noble State. Another great battle is reported to have been fought at Manassas Gap.[18] 30 or more it is said belonging to the 14th Reg. were killed at the Culpepper C H battle, Leut. Col Harold[19] among the number. Mr. Homer is telling me so much about the battles I must close and listen.

New Providence, Tennessee, Thursday night, September 4, 1862

Resumed my usual trade this morning. Went over to Mrs. Wilson's before 8 o'clock, my first visit to the young lady stranger. She's just three weeks old today and a very fine looking child. Came home from there and as the buggy and horse were at the gate idle I drove down to Cousin Jane's. This evening I've been crocheting and looking at the Soldiers pass. Woodward's men have all returned to Clk.

New Providence, Tennessee, Friday, September 5, 1862

Left home early this morning with the intention of spending the day; to the letter I carried it out. First to Mary Smith, then to Mrs. Pat Riggins, and from there to Alice's where I dined and spent the evening. From there this evening we had a full view of Woodward's company passing out. The latest news by "Grapevine" reports 1,500 Yankees not more than 12 miles from Clarksville on their way to retake Clarksville.[20]

New Providence, Tennessee, Saturday night, September 6, 1862

The rumor in circulation yesterday in regard to the near approach of the Federals has been fully credited today. As Capt. Marr[21] came up this morning early from a reconnoitering expedition, and in a very plain and unmistakable language represented the case as it was and is. He with his company on yesterday saw the "Yanks," counted them, and left immediately to report to Woodward. But as he had left, a courier was sent soon after his arrival here and by 10 o'clock the Regiment (Woodward's) was stationed not more than two miles from here ready to give them a most cordial reception. Marr reported them 10 or 12 miles distant yesterday. Today went down, met with the advance guard, and had a skirmish with them not more than 7 or 8 miles from here. Tonight it is said they have fallen back a mile or two so that they might have the advantage of a good spring. So tomorrow we may expect a continuation of the confusion and excitement of which we have had such an abundant share today. Many suppose they intend to make their appearance in Clarksville early in the morning, but if Woodward stands to his post, their progress no doubt will be a little impeded. Mr. Pettus was up tonight and has seen papers up to the 4th. He says the Yankee papers all unite in giving to the Southerners the praise for their brilliant success in the late battles. Our arms from every quarter are represented as carrying with them victory & success.

New Providence, Tennessee, Monday evening, Sept 8, 1862

As we expected and as we feared, Woodward with his few men came in contact with the "Yanks" (if they are deserving even that hateful name) yesterday morning about 2 miles from this place and with the loss of some 4 or 5 men was compelled to retreat soon after the firing of the enemy commenced.[22] We hadn't a single piece of artillery while they had as many as 6 or 7 canon besides small arms of the most superior kind. They planted their canon and commenced the attack by throwing shell over among our soldiers so that to charge the battery with Woodward's few men would have resulted in great sacrifice of life. He saw what the consequences would be and without giving his men a single order to fire he gave the command to retreat, which they did in good order. 2 men were killed and three or four wounded by shells bursting near them. The morning (yesterday morning) passed in most dreadful suspense. The canon ceased firing about ½ 11; by 12 our men were passing in the greatest haste in their retreat to Clarksville; and I suppose by 1 or half after 1, anyway the "Yanks" were passing if possible in greater haste. The cavalry were pursuing our men while the infantry were scattered on either side of the road some distance out in search of any who might have halted by the wayside from fatigue or other cause.

None that I have heard of were overtaken though Jo Jones[23] and G Marr,[24] two officers under Col. Woodward, were standing within ten steps of our gate when the advance guard came in sight. As they came rushing by, the road full, the back yard strewn with them, and on all sides, they so completely seemed to surround us each looking so blood thirsty and bent on some such dreadful purpose that Xerxes' army wouldn't have appeared larger. Never may I experience again such feelings. One oath after another was uttered in such quick succession when they called to ask for water, and the abuse heaped on "Secesh" so shocking that it made my blood run cold and I scarcely dared to make any appearance even at the window. Demons attired in blue cloth and jingling with sword and pistol on either side would scarcely have presented a more shocking appearance. May it be my fortune never, never to be brought in contact with such again.

The Southerners as they passed over the bridge attempted to destroy it so as to impede their progress, but they soon repaired it and all crossed over. Today until about 2 o'clock they spent in breaking open and robbing business houses. About that time they left again for Ft. Donelson, carrying with them Denison[25] with his family and 1 or 2 other Lincolnite families—also about 39 or 40 negroes and as many loose horses as they could find on the way. Elie says they took Dick out of the pasture as they passed on Aunt Tabbie's buggy horse,[26] and though he was my dependence for visiting, on her account he was dearer to me than anything belonging about the place. I could have parted more readily with any servant on the place anything, anything before Dick. To think he has been so tenderly cared for the whole of his life time-and now that he's growing old had to meet with such a fate. It is more than I can bear without begging for something to rest on them other than a blessing. They all halted in front of here for an hour or more for water; and some of them say that Buell is expected to fall back to Clarksville— is why they left. Others that Morgan or Forrest were expected.[27] So we are left to wait the result and it may be more dreadful than ever.

New Providence, Tennessee, Wednesday night, September 10, 1862

Spent yesterday morning with Mrs. Pollard. Bettie Helm called in soon after I did. So with Fannie and Mrs. P with her loud tongue the Yankees were all carried to the stake, burnt, and then their ashes carried through a chemical process to be sure the "Yankee" was all gone. We "put them all through"—in imagination. After dinner Fannie, Bettie, Mr. Homer, & I went down to the battlefield if it may be so termed. We saw where the two men were killed, where the balls passed through the frail breastworks of the Southerners and from thence through a large barn nearby, the graves where the dead were buried, the eminence on which were placed the artillery of the Enemy. In a word the whole space [was] occupied both by friend and foe and though but little was presented calculated in the least to interest a veteran used to scenes the most horrible. Every spot to us we associated in our imagination with something of more than usual interest.

From there we went down & spent an hour or two with Mrs. Howard. She entertained us with many little circumstances relative to thieving expeditions of the Yanks. They camped near her house. Some of her neighbors she said had been robbed of everything, even their wearing clothes, silver ware, china ware, &c. Some will be compelled to break up housekeeping for the want of necessaries. Just as we drove up home Jo Jones captured a stray Yankee soldier going into our gate. He disarmed him, took him out to the country, and says he paroled him. But many think his parole took him to another world. If so and Yanks find it out, the citizens of our little town may have to pay the penalty. "Oh, the horrors of war." Stayed with Mrs. Pollard last night. Went out this evening to see Mrs. Pettus. Negroes continue to follow after the Yanks. Several hundred will probably be led off. That trip up here was only a negro stealing expedition. Some families are left with only one [or] two, and they are old and decrepit enough to die a natural death.

New Providence, Tennessee, Thursday night, September 11, 1862

Fannie Britton and I went out to Mrs. Britton's, her mother's, and spent the day today. Drove an old horse of Mrs. Pollard's and if we had have walked I would scarcely have been reminded of Dick oftener. Poor fellow. Some Yankee by this time no doubt has nearly rode him to death. Mrs. B and Mary had but little to tell us excepting of some poor family's destitution who had been robbed of almost everything except existence and that would not have been spared them had they ventured to call it "their rights." Mrs. B abused them to all intents and purposes, though she was fortunate enough not to lose a thing, unless it be a negro she had hired out. Several of the pressed wagons came in this evening, and all say that Horace remained of his own free will and accord. Mr. Ware[28] came up and said they hired Horace for his services and mules — 5 dollars a day in gold — and that he left for Paducah this morning before day. The thought of such a state [of] affairs is too provoking. I will close.

New Providence, Tennessee, Friday night, September 12, 1862

Rose this morning in time to make up my bed and sweep before breakfast. "Getting better" — the cause not altogether unknown to myself. After breakfast asked Miss Fannie for a pair of Uncle Trice's pants to make. As usual she denied me but said I liked I could make a pair of shirt bosoms. Strange, she never seems inclined to encourage me in doing work for the family. Sewed busily until the bosoms were finished; then walked down to the store and to Mrs. Staton's. Mrs. S thinks after all the Yanks didn't serve her as badly as they might. They only took her preserves, a pair of pants of Mr. Staton's, a pair of shoes, and Ann Mary's picture. Well, of course, they robbed the safe of all that was cooked. The late papers still give a more encouraging [report] of the late battle at Manassas. The last fight at Manassas, like the first, is destined no doubt to embellish and throw an additional brilliancy around many of the other great achievements of the South. Jackson it is said has certainly crossed over to Maryland while Rumor reports Kirby Smith in possession of Louisville.[29]

New Providence, Tennessee, Monday evening, September 15, 1862

According to arrangements made last week, Fannie Britton and I, Saturday evening went down to Mrs. Ogburn's to attend a meeting held at Mt Pleasant. Mr. O'Neal came on just in time to go with us down. These Yankee times we are a little afraid to carry our independence too far and we are oftener than otherwise forced to go with a pleading face to some of the old widowers notwithstanding our promise to the volunteers to have nothing to do with any such characters (at least until after their return). And then doubtless; an old widower will be just in place with many of us, for from accounts but few will be permitted to return. And as a matter of course there will be more girls than the boys will feel disposed to take care of. Well, my visit, and not the war with its consequences &c., I believe I commenced to say something about. Though we were until 4 o'clock getting down there we were in time for evening service as the members decided that service late in the afternoon would perhaps be better than by candle light, taking into consideration the impropriety of leaving home [at] such an hour and under existing circumstance. This morning I sit with Ann until F came by for me. War news both sad and good. Jackson is said to have fought a battle in Maryland at which we lost 15,000 men;[30] while the Federals lost in killed wounded and taken prisoners, 30,000. Gen. McClellan is reported killed.[31]

New Providence, Tennessee, Tuesday night, September 16, 1862

Walked up town this morning to get some cruel,[32] but as usual was disappointed. Came home. Went to work on my new calico and by 4 this evening the body was finished. Mary Britton called twice to see if I would go out home with her, but I had no way. Dick is gone and Mr. Homer hadn't time to take me out. Something a little startling and not "war news" either. Sylus Trice and Mary Trice are to be married tonight, two first cousins and these hard times too.[33] What will happen next? I prophecy just here, if her disposition remains as it is and he lives, in less than three years they will be separated or living wretchedly together. She is as little calculated to discharge the duty of a wife or mother as anyone I know of, not that I know so much of her these late years as during her school days except from others. While I know for myself her character as a school girl, and as the twig is bent they say so the tree's inclined. The good news of yesterday was brought, many think, by "grapevine."

New Providence, Tennessee, Saturday night, September 20, 1862

Wednesday morning bright & early I was ready to go with Uncle Trice out to Mrs. Britton's. He had business at the mill and I made use of the opportunity; the first ride I've had with him in some time. Found Mrs. B and the girls looking. My visit was made very pleasant. Mary and I took a long ramble one evening looking for sweet gum,[34] and then we went fishing. Spent the entire evening and caught one little fish. This morning Mr. Homer went out and the greater part of the day we spent on the creek. And though we had better success, we have nothing to brag of.

New Providence, Tennessee, Sunday night, September 21, 1862

Mr. Homer came up this morning while we were at breakfast to find out the "program of the day." After some little hesitancy, we decided to go down to Sunday school and return in time to go out to West Fork. From Sunday school Cousin Jane came up to go with us out. She and Cousin Alley went in the rockaway,[35] while I was honored with a seat in Mr. H's new buggy. Uncle John Mallory preached a real war sermon. The congregation was unusually good for West Fork.[36] After dinner we went down to hear Mr. Johnson; he gave us Campbellism[37] in all of its purity. After service I walked with Cousin A over to Mr. Howell's where she will remain all night. After being in so much company I feel so lonely. Lilly's company would be very agreeable just now.[38]

New Providence, Tennessee, Tuesday, September 22, 1862

Handed over my dress to Cousin Lou this morning and took a bonnet in hand for her. Both have worked busily all day and still both jobs remain unfinished. At last we've something at least reliable although only a partial history of the 14th Tenn. Reg. — since the battle of Manassas the 28th, 29th, and 30th of August. The Jeffersonian sent out an Extra today. Mr. Edings was kind enough to bring the news from Virginia. And though the list is incomplete, he having to leave too soon after the battle, it is too full of names dear and familiar to us all to allow one moment's exultation over a victory so dearly bought. Under the head of "killed" comes first the Col of the Reg., Wm A Forbes.[39] Though not a personal acquaintance, his name will ever be held as sacred on account of its intimate association with the welfare of the South and with the history of many dear friends. Adjt. Hutchinson[40] and Maj King;[41] (Staff Officers) were wounded. Among the members of the Reg. under the heads of Killed and wounded, I recognized the names of many friends and acquaintances. Robinson Brown,[42] for one, killed; John Mallory and Tom Taylor severely wounded. Poor John, they say, has his thigh broken. His health is already so delicate that his recovery, I think, extremely doubtful. If he could only be at home and have the attention of friends and relatives, some hopes might be entertained, but as it is we are left only to fear the worst. The dreadful consequences of war! Each day but brings some more horrible pictures to our view, some new scene in which we see all that makes life pleasant snatched from our gaze and laid a sacrifice on the bleeding altar of our Country. From Manassas Mr. E says our Reg. was ordered to Maryland, where a severe struggle has been going on for some time.[43] And perhaps the next news will come accompanied with another list similar to the one received today. Already the Reg. is greatly reduced, and soon I fear all accounts of the noble 14th will be lost to us forever as prospects promises soon to bring the sad tidings of the sacrifice of the last of that heroic band. But will their names, their noble deeds, their death in the cause for which they have so long fought be forgotten? By a few, perhaps they may, but by many and particularly by those still claiming homes in their own loved Tennessee will their memory be cherished with a feeling nearest akin to idolatry — and second only to that adoration acknowledged by all as belonging to the Creator of the Universe. Our victory at Munfordville, Ky., has revived the drooping spirits of our citizens considerably. Report says we took 5000 prisoners, captured 7000 stands of arms, and 11 or 12 canon.[44]

New Providence, Tennessee, Sunday night, September 28, 1862

Wednesday: Cousin Lou and I finished off the dreaded job, Blanche's[45] bonnet. Mr. Homer came up that night, talked us to sleep. And too drowsy to write a line, I very readily concluded to dispense with my usual task. Thursday: Cousin Alley came from Clarksville and according to previous arrangements after dinner we went over to Mr. Frank Waller's.[46] I drove Gray in Mr. Homer's buggy, and though he's generally driven gently enough, I was far from feeling that ease that I always did while using Dick. Cousin A's horse backed that evening, and locking wheels with our buggy. A collision dreadful in its results was feared. But fortunately for us all, the fence stopped the backing of Gray and we escaped unhurt. We stayed all night and the next day [Friday] at Mrs. W's. Visited while there Dunbar's Cave,[47] and the Springs nearby, both places of considerable resort for many years past. Friday night we stayed at Mr. Dudley's.[48] In the rain yesterday [Saturday] we left for Mr. Whitefield's where we spent the day. Last night and today until after dinner we spent with Cousin Marion. From yesterday evening late Cousin A has been quite sick, seriously so. Came home, vomiting frequently on the way. Dr. Harrison called this evening and gave her some medicine which I hope will give some relief.

New Providence, Tennessee, Thursday night, October 2, 1862

Eugene and I have spent yesterday and today digging a pit for my geraniums and now that it is done it seems as fit a place for the dwelling of a hog or something on the same order as for hot-house plants. We made an awful "botch" of it. Cousin Alley, notwithstanding she spent such a dreadful night of it last night, was up and ready to be off for home this morning by 8 o'clock. Mr. Homer went with her. This evening late concluded I would walk down to Mrs. Pollard's to come up with Cousin Lou. What was my surprise just before entering the gate to see Cousin Nat Mills. More than two months ago he left home with the intention of with the 14th Reg. and though he told us not to look for him under two months we have been anxiously and impatiently looking forward to his return for more than a month. I saw him but a few minutes. He brought but little in the way of news, but something of considerable importance under a different head (to me all so important)— a letter from John. Though brief and written with a pencil and such a nervous hand, the superscription was his, the language was his, and in all was recognized that same kind loving feeling so characteristic of himself and his productions.

Between this and Dec. he says, being able to travel and nothing prevents, he intends getting a furlough permitting him to spend the winter at home. His thigh bone as we heard is entirely broken though the danger is not so great as we had supposed. A letter from Va. seems so like old times. This is the first from John and the second one I've received from Va. since the fall of Ft. Donelson in February. (Another attack by the Ft. D Yankees is greatly feared both by our citizens and the Clarksvillians. If they do attempt it we are ruined, for they say the next raid will not compare with the last. The destruction of both life and property will be so much greater.) On Sunday last a number of the wretches surround a church in which Uncle John Mallory was preaching down in Stewart Co;[49] and captured him with another preacher and all the gentlemen of the congregation, also buggies, horses, &c. The ladies after taking the oath[50] (this later may be untrue) were permitted to get home as best they could. Some families near them they have robbed both their food & clothing; not even a second suit is left them.

New Providence, Tennessee, Monday night, October 6, 1862

Was at Sunday-school yesterday morning and the school going down so rapidly is really distressing—just as everyone prophesied when Mr. Hirst left. Dr. H preached at 11 on the subject of death, 2nd Cor, 5 chap and 8th verse.[51] Today I've been engaged in mending up old stockings, a job quite new to me, more novel decidedly than interesting. I have taken time too to run round to several of the stores, but at every place the cry "just sold out" was heard. Mr. Glen from Clarksville has been over & bought out at wholesale every merchant in the place. He is buying for the South. Goods there they say cannot be had scarcely at any price. Coffee is selling for 4 and 5 dollars a pound; calico from 1.00 to 1.50 to 2.00 per yd, but the cotton is there, if not the machinery, and in a short while I hope the Southern people will be in possession of both and then farewell to Yankee goods, and Yankee tricks.

New Providence, Tennessee, Tuesday night, October 7, 1862

For once I feel as if I had nothing particularly to employ me, and still I have plenty to do too, as many as three bed quilts to quilt and other sewing necessary for myself. But these Yankee times we feel that clothing and everything else is liable to be taken from us at any time and there is nothing to encourage us in working or preparing for the future. Scarcely a day passes without a message reaching us that "the Yankees are coming." Mrs. Pendleton called today—the first time I've seen her since the death of Aunt Tabbie.

New Providence, Tennessee, Wednesday, October 8, 1862

Busy all morning most with my geranium slips; Mrs. Wilson was kind enough to give me a fine lot. This evening I fell back on my mats again. Miss F has been out at her mother's all day. The citizens of our town & the surrounding neighborhood are still in hourly expectation of the Yankees. The last reports say they are at Outlaw's Springs,[52] but some seem to think it is only a foraging party and will come no farther up. Mr. Pettus closed out his business today (dry goods) and Mr. Homer seems no little delighted at the idea of being free again. Already he has a fishing spree in view with one or more visits.

New Providence, Tennessee, Thursday night, October 9, 1862

Will the Yankees never cease troubling us? Last night between 1 and 2 o'clock a messenger came telling us they were but a few miles off. They had certainly been seen and would without a doubt be here in a very short while. The whole town in a short while was all excitement. A few before day packed

& sent to the country their bed clothing, wearing clothes, &c. As the Vandals have declared to destroy everything on their next trip, such precautions are not altogether useless. And as Uncle T would take nothing for Miss Fannie or I, we decided to hunt out if possible a secure place where we could at least store away a few of most valuables. No place could be thought of but where on some occasion we've heard of the searching, excepting up the chimneys. So as quietly as possible we went to work and in a short while my chimney was full, yes, running over almost with what I thought I cared most for. But on turning around, I found in everything most that met my gaze something that I valued as much or more than anything I had given the "old man living in the chimney." Here were my pictures (They always take a delight in breaking them), there a dress, and somewhere near a trinket valued above its real worth on account of some association. And so after all I concluded the "Yanks" might probably take pity on me and my scant possessions and I would not take the trouble of hunting up either chimney, leaving the consequences for chance and the "Yanks" to govern. My jewelry I have put in a long pocket of an old rapper, and if they do come, I intend dressing out in that with skirts underneath about 5 deep. My two tucked skirts, if they get at all, I'm determined they will have to tear them off. Miss Fannie is looking to the negroes for protection—a pretty pass we Americans[53] have come to. To one she has given her blankets, to another something else; just here and there where she finds one she can trust, she gives them up something, thinking out of all she may save a little. Rumors still came in this morning that they were very near until some of the citizens went down some distance to see for themselves and returned with the glad news that they were nowhere near nor had been excepting a few—about 30 who came up from Ft. Donelson on the road a piece to arrest one or two secessionists. And out of this has grown about 1 thousand reports as to their number, their intentions, &c.

New Providence, Tennessee, Friday night, October 10, 1862

Yesterday muslins and fans were in requisition. Today woolen wrappings and fires. And tonight, since the rain we're even chilly while sitting by the fire. Spent the day making a riding skirt and replacing dresses &c that were so carefully concealed night before last. The Yanks have not yet made their appearance.

New Providence, Tennessee, Saturday night, October 11, 1862

The weather continues very cool—fires with the doors closed have been exceedingly comfortable all day. Finished a black body[54] commenced yesterday and renewed the task of putting things to order so completely disordered the other night. We seldom get even "grapevine" news these days. I should like very well to hear something from our Army in Va. and Maryland.

New Providence, Tennessee, Tuesday night, October 14, 1862

Rose this morning determined to commence my quilted silk quilt. The frames were sent for and [with] the cash went up town myself and paid 30 cts a lb for cotton. And though I have been hard at work all the evening trying to finish the bats, they are yet to finish and the quilt to put in the frames. So not a stitch has yet been made notwithstanding my resolution [and] sure calculations. A "Journal" of the 9th brings news of another battle at Corinth[55] and of another retreat to Pittsburg Landing. Price[56] and Van Dorn[57] made the attack and as usual were successful. A fight in Ky is also reported between Bragg and I think Buell[58] (not certain however). The notorious Jim Jackson[59] at Hopkinsville, it is said, was killed during the engagement.

New Providence, Tennessee, Wednesday night, October 15, 1862

Hard at work on my quilt all day and only two hexagons have been finished. Jack Gold came by late walking and as my limbs were considerably cramped I concluded to join. We called by to see Mr. Magaren's flowers again, to see Mrs. Harrelson also. She gave us some beautiful geranium slips. Through an invitation from Jack, Mr. Gold, and "Uncle Kit," I went with them up to eat oysters. The oysters were fine but the richest treat was the meeting with a Mr. Kellogg,[60] a member of the 14th Reg. and of John's Co. For hours he has been entertaining us with stories of camp life, Soldiering, &c — from the most trivial little circumstance (such as making a pint of coffee of six grains) up to a ground fight at which the Yankees would be forced to run or something else equally as interesting occur, for instance their retreat at Romney.[61] He certainly is gifted with an excellent memory as well as with language to tell what he knows.

New Providence, Tennessee, Thursday night, October 16, 1862

My fingers are too sore to hold a pen with comfort, and of course to hold a needle must be a great deal worse; quilting is such hard work. Members of the 14th Reg. are coming rapidly. I've heard of as many as three or four today. Mr. Prichet[62] brings word that our wounded were all captured by the Yanks at Warrington,[63] John Mallory among the no, but thinks they will be paroled. Mr. Homer has just gotten back after an absence of three or four days and seems to me has been gone at least a week. He is in the smuggling business now to a small extent.

New Providence, Tennessee, Friday, October 17, 1862

So much of my time was idled away this morning with my flowers that the dreaded job was for a while almost forgotten. Mr. Whitefield and Mr. Homer were both in, giving me instructions as to raising slips. This evening Mr. H went up to Oak Grove, and since he left we've heard of Woodward's complete rout by the Yanks this morning, and that both the Federal and Southern troops were on or very near the road between the Grove and this place. He left so early, however, that I hope he managed to avoid them entirely. His contraband may yet pay him anything but money. Really, I'm at a loss to know which is giving us the most trouble — Woodward with his "Guerillas," as the Yanks call them, or the Lincolnites with their frequent raids. We are expecting them now almost hourly. They are pursuing Woodward (at least his men — they think he is prisoner or killed)[64] and no doubt they will be in Clarksville very soon. And as usual no limit will be to their plundering, searching, stealing, &c.

New Providence, Tennessee, Saturday night, October 18, 1862

The day has come and gone and the Yanks have not yet made their appearance. Woodward's men are camped not far from here while the "Fed's" they say have gone on to Hopkinsville. Mr. Homer came in about 3 "right side up with care" as poor Dr. Neblett used to say. He brought me such a handsome present and one that I've so long been wanting. How could I get along without "rebelling" these hard times were it not for Mr. H's thoughtfulness?

New Providence, Tennessee, Tuesday night, October 21, 1862

Sunday morning as usual I went to Sunday school and church, but very few of the scholars were present, only one in several of the classes. Dr. M preached on the subject of Charity. After dinner I read and tried to sleep a little, but making a poor out at both I concluded to walk down to Cousin Jane's. Mrs. Herring was there for a while but soon we had the time to ourselves, and after talking for some time, took a walk. Found some hickrenuts by the way, which Mr. Homer was kind enough to knock from the trees and the scarcity of them only added to their sweetness. Stayed all night. Had the pleasure through Mr. H's direct influence of sleeping between a pair of his new blankets. That night we had the first heavy frost and to say as little as possible they were not at all out of place. Came home early [Monday]. Quilted all day and last night went out and stayed with old Mrs. Pettus. They are all so kind and good out there. I would almost be willing to exchange homes. Here I'm one alone; not one on the place cares for my existing, and if the truth were known, my room is always preferable to my company. Will I ever have another home—one among friends as this used to be—is a question that so often forces itself.

New Providence, Tennessee, Wednesday night, October 22, 1862

Quilted all morning. Before dinner a while Mr. Homer came up, and from his description of a hicrenut tree seen this morning while hunting [on] Old Gray, I was induced to go and see for myself the prospect of getting a few hicrenuts. Cousin Jane, Inez, and Bobbie[65] went with us, and off of the tree I'm certain we gathered as many as two doz. They were too green to fall; at another place we gathered a good many. "Jeff Davis" gave us some news today in regard to the engagement between Buell & Bragg. Our victory is represented as very decided—18,000 prisoners, wounded, &c, with 40 pieces of artillery captured.[66]

New Providence, Tennessee, Thursday night, October 23, 1862

A little help on my quilt is very much appreciated: Mr. Homer drops in now and then and does a stitch or two and it always seems just in place. How long it would have taken me to have done the same. Cousin Nat dined with us today but I was too busy to talk to him much. This evening Mary Britton, Fannie came in and just as I was finishing off my task, so for once I was at leisure just at the right time. Before they left, several of the 49th Reg. passed, among the number Billie Mallory, Cousin Will, and others of my acquaintance. They, however, were the only ones that called. Through request, a kiss was given each or rather given at them. Their mustaches are so long that I'm sure it would take better eyes than mine to find their mouths. They in reality wear the appearance of prisoners of war, their persons so neglected and their appearance in every way so changed.[67] Cousin Will,[68] I really fear, has consumption.[69]

New Providence, Tennessee, Friday night, October 24, 1862

Seated myself to do a long day's work this morning, but before I had taken many stitches, Mr. Pollard came in and gave me an invitation to go hicrenut hunting with he and the girls, Mary and Fannie. (Miss Myers was along too.)

We went, spent the whole morning and returned altogether with something less than half bushel. We were poorly paid for the jostling ride in that old wagon over rough roads. But pleasure took the place of disappointment soon after getting home. For Efe Manson called just from the 14th, full of news and looking as well as I ever saw him. I was so glad to see him; he says he left John improving rapidly and will if nothing prevents be home soon. So many of the soldiers are coming in now I'm scarcely over the excitement of meeting with one before another comes in.

New Providence, Tennessee, Saturday night, October 25, 1862

Yesterday and last evening were so warm and pleasant that I decided once to let my slips remain out and take the dew, but then I thought perhaps the weather would change and in that event they would fare better protected a little. And fortunately for me I decided right at least once, for this morning before rising I felt the change. And after breakfast Mr. H, Inez, and I took a walk over to a hicrenut tree when I felt more severely the sharp wind. Really, I never felt much colder in December. Since dinner we've had both sleet and snow. The snow continued for several hours, and little are we prepared for so sudden a change. Only last week we had our first frost. Tommie Grinstead called this evening, looking like the very picture of hard times. He has recently entered service under Woodward and though his commander has played everything else lately but the General, he seems to have great confidence in him.

New Providence, Tennessee, Wednesday night, Oct 29,

News! Certain at last and not "Grapevine." Morgan with his forces are in Hopkinsville and are expected here soon.[70] Several of his men have already passed through and around the neighborhood. "The noted Rebel Chief" is so near us. How can we realize that such is the case and just when we need him most? How I hope he will make the Yanks skedaddle from Ft. Donelson.

New Providence, Tennessee, Thursday night, October 30, 1862

Early this morning Mr. H, Bettie, and I left for the country. Our object was to gather up something to eat. Fishing, however, was the principal thing in view, and as usual we met with—anything but fish. Failing in every attempt we turned our attention to hicrenut and apple gathering, in both of which we met with a decided success. The apples are very good and just the thing I wanted. Apples are a luxury to me the year round (peach season excepted). As a reward for my round, my feet and limbs are no little wearied and, of course, a good night's sleep is in anticipation.

New Providence, Tennessee, Friday night, October 31, 1862

Mrs. Jo Gold was down to see me this evening. She and Mr. G are visiting Ben's family. She dreads the Yankees I believe as much as anyone I've seen. They treated her so badly their last trip up from Ft. D it is not to be wondered at. The Southern troops are all fast retreating from Ky and soon no doubt Tenn. will be flooded with the Yankees. Several thousand it is said are in Bowling Green with their faces set toward Nashville. A battle is expected there soon,[71] and if we are unsuccessful, the story is told, we are doomed with our property to destruction.

New Providence, Tennessee, Sunday night, November 2, 1862

Mr. Garrett and I went fishing yesterday [Saturday] & I'm so tired of writing "went fishing today but came home without any" that I concluded to dispense with yesterday's record. This morning went to Sunday school but very few scholars were present, in consequence of which Dr. M gave both scholars and teachers a long lecture.

New Providence, Tennessee, Monday night, November 3, 1862

Commenced sewing early on my quilt but pieces soon gave out and I run up town to buy more. Called on the two Mrs. Rigginses and Mrs. Smith. Mary gave me a few scraps like her dress and with those my begging expedition ended (my fate always). This evening went down to Mr. Helm's. Met with Mrs. Magaren and two Mr. Blakemores. Nothing but war news can be talked of now; no other subject can come in even edgeways, and all seem to fear a return of the Yanks to Clarksville. If so large a force as we hear are going to Nashville, we may expect nothing else but for Tenn. to [be] occupied by them during the coming winter and of course be in their midst and subjected to everything that is fiend-like and revolting to a civilized people.

New Providence, Tennessee, Tuesday night, November 4, 1862

The weather is very pretty now — so pleasant. I make from one to three visits most every day. This evening paid Mrs. Pollard a good long visit, gave Mrs. Davis a call, and took tea with Jack Gold. She moves tomorrow to her new home. Mr. Baynham will occupy the house they leave. Cousin Will Trice was to see us this morning, his first visit since getting home. He had but little to say of prison life. What he did say, however, was more favorable than one might suppose. The Yanks are reported at Garrettsburg[72] today. Davis' company came through this morning — on a retreat I'm left to presume. Another report says Woodward has engaged them at Lafayette, but pshaw that's grapevine.

New Providence, Tennessee, Thursday night, November 6, 1862

Yesterday Uncle 'T' and Miss Fannie spent the day out at Mr. Osborne's. I was alone the greater part of the time and really, the day was so gloomy and everything wore such a woebegone look that my spirits were no little depressed. And notwithstanding a trip down to Mrs. Howard's with Cousin Will last night and today they have undergone but little change. A seriousness has taken hold of me — ominous I fear of something dreadful yet to come. On our way home we heard the Yanks from Ft. Donelson were but a few miles from us. Later this evening Soldiers have come in and report a fight between Woodward's men and the Yanks which commenced at Garrettsburg and was continued for several miles on the road leading this way. The Yanks are said to be now within seven miles of the place, having played destruction with W's cavalry from the commencement of the fight. One soldier reports that half of W's men have been killed, and we have but little reason to hope to the contrary when we think of the heavy cannonading that has been going on for several hours past. Oh, what have we to look forward to? What have we to hope for? Distress, destruction, and destitution are now almost at our doors and soon the worst will be realized. Sooner or later we will be compelled to share the fate of some of Virginia's and Missouri's downtrodden citizens and then indeed will we know something of the "horrors of war."

New Providence, Tennessee, Friday night, November 7, 1862

The weather continues very gloomy; a small snow fell this evening. Indoors all day. My quilt is growing rapidly; Mr. H was up today and says he admires it extensively. The fight between Woodward and the Yanks we've heard today was not half so bad as represented, though bad enough as it is. Last accounts the Yanks had gone to Hopkinsville; the Southerners had crossed the river and we all hope have gone south.

New Providence, Tennessee, Saturday night, November 8, 1862

Concluded to put away my quilt and rest for a day. So early I sent down for old Gray and went out to spend the day with Mrs. Britton and the girls. They had just commenced a soldier's coat and were up to their elbows in work. An invitation was soon given me to join them. Of course, as it was a soldier's coat, I could not refuse, and so when dinner came my shoulders were aching worse than if I'd been at home sewing on my quilt. My dinner though excellent was but little enjoyed. An excuse was at hand for coming home early. Bettie was at Mrs. Williams' and I had promised to go by for her. At 3 I left but not until the girls had given me some pieces for my quilt, which I appreciated no little. One of the Ft. D negroes came in today, George belonging to Mr. Pettus. They say he seems heartily tired of his trip and with permission will cling closer to home than ever. He also says Horace with many others that run away are anxious to come home but the Yanks will not allow it.

New Providence, Tennessee, Sunday night, November 9, 1862

Went down to Sunday school this morning but for once Dr. M was absent. His excuse was sickness. Miss Lelia came up home with me and we decided on going down to hear Mr. Taylor. He discoursed a little on the 1st Psalm, the Yankee excitement keeping him from preaching a regular sermon. Unexpectedly I went down home with Mrs. Magaren and Mollie Harrelson — took dinner and spent most of the evening. Mr. M took me around to see all of his flowers. He has two pits now filled with a very fine collection of flowers. Some of our citizens are again looking for the Yankees but all join in the hope that they will stay away.

New Providence, Tennessee, Wednesday night, November 12, 1862

At last we've a prospect of rain; the dust is so deep and the wheat is needing it so badly that both the farmer and merchant alike will welcome it. Sewed so constantly today that my shoulders are giving me particular hardship tonight. Laura is with me tonight. I'm so glad of her company since Mr. H has dispensed with his calls. Bed time comes entirely too soon and I sleep too much for comfort.

New Providence, Tennessee, Thursday night, November 13, 1862

Laura left early for school. Sewed steadily on my quilt until dinner; then walked down to Cousin Jane's. While there Mr. H brought in such a nice lot of birds; he and Mr. Helm had netted[73] them. Cousin Jane seems quite from home over at the "Mallory house."

New Providence, Tennessee, Friday night, November 14, 1862

Mr. Homer and Mr. Helm went out partridge netting today and I rode with Mr. H out as far as Mrs. Brunty's. Spent the day and not a stick of work did I have. Of course time could have passed a little more agreeably with something to keep my fingers employed. But after all, Mrs. B made herself very entertaining and I left more impressed with a sense of her true ladyship. She gave me some such nice pieces for my quilt that greatly exalted her in my estimation. Bettie & Laura Helm were up tonight. What a difference in the two. B is affection itself while [Laura] is one of nature's own daughters.

New Providence, Tennessee, Saturday night, November 15, 1862

It seems a week since yesterday—how drearily time passes now. To pass through a day without being so intensely interested in a piece of work as to be forgetful entirely of myself is almost a task. Yesterday and today I've had the "blues" too bad to talk about. But who could help it? Let me look where I will, something meets my gaze that tells me this was once my home, something that tells of "pleasures past," something that once formed a link in the chain of household treasures; yet with all these to look upon a piercing glance is sometimes given me that for the moment is heart breaking and tells but too plainly all is more welcome than myself. My presence I've every reason to believe is an annoyance and my room always preferable to my company. Under the circumstances who but me would even smile, much less enter into the hearty laugh so much enjoyed by a certain acquaintance of mine.

New Providence, Tennessee, Sunday night, November 16, 1862

Dr. M was well enough to be over this morning—Sunday school as usual. He preached at ½ 10 from 8th Romans 1st verse.[74] Both school and congregation were small. Mr. H dined and spent the evening with me. Some of my trials were talked over but little relief is felt from it.

New Providence, Tennessee, Thursday night, November 20, 1862

After a rainy morning yesterday the clouds cleared away and the evening was so pretty that I sent down for Bettie Helm and we walked out to old Mrs. Pettus' to spend the night. Met with Miss Nannie Davidson; Miss

Moder was as agreeable and laughable as usual, so of course time passed
more pleasantly than setting here at home alone. No company today excepting Archy Ferguson (Lieutenant I should say).[75] He has many wonderful stories to tell of his adventures with the Yankees. Went up to see
Mrs. Baynham this evening. Her children were dreadful I must say.

New Providence, Tennessee, Saturday night November 22, 1862

Soon after we left the breakfast table this morning Efe came in almost
breathless to tell us 'the Yankees are coming." Three hundred were already in Clarksville. "Better hide your things," "send your horse away,"
and such expressions were uttered almost in the same breath. Poor idiot,
his little money and what few confectioneries he has on hand give him
as much trouble as all of old Dr. Drane's wealth.[76] For once we heard
the truth. The Yanks were in town, but only about a hundred, and they
passed this evening on their way to Hopkinsville. Many suppose they
were the advance guard of the forces to be sent to Clarksville and that the
main body will be in tomorrow or perhaps earlier. A straggler belonging
to the company that passed this evening called at Mrs. Atkinson's gate.
Unable for a while to proceed farther on account of some wounds in his
head, caused he said by his officer striking him with his saber for getting
drunk, the very thing he himself had done yesterday. He gave the officer
a blessing over the left.[77] Mr. Wills and another gentleman offered their
assistance in guarding him out to where the other soldiers are but long
before this I guess. He is without gun, pistol, or any other weapon of
defense. Spent the evening with Mrs. Riggins. Alice had much to tell me
about the Yankee raid through her father's neighborhood.

New Providence, Tennessee, Tuesday night, November 25, 1862

Our school Sunday morning was reduced almost to the last extremity—
but one scholar in Dr. M's class and she had to take a teacher's place. The
prospect was so dull that preaching was dispensed with and we all had
an opportunity of going down to hear Mr. Taylor.[78] He preached from
the text "Oh taste and all how good the Lord is."[79] Mr. Homer dined
with us and after I had quarreled with him, as long as circumstances
would permit, about not bringing me some partridges. We walked down
to Cousin Jane's. Unexpectedly I stayed all night and until the next day
after dinner. Cousin J did have such a good dinner—broiled partridges,
baked sweet and Irish potatoes, broiled ham, etc., just the very thing my
appetite called for. She makes everything good she cooks. Mrs. Magaren

and Mollie Harrelson came home with me. Found Miss F had gone up to Mr. Grinstead's to stay until this evening. Returned with them and spent the night with Mrs. Harrelson. Mr. H was absent, and not a little uneasy did I feel just with Mrs. H and the girls. Mr. Homer and Laura Helm have been with me today. Miss [F] came about sunset. Woodward and his men have again made their appearance on this side the river well-armed with Enfield rifles,[80] but, pshaw, they'd better go south.

New Providence, Tennessee, Wednesday night, November 26, 1862

Have been busily sewing all day on a dress commenced yesterday. Took a walk late this evening with Mrs. Wilson. Called by to see her pit; her slips are doing finely. A continual battle has been kept upon the pike today by the soldiers. Some of Woodward's men almost certainly {*indecipherable*}.

New Providence, Tennessee, Thursday night, November 27, 1862

After spending another day working on the sleeves of my dress, they look somewhat to my liking. Mr. Homer went out to the country today and brought in some such good apples that I've been in a good humor ever since, notwithstanding my trials over the old dress sleeves. Laura brought me some very fine rose slips this evening from Mrs. Couts,[81] and after getting here I forced her to stay all night. With the addition of Mr. H's company, we've had a right lovely time—considering the war's going on.

New Providence, Tennessee, Friday night, November 28, 1862

Laura left early for school. After keeping such late hours last night we hardly expected to breakfast so early, but at the usual hour we were up and, with Miss Fannie and Uncle Trice, prepared for breakfast. (We talked until 12, notwithstanding we felt so drowsy about the time Mr. Homer left.) This morning Mr. H was up again. Brought me some such nice boxes for my slips. After chatting with him a while I put a pocket in my dress and with a few other additions near about made a finish of it. Old Mrs. Pettus dined with us. She and Miss [*Serepta did not write a name*] spent the evening with Mrs. Leonard. Mr. L was arrested last Monday by the Yankees and is expecting to be sent soon to Camp Chase[82] as prisoner. Mr. Wilson came over this evening and assisted me in setting out my slips. Ross Donaldson called before we had completed the job, but as it was his first call since his return from Va. and "the 14th," small matters were done away with and we "set ourselves up" to hear the latest from friends absent. He was too hoarse to talk much but still a little piece of news now [and] then just fitted in, and he left us feeling a little more decided.[83]

New Providence, Tennessee, Saturday night, November 29, 1862

Cut the lining out for a cape to my dress this morning but concluded these hard times the piece would be more serviceable in another pair of sleeves. So I went to work on my net but soon concluded to go down and see Mrs. Edwards and Mrs. Pollard. And after getting there, concluded again to spend the day. Mrs. E and Mr. Edwards left for home about 2. Later in the evening Mary Boston[84] came in and from her we learned the Yanks were in Clarksville. How many no one seems to know. On my way home two of them passed me. A part of Bruce's[85] command has been expected there to spend the winter.

New Providence, Tennessee, Sunday night, November 30, 1862

The morning was so unfavorable that few of the children were out at school although this was the day set apart to preach to them particularly. So many being absent Dr. M decided that probably next Sunday would be better and so preached to the "grown folks" on the subject of Christ as an example for us. During the first prayer a crowd of Yankee soldiers passed, variously estimated at from 300 to 1,000. I was not a little uneasy for fear that Dr. M as is customary would send up a petition for the Confederacy. But for once he did not. Two acquaintances of mine—ministers of the gospel— were thrown into the prison for such an offense not long since, and while there one of them took such a deep cold that he has since died & we've heard the other has also. So we find those they do not instantly kill are almost as certain of death.

New Providence, Tennessee, Wednesday night, December 3, 1862

While I finished off my cape this morning, some old magazines were brought out for Mary, and I might have known not another word would she speak (without accident) until every story had been read. But for- tunately for once an accident occurred. Mr. Homer came along about dinner and we determined after dinner to go with him netting. We went, saw only one drove of birds, didn't catch one of them. At our return, Mary and I on old Gray, both had a nice fall backwards. We were so glad Mr. H was not near enough to see it. I know he would have teased us a week. My head aches too badly to write another line but I must say Mr.

Barbee was married to his fourth wife[86] this evening, sister to his last wife. Efe says "there is one more Fields girl left and she'll be his next second wife."

New Providence, Tennessee, Thursday night, December 4, 1862

At home alone all morning. Though busy with my net, took time to go in and see the cooking of a partridge pie. As is usual, Miss Fannie thought I used the butter too extravagantly. Inez, unasked for, told me what she said, while I saw for myself actions that went to prove her displeasure. Was ever such stinginess known? For I can call it by no other name. What else can it be called when during each week she makes from one to two lbs. more than is used? At least she sells near about that much, for this I know and, of course, if she sells it, more a good deal is used than is required for the use of the family. The idea of a lady with a husband to supply each and every want and with an income independent of his assistance to stoop to anything so little. In how many instances daily and almost hourly am I forced to compare Aunt Tabbie's goodness and kindness to me with the strict and parsimonious dealings of others? Spent the evening at Mrs. Davis' and Mrs. Pettus'. Met with Jimmie Donaldson,[87] an exchanged prisoner, at Mrs. D's; he is looking badly from {*indecipherable*}.

New Providence, Tennessee, Friday night, December 5, 1862

The snow commenced falling this morning about day and continued until near 12. It is now so deep that sleigh riding would be excellent, splendid. How I wish some kind out-of-the-friend would offer a seat; really, it would be a treat—better than partridge netting or a ride on old Gray. Spent the morning reading Anna Clayton,[88] a book kindly lent me by Mrs. Baynham. She is so very kind in offering me of her books. This evening I spent with her and she gave me access to her library with the privilege of selecting any book that I chose to read. The first series of "Grace Greenwood Leaves"[89] was the one I chose, and I'm so delighted with it. Since tea I've done nothing but read it. Mrs. Gregg Baynham[90] is visiting Mrs. B now and really, she's the greatest curiosity in her manners that I've met with for many a day, so perfectly childlike in all ways and yet the mother of two children and only 19 years of age.

New Providence, Tennessee, Monday night, December 8, 1862

Mary left early this morning. After some deliberation as to what kind of work should be brought out I decided on commencing a gown—quite a task these days of "jobbing" and patchwork. After dinner the snow having nearly all melted off my pit I went out to see about my flowers, and what a sight they presented. Not one of them but was froze stiff and limber. The dirt hard as rocks; the geranium leaves limber as rags. I took it on myself after watering them with warm water if not hot to go down and ask Mr. Magaren, the flower doctor, if no remedy could be applied. "Without exposing them to the light, water them with ice cold water and keep them for some time in the dark" was all that he thought would save them. And now what will become of them? The sun has shone on them, the water with which they were sprinkled was warm, and everything done for them but the right. Oh, if I only had a nice pit. "Greenwood Leaves" have failed to interest me since my geraniums look so droopy and forsaken.

New Providence, Tennessee, Thursday night, December 11, 1862

Tonight a week ago Mrs. Tom Pettus[91] was taken very suddenly with severe pain in side & head. The Dr. was sent for and immediately pronounced her disease pneumonia. She has been growing alarmingly worse ever since. Yesterday I spent the day with her. So many were calling that the Drs thought it to her disadvantage so I came home — at least started. But called at Mrs. Pollard's and there concluded to tarry for the night. Mary, Fannie, and I all slept together. I told this morning that I had to sleep so straight it gave me the backache and so it did without jesting. For these cold nights when sleeping alone I draw up in a knot. And my spine, of course, is always in a curved position. No wonder it aches when straightened. This evening I went down to see Cousin Jane, Jack Gold, and not neglected were the sweet gum trees. Mary Britton came and Miss F sent for me. She went down to sit up with Mrs. Pettus. Woodward has disbanded.[92] Who ever heard of such?

New Providence, Tennessee, Sunday night December 14, 1862

Finished off two or three unfinished jobs yesterday morning, and about 3 in the evening Miss Meda Pettus came along. And with a little persuasion I soon decided to go out & spend the night with she and Miss Nannie. Miss N I find a better day companion at least more agreeable during the day than at night. In a word she proved a little selfish last night I thought in not wanting my feet to sleep with hers. However, the night was not very cold and of course the disappointment was not very great. This morning we walked up to see Mrs. Brunty; found her very ill. Miss N as well as myself enjoyed the walk extensively. Mine continued down home but only with Harriet as a companion. Uncle T had but little news. Morgan's exploits are still talked of with much "interest; his capture of 3 Regiments near Hartsville[93] the other day has created no little excitement. The Northern papers allude to the affair as "another disgrace to our Army." At home all evening, honored with a visit from Mr. Homer. He is still present and I'm doing him the honor of writing in his presence.

New Providence, Tennessee, Monday night, December 15, 1862

The rain has fallen in torrents nearly the whole day; notwithstanding Mr. Homer spent nearly half of it on the pond side catching minnows to go fishing tonight. Certainly he is a very imprudent man. Uncle Trice brought us in some papers today, but very little of interest was contained in the telegraphic column. Rather an interesting incident was related to me the other day of John Morgan while passing through Christian Co., Ky.[94] It is said he called at a Union man's house and in the disguise of a Federal soldier made himself so very agreeable that comfortable quarters were offered him for a whole night. (John Morgan and a feather bed, could two things be more suggestive of things directly opposite?) During the evening Morgan managed to introduce the "celebrated Rebel Chief" by referring to some of his late exploits, and of course advocates in favor of his course were few. One young lady, however, daughter of the gentleman with whom he was spending the night, ventured her opinion and boldly declared her approval and worthily defended the course hitherto pursued by the "noted horse thief." He drew her out at the same time. From the depth of her argument drawing himself to the conclusion that the beauty of her person was only excelled by the beauty of her mind. Very gravely next morning he bade her prepare for Camp Chase as she might consider herself his prisoner, the offense being of a character highly deserving punishment. He said, as she looked up at him with surprise and tears gathering in her eyes, he thought he never beheld a more lovely object in his life. He then revealed himself the very man whose cause she had so nobly defended and making her a present of all her father's fine horses which he had intended pressing. He made his exit leaving her with the rest of the family rejoicing in the fortunate escape.

New Providence, Tennessee, Tuesday night, December 16, 1862

Went up first thing this morning to see Mrs. Trabue, but as she and Mrs. Atkinson were going out to the country I soon returned promising to call after tea. I have just gotten back. Mrs. T. laughed no little about the whipping she gave the toll gate man today. She says he attempted to take hold of her bridle and she actually gave him several hits with the whip.

New Providence, Tennessee, Wednesday night, December 17, 1862

My shoulders ache so from sewing all day that I should not have taken up this old book. But neglecting to record a very important item last night, I will improve the present opportunity. Mr. John Helm and Miss Rebecca Buck were married yesterday,[95] so the Helm girls told me. It may be false. I've yet to see them to hear "the straight of it." The "Grand Army of the Potomac" has met with another grand failure[96] if we are to believe the reports published by the Northerners themselves."

New Providence, Tennessee, Thursday night, December 18, 1862

Late went up to see Mrs. Baynham. She got home from Louisville about 8 last night. Calico is selling now for 25 cts. Soon I know it will be 1.00 here. Laura is with me tonight. She was an eyewitness to the marriage of her Uncle John. Miss R., she says, turned pale, turned red, and of course spotted.

New Providence, Tennessee, Saturday night, December 20, 1862

Commenced another net for the hair this morning; worked steadily on it all morning. Mrs. Wilson sent for me after dinner; spent the greater part of the evening with her. Found Mr. Homer here on my return; he had considerable to tell us of the Yankees and their capers over in Clarksville this morning: they arrested 3 or 4 soldiers over there. Young Ritter is said to be at the head of the band; they grossly insulted several of our citizens as they passed today.

New Providence, Tennessee, Sunday night, December 21, 1862

Our school is still on the decline. Notwithstanding the pretty morning, but very few of the children were out & nearly all of the teachers were absent. Dr. M preached from the text, "For there is no other name given whereby man can be saved &c." Ross Donaldson came home with me after dinner. We went down and spent the remainder of the day with Cousin Jane. Mr. Homer happened to get into one of his old moods and destroyed to a great extent the pleasure of the evening. Made a remark that wounded Cousin J's feelings. The result of which was a long cry and not another word from her. I regretted so much Mr. H's thoughtlessness. Great joy in our family—Mr. Gregg brought in Uncle T's mules today; so much for having a good Union friend. Horace, he said, seemed to have no notion of coming home and was very much opposed to separating with the mules.

New Providence, Tennessee, Monday night, December 22, 1862

Commenced a watch pocket as a gift for someone this morning, but made an admirable failure. Mrs. Harrelson and Mary spent the morning with me. Mr. Homer brought in a Southern newspaper; when did such a wonder appear before. He was over in Clarksville this evening when a company of Yankees went in. As usual they sent in before them what they call "the Butternut."[97] A man, however, is he nothing more dressed in Southern uniform, brown. Just in advance of the company he rushes in, pretends that he's being pursued by the Yanks, inquires for someone whom he knows to have been in the Southern service and if a "Greeny" happens to be present he's immediately conducted to the one, the very one, inquired for. And that moment he lays eyes on him, he grabs him and claims him as a prisoner. This trick they've been playing off frequently since Woodward's Reg. disbanded and so many of the soldiers have been in and around Clarksville. But this evening two of W's men were up to them. When the "Butternut" came in, they walked up and claimed the right of protecting him. Of course if he was a "rebel running from the Yankees," they thought it brotherly to conduct him to some safe place. But he hesitated a little at first, and one of them presented a pistol and so urged his solicitation that the Yankee in Rebel disguise was compelled to obey. And without another word accompanied them across the river. Not a little chagrined was the company when they entered and found Butternut missing. Some say he returned late this evening "flooded with tears" as a certain friend would say. Others suppose that he met with a spy's fate. One thing is certain—the Yanks threatened to burn Clarksville on the strength of it.[98]

New Providence, Tennessee, Tuesday night, December 23, 1862

Went out to old Mrs. Pettus this morning early; spent the day. Miss Nannie is still out there; had quite an agreeable time with her. Miss Meda was busy making cake for Christmas, the only preparation I've seen making for Christmas at all. Miss M and I employed ourselves in making watch cases. I crocheted two, called at the store this morning and supplied myself with cruel.

New Providence, Tennessee, Wednesday night, December 24, 1862

Went to work to finish off a pair of gloves for little Marion this morning before breakfast. Worked on them until about 9 when I went in to assist Miss
Fannie about making some cakes. Belle Dunn came in about ½ 10 and again
my seat was taken. Miss F was too deeply engaged to let go all of a sudden.
She left before dinner. The cake turned out admirably. This evening finished
off some little Christmas presents. Mr. Homer is up tonight, slightly touching on the subject of matrimony. I wonder if he has thought about how time
passed with him about this time last Christmas Eve.

New Providence, Tennessee, Saturday night January 3, 1863

Christmas morning [**Thursday, 25th**] according to custom we were up a
little earlier than usual. Miss Fannie made an egg nog. Mr. Homer concluded to accept the invitation offered the night before and was up bright
& early. "Felt badly; thought something stimulating would improve him."
Greatly to my surprise "Kris Kringle" or some of his agents left in baskets &
other places for me several presents. In Inez's basket was a toy tureen, in Mr.
Homer's overcoat pocket was a nice pair slippers and pair of kid gloves, and
Miss Fannie in return for my pitiful pretense of a present sent in a nice calico
dress. I could scarcely believe my own eyes. That evening Fannie Britton
came by for me, and notwithstanding Clarksville was full of Yankees and
pickets out at the toll gate, (all of whom by the way made their appearance
that day), she would have me go out home with her. The next day [**Friday,
26th**] according to the program we were to take a horse back trip up to old
Mr. Len Johnson's;[99] but wind and weather preventing, we contented ourselves with reading, talking, laughing, and other indoor amusements, thinking maybe fortune would favor us next day. But [**Saturday [27th]** came and
still as Fannie would say no "boo sky" could be seen, while the rain fell in
torrents until about 12, thus too late for us to start. We determined on a ride,
however, and off we put for Mr. Mills'. Cousin Mary not being home, we
rode down and paid Tom Long a short visit. Found Cousin Mary with her.
We sit only a few moments, but those few should have been passed on the
road for we were very late getting home. Next day [**Sunday 28th**] through
persuasion Fannie & I came down home that I might get a fresh supply of
clothing, still determined to pay our visit to Mr. Johnson's. We talked such
good Union talk to the pickets that we were permitted to pass and repass
without the trouble of getting papers. Mrs. Pollard went out home with us
that evening. Next day everything being favorable we went up to Mr. J's.

To our regret found Inez Ogburn and Jane Johnson[100] both from home. We soon knew our fate, to sit up like wall flowers all day now and then laughing to ourselves at some drollery of Mrs. Duncan or at some of old Mrs. J's eccentric ways. Dinner was scarcely over with when we ordered our horses, but Fannie must spoil the day's monotony by falling from her horse just as we were starting, injuring herself considerably. Her saddle turned and backwards she fell, nearly bursting her head. As soon as she recovered sufficiently from the shock we made a second start, which was not interrupted until we found ourselves safely at Mrs. Britton's. The trip had been made and I for one was not sorry of it. The next day [**Tuesday 30th**] Mr. Ike Howard spent with us. With none do I think the day passed so agreeably as with Mary. The next day [**Wednesday 31st**] Mrs. Collins and Jones spent with us. Mary and I went home with them leaving Mrs. Pollard quite ill. We spent the night & next day, and a very pleasant visit it proved. The girls are so interesting. In the evening [**Thursday, January 1st**] we separated. Mary went home; I over to Uncle Wm Mallory's. Cousin Nat, Uncle Wm, and all are living together now. Mr. Homer came in soon after I got there. Had been out hunting. He has spent the week out there. Yesterday [**2nd**] Cousin Mollie & I went up to Garrettsburg, that long heard of city. We went up shopping but found nothing we went for, excepting a pair of boots for Bobbie. This evening I intended going over to see Jennie Mallory but the rain prevented. Came home after dinner.

New Providence, Tennessee, Monday night January 5, 1863

No Sunday school, no service yesterday, so much for the presence of the Yankees. Read all morning; spent the evening & night with Cousin Jane. Florence & I carried Bettie out to school this morning. Not having a pass, the pickets turned us back. Another road not guarded was taken and we made the trip. Dined with Mrs. Pettus & Miss Meda. Went over this evening to see Mrs. Wilson.

New Providence, Tennessee, Tuesday night January 6, 1863

Commenced Mr. Homer a pair of gloves this morning. Have knit steadily all day on one and it is yet unfinished. Mr. H, being out of employment, spent half the day with us. He read for me two or three chapters in "Miriam," Marion Harland's last novel[101] dedicated to "George D Prentis,"[102] one of Ky.'s "noblest sons." A good many seem to dislike the work on this account. They forgot how short a time has elapsed since they would have thought a work dedicated to him would have been a sufficient recommendation and devoured its contents the first opportunity. Went down to Mrs. Pollard's this evening. Mr. P has seen a paper of the Gov. in which Lincoln specifies in which of the Southern States his proclamation shall be carried into effect.[103] The fight which has been going on for the last 6 days between Nashville and Murfreesboro is still going on. The loss it is said on both sides amounts up to this time to 50,000. Rosencrantz [at] last accounts was in sight of Murfreesboro, the stronghold of the Confederates.[104] Morgan's tearing up the Louisville RR and cutting off supplies from Nashville[105] seems to have enlarged the combative organ of some of the Yanks. I made Fannie come up home with me this evening and I know she thinks I'm writing unnecessarily long.

New Providence, Tennessee, Wednesday night, January 7, 1863

After breakfast Fannie and I walked up town; we parted at the gate on our return. Miss Nannie and Miss Meda called soon after and I promised to spend the evening with them at Mrs. Pettus'. For once my promise was kept, and the evening would have passed very pleasantly indeed but for the presence of that old long faced Mrs. Kirby. Mr. P leaves for Louisville tomorrow. His business is to get the money for flour sold to the Federal Government, rather a strange errand for a man with two sons in the Confederate army and professing strong Southern sentiments himself. Knowingly he has sold flour which will go [to] the support of an army now invading his own country and one against which his own sons have taken up arms. Surely man is a strange bundle of contradictions.

New Providence, Tennessee, Saturday night, January 10, 1863

Thursday I commenced a calico dress, but my patience soon gave way because of its not fitting, and I threw it by, vowing I would not pick it up until in a better humor. I walked down to Mrs. Magaren's. Found Laura Helm and Mrs. M. enjoying a social chat. Mr. M being absent I was persuaded to stay all night. Next morning L came home with me. In the evening she, Bettie and Mary Harrelson, and I walked down to Mr. Smith's thinking we might possibly see a gunboat, that great curiosity to all not too strongly "secesh" in their views to look at an object so "Yankish." To our disappointment a boat of no description passed either up or down. Inez told me after getting home that Mary & Fannie Britton had sent for me to go down & stay with them at Mr. Pollard's. Unhesitatingly, I went. Mary had a great deal to tell me about the party up at Mr. Johnson's. My invitation came too late or I should have been there. Without a doubt busy all day today sewing on my dress. The fight between Bragg and Rosecrans is supposed to have been decided and in favor of the Southerners. The fact of Bruce's being ordered from Clarksville and Rousseau's[106] coming to take his place has a tendency to lead us to that conclusion. It will certainly be a retrograde move if so important a general as Rousseau falls back to Clarksville. We've had no papers since the 4th. In papers of that date a minute account of the fight was given up to New Year's day. The Federals have lost a great many officers, two or three Gen's among the number. Gen. Sill's death[107] seems to be greatly regretted.

New Providence Tennessee, January 11, 1863

What a beautiful day this has been, so clear, so calm, so Sabbath-like indeed as far as the beauty & stillness of a day will suggest, but our churches have presented quite a different appearance. Not a sermon has been preached at either of the churches since the Yanks took possession of Clarksville. 27 foraging wagons passed through today and it is said all of them loaded at Dr. Thomas'. He'll thunder down his curses on someone else now I guess rather than on Woodward.

New Providence Tennessee, January 12, 1863

Busy sewing on my dress all day and after all my trouble it doesn't fit. The red cord is quite becoming and the yoke would have fitted elegantly if it had been cut a little smaller; however, it is cut after the "Confederate fashion" and will have to do.

New Providence, Tennessee, Tuesday night, January 13, 1863

Left home very soon after breakfast; went down to Mr. Helm's. The morning was too cloudy & windy to think of going fishing. Bettie and I went up to see Ann Ogden. Found she and Jack both absent. Through an invitation from Mr. H we called in at Cousin Jane's. He helped us to some fine hickory nuts. We ate very heartily, made our "bow," & left. Called a few moments to see little Sarah Jackson;[108] she is still quite ill with scarlet fever. I had forgotten to say on our way up to Mr. Gold's we met three elegantly dressed Federal officers. One of them we supposed to be Col. Bruce himself. He made a very low bow with a loud "good morning ladies" as we passed, but neither of us spoke. We Southerners consider an animal dressed up in a Lincoln uniform calling himself a man unworthy of being spoken to. Though the

"Providentials" have not gone so far as to turn their noses up as they passed as some of the ladies of the more southern cities do. Even in Clarksville they cross the street frequently to keep from meeting with them. After dining heartily at Mr. Helm's on wild goose & blackberry rool & other good things, Mrs. Magaren, Laura, Bettie, & I walked down to Mrs. Harrelson's. We nearly met all Providence there. We said our say & left early. Laura came home with me. We've had quite an interesting time since tea talking over our early love scrapes &c &c.

New Providence, Tennessee, Wednesday night, January 14, 1863

Such an unceasing rain as we have; but 5 minutes hardly has it ceased today. Laura was compelled to spend the day but left late through rain and mud up to her ankles almost. Shackleford's cavalry[109] passed through this evening on their way to Clarksville. Bruce is smartly scored up. Wheeler's' cavalry captured 8 of the Federals' transports the other day as they were attempting to pass Harpeth's Shoals.[110] Robbed them of all that was valuable. Then burned the boats and sunk the gun boat that was along as a protection (so the story goes), and unconditional surrender was made of everything—officers, commissary stores, & everything.

New Providence, Tennessee, Thursday night, January 15, 1863

The snow has fallen as unceasingly today as the rain yesterday. I thought this morning when I first peeped out that such a snow had not fallen for many years. It seemed so deep and in reality, was as deep as any we had had for several years, but tonight I think I may be safe in prophesying that this snow will long be referred to as "the deep snow." Not five minutes I'm certain has it ceased falling today. Read a while in some of Mr. H's interesting books this morning. Spent the remainder of the day altering an old gown. The "Yanks" have planted 6 canon on the fort this side of the river and declare they will shell Clarksville if taken by the Southerners.[111]

New Providence, Tennessee, Friday night, January 16, 1863

This morning the prospect was promising for another snowy day, but it soon ceased and has continued to fall only by spells. Mr. Homer spent the morning with me and promised to come up again this evening & bring me a bird trap,[112] but as usual a disappointment came in in the place of the trap. The Yanks are still looking for the "Rebels." Several canon have been fired over on the opposite side of the river.

New Providence, Tennessee, Saturday night, January 17, 1863

The weather continues very cold though the clouds have mostly disappeared, but neither rain or snow is looked for several days. Finished off my gown today and read several of Grace Greenwood's letters.

New Providence, Tennessee, Tuesday night, January 20, 1863

Another constant day's rain. The snow will soon have all disappeared. Indoors all day piecing my worsted quilt. Did venture out a few moments to see about my flowers. Found them unexpectedly untouched by the freeze. Took some of the geraniums up and brought them in the house. Mrs. Baynham was down [a] few minutes late; she had considerable to tell me of her trip over to Col. Bruce's headquarters this evening — 500 lbs of meat she had sold to Gregg Baynham was pressed by a drunken officer while being weighed today and she was sent for to prove that it was his meat & that she sold it to him. The same officer arrested several other citizens & ordered them over. Col B. learning the true state of the case permitted them to return without taking the oath. In reality I'm convinced that Miss Fannie has just encountered her first heart trouble since her marriage. I've not heard her speak today except when spoken to.

New Providence, Tennessee, Thursday night, January 22, 1863

Sewed busily on my quilt until yesterday 3 o'clock. Walked up to see Mrs. Baynham & Miss Bettie B—met with Mrs. Grigg B—also. She's just as childish as ever. I had not been in the house half an hour before she was in for a romp and notwithstanding my hair before going up had cost me no little trouble in trying to arrange it. It seems to me after taking off net, comb, and everything belonging thereto, that she tried to see if it really [was attached] to the skin and, like the most of people's, would hurt from jerking. Went from Mrs. B's down to Mrs. Staton's to sit up with the corpse of little Norah.[113] She died about 11 yesterday. Though the most of the young ladies round town were present, the amusing stories told of old Mrs. Sisco would become uninteresting ever now & then. And despite our efforts to the contrary, the broad grin would give place to the yawn and sleepy gape. I came home at 12, not having any way of going over to the burial. Everything looked so lonely. Although Miss Fannie had resumed her happy appearance and perfect contentedness, I could not stand the dull prospect so I jerked up my bonnet & walked over to Mrs. Wilson's. Spent the entire evening.

Supped dinner with them. She had a fine turkey & elegant fritters. Met with Mrs. Pollard.

New Providence, Tennessee, Sunday night, January 25, 1863

Read all morning & [a] while after dinner; then walked down to Mr. Helm's and from there the girls and I, with the addition of Mollie Harrelson & Mr. Homer's company, walked down to the fort. We expected to see one or two gun boats but were disappointed; 15 or 20 transports were up at Clarksville, a considerable number to be landed there at once. Mr. H would have us to come by with him to get some water and hickrenuts. Mrs. West was buried today. She has been very low for weeks with typhoid fever.

New Providence, Tennessee, Wednesday night, January 28, 1863

The morning was so very cold that Bettie and I concluded still to postpone our visit out to Mrs. Pettus. She left for home about 10. Mr. Homer has been in the greater part of the day. If the war continues much longer he will have become so loferized that business habits I guess will be resumed with some little reluctance. Went up to see Mrs. Baynham few moments this evening. She says that report says that a party was to be given to the negroes tonight at the Ware house by the Yankees. And that the object she thought was to collect as many as possible and send them off on some boat appointed for the purpose, thereby carrying out "Old Abe's" proclamation to the letter. Officers under Bruce are going round & pressing negroes wherever they find them pretending that they want them to work on the fortifications. But the citizens say that no less than a hundred were sent off last night in the direction of Ft. Donelson, and when once they are there goodbye to them. Many believe that it is a move for the sole purpose of carrying out old Abe's proclamation and I should not be surprised if such indeed were the case.

New Providence, Tennessee, Thursday night, January 29, 1863

At last Bettie Helm and I have made our visit out to Mrs. Pettus. The morning was clear though rather cool. So Mr. H thought as clear mornings were not all way convenient we had better make use of the opportunity and very early brought the buggy up for us. Miss Nannie is still out there. The day passed very agreeably. But for my haste to finish Mrs. Harrelson's net it would no doubt passed still more agreeably. On my return found Cousin Lou here. Really, it seems like old times to hear her blustering around. Her abuse of the Yankees is unlimited. She says she wishes them everyone at the devil and that every true Southerner at heart agrees with her. Col. Bruce continues to send out his forage wagons; the country for miles around is being stripped of everything eatable either for man or beast. Some of the poorest of families are left almost without a sufficiency for the next month, much less during the coming year.

New Providence, Tennessee, Sunday, February 1, 1863

After no little confusion in getting up my chickens for "old Charlie" to sell yesterday morning, Cousin Lou and I through Mr. H's kindness got started off to Mrs. Britton's. Were until 11 getting there but not too late to share a mighty good dinner such as Mrs. B always has. We stayed until this evening. Left Fannie mad, the jokes Cousin Lou run her with were most too severe. Mary's about the same, too good & sweet to care for jokes or anything else. My chickens brought me 9.00. What a sum—enough to buy me two pair of good winter shoes. My head aches too bad to write.

New Providence, Tennessee, Tuesday night, February 3, 1863

The weather is very cold; within the last two months we've had more cold weather than we had all together last winter & the winter before. Have been busy with my quilt all day. Did take time too to run to the window to see all the bridal company as they passed out. Miss Ada Kelly & a Mr. Hirch[114] were, I believe, the most important of the party. I wonder if a magistrate married them? The minister from Clarksville can't come over without taking the oath, and that they say it is not according to gospel. The Southerners, report says, are still concentrating in large numbers on the opposite side of the river. The "Yanks" are expecting an attack on Clarksville almost hourly.

New Providence, Tennessee, Thursday night, February 5, 1863

About 3 yesterday evening Mary Britton came in. I was not sorry of an excuse to put away my sewing, and very soon a walk was proposed, which was equally as agreeable. Our walk extended as far as the drug store, and on our return we called at the pond where Uncle Trice with several hands were hooking out ice to put up.[115] We helped ourselves bountifully to some very clear, nice looking pieces, notwithstanding the warning so often given by mothers and seigniors[116] generally. Mr. Homer was with us and, unexpectedly to me, didn't say a single time "don't eat it, it will be sure to make you sick." This winter we've had the first ice season for two or three winters in succession. Another heavy snow has fallen. Went down home with Mary last night and was compelled to wade through snow to get home, nearly ankle deep. At least twenty rumors have been afloat within the last 48 hours relative to the late attack of the Southerners on Ft. Donelson.[117] Some really believe that Forrest with Wheeler & others have captured it while the "Yanks" say that 8 gun boats came up and so completely rousted the "Rebels" that they retreated almost simultaneous with the attack. One thing is sure: Col. Bruce nor his command either are entirely at ease. He has moved ever so many of his troops over to the fort this side of the river, and rapid preparation is being made in case the "Rebels" do hold Ft. D and come on up to take Clarksville as the Yanks did.

New Providence, Tennessee, Friday night, February 6, 1863

The ground is still covered with snow though the sun shone out very prettily for a while today. The citizens are still gathering ice. Uncle Trice made a finish today about 11. Eating ice & snow together gave me the toothache so that it seems to me I didn't sleep two hours last night. Mr. H treated me to a lb of candy this evening and that, added to another lump of snow this evening, is enough to set my tooth again. And what will I do? The pain is so severe.

New Providence, Tennessee, Saturday night, February 7, 1863

Sure enough my tooth gave me particular trouble again last night, though it was not as bad as night before last. Through Uncle Trice's advice this morning, I decided to go over to Clarksville this evening & have it extracted. Went up before dinner & made arrangement with Bettie Baynham to go over with me. Mr. Baynham being one of the "loyal citizens," we made use of his "family pass" & so had but little trouble with the pickets. Mary Britton was here when I came back from Mrs. B's so we all concluded under the favorable circumstances (passes to Clarksville are something rare to we poor Rebels) to make use of the opportunity & so crowded into one buggy. Dr. Castney being absent, we went round to Dr. Acree's & I must do him the credit to say I never had a tooth drawn attended with less pain.

New Providence, Tennessee, Monday night, February 16, 1863

Yesterday week ago [Sunday, February 8] Mary Britton called in about 12 o'clock; and without allowing of an excuse of any kind bade me bundle up my duds & go out home with her. I had been in an unusually blue way ever since she had left me early in the morning. (And why my case is not chronic is strange to me. I've enough just such cases as I had that morning) Mr. Homer had called in to spend the evening with me and I had calculated through him to find something in the shape of relief. At least he generally makes an effort of the kind when I lay before him some of my most serious troubles. But Mary would listen to nothing, so I went out with her and during the ride scarcely a topic was introduced or continued beyond a reply to some question directly asked by her. The next day [**Monday, February 9**] we would have gone to Garrettsburg but for the appearance of rain. Mr. H called [a] few moments on his way to Wm'stown. [**Tuesday, February 10**] We did go to Garrettsburg shopping. We found but few goods, though those few were what we call cheap nowadays. Calico was only 30 cts while the merchants here sell it for 50 cts. I bought a very nice pair of Balmoral[118] shoes for 3.50 for which I would have given 4.50 here. My bill amounted to 13.00. Independent of the shoes I've scarcely anything to show for it. We bought for Mrs. Britton a sack of coffee, 174 lbs, for which she paid 80 or 90 dollars. Sugar we paid 50 cts for — very cheap. After our trip there, the week we passed mostly indoors. Went over one evening to see Tom Long, & one evening Mr. H called by & we went partridge netting with him. As usual when Mary and I are along, we had no success. Mrs. Pollard came out [**Saturday February 14 morning, & Sunday February 15**] morning Mr. H brought me in, notwithstanding we had heard the town was so closely picketed that citizens were not allowed to pass back & forth from business without passes. We found after getting here that such had been the case but that several of the pickets had been called in, and with no difficulty at all we came in. Since Col. Bruce's last proclamation, a third of the citizens have gone in to Clarksville and taken the oath. Many still declare they will refrain from taking it until forced. This evening I went down to see poor Mrs. Staton. Mr. Staton came home Saturday from Jackson with the sad news of Jo's death, the idol of the family.[119] He did not reach Jackson in time to see him before he died being just two days too late. Never was a nobler sacrifice made in the cause of freedom. Never died a truer friend to home and country. In his death his friends have sustained a deep loss and from his family has been taken one of its brightest ornaments, while the Confederacy is left to mourn the loss of one too eager to pour out his blood in its defense. To Mrs. Staton it seems useless to offer consolation so great is the grief which has overtaken her. But while we blend our tears with hers, forgetful of the same deep sorrow that is crushing the hearts of so many mothers, should we not remember that they are spilling their blood in a noble cause and that posterity will yet rise up and bless both them & their mothers for this unflinching adherence to the cause of freedom? Oh, the deep, deep distress this war is hourly bringing on our country, and years on top of years will have to pass before peace will again smile upon us as a nation

New Providence, Tennessee, Tuesday night, February 17, 1863

Finished "Moss Side," one of Marion Harland's novels.[120] The style did very well, but some of the characters turned out contrary to my wishes. After laying that aside, my quilt was again brought out and with equal pleasure I record its completion. The greater part of the evening I spent with Mrs. Wilson in company with Mrs. Baynham & Bettie. Would have stayed all night with Bettie but Mr. Homer had called in to spend several hours. He with several others went over to Clarksville in compliance with Col Bruce's order to register their names. They were not required to take the oath and were given papers to pass during the day. His object for calling in the citizens remains yet to be found out.

New Providence, Tennessee, Thursday night, February 19, 1863

This morning I finished my quilt. Since dinner Mr. Homer has called in & late the two Mrs. Baynhams with the two children. Never did I try harder to gratify children in everything, knowing Miss Fannie's aversion to them. But after all, Willie raised a yell which lasted it seemed to me one hour, but finally after at least 50 licks (over his pants), his mother succeeded in conquering him. As expected Miss Fannie spared neither them nor Mrs. Grigg Baynham. At the supper table she took particular pains to express her opinion of Mrs. B. but didn't look at me during the whole time, which is her way always when vexed with me & still wants me to know her sentiments. May my tongue cease to speak when I can't boldly look a man or woman in the face & tell them (not someone else) what I want them to know.

New Providence, Tennessee, Friday night, February 20, 1863

By times this morning I went out to old Mrs. Pettus to spend the day. To my surprise Mr. Newell[121] was among the first to meet me but to my journal alone must I breathe this secret, as more than one of the family charged and almost swore me not to let a soul know that he is there. He is just from the Southern army & recruiting for Capt. Bell's company.[122] Mary Grinstead, Miss Nannie Davidson, Mrs. Barksdale, and Mrs. Pettus were all busy piecing on a quilt for Mary, which they nearly finished. They walked with me as far as the toll gate where we heard that the Abolitionists & Democrats were fighting at Russellville.[123]

New Providence, Tennessee, Saturday night, February 21, 1863

A longer evening it seems to me I never spent. After finishing *Nellie Bracken*,[124] I was at a loss of employment.

New Providence, Tennessee, Sunday night, February 22, 1863

This morning when I awoke the canon were firing at such a rate I didn't know but Forrest had made his appearance again, but after the day was well nigh spent, someone reminded me that it was the 22nd of Feb., Washington's birthday.[125] Spent the morning reading & ———. I believe I'll keep it to myself though an employment, however, I was going to mention that will do myself nor no one else very great credit. Mr. Homer came up after dinner & late we walked up to Mr. Baynham's. He has just returned from Louisville. On entering the parlor what was my surprise to find two Lincoln soldiers sitting back with their old blue coats and pants on. After some enquiry I learned they were old acquaintances. With me, their uniforms would be sufficient reason for cutting their acquaintance.

New Providence, Tennessee, Thursday night, February 26, 1863

Another heavy rain has fallen. From 3 last night until 12 today it has been raining almost constantly. At 10 this morning a large body of cavalry passed. The late papers state that heavy Confederate forces under Marshall, Longstreet, and Floyd have crossed over into Ky. and that they threaten an immediate attack upon Lexington, the State Capitol, and probably upon Louisville.[126] The command that passed today, we suppose, have gone to defend Hopkinsville. The taking of Richmond is said to have been abandoned by the Federals and if such is the case some of our ablest Gen'ls will no doubt be removed to the West and in a short time we may listen for some unparalleled victories to have been gained by them. If "Stone Wall" Jackson could only show off some of his Virginia exploits in this Western country, how reviving it would be to us poor crest fallen Rebels of Tenn. The Nashville Union says we have captured the great Queen of the West with all of her officers.[127] This is almost too good to be true but we will enjoy the belief for a while at least. She was captured while making an attack on the Red River fortifications.

New Providence, Tennessee, Friday night, February 27, 1863

Once more the sun has risen clear, and for a whole day the sun has shone out beautifully. Mary Grinstead came in early for me to go over to Clarksville with her. She went to sit for a picture and by her request we sit together for a picture for Tommy, a poor soldier at present somewhere in Rebeldom fighting for his country. The gallery was filled with Yankees, and for two hours we were compelled to wait. The pictures we had taken separately are very good. Laura and [I] went fishing this evening, and for one hour while on the water heard heavy cannonading in the vicinity of Ft. Donelson.

New Providence, Tennessee, Monday night, March 9, 1863

Saturday week ago [**February 28**] Laura Helm, the children, and I spent down at the backwater fishing. Late in the evening we walked up to the Fort to see the fleet of boats go down. After getting there I was so fatigued that I decided to stay all night with Cousin Jane. The next morning [**March 1**] Bettie Helm and I went to hear Mr. Taylor preach, the first sermon I have heard for months. He has been prevented from coming over hitherto by the Yankees. That evening Mr. Homer said he was going to Uncle Wm Mallory's to spend the week. I accepted the opportunity & went with him. Found Cousin Mary still with Mr. Cowherd's little boy—and a time she is having with him—he is so troublesome to nurse. I stayed there until Thursday [**March 5**] evening when Jennie Mallory came over and I went & stayed with her until Saturday [**March 7**] evening. While there I read John's last letter to the family dated Jan. 9th, '63. He has had the misfortune to have his leg broken again and it will be months before he will be able to walk without the aid of crutches, and his lameness no doubt will continue his life time. Poor fellow, his trials are indeed severe. He gives the ladies of Va. unlimited praise for their kindness & attention to the wounded & suffering of the Southern Army. And not for once, as he used to do, referred to the "noble & heroic daughters of his own much loved Tenn." I had a delightful ride on his pony "John Bell" and saw much that reminded me of him & of hours we had passed so pleasantly together. What changes can be wrought in two short years?

New Providence, Tennessee, Tuesday night, March 10, 1863

Mary spent the morning reading aloud while I was intent on my calico quilt. She likes "Mabel Vaughan"[128] and yet dislikes her and all because she's about to become a convert to Christianity, on consequence of which she will have to give up her former gay way of living and become so sedate and unsocial. She says she does hate to read a story in which preachers and such saintly women have so conspicuous a part to perform.

New Providence, Tennessee, Wednesday night, March 11, 1863

Today has been clear. Bettie Baynham spent half the morning with us and we the other half with her. This evening we went over to Clarksville. Mary went to Dr. Acree to have her teeth examined; as she didn't have one extracted I hadn't the pleasure of laughing at her. The late Yankee papers acknowledge the brilliant success of Van Dorn at Spring Hill.[129] He captured more than three Regiments.

New Providence, Tennessee, Monday morning, May 25, 1863

Once more I'm at home after an absence consisting not of weeks but months and to say that those months have flown like weeks and weeks like days would scarcely express it. Time has been so rapid in his march. Still the above date and the one under which I'm writing includes a lapse of time amounting to months and of course my visit must have proved as pleasant as it seems brief. Since leaving home, many things have occurred which for the present have escaped my memory yet deserve to be remembered in this book as much as anything that has occurred during the past year, a truth which leads me to the determination never again to leave home for so long a time without taking with me my journal, inconvenient though it may be.

The first 4 weeks after leaving I spent with Mr. Waller's family. Cousin Alley and I passed the time as usual in talking over "old times," making our fingers work as well as our tongues that we might be prepared for any visit that happened to step in our way. About the close of the 4th or 5th week Mr. Homer came up, not very unexpectedly however, as Gen. Burnside's order for the arrest of all secret carriers of mails &c &c had not been issued then.[130] He remained with us then for several days and on his return carried Cousin Alley and I down as far as Mr. Slaughter's before leaving there for home. He carried us over to see Mr. Downer's[131] garden, a place I think more celebrated than beautiful. Mr. H bought of him several very fine roses, a heliotrope, and lemontrifolia.[132]

Our return home will long be remembered as we lost our way something less than a doz. times. I spent more than a week at Mr. S's, went back to Cousin Alley's, spent a week, and went over to Cousin Willie's to spend the week. Cousins Nannie and Willie were so agreeable my visit couldn't be otherwise than agreeable. A butternut breast pin with other things while there were presented me, but the pin I prize most more on account of its novelty and political association than real worth.[133]

The Sunday after we came in from Mr. S—Donie[134] and I concluded to go round to the Episcopal Church. Cousin A went with us and we all rendered ourselves ridiculous laughing at old Mr. Webb[135] praying for the President of the U States. For several Sundays previous he had been in the habit of omitting that particular part of his prayer some of his Southern rights members objecting to it, but Gen. Shackleford[136] happening to hear of it, ordered him round to headquarters and, after investigating thoroughly the case, bade him the next Sunday (which was the Sunday we heard him) to pray according to the Episcopal form of prayer for the Pres'nt., telling him that some of his soldiers would be present to see that his orders were carried out, which sure enough was the case. And we laughed as immoderately at an officer that sit just before us as we did at Parson Webb. "Sweet land of Liberty"—this is must pray and not pray for just whoever a Lincoln commander says.

We found Mr. Homer at Cousin Louis' that evening after getting home from church; he spent the week. We made him take us to Pilot Rock,[137] a place long heard of but one we had never seen before, consequently of great importance to us. The rock of course we found a great curiosity, but for a minute—- description I have to [leave] to abler pens. The dinner we had previously prepared we enjoyed next best, I believe, to the view from the rock. Messrs. Brenough & Holmes called on us a night or two after we had been up to the Rock and enjoyed no little a description of our trip, particularly the mistake we made in hunting the place of ascent. We also pressed Mr. H in service long enough to go with us over to see Mr. Goodall's[138] and Mrs. Callis's[139] flowers. They both have lovely gardens and finer strawberries I never saw. We brought several very fine roses and Geraniums.

Last Saturday morning we left for home and though I felt sad at parting with them all, I regretted to give up the society of none worse than Lilly. She is truly one of the most interesting children I ever knew. I brought home with me a blue merino dress to embroider for her and if possible, I intend having her photograph so soon as it is finished. Found Cousins Jane, Bet, and Marion here Saturday evening when I came. They had bushels of news for me. The first thing, however, was that I would have to go over according to Bruce's late order and sign a parole of honor. The next, that all the negroes round were flocking in to the abolition negro thieves down here at the Fort and that Winnie, one of Uncle T's women, had gone among the rest— She left a good home and will, I hope, have cause to regret it.

It has been since I left home that Hooker[140] has given orders for another "on to Richmond," but like his four predecessors Scott, Pope, McClellan and Burnside, he has met with a most miserable failure and leaves the task yet unaccomplished. And may all future attempts meet with the same result is my honest wish. Yes, the great battle (to be known in history as the battle of Chancellorsville)[141] and fought between Hooker with "his Grand Army" and the Confederates under Lee and Jackson is over with. And while we rejoice over it as decidedly the most brilliant achievement of the war, we are forced to mourn at the same time the loss of some [of] the most distinguished and heroic generals that ever lived. Stone Wall Jackson, it is said, received there the wound that terminated his existence.[142] And though it is some consolation, if we are to credit the papers, to know that his wounds were inflicted accidentally by his own men. Yet we feel that in his death we have sustained such an irreparable loss that nothing can be said or done that will in the least reconcile us to such a misfortune. But we forget there is one above who doeth all things well and, but for our good, he would not have permitted so great a calamity to have befallen us. It is said the Federal loss at Chancellorsville amounted to 24,000 while ours is much less though the exact number is not known.

New Providence, Tennessee, Wednesday night, May 27, 1863

Yesterday morning I finished off a quilt commenced before I left home. In the evening Mrs. Magaren and Mary Britton called. Mary insisted that I should go over to Clarksville with her. Notwithstanding my aversion to signing the parole of honor as ordered by Col. Bruce, I went and of course was forced to "become loyal" before a pass was granted me with [which] to come out. Such paroles I consider worse than useless and will no doubt injure the Federal party, as neither lady or gentleman seem to regard either the parole or oath. At home I'm always unhappy. Why Miss Fannie treats me as she does is a mystery never I fear to be solved. The soldiers down at the fort have fired near 1,000 guns in honor of their victory down at Vicksburg and how it is that Grant is cut all to pieces and still Vicksburg captured is strange to me.[143]

New Providence, Tennessee, Thursday night, May 28, 1863

Commenced a mull[144] dress this morning. It may answer for a bridal occasion or it may be used as a shroud. On one or the other occasion it will certainly be brought into requisition. Mr. Homer spent a while this morning. His mania for flowers still continues. The news relative to Vicksburg has been contradicted.

New Providence, Tennessee, Friday night, May 29, 1863

The rain so much hoped for has come at last, and we've had it in the greatest abundance. It only ceased long enough this evening for Mrs. Baynham and I to take a walk. In passing down street the hotel is missed so much; by some accident it caught fire and was burned while I was in Hop'sville.

New Providence, Tennessee Monday night, June 1, 1863

Miss Fannie never speaks to me unless in reply to some direct question and all the while looks mad enough to crush me into atoms.[145] Surely hatred was never more intense than hers for me. My life at home is one of misery, whereas in times past only here could I find any real happiness.

New Providence, Tennessee, Wednesday night, June 3, 1863

Have done but little work today. Walked with Mrs. Wilson and since tea walked up to Mr. Baynham's a while. He says no goods, however small the bundle, are permitted to leave Clarksville now without giving 20 cts for a permit—a making business to Old Blackman.[146]

New Providence, Tennessee, Friday, June 5, 1863

Sewed & chatted with Mrs. Baynham all yesterday [**Thursday, June 4**] morning. After dinner Mary Britton called in a while. I walked with her down as far as Dr. Herring's. From there I walked down to Cousin Jane's and as usual (through persevering) I consented to stay all night. Cousins Jane and Bet came in late. They had been over to Maj. Henry's[147] residence and were loaded with wildflowers. After tea Marion gave me a nice swing in Mr. Homer's hammock out in the new porch. Mr. Kelly gave the porch the finishing touch this morning. This evening, notwithstanding Gray's lameness, I went out to Mrs. Williams' for Mattie Carneal and Bettie Homer. Both seemed in ecstasies at the thought of a short absence from school,[148] and Mattie even now seems scarcely to realize that she is here. She speaks as affectionately of Aunt Tabbie and seems to miss her so much. Surely a better girl never lived, so thoughtful about every little thing. During the short time she has been with me she asks almost a thousand and one questions about how I have been getting on, how Miss Fannie treats me, whether she ever speaks of Aunt T, and many such thoughtful questions that to one less interested in my welfare would perhaps never be thought of.

New Providence, Tennessee, Saturday night, June 6, 1863

Mattie C and I have chatted the day out, except a short while we were napping. She amuses me with her remarks about the Yanks as they pass; her abuse is almost unlimited. We walked down late this evening to see the Ky. Regiment drill. Bettie Helm came up home with us. Oh, I'm so miserably low spirited I can't write.

New Providence, Tennessee, Sunday night, June 7, 1863

Mr. Taylor preached one of his dry sermons to a medium congregation. About 1, the Yankee cavalry from Ft. Donelson commenced passing on their way to Murfreesboro. About 500 passed.[149] Last reports say already Johnson and Rosecrans have commenced the long expected fight.[150] These forces were going up to reinforce. The wretches could not pass without indulging a propensity that seems to be second nature with them. Stealing seems to be indispensable with them. Several have passed through in pursuit of them with the hope of recovering stolen property. We all walked down and sit a while with Mrs. Magaren this evening. Mr. M is still absent and she is looking really low down.

New Providence, Tennessee, Monday night, June 8, 1863

This evening Mollie Harrelson and Mrs. Staton called for a while. Mary came very near being left in the road yesterday without any way of getting home. She together with some other young ladies and gentlemen were on their way to church, when they met up with a squad of Yankees out on a thieving expedition. One of the young ladies being on horseback was ordered to dismount which she did begging all the while that they would not take her horse. Her words were all in vain, so her only alternative was to get in the carriage with Mary and one other young lady and drive back home as quick as possible. They spoke of pressing the mules belonging to the carriage, but the driver was rather too fast for them. As expected they have stripped the country of horses almost between here and Ft. Donelson. They still continue to pass on their way to Murfreesboro, and after each company, is sent up a fervent prayer that they will never return.

New Providence, Tennessee, Tuesday night, June 9, 1863

One whole day I've had to myself. I've walked, talked, and went out where I pleased and felt no restraint. No searching eye has followed me "noticing" every movement, as though it was feared I would touch something that didn't belong to me. At the table I partook heartily of the butter and no one was near to gaze at each mouthful as though it were precious jewels being cast before swine. The servants received no withering looks so that confusion instead of presence of mind prevailed. All went off quietly and feelings similar to those experienced in better days crept over me, but with the last meal of the day all such feelings vanished. Miss Fannie went out to her mother's only to spend the day.

About 10 o'clock this morning Mrs. Trabue called at the gate. I saw in a moment that trouble of some kind had overtaken her and what was my surprise to find that it was Tom's death. Yes, she said he was certainly dead, but so choked with grief was she that she could only tell he died last August at West Point, Ga., and that the news did not reach her until March though her brother had written her in regard to it in December, the letter being miscarried.[151] Since tea I was up to see her when she gave me a more minute account of his death. Though greatly grieved, it has not entirely taken the place of inquisitiveness. She came out in plain language and asked if he and I were not engaged. For once, as Cousin Louis Meacham[152] would say, I was "smartly stumped," but finally succeeded in answering "partially." Poor fellow. I may have wronged him but it was unintentional and with his mother, I sincerely grieve that more exertion was not made to promote his happiness while he lived and that his last hours were passed with strangers in a strange land far distant from his boyhood's home and those friends who knew and loved him best. Another sad piece of news was Hock Ogburn's death; he was buried today, the last of 4 sons, the oldest of whom did not exceed 23 years. I had almost forgotten to mention the serenade given us by the Yankees last night. The music was splendid. Though as usual with their exploits, they capped it off with a little roguery, stole one of my favorite wineglasses.

New Providence, Tennessee, Wednesday night, June 10, 1863

A heavy rain commenced this morning which continued until 10 o'clock. About 11 according to promise I went over to dine with Mrs. Wilson. The nicely fried chicken and potatoes were excellent. I left rather early to go down with Mrs. Trabue to see Mrs. Drane. We spent an hour or two with her. Since tea I have walked up to Mr. Baynham's. Saw today's papers; everything in them goes to prove that Vicksburg and Port Hudson are still in the hands of the Confederates and that the rumor in regard to Grant's retreat is very probably true.

New Providence, Tennessee, Thursday night, June 11, 1863

Having been busy sewing all day; my shoulders ache dreadfully. Very late Mrs. Wilson and I took a walk. Called to see Mary Smith a short while. A Wisconsin Reg. passed this evening on their way to Murfreesboro.[153] Condemned horses are being sold in Clarksville this week,[154] and certainly Uncle Trice bought the shabbiest looking one "perhaps," though he says it will make a useful work horse. Mr. Howard was up today and says he is after a pony. If could only keep it, the idea would be delightful.

New Providence, Tennessee, Friday night, June 12, 1863

Finished a body for Inez this morning and went down to see Cousin Bet about going to Uncle Wm Mallory's. As usual spent most of the day there. Came by and paid Mrs. Staton a short call on my way home. Mr. Slaughter is with us tonight. He has been over to buy the worth of his receipt for Donie's horse in old broken down stock.[155]

New Providence, Tennessee, Tuesday evening, June 16, 1863

Saturday [June 13] morning after waiting an age it seemed to me, Cousin Bet came up and we drove out to Uncle Wm Mallory's. We were there just in time to save our dinner. The ride was very warm. Uncle Wm as expected was rather low spirited from taking the oath. Cousin Mary walked with us to the sulpher spring that evening where we met with the Miss Collins. They were preaching the funerals of the Yankees the whole time we were there. Sunday [June 14] I was quite unwell all day. Jennie Mallory stayed with us that night and yesterday [June 15] we spent with her. Came home this morning; found Mattie Grinstead here. She will leave this evening and I guess she will not regret when the hour arrives as it will certainly be agreeable to be relieved of Miss Fannie's gapes and "humphs hums." The Yanks are considerably scared up today. The Rebels are reported again on the opposite side of the river. They stood in line of battle half the night last night. Mr. Homer has just stepped in and I must hear some news if possible.

New Providence, Tennessee, Thursday night, June 18, 1863

Two warmer days we've not had this year than yesterday and day before were. Sewed yesterday until 3. Mr. Homer came up and drove me out to old Mrs. Pettus' where I remained until this evening. Mattie Grinstead is still out there. We had fine times today eating apples, goose berries, raspberries, &c &c. Time passed so differently out there from what it does at home. Out there all seemed cheerful; here just the reverse is the case whenever I am present. Not one word has been spoken to me since my return home except by the servants. Home is not home when happiness can be found anywhere else than there. What have I done that such a fate should be mine? The papers today speak of Lee's advance into Pennsylvania as being certain.[156] Lincoln has called for 100,000 more men. They are called to defend their homes, their firesides, their families. They are badly frightened no doubt of it. Kirby Smith's[157] victory in the South is also very cheering to the Southerners.

New Providence, Tennessee, Thursday evening, June 25, 1863

Last Friday Mary Britton came down for me to go out home with her. I stayed until this morning. Mary and I decided to make a trip up to Hopkinsville. She had a few purchases to make and I, of course, wanted to see Cousin Ally. Mrs. B gave us the carriage for two days and we just did come up to the time, as the rains detained us and we were until dark getting home last night. Had the good fortune to meet with Cousin Ann—Mr. and Mrs. Smith while there. Goods are still dear up there, though some cheaper than when I left there. I can't write. My mind is otherwise engaged. If I could only once come home and find everything as it used to be, but change is too deeply written on everything I see and never more is it possible for such a pleasure to return.

New Providence, Tennessee, Saturday evening, June 27, 1863

I stayed all night and in the society of Cousin Jane and the children I felt partial relief from those sad feelings known only to those who have unpleasant homes. Florence is attending very carefully to the pet Mrs. Pollard gave me, a young calf the mother of which died and left it only three days old. It is really amusing to see its actions with Florence and the bottle. Called at Mrs. Magaren's this morning. She is still a widow, Mr. Magaren having gone from Louisville to New York to see his mother. The war news is about on a stand. Grant is still driving away at Vicksburg, while Lee has ceased to annoy the people of Washington with his threatened attack and gone into the harvesting business in the valley of Va. Mary Britton has stepped in and I must chat her a while.

New Providence, Tennessee, Monday night, June 29, 1863

Rainy weather continues. Nearly finished embroidering Lilly's dress today. If nothing prevents will finish tomorrow. Went over about ½ 4 to see Mrs. Wilson. From there went down to see Mrs. Pollard few minutes. She seems some better. Found a Mr. Kay here at supper. He has come for Uncle T's assistance in what he thinks a very important matter. 7 of his negroes left yesterday or last night for the Fort and he is trying to arrest them before they get in too safe quarters. 3 soldiers were here since tea who say, if they are to be found, the owner shall have them. Uncle Trice, I think, is making himself too officious. His house, the first thing he knows, will be burnt down over his head or some other mischief equally as great.

New Providence, Tennessee, Tuesday night, June 30, 1863

At last I have finished Lilly's dress and really, I feel relieved. It has proven such a tedious job. My first piece of embroidery, I think, will probably turn out to be my last. Mary Britton came up early this morning and is still with me. Mr. Homer had the kindness to drive me out this evening. We went down to Mr. Howard's where we helped ourselves to some very nice apples and on our return to some dew berries. Uncle T's Yankee horse promises to be something superior in the way of a buggy animal. He drove very gently this evening. One fault, however, is his wanting to stop and have a social meeting with everyone he passes. Rainy weather continues.

CHAPTER SIX

July 1863 – June 1864

DESPITE GREAT TREPIDATION and uncertainty, Serepta married B. B. Homer although she never wrote of love or joy. Serepta quarreled with the Trices about what possessions she could take to her new home. Finances were difficult for the Homers. Serepta traded with the Union troops and took in boarders. Young Inez proved adept at selling eggs and produce and contributed essential income to the household. Serepta chronicled the breakdown of slavery as enslaved people fought for emancipation. There was no consistent enforcement of emancipation. Some Union soldiers assisted the enslaved. Others helped the enslavers. Uncle Trice violently beat his enslaved people in a futile attempt to maintain his mastery. His enslaved woman Winnie escaped and tenaciously fought to gain possession of her child. Trice physically fought Union troops to keep her. Homer severely beat Inez on several occasions to force her submissiveness. Serepta was unhappy about the end of slavery and expressed her disapproval using racist comments. Ironically, the Homers took in a boarder who was a white officer for the US Colored Troops.

Serepta never mentioned that she was pregnant, only commenting about not feeling well. The diary contained a surprise when she wrote about the birth of her baby girl, named after her deceased aunt, Tabitha.

New Providence, Tennessee, Saturday night, July 4, 1863

Thursday last I spent with Cousin Jane. That day, two years ago during which the saddest event of all my life occurred, has proven what many prophesied, the commencement of a series of sorrows and troubles which will end only with the termination of this existence. Late that evening Cousin Bet and I drove up to Uncle Wm Mallory's. Billie Donelson was kind enough to drive me down home, and a very pleasant ride it proved. Being one of John's confidants, old times were intentionally referred to and from that discussed fully and lengthily. Poor John, love such as his is seldom to be met with and much to be admired. After dinner went down to Cousin Jane's. Was sorry to find that Mr. Homer had gone over to Clarksville as I feared he would be prevailed on by some of the Yankeeized citizens to attend a barbecue given in honor of the day, by the Federals,[1] an honor which I hoped none of our respectable citizens would confer on the wretches. But as might have been expected, they "had a desire to hear Col. Given's[2] speech" and first one excuse and then another was offered—all of which were worse than none with me. Mr. Homer remained only a short while and seemed to like what he heard of the Col's speech very well. The beauty of the day's performance was the inviting of the brass band from this place to perform for them, then neglecting to send for them. I was really glad of it. They continued at intervals all day firing canon and tonight sky rockets have been whizzing from the fort in every direction for about an hour. Bettie and Florence are on hand tonight and, of course, all mistakes are excusable.

New Providence, Tennessee, Tuesday night, July 7, 1863

Met up with Mary Britton and nothing would do but I must stay with her all night. Came home early yesterday morning. Went to work to clean up my beds and room. Having completed my task, walked down again to see how Mrs. Pollard was getting on; found worse than when I left her in the morning. The rain detained me until it was too late to come home, so Mary was troubled with my company again. Mrs. Edwards and Mrs. Magaren were there during the evening, and really, I thought Mrs. E introduced very inappropriate subjects considering Mrs. P's extreme illness. The Yankees, their wives, way of dressing &c seemed [to] be her favorite theme. She expressed herself rather favorable to the Southern cause once or twice, which greatly surprised me as her strict adherence to the "Old Union" has of late days created no little excitement among the gossiping class of our town. "Sentiment" still comes in very conveniently about every other word.

An Extra came out yesterday containing the great news of Meade's[3] (Fighting Jo Hooker's successor) brilliant victory "in Pennsylvania.[4] Yes, the Yankees have at last a foretaste of what we've been enduring for more than two years. A battle has been fought, the most terrific of the war, (they say) on their own soil. And yet from their own accounts we are led to the conclusion that Lee's army is by no mean demolished. And, of course, the inference is that when the last dispatches came, the ball had only commenced, and that we may yet hear of one of the most decided victories ever gained by the Southerners. The fight was still raging on the 3rd. Since then we've had nothing reliable. Morgan has made another dash into Ky. capturing at Lebanon 1,000 men, all of whom I think were members of Col Bruce's old Reg.[5] The "Rebels" are reported also to have captured Brashear city, near New Orleans, with 1,000 men, several siege guns. Three cheers for the brave Southerners. News of victories come crowding in from all quarters. Mr. Pollard bet with Mary B. yesterday that the Crescent city would be recaptured by the Southerners by the 20th of this month.

New Providence, Tennessee, Thursday night, July 9, 1863

This morning early Mr. Homer, Florence, and I went blackberrying. Succeeded in getting enough to have a splendid pie for dinner. Cousin Jane does make such good cobblers. Came home late this evening; found Mary Britton and Bettie Helm here. We took a long walk; parted with them both about sundown. Since then all the soldiers from Hopkinsville have come down, both infantry and cavalry. They expected Morgan in Hop'ville and have come to the fort, I suppose for protection.

New Providence, Tennessee, Friday night, July 10, 1863

Soon after breakfast went down and spent an hour or so with Mrs. Pollard, came home, crocheted lace until dinner, and then went down to Mrs. Magaren's. From there drove out to Mrs. Howard's after Miss Lou Peterson. As I feared, found her absent and I was so disappointed. Really, I wanted to see Cousin Lou. Ike was out on the farm at work. Out of 6 or 8 negro men, he has one remaining—Everywhere the farms seems miserably neglected. The wheat crop will prove almost an entire failure on account of the long continued rains; it sprouts standing in the field.

New Providence, Tennessee, Saturday night, July 11, 1863

Sit myself down for a day's work this morning, but Mr. Homer came by going out to Mrs. Williams for Bettie's trunk, and through his persuasion

I consented to go out to Mrs. Britton's to spend the day. Found Mary and Fannie at home with Blanche Howard. Fannie had prepared for us a very nice dinner. She had such a variety of vegetables, besides meats that were excellent. This evening Mary and I went hunting with Mr. Homer. He killed two squirrels and a ground hog. The first squirrels I ever saw fall to the ground; the amusement was quite novel to me. Coming home Mr. H shot a beautiful partridge which I intend broiling for Mrs. Pollard.

New Providence, Tennessee, Tuesday evening, July 14, 1863

After dinner Sunday [July 12] walked down to Cousin Jane's. Sit for an hour or two with her, when we both walked up to see Mrs. Magaren, where I stayed all night. Mr. Homer carried Bettie up to Uncle Tom Campbell's that evening. Yesterday morning I called to see Bettie Helm and Mrs. Pollard, came home, and late in the evening walked over to see Mrs. Wilson. As I came in, Uncle Trice was sitting in the porch. I asked him for money to buy myself a braid. The scene that followed I would rather remember than record. Today I've been tempted to wish myself out of existence, and if the present state of family affairs continues, I'm sure it will not be long before life for me will be done.

New Providence, Tennessee, Wednesday night, July 15, 1863

Left home early this morning resolved to spend the day; went to several places, but only in Mrs. Magaren's company did I feel much interest. Whenever I get as miserably low spirited as I've been today, but few persons have the power to interest me. Even Ann Amelia Helm[6] failed to amuse me today with her budget of news—the town gossip in regard to the Yankees waiting on the southern girls &c. She really told me of several very ugly cases in regard to the girls permitting the Yanks to ride with them, walk with them, and so on.[7] Even May Scott has accepted a photographic album from one of them as a present, and report goes so far as to say that she is engaged to be married to the same one. What would our Southern boys say to such conduct? What would these girls have said of such a course one year ago? Surely, there is no accounting for the fickleness of the human family. Mary Britton and Nannie Grinstead are with me tonight. Old Mrs. Pettus with Nannie spent the day here. Today's papers confirm the news of the surrender of Vicksburg and Port Hudson,[8] and yet we Rebels will not believe it. Morgan is said to be playing the mischief in Indiana and Ohio. May he have success and a safe return.

New Providence, Tennessee, Friday night, July 17, 1863

Nannie G spent the day yesterday and what a time I did have of it. There was
not quite as much gaping at Nannie going on as usual, but more assurance
than "Old Scratch" need care about. To my great relief Mary Britton came
up in the evening for me to go to Clarksville with her. Mr. Homer drove us
over. Made no purchases for myself at all, but prevailed on Mr. H to buy a
coal oil lamp which I thought very pretty indeed. Mary made several small
purchases. Stayed with her all night. Found Mrs. Pollard uneasy about our
staying out so long with the "Yankee horse." She was not aware of the exchange that had been made. This evening Alice Riggins and I went up to
see Bell Dunn, my first visit for nearly two years. Met with deceitful old
Mrs. Kirby up there. Late papers confirm the news of the surrender at Port
Hudson and Vicksburg. How can we believe it?

New Providence, Tennessee, Tuesday evening, July 21, 1863

At home all day Saturday until about 3 in the evening, when I walked down
to Mrs. Pollard's, finding her, Mr. Pollard, and the babe all asleep. Mary and
I carried on a whispering conversation for a few minutes and then I left for
Mrs. Magaren's; found her sick with the head ache and too much "hippoed"
to be much company, so I went on down to Cousin Jane's where I remained
all night. Next morning we decided to go in the afternoon to see Cousin
Marion, notwithstanding my promise to Mr. Homer to become his wife
the first of this week provided [in] these Lincoln times the license could be
procured.[9] But with me pleasure before business. So the visit was made and
he says now, with my consent, tomorrow is the day set apart for the commencement of our united happiness or misery. But how can I realize that
such is the case? Never have I felt so undecided on any one subject as I have
on the subject of matrimony. True more than once or twice have I brought
myself up to the point to be "engaged," but to marry was something too far
off ever to engage my serious thoughts. So I find myself even now undecided
in regard to what course I should best pursue. To remain at home, I know
would be to increase a weight of sorrow already too heavy to be borne by
one so unused to anything in the shape or form of family discord. While to
bring my disposition in contact with those strange and untried events may
prove to be a step taken equally as injurious to my welfare and interest. But
fate will have its way and life even when made up of sorrows and troubles is
but a short duration anyway. So my determination at present is to make the
best of it.

Cousin Jane and I had a very pleasant visit over to Mr. Osborne's indeed. Cousin Marion yesterday gave us such a nice dinner — fresh shoat and such nice ice cream. Really, both and all were so good that it was difficult to decide which to partake of most heartily. Mr. Homer met us on the way yesterday evening and it was so late after getting to Cousin Jane's I stayed all night. Came home this morning and finding that Mr. Baynham had selected me such a nice braid, went up immediately to thank him for it. Since then I've packed one trunk (in the event I should need it) and spent the rest of the time in crocheting. Uncle Trice has at last succeeded in getting Ida, Winnie's baby, and Col. Bruce has given him an order for Winnie herself, though I think his getting her is rather improbable, as the abolition Yankees have sworn vengeance against him for taking the child. It would not surprise me to hear at any time that they had attempted to take his life or burn him out. During his sprees of dissipation he says and does so much to excite their hatred that I live in constant dread.

New Providence, Tennessee, Saturday evening, July 25, 1863

Crocheted the greater part of the day last Wednesday, and I'm pleased to say that that all important piece of work is at last finished. Mr. Homer came up during the morning. Said but little to me, though he had a conversation with Uncle Trice that lasted for some time. Mary Britton came in that morning and feeling so miserably "low down" I went out to the gate determined to ask her to remain with me all day — at least until after 6 o'clock that evening. But my heart failed me and I let her go thinking perhaps she would call again in the evening. But as before I let her pass and for the life of me couldn't tell her why her presence was particularly desired. And until this moment have I found courage to tell a single being that I expected to be married, not even Uncle Trice. As a natural consequence I was perfectly alone during the whole day feeling that it would be wrong to even think aloud or stir from my seat for fear of breaking the dead silence that seem to forebode something so strange and unnatural. The occasional hum or laugh of Miss Fannie seemed like mockery on the occasion, though I knew that it came from her heart and next to the day of her own marriage that was her second happiest.

She asked me that morning as an evidence of her pleasure of the occasion if I would have her to make any preparation. This I am sure was the first kind word or look she had given me for months, and knowing as I did her unwillingness to my eating at the table as much as my appetite sometimes called for, I very politely requested her not to do a thing. But so overjoyed was she at the thought of being rid of my presence, she went ahead anyway and baked several cakes and made some ice cream. And to her surprise, no doubt, only Dr. M was present to enjoy it. Soon after the ceremony was over we came down to Cousin Jane's where I have been ever since. Found Cousin Jane and the children looking as I had been feeling all day, as though a corpse was present and to smile was death by the law. Oh! such a doleful time as I did have of it. Mrs. Magaren was here and but for her presence scarcely a word would have been spoken during the evening.

The marriage ceremony I consider the most solemn scene in the world and under some circumstances equal to a funeral itself. Next morning Mrs. Magaren left early. Bettie Helm soon came in and after her Jack Gold. When B left, she remarked that I must make my visits frequent, not to consider myself an old married woman too soon. Jack says, Married! why whoever heard tell of such a thing. Not a word had she heard of it, and for some minutes she [was] incredulous, notwithstanding Bettie and Marion were both intent in convincing her to the contrary. That evening we went blackberrying and for two or three days Cousin Jane has given us some excellent cobblers. The peach cobbler today was very fine indeed. Laura Helm and Ann Mary Staton were to see me yesterday evening and today Mrs. Herring and Jack again. They all seem bent on knowing my plan for keeping a secret.

New Providence, Tennessee, Sunday evening, July 26, 1863

The weather is very warm indeed. Florence and I walked to the sweet gum tree early this morning and though [we] were absent but a short while, it seemed that the sun would almost bake us before our return. Such weather as we have now we do little but lounge, Cousin Jane excepted. She will exert herself to give us something good to eat today. I thought the peach cobbler she gave us was, if possible, better than the one yesterday. She went up to see Bell Dunn this evening, and since she left, Mrs. Blakney and Cousin Lourane Donelson have spent an hour or two with us. Cousin L very frankly acknowledged that her business was to see if I had married, while Mrs. B, I inferred, came on the same errand, though she said nothing. Mr. Homer took great pains in showing them his flowers, and as a reward for his trouble, Cousin L gave him a hint of his advanced years in comparison with mine, an allusion not by any means the most agreeable to either party.

New Providence, Tennessee, Monday night, July 27, 1863

Rose in time this morning to dress, make up my bed, and then sit a while before breakfast. Cousin Jane's breakfast hour is not likely to interfere with morning's nap and for that I like it all the better. Soon after breakfast Ann called for my clothes, and after getting them up, Jack Gold came in. She spent the greater part of the morning with us. She is indeed a great talker. I went over to see her this evening and from there we all went after apples, but we were scarcely repaid for the trip the roads were so rough. Since getting back, Mr. H has shown me a ticket to a picnic addressed to Mr. B. B. Homer & Lady. It may be that it was intended for me but I can scarcely believe it.

New Providence, Tennessee, Tuesday night, July 28, 1863

Commenced another piece of crotchet edging a day or two ago, and in the absence of something of more importance, I find myself quite busy with it. Such was the case until this morning until about ½ 10 when Florence and I drove up home after some of my clothing & flowers. Miss Fannie watched me very closely while packing the things in the buggy and I'm not certain but she thinks half I brought away was stolen. She only spoke to me twice while there, and the deceitful old thing had the face to speak kindly after having frowned on me for the last 6 months. This evening Mr. Homer drove me up to Mrs. Magaren. While there Mary and Fannie Britton came down here to see me, but finding me absent, went up to Mrs. M's. They both, with Mrs. Magaren's assistance, did their best in trying to tease me, and in regard to the "plow and new ground" case carried it out pretty well. They had a great deal to tell me about what people said about my marrying, among other things that Uncle Trice was violently opposed to the match and cursed around no little about it. That, of course, I could flatly contradict, knowing his entire willingness as I did. Uncle Trice and Mr. Homer had a conversation this evening, and Mr. H thinks what he said was greatly in my favor, but pshaw, I've heard him talk before.

New Providence, Tennessee, Wednesday night, July 29, 1863

Mr. Homer called old Mr. Duncan in this morning to do some painting, and as a natural consequence this room has been in utter confusion throughout the day. Painting the mantle has made a decided improvement in the appearance of things. Uncle Trice, according to his conversation with Mr. Homer, sent a cow and a calf down this morning. He speaks of her as being very superior, but if she proves so I shall be greatly disappointed in her. If much "butter" had been contained in her milk, Miss Fannie never would have parted with her in the world. The calf Mrs. Pollard gave me about 2 months ago is now my only hope in the way of making a fortune in the milk or butter line. Marion really amused me in pretending to milk her when Cousin Jane goes down to the cow-pen of evenings. She stands so gently while Marion pulls away at her little nipples as though she was the mother of ½ doz. calves. Having been used to the bottle all her life, her gentleness is very easily accounted for. Mr. Rice Oldham[10] was brought down from Nashville today, and is now over at Ben Gold's. Mr. H says he is nothing but skin and bones; he is so wretchedly poor, [a] few more days at the hospital would no doubt have finished him.

New Providence, Tennessee, Thursday night, July 30, 1863

Slept this morning until near 8 o'clock. After breakfast spent an hour or two in cleaning up; then went to walk and continued at it until 11 when I assisted Cousin Jane in a small way about dinner. The berries we gathered yesterday evening made a splendid pie. After dinner slept a while and from that time until late crocheted on some edging. Late papers contain but little news in favor of the Southern cause. An attack has been made on Charleston by Gillmer[11] and this time they say they have the man to go forward and they will have it. It may be that Charleston will share the fate of Vicksburg and Port Hudson, but true Southerners feel about that as they do about Lee's success in Va. — there is yet hope. Jack has been relieved of one of her boarders. Mrs. Brooks left this morning for Louisville and no doubt to the great satisfaction of the Capt. as he can resume his old way of getting along now. He passed here just now singing at a high rate, at least I thought it was him.

New Providence, Tennessee, Friday night, July 31, 1863

Mr. Homer had the buggy in readiness early this morning for me to go up home and pack up the rest of my clothes. I went by Mrs. Pollard's and Mary B went with me up, but Uncle Trice thought in the morning would be a better time for sending them down. He gave me a considerable chat in regard to his "piece of perfection" and about what he intended to give me (My start in life). In addition to the cow, I'm to have Aunt Tabbie's wardrobe, one bed and such other things as he saw proper. The "other things" I suppose meaning a quilt or two or a couple of pillows to go with the bed. In everything he seemed to say I'm giving you this not because you deserve it, or because it was your Aunt T's and she wanted you to have it, but to feel that I've done my duty so far that the world will not censure. From his heart I don't think as much as a pin's worth was given freely. Called a little while at Mrs. P's as I returned. This evening Mary Smith and Alice have been to see us. They spent most of the evening. Since tea Mr. H and I have taken a long walk, and since then Cousin Jane and I have had a long conversation out on the back porch. The drum and fife music so distinctly heard from the camp, that but acted their part in adding solemnity to the occasion, we conversed on grave subjects, and all around seemed to assume a melancholy aspect.

New Providence, Tennessee, Saturday night, August 1, 1863

Agreeable to Uncle Trice's request, this morning first thing we went up after my remaining interest in the estate. We brought down the wardrobe, Aunt T's chair, my rocking chair, and the remainder of my clothing. The bed and Aunt T's chest with her clothes are still there. Since coming home we've tried to straighten up, but still everything seems to be in confusion. The band over at the camp gave us a real benefit tonight. They perform very well indeed.

New Providence, Tennessee, Sunday night, August 2, 1863

Read the bible a while after breakfast this morning. Then went into Cousin Jane's room. Sit until just before dinner when I took a small nap and rose almost too lazy to enjoy the good apple dumpling Cousin J had made. After dinner it was too warm to sleep, so we chatted until about 4 when we walked down to Mrs. Herring's, and finding that she had so much company, walked over to Mrs. Staton's. Found her very low spirited about Charlie.[12] Woodward's command was engaged in that cavalry fight at Winchester,[13] and she of course feels uneasy about C, until something definite is heard from him. Late papers confirm the news of Morgan's capture[14] and state that he has been sent to the penitentiary [at] Columbus, Ohio.[15] We Rebels are loathe to believe it.

New Providence, Tennessee, Monday night August 3, 1863

Mended Mr. Homer an undershirt this morning. Found the job rather a tedious one, but if that proves the worst, I shall consider that I'm doing well. I never did like patching in my life. Inez came down this morning. Having no other employment for her, I set her to pulling up weeds, but Marion and she have such a fancy for playing she has accomplished but little. Old Mrs. Sisco called on us this evening. Her direct business was to sell some damsons; her indirect to see what our calculations were for the future. The soldiers are cheering at a high rate over at camp this evening. They've certainly heard of the capture of Charleston or Richmond. I believe they are about the only two places the Southerners have much claim on now. Poor Confederacy, your prospect is indeed dull for the present. Even friends think your case "gone up for 90 days."

New Providence, Tennessee, Tuesday night, August 4, 1863

I can afford to assist Cousin Jane in milking of an evening, but these mornings are so fine for sleeping that I give way to laziness and leave her to go only with the children. The rain today made the weeds so wet that we presented quite a ludicrous appearance this evening when we started out with our dresses and skirts raised above the elbows of our feet. I milked Lilly tonight all by myself. Cousin Jane said she thought it was right smart for me to do, and it helped her a long so much as Bobbie went to camp with milk and made it so late getting back. My little calf Nannic Pollard is growing off finely and it is certainly the prettiest little thing I ever saw in the shape of a calf. Inez and Marion are scratching my feet at such a fast rate I will have to close the milking business. But I forgot to say that Cousin Jane sold a soldier a pound of butter yesterday for 20 cts and gave me the money. She has the milk money and I the butter; both have a fortune in anticipation though it is some distance off. Cousin Jane makes over a dollar a week sometimes, selling butter milk at 5 cts a quart.

New Providence, Tennessee, Wednesday night, August 5, 1863

Finished a piece of edging this morning for pillow slips. Mr. and Mrs. Daniel Gold came in early from the country. She and Jack sit with me for an hour or two before dinner. She like all the other ladies from the country has too great an aversion to the Yankees to treat them with civility. Her conversation, while here, almost entirely was about the "Yanks" and their meanness. 3 or 4 of her father's negroes have gone to Ft. Donelson, and that particular feature of Yankee rule I think she objects to more than anything else. The negroes through the country round far and near are flocking in to the abolition Union soldiers, more rapidly than ever, from this place and Clarksville too. They are constantly leaving. Just in time for her dinner Cousin Marion came today. She tells most horrible tales of Yankee tyranny down in Miss., as related and witnessed by Mrs. Clayton, who is just up from that state. She says down there it is not at all uncommon for Grant's soldiers to turn out of doors helpless women and children, burn their houses down over their heads, and leave them without one mouthful of bread to eat and perhaps miles and miles from where there is any bread, meat, or anything else with which to sustain life. Children scarcely knowing how to walk have been seen trudging along some public road in search of something to eat, whose parents have once commanded all that ease and luxury would call for, and yet after all

this talk about uniting with the North again the idea is indeed absurd.
Though Vicksburg, Port Hudson, and Richmond even were to fall, still
as long as one man is left to tell of their cruelty, so long may we expect to
live a disunited people.

New Providence, Tennessee, Thursday night, August 6, 1863

Soon after Mr. Homer rose this morning, he was out in the yard and
Esq. Oldham beckoned him to come over to Mr. Gold's. And as we all
expected, he just did get over in time to see Mr. Rice Oldham breathe
his last. He lived but a few minutes after Mr. H got [there]. Cousins Jane,
Marion, and I went over about 9 to see the corpse, and certainly I never
saw a poorer frame, nothing but a regular skeleton. Jack seemed entirely
composed. After coming home from there, Cousins Jane and Marion
went up to Mr. Howell's, where they spent the day. Cousin M stayed up
at Uncle Trice's tonight. The rain and the lateness of the hour prevented
Cousin Jane from going in, but no excuse satisfied Uncle T. Cousin Jane
said he gave her one of his sarcastic laughs, as much as to say your company is not particularly desired.

Florence and I got dinner today, and as no one else will praise us, we
will say for ourselves that everything (the cabbage excepted) was cooked
very well. Really, I relished everything I ate more than usual though I acknowledge (to myself) that it may have [been] the exercise taken [not] the
excellence of the cooking that sharpened my appetite at such a high rate.
We were so smart that Cousin Jane came and found us nearly through
with the milking, and to milk Pink (her cow) is quite a feat for any of us
to perform. One of the Regiments, or a battery at least, moved over this
side of the pike this evening and have camped but a few steps from where
we milk. We are opposed to having our rights invalid to such an extent,
and if they take possession of Mr. H's stable, which I expect they will,
they may listen for a fuss in camp. [He] says our Old Gray and his rights
must be respected as well as Old Abe and his rights.

New Providence, Tennessee, Friday night, August 7, 1863

Mr. Homer with several others went with Mr. O's {*indecipherable*} out this
morning and did not return until nearly dark. About {*indecipherable*} Mrs.
Magaren came in and though she came only to spend the morning, we prevailed on her to spend the day. I always enjoy her visits. Cousin Bet and Mr.
Mills went over to town, came by, took dinner, and spent some time with

us. Cousin Bet brought down 12 lbs of butter to sell for Aunt Kit Collins. Bobbie only got 25 cts for it. Yesterday, or this evening it was, Cousin Jane got 25 cts for some. Cousin Nat was more friendly than I anticipated. He even called me "Cousin Rep," but why should I expect to see him changed? Received very unexpectedly today such a nice present. Cousin Nannie Layne sent me a feather fly brush, done up so nicely. Really, I appreciated the gift coming from such a good friend, and under the circumstances, I shall ever remember it with much pleasure. Started Lilly's dress home today. Cousin Steve and Annie Trice[16] are up at Uncle Wm's and through him I expect Cousin Alley to get the dress.

New Providence, Tennessee, Saturday night, August 8, 1863

Almost by force Mr. Homer made me go with [him] after minnows this morning. I had made up my mind to go blackberrying and no other jaunt was preferable to it; however, I assisted him in catching the minnows and after so long a time we were started—he to the creek, Florence, Inez, and I to the blackberry field. We succeeded in gathering a good many, such as they were, but they cost us many a long breath, with the loss of a few drops of perspiration. And such an intense thirst that we could scarcely wait to get home before almost giving up, we were so very thirsty. Mr. H didn't catch any fish, but chanced to meet up with a spring of the very best water. I quarreled and quarreled with him for not bringing us some water or telling us where the spring was. In attempting to find him, we drove Old Gray into a ditch, and but for the assistance of a Yankee soldier, we would have been upset. I was so mad it would have made but little difference with me. After my nap this evening I was just going about bottling the berries[17] when Mrs. Wilson came. She only sit an hour, and after she left, Cousin Jane and I put up the berries in a hurry. Had supper over directly and went to milking in time to have a good long rest spell before bed time.

New Providence, Tennessee, Sunday night, August 9, 1863

Read this morning until about 9, when Mr. and Mrs. Edwards came along and I walked over to Mr. Gold's, and spent the rest of the morning. Mr. E is just from Louisville and he had a great deal to tell us about the interference of England and France in behalf of the Confederacy. It is an evident fact that, as Baldwin[18] says, every nation will have been engaged in this war before it closes. Mrs. E spoke of "Lieutenant" as often as ever, though it was only night before last that one of [the] Negro women left and went, if not to his Regiment, some of brother soldiers. This evening we had another hard shower, and notwithstanding the frequency of the shower, this weather remains very warm.

New Providence, Tennessee, Monday night, August 10, 1863

After seeing Mr. Homer off for Ky. this morning, I had sit me down quietly to work, little thinking I would be disturbed again during the day, but to my surprise, the children soon came and told me that Miss Lou Peterson was coming. To meet with her was an agreeable surprise indeed. I have not seen her before for months. Her school is out now and she says she intends paying me several good long visits before returning to her labors. Her sneers and remarks in regard to the deserters that have recently come home from the 49th were really amusing. She has conversed with John Fletcher[19] and says that he can scarcely hold his head up long enough to answer a question. I'm so sorry that Tennesseans ever acted so disgracefully, but none of the first class, those that deserve the name of Tennessean, have acted so, and in this there is consolation.

New Providence, Tennessee, Wednesday night, August 12, 1863

Agreeable to my promise yesterday I started out early this morning to spend the day with Mrs. Magaren. But having a desire to see Mrs. Harrelson's fine gold-starred tucking comb,[20] I concluded to call in there awhile and, without hardly knowing it, a good part of the evening had passed before I got over to Mrs. H's at all. However, I was in time for a good dinner and a long social chat before walking over to Mrs. Herring, which was about 4 o'clock. While there, a gentleman passed and bowed and bowed and took off his hat and seemed so pleased at the idea of seeing us that no few wonders were expressed as to who he was. But without satisfying curiosity I started home, but had proceeded no farther than Mr. Harrelson's when they told me it was Mr. Hargrave,[21] a Rebel soldier just from Port Hudson and a member of the 49th Tenn. Regiment. Nothing more was necessary. I immediately retraced my steps, told the news, and "with one accord," Mrs. Magaren, Dr. and Mrs. Herring, the children, and I all started to see him. We were not disappointed in him. He bore the marks of a "war worn" soldier. His bruised face and rough clothing all spoke of hard service. He looked the soldier, not the military gentleman showing off under blue cloth and shoulder straps. And from his lips we heard that Port Hudson had surrendered. Now we believe it. He says, however, that for the Federals it was a dear bought victory. They during the two months they were endeavoring to take it having [lost] from 8 to 10,000 men while we only lost in killed and wounded about 6,500.

New Providence, Tennessee, Friday night, August 14, 1863

Yesterday morning [August 13] determined to employ my time more usefully, I cut out a pair of pillow cases (my first attempt toward housekeeping,) and went to work in real earnest. But, as usual, my good intentions were frustrated. About 10, Eugene brought a note from Miss Fannie saying that Cousin Nannie Layne was there to spend the day & desired me to go up and spend it with her. The walk was very warm & tiresome, but I was fully repaid in seeing Cousin N and the children and listening to her old familiar laugh. Though I felt but little like joining her. Somehow a gloom comes over me when I go up home and a sadder feeling I never wish to have around the deathbed of a friend. Cousin N and I had only one private conversation, though that did me a great deal of good. When she left, it was with the promise that I would come out before long and spend a week or two, which I intend doing, for invitations from such a friend as she is, should not be slighted.

Cousin Lou was up there staying while Uncle Trice was gone to Ft. Donelson, after Horace I recon. What love some people have for a negro. I'm glad I know that my cow and calf, wardrobe and will-be bed didn't consist in woolly headed negroes. Just as I was ready to come home, I spied Mr. Homer passing. He called for me to come home with him. Out of the buggy I should scarcely have recognized him. He had bought what the men call a duster, a long linen sack coat and "pon my word" it nearly touched the dust sure enough. In the buggy he had tin ware, roses, and my fuchsia that I've so long been wanting. While at Uncle Tom's, they went to Hopkinsville and at Mrs. Goodall's[22] he purchased the flowers. A while after we were at home yesterday evening, Cousin Steve Trice drove up. He came down to Clarksville on business, and spent the night with us. Our sleeping arrangements are not very convenient when gentleman company come, but Mr. H will have his own way. Today it has been too warm for any use; still I've been trying to sew. The "Yanks" I know are having a warm time down South.

New Providence, Tennessee, Saturday night, August 15, 1863

Jack Gold gave up her Yankee boarders today on account of sickness among the servants. I know they will miss the many accommodations met with at Ben G's.

New Providence, Tennessee, Tuesday night, August 18, 1863

The weather continues almost insufferably hot. Last night I could scarcely sleep for the heat. Uncle Trice came down to the gate this morning for Mr. Homer to go over to town with him. He was still to some extent under the influence of yesterday's "bust," as he was pleased to term it. With Mr. H he is in a might givy way; says when he went down to Ft. D last week he told Horace if he would come home, he could come and live with "his" Miss Rep and Mr. H if he wanted to. I know something of Horace's desire to come, and of the conditions of which he would come here to live. And so, taking all things into consideration, I had about as live he were at Ft. D as here. Jack Gold spent this evening with us, but has as much gab as ever on her.

New Providence, Tennessee, Wednesday night, August 19, 1863

I haven't the slightest recollection of how the morning passed except I made a cake—oh yes, and peeled peaches to make a cobbler for dinner. Sent Mrs. Pollard some of both. This evening went over to see Jack, and tonight ground cucumbers to make catsup.[23]

New Providence, Tennessee, Thursday night, August 20, 1863

My ankles are "slightly" aching tonight. I was standing up the greater part of the morning, putting away cucumber ketchup[24] and tomatoes. This evening after taking a nap I assisted Florence in churning, and without Cousin Jane's assistance, we milked. This we consider a very great achievement, though we have once before done the like. The late papers confirm the news of France's recognizing the Confederacy.[25] War with foreign powers is now all the talk and I may say all the prospect.

New Providence, Tennessee, Friday night, August 21, 1863

Unexpectedly to Mr. Homer and I, Cousin Jane came in this morning to tell us of her intended visit to the country. She and the children all left for Mr. Osborne's about ½ 8. Notwithstanding she had an offer of the buggy and Old Gray, she insisted on walking and walk she would. Jack came over about 10 and sit until 12, and after that Inez and I prepared dinner, but everything was cold before Mr. Homer came from town. So he had but little chance of judging of my cooking qualities. However for myself, I will say everything did very well for the first attempt. The bread, it is true, was slightly scorched, the corn so dry that it would choke the cows, and the biscuit so tough, that one mouthful would last long enough for the cream to curdle in the peaches before tasting them. The middling meat and cucumbers were my favorite dishes and both of them did very well. I was so fatigued that after all was over I tried to sleep for an hour or two but after all did not make it out. Since milking, which well nigh exhausted my patience as well as strength, I've concluded that hot suppers were injurious, and so decided that for a season at least we would all be as healthy as possible. For supper our bill of fare was fresh buttermilk, cold light bread, butter, & honey.

New Providence, Tennessee, Saturday night, August 22, 1863

Well, we've managed to get through with another of the warmest days that it seems to me I ever felt. After getting through with the morning's work, I went over to Jack's and sit until about 11. Mr. H went out after peaches and such an attempt as I made at a cobbler nobody ever saw. All the rest of the dinner turned out tolerably well. Mr. H said this evening the batter cakes[26] were as good as Cousin Jane's, but perhaps I expect he said that just to flatter me. This evening I was too lazy to do a thing but milk and attend to the churning. This weather is warm enough to break a mule down and after the Yankees' attack on Aunt Lucy[27] last night, we'll be afraid to sleep with the windows open.

New Providence, Tennessee, Monday night, August 24, 1863

Rose this morning feeling but very little refreshed. Mr. H passed a very restless night. His fever and headache continued until late. This morning he seemed some better until about 9 or 10 o'clock when his fever rose again and shortly afterward his disease manifested itself in unmistakable characters. The nettle rash[28] broke out [on] him so thick that a pinhead could scarcely be placed in a clear place. This evening Dr. Herring came up and from the effects of morphine and quinine given, he seems a great deal better. Through all his sickness and grunting today, I've had company and had to get dinner too. Laura and Gerty Helm spent the day with me. Uncle Steven Mallory called long enough to dine and sit a while with us.

New Providence, Tennessee, Tuesday night, August 25, 1863

Was awakened this morning about 2 o'clock. From that until day Mr. Homer kept such a complaining that sleep was impossible. Today until 4 this evening he has been very sick. Cousin Jane and the children came this morning, and with their assistance I have done much better. The tomatoes Mrs. Pollard sent me yesterday, I bottled this morning and am not sorry the job is off of hand. The battery left yesterday for parts unknown to us, and tomorrow they say the 28th Ky. leaves.[29] What good old times we would have if the 102nd Ohio[30] would leave and no worse villains were sent in their place. Aunt Mary says she had to take a good cry when her boarders left. I expect she died over Mr. Laney's leaving, and no doubt they will miss their "Cousin Mother."

New Providence, Tennessee, Wednesday night, August 26, 1863

Mr. Homer rested so much easier last night that he concluded this morning he was well enough to be up. So he dressed, and about 8 o'clock Jack Gold came over and we all walked over to the vineyard to get some grapes to put up and jelly. Notwithstanding my efforts to induce Mr. Homer not to go, he not only went with us over there but walked over to Mr. G's, the picket post, to see the pigs and round generally. As a natural result he is quite sick again tonight and threatened with another attack of the nettle rash. We rejoiced at the leaving of the battery Monday, but grieve today at the appearance of another—and from Ft. Donelson that horrible of all places. Jack's boarders sup with her tonight for the last time perhaps—Galt and Loyal Brooks.

New Providence, Tennessee, Thursday night, Aug 27, 1863

After sealing up my jelly this morning, went over to see if Jack's was any nicer than mine. Found it to be about the same quality. While there, Lieut. Loyal came in for his haversack[31] of provision. The 28th Ky. have indeed gone and left us with only the Ohioans for protectors. Jack with some others seems greatly distressed at their leaving, and even went so far as to let the Yankees know it. How strangely fickle some people are. She and I drove over to town this evening for some fruit & such but were disappointed. Mr. H still has some fever.

New Providence, Tennessee, Friday night, August 28, 1863

Went to work early this morning on my damsons. Sent Inez up to Alice Riggins for another basketful. It rained so, I regretted sending her. Before we were through at breakfast Mr. Gold came over. He told us of the circumstance of two soldier robbers arresting Mr. Woods and others down on the Dover road and robbing them of all valuables such as watches, money, &c. They were traced here within the lines and were found to be two of the 28th Ky. who, of course, expected to leave yesterday and thought before leaving to make an impression of some kind on the citizens if it had to be done over the head with a pistol that proved to be tricky in the act of being fired. Such circumstances in the neighborhood are of almost weekly occurrence, and we have nothing but to look forward to the time when they will be of even more frequent occurrence. One of the battery over here had the impudence to come in this evening and take his seat with Mr. H—I felt all the while rather doubtful of the real object of his visit.

New Providence, Tennessee, Sunday night, August 30, 1863

Through some means I made a very great mistake. Friday night [August 28] turned over two leaves in the place of one, but, as paper is scarce, I shall not lose anything by it, and only turn back and take a fresh start. Were it not that this is August I should certainly expect frost the weather is so extremely cold. Florence and I went after sweet gum early this morning and really, a blanket shawl would have been comfortable. Cousin Jane and I walked down to Mrs. Magaren's this evening; found her looking very badly indeed. Mr. M. has again disappointed her about coming home, and disappointment or its effects begin to tell as much in her countenance as in her words.

New Providence, Tennessee, Monday night, August 31, 1863

Commenced a new pair of pillow slips today and finished them with the exception of the trimming. Mr. Homer went for peaches this morning and I expected to spend the evening making jam. But Mr. H disappointed me about bringing soft peaches and so I find that he, like other men, thinks he knows better what women want than they do themselves. I begged him before he left and my last words were (bring the soft peaches), but I suppose they were a little more trouble to get, and "I didn't know what I wanted any way." One thing is certain, the lover is more attentive and more apt to try to please than the husband. My experience though short has taught me that much. If a little crying would have helped me out today in my disappointment, trivial though it was, I would certainly have given way to my tears, for as it was, they were somewhat troublesome to control.

New Providence, Tennessee, Tuesday night, September 1, 1863

Rose this morning determined to have enough peaches to make at least a little jam. Asked Mr. H. to lend me old Gray but he offered as he did yesterday some trivial excuse. I went up to Mrs. Magaren's thinking perhaps she could drive me out to the country, but her buggy was broken and there was none to be borrowed. I then watched for old Mrs. Gregg. She soon came in with some old green things hard enough to knock a Negro down. But determined to the last, I bought some of them and such jam as they did make. I grieve more and more about not getting any of those out at Mr. Jenkins'. I dined with Mrs. M but was home in time to eat some of Cousin Jane's apple dumplings. About 4 this evening an old drunken Yankee staggered in. Through fear, I made him welcome to some peaches that were setting by, and during his stay he just showered the compliments down. With Cousin Jane he was not so profuse, owing no doubt to her telling him in the first instance the peaches were not hers. Left with me I was afraid of him, he might have had all of the peaches in the basket. The children amuse themselves very much at his conversation with me.

New Providence, Tennessee, Wednesday night, September 2, 1863

Mr. Homer went fishing this morning. He and Bob spent the live long day and came home with about as many fish as I could eat — at two meals. Told him and Bob both to bring me some pears, but they turned out like the peaches. After a while I suppose I'll get used to such disappointments. He called at Uncle Trice's this morning where he learned that Winnie, escorted by two Yankee soldiers, walked up to the gate and demanded her child.[32] Uncle Trice came up in the meantime, took possession of Winnie, and in the face of the Yankees has succeeded in getting her off somewhere — the place is yet unknown to me. She called him a liar and almost cursed him. Such independence, I suppose, never escaped a Negro's lips. I expect he was almost, if not quite, killed.

New Providence, Tennessee, Thursday night, September 10, 1863

This morning a week ago [**Thursday, September 3**] Mr. Homer and I went out to Mr. Layne's. The clouds threatened rain all the way, but with no damage done either to ourselves or baggage, we safely landed at the point of destination about ½ 11 o'clock. Found Cousin Nannie sick, but to our great surprise, Mary and Mattie Carneal were both there, and both I feel safe in saying were equally surprised at meeting with us. About the middle of the afternoon Uncle Trice drove up. All were eager to know the cause of his sudden appearance, and soon we were informed he had taken that long ride to get Mr. Homer to go up to Hopkinsville to see something about Winnie. Of course he went, stayed at Mr. Layne's that night, and left early the next morning [**Friday, September 4**]. After he left I went home with Mattie. Had the headache slightly when I left, but it continued to grow worse all day. Through Mattie's advice I went to the dinner table where imprudence in eating no doubt caused it to terminate in real sick headache. Mary and Mattie seemed very much interested, but didn't succeed in forcing me to the supper table as they did at dinner. I was too sick. The next day [Saturday, September 5] to my great joy I found myself almost well. We lounged, at least I did, the most of the day, and late Mattie and I took a ride but I was so sore from vomiting that I failed to enjoy it much. [Sunday, September 6] Were to have gone to church [but] the prospect of rain prevented. Read and slept, eat peaches and drank cider, until about 5 when Mary's beau came (Mr. Harris) and we all concluded to be dignified for a while. The next day [Monday, September 7] we sewed, made jelly, and talked over our reasons for not going to Mr. Grinstead's until 4 in the evening when Mattie and I with her little brother and a servant for company went up to Mr. Layne's. I was a little surprised at not meeting with Mr. H that evening but was more so when [Tuesday, September 8] passed and [Wednesday, September 9] came and brought Dud Magaren and Old Gray without Mr. Homer. He soon told me that Mr. H had been quite sick and was still too weak to drive out for me. Mattie left that morning just before Dud came. When we started yesterday evening Cousin Nannie waded me down with cakes, peaches, mutton, knitting yarn, and many things that will be of great use to me and that will be but little missed by her. I wish all country people were so thoughtful.

New Providence, Tennessee, Friday night, September 11, 1863

After seeing Mr. H off for a day's fishing this morning, I went to sewing, and kept it up until nap time when it was too warm for anything else. Jack Gold came soon after I rose and nothing but the great picnic at Davis' Spring[33] tomorrow seemed to engage her interest. Mr. Homer and Bob to our surprise came home this evening loaded with squirrels & fish.

New Providence, Tennessee, Saturday night, September 12, 1863

After knitting a while this morning I went over to see Jack Gold. She was dressing in great haste for the picnic, had on her blue silk skirt with small muslin body trimmed off with black velvet and brass buttons on the sleeves, on the shoulders, on the neck and up nearly where {indecipherable} the black velvet was strung around. Some people may follow fashions because they are fashions, but that is one I think I should slight all the time, it seems so out of taste. I came home and to my surprise Cousin Jane was preparing to go to the picnic. Florence and Bob had both taken contrary fits and to prevent Marion's being disappointed, she went with her. F's excuse was she had no hat pretty enough to wear and, Bob if he had to have "Little sister" at his heels all the time he didn't want to go. Cousin Jane says there were a great many there from the country all round. As many as four sets danced at one time, but a severe storm came up between 2 and 3 and, with but little warning, the crowd adjourned to the hall above the "Big grocery" where I suppose the dancing is still going. What mockery it seems for people to engage in such amusements times like these. Late papers say that Bragg has been driven from Chattanooga and the Yanks have now possession of it[34] and that Charleston will be theirs soon. It does seem that the Confederacy is fast dwindling to nothing.

New Providence, Tennessee, Sunday night, September 13, 1863

After cleaning up this morning I read until near dinner time; then teased Mr. Homer until he thought or called me deranged. Took a short nap and dined heartily on Irish & sweet potatoes, corn and other things in proportion. I walked down to Mrs. Harrelson's and Magaren's. Mrs. H — had considerable to tell of the picnic and dance last night, but to cap it all the negroes and Yankees had a real break down at the cave spring today in imitation, I suppose, of the (whites' picnic) yesterday.

New Providence, Tennessee, Friday night, September 18, 1863

The rain and blow yesterday brought up such cold weather that fires and winter clothing have scarcely made us comfortable today (wood being rather scarce). I have nearly knit Inez a stocking today.

New Providence, Tennessee, Saturday night, September 19, 1863

Cousin Jane and I were going to Oak Grove all so fast this morning, but Mrs. Howell sent her word to go with her out to see Cousin Marion, and of course that invitation before any other was accepted. Jack Gold and I then concluded to go with Mrs. Dan G over to Clarksville to have her children's pictures taken. As usual the gallery was crowded, but "first come first served" with Mr. McCormack, and so we were fortunate enough to get off rather early. Mrs. Sears[35] and nearly the whole Major family were there. Miss Bobbie Killebrew[36] was along, I suppose, to see them well taken care of. Miss Robb[37] with Juliet McDaniel[38] and the other young ladies were there, having pictures taken in fancy dresses, and indeed some of them were fancy. Went down town and it seemed that the citizens for miles around had concentrated there; so many were in from the country. We had to wait on the provost marshal until 2 o'clock for a pass[39] and our patience was no little tried, as the weather is too cold for us to be comfortable anywhere except before a large fire.

New Providence, Tennessee, Sunday night, September 20, 1863

This evening I walked down to Mrs. Helm's. While there, the Ft. Donelson crowd came in; the long dreaded "scarecrows" have certainly arrived. And if we are not literally to pieces by the savages, we shall think our case not so hard after [all]. The Ohioans have taken great pleasure for some time past in threatening us with the "Jay hawkers"[40] as they call them, and we will now see whether or not their threats were in vain.[41] The 102 Ohio leaves tomorrow.

New Providence, Tennessee, Tuesday night, September 22, 1863

Gathered and put up a jar of corn yesterday morning, and as a result of my trouble and exertion in the hot sun, suffered all the evening with sick headache. Cousin Jane and Jack Oldham[42] were so interested in the exit of the Ohioans that they walked down near the camp to see the last of them, and by the way met with and entered into a confab with two or three of the Ft. D set. Jack will talk to any of them, while their very appearance satisfies me. Some of them were here yesterday and today to have their meals cooked, but all alike met with a refusal, and what the consequence will be we yet have to learn. We are here in their power. The last Ohioan left yesterday, and with such protection as they are a mind [to] extend, we are to put up with, be that good or bad.

New Providence, Tennessee, Friday night, September 25, 1863

That evening Miss Mary and Gold Collins[43] came in and spent the evening. Miss M was the only one I saw while there that gave me much reason to believe myself well and able to look and act as other people. Everyone was ready to tell me of how badly I was looking; to have listened to them and without the presence of a mirror I might very easily have considered myself a ghost or some walking shadow. Mete Sypert[44] is boarding with Mrs. B and even he had to speak of my ethereal appearance. Cousin Will Trice, while we were at the store, rendered himself quite disgusting indeed. Yesterday Mrs. B as usual had us all at work for Fannie. She is going to school in Clarksville and, of course, must have a supply of everything fashionable and nice.[45] Late Mrs. B was taken with a chill which

terminated in palpitation of the heart, and from both she was so ill that we
sent for Dr. Thomas. Today she seems better. Mary drove me in this evening
after dinner. Found Cousin Marion here. Late papers confirm the news of
Rosecrans' defeat and the victory of Bragg.[46]

New Providence, Tennessee, Monday night, September 28, 1863

Went to work towards putting a quilt in the frame this morning, but the
Yankees were taking the corn so fast I stopped to put up some more in brine.
In a few more days I think the patch will be stripped. Before our eyes in the
broad daylight they walk into the garden and help themselves to both corn
and potatoes, nor do they seem to think for once that they are taking that,
that doesn't belong to them. Many Yankees have been stationed here in our
midst, but never before such a set as these are. Set out some roses this evening and really, I feel so tired that it is a task for me even to write

New Providence, Tennessee, Saturday night, October 3, 1863

Tuesday morning I thought nothing should prevent my quilt being in the
frame by night, but about dinner Mr. Mills came in, and as it was not convenient for Cousin Jane to go out with him, her persuasion added to his
induced me to take a seat with him myself. So very unexpectedly at tea
time I found myself enjoying some of Aunt Kit's good toast and coffee. Mr.
Homer, as usual, was out fishing when Cousin Nat came down, but came out
the next morning—according to Cousin Mollie's orders. He went turkey
hunting that evening and brought back with him a very fine old hen. He
laughingly told her that he intended to bring one back with him if he had to
kill a tame one.

New Providence, Tennessee, Sunday night, October 4, 1863

In this end of town so little seems, particularly on Sunday, worth recording
that sometimes I'm almost persuaded not to write at all. To write just of myself and my performances is of all things to me the most irksome task, and
for that reason I like to write of other things. Preaching and church service
seems to have been given up, at least in this place. Rosecrans, rumor says, is
being heavily reinforced and another clash is expected soon between he and
Bragg.[47] The cars[48] have been pressed and we get no more papers for some
time. The negroes are flocking into the Yanks here at the Fort by droves. It
is thought this will be made a recruiting post for them.[49] Old Mrs. Trice's[50]
two maids, her dependence almost for cooking and homework, left last week,

and Mr. Homer has been lecturing Cousin Jane and I ever since we heard of it, for rejoicing over the old lady's downfall.

New Providence, Tennessee, Monday night, October 5, 1863

Rose this morning early. Commenced putting my quilt in the frame before breakfast and thought after getting it in I would go out to Mr. Jake Wilson's burial, but Cousin Jane couldn't go and Mr. H wouldn't go, so I had no company. I drove up as far as Mr. Magaren's and Mr. Helm's. Mr. M just helped me to flowers of most every description. I brought a great many slips with me home including gooseberries with the rest. I expected to quilt all the evening, but the Yankees came very near stealing all of Cousin Jane's potatoes last night, so we decided to join forces and bring in the few remaining ones. We were busy the whole evening. Mr. H and Jack Gold were the overseers. Jack sit out in the patch most all the evening.

New Providence, Tennessee, Tuesday night, October 6, 1863

Went to work early on my quilt. Laura Helm came about 9 to assist me, and with all our efforts, we made very slow progress. Cousin Jane helped me a while this evening, and what she did seemed to show off better than all Laura [and] I both did. Florence started to school yesterday to Miss Turbyville, and without her help Cousin Jane hasn't much time for sewing. Cousin Marion came today just before dinner and left about three, the rain just pouring down. No doubt her clothes were saturated by the time she got home. She says the Yankees from here have been all through her neighborhood pressing negro men, and Mr. Osborne expected them at his house today. They pretend they want them to work on railroads, breastworks, &c-but it is all a scheme to force them away from their owners, and they will live to find {indecipherable}. As many as 175 were brought in today I've heard.

New Providence, Tennessee, Wednesday night, October 7, 1863

Have quilted so hard today that my back aches, my fingers ache, my elbow and even my feet feel uncomfortable. Cousin Jane has helped me a great deal. If nothing prevents, it will be ready to leave the frames tomorrow. The weather remains very gloomy; heavy showers have been frequent for the last two or three days. Mr. Homer has been so busy yesterday and today converting the reservoir into a pit that I fear the cistern will be neglected until the rain is over with. I wish that snake had been somewhere else anyway when he crawled into it. Then we need not have been in such haste about cleaning it out. Went with Florence to milking this evening and it is really heart sickening (to say nothing of the stomach) to find how rapidly the cows were failing in their milk. The prospect for winter is indeed gloomy.

New Providence, Tennessee, Thursday night, October 8, 1863

Finished my quilt between 3 & 4 o'clock this evening. Up to that time only a few moments were spent at meals and about 15 minutes with Jack Gold. I had a real pain in my shoulder from sitting so constantly. Jack told me while over there, that Jane and Paralee[51] had sent up for their mother & Jane's two children, so old Mrs. Trice and Mary are left without a single maid. Tom, they say, does their cooking and as for washing that has to be done from home just whoever will, may. One thing certain Mary won't put her hands to the tub nor pot either if there can be found a preventative. I heard they called in a neighbor to turn a hoecake for them. The pressing business is still going on. Mr. H and Ben Gold were over in town this morning and say over a hundred were sent from there today—to reinforce Rosecrans I suppose. Some laugh and some cry when they are sent off. A great many round here have run off to avoid the draft—Uncle Billy for one, I heard. Mr. H also brought news that Forrest had taken Murfreesboro.[52] If that be true, we may expect him here soon. Cousin Jane and I have been putting up tomato pickle tonight and I'm so tired.

New Providence, Tennessee, Friday night, October 9, 1863

Worked over my pickle this morning until Jack Gold came over and reminded me of our trip to old Mrs. Pettus'. We went out expecting to return before dinner, but Mrs. P and Miss Meda just wouldn't listen to it, so we concluded to remain and came home soon after dinner. But the stereoscopic views and Miss M's flowers engaged our attention so that we made it 3 o'clock getting home. While there we heard heavy cannonading in the direction of Ft. Donelson. We are anxious to know the object of it. Bragg it is said has had another engagement with Rosecrans and whipped him if possible worse than before.[53]

New Providence, Tennessee, Sunday night, October 11, 1863

Have been so mad all day that not one line in the bible have I read. As usual when I want Old Gray he is engaged. A Baptist minister preached in Clarksville this morning and I wanted to hear him, but no, a Yankee, a Ft.

Donelson Yankee at that, wanted Old Gray this evening and so much afraid was Mr. H of disappointing him that I must stay from church this morning. Before I would lend a Yankee, particularly one who had ever been to Fort D, I'd see them crawling on their knees and their hands. The only horse I ever had the slightest claim to or ever expected to have, a rogue from Ft. D stole from me. Even now they would take from me or from Mr. Homer the last crumb, the last drop of anything that goes toward keeping us alive, and still Mr. H will put on a smile and tell them "oh yes they are entirely welcome." May it be my lot to show independence to the last and though we may be subjugated in the end, in every word, look, and action may I prove to the day of my death that I scorn, I despise, I detest a Yankee. Cousin Jane and I walked over to her old home this evening. Time has brought many changes over the old place, but the Yankees bid fair to make greater havoc still. They have commenced tearing the old house to pieces and if they do that as they do all the other vacant houses round, there will be but little left to tell where the old homestead once stood.

New Providence, Tennessee, Monday night, October 12, 1863

Made a complete finish of my quilt today; finished hemming it before dinner. The rain came down so constantly and in such torrents, today that Florence had to defer milking until noon. Since dinner Mr. H went over to see about his sow and pigs. Out [of] the eight, the Yankees have stolen six. That looks very much like they were "gentlemen" and deserved to be "accommodated." I hope and trust that every Yankee that tastes a piece of those pigs may be paralyzed from head to foot. Some of the officers went out pressing negroes again today. From the noise they made coming in they had a considerable drove. They said they selected today because it was rainy and they would find them in the houses.

New Providence, Tennessee, Tuesday night, October 13, 1863

The rain still continues. I regret so much the cistern isn't prepared for it. Jack came over this morning with a face as long as the moral law; 4 of her father's negro men were pressed yesterday. Not until this evening did she know that any of them had been released. Through Mr. Pettus' influence, our most prominent loyal citizen, two of them were gotten — so she told me this evening when I was over to see her a short while. To Mr. Oldham's astonishment when they were called up, not one of them seemed willing to return with him home, notwithstanding yesterday evening when they left home they feigned great reluctance, took a cry,

&c &c. Mr. O says now that he hasn't any confidence in those that came back nor in any of the others. He thinks the last one will leave so soon as he gets his little business matters adjusted. Even 3 of Uncle William Mallory's left today and when they run from freedom, as they have surely done, no confidence is to be placed in the rest. A good many prophesy that by Christmas, scarcely a negro man will be left in the State. 11 out of old Mr. Buck Davy's 12 have gone.

New Providence, Tennessee, Wednesday, October 14, 1863

Mr. Homer went out this morning to spend the day getting up wood, but the rain at 12 o'clock prevented farther operations and so he with all hands were stopped with only half a day's work done. I expect the Yankees from the post just below us will get the better half of what he did get. He heard one make an inquiry about wood yesterday and another remarked "Oh there's a dam good wood pile near us." They take the wood, they milk the cows as they pass the post, they steal potatoes, they kill and eat suckling pigs, they do everything it seems that's mean and Yankee like. Jack sent us over a piece of fresh beef today. It was a real treat; we had been without fresh meat so long.

New Providence, Tennessee, Saturday night, October 24, 1863

After milking this morning, went to work on some onion pickle and not until dinner were they finished. Since then I've been so sick with cold that I haven't engaged in anything bearing a resemblance to work. Uncle Trice came down this evening & brought my bureau. He was pretty high up in the pictures, at least Cousin Bet thought so. Cousin Jane came about 3 o'clock. She came by Pea Ridge[54] and says a band of robbers were there last night and took goods to the amount of $12.00 worth. Bands of highway robbers are becoming so common in this part of the country as they ever were in Murrell's[55] time. Every country store round with few exceptions have been robbed within the last two or three months.

New Providence, Tennessee, Monday night, October 26, 1863

Went to work at my old trade this morning, altering an old dress. This evening I trimmed up an old hat for sale, went down to Aunt Lucy's to sell it, but failed of course. Aunt Lucy was telling me of one of Mr. Holland's negro men that came down this morning in search of freedom, but met with his master before getting in possession of it. He had stolen $4000 in gold from Mr. Holland. He found only $60 of it about his person.

The negroes are coming in to the Yankees, if possible, faster than ever. 4 and all of Mr. Layne's came in last night. He succeeded in getting his horses back. 4 horses out of 6 were captured Saturday night that negroes had stolen from their masters to ride in. Citizens who have been round in camp say the place seems literally alive with them.

New Providence, Tennessee, Tuesday night, October 27, 1863

"Quite an important" day in our little family at least, (Mr. Homer and Uncle David and Bobbie) killed one of Old Peggy's little pigs this morning before breakfast. We all thought it a great pity that such a pretty little thing had to be butchered. Still at dinner our admiration was as extensive as ever even though his features wore something of a deathly character. Laura & Bettie Helm were to see me this evening. They have seen a New York paper in which Meade's defeat is acknowledged and also that he has been driven back to Washington City for protection.[56] His "On to Richmond" has turned out, if possible, worse than his predecessor's. The paper tonight seems very quiet on the subject. It is no longer a matter of doubt about the negroes being called in to the field.[57] From Maryland, Ky., Tenn., and Missouri the negro men have been called, (all that are willing) and if volunteers do not come forward, they are to be forced—their owners, if loyal, being paid $300 for each. From the day of this enlistment they are free, so considered by their brother Yankees.

New Providence, Tennessee, Thursday night, October 29, 1863

Worked hard yesterday and today on an old dress and it is yet unfinished. How I wish old dress could be replaced with new ones every time. Last night Mr. Homer went over to take a game of cards with Ben Gold, and while there Inez had some miraculous tale to tell of someone rapping at the door. So fear took the place of better sense and she took up quarters with Cousin Jane for the night. Her feather bed is somewhat more inviting anyway than our old mattress, and then Cousin J is such a good bed fellow. Mrs. Magaren and Mary Harrelson were here this morning. They had but little news except that there seemed to be a general ingathering of the few remaining negroes in the country. Last night Mrs. M said they sounded like cavalry coming in. Yesterday 2 forage trains were sent across the river and before getting far from town they were fired into by the guerillas. One or two are reported killed and several wounded. After returning, a constant firing of the canon was kept up nearly all the evening. The woods were shelled far and near.

New Providence, Tennessee, Monday night, November 2, 1863

Rose in time this morning to have breakfast before 9 o'clock. After milking I went down to see my roses. To my horror I found the old sow had taken them by the row and entirely rooted ever so many of them up. If ever I was tempted to curse, then is the time. I tried to kill her and took the rest of it out in crying. Altogether I made myself sick with the headache so Inez had the most of the dinner to get.

New Providence, Tennessee, Tuesday night November 3, 1863

I have been busy all day raising yeast and making light bread. For once my efforts were not fruitless. We had very nice rolls for supper and for breakfast I have a very inviting pone.[58]

New Providence, Tennessee, Wednesday night, November 4, 1863

Mr. Homer went out partridge netting again this morning, and being alone he came out much better. Out of 2 flocks he brought home 18. The last of the Burgess family[59] has returned. They are all now as in other days clustered around the same hearthstone, each reflecting glory on the other from laurels gained since the commencement of the war.[60] George[61] they say has made so many miraculous escapes that it really seems for the moment that his ghost and not he himself is present. For three days I believe they say he was buried beneath the sand at Charleston, from one of the enemy's shells busting near him, (poor boy, will he ever get forgiveness for such tales).

New Providence, Tennessee, Thursday night, November 5, 1863

Rose so early this morning that Mr. H seemed no little astonished and done away with my industrious fit to some extent by laughing at me. The partridges for breakfast were broiled so nice that he even noticed them enough to praise them, and on that account I half way excuse him for laughing at me on the former occasion. He has been out all day hunting again but came home without any birds. But for the fact of having no cooking of importance to do in his absence, I should feel inclined to grumble a little at him for leaving me alone all day. Today Inez and I dined on cold light bread, ham, and pie left over yesterday, and Mr. H came in about 4—so hungry that he joined dinner and supper by which I was saved the trouble both of preparing dinner & supper. If the Yankee women can beat me in economy when it comes to cooking, I should like to know of the gone about it. The Democrat[62] of yesterday contains such an excellent speech of Gov. Seymour of New York.[63]

New Providence, Tennessee, Saturday night, November 7, 1863

Didn't write last night because I had nothing worth writing, and tonight I think I might bring up the same excuse. But I forget, Old Aunt Mary has gone to the Yankees. Not exactly that way either, they say "she has gone North." Well done, I suppose as she had no one to run from. She concluded to change the common way of doing up things and has "gone North." Mr. Homer says he is really glad to get her out of the way. But for the way she or someone else did Cousin Jane's cabbage, I should not regret her leaving one moment—went into the patch and twisted all the heads out of the nicest ones.

New Providence, Tennessee, Monday night, November 9, 1863

Yesterday evening and last night the weather turned so cold that fire will scarcely keep us warm (little ones as I keep). I've spent the whole day mending up old stockings and have not yet finished. Mr. H killed the other little pig this morning, so we are done "killing hogs" for the season. Up town he learned that a large fire over in Clarksville had destroyed a great many valuable buildings both public and private.[64] It is supposed they were set on fire by the negroes, offended of course because they were refused permission to go in and take possession. We will not be surprised when they order us out of homes—they are getting at such a high pop. Maj., Col., or Gen. Stones,[65] whichever he is, the Journal say[s] is to be the recruiting officer for the blacks at this place.

New Providence, Tennessee, Thursday night, November 12, 1863

Yesterday and today I've been mending up Mr. Homer's old shirts, a job equally as tiresome and altogether as prosy[66] as darning stockings. This evening I went with Bob walnut hunting—walked two or three miles and found about a peck. Mr. H has made repeated promises to go with me in the buggy, but like all his promises of late, they have availed nothing. He always has to see about "something to eat" and that something to eat turns out to be the same old meat and bread we've had at the meat-house all the year. Through old Crippled Charlie, old Donel, or some such is the only way I know to get him to do one of the family a favor.

New Providence, Tennessee, Friday night, November 13, 1863

Made Inez two skirts today. Jack Gold spent most of the morning with us. She and Mr. G speak of moving to the country. We shall miss her visits so much if she does go. No news except Meade is whipping Lee back to Richmond.[67]

New Providence, Tennessee, Sunday night, November 15, 1863

The weather this morning was dark & gloomy & this evening the wind blew up so cold and the prospect for snow was so favorable that we rather looked for it. Before dinner a while Mr. Allen came in with a horse for Cousin Jane. Mr. Osborne is very ill and Cousin Marion got Mr. A to come over for Cousin Jane. While at dinner he gave us a history of his trial with the robbers the other night. He attempted to defend himself when they collared him. But for the assistance of his family & the two sisters, [he] would have made a poor defense, being a cripple and badly frightened too. They entered his house about 12 o'clock at night and pretended to be Southern soldiers wanting to know the route to some place not far off. On his refusing to accompany them, they cursed him, took hold of him, and one of them tried to drag him out of the house. The others I suppose had some sense of humanity left, and after the extraordinary bravery exhibited on the part of his sisters, they consented to release him, provided he would give them $5,000. He said then for the first time the thought occurred that they were robbers and with it his courage returned and almost in an instant he had one of them thrown to the floor. But for being overpowered by superior numbers, he says he could have whipped that man good. He talked to them very roughly. At the same time, he took hold of the man and with that they left. I think the only thing that saved him from being murdered was the influence of his sisters and children.[68] He had not heard of Mr. Wray's marriage last Wednesday to Miss Lettie Jenkins.

New Providence, Tennessee, Monday night, November 16, 1863

After breakfast a while old Mrs. Sisco came in, on business of course. She said "the Yankees or somebody else was perusing round her house every night and that altogether they had stolen 50 cabbage from her." Have finished Inez's dress at last with red cord and buttons to match. She seems very proud of it. In the culinary department I am making rapid progress. Tonight we had some of the most splendid rools and the best broiled partridge imaginable.

New Providence, Tennessee, Wednesday night, November 18, 1863

Had the headache all day yesterday & didn't feel like writing last night. When Mr. Homer came in from partridge hunting he told me that Efe Fairfax[69] was married day before yesterday.[70] I could not, would not, believe it, but today he went uptown, saw Efe himself, got all the particulars, and to my astonishment came home with not a shadow of a doubt remaining as to the certainty of his marriage. He says he and Miss Mary Trice were certainly married at Mr. Williams', his brother-in-law, on Monday. Went from there up to Uncle Tom Campbell's where a supper was given them, stayed all night that night, slept with her, and came home yesterday morning "to make preparation for her." He says she told him to leave her up there — and no doubt she did, for well she knows the world will say money, not love, prompted her to marry an idiot. Under the circumstances she is excusable for not showing her face. Surely she has paid dearly for the mere prospect of someday possessing what Efe's father and mother now own and are likely to own for some time to come.

New Providence, Tennessee, Friday night, November 20, 1863

Nothing for the last week in the way of news (Efe's marriage excepted) has occurred — I mean within the borders of our little village. Uncle Wm Mallory called yesterday on his return from Clarksville, but brought with [him] neither telegraph or "grapevine" news. Mr. H's telling him of the Negro Regiment that is being organized in Clarksville was news to him though he is now fresh from the city. Mr. Homer's "Yankee tenant," a negro man of some distinction as preacher, cook, &c, was telling him yesterday morning that the recruiting business here now was progressing finely.[71] He thought there had & would be about 175 blacks down at the fort that would enlist.

New Providence, Tennessee, Saturday night, November 21, 1863

The Democrat tonight confirms the news of Burnside's defeat in East Tenn. and says that he is confined in Knoxville on half rations.[72]

New Providence, Tennessee, Monday night, November 23, 1863

What a shame! Jack Gold came over this morning before I was even dressed. She pretended as though she was late enough rising, but I told her I knew it was not a common occurrence. Before she left, I went up to Mrs. Pollard's expecting to go out to see Mrs. Wilson, but the morning was so unlikely we decided not to go, so I spent the whole day with her. Sandy told her this morning he believed he would enlist and it made her so mad that she was blue when I got there

New Providence, Tennessee, Tuesday night, November 24, 1863

Made Inez an apron today. Jack Gold spent most of the evening with us. She came over to get Cousin Jane to cut out some work for her. Tomorrow she expects to have another grand sewing. She says if they move to the country, which they expect to do next week, she never will get any more sewing done. Mr. H and I sit with them until 9 tonight. The new trade regulations seem to interfere with Mr. Gold's tobacco speculation to some extent. A man now has to get licenses and pay for them for everything he buys or sells, and even has to pay tax on his cattle, such as hogs, sheep, calves, &c. The next move will be to make a man pay for each breath drawn, and they must not consume too much oxygen or destroy too much carbonic acid gas.[73]

New Providence, Tennessee, Wednesday night, November 25, 1863

Attended today for the first time what the ladies of late have been pleased to call "a sewing." They will have a new name for meeting together now & then and going over the news of the day, the late fashions, and other subjects of equal importance. Yes, as expected, Jack Gold had her sewing. Bettie Helm came by for me and though it was near 10 when we went over, the company had not all assembled. Old Mrs. Fairfax (first on the list of course), Tishy Barber, Mrs. Hargrove, Mrs. Manson, Mary Harrelson, Mrs. Harrelson, Anna Staton, Bettie, and myself composed the crowd, and as many of us as there were, Jack didn't get much more sewing done than one ought to have done during the day. She gave us a good dinner, however, and that to most of us proved more interesting than Clarence's little aprons, skirts, or her good music, though the latter was very much appreciated. Mr. H went over tonight to finish off the day's entertainment by taking a game of euchre with Mr. Gold. Tonight's paper confirms the news of a fight going on near Chattanooga. Thomas, they say, so far has met with brilliant success.[74]

New Providence, Tennessee, Thursday night, November 26, 1863

Papers tonight say that Bragg is on the retreat and that Thomas has given him a most terrible whipping.[75]

New Providence, Tennessee, Sunday night, November 29, 1863

The weather was so cold last night that nearly all of Mr. H's plants froze in the pit, and even plants that I had in the room here setting near the fire. The river really looked as if it was frozen this morning. Sit with Jack Gold most of the morning. She and Ben are grieving terribly over Bragg's defeat. Came home and Mr. H had cut two of my geraniums down to the ground. Have been too mad to speak pleasantly ever since.

New Providence, Tennessee, Monday night, November 30, 1863

Nearly finished another collar today. The weather is still so cold that I can get my consent to do nothing but sit over the fire and sew or chit chat. Mr. H brought home today glorious news together with two turkeys. He says it is certainly so that Morgan with several of his men have cut their way out of prison. They dug out an underground road some way and so secretly that their escape was not found out until they [were] good and out of reach. A reward as high I think as $6,000 has been offered for him.[76]

New Providence, Tennessee, Wednesday night, December 2, 1863

Rose rather early this morning. Went to work to burn out a hominy mortar[77]—to me quite a novel proceeding, as I never even saw one that I know of. Have kept up a good fire in it all day and agreeable to my opinion it is doing very well, notwithstanding Mr. H's prophecy that I would be six months burning it out. This evening I went with the children to the woods after chips, brush, &c. Mr. Homer, Bobbie and Uncle Donel[78] have been out there all day and it is really distressing to see the destruction of timber made by the Yankees. They are cutting and hauling [it] into camp all the time, regardless of the owner's wishes or circumstances. Three or four of their teams were frightened at our wheel barrow this evening, and Florence is Yankee hater enough to say she didn't care if they were.

New Providence, Tennessee, Saturday night, December 5, 1863

Thursday Cousin Marion & Johny came in. They came in time for dinner & left soon afterwards. As usual Cousin M was in a hurry. Mr. O, she says, is improving. Yesterday I spent nearly the whole day making Mr. Homer a watch case. Late went over to take Jack Gold's new dress to her. While there Mr. G came in with two very fine cans of oysters and insisted that I would stay & take supper with them. Of course much persuasion was not necessary.

Mr. H was sent for and with "Uncle Kit" the repast was enjoyed to the greatest extent. The card playing until 10 o'clock was all the objectionable part. Not exactly all either—Mr. Brown, one of Mr. G's and Jack's Yankee friends, came in and sit until 8 o'clock, and that I will say was my first meeting with a Yankee around the social fireside.

New Providence, Tennessee, Sunday night, December 6, 1863

Inez went up home this evening and says Uncle Trice threw Elick's working tools into the fire the other day. I suppose from that, he has played out. I suppose since the order from old Col. Smith[79] for the ministers all to pray for Old Abe Lincoln and his government or else have the church doors closed, the members have concluded to close doors.[80] I've heard no bell at the church today.

New Providence, Tennessee, Tuesday night, December 8, 1863

Yesterday I made a little hood for Marion's doll and commenced another collar. Inez calls them Christmas collars that I've been making because I design them for presents at that time. Cousin Jane spent the day out at Mr. Jenkins'. Coming home she called at Uncle Trice's and from him she brought what I called an insulting message. When Mr. Homer and I married he told me when I had room for it he would give me a bed and such bed clothing as he "saw proper." Since then I've said nothing to him about it, though he has mentioned it time and again to Mr. H and urged the necessity of sending for the things as the Yankees he thought very soon would go round pressing such articles for the negroes that were daily coming into their lines.[81]

So yesterday Mr. H thought as he was going over to take possession of Mr. Gold's house and had room for the bed that he would send up for the bed and a mattress of his own that was there. The mattress came without the bed and the message by Cousin Jane, "Mr. H had sent up there for a bed" and "he didn't know what to make of it," as though he never had heard of such a thing before, and that if I wanted anything from there I must come up & select it—after saying to me that he expected to give me what he saw proper. Other things more cutting still he said to Cousin Jane. And that, added to her looks for the last two or three days,[82] gave me a sufficient excuse for a long cry, and so after supper I freely indulged in what is always woman's standby in time of trouble. Today Cousin Jane has seemed in a better humor. Mr. H has been over at Mr. G's most of the time, preparing things for our reception tomorrow.

New Providence, Tennessee, Wednesday night, December 9, 1863

As expected Mr. Homer and I with part of our effects (such as a coffee pot, two spoons (& they borrowed), a few little napkins to use in place of table cloths, &c) "moved" over to "Mr. Gold's" today. We dined with Cousin Jane and so our first meal was supper tonight. Mr. G's Fannie is still here and with her assistance & Inez I made out to have a little coffee and some biscuits. Supper was ready & waiting and I happened to think we had no sugar. It was then too late to send to Cousin Jane & so the last resort was to borrow from Fannie.[83] Mr. H met with Uncle T up town this evening. The bed question was talked over again. Of course, Mr. H came home with a long lecture for me. I despise to see a man so fickle, at least so credulous. His last request was for Mr. H to come up in the morning & select what things he intends for me.

New Providence, Tennessee, Thursday night, December 10, 1863

Mr. Smith came in this morning before we were through breakfast for Mr. H — to go partridge netting. They spent the day and returned without a bird. Our partridges gave out tonight and I don't know where our supply of meat is to come from tomorrow. I hope to rest a little better tonight as we have some pillows.

New Providence, Tennessee, Monday night, December 14, 1863

As Mr. H prophesied, a northwester came up last night and brought such a change over things that we were not in the least prepared for it. So cold has it been that I have not been out but once today. Laura & Gerty Helm came this evening to stay all night with us. They have been packed up for the last few days expecting to move to the country, but bad weather prevented and they are staying round with friends. Providence will soon be altogether unlike itself. Mr. Helm is going to the country, & Tine Smith[84] and Ben Gold & Mr. Harrelson have already gone, and by the time the others that speak of going have gone we will find ourselves settled round by new neighbors altogether, and [if] they do not prove to be Yankee negroes I shall be glad. Mr. H was up town this morning and says the last negro of Mr. Pollard's left last night — Rhoda & her tribe, Armistead & his tribe. Mrs. P is without even a nurse.

New Providence, Tennessee, Tuesday night, December 15, 1863

After so long a time we had breakfast this morning after which Gertie went to school and Laura decided to stay all day with me. Our pork came in just before dinner, and for the sake of having spare ribs, I concluded to unite the two meals and have dinner & supper together. I like the plan very much and think I will continue it at least until sausage and drying up lard[85] time are over. Sit until bed time over at Cousin Jane's tonight. Cousin Marion has been over to Clarksville today and had on exhibition her purchases when I stopped in.

New Providence, Tennessee, Wednesday night, December 16, 1863

Thought I was getting up very early this morning. Made up my bed, made up light rolls for breakfast, fried some brains[86] (my first attempt), and made coffee, and so breakfast was over. Left Inez to clear the table while I churned. After that, straightened up things generally a little, looked at the watch to see what time my first boiler of lard would be put on, and lo and behold it was 11 o'clock. And had Old Aunt Delony, one of Mr. H's acquaintances, to come in about 10 to help me. She stayed until dark and only one boiler of lard was finished. Bob went to camp and made 40 cts off my butter milk, and that helped out considerably. The rain has been pouring almost ever since last night some time. Will good weather never return?

New Providence, Tennessee, Thursday night, December 17, 1863

Well, Old Aunt Delony, or Demuslin,[87] whatever she is, has gotten through with the lard at last. She stayed until dark finishing off the sausage meat, and tonight I feel almost as much fatigued as if she had stayed at home. She was so slow and I was so impatient to see the business through with that, I felt as if it would make me sick to have to wait with her. A cold N. Wester has been blowing all day, and tonight it is cold enough to wake up the snakes.

New Providence, Tennessee, Friday night, December 18, 1863

Rested nearly all of day. Inez prepared most of the dinner and a right good cook she makes. Two Yankees came in today just before our dinner-supper, but they got what they came for, sausage meat, without being invited to dine. By the by I have made a whole dollar today selling sausage meat, and all of 95 cts off my butter milk. Fannie let them cheat her down at camp, else I would have made more on my meat.

New Providence, Tennessee, Saturday night, December 19, 1863

Churned, cleaned up my room, and ordered things generally this morning in time to make Fannie a dress body before dinner. Dined at 3. Fannie went to camp this evening and made for me 63 cts on milk. I say for me, but if it goes like the milk money—generally it will be for anyone else before me. Mr. H goes into my pocket money by the time I have accumulated a dollar or two and robs it of nearly the last cent. We've just had a long quarrel about it.

New Providence, Tennessee, Sunday night, December 20, 1863

The weather still is very cold, though it has been clear most of the day. After cleaning up this morning, read until 12, then took a short nap. At 3 we dined, though everything was cold. I have always thought it wrong to have cooking going on Sunday and now that I am cook and bottle washer in chief I am more of the opinion than ever.

New Providence, Tennessee, Monday night, December 21, 1863

It wouldn't do for me not to record the events of [today], for strange to say I have made one more trip uptown. Mr. Pettus, I thought, let me have right cheap bargains. I traded with my milk money, "our kind of money" he called it. Some shoes for Inez were the only things I bought with Tenn. Money; they were 2.75. Pie pans, pint cup, &c, he let me have for 10 cts each, which I thought cheap enough. I called at Cousin Jane's and I thought the children would see anyhow what I had gotten for their Christmas presents. The candy was so nice I expect to enjoy that as much as they do.

New Providence, Tennessee, Tuesday night, December 22, 1863

Before I was done churning this morning Betty Helm came in. They have not yet moved unless they went out this evening. Bettie's whole conversation nearly was in regard to their negroes leaving. Some of them have left, and the others have given them to understand that they would leave. She seems to dread cooking bad enough, but having to wash—the thought almost makes her sick.[88] Mr. H tells me the negro soldiers from Clarksville will be over tomorrow to camp near us.[89] What will we do? Already someone has frightened Cousin Jane nearly to death, and she thinks they were negroes.

New Providence, Tennessee, Wednesday night December 23, 1863

Dinner was so late yesterday that I ate entirely too much and as a natural consequence was sick all night. And until late this morning though I went to work early to baking some cakes for Christmas and did not finish until dark tonight. Bettie and Laura came to stay all night with me just as I was commencing some doughnuts. Excused myself until they were finished, which was a good while. With them I have a Gold & Silver cake[90] and a jelly cake. Whether I've a chance of baking any more or not, they, I think, will last at least during one day of the Christmas. Mr. H tried to laugh me out with my cakes. Said I had too much butter & too much sugar, and everything else, but I notice he takes occasion to taste them regularly.

New Providence, Tennessee, Thursday night, December 24, 1863

Breakfasted this morning about 9; in the place of getting better, I believe we are getting worse in the getting-up line. While at the table Uncle Trice came with the long talked of bed and "such bed clothing as he saw proper." The whole consisted of a feather bed & stead[91] with a pair of pillows and bolster, two pair of slips for each, a pair of sheets, a pair of blankets, one quilt, one comfort, one counterpane, and an old bookcase with some of my school books. Though "the best of Aunt T's bed clothing," as Miss Fannie said she intended for me, would seem to be a very few articles, yet not a thing was sent for which I was not thanking and not a thing but what will prove most useful to me. Mr. H had a feather bed & two mattresses it is true, but for company we have scarcely enough covering for an extra bed (that borrowed)—indeed nothing over change for our own.

Bettie & Laura left early after breakfast. Put on a hogs head & some chive[92] to cook about 11. Went over to Cousin Jane's and sit until ½ 12, when Jack Gold came in and stayed a short while. She says Mr. G is quite ill with neuralgia. About 3 took off my meat and it was so cooked to pieces that I could scarcely take it up. This evening Cousin Jane made me some such excellent potato custards. When Inez went over for them, I sent the children some little Christmas presents. They suspected directly what the basket contained and Bobbie, I think, is making grand expectations. Poor fellow, he will soon find that they are indeed "hard time" presents. Ed Pettus was up tonight to invite us to an egg nog in the morning and to dinner tomorrow. I think we will split the difference as these are Yankee negro times. Mr. H may partake of the egg nog while I would prefer the good dinner.

New Providence, Tennessee, Friday night, December 25, 1863

What have I to write of today? I woke Inez so early she had to light the candle to see what "Old Kris Kringle" had brought her. She seemed highly delighted with everything. It did me good to see how she enjoyed the presents, simple though they were. I felt how I had and would enjoy just such things now, but Mr. Homer says I must be a woman now and put away "childish things." And to bring about this change he seems resolved. I made him a very pretty & neat little watch case, hoping in return he would at least make me a present of some little something similar to what Aunt T was always in the habit of giving me. The name of husband seems with some to hold the dearest place in the affections, but with me, her name before all others. From her have I received the kindest words, and by her have my wishes though "childish" been oftenest gratified. If in making a woman of me, as Mr. H calls it, he has to resort to such means as denying me little presents, forcing me with the dark alone, and such like, he may expect the task to be accomplished with my death. For not until then do I expect to be less "childish" in my notions. I surely think sometimes that he forgets there is a difference of nearly 20 years in our ages, and then I remember how he used to tell me he would do if only I would become his wife—that he would have treated me like I was a baby, a spoiled child and all that. And I remember that he has known the difference if he does not now. Men's vows as well as women's, I find, are often traced in sand. I was so disappointed this morning that I declined going to {indecipherable} Mrs. Pettus, and have stayed at home the livelong day pretending to sew {indecipherable} but doing more crying than anything else. Cousin Jane about 11 sent me over some pickle apples and other little things and I'm sorry to say I was in no frame of mind to even enjoy them. Some of the Yanks, or Negroes one, came and took Mr. H's prettiest pig out of the pen last night, and I haven't grieved one bit, because I thought if all the care and attention that he had been bestowing on that had been invested with me, perhaps he would have come nearer his object of making a "woman of me."

New Providence, Tennessee, Sunday night, December 27, 1863

After going through with the regular routine yesterday morning, I concluded to give my room a scouring (another novel employment which will tend, I suppose, "to make a woman of me"). I tucked up my dress, borrowed Cousin Jane's broom, and waded into it. And strange to say after it dried off and the chairs & furniture were rearranged, several of the grease spots that had so long been giving me such impudent looks seemed so utterly surprised at the attack, that several of them turned ghastly pale, while others almost entirely disappeared. Just as I was finishing, Cousin Jane came over to tell me of the Yanks or negroes or both going to Uncle Trice's the night before and stealing from one of the little bedrooms, the most of Miss Fannie's bed clothing, at least the most of what used to be Aunt Tabbie's bed clothing (Miss F I've heard had sent the most of hers to the country) besides other articles of clothing equally valuable. Uncle T yesterday morning told Mr. H there were 8 counterpanes. Those I'm certain were all Aunt T's, and if in the place of the one they sent me they had sent some of the 8, perhaps they would have done them as much good as for the negroes to have them, though Fannie was telling me today, that Uncle T had paid some of the Yanks to make a search and that they had found the things among some of the "free negroes" who have recently located up in "Meacham Town." He gave, she says, $1.00 to the Yanks to find what he thought would amount to $200 worth of goods. It is no longer a disputed fact about the negro Regiment coming over to our side of the river. They came over yesterday morning and are now camped within a few hundred yds of us. They sent, so Fannie says, 350 with their new uniforms out through the country yesterday, pressing more into the service.

New Providence, Tennessee, Monday night, December 28, 1863

My employment today has been mostly churning. I churned both this morning & this evening. Fannie and Inez sold a dollar's worth of milk for me. Inez made her first trip over to camp. She seems highly delighted with the appearance of things. The weather is very cold & disagreeable again.

New Providence, Tennessee, Tuesday night, December 29, 1863

Three Yankee women have come to see me today to buy butter. They seemed ladylike in their manners. Walked with L[aura Helm] & Bettie as far as Mrs. Magaren's this evening. Mrs. Herring was there & of course but little was talked about except the negroes leaving and the arrangements they were making about cooking. Saw a squad of Negro soldiers coming in, in full uniform. Been out pressing I suppose.

New Providence, Tennessee, Wednesday night, December 30, 1863

Went to work early on my quilt and since dark I have made a complete finish of it. Mr. H went out to see Mr. Gold this morning about having this clan of negroes moved out of the cabin and didn't return until 4 this evening. Mrs. Magaren came about 2 and stayed until he came. I really enjoyed her visit. While she was here, Mr. Holland came and spent a short while. When did a visitor surprise me more? I heard him knock and remarked to Mrs. M. "That's a Yankee." I didn't dream of its being anyone else, and my surprise may be imagined at seeing Mr. Holland instead. I was so glad to see him it seemed like old times. He came down to get a receipt for a negro of his that run off a short time ago. The negro soldiers that went out in the country pressing the other day went to old Mrs. Hutcheson's one night, threatened to kill her and two of her nieces that were with her, ransacked her house, took all of her valuables, and frightened them so that they stayed out in the woods all night. They attempted rape on one of the young ladies but were prevented by some cause. I didn't hear the particulars.

New Providence, Tennessee, Friday night, January 1, 1864

Surely, surely such cold weather never was felt in this region before. It seems that the "Yanks" have brought their climate with them, while the negroes have not enough of their natural heat about them to counteract the effects of the other. They look as cold and dreary over on the hill as I feel, notwithstanding they are burning the fencing all round and packing wood all the while. One of the battery men was here this morning and said "I guess they'll miss their warm homes this winter." Cousin Marion was here and replied that they had rather be there freezing to death than at home in good warm cabins. She stayed with us until 12. After that I went over to Cousin Jane's and we all concluded to "throw in" and have an oyster supper. Johny and Bob went up town and bought us two very good cans and some nice crackers. I just "stuffed" myself so that I haven't gotten over it yet.

New Providence, Tennessee, Tuesday night, January 5, 1864

Had the colic last night with other complaints so that I slept but very little. Inez prepared most of the breakfast, and since has done a "big day's washing." She's learning fast. Mr. Gold was in today and Mr. Clardy. Mr. G has finally decided to give his negroes their freedom {*indecipherable*}.

New Providence, Tennessee, Wednesday night, January 6, 1864

Commenced a bolster case this morning, and as Inez found time to churn, I have had but little to do. So for once more I have spent the day sewing; finished the slip late this evening and commenced the edging for another. Mr. H makes slow progress with his pants. He has been busy today helping Uncle Donel to move. He and Aunt Lucy will occupy the kitchen until Fannie leaves the cabin. So we are destined to live with the negroes, be the circumstances what they may. It may be for the best—negro protection these times I believe is better than the military can afford.

New Providence, Tennessee, Thursday night, January 7, 1864

What a dreadful spell of weather we are having. Nearly a week now has passed since the snow and sleet set in and still the snow continues and the weather too cold to talk about. Mr. H says the ice on the ponds is 6 inches thick; such an ice season we have not had for years. He has been out today with Uncle Donel trying to get up some wood and tonight he is almost sick from the effects of the cold and raw wind that has been blowing all day. It seems to me that I take cold sitting right in the fire all the time. Made another bolster case today, and 50 cts on milk.

New Providence, Tennessee, Friday night, January 8, 1864

Have been busy all day receiving Yankee calls. Women, men, and children have all been in. Some wanted milk, some butter, and some one thing, & some another. I wish I had milk & butter to supply them all as "Greenbacks"[93] seem to be pretty plenty with them. I'd soon have money enough to buy my spoons and a new dress besides. Went over to Cousin Jane's this evening, but with fear & trembling I took every step. The ice and snow together have made a perfect skating place of "all out doors." The Yankees with their jumpers,[94] sleighs, and bells may be seen on all occasions. I saw today for the first time the "Colored Regiment" drilling. They seem to get on tolerably well with their bowlegs over the ice and snow. I fully expected to see some of them fall but was denied the pleasure.[95] We received two new barrels of flour today. How glad I am—batter cakes for a while at least with me have "played out."

New Providence, Tennessee, Tuesday night, January 12, 1864

After churning yesterday morning I set to work on Mr. Homer's pants, and continued to sew on them until between 3 & 4 in the evening when someone

knocked at the door, and to my surprise when I rose to receive them, it was
Mrs. Pendleton and a young Mr. Reeves. I expected business of some kind
had brought her down on such a cold disagreeable day, and was not surprised
when she told me that Susan with 3 of her negro men were down here. She
had been over to Clarksville to hunt them up or get a receipt for them, but
failed either to find them or to get the receipt. She seemed very much disappointed, and altogether as much grieved at the loss of her negroes as anyone
I've seen. She left soon after breakfast, fully satisfied after watching a
company of negroes drill just across the street for an hour, that her men
at least were clear out of her reach. Been sewing busily all day; nearly
finished Mr. H's pants. It is much warmer. The snow and ice have nearly
disappeared.

New Providence, Tennessee, Wednesday night, January 13, 1864

The weather is again mild and pleasant. The snow is melting so fast that
it makes it very disagreeable under foot. Nearly made a finish of Mr. H's
pants today. Done nothing this evening because Mr. H concluded under
existing circumstances that it would be best for us to take in a boarder or
two among the Yankee officers. So as Adjutant Perkins was first to apply,
he was first accepted.[96] He dined with us today, and not being used to
dinner, I made myself so dull and stupid from eating that I was in bed
most of the evening. Mr. H thinks for our protection it will be better to
have boarders but as for my part I detest the idea of ever being brought
in such close contact with a man for whom I've no more use than I have
for one dressed in Federal uniform. Aunt Lucy is to assist me in cooking
and even with her help, I shall have so much more trouble than when I
got up this morning and prepared enough to last Mr. H and I all day.
Enjoyed a cold snack in our fingers as much or more than we ever did
warm & extensive meals.

New Providence, Tennessee, Friday night, January 15, 1864

Getting three meals keeps me busy all day long. I haven't time between
either meal to hem a pocket handkerchief. I wish Mr. H had sent his
"Adjutant" somewhere else. $20 a month never will pay me to board any
Yankee I don't care who he is, and as for his protection, that I'm thinking
won't "pay much." I went over to see Cousin Jane this evening muddy as
it was. She looks quite easy in her rooms. I didn't get through telling her
all I know before supper time came round.

New Providence, Tennessee, Saturday night, January 16, 1864

Mr. H was just ready to start out to the country this morning, when an abolition Yankee came and applied for {*indecipherable*}. I suppose they are all abolition Yankees, but he certainly headed any {*indecipherable*} yet. He was denied of course. After his harangue Mr. H left and has been absent almost all day. Florence spent good part of the morning with me. Made a whole dollar on my milk today.

New Providence, Tennessee, Monday night, January 18, 1864

Yesterday we had rain all day, and today snow all day. It seems that one disagreeable spell of weather only gives place to another of possible a little worse. The Yankees, judging from this winter, "guess" they never have more disagreeable weather up "North" than we have here during this season of the year. Mr. H's Adjt. yesterday after eating a cold dinner, "quipped" he wouldn't be to supper. He'll never get any butter from me on Sunday. Today I've been busy all day, and when I come to look over my work tonight, I find I have faced an old calico dress. Yes, done all of that today. Between breakfast and dinner I have ½ an hour to sew, between dinner and supper 1 or 2 hours. In the morning when I finish churning it is 10 or ½ 10 o'clock. By then it is hurry about dinner. How little did I appreciate the good time I used to have to sew in.

New Providence, Tennessee, Wednesday night, January 20, 1864

Again we have had two pretty days in succession — yesterday and today the sun has shown out beautifully. Aunt Lucy took advantage of the sun and has finished her washing for the week. Tonight she is going to make some hominy, and really, I shall be glad of the change. For the last week Mr. H has kept us in nothing but beef — beef for breakfast, for dinner, and for supper. He works with the cows so much that it is not to be wondered at however. Old Reed and the white cow are slopped so highly that their milk and butter brings in over a dollar a day, but Mr. H says that is owing to his good milking. "No one else would get the same quantity from the same cows." His "Adjt." offered to pay for his week's board tonight but we hadn't decided on the price so the money was not accepted. Money don't seem to be much of an object with him.

New Providence, Tennessee, Thursday night, January 21, 1864

Commenced with my regular routine of business this morning hoping to get through in time to sew a little on my new calico dress. But to my great disappointment the hot water was poured into the churn too soon, and not until 4 o'clock this evening did the butter come. I churned until near 11, and after dinner I gave it up to Inez. Bell Dunn and Cousin Jane were over this morning and Cousin Marion for a few minutes. They all had great tales to tell of how the negroes were carrying on, but the most surprising was the leaving of Dr. Herring's Mary. Mrs. H has had such great confidence in her all the while. She and Uncle Billy will set up to housekeeping now I guess. Two or three companies of the Negro Regiment were sent out today recruiting. Cousin Marion says they were out the other day in her neighborhood and had pretty good success. Took four from Mr. Ferguson.

New Providence, Tennessee, Saturday night, January 23, 1864

Since that Yankee has been here I can get nothing done but a little something cooked for him to eat. Yesterday & today I've not done 3 hours' sewing, I feel too sick and tired to set up tonight. I will wash, put on my clean clothes, and go to bed to read if nothing else.

New Providence, Tennessee, Sunday night, January 24, 1864

Had the colic last night so that I scarcely slept an hour. After reading a while this morning I made me a pallet and tried to go to sleep until ½ 12, when I gave up the idea all together. Had cold dinner set for that Yankee, and then he didn't come. It was too provoking. His excuse at supper half way relieved the case. Spent most of the evening with Cousin Jane. Inez went up home, says that Uncle Billy & his wife have "set up" in my residence. Effie, I suppose, occupies one room and they the other. Mrs. Herring now that Mary has left her has the pleasure of doing her own work. She has seemed to look forward to the period as being a very happy one, but Uncle Trice, rather than give up Uncle Billy, would set him up to housekeeping, and if old Mary requested it, give them a deed of gift to the house & lot. Negroes of every description are coming in to the Yankees now very fast, and recruiting among the men is going as rapidly as could be desired. The Regiment, I suppose, will soon be filled.

New Providence, Tennessee, Monday night, January 25, 1864

Rose so early this morning that Inez had time to finish nearly the second churning before we ate breakfast. "Mr. Homer's Adjt" hinders me terribly by coming to breakfast so late, and this morning particularly. Mr. H wanted to go out to Mr. Osborne's and I wanted him first to go up town and get my spoons. He went and in a short time returned with them. They are really very fine—so heavy & stout. According to my request there are no initials engraved, but simply "Rep" in large legible letters.[97] I tell Mr. H his next wife, if she ever uses them, shall certainly know whose they were. The ½ doz. cost 12.00 in "Greenbacks"—the very spoons that once could have been bought for 7 or 8. Nevertheless the money goes willingly as they will profit me more than that ever will. But while I rejoice over them I have to regret the loss of my nice chamber.[98] Inez set it out in the yard today and some of those stinking little negro brats broke it. I was really grieved about it for it was such a nice one. Florence came over today and recited her first lessons. She will continue so to do until other arrangements are made for her education. I was over tonight to take Cousin Jane some {indecipherable}.

New Providence, Tennessee, Wednesday night, January 27, 1864

My birthday, and I had clean forgotten it until I went over to Cousin Jane's this evening. But pshaw, what have I to care for birthdays? The reflection that I am growing old is anything but pleasant, and as for presents being given as they once were, I must never more think of that, but go to work to "make a woman of myself." I think of all those little things sometimes and wonder how I am to worry through the remainder of my life, cut off from every indulgence, forced to forget that any pleasure was ever looked forward [to] on the coming of certain annual days. Passing into what Mr. H calls the "woman's stage" has cost me too many tears and pains for me to ever appreciate the change. Cousin Jane heard from Sy Crabtree today. He is at Ft. Donelson and is anxious for her to go down as he is badly wounded and thinks he will never recover. I wish some way could be provided for her to go.

New Providence, Tennessee, Thursday night, January 28, 1864

Have been busy the day throughout, and not one stick of sewing have I done. Inez has been to sell milk twice today and in her absence I have to take her part. So my whole time is consumed in cleaning up and running round.

New Providence, Tennessee, Friday night, January 29, 1864

Cousin Jane and Mr. Dunn started for Ft. Donelson about 8. Florence and Marion are with me tonight. At last Fannie and her tribe have moved. Aunt Lucy and Uncle Donel are in the cabin tonight which leaves us to ourselves to a certain extent. Lu Ella and Inez are our only "safe guards."

Mr. H went out to Mr. Pollard's today and bought a doz. chickens. I'm so proud of them.

New Providence, Tennessee, Saturday night, January 30, 1864

Mr. Homer had to come over and awaken us this morning. We were so late rising that everything has been behind hand today. It was after 3 this evening before Inez had time to go to camp. She sold 49 cts worth of milk for me—doing quite well for a little thing like her. The whipping Mr. H gave her this morning had a very agreeable effect. The children are popping corn; I must stop anyway to eat some.

New Providence, Tennessee, Sunday night, January 31, 1864

Cousin Jane came about supper. She found Sy not half so badly wounded as she had heard and returned pretty relieved in regard to his condition.

New Providence, Tennessee, Monday night, February 1, 1864

Thought this morning that I would sew nearly all day, but commenced washing one or two of the milk vessels and found they all need scouring so badly that I didn't stop until I had finished them all, even the churn and dish pan. Cousin Jane came over about 11 and sit until 12. She says she came down the pike and then across yesterday evening to avoid showing her pass to Negro pickets. They were put out Saturday while she was gone. We can't go up town now without being halted by the black face wretches. Mr. H went over to Clarksville this evening and the pass he got for February has C. O.[99] on it. I suppose the negroes will understand it, but if they do it is more than I do.

New Providence, Tennessee, Tuesday night, February 2, 1864

Aunt Lucy washed today, and I had scarcely gotten through with the morning routine of duties before I had dinner to commence—Lu Ella my only help. Inez went to camp with the milk, and but for the money she makes me, I could by no means give her up. Lately I have averaged a dollar per day on milk and butter. Have been sewing on my ruffled pillow slips today, but fear I shall have to stop for the want of more nainsook.[100] Mr. H has been up town all day, and says negroes are still coming in very rapidly. Last night a great number from Ky., as far down as Uncle Tom Campbell's, came in. How on Earth people here are to live I can't see. The roguish things from all directions just concentrating here on this poor spot. I see no chance but for all to {*indecipherable*} together.

New Providence, Tennessee, Thursday night, February 4, 1864

We have a visitor tonight. Notwithstanding the Negro pickets, Mary Britton is with us. Really, I was so surprised to see her and so glad. She has so much to tell us of things she has seen & heard since we last saw each other. She's "Rebel" still, and I guess "Mr. H's Adjt" found it out.

New Providence, Tennessee, Friday night, February 5, 1864

Rose, I thought, in excellent time this morning considering Mr. H was not present to hurry me, but after all, we did eat breakfast before 8. While I was in the kitchen, Mary attended to the rools and she raised them very well indeed. She left soon after breakfast. Mr. H went with her up as far as the store. Bought Inez two cotton dresses, thin almost as muslin, and gave nearly 6.00 of my "Greenbacks" (milk money) for them. Indeed it is too bad—Col. Smith issued an order today compelling every citizen to subscribe to an oath recently laid by Governor Johnson,[101] before making purchases of goods or anything in Clarksville. The Adjt. brought the order over tonight and seems to think it "just the thing." Went over to Cousin Jane's this evening. She didn't get much news up town yesterday. The negro pickets were stationed just across the street from us today—and a more contemptible sight I didn't care to see. I thought a view of the Regiment at a distance was bad enough. They were practicing this evening for tonight I suppose, trying to mimic the Yankees. "Halt," they would say with the Yankee brogue, and then "who comes there?"

New Providence, Tennessee, Saturday night, February 6, 1864

Have been busy all day making Inez's dress. Finished it late this evening. She has been unusually sweet since the whipping this morning. Went to camp and made for me 95 cts. This week my milk & butter has brought me in over 6.00. Soon I will have made 50.00 and where has it all gone to?

New Providence, Tennessee, Monday night, February 8, 1864

Yesterday we had quite a quiet time. Mr. H's Yankee boarder did not come in until supper, and so we ate when we felt like it; slept and read when we felt like. So much relieved do I feel when we are alone that I offered Mr. H. 4.00 of my milk money (the amount of his board) per week to dispose of him. This morning I took Inez's place—we were so late rising—and swept the room, made up my bed, set the table, & made batter cakes for breakfast, while she made the fires, swept out the hall, and did other little dallying around. After breakfast I churned, poured up the milk, and prepared it for market. Sold 1 gallon at home, and prepared two plates of butter, all in time to sew up the skirt of Inez's dress before dinner. This evening I sewed until 3, heard Florence's lessons, and entertained Laura Helm and Anne Staton until supper time, when I went to brown a skillet of coffee[102] and they left for a candy stew[103] to be given at Mrs. Parker's.[104] Since supper I have quietly given up the duties of the day and entered into a hearty quarrel with Mr. Homer, which was not ended until I had said the last word.

New Providence, Tennessee, Wednesday night, February 10, 1864

Finished Inez's second dress yesterday besides helping her to get dinner. Aunt Lucy was washing and, of course, no help from that source. Cousin Jane for a rarity spent most of the morning with me. Late in the evening Laura Helm and Anne Staton came. They spared not the Yankees or their cause from the time "Mr. H's Adjt" came in until he left. Anne S left early this morning. Laura is still with me, and I think seems a little more favorably impressed with the Yankee. His candor with her seems his most admirable trait.

New Providence, Tennessee, Friday night, February 12, 1864

Cousin Marion came over yesterday in a great way about going to Louisville. She intends starting Monday. Borrowed my cloak and promised in return to select for me a nice set of table spoons. Not having a sufficient amount, I had to borrow from Mr. H and I shall be very impatient until it is replaced. "Mr. H's Adjt" was telling us today that a contraband camp had been established at Nashville and the women and children would be sent from here soon. How glad I will be. Every hole and corner is stuck so full of them and filth is accumulating so fast as a result that disease will undoubtedly break out soon,[105] and then the suffering that will come none of us can depict. The poisoning process among the negro soldiery seems to be proving pretty successful. 9 out of 11 cases, it is said, has proven fatal. Strange to say, negroes have been classed with the white people as the guilty ones. Cousin Jane was telling me yesterday that Winnie had gotten back to camp. What will Uncle T and Miss F do now? They are leaving Christian Co., Ky., almost by the hundred.

New Providence, Tennessee, Monday night, February 15, 1864

I felt so fatigued yesterday & today from last week's work that I decided to rest today. Inez swept this morning, churned, helped Aunt Lucy about dinner, and this evening came back from selling milk in time to scour the {*indecipherable*}. While she was at that, I went home with Florence and sit until sunset. Met up with Mr. Homer on his way home as I returned, and to my surprise he told me that he had a present for me. I was all impatience to get into the house to see what it was, and I could scarcely believe my own eyes when I saw it—the very thing I had this day been planning about how I would get it, two sets of silver plated forks & knives. The desert set are the tiniest, prettiest little things, so exactly in accordance with what I had been wishing for. Surely a present with me never came in better time. I shall thank Mr. Pettus to my dying day, for to him I owe the debt of gratitude.

New Providence, Tennessee, Wednesday night, February 17, 1864

Mr. H was up town yesterday & today all day. The pressing business, he and "his Adjt" say, is progressing admirably. Not only are the farmers being bereft of all they hold as dear, but the orders from the Secretary of War is to press every able bodied negro man they see, and under this head are placed some of the "gentlemen" round town that have been stealing and pilfering from every honest man that chances to be about. Charlie Jackson,[106] they say, and Jim Meacham[107] are included. How relieved I would feel to know that Charlie especially had marching orders tomorrow.

New Providence, Tennessee, Thursday night, February 18, 1864

Going out to help Mr. Homer milk yesterday evening gave me such a cold that I was sick all night from it—at least too sore to move with comfort. Today I have felt better. Aunt Lucy was washing and I was compelled to feel well enough to get dinner, such as it was, some oysters & soup, potato stew, some pies and custards were all that we had. Apologies were made, which pretendingly, "Mr. H's Adjt" thought unnecessary. Cousin Jane for a rarity spent the evening with me. Two Yankees came for milk while she was here and I began to think they had come to make a visitation they sit so long. They are dropping in now all through the day and say that since the order in regard to poison was issued they scarcely get anything in camp. People are afraid to send in for fear of some accident and they be brought up as the guilty ones.

New Providence, Tennessee, Friday night, February 19, 1864

This morning at the first tap of the drum over at camp awakened Inez, and as usual she dressed, made the fire, and had the room half swept before going out. I waited, of course, thinking she would be in directly, but to my surprise she kept staying and after 15 or 20 minutes, I remarked to Mr. Homer that she had gone to the Yankees. He went down to the cabin and came back in the same notion. So soon as I went into the dining room & kitchen the case with me was decided. I found everything helter skelter, and knew from the very appearance of things, that she intended going last night. At dinner Margaret came to let me know that Inez had gone up to her house and that she had gone with great tales in regard to my treatment. She couldn't please me and I couldn't tell what all. I simply remarked that Inez had left without any good excuse whatever, agreeably to my notion, and that she should never again set foot on the place when I could prevent it. At this she seemed to take offense and not very pleasantly asked for her clothes. I readily gave them to her. She left mad, went up home, told Uncle Trice a great tale, and tonight I suppose I have the name worse than ever of being "sharped nose for nothing." Have done more sewing this evening than I have for a week. Tonight the table was cleared and I had time to sit with Cousin Jane two hours.

New Providence, Tennessee, Saturday night, February 20, 1864

Mr. H had a booming fire by times this morning. I went to work after dressing without waiting for "Inez to sweep." While setting the breakfast table Margaret came in again to see if I would take her back. I positively refused telling her as I did yesterday that she had left without a cause, and that I should never consent to her return. No doubt one negro, if not a few white men, have been disappointed since the commencement of the negro excitement. By 9 I had the churning, the dishes, and nearly all the house cleaned up. Lou Ella is considerable help to me. Laura Helm sit with me from 10 until near 12. This evening I went over to Cousin Jane's.

New Providence, Tennessee, Tuesday night, February 23, 1864

Cousin Nat was in yesterday. All of his negro men have been pressed into service except one. He looks quite long faced over it. As Mr. H is afraid the rain will drown his flowers out, I must go with him over to see about covering them. I can't stay alone after dark.

New Providence, Tennessee, Wednesday night, February 24, 1864

Notwithstanding Mr. H's promise to himself last night, he rose later this morning than usual. So churning was postponed until after breakfast and I had it all to do by myself. The assistance that he gives me before breakfast is my greatest inducement for rising early, but yesterday and today he has been so busy plowing & planting potatoes that my interest has been almost entirely forgotten. I'm very much afraid as his own business increases that milking will finally be left off. If that is given up, no more money for me. Today I have made 90 cts on milk alone, and 90 cts on butter. Nearly 2.00 during the day from 2 cows, but few can say as much for cows

New Providence, Tennessee, Friday night, February 26, 1864

Yesterday I was busy cleaning up until near dinner when I went to sewing and by night had finished making one corner of my pillow slip. Before breakfast Mr. H no doubt in an ill humor from being fatigued himself, remarked in reply to my saying that I was so tired, "that he could see nothing I did except dress myself." It made me so mad that I studied all day how I might take revenge. Finally, I decided on staying in the bed and getting up in time to just dress myself before breakfast, and by that means letting him see how things went without my attention. I rose at 7. While dressing, that light shone so brightly through the window that I had the curtains lowered to darken what seemed to be the image of a housekeeper's neglect. I took my chair and acted the lady plum through — didn't sweep, didn't make up the bed, didn't go out to see about breakfast, didn't prepare the churn for churning, didn't strain or put away the milk, didn't do scarcely one of the thousand things that call for my attention almost any second. The appearance things presented mortified him I know, but not sufficiently to induce him to lend a helping hand. He went off, out to the country on business, and spent the day, while I was left to go through with my regular routine of duties, though it took me until 12 o'clock. Cousin Jane spent most of the morning with me. During her visit, churning was my employment as that required more setting down than my other work. This evening heard Florence's lessons and devoted the rest of the time to a rest spell.

New Providence, Tennessee, Monday night, February 29, 1864

Saturday morning after much persuasion from Mr. Homer I concluded to go with Cousin Jane over to see Cousin Marion. To see my spoons, however, was almost a sufficient inducement of itself. We found Cousin M quite complaining from her trip to Louisville & back. She brought my tablespoons and very nice ones they were. She only gave 22.00 for them. We stayed with her until yesterday evening, came home late, and if we had stayed until today, our trip perhaps would have been prolonged for several days longer for since yesterday morning we have had every variety of falling weather. Sleet seems, however, to have the ascendency. Mr. H started hunting this evening on his new horse. His feet slipped and away they both went. The horse ran home and frightened me like everything, but soon Mr. H came in sight, "all setting up" as the boys of the 14th used to say, and my fears were done away with. He sent over today & got a jug of Lager beer and I a box of sardines, and don't know which is feeling the worse from having indulged too much.

New Providence, Tennessee, Tuesday night, March 1, 1864

The first day of the first spring month, and a deeper snow has scarcely fallen this winter than the one that now covers the Earth. The weather above it not so disagreeable, but ice & snow covers everything under foot. Mr. H has been up town all day helping Mr. Pettus to invoice his goods. He brought home good news, a Southern victory has been achieved! How can we believe it? Seymour was advancing into Florida, the taking of Charleston having been abandoned, and to his utter surprise, Beauregard, finding out his plans, advanced just a little ahead [of] him and waiting in ambush made a complete rout of his whole force.[108] They say the victory is complete. How glad I am that once more we can hear of the success of Southern arms.

New Providence, Tennessee, Friday night, March 25, 1864

Such a long, long time has elapsed since I wrote last, and yet I've no excuse for myself but laziness. During the long silence many things have happened. Two of my hens have hatched and between them I have 16 of the prettiest little chickens. Mr. Homer's last hog, the old sow, has been stolen by the "Yanks." Cousin Marion has been down and spent a week with Cousin Jane. They went over to Clarksville and purchased for me something—the future only must reveal. Today two weeks ago, Uncle Tom brought Bettie home. She seemed glad to see us and assists me a great deal in the way of housekeeping. The worst of all is—the Yankee still boards with us and Grant has been made Lieut. Gen'l. of the U States [Army].[109]

New Providence, Tennessee, Saturday night, March 26, 1864

The morning promised such a pretty day that I tried to get a "contraband" to come and assist me in having a general "cleaning up," but failing, I concluded to sit down and sew, and from 9 until milking time this evening I was busy. The old setting hens were all that claimed much of my attention outside of my room. Aunt Lucy and Bettie had the management of dinner. Mr. H passed the day hunting—killed four squirrels.

New Providence, Tennessee, Sunday night, March 27, 1864

After getting through in the dining room this morning I walked with Mr. Homer out as far as the new ground. We remained so long and the walk was so fatiguing that I could scarcely wait to get in the house to rest. I laid down from 12 to near 3. Then went over to Cousin Jane's of course. Mr. H, for a rarity, went up town, heard the news that Forrest had burnt Paducah,[110] hung the negroes contained therein, and much more. From appearances the Yanks expect him here soon. The wagons are bringing over from Clarksville in great haste commissary stores and other valuables and placing them in the Fort for security. Perkins didn't come to supper tonight and this morning made me a present of a bottle of honey. Bettie says she knows something is going to happen.

New Providence, Tennessee, Tuesday night, March 29, 1864

Yesterday was the appointed day for Forrest to make his entrance into Clarksville, but in his place a hard wind came up which for a while seemed intent on taking many people's houses and everything else. Several houses occupied by soldiers & contrabands were entirely destroyed by fire. The news relative to Paducah has been confirmed. Today winter seems to have set in again. A snow storm has been threatening all the evening. Went to lock the hen house this evening. Someone had stolen the lock. My chickens, I suppose, are to follow Mr. H's sow & pigs. Bettie was telling me this evening that Miss Lou Peterson started down to see me the other day, but being halted by the negro pickets and required to show her pass, she refused, cursed them, and returned home. "The Rebellion" from this, it seems, has not quite "played out."

New Providence, Tennessee, Wednesday night, March 30, 1864

Mr. H spent the day up town. What is going to happen? He came home dreadfully low spirited. The war news he seems to think very discouraging indeed. Forrest, it seems from late accounts, has turned his attention to Smithland in the place of Clarksville.

New Providence, Tennessee, Monday, April 4, 1864

Saturday, yesterday, and part of today I have been too sick to sit up— a severer cold I have not had for years, and for years before. I had not kept my bed two days in succession. Mrs. Wilson spent the day with me yesterday and she could scarcely believe it—we all smothered up in bed, but who would stay ill under present circumstances? Our Yankee boarder has certainly left and not only him but the whole Regiment, the "gallant colored 16th." Isn't it news too good to be true? I watched their departure with eager interest, but for other duties I would've remained a while longer. They left about 2 o'clock this evening, they say, for {*indecipherable*} for accommodation, I suppose.

New Providence, Tennessee, Sunday night, May 1, 1864

Yesterday three weeks ago, I sent down and got a "contraband" to come up and scour for me, but she, like all the rest of them, seemed to think if she merely went through with the motion that all was done that was necessary. And so after spending most of the day, went home with her pay, feeling quite as well as if she had been hard at work all day. When in reality I did more towards getting the dirt up than she did. I felt very much fatigued at the close of the day and retired early hoping to find relief from slumber. But no, I felt worse and worse, so that by light, almost, I made Mr. H go for Cousin Jane and by 9 o'clock Dr. Herring's presence was considered indispensable. I grew sadly worse until about 11, when to make short of a long matter, I gave birth to a little "wee bit" of a girl babe, which after including clothes & all only weighed 5 lbs.[111] Mr. H with the rest of us seemed disappointed that it was not a boy. However, just for the time, I was very well pleased. I kept my bed for a week, then got up, went to sewing for "the baby," and sewed for a week.

This last week has been employed, rather difficultly, in cooking, washing, & such like. Aunt Lucy not being able to cook, I have had to take her place. During the three weeks of her existence (the baby's), oh pshaw, I have to [abreast] her so often. Several ladies have been in and they all join in the opinion that she is the smallest thing they ever saw for a human. We went visiting today for the first time over to Cousin Jane's. Cousin Marion has been down for a day or two. We were there when they left. A thousand things I could write about the little treasure, but the want of time and her immediate presence forbid. To write with her in my lap and this great book too is quite a serious undertaking. I shouldn't wonder if the business had to be done away with now.

New Providence, Tennessee, Monday night, May 2, 1864

Was so lazy this morning that breakfast, business, & everything was behind hand. The churning arrangement detains me now longer than anything else. The butter is so long coming these warm mornings. This evening I overcasted the baby a little gown up in front, and had supper in good time, so some amends were made for negligence this morning. Mr. H failed to get a paper this evening. We were anxious to hear farther particulars of the Southern victory at Chattanooga[112] and also of the great victory in Texas over Banks.[113] The baby hollows so loud that she almost deafens me. I wish Bettie would hold her a little while that I might say something of her smartness during the day (her lungs are "all right" I'm sure).

New Providence, Tennessee, Wednesday night, May 4, 1864

Mr. H was up town this evening and says the "contrabands" are pouring in from every direction. From Ky. they come by the wagon full. No decided news from Chattanooga, which speaks badly for the Federals. Strange the papers are so silent on the subject. The baby has been sick all day with colic. Though she suffers with it so much, she is growing very fast.

New Providence, Tennessee, Wednesday night, May 11, 1864

A week has elapsed since a half an hour's time has been given me to write. Since Aunt Lucy stopped cooking for us two weeks ago, that with other housekeeping arrangements keep me almost steadily on my feet from the time I rise until late in the day. At 4 o'clock every evening the baby takes the colic and she, with her screams, keeps me busy trying to relieve her until 10 in the night. Cousin Jane gave her a bath the other night. That has seemed to do her more good than anything else. Yesterday she was a month old, and Sunday when we were over at Cousin Jane's we weighed her and she still weighs 7 ½ ℔s. She begins to notice considerably and grows sweeter every day. I lay [her] in the rocking chair & sit her by the stove, and there she rests quietly of a morning until I get breakfast. Mr. H got two papers this evening in which were given long accounts of the great battle now in progress between Grant & Lee.[114] They have been fighting now for a week or more, and think of the terrible slaughter & bloodshed no human tongue can give a description. Grant has as many as 23,000 wounded already. Longstreet on our side, it is said, is badly wounded.[115] Sedgewick[116] on the Federal side killed, with several of Grant's staff. This will in the end no doubt prove the hotly contested and bloodiest battle of the war.

New Providence, Tennessee, Friday night, May 12, 1864

Cousin M. had on a beautiful "butternut" bonnet and only gave ten dollars for it. As usual, she seemed confident of Lee's success in Va. She has never yet given up the Confederacy.

New Providence, Tennessee, Saturday night, May 13, 1864

Hurried through with breakfast this morning that I might have some milk & butter ready for Mrs. Poindexter. Aunt Lucy came in and kindly offered her assistance so that for once butter & milk were both ready for "Uncle Sy." This week my milk & butter averaged 1.00 per day. This is doing some better. Made slow progress on Mr. H's second shirt today. Bettie Helm and her Pa came in about 3 o'clock. Bettie is with us tonight; this is her first visit since Christmas. The last papers bring unfavorable news from Virginia. They represent Grant as having met with a series of successes. From his first encounter with Lee, Mr. H says he has counted as many as 8 or 10 generals that have been killed on the Federal side since the commencement of the fight.

New Providence, Tennessee, Sunday night, May 14, 1864

The morning was clear and pleasant, but this evening a gentle rain commenced falling which bids fair to continue for a good while. After dressing the baby this morning, I excused myself to Bettie and laid down to rest a while. I went to sleep, and I do believe it was 1 o'clock or near it before I woke. This evening the baby has kept us all employed nursing her. While Bettie and I took a short walk leaving her in Mr. H's care, he took her over to Cousin Jane's and there she remained for an hour or two, quite young to be taking advantage of her mother's absence. The contrabands have commenced a protracted meeting and they say every church was full to overflowing — no wonder when every hole and corner is rammed and jammed with the lousy lazy things. They come in now from the country by the wagon load. What on earth they are to do for something to eat is a mystery to me.

New Providence, Tennessee, Saturday night, May 21, 1864

Bettie Helm has spent the week with us; left this morning with her Pa. She went calling one or two days. The rest of her time she spent knitting when not assisting me on the baby's skirts. I have made her two flannels and one cotton one and finished Mr. H's second shirt. The late papers came out and acknowledge for the first time Grant's defeat before Richmond.[117] Lee is now without a doubt the renowned General of the world. He is now driving Grant toward Washington city. The baby, after sleeping all day, is paying up now, and Mr. H is all out of patience. He says she grows so fast that it stretches her skin and gives her pain and for that reason she cries so much. Tomorrow she is 6 weeks old and she is double her weight almost.

New Providence, Tennessee, Monday night, May 23, 1864

Florence stayed with Bettie Saturday night and yesterday morning early she
came down to see the baby weighed. All had silently concluded that she was
nearly grown and of course would weigh heavily, but to our surprise she
only weighed 9 lbs, and we were forced to believe her still a babe though all
of 6 weeks old. She begins to notice considerably, and though she smiles for
us occasionally, they are like angel visits—few & far between. Yesterday
morning I went over to Cousin Jane's and unexpectedly stayed all day. In the
evening Laura Helm came and stayed until this morning. Mr. H and Bobbie
have been plowing tobacco ground today, and but for Bob's being engaged
I could have sold 1.50 cts worth of milk. I was so sorry. I wanted to make
money enough to go to Oak Grove this week.

New Providence, Tennessee, Thursday night, June 2, 1864

I have a few moments to write tonight, and would like to have something to
write, but to commence where I left off would take me too long, and to record
only today's events would scarcely pay me for lifting this old book. So little
home matters in this case, as in many others, must be neglected, and I will
just say that the mighty General Grant has not yet taken Richmond nor is
there a prospect of his taking it soon. The Southern cause is progressing
finely it seems most everywhere but here. Here the contraband negroes are
overrunning the place and still coming in averaging 50 a day. Every hole
and corner seems to be alive with the filthy things and disease in every form
almost has taken hold of them. Many of the older ones have died and are
dying from the smallpox while the children suffer dreadfully from measles,
whooping cough, and similar diseases. The citizens are hiring them now to
a great extent, both men & women. Mr. H had as many as 5 today in his
tobacco patch. Uncle Trice was down this evening and said Gilbert had 15
in the same employment.

THE JOURNAL ENDS HERE. It is unknown whether there was another volume that has been lost, or whether burdened with the trials of the war and
a new baby, Serepta did not have the energy to continue. Serepta and B. B.
Homer had another daughter, Evaline, in 1867, in 1869 a son, Baily, who
lived only a short time, and a daughter, Janie, in 1870. B. B. Homer died
in 1873, leaving Serepta a widow with three daughters under the age of 10.
Janie (1870–1937) married Parker G. Dibble (1866–1938) in 1894 and the

couple had one son, Parker J. Dibble. Eva (1867–1934) married Christopher Kropp Smith (1864–1957) in 1889 and the couple had four children, Homer, Christopher Jr., Mildred Louise, and Sory. Tabbie (1864–1926) married Hart W. Myers (1863–1937) in 1901. At some point Serepta began spending her winters in Weir Park, Florida, where she managed a boarding house or small inn. Serepta ended a February 2, 1892, letter from Weir Park to her first grandson, Homer, on his first birthday, with, "May he live to see many returns of his natal day, and with a life long and useful may he so number his days that his heart may be applied into wisdom is the prayer of his loving Grand Mother Homer."[118] She lived two more years, dying on September 25, 1894. The *Daily Tobacco Leaf Chronicle* ran her obituary on their front page that same day, writing, "When Mrs. Serepta M. Homer passed away at her home in New Providence this morning at 2 o'clock, one of the best women who ever lived in Montgomery County died."

NOTES

Introduction

1. Catherine Clinton, *Step-Daughters of History* (Baton Rouge: LSU Press, 2016).

2. Mary Chesnut, *Mary Boykin Chesnut*, edited by C. Vann Woodward (New Haven, Yale University Press, 1981).

3. Daniel E. Sutherland, ed., *A Very Violent Rebel: The Civil War Diary of Ellen Renshaw House* (Knoxville: University of Tennessee Press, 1996).

4. Nancy Dasher Baird, ed., *Josie Underwood Civil War Diary* (Lexington: University of Kentucky Press, 2009).

5. Minoa D. Uffelman, Ellen Kanervo, Eleanor Williams and Phyllis Smith, eds., *The Diary of Nannie Haskins Williams: A Southern Woman's Story of Rebellion and Reconstruction, 1863–1890* (Knoxville: University of Tennessee Press, 2014).

6. The diary is housed at Customs House Museum and Cultural Center, Clarksville, Tennessee.

7. Heirs of John Trice, Guardian Report (Henry Frey, Guardian). (*Robertson County Probates: Will Book 9*), pages 367–368. Office of the County Clerk (originating office), Robertson County Archives, Springfield, Tennessee.

8. See Chapter 1, Note 57.

9. Trice Guardian records, Robertson County Probate.

10. Serepta's family loaned books to Fort Defiance in Clarksville, Tennessee. Some of ones she discusses reading in this diary were in the collection that was on display in the Interpretive Center. These books she mentioned in the diary are in possession of the family.

11. Jordan diary, June 23, 1863.

12. Jordan diary, November 19, 1861.

13. For a good overview of southern agriculture see *Agriculture and Industry*, edited by Melissa Walker and James C. Cobb (Chapel Hill: UNC Press, 2008) p. 3–29, Julie A. Avery, ed., *Agricultural Fairs in America: Tradition, Education*, published by Michigan State University Museum on behalf of FairTime Project, 2000, "One Hundred Years of County Fairs in Montgomery County, Tennessee," by Paul Hyatt, Marie Riggins, Ralph Winters, and Thurston L. Lee (Clarksville, TN: Clarksville-Montgomery County Historical Society, 1960).

14. Jordan diary, October 23, 1860.

15. Jordan diary, October 24, 1860.

16. Jordan diary, October 25, 1860.

17. *Clarksville Chronicle*, October 26, 1860.

18. Jordan diary, October 26, 1860, Hyatt, *et al.*, 10.

19. Hyatt, *et al.*, 7–11.

20. Jordan diary, October 29, 1860.

21. Jordan diary, November 6, 1860.

22. Richard Gildrie, "Dilemma and Opportunities, 1860–1900" in Charles M. Waters (ed.), *Historic Clarksville, The Bicentennial Story, 1784–1984*, (Clarksville, TN: Jostens Publications, 1983), 64–65.

23. Stephan V. Ash, "A Community at War: Montgomery County, 1861–65," *Tennessee Historical Quarterly, 161–176*; Ash, *Middle Tennessee Society Transformed*, 18, 25.

24. *Clarksville Chronicle*, May 10, 1861, 3.

25. Gildrie, "Dilemma and Opportunities," 66.

26. Ash, "A Community at War," 34.

27. Jordan diary, February 16, 1862.

28. Jordan diary, February 23, 1862.

29. Jordan diary, February 23, 18862.

30. Gildrie, "Dilemmas and Opportunities," 67.

31. See Leeann Whites and Alecia P. Long, eds., *Occupied Women: Gender, Military Occupation, and the American Civil War* (Baton Rouge: LSU Press, 2012). This collection of articles explores the different ways women in occupied South aided the Confederacy. It was a fine line between traditional female labor of feeding, nursing, providing clothing, sharing support and news—and subversion to the USA and treason.

32. Jordan diary, March 15, 1862.

33. Jordan diary, May 5, 1862.

34. *Clarksville Jeffersonian*, July 8, 1861.

35. Jordan diary, November 12, 1861.

36. Jordan diary, May 6, 1862.

37. After the fall of Fort Donelson, Nashville surrendered. Union troops built Fort Negley south of the city. Newly freed African Americans helped with the construction.

38. *Dear Rep: Letters to Serepta Jordan Homer of New Providence, Tennessee.* Privately published book, Genealogy Room, Clarksville-Montgomery Public Library, Clarksville, May 15, 1862.

39. The 1850 Logan County, Kentucky, Census lists Tom Trabue as the son of Dr. John E. and Elizabeth Atkinson Trabue.

40. The 1850 Montgomery County, Tennessee, Census lists John Mallory (ca. 1835–1868), in the household of Stephen Smith Mallory, 47, with Eliza Mallory, 50.

41. Bladen Beverly Homer, who went by B. B. Homer, was a New Providence merchant.

42. Jordan diary, December 24, 1861.

43. Jordan diary, December 23 and 24, 1862.

44. Jordan diary, December 24, 1863.

45. Jordan diary, December 24, 1863.

46. Jordan diary, January 25, 1864.

47. See photo on page 152.

48. Jordan diary, May 1, 1864.

49. Jordan diary, May 1, 1864.

50. Jordan diary, May 11, 1864.

51. Jordan diary, June 2, 1864.

52. Jordan diary, February 20, 1858.

53. Jordan diary, March 24, 1862.

54. Jordan diary, February 28, 1861.

55. Jordan diary, December 25, 1863.

56. Jordan diary, February 26, 1862.

57. Jordan diary, March 25, 1862.

58. Jordan diary, March 12, 1862.

59. Jordan diary, March 12, 1862.

60. Jordan diary, February 12, 1864.

61. Jordan diary, October 9, 1862.

62. Jordan diary, July 10, 1863.

63. Jordan diary, October 4, 1864.

64. Jordan diary, October 8, 1864.

65. Jordan diary, February 5, 1864.

66. Jordan diary, May 25, 1863.

67. Jordan diary, July 21, 1864.

68. Jordan diary, September 2, 1863.

69. Jordan diary, February 12, 1864.

70. Jordan diary, August 14, 1863.

71. Jordan diary, January 30, 1864.

72. Jordan diary, February 6, 1864.

73. Jordan diary, February 19, 1864.

74. Jordan diary, June 2, 1864.

1. November 1857–June 1860

1. Serepta's aunt, Tabitha Trice (ca. 1812–1861), was the sister of Serepta's mother, Damaris Trice Jordan Bennett (ca. 1814–1852). Tabitha Trice, born in North Carolina, was daughter of John Trice and Nancy Castleberry Trice Travathan. She married Elsey Trice, date unknown but prior to 1850. In the 1850

Montgomery County, Tennessee, Census, she was in the household of Elsey
(sometimes spelled Elsy, Elsie or Elry) Trice, 40, with Serepta Jordan, 11, in New
Providence. Tabitha died on July 2, 1861, of apoplexy and was buried in City
Cemetery (now Riverview Cemetery, Clarksville). Elsey Trice (ca. 1810–1877)
married Fannie Pettus on April 8, 1862. Damaris is buried near Fredonia,
Kentucky, on Cumberland Landing near Dycusburg, Kentucky. Division of land
of John Trice, deceased. Montgomery County, Tennessee, Record Book F, 215;
1850 Caldwell County, Kentucky, Census, family 470; 1850 Montgomery County,
Tennessee Census, family 1370.

2. The 1850 McCracken County, Kentucky, Census lists James L. Riggs, merchant, 32; Eliza C., 21; Martha A. (Mattie), 5; Benjamin, 1, family 9. Eliza received
property in New Providence in 1854. Montgomery County Deeds, 3:121

3. Mrs. Hendrick was probably Mary A. Cooke Hendrick, second wife of the
Reverend John T. Hendrick, pastor of First Presbyterian Church, Clarksville,
Tennessee, from 1847 to 1858. The 1850 Montgomery County, Tennessee, Census
lists J. T. Hendrick, 39, with J. E., female, 33; J.T., male, 15; J. A., male, 13;
C.S., male, 12; Mary C., 10; Luther W., 8; Melanthon J., male, 6; Robert G., 3;
Samuel F. Dallam, 16, family 28. Eleanor S. Williams, *Worship along the Warioto:
Montgomery County, Tennessee* (Clarksville, TN: First Federal Savings Bank,
1995), 281.

4. Louisa V. Peterson, 27, was the sister of Minerva Peterson Howard, wife
of Meredith Howard. The 1850 Montgomery County, Tennessee, Census lists
Meredith Howard, carpenter, male, 60, with Minerva H., 39; Jane B., 13; James B.,
12; Isaac, 10; Blanch, 5; Louisa Peterson, 27, family 1469. Louisa and Minerva
were daughters of Isaac Peterson Jr., and Nancy Farrier Peterson.

5. Mrs. Meacham may have been the mother-in-law of Serepta's Cousin Mat,
Martha Leonora Galbreath Meacham, wife of M. L. Meacham. See Chapter 1,
Note 21 for more information on Cousin Mat.

6. In December of 1856, a general panic spread throughout the South about a
possible slave insurrection. The panic was apparently brought on by black interest in claims that if Republican candidate John C. Frémont had won the 1856
presidential election, he would have freed the slaves. Insurrection fears were most
severe in Montgomery and Stewart counties in Tennessee and centered on the approximately 2,000 to 3,000 slaves who worked at the local iron furnaces. Charles P.
Dew, "Black Ironworkers and the Slave Insurrection Panic of 1856," *The Journal
of Southern History,* Vol. 41, No. 3 (Aug., 1975), 321–338, argues the panic was
caused by white fears rather than actual rebellion plans. He suggests six or seven
slaves were hanged in Dover, one was shot to death and another beaten to death.
Anita S. Goodstein writes, "Nine of the 'confessed' rebels were hanged at the
Iron Works and another nineteen at Dover." Anita S. Goodstein, "Slavery," *The
Tennessee Encyclopedia of History and Culture,* 855.

7. The 1850 Montgomery County, Tennessee, Census lists M.G. Beaumont, 22, female, in the household of Henry Beaumont, tobacco merchant, family 10.

8. The 1860 Montgomery County, Tennessee, Census, lists John B. Fairfax, 55, male; Tennessee Fairfax, 44, female; and E.B. (probably Ephraim, or Efe as Serepta called him), 22, grocer, in a household with Frank Hacking, 52, mulatto; H. Anderson, 46, female, mulatto; Lucy J. Anderson, 12; J.O. Anderson, 10, male; R.O. Anderson, 7, male; and J.F. Anderson, 2, male, family 712.

9. Inez was Serepta's slave, about age 7. 1860 Census Slave Schedule Montgomery County, Tennessee. Slave Schedules only listed the gender and age of the enslaved person. The census listed Serepta owning one slave, female, about age 10 in 1860.

10. The 1850 Montgomery County, Tennessee, Census lists G. B. Trice, 44, with F. Trice, 43; E. M. Trice, 20; T. Trice, 18; E. Trice, 15; A. Trice, 13; M. Trice, 9; and Nicholas Manby, 52, mulatto, family 28.

11. Dr. Joseph Franklin Alsup (1833–1863) was the son of Methodist circuit-riding minister, Asaph Alsup, and Mary Hill Alsup. "Thetford-Meyer Family Tree," accessed January 10, 2019. http://www.ancestry.com.

12. Trice's Landing on the Cumberland River was near Serepta's home. It was established by the Trice family in 1832 and was an important riverfront shipping landing for area farmers and merchants. Today it is a 30.5-acre Clarksville city park with a boat ramp, restrooms, picnic area, and walking trail.

13. Linwood (or Lynwood) Landing was near Trice's Landing. Linwood was owned by J. M. Jones and Company, J. W. Edwards and Company, and George P. McMurdo. Paul Wyatt (1865–1927) recalled in "History of New Providence" going with his father in the 1870s "to see the steamboats land at Red River Landing, Trice's Landing and Lynwood Landing and have seen great quantities of tobacco loaded at these places. At each of these landings there were immense brick warehouses near the river, and well paved wharves, with good roads leading to town." Unpublished paper, Clarksville-Montgomery County Public Library Genealogy Room, Clarksville, Tennessee, 1923.

14. The 1850 Montgomery County, Tennessee, Census lists W. L. Neblit, 31, farmer; Mary A., 27; Thomas W., 2; Jesse W., 5 months, family 1505. William L. (Buchanan) Neblit married Mary J. Randolph in Cheatham County, Tennessee, in 1857. His first wife, Mary A. (Jessia), whom he married in 1844 in Montgomery County, died in 1856.

15. Mrs. Crabtree may have been Serepta's Cousin Jane Crabtree. Laurena Jane Trice Crabtree was the widow of J.M. Crabtree. The Crabtrees married on August 5, 1847, in Montgomery County, and by 1860 Laurena Jane Crabtree was widowed. The 1850 Montgomery County, Tennessee, Census lists J. M. Crabtree, merchant, 26, with Laurena J., 22, and Florence, 0. The 1860 Montgomery County, Tennessee, Census lists Jane T. Crabtree, 32, housekeeper, with Florence,

11; Robert, 8; Mary, 5; Charles Dunn, 26, clerk; A. [*sic*], 23, female; and Bettie Lynes, 28. Bettie Lynes and Jane Crabtree were daughters of Nace Trice and Elizabeth Mallory Trice. Irene Griffey, *Riverview Cemetery* (2002, Montgomery County Historical Society), 65–66.

16. Serepta's maternal grandmother was Nancy Castleberry Trice Travathan (1796-March 22, 1857), married first to John Trice (either 1763 or 1794- ca. 1824). She was the daughter of Paul Castleberry. After John Trice's death, she married Lyon Travathan. The 1850 Montgomery County, Tennessee, Census lists Nancy Travathan, 54; Ailey Trice, 12; Emily Woodmore, 35; Mary Woodmore, 14; Eliza Woodmore, 12; Ellen Woodmore, 9; and John Woodmore, 6, family 1478. Emily was Nancy Castleberry Trice Travathan and John Trice's daughter, who married William W. Woodmore.

17. Cousin Mollie was probably Mary E. Mills, daughter of William Mallory and his first wife Lucinda Draper Mallory (deceased) and wife of Nathaniel Mills. 1850 Montgomery County, Tennessee, Census, family 287; *Montgomery County, Tennessee, Marriage Book* 3, 21. The 1860 Montgomery County, Tennessee, Census lists N. J. Mills, 35, with M. E. Mills, 32, and Wm. Mills, 3, family 868. In her October 7, 1861, entry, Serepta recorded the death of 4-year-old William.

18. Two Noel families are listed in the Davidson County, Tennessee, Census: John Noel, 32; Huda Fox, 30; Fermina, 24; Simms, 2; Nancy, 1, family 27, and O. F. Noel, farmer; Sarah, 21; Achilles, student, 16; Edwin T., 2.

19. Perhaps Serepta was referring to an English dessert call Fruit Fool or perhaps she was misspelling *roux*, pronounced "roo," a flour and fat sauce.

20. Cousin Mildred may have been Mildred Trice Jeter (1829-aft 1870). She was the daughter of May Trice (1798–1855), brother of Bingham, Elizabeth, Leigh, Jesse James, Nace, Jane, Thomas Alexander, Greenberry, Mary "Pollie" Campbell, Elsey, and Nancy Barbee—all children of James and Susannah Leigh Trice. James was probably a brother of Serepta's maternal grandfather John Trice. Mildred Trice married Mathew A. Jeter in 1852 in Montgomery County, Tennessee. "Buchanan Family Tree," accessed January 18, 2019, http://www.ancestry.com. "Garner Family Tree," accessed February 11, 2019, http://www.ancestry.com. While these family trees list Elsey with these siblings, no official sources could be found to corroborate this information.

21. The 1860 Shelby County, Tennessee, Census lists Margaret L. "Mattie," 38, in the household with Majors Louis Meacham, 40, wholesale merchant, and their children, Eugene, 11; Ida, 9; and Annie G., 1, family 1031. The family was wealthy with property valued at $9,500 and a personal estate of $60,000. Unpublished letters to Serepta Jordan are in Special Collections of Clarksville Montgomery County Library and contain six letters from Mat written from Memphis. Mat Meacham lived in Montgomery County in the 1850 Census and had moved to Shelby County sometime before 1860. Several unpublished transcribed letters

from Mat to Serepta are in *Dear Rep: Letters to Serepta Jordan Homer of New Providence, Tennessee.* Genealogy Room, Clarksville Montgomery Public Library, Clarksville, Tennessee.

22. The 1850 Montgomery County, Tennessee, Census lists T. B. Yancy, 22, farmer; Sarah Yancy, 19; Pliety Yancy, 1; Eliza Gossett, 24; Wm. Pass, 25; Whitmel F. Greenfield, 18; and Catherine Fort, 14, family 409.

23. "She" was probably Serepta's stepsister Mary Elizabeth Bennett Groves, daughter of John Bennett and Elizabeth Wade Bennett. She married William J. Groves in 1855 in *Caldwell County, Kentucky. County Marriages, Kentucky, 1783–1965.*

24. The 1860 Caldwell County, Kentucky, Census lists B. Brashears, 32; Julia Ann, 25; Serelda, 2; and S. Hopper, 70, family 577.

25. Serepta's stepfather John Bennett married Amanda Knower after Damaris died, and the couple had five children. However, the children mentioned in this entry were Serepta's half siblings. The 1850 Caldwell County, Kentucky, Census lists Serepta's younger half-sister and brother as Judson, 3, and Anne, 1. The Jordan-Homer Family Tree on ancestry.com lists a daughter, Susan, being born to Damaris and John Bennett in 1851.

26. Nehemiah W. Nixon was pastor of Spring Creek Baptist, Clarksville, Tennessee, from approximately 1850 and served for twenty years. Williams, *Worship along the Warioto,* 346.

27. The Reverend R. L. Fagan was a circuit riding pastor who served what is now Chapel Hill United Methodist Church and Antioch United Methodist Church in Montgomery County, Tennessee, from 1854 to 1858. In 1859 Woodlawn United Methodist Church in Montgomery County was organized and was first known as Fagan's Chapel in honor of Fagan, who died in 1884. Williams, *Worship along the Warioto,* 26, 77, 124, 263.

28. "Then said Jesus to his disciples, If any man will come after me, let him deny himself, and take up his cross, and follow me." Matthew 16:24 KJV.

29. C. M. Day served as minister at First Christian Church, Clarksville, after 1865. Williams, *Worship along the Warioto,* 346.

30. Springfield, Tennessee, is the county seat of Robertson County, adjacent to and east of Montgomery County. Springfield is approximately thirty-five miles from Clarksville.

31. The 1860 Montgomery County, Tennessee, Census lists B. N. Herring, 39, with H. E. (Hester), 34; H. E., male, 11; E. H. female, 8; A. E. Ricks, female, 35; and S. W. Trice, male, 23, family 744.

32. Mrs. Gordon may have been Sarah Ann Ogburn Gordon, wife of Robert B. Gordon and daughter of Josiah (1793–1829) and Susan Howell Ogburn (1796–1860). Josiah was the brother of John, Thomas, and James Ogburn.

33. There are two possibilities for the identity of Mr. McDaniel. He may have

been the J. McDaniel Serepta mentioned in discussing the marriage of Sue Barbee. *The Tennessee, Compiled Marriages, 1851–1900* lists her marriage to A. (Alsa) McDaniel on December 22, 1857, and the 1870 Montgomery County, Tennessee, Census lists A. McDaniel, 41, and Susan McDaniel, 33, in the same household. It is possible this J. McDaniel was a relative of the groom or Serepta miswrote the initial. Or Mr. McDaniel might have been William McDaniel, listed in the 1860 Christian County, Kentucky, Census, family 74, as age 28 and overseer in the household of Shandy Holland, a friend of the Trices.

34. In this chapter, David gives his son, Solomon, the plans to build the temple and tells him to be faithful to God.

35. Mrs. Neely may have been Agnes Neely, 24, wife of T.J. Neely, 40, preacher, listed in the 1860 Montgomery County, Tennessee, Census, family 285, with their son George, 2.

36. Jennie was mentioned throughout the early part of the diary. Perhaps she was Virginia Caroline Ogburn, daughter of Mary Ann Caroline Hunt Ogburn and the late John Ogburn. She may have been a first cousin to Sarah Ann Ogburn Gordon.

37. J.H. Nichols served as pastor at Liberty Cumberland Presbyterian Church in Montgomery County from 1857 to 1859. Williams, *Worship along the Warioto*, 130.

38. Mount Pleasant United Methodist Church, in what was known as Seg Community before 1838, is one of the oldest churches in Montgomery County. Williams, *Worship along the Warioto*, 166.

39. Dr. Joseph Burris West, Methodist minister, taught at the Clarksville Female Academy from 1866 to 1872. In 1860, he was the presiding elder of what is now known as Salem United Methodist Church in Montgomery County, Tennessee, Williams, *Worship along the Warioto*, 264.

40. John Mallory, along with Tom Trabue and Quint Atkinson, first cousins, seemed to be interested in courting Serepta. She recorded their visits and when she received letters from them. The 1850 Montgomery County, Tennessee, Census lists John Mallory (ca. 1835–1868), in the household of Stephen Smith Mallory, 47, with Eliza Mallory, 50, and children: Mary, 19; William, 18; Jane (nicknamed Jennie), 14; Ann, 12; along with T.D. Rucker, male, 26. John Wilson Mallory was the son of Stephen Smith Mallory and his first wife Nancy Wilson Collins Mallory (deceased). Gladies Higgins, "Some Descendants of George Sims and John Mallory, Caswell County, N.C." *The Montgomery County [Tennessee] Genealogical Journal 9* (June 1980): 104.

41. A number of Mockbees lived south of the Cumberland River in Montgomery County. Miss Mockbee could have been one of the daughters of Risden Mockbee, 56, and his wife Margaret, 48, listed in the 1850 Montgomery County, Tennessee, Census, family 1104, with children, John, 28; Henry, 18;

Elizabeth, 20; Lucy A., 14; Mary D., 12; Josiah, 10; Louisa, 8; and Margaret Mastin, 8.

42. Antioch is a small community on the south side of the Cumberland River in Montgomery County, Tennessee.

43. West Fork Baptist is in Ringgold, Montgomery County, Tennessee.

44. Perhaps Mrs. Pollard was Susanna C. Herndon Pollard. Serepta wrote on January 29, 1861, that Elsey Trice co-signed a loan with B. Pollard, probably her husband, Byard T. Pollard. The 1860 Montgomery County, Tennessee, Census, lists B. T. Pollard, 33, farmer; S.C., female, 35; J.W., male, 15; E.H., female, 10, family 468. Byard T. Pollard married Susanna C. Herndon on September 17, 1844, in Montgomery County, Tennessee. Or Mrs. Pollard could have been N. B. (Nancy Britain) Pollard, listed in the 1860 Montgomery County, Tennessee, as age 26, female, in the household with R. T. (Reuben) Pollard, 35, male, merchant, and Susan, 7 months. Serepta may very well have known this family as she mentioned one of their boarders, W.H. Garrigus, 19, male, clerk, in her December 25, 1860, entry.

45. Florence Crabtree was the daughter of Cousin Jane Crabtree; she would have been about 7 years old in 1857.

46. There are two possible men to whom Serepta may have been referring. Dr. Lindsey may have been Livingston Lindsey, who moved from Cadiz, Kentucky, to Clarksville and practiced medicine and served in the 49th Tennessee Infantry, or he might have been L. Linsay, who enlisted as a private and surgeon in Company F, 49th Tennessee Infantry. Wallace C. Cross, *Cry Havoc: A History of the 49th Tennessee Volunteer Infantry Regiment, 1861–1865* (Franklin, TN: Hillsboro Press, 2004), 151.

47. The 1850 Montgomery County, Tennessee, Census lists Eliza Dicks, 10, in the household of John B. Fairfax, family 1262.

48. Although Serepta spelled the last name "Dirett," she probably meant "Miss Durrett." Miss Durrett could have been Susan Ann Durrett, who married D. A. Elliott on September 16, 1858, in Montgomery County, Tennessee. The Elliott household is listed in the 1860 Montgomery County, Tennessee, Census: D. A., 39, carpenter; Susan N., 39; A. A., 13, female; J. R., 11, male; Gertrude, 4; and Richard Durrett, 75, family 611.

49. Dawson F. Ogburn, son of Major Thomas Ogburn (1800–1889) and Sally Bayliss Ogburn (1805–1856), died of consumption on December 26, 1857. "Dawson F. Ogburn," US Find A Grave Index, 1600s–Current, http://www.search.ancestry.com. The 1850 Montgomery County, Tennessee, Census lists him as age 12 in the household of Thomas, 50, farmer, with Sally, 44; Adeline, 18; Harriet, 16; Benjamin, 14; Hockett, 10, and Ethalinda, 6.

50. Serepta mentioned Mr. or Mrs. Atkinson numerous times throughout the diary. Mrs. Atkinson was probably Sarah Elizabeth Tuck Atkinson (1818–1859),

wife of Quintus Atkinson Sr. (1802–1864) and mother of Quintus Atkinson Jr. (1828–1902). Quintus Atkinson Sr. was the son of Thomas Walton Atkinson Sr. (1778–1862) and half-brother of Thomas Walton Atkinson Jr. (1825–1860), who had married Serepta's cousin, Henrietta Trice (1827–1852), daughter of James Pinhook and Zelpha Mallory Trice. "Bordewick Master 2012 Family Tree," accessed January 10, 2019, http://www.ancestry.com; "Nelson Family Tree," accessed January 21, 2019, http://www.ancestry.com.

51. Dr. Walter Harding Drane (1824–1865) was a physician and later tobacco farmer in Montgomery County. In 1843, he moved his family from the College Street home in Clarksville out to a farm on the Hopkinsville Road. Three of his sons fought for the Confederacy, and Drane himself volunteered his services near his sons' units in Virginia and West Virginia. The Drane Family Papers are housed in the Tennessee State Library and Archives in Nashville, Microfilm Accession Number 1143a.

52. Tobacconist John K. Smith (1822–1911) operated a warehouse/stemming house in New Providence in the Trice Landing area before the Civil War. He married Mary Bowman (1849–1871), daughter of John Bowman. Paul J. Wyatt described a two-story brick tobacco factory "used by John K. Smith for a wholesale grocery . . . it is said this house would sometimes unload a steamboat up from New Orleans with a full cargo of sugar and molasses and give the boat a return trip of tobacco, flour and bacon." Wyatt, "History of New Providence."

53. This entry is the first of several in which Serepta mentioned toothaches. Because most dentists used no anesthetics other than strong drink until the late 1800s, tooth extractions, or indeed any attempt at dental treatment, would have been acutely painful. Nineteenth-century toothbrushes and toothpastes were relatively ineffective in preventing tooth decay. Women were likely to lose a tooth or two during pregnancy. In fact, age in general inevitably brought with it an increasing lack of chewing power, frequent discomfort, limited food choices, shame about appearance, bad breath, and periodic bouts of acute pain and swelling. Even worse, in the pre-antibiotic era these ailments often led to systemic infection and even death. "Dental Health and Diseases in the Past," accessed July 21, 2017, http://www.digitiseddiseases.org/dental_health_and_disease_in_the_past.php.

54. Mr. Watts may have been H. W. Watts. The 1860 Montgomery County, Tennessee, Census lists the household of H. W. Watts, 38, merchant, with S.O., 18, female, and W.W., 17, male. He operated Watts Brothers Dry Goods Store in New Providence.

55. The 1850 Sumner County, Tennessee, Census lists George Sawyer, 4, in what was probably a boarding house with twenty people, including Thomas Sawyer, 40, teacher; Henryetta, 35; Clarintine, 9; George, 4; and Edward, newborn, family 337.

56. The diary says Skipwith; Serepta probably meant Skipworth. The 1850

Davidson County, Tennessee, Census lists Austindar Skipworth, 29; Caroline, 26; and Eli, 2.

57. Elsey Trice was married to Serepta's aunt Tabitha, who was her mother's sister. The couple took Serepta in when her mother died. Serepta seems to have been close to her aunt before her mother's death. Serepta was listed in the 1850 Caldwell County, Kentucky, Census, recorded August 29, 1850, in the household of John and Damaris Bennett along with Mary E. Bennett, 13; Judson Bennett, 3; and Anne Bennett, 1, as well as in the 1850 Montgomery County, Tennessee, Census, recorded November 18, 1850, with her aunt and uncle, Tabitha and Elsey Trice. John and Damaris Bennett had another daughter, Susan, born in October 1851. Serepta's mother, Damaris Trice Jordan Bennett, did not die until 1852.

58. Typhoid is a bacterial infection with symptoms including bloating, constipation, diarrhea, nausea, vomiting, fatigue, fever, chills, loss of appetite, headache, muscle weakness, rash with small red dots, or weight loss. During the nineteenth century, typhoid could be fatal. It killed more soldiers than battle wounds. The severity of the disease was diminished after the development of vaccination and understanding that bad sanitary conditions contribute to infections.

59. Mrs. Mullins and son may have been Ann Mullins and her son, Dr. Charles Mullins. The 1860 Davidson County, Tennessee, Census, family 198, lists the household of Wilson Mullins, 45, clerk; Ann Mullins, 40; Charles, 22, physician; Willis, 19; Nathaniel Smith, 22, physician; Sarah Smith, 16; and C. K. W. Smith, 9 months.

60. In the nineteenth century, it was popular to visit asylums and prisons. These institutions touted themselves as modern and scientific, and people were curious to see them. Jennifer L. Bazar and Jeremy T. Burman, "Asylum Tourism," *Monitor on Psychology*, 45, no. 2 (February 2014): 68; accessed May 10, 2017, http://www.apa.org/monitor/2014/02/asylum-tourism.aspx. The Nashville Insane Asylum opened in 1840. It operated over-budget for several years and eventually became overcrowded with poor conditions. Mental health reformer Dorothea Dix visited the asylum and her report of bad conditions prompted the Tennessee Legislature to build on Murfreesboro Road a new facility that operated from 1851 to 1995. Robert Oliver, "Tennessee Lunatic Asylum," *Tennessee Encyclopedia of History and Culture*, 938.

61. The state capitol sits prominently on a hill in Nashville. It was designed by renowned architect William Strickland and is modeled after a Greek Ionic temple. Construction was done by commercial, convict, and slave labor and the capitol was completed in 1859. Serepta would have seen the building under construction.

62. Edgefield was a community in Davidson County, Tennessee. Today, Historic Edgefield is one of the oldest neighborhoods in Nashville, east of downtown, overlooking the Cumberland River.

63. Mrs. Carneal was probably Lucy Jane McQuary Carneal, third wife of

Josiah Carneal. Josiah and his first wife, Mary Catherine Galbreath Carneal, had seven children: Henry Wright, John Duncan, Mary Ellen, Martha (Mattie), Walker C., Eliza Catherine, and Robert Patrick. He had one child with his second wife, Nancy Jo Rice Carneal: Josiah R. Lucy and Josiah had eight children: Virginia, Isaiah Thomas, Victoria Reid, William Silas, Wesley Monroe, Demetrius Stout, Paul and Frances. "K-Kingins Family Tree," accessed January 10, 2019, http://www.ancestry.com.

64. Mary Harrelson was the daughter of William Harrelson, a former innkeeper in New Providence, and Eliza A. Harrelson (deceased). The 1850 Montgomery County, Tennessee, Census lists William Harrelson, innkeeper, 45, with Eliza A. Harrelson, 35; William C., 17, student; Mary E., 9; William Poindexter, 23, clerk; L.L. S. Whitfield, 25, merchant; William Bryarly, 21, merchant; H.W. Hibbs, 35, merchant; Samuel Frazier, 18, clerk; and R. McDaniel, 18, clerk. In August 1857, in Christian County, Kentucky, William Harrelson married Permelia A. Watson. The 1860 Christian County, Kentucky, Census lists William Harrelson, farmer, with Permelia A. Harrelson, 49; Leroy D. Watson, carpenter, 21; Frank O. Watson, farmer, 18; Nathan T. Watson, farmer, 16; Anna C. Watson, 8; Mary E. Harrelson, 20; and Shelton Watson, 50.

65. Tennessee School for the Blind was first conceived by James Champlin, who was blind from birth, after visiting Boston Asylum for the Blind. In 1843, Champlin established a small private school for the blind in Nashville with the financial help from First Presbyterian Church women. In 1844, the Tennessee Legislature voted to underwrite the establishment of a state school for the blind. In 1853, a permanent facility was built on Lebanon Road at Asylum Street in Nashville. The school, though in different locations, has continually operated until today. "Tennessee School for the Blind," Historic Nashville, accessed May 25, 2017, https://historicnashville.wordpress.com/2009/03/05/tennesse-school -for-the-blind/.

66. Mrs. Johnston was probably C. Johnston, listed in the 1850 Montgomery County, Tennessee, Census as age 45, female, in the household of James Johnston, 43, cabinetmaker, and Elizabeth Felin, 74, family 423.

67. Edward Branch Haskins (1813–1868) came to Clarksville to practice medicine and eventually served as president of the Montgomery County Medical Society. His daughter, Nannie, kept a diary published by the University of Tennessee Press in 2013, *The Diary of Nannie Haskins Williams: A Southern Woman's Story of Rebellion and Reconstruction, 1863–1890*.

68. Perhaps Serepta meant the plural of "Mrs." when she wrote "Misses." The 1850 Davidson County, Tennessee, Census lists Sarah Story, 24, in the household of Jesse Story, 27, with William, 2, and Elija 1, family 1044. Sarah Cartright married Jesse Story in Davidson County, Tennessee, on February 18, 1847. Amy Cullom married William H. Story in 1846. Amy, 20, is listed in the household of William H. Story, 35, family 63.

69. In addition to Serepta's mother, Damaris Trice Jordan Bennett, married to John Bennett, four other children of John and Nancy Trice had died: Susannah Trice Dycus, married to Berry (Greenberry) Dycus; Nancy Trice Anderson, married to Abraham Anderson; Milly Trice Chisenhall (d. 1849), married to Leigh Chisenhall; and Harriett Trice, never married. Still living were Tabitha Trice Trice (d. 1861), married to Elsey Trice; Benjamin Franklin Trice—later perhaps known as Franklin Castleberry Trice (1810–1883), married to Sarah (last name unknown); and Emily Trice Woodmore (died before 1860), married to William M. Woodmore (deceased). Emily Woodmore and her children were living with her mother, Nancy Castleberry Trice Travathan, in 1850.

70. Serepta may have been referring to Dawson Ogburn, who died December 26, 1857. His brothers, Benjamin (1832–1858) and Dr. Josiah H. Ogburn (1833–1858) died after lingering illnesses, probably tuberculosis, as Serepta suggested. Benjamin, Dawson, and Josiah are all buried in Mount Pleasant Cemetery, Montgomery County, Tennessee.

71. Consumption, the nineteenth-century name for tuberculosis, was a major disease among all ages and classes of society. See Sheila M. Rothman, *Living in the Shadow of Death: Tuberculosis and the Social Experience of Illness in American History* (New York: Basic Books, 1994) for a discussion of its effects on patients. Tuberculosis, typhoid fever, scarlet fever, and smallpox were major killers in the nineteenth century. Serepta mentioned friends suffering from all of these in various journal entries. William S. Joyner, "Infectious Diseases, 2006," accessed July 21, 2017, http://www.ncpedia.org/infectious-diseases.

72. Cousin Lou was Louisa V. Peterson, sister of Minerva Peterson Howard. See Chapter 1, Note 4 for more information on the Peterson and Howard families.

73. Cousin Lou's brother may have been Isaac Peterson.

74. The 1850 Montgomery County, Tennessee, Census, family 398, lists Lucy V. Helm, 10, in the household of P.N. (Presley Neville) Helm, 48, farmer, and Ann E. Helm, 35, with children George M., 12; Anna A., 7; Elizabeth, 6; Laura, 5; and Gertrude, 3. By the 1860 Montgomery County, Tennessee, Census, family 700, Presley Neville Helm was listed as a lumber merchant and the family had added three children: Walter, 9; Martha, 7; and Anise, 2.

75. Hopkinsville, Kentucky, is the county seat of Christian County, and is about 30 miles north of New Providence, Tennessee.

76. The *Montgomery County, Tennessee, Marriage Book* 3, 21, recorded Sue Barbee married to A. (Alsa) McDaniel on December 22. J. McDaniel was possibly a relative of the groom, or Serepta miswrote his first initial.

77. Mr. Leigh was probably William Henry Leigh, son of Henry Leigh and his first wife Nancy Lucinda Trice Leigh. Eleanor S. Williams, *Cabins to Castles, Historic Clarksville* (Oxford, MS: Guild Bindery Press, 1994), 163; 1850 Montgomery County, Tennessee, Census, family 1455.

78. The 1850 Montgomery County, Tennessee, Census, lists the household of

Solomon, 38, and Nancy Trice Barbee, 38, with children Susan, 16; Mary, 14; and George, 11; Eliza, 7; James, 2, family 73.

79. S. A. Holland was pastor at New Providence Baptist Church from 1854 to 1858. Williams, *Worship along the Warioto*, 187. The 1860 Christian County, Kentucky, Census, family 74, lists Shandy A. Holland, 44; Almeda, 39; Fannie, 20; Sarah T., 15; Almeda W., 8; George B., 5; Susan P., 3; Mary, 7 months; William McDaniel, overseer, 28. Shandy Holland was also a farmer.

80. Edward Hewitt, a teacher, became the first captain of Company L, 14th Tennessee Infantry. He retired at the reorganization of the company in 1862 and was replaced by John Mallory. Wallace C. Cross, *Ordeal by Fire: A History of the Fourteenth Tennessee Volunteer Infantry Regiment, CSA* (Clarksville, TN: Clarksville-Montgomery County Museum, 1990), 139, 159.

81. Will Trice may have been William Trice listed as age 14 in the 1850 Montgomery County, Tennessee, Census, family 1333, in the household of Bingham Trice, 61, and Eleanor Trice, 45, with John, 19; Judith, 17; George, 16; Frances, 14; Martha,11; Mary, 10; and Margaret, 7. Bingham Trice was a brother of Elizabeth, Leigh, Jesse James, Nace, May, Jane, Thomas Alexander, Greenberry, Mary "Pollie" Campbell, Elsey, and Nancy Barbee. Or he may have been William Lewis Trice, age 38 in 1858, son of James Pinhook and Zelpha Mallory Trice. Serepta was closer to the latter's family; however, the former was closer in age to Serepta.

82. Mollie Barbee was the sister of the bride, Susannah E. M. Barbee. Mary (Molly) Barbee was 14 in 1850.

83. Arabella A. Jenkins is listed as age 13 in the 1850 Montgomery County, Tennessee, Census in the household of James Jenkins, 46, farmer, with James, 14; Susanna A., 10; Ann T., 7; and Virginia, 3. Bell Jenkins married a man named Dunn and Serepta later referenced Bell Dunn.

84. Both Osborne and Lynes are married names of Nace Trice's daughters, sisters of Jane Trice Crabtree. Marion Trice married John Bryan Osborne, who died in 1852; perhaps this Mr. Osborne was their son, John Bryan Osborne Jr. Betty Trice married Auselme (possibly Anselm or Ansden) Lynes (No dates found).

85. Dr. Joseph Franklin Alsup had six brothers: Elijah Beam, Gideon McKnight, Daniel Nelson, William F.M., Asaph Hill, and Samuel Thomspon. "Thetford-Meyer Tree," accessed January 10, 2019, http://www.ancestry.com.

86. "Of consumption on the 1st inst. at the residence of her mother, Miss Susan A. Boatwright, in the 29th year of her age." "Died," *Clarksville Weekly Chronicle*, January 8, 1856.

87. Mrs. Staton was probably Clarissa Staton, wife of Joseph T. Staton, Sr. The 1860 Montgomery County, Tennessee, Census lists Joseph Staton, Sr., 49, stable keeper, C. A (Clarissa), female, 45; E.A. Jackson, female, 22; J. W. (Joseph) Staton, male, 20, merchant; C.W. (Charles) Staton, male, 15; Ann M. Staton, 13; Senora

(perhaps Lenora) Jackson, 4, family 741. Serepta reported the second marriage of Emily Staton Jackson in her January 16, 1862, diary entry.

88. Mrs. Davis was probably Amanda Davis. The 1860 Montgomery County, Tennessee, Census lists Thomas Davis, 34, grocer; Amanda, 34; S., female, 7; Minna, male, 5; Patsy, 4; Ann Donaldson, 15; and James Jenkins, male, 23, clerk, family 703.

89. Death was an everyday occurrence in the nineteenth century. While mortality is inevitable, today, we are, in fact, dying of different things and less frequently — life expectancy has dramatically increased in the past century, partially because of a decrease in infant mortality. Medical historians suggest mortality was not under significant human control until around 1880 when vaccines began to come into widespread use. Sulfonamides did not appear until 1935, and penicillin, discovered in 1928, was not available as a treatment until 1950. Antibiotic drugs did not exist until the middle of the twentieth century. A.M. Stern and H. Markel, "The History of Vaccines and Immunization: Familiar Patterns, New challenges," *Health Aff*airs, 24, no. 3 (2005): 611–21; George Dvorsky, "How We Died 200 Years Ago, Compared to How We Die Today," *The New England Journal of Medicine*, (2012) accessed July 21, 2017, http://io9.gizmodo.com/5920871/how-we-died-200-years-ago-compared-to-how-we-die-today.

90. Townsend A. Thomas and brother, John N., opened Thomas and Brother Drug in New Providence in 1858. Ursula Smith Beach, *Along the Warioto*, (Nashville: McQuiddy Press, 1964) 134.

91. John Ogburn was the 18-year-old son of Mary Ann Caroline Hunt Ogburn and the late John Noble Ogburn. The 1850 Montgomery County, Tennessee, Census, family 1336, lists the household of John, 53, and Caroline, 43, with children, William, 20; Samuel, 18; Sarah, 14; Richard, 12; John, 10; Elizabeth, 8; Mary A., 6; and Caroline V., 3 (probably the Jennie Serepta often referred to); and William Hunt, 72.

92. Scarlet Fever is an infection which causes sore throat, fever, headaches, swollen lymph nodes, and a red rash that feels like sandpaper. It most commonly affects children between 5 and 15 and, in the nineteenth century, could have caused death.

93. James Ross was the elder son of Elder Reuben Ross and Mary D. Baker Ross. He opened a school in January 1858, seven miles northeast of Clarksville. Williams, *Cabins to Castles*, 203.

94. The 1860 Montgomery County, Tennessee, Census lists George Trice, 25, merchant, living in the household of Moses Sally, 68, cooper; E. Sally, female, 65; and J. E. Ray, male, 22, family 706. This George may have been the son of Bingham Trice and nephew of Nace Trice. The census also lists George A. Trice, in the household of Harriett Trice, 56, with J.E. Trice, 20, male; L.S. Trice, 17, male; and M.A. Trice, 37, female.

95. A hackney carriage was hired for transportation.

96. Greenberry B. Dycus married Serepta's aunt Susannah Trice, Damaris Trice Jordan Bennett's sister, on September 9, 1841, in Montgomery County, Tennessee. The couple had two daughters, Elsey (1840–?) and Cassus (1843–?). The 1860 Indianola, Calhoun County, Texas, Census lists G. B. Dycus, 41, steam boat captain, with M.E., 25; D. E. (Elsey), 15, and C. A. (Cassus), 12. From Serepta's comments, one assumes soon after Susannah's death Berry Dycus remarried the much younger M.E. Dycus, who remained in the hackney during the visit. *Montgomery County, Tennessee, Marriages*, Book 2.

97. "In the early history of the town, New Providence was, in fact, two towns, the upper end, or western portion, being incorporated under the name of 'Meacham Town,' while the eastern, or lower end, was called 'Cumberland Town.'" Paul J. Wyatt, "History of New Providence." Today, both New Providence and Meachamville are within the bounds of north Clarksville. Montgomery County, Tennessee, Deed Book 3, 149–150.

98. Mr. Slaughter was probably Armistead G. Slaughter of Pembroke, Kentucky. The 1860 Christian County, Kentucky, Census lists Armistead C. Slaughter, farmer 55; Ann R., 43; Ellen (Possibly Helen), 19; Donay C., 16; and Gabriel L., 24, family 31. The 1850 Christian County, Kentucky, Census lists A. G. Slaughter, 40; Ann, 34; Mary St. C., 12; Ellen L., 10; Cladonia, 7; and Gabriel L., 4. Serepta called his wife Cousin Ann.

99. Serepta included the designation of "Junior" to distinguish William S. Mallory from his Uncle William Mallory. William S. Mallory was the brother of Mary Elizabeth, John Wilson, Lorinah Jane (Jennie), Zilpha Ann (deceased), and James S. (deceased) Mallory and son of the Reverend Stephen S. Mallory (1801–1883) and Nancy Wilson Collins Mallory (1813–1841). The 1850 Montgomery County, Tennessee, Census lists the household of Stephen Mallory, 47, with his second wife Eliza Mallory, 50, and children: Mary, 19; William, 18; John, 15; Jane (Jennie) 14; Ann, 12; along with T. D. Rucker, male, 26.

100. A manager in the firm of William Gray & Company, a tobacco manufacturing and shipping firm in Manchester, Virginia, Joseph H. Harris came to New Providence in 1856 to establish a tobacco stemmery. In February 1858, he was murdered by a slave that had been mistreated. The enslaved worker was charged with splitting Harris's head with an axe on February 19, 1858. Suspicion centered on this man due to his excessive demonstrations of grief at his owner's death. This behavior was especially notable since the slave had been severely punished the day before for theft and disobedience. A twelve-man committee tried and sentenced him to death. When they hung the rope over a limb and kicked the bench away, he caught the trailing rope with his feet, upholding his weight. He was let down, whereupon he made a full confession. After his confession, he was hanged by those assembled. *Clarksville Jeffersonian*, February 25, 1858; Beach, *Along the Warioto*, 92.

101. This sentence refers to Job 14:1. KJV, "Man that is born of a woman is of few days and full of trouble."

102. John Andrews Murrell, commonly spelled as Murel and Murrel (1806–1844), was an infamous bandit as a horse thief and slave stealer. He was imprisoned in the Tennessee State Penitentiary and died of tuberculosis several months after release from prison.

103. Vol Harris was the younger brother of Joseph H. Harris.

104. A stemmery is a large building in which tobacco stemming process occurs. The leaves are stripped from the stems.

105. Joseph Ridley was rector at Trinity Episcopal Church, Clarksville, Tennessee. Williams, *Worship along the Warioto*, 331.

106. Christian County, Kentucky, borders the Kentucky-Tennessee state line with Montgomery County, Tennessee, to the south. Hopkinsville is the county seat.

107. Brilliantine is a cotton fabric blended with a worsted fabric. Because it does not wrinkle, it was popular as a summer dress fabric in the nineteenth century.

108. Alexander Smith Jr., began medical practice in Montgomery County in 1854 in the McAdoo community, approximately seven miles southeast of Clarksville. The community is named for nearby McAdoo Creek.

109. On January 14, 1858, Italian pro-unificationists threw three bombs at Napoleon III and wife Eugenie of France as they were on their way to the opera. The Italians were led by Fleice Orsini, who was arrested and executed.

110. Serepta was mistaken. Queen Victoria's oldest daughter, also named Victoria, (1840–1901) married in 1858 Frederick, Crown Prince of Germany and Prussia and later Frederick III, German Emperor and King of Prussia (1831–1888).

111. Charles Babbage (1791–1871) was an English mathematician, philosopher, inventor, and mechanical engineer. He invented the first mechanical computer and is known as the "father of computers."

112. French inventor Thomas de Colmar patented the arithmometer, the first commercially successful digital mechanical calculator. It was manufactured from 1851 to 1915.

113. The 1850 Montgomery County, Tennessee, Census lists Nace F. (possibly Ignacius Fred) Trice, 56; Alley, female, 33; Dolatha M, 17; Eliza J., 9; Mary, 7; Martin C., 6; Eugenia, 1. Three more children were born to the couple after 1850: Harden N. in 1853, James C. in 1855, and Valentine in 1859. Nace Trice married Alley Alice Allen in Montgomery County in 1841. He died in 1858 and was buried in the Trice Cemetery. The children born after 1841 represented a second family for Nace Trice. He was first married to Elizabeth Mallory (1792–1831); Jane Trice Crabtree, Bettie Trice Lynes, Marion Trice Osborne, and B. B. Homer's first wife, Harriett Trice Homer, were their daughters. "Hunter-Worley Family Tree," accessed January 20, 2019, http://www.ancestry.com.

114. A bitters is an alcoholic concoction flavored with plant matter and is characterized by bitter, sour, or bittersweet flavor. Bitters were originally developed as patent medicines. Silkweed, another name for milkweed because its pods contain a silk-like down, may be eaten by humans but does contain poisonous toxins that vary in strength.

115. William Lewis Trice (1825–1891) was the son of James Pinhook and Zelpha Mallory Trice. He was born in Montgomery County and died in Hopkinsville.

116. Bettie Homer was the daughter of B. B. Homer and Harriet Trice Homer (deceased). Griffey, *Riverview Cemetery*, 66.

117. While Serepta was concerned about the welfare of her cousins Marion, Jane, and Bettie, all of whom were widowed and probably struggling to survive, one must also feel concern for their stepmother and seven half siblings, four of whom were under age 10 when their father died. In fact, Alley Trice was pregnant with the fourth, Valentine, who was not born until 1859.

118. The Reverend John B. Duncan, from the First Baptist Church in Clarksville, served as pastor of New Providence Baptist Church from May 1858 until March 23, 1861. Williams, *Worship along the Warioto*, 187.

119. Mathew 1:21 "And she shall bring forth a son, and thou shalt call his name JESUS: for he shall save his people from their sins." (KJV).

120. *The History of Napoleon Bonaparte* by John S. C. Abbott was published in 1855 by Harper and Brothers. This book is still in the family's possession and has been displayed at Fort Defiance in Clarksville.

121. HHDS is an abbreviation for hogshead, a very large wooden barrel. A standardized hogshead measured 48 inches long and 30 inches in diameter at the head. Fully packed with tobacco, it weighed about 1,000 pounds.

122. Although Serepta used honorific titles of Uncle and Aunt for a number of members of the Mallory family, she probably was not directly related to the Mallorys. Two Mallory siblings did marry Trices: 1. Zelpha (Zilpha) Mallory (1793–1860) married James Pinhook Trice (1787–1853), and 2. Elizabeth Mallory (1792–1831) married Nace (possibly Ignacius) Fred Trice (1794–1858), probably a first cousin of James Pinhook Trice. The older Mallory siblings were William (1791–1874), Elizabeth, Zelpha, George Sims (1796–1823), Stephen Smith (1801–1883), Henrietta (1802–1860), Allatha (Alley) (1802–1890), Lorainah Sims (1811–1831), Zebiah (1813–1852), and Ann Zinah (1816–1849). "Blackman Family Tree," http://www.ancestry.com, accessed January 20, 2019. While Uncle John Mallory was not a member of this immediate family, he appears to have been a contemporary of these siblings and may have been a cousin. The "Futrell Family Tree," accessed January 14, 2019, http://www.ancestry.com, lists a John Mallory (1795–1873), who was buried in Big Rock, Stewart County, Tennessee. Williams in *Worship along the Warioto*, 144, mentions John Mallory as a trustee of Little West Fork Baptist Church.

123. Eliza Trice was the daughter of Nace Trice and Alley Alice Allen Trice.

124. Aspen Cottage was apparently the name given to the home of Elsey and Tabitha Trice.

125. The 1870 Montgomery County, Tennessee, Census lists Valentine W. Smith, 35, druggist, with Mary Ann Leigh Smith, 27; Mediceas A., 9; Blanche, 8; Ada E., 6; James F., 4; and Valentine H., 1. Valentine (Tine) was the son of James N. Smith and Nancy Collins Smith, and Mary Ann was the daughter of Henry Leigh. 1850 Census Montgomery County, Tennessee, family 1455.

126. The 1850 Christian County, Kentucky, Census lists Annis Buck, 17, in the household of Samuel D. Buck, 46, druggist, with John, 11, and Henry C., 2, family 46.

127. J. F. Alsup married Eliza Trice, daughter of Nace and Alley Trice, on June 15, 1858, in Montgomery County, Tennessee. Tennessee, *Compiled Marriages, 1851–1900.*

128. Mildred Ray was perhaps Mildred Wray, age 18, listed in the household of Joseph Wray, 44, farmer in 1850 Montgomery County, Census, along with Elin, female, 86; Ann, 16; and Joseph, 12, family 89.

129. Plutarch's *Lives of the Noble Greeks and Romans*, commonly called *Parallel Lives* or *Plutarch's Lives*, is a series of biographies of famous men, illuminating their common moral virtues or failings. They were probably written at the beginning of the second century AD. The book is in the family's possession.

130. *Macaulay's History of England from the Accession of James II* by Thomas Babington Macaulay was first published by J. M. Dent and Sons in 1848. The book is in the family's possession.

131. *The Ancient History of the Egyptians, Carthaginians, Assyrians, Babylonians, Medes and Persians, Macedonians and Grecians* was written by French historian Charles Rollin (1661–1741). The book is in the family's possession.

132. Wig wag is a system of communication employing flags used by ships and railroads. Perhaps Serepta and her friends were playing a game involving signaling.

133. Mrs. Pirtle was Nannie H. Rogers Pirtle, age 28 in 1860. Mrs. Rogers was probably her mother, Susan Rogers, listed as age 59 and a farmer in the 1860 Montgomery County, Tennessee, Census, family 101. Dr. John Milton Pirtle, age 31 in 1860, was listed in the *Minutes of the Tennessee Conference* and was assigned to the Red River in the Clarksville District. A Methodist minister and a medical doctor, he was elected chaplain of Company F, 14th Tennessee Infantry. The July 5, 1861, *Clarksville Chronicle* reported on his election: "The gentleman thus honored is a regular M.D., and 'on the pinch,' can be useful to the body as well as the soul, of the men." The couple had three children in 1860: A. Pirtle, 4, male; Pete, 2; and Elizabeth O., 5 months.

134. Janie and Gertie Helm were daughters of Presley Neville and Ann Helm. See Chapter 1, Note 74 for more information about the Helm family.

135. Sarah was Sarah Ann Ogburn Spence, daughter of Mary Ann Caroline Hunt Ogburn and the late John Noble. Sarah married Joseph Spence in 1858.

136. Palmyra is one of the first communities established in Montgomery County, Tennessee, located twelve miles south of Clarksville on the Cumberland River.

137. The steamer *Huntsville* sank on May 12, 1858, in the Cumberland River hitting a snag at Palmyra Island which broke the hull and sank in minutes with five or six people on the deck. *Clarksville Chronicle*, May 14, 1858.

138. The *Clarksville Chronicle*, May 28, 1858, p. 3, reported the death of Mrs. William Young, "On the 26th inst., in this County, Mrs. Mary P. Young, consort of W. F. Young, age about 26 years."

139. The 1870 Montgomery County, Tennessee, Census lists Jno Morrison, 46, physician, with Martha, 44; Robert, 20; Joseph, 19; and Mattie, 16, family 73.

140. Alley, Gibbie, and Ann Donaldson were daughters of William Donaldson and Allatha Mallory Donaldson. The 1850 Montgomery County, Tennessee, Census, family 288, lists William Dollanson [*sic*], 48, tailor, with Alatha, 47, and children Laurana, 25; Amanda, 23; Zilpha, 22; Adelina, 21; Zebiah (Gibbie), 18; Lucinda, 16; Allatha, 14; William, 12; Rebecca, 10; James, 8; and Ann, 6. Allatha Mallory Donaldson was the sister of William, Elizabeth, Zelpha, George Sims, Stephen, Henrietta, Lorainah Sims, Zebiah, and Ann Zinah Mallory. "Hille Family Tree," accessed January 14, 2019, http://www.ancestry.com.

141. Trenton, Kentucky, is a city in Todd County. It is about fifteen miles northeast of New Providence.

142. Mr. Waller was Lewis Waller, a tobacco buyer married to Serepta's cousin Alley Trice, daughter of James Pinhook and Zelpha Mallory Trice. The 1850 Montgomery County, Tennessee, Census lists Alley J. Trice Waller, 18, wife of Lewis A. Waller, 28, merchant, with William L., 2 months. The same census also lists L.A. Waller, 28; A.J. Waller, 18; and William A. Waller, 2, in the household of James Trice, 60, and Zelpha Trice, 50. By 1858, the Wallers had two more sons, Frank, born in 1850, and Bailey, born in 1855. "Choate Family Tree," accessed January 18, 2019, http://www.ancestry.com.

143. Pembroke, Kentucky, is a city in Christian County that was settled in 1836. It is located between Oak Grove, Kentucky, and Hopkinsville, Kentucky, but to the east of both towns. It is about 6 miles from Trenton, Kentucky.

144. Cousin Ann was probably Ann Slaughter, wife of Armistead G. Slaughter. Hellen and Mollie were their daughters. See Chapter 1, Note 98 for more information about the Slaughter family.

145. Serepta was referring to a nursery owned by John S. Downer. The 1860 Todd County, Kentucky, Census lists John S. Downer, nursery man, 52, Elizabeth W., 42; Press, 2; and Robert, 16, family 308.

146. Zelpha Trice is listed in the 1850 Montgomery County, Tennessee Census, age 50, in the household of James Trice, 60, farmer along with L. A. Waller, 28; A. J. Waller, 18; and William A. Waller, 2, family 1365. Zelpha Mallory Trice was the sister of William, Elizabeth, George Sims, Stephen, Henrietta, Allatha, Lorainah Sims, Zebiah, and Ann Zinah Mallory. "Hille Family Tree," accessed January 14, 2019, http://www.ancestry.com.

147. Stephen E. Trice was the son of James Pinhook and Zelpha Mallory Trice and brother of William Lewis Trice and Alley Trice Waller. Will of James Trice, Montgomery County Tennessee Will Book M, 563. The 1860 Christian County, Kentucky, Census, lists Virginia "Jennie" Buckner Stewart Trice, 42, wife of Stephen Edward Trice, 40, tobacco stemmer, with John B., and Annie, 9. Jennie was the widow of Clement Stewart, family 1037; Cordelia C. Gary, *Christian County, Ky., Marriage Records 1797-1850* (Hopkinsville, KY: Christian County Genealogical Society, 1997), 13 and 127. *Clarksville Leaf Chronicle*, April 26, 1904.

148. The 1860 Edmonson County, Kentucky, Census lists Marcellus N. Drake, 38, doctor, estate value $300, living with the Shaggs Family: Henry, 81, and Frances, 61, family 725.

149. Western State Lunatic Asylum opened in 1850, two miles outside of Hopkinsville, Kentucky. Today it is Western State Hospital. The original building is on the National Register of Historic Places.

150. There were two Dr. Winstons (not Winstone) in the 1860 Davidson County, Tennessee, Census: John D. Winston, physician, 54, family 473, and C. K. Winston, 47, family 215.

151. Neuralgia was a type of nerve pain. Nineteenth century doctors debated the cause of the condition.

152. *Kentucky Will and Probate, Volume 1-4*, 1831-1979, 86, records indicate that Drake left part of his estate, probated September 8, 1892, to "my beloved wife Margaret Jane Drake."

153. Serepta must have been reporting on the birth of Ella Riggins, daughter of Thomas and Alice M. Garrett Riggins. The 1860 Christian County, Kentucky, Census, family 216, lists Thomas, 39, a grocer, with Alice, 23; Ella, 2; and William, 1. Riggins married Alice M. Garrett on April 14, 1857.

154. Jane Crabtree and Marion Osborne were sisters, daughters of Nace and Elizabeth Mallory Trice.

155. Dycusburg, Kentucky, is located near the southern tip of Crittenden County on the east bank of the Cumberland River. The town was laid out by William E. Dycus and became a shipping port on the Cumberland River. A post office was established in 1848.

156. The 1860 Montgomery County, Tennessee, Census lists G. W. Rogers, 22, laborer, living in the household of James Heathman, 52, carpenter, family 1049.

157. The 1860 Montgomery County, Tennessee, Census, family 821, lists J. W. Cabiness, 28, dentist, with Lucy, 23; Edwin, 3; and Ellen, 2 ½. Cabiness

became a leading dentist in Clarksville, died in 1894, and is buried in Greenwood Cemetery.

158. Fredonia, Kentucky, is in western Caldwell County.

159. *Minatonce* seems to be the name of the boat on which Serepta and her party traveled. *Minatonce* may have been a misspelling for the passenger vessel *Minnetonka*.

160. There are two Mrs. Blues in the 1850 Caldwell County, Kentucky, Census: Mary E. Blue, 24, in the household of William E. Blue, 29, farmer, with William T., 2. The second is Plemsey Blue, 23, in the household of John C. Blue, 26.

161. John Bennett married Amanda Knower after Damaris died, and the couple had five children, in addition to the three John Bennett had with Serepta's mother Damaris. The 1870 Livingston County, Kentucky, Census lists John Bennett, 57, with Amanda, 34; Judson, 23; Susan A., 18; Isabell, 12; Robert, 11; Forest, 8; La, 4; and Minnie, 9 months. "Bennett Family Tree," accessed January 10, 2019, http://www.ancestry.com.

162. Murfreesboro, Tennessee, is the county seat of Rutherford County. It is eighty miles southwest of Clarksville in Middle Tennessee. It was home to the Stones River Battle during the Civil War.

163. *The Clarksville Weekly Chronicle*, July 2, 1858, p. 3, listed the obituary of N. B. Whitfield, who died of "flux" and was a "member of the Masonic fraternity."

164. A cordial is a comforting or pleasant-tasting medicine. Nineteenth-century homemakers often distilled cordials, or sweet liqueurs, from fruits like blackberries, cherries or elderberries.

165. Arabella Trabue (1840–?) was the daughter of Dr. John E. and Elizabeth Atkinson Trabue, sister of Tom Trabue, granddaughter of T. W. Atkinson and his first wife Elizabeth Hundley, and niece of Quintus Cincinnatus Atkinson Sr.

166. Keysburg, Kentucky, is a community between and to the north of New Providence and Springfield, Tennessee.

167. Sue Barbee McDaniel was the daughter of Solomon Gray and Nancy Trice Barbee. The 1860 Montgomery County, Tennessee, Census lists Sue E. McDaniel, 23, in the household of A. (Alsa) McDaniel, 30, with T. A. McDaniel, 1, male.

168. The Atlantic Telegraph Company laid the first transatlantic telegraph cable. The project began in 1854 and was completed in 1858. The first official telegram to pass between two continents was a letter of congratulations from Queen Victoria to President James Buchanan on August 16. However, the cable functioned for only three weeks. Signal quality declined rapidly, slowing transmission to an almost unusable speed. The cable was destroyed the following month when excessive voltage was applied to improve the operation. A second attempt was undertaken in 1865 with much-improved material and the cable functioned after 1866.

169. Little West Fork Baptist Church was organized in 1818 on the banks of Little West Fork Creek by Elder Reuben Ross, who served as its pastor for forty-two years. Williams, *Worship along the Warioto*, 144.

170. Comet Donati was named after the Italian astronomer Giovanni Battista Donati, who first observed it on June 2, 1858. It was closest to the earth in October of 1858 and was the most brilliant comet that appeared in the nineteenth century. It was the first comet to be photographed.

171. This quote may have come from "Letters from Italy, No. III," *Blackwood's Magazine*, Vol. 12, 1822, 583, "The great difference between the distant view of an English and of an Italian town, besides the essential one of clearness of sky, is, that from the latter lofty square towers are seen to rise, in place of our subtle steeples."

172. The 1860 Montgomery County, Tennessee, Census lists the household of E. (Ezekiel) J. Wilson, 26, merchant, with Irina Wilson, 20; Eunice W., 6 months; R. (Robert) A. Wilson, male, 23, family 709.

173. *A Pictorial History of England* by Samuel Griswold Goodrich was originally published in 1845.

174. The 1850 Montgomery County, Tennessee, Census lists Ellen Pettus, 8, in the household of Thomas F. Pettus, 31, merchant, with Martha A. Cowherd Pettus, 29; John H., 6; Stephen, 4; and Edman H., 1. B. B. Homer, clerk, 30, is also listed in the 1850 household. Thomas H. Pettus was the brother of Frances Pettus, who married Elsey Trice after Serepta's Aunt Tabitha Trice Trice died. See Chapter 1, Note 266 for a fuller discussion of Thomas Pettus's birth family.

175. Serepta had two friends named Ephraim, whom she called Efe: Efe Manson and Efe Fairfax. See Chapter 2, Note 215 for more information on Ephraim Manson and Chapter 1, Note 8 for information on the Fairfax family.

176. The *Clarksville Jeffersonian* was a weekly newspaper published from 1843 to 1873. The article she quoted was published September 29, 1858, 2.

177. A charivarie is a folk tradition of a noisy mock serenade banging pans and making noise to a couple when they marry. Sometimes pranks could become violent.

178. In the nineteenth century, conjoined twins were displayed as curiosities in fairs. Chang and Eng Bunker (1811–1874) were brothers born in Siam, now Thailand. They traveled with P. T. Barnum's circus for many years and were labeled as the Siamese Twins, a term that was commonly used for all conjoined twins.

179. The 1860 Concord Township, Clinton County, Missouri, Census lists John H. Trice, 44, farmer, with Eliza, female, 31; N. B., 20; Samuel T., male, 10; and Francis, female, 10, family 78.

180. The 1850 Montgomery County, Tennessee, Census lists David T. Porter, 22, druggist, in the household of E. C. Dycus, 30, physician, with Atalanta G. Dycus, 25; Francis A., 22; and Francesca, 0, family 1429. Elijan Carroll and

Atalanta Mary Dycus were married in Montgomery County, Tennessee, on
April 30, 1849.

181. This appears to be "C/O," an abbreviation for "in care of."

182. Before the days of refrigeration, several days of cold were necessary during
hog butchering season to prevent meat from spoiling from temperatures above
freezing. Therefore, slaughtering happened in the fall to minimize any chance of
unseasonable warm weather ruining valuable meat.

183. Mr. Smith was probably Valentine (Tine) Smith. See Chapter 1, Note
125 for more information on the Smith family . The 1860 Montgomery County,
Tennessee, Census does list another Smith, who is a druggist: B. W. Smith, 25,
in the household with Mary, 19.

184. *The Sketch Book of Geoffrey Crayon, Gen.*, commonly referred to as *The
Sketch Book*, is a collection of thirty-four essays and short stories written by
American author Washington Irving. It was published serially throughout 1819
and 1820.

185. *The History of Napoleon Bonaparte* by John Stevens Cabot Abbott
(1805–1877) was published in 1855.

186. Samuel Ogburn was the son of Mary Ann Caroline Hunt Ogburn and the
late John Noble Ogburn. He was 18 in 1850.

187. A melodeon was a type of button accordion or also a type of nineteenth-
century reed organ.

188. Turpentine can be used in explosive devices. Perhaps the children were
making a type of fireworks for Christmas.

189. Threnology, or more popularly referred to as phrenology, was a theory
which claimed to determine character, personality traits, and criminality based on
the shape of the head. Developed by German physician Franz Joseph Gall around
1800, it was most popular in the first half of the nineteenth century. Phrenology
posited four temperaments, accompanied by different degrees of strength and
activity in the brain. The lymphatic temperament is caused by glands and assimi-
lating organs being the most active in the body. The nervous temperament comes
from the brain and nerves being strongest. Strong muscular and fibrous systems
lead to the bilious temperament. The sanguine temperament occurs when the
lungs, heart, and blood vessels are constitutionally predominant. John van Wyhe,
"The Four Temperaments," The History of Phrenology, accessed January 14,
2018, http://www.historyofphrenology.org.uk/temperament.htm.

190. Ambrotype is a type of photography that replaced daguerreotype and
involves coating a positive image on a piece of glass. Ambrotype was introduced in
the 1850s. During the 1860s, it was superseded by the tintype, a similar photograph on thin black-lacquered iron.

191. The 1850 Montgomery County, Tennessee, Census lists Sally B. Cowherd,
female, 10 in the household of Anah Cowherd, female, 52; with Richard, male, 19;
Frances, female, 21; and Benjamin, male, 13, family 118.

192. *Godey's Lady's Book*, also known as *Godey's Magazine and Lady's Book*, was a women's magazine published in Philadelphia from 1830 to 1878. Sarah Josepha Hale was the editor. It was the most popular magazine in the years before the Civil War. Each issue contained poetry, articles, and engravings created by prominent writers and artists.

193. Bud Trice was James T. Trice. The 1860 Montgomery County, Tennessee, Census lists J. T. Trice, farmer, 26, with M.J. (Margaret Smith) Trice, 21. Margaret was the daughter of James N. and Nancy Allen Smith and sister of Valentine (Tine) Smith.

194. *The Clarksville Weekly Chronicle*, February 11, 1859, noted on page 3 "Died, On the 4th inst, at his residence in this county, Mr. Bingham Trice, about 70 years of age." Bingham Trice was the brother of Elizabeth, Leigh, Jesse James, Nace, May, Jane, Thomas Alexander, Greenberry, Mary "Pollie" Campbell, Elsey, and Nancy Barbee.

195. Samuel Daley Ogburn did marry Mary Ann Hutcheson on February 24, 1859, in Robertson County, Tennessee.

196. The hymen is a membrane that is broken the first time a woman has intercourse.

197. Corns and calluses are thick, hardened layers of skin caused by friction or pressure, usually on the feet and toes or hands and fingers. Corns are smaller than calluses and can be painful when pressed.

198. Acts 19: 15–16: But the Lord said unto him, Go thy way: for he is a chosen vessel unto me, to bear my name before the Gentiles, and kings, and the children of Israel: For I will shew him how great things he must suffer for my name's sake. KJV.

199. The Reverend J. B. Duncan served as pastor at New Providence Baptist Church and First Baptist Church in Clarksville before the Civil War. Williams, *Warship along the Warioto*, 187, 311.

200. Numbers 10:29: And Moses said unto Hobab, the son of Raguel the Midianite, Moses' father in law, We are journeying unto the place of which the LORD said, I will give it you: come thou with us, and we will do thee good: for the LORD hath spoken good concerning Israel. KJV.

201. Richard Ogburn was the son of Mary Ann Caroline Hunt Ogburn and the late John Noble Ogburn. He would have been about 21 years old in 1859. See Chapter 1, Note 91 for a full listing of the John Noble Ogburn family.

202. *The Clarksville Weekly Chronicle*, reported that Waller and Smith upon purchase became Ogburn and Brothers, selling "toys, Christmas tricks, music boxes, hand organs &c.," December 10, 1858, 2.

203. Mr. Burgess was probably J.M. Burgess, hotel keeper. See Chapter 2, Note 30 and Note 31 for more information on the Burgess family.

204. Mrs. Gold may have been Clarissa McDough Gold, second wife of John Gold (1791–1868). Or she may have been Clarissa Gold's daughter-in-law, Sarah A.

Davie Gold, wife of Daniel Gold. *The Tennessee Compiled Marriages, 1851–1900* lists Sarah and Daniel's marriage as March 5, 1856. The 1850 Montgomery County, Tennessee, Census lists the household of John Gold, 58, farmer, and Clara Gold, 30, with children, Daniel, 21; Susan, 14; Benjamin, 12; Lewis, 8; and Elizabeth, 5, family 322.

205. The 1859 Clarksville City Directory lists Dr. James F. Johnson as a partner with Dr. Edward Branch Haskins. Their office was on the southwest corner of Second and College streets, Clarksville, Tennessee, where the Haskins residence was also located. *Williams' Clarksville Directory, City Guide and Business Mirror, Vol. 1, 1859–60.* (Clarksville, TN: C.O. Faxon, 1859. Reprinted by Ursula Beach, 1976). The September 15, 1877, *Clarksville Weekly Chronicle,* 3, reported that Johnson died on September 12 in Guthrie, Kentucky, of a morphine overdose. His obituary noted he had served as a surgeon in the 14th Tennessee Infantry.

206. The 1850 Christian County, Kentucky, Census lists David Jameson, 18, clerk, in the household of Robert C. Jameson, 27, farmer, family 223.

207. William Mallory (1791–1874) was the brother of Zelpha Mallory Trice, Elizabeth Mallory Trice (deceased), George Sims Mallory (deceased), Stephen Smith Mallory, Henrietta Mallory Collins, Allatha "Alley" Mallory Donaldson, Lorainah Sims Mallory (deceased), Zebiah Mallory (deceased), and Ann Zinah Mallory (deceased). Higgins, *The Montgomery County [Tennessee] Genealogical Journal 9,* 104; "Hille Family Tree," accessed January 14, 2019, http://www .ancestry.com. The 1860 Montgomery County, Tennessee, Census lists William Mallory, 68, with Henrietta, 59; John Sawyer, 18; and Lorena Sawyer, 10. William married first Lucinda Draper on April 24, 1821, in Caldwell County, Kentucky, and second Henrietta Sawyer (1800–1881) on February 14, 1845, in Montgomery County, Tennessee. Henrietta Sawyer Mallory was the daughter of Nathan Sawyer. Their nephew and niece, John and Lorena Sawyer, were the orphaned children of John and Zebiah Mallory Sawyer. *Caldwell County, Kentucky, Marriage Index, 1809–1828; Kentucky County Marriages, 1793–1965.*

208. Tatting is a kind of knotted lace made by hand with a small shuttle. Tatted lace was used chiefly for trimming clothing, table runners and cloths, bedding, and towels.

209. The 1860 Montgomery County, Tennessee, Census lists Alexander L. Hamilton, 33, teacher and preacher; Dollie, 23; Ida, 3; and Eason, 6 months, family 1162. The census also lists faculty, staff and families in the household.

210. Clarksville Female Academy was chartered in 1846. It was re-chartered in 1854 and had an extensive building expansion including study hall, classrooms and a dormitory; 170 students were registered with 60 girls living in the dormitory and room for 100. The Academy was located on the corner of Madison and Fifth streets. After the fall of Fort Donelson, the school closed and was used as a hospital.

211. Sarah was probably Sarah Ann Ogburn Spence, daughter of John Noble and Mary Ann Caroline Hunt Ogburn and wife of Joseph Spence. Their son, Brent, was born March 20, 1859.

212. Mr. Blakeney was probably Robert Blakeney. The 1860 Montgomery County, Tennessee, Census, family 733, lists R. J. Blakeney, 30, carpenter, with V. [Z.?] M., 30, female; L. E., 8, female; and Isabella, 83. R.J. Blakeney was married to Zilpha Donaldson Blakeney, daughter of William and Alley Mallory Donaldson.

213. Margaret seems to have been one of Serepta's Uncle Trice's slaves. It is impossible to check the census for slave names because the government in its Slave Schedule, only listed slaves by gender and age. This entry indicates that Trice had a hard time controlling Margaret. Enslaved people resisted in many ways and enslavers resorted to many strategies of oppression to control their slaves.

214. George Barbee was the son of Solomon and Nancy Trice Barbee, listed as age 11 in the 1850 Montgomery County, Tennessee, Census. Nancy Trice Barbee was the sister of Bingham, Elizabeth, Leigh, Jesse James, Nace, May, Jane, Thomas Alexander, Greenberry, Mary "Pollie" Campbell, and Elsey. See Chapter 1, Note 78 on the Barbee family.

215. Ann Johnson Ogburn was the widow of James Ogburn, brother of John Noble Ogburn. She was the sister-in-law of Mary Ann Caroline Hunt Ogburn.

216. Kate and Eugenia Fauntleroy were the daughters of Butler E. and A.M. Fauntleroy. The 1860 Montgomery County, Tennessee, Census, family 805, lists the household of B.E. Fauntleroy, 59, merchant, with A.M., 38; Kate, 22; Eugenia, 18; Florence, 16; and T. B. (Thomas), 14. Butler Fauntleroy was appointed postmaster for New Providence on March 2, 1847, and postmaster for Ringgold, Montgomery County, Tennessee, on April 22, 1856.

217. Georgia Smith was Georgina Smith, daughter of Catherine Smith of Todd County.

218. Canton, Kentucky, is a community in Trigg County, Kentucky. It is eight miles west-southwest of Cadiz and today is on Lake Barkley.

219. The 1860 Montgomery County, Tennessee, Census, lists B. H. Thomas, 26, doctor, in the household of N.L. Thomas, 55, with E.E., 50, and N.G., 14, family 768.

220. The *Clarksville Weekly Chronicle* noted on May 6, 1859, that Ellen Carter, "an interesting young lady" drowned trying to cross the Little West Fork of the Red River. Her horse plunged into deep water and she was thrown off. She was pulled out twenty minutes later, but her rescuers could not resuscitate her.

221. Sarah Ogburn Spence was the daughter of Mary Ann Caroline Hunt Ogburn and the late John Noble Ogburn. She was 14 in 1850. See Chapter 1, Note 91 for more information on the John Noble Ogburn family.

222. Jennie may have been Caroline Virginia Ogburn, daughter of Mary Ann Caroline Hunt Ogburn and the late John Noble Ogburn.

223. Serepta was to see more of Tom Trabue over the next several years as he became one of her suitors.

224. Jane was the daughter of Meredith and Minerva Peterson Howard.

225. P.T. Boatwright owned Oakford Clothing store in New Providence, *Clarksville Weekly Chronicle*, June 17, 1859, p. 4.

226. Serepta was expressing dislike at being stared at by men in the public space.

227. Dr. George Hightower Swift and Adeline Agnes Ogburn Martin were married on June 8, 1859, in Montgomery County, Tennessee.

228. Cousin Mollie was probably Mary E. Mallory Mills, daughter of William and Lucinda Draper Mallory. See Chapter 1, Note 17 for more information on the Mills family.

229. Although the 1860 Montgomery County, Tennessee, Census lists Jane Crabtree's younger daughter as Mary, Serepta referred to her as Marion.

230. Mary Duff, 13, is listed in the 1850 Montgomery County, Tennessee, Census in the household of Thomas M. Duff, 45, jailor, with S.W., 43, female; J.M., 19, cabinet workman; A. F., 15, female; S. F., 12, female; C.F., 8, female; J.W., 3, male.

231. For a social gathering to be "a squeeze," it would have been well-attended, even crowded.

232. Bowling Green, Kentucky, about sixty miles northeast of New Providence, is the county seat of Warren County.

233. Adaline Howell was the daughter of William and Allatha Donaldson and wife of J. W. Howell. 1850 Montgomery County, Tennessee, Census, family 288; *Montgomery County Marriage Book 2*, 158.

234. Laura was probably Laura Helm, daughter of Presley Neville and Ann E. Helm. She was listed as age 5 in the 1850 Montgomery County, Tennessee, Census.

235. Zilpha Blakney was the daughter of William and Allatha Donaldson and wife of Robert J. Blakney. *Montgomery County Marriage Book 2*, 122; 1850 Montgomery County, Tennessee, Census, family 1367.

236. A pedobaptist is one who practices infant baptism.

237. Mrs. Trabue and Mrs. Atkinson may have been Elizabeth Atkinson Trabue and her sister-in-law Sarah Elizabeth Tuck Atkinson, who died in November 1859. Or Mrs. Atkinson could have been Elizabeth Atkinson Trabue's stepmother Elizabeth Carlisle Atkinson, second wife of Thomas Walton Atkinson Sr.

238. Sylus Trice would have been 20 years old in 1859. The 1850 Montgomery County, Tennessee, Census lists Silas, 11, in the household of May, male, 51, farmer; Frances M., 21; Thomas J., 17; Leona, 5; Henry F. Trice, 23, carpenter. May married Jane (Trice) Trice (deceased), family 80. Sylus was living in the household of Dr. B. N. Herring when the 1860 Census was taken in September. By 1870, he was in Ballard County, Kentucky, with "physician" as his profession.

He was the son of May and Jane Trice and brother of Mildred and George May Trice. 1860 Census Montgomery County, Tennessee, family 744; 1870 Census Ballard County, Kentucky, Lovelaceville District, family 37.

239. Serepta was recording the birth of Alma Gold, daughter of Sarah and Daniel Gold and granddaughter of Clarissa and John Gold. The 1860 Montgomery County, Tennessee, Census lists Daniel Gold, 31, merchant; L.A. (Sarah A. Davie Gold), 20, with C.A. (Alma), 1, female.

240. The 1860 Montgomery County, Tennessee, Census lists A. Colishaw [*sic*], 63, housekeeper, with William Leo, 14; James Leo, 12; and Thomas Leo, 10, family 688.

241. *The Jeffersonian*, October 5, 1859, reported on the third trial of a Dr. Rutland for killing his wife. The first two trials were appealed to the Supreme Court and overturned. The third trial resulted in a guilty verdict and a sentence of three years in the penitentiary.

242. George Trice could have been any one of these four: George (1834–?), son of Anderson and Harriett Trice; George (1834–?), son of Bingham and Eleanor Trice; George Washington (1838–?), son of Leigh and Sarah Trice; George May (1825–1879), son of May and Jane Frances Trice. Anderson was first cousin to Bingham, Leigh, and May, who were brothers.

243. The 1860 Montgomery County, Tennessee, Census, family 92, lists H. M. Acree, dentist, 29, with Caroline, 29, and Sue, 2 months. Horace M. Acree (1828–1923) married Caroline Allen on September 12, 1859, in Montgomery County, Tennessee.

244. Uncle Steven was probably the Reverend Stephen Smith Mallory.

245. Valentine W. Smith married Mary Ann Leigh on November 1, 1859. Valentine (Tine) was the son of James N. Smith and Nancy Collins Smith, and Mary Ann was the daughter of Henry and Nancy Lucinda Trice Leigh. Nancy Leigh may have been the sister of Bingham, Elizabeth, Leigh, Jesse James, Nace, May, Jane, Thomas Alexander, Greenberry, Mary "Pollie" Campbell, Elsey, and Nancy Barbee.

246. The 1860 Montgomery County, Tennessee, Census lists T. J. Neely, 40, preacher, with Agnes, female, 24, and Geo, male, 2, family 285.

247. Robert A. Wilson was the son of John Wilson and Mary T. Jones Flemming Wilson. *Goodspeed's Histories of Montgomery, Robertson, Humphreys, Stewart, Dickson, Cheatham, and Houston Counties of Tennessee* (Chicago and Nashville: Goodspeed, 1886. Reprinted Columbia, TN: Woodward and Stinson Printing Company, 1972), 1119.

248. Euchre is a popular card game most commonly played with four people in two partnerships with a deck of 24, 28, or sometimes 32.

249. Flavius Josephus (37 AD–100 AD) was a member of the priestly aristocracy of the Jewish people. He was held as a Roman hostage after the Jewish revolt of 66–70 AD. He became a historian and his writings provide insight into ancient Jewish history.

250. Until pavement of roads, the weather often made travel difficult or impossible. Heavy rains caused mud that made roads impassable. The Southern expression, "Good lord willing and creeks don't rise," reflects the reality of mud roads and inability to cross bridges due to floods.

251. Amos 14:12: Therefore thus will I do unto thee, O Israel: and because I will do this unto thee, prepare to meet thy God, O Israel. KJV.

252. Birdsville, Kentucky, is in Livingston County and is about ninety miles from Clarksville, Tennessee.

253. Dr. Samuel A. Neblett had boarded with the Trices earlier in the year. He had graduated from University of Nashville Medical School that spring. *Diary*, November 20, 1859; Obituary, *Clarksville Weekly Chronicle*, November 7, 1860, 3.

254. Skyrockets are among the oldest fireworks. They consist of a paper tube that, when lighted, propels into the air and explodes in a burst of color and sound. Setting off fireworks to celebrate Christmas is a Southern tradition.

255. The 1860 Federal Census Mortality Schedule, Montgomery County, line 14, records that A. E. Stanton, 7, male, died January 1860, listing the cause of death as fever.

256. According to a quasi-historical account of Norman England by the poet Wace, the powerful Saxon thegn Brictric, son of Algar, as a young man, declined Matilda's advances. Whether this account is true or not, years later she is said to have used her authority while acting as regent for her husband William in England to confiscate Brictric's lands and throw him into prison, where he died. After Matilda's death, her son William Rufus gave part of this property to Robert Fitz Hammon, whose daughter and sole heiress brought them to her husband Robert de Caen, 1st Earl of Gloucester, a natural son of Matilda's younger son King Henry I. Thus, Brictric's fiefdom became the feudal barony of Gloucester, one of the largest of the medieval English feudal baronies. Edward Augustus Freeman, *The History of the Norman Conquest of England*, Vol. IV (Oxford: Clarendon Press, 1871), 761–64.

257. Serepta did not give the reasons for her dissatisfaction with the reign of William Rufus (William II of England); however, William has received mixed reviews from historians. He maintained order in the England he inherited from his father thus unifying the kingdom; in addition, he extended his father's conquests further into Wales and Scotland. On the other hand, he pushed the archbishop of Canterbury into exile and claimed the revenues of Canterbury to the end of his reign.

258. *The Clarksville Chronicle* of March 16, 1860, carried an advertisement by J. F. Shelton & Co.'s Railroad and City Omnibus Line that would run regularly to and from the Railroad Depot.

259. The name of a passenger vessel, *Minnetonka*, means "great water" in Dakota Sioux, *mni tanka*. The *Minnetonka* was built in California, Pennsylvania, in 1857 for Captain W. W. Williamson and others. During the Civil War, it was a

victim of Morgan's Raiders on February 23, 1862. The *Minnetonka* was moored in midstream a few hundred yards above the Federal fleet when Morgan's men fired it. It was owned at the time by James Miller, Clarksvillian George Stacker, and B.M. Runyon. Frederick Way Jr., *Way's Packet Directory, 1848–1994* (Athens, Ohio: Ohio Univ. Press, 1994), 323.

260. Horsehair was a common material used to make hair ornaments and chains for watch fobs.

261. The Louisville and Nashville Railroad would have been in operation for only seven months. Its first full-length 187-mile run was on October 27, 1859. Scheduled trains began running a few days later. Cost of its original construction was $7.2 million.

262. The greenhouse was probably on the property of Adelicia Hayes Franklin Acklen and her second husband, Colonel Joseph Acklen. The couple hired noted architect Adolphus Heiman, who had designed the Tennessee Hospital for the Insane, to enlarge their existing house. Heiman also planned their extensive formal gardens, with walkways, statuary, and gazebos. Named Belmont, the home had thirty-six rooms, an art gallery, bowling alley, billiards parlor, water tower, green house, conservatory, lake, zoo, aviary, ornamental gardens, and its own gas lighting system—all on 177 acres.

263. Old Mrs. Blakney was Isabella Blakney, mother of Robert Blakney. See Chapter 1, Note 212 for more information on the Blakney family.

264. Mrs. Ed Ogburn may have been Mary Hart Ogburn, wife of Edwin Ogburn. Ann may have been Ann Ogburn, widow of James Ogburn. Edwin Ogburn was the son of Josiah and Susan Howell Ogburn. Josiah and James were brothers, both deceased.

265. The 1860 Montgomery County, Tennessee, Census lists George J. McCauley, 62, farmer; E., female, 55; E. J., female, 22; E. G. female, 20; W. A., male, 20; G. B. male, 18; P. A., female, 12, and living next door was B. B. Homer, 42, merchant.

266. Mrs. Pettus was probably Mary M. Watson Pettus, widow of Stephen Pettus. S. Emmett Lucas Jr., ed., *Marriage Record Book 1, January 2, 1789-December 13, 1837, Davidson County, Tennessee,* (Easley, S.C: Southern Historical Press, 1979) 32. The 1860 Montgomery County, Tennessee, Census lists the household of Mary Pettus, 66, farmer, with daughters Almeda (Meda), 35, and Frances (Fannie), 33. Mary and Stephen Pettus had at least two other daughters, Sallie E. Pettus Grinstead and Mrs. R.T. Pollard, as well as a son, Thomas F. Pettus.

267. Joseph Hatcher, 20, is listed in the household of Richard Grinstead, 47, and Sallie E. Pettus Grinstead, 44, with children W. T., male, 21; M. C. female, 18; M. F., female, 16; and N. P., female, 14. Sallie E. Pettus Grinstead was the daughter of Mary and Stephen Pettus. 1860 Todd County, Kentucky, Census, family 625; *Montgomery County, Tennessee., Marriage Book 1,* 12.

268. The 1850 Montgomery County, Tennessee, Census, family 78, lists
F. Herblin, 35, teacher, in the household of Eli Lockert, 55, farmer. In addition to
Lockert's family, were listed A. Herblin, 22; Anna Herblin, 3; and Frank Herblin,
6 months. F. Herblin taught piano, guitar, and vocal exercises. Lockert was
proprietor of the Franklin House, a three-story, frame hotel on Public Square in
Clarksville, Tennessee.

269. *The Clarksville Chronicle* on June 29, 1860, noted on page 3 "Married, In
New Providence, on the 27th inst., by Elder W. C. Rogers, Mr. S.H. Monroe and
Miss Lou F. Everett."

2. September 1860–May 1861

1. Williamstown was an area northwest of New Providence along Fletchers
Fork Creek. The name was a localism referring to the number of family mem-
bers named William who lived in that area. The land is now on Fort Campbell,
Kentucky, Military Reservation.

2. William Mallory (1791–1874) was the brother of Stephen Smith Mallory,
Zelpha Mallory Trice, Elizabeth Mallory Trice, George Sims Mallory, Henrietta
Mallory Collins, Allatha "Alley" Mallory Donaldson, and Zebiah Mallory Sawyer.
Higgins, *Montgomery County Genealogical Journal 9*, 104. See Chapter 1, Note
207 for more information on the William Mallory family.

3. Aunt Brit was William Mallory's second wife, Henrietta Sawyer Mallory.
Montgomery County, Tennessee, Marriage Book 1, 76.

4. Cousin Mollie was probably Mary E. Mallory Mills, who was probably the
daughter of William and Lucinda Draper Mallory.

5. Jennie Mallory was John Wilson Mallory's sister and the daughter of the
Reverend Stephen Smith Mallory (1801–1883) and Nancy Wilson Collins Mallory
(1813–1841). The 1860 Montgomery County, Tennessee, Census lists L. J. Mallory,
23, in the household of Stephen and Eliza Mallory. Elizabeth Draper Rucker was
Stephen's second wife. Jennie married William D. Taylor on January 26, 1865,
in Montgomery County, Tennessee. W. D. Taylor (1835–1910), son of W. H. and
Lucinda Duncan Taylor, served during the Civil War. William and Jennie Taylor's
children were John, Mary, and Annie. *Goodspeed's Histories of Tennessee*, 1106.

6. William Donaldson was the husband of Allatha "Alley" Mallory Donaldson.
Higgins, *Montgomery County Genealogical Journal 9*, 104. Allatha "Alley"
Mallory (1802–1890) married William Donaldson (1802–1878) on December 24,
1822. The 1860 Montgomery County, Tennessee, Census lists the household of
William Donelson [*sic*], 62, farmer, with Lorane, 30; William, 24; Ally, 25, Ross,
21; James, 19; and Ann, 17. See Chapter 1, Note 140 for more information on the
Donaldson family. Census takers seem to have had trouble recording the last name
of this family: the 1850 census recorded them as Dollanson and the 1860 census

as Donelson. In addition, the 1850 census listed Rebecca, 10, and the 1860 census listed Ross, 21. "The Hille Family Tree," accessed January 14, 2019, http://www.ancestry.com, gives this child's name as Ruben Ross Donaldson.

7. John Bell of Tennessee and Edward Everett of Massachusetts were nominees for US president and vice president of the newly formed Constitutional Union Party. A Whig and former US senator, Bell believed Tennessee should remain in the Union. However, following Fort Sumter, he reluctantly supported Tennessee's secession. He carried only the popular vote in the border states of Tennessee, Kentucky, and Virginia. Jonathan M. Atkins, "John Bell," *Tennessee Encyclopedia of History & Culture*, 56–57.

8. Mollie Frank was Mary Frances Mallory, wife of William S. Mallory, who was the brother of John Wilson Mallory and son of Stephen Mallory. She was the daughter of Archibald and Ann Donaldson of Logan County, Kentucky. The 1860 Montgomery County, Tennessee, Census lists W. S. Mallory, 27, with Mary, 26; Edward, 5; and Rose, 1. Mary Frances is listed in the 1850 Logan County, Kentucky, Census with Archibald Donaldson, 56, farmer; Ann, 40; Mary F, 16; James, 14; Archibald, 12; Sarah, 11; William, 10; and Henry Bell, 22. 1860 Montgomery County, Tennessee, Census, family 333; 1850 Montgomery County, Tennessee, Census, family 290; Logan County Genealogical Society, *Abstracts of Wills and Settlements, Logan County, Kentucky 1856–1874* (Russellville, Kentucky, 1989) 45; Logan County Genealogical Society, *Logan County, Kentucky Marriages, 1790–1865* (Russellville, Kentucky, 1981); Additions and Corrections, 1985).

9. Alley was probably the daughter of William and Allatha Mallory Donaldson. She would have been 25 years old and unmarried in 1860 and could have competed with Serepta for the attention of others in the family. Alley Donaldson married Jacob George Torian on April 9, 1863, in Montgomery County, Tennessee. "Hille Family Tree," accessed January 14, 2019, http://www.ancestry.com.

10. Cousin Mary may have been Mary Elizabeth Mallory Morris, daughter of Stephen Smith Mallory and his first wife, Nancy Wilson Collins Mallory, and sister of William, John, Jennie, Zilpha (deceased), and James (deceased) Mallory. She married George Nathaniel Morris on November 7, 1855, in Montgomery County. "Hille Family Tree," accessed January 14, 2019, http://www.ancestry.com.

11. Frances and Ann Collins were daughters of Daniel and Henrietta Mallory Collins. Frances, 12, and Ann, 16, are listed in the 1850 Montgomery County, Tennessee, Census, family 306, with Daniel Collins, 45; Henrietta, 49; James, 18; William, 15; Stephen, 13; Alex, 8; and John, 7. Henrietta Collins was the daughter of Stephen Mallory (1766–1836) and Loriana H. Sims Mallory (1772–1846) and sister of William, Zelpha, Elizabeth, George, Stephen Smith, Allatha, Lorainah, Zebiah, and Ann Zinah Mallory.

12. Henrietta Jane Collins Weaver was the sister of Frances and Ann Collins and wife of Thomas J. Weaver of Stewart County. She married Thomas J. Weaver

on September 30, 1851, in Montgomery County, Tennessee. The 1860 Stewart County, Tennessee, Census lists Thomas Weaver, 32, farmer, with Jane, 27; Mary, 7; Willie, 4; James, 2; Thomas, 2; and Miles Griffey, 45, farmer. Thomas J. Weaver (1828–1901) was buried in William Collins Cemetery, Montgomery County, Tennessee. *Montgomery County, Tennessee, Marriage Book 2*, 156; 1860 Stewart County, Tennessee, Census, family 264.

13. Damson is a variety of plum.

14. Ornaments woven of human hair were fashionable for both men and women during the mid-to-late 1800s.

15. William A., James, and Ross were sons of William Donaldson and Allatha "Alley" Mallory Donaldson. 1860 Montgomery County, Tennessee, Census, family 289.

16. Mary Harrelson was the daughter of William Harrelson, a former innkeeper in New Providence, and Eliza A. Harrelson (deceased). By 1860 the family was living in Christian County, Kentucky. 1860 Christian County, Kentucky Census, family 15. See Chapter 1, Note 64 for more information on the Harrelson family.

17. Elizabeth was the wife of William McGowan [Gowans], a shoemaker from Scotland. The 1860 Montgomery County, Tennessee, Census lists William Gowans, shoemaker, with Elizabeth S. Gowans, 40; Sarah J., 11; J. W., 9; P. C., 7; and Lizzie, 4, family 885. There is still a bridge on Peacher's Mill Road across Little West Fork Creek known as Gowan's or McGowan's Bridge.

18. Thomas Ogburn was a close family friend of the Trices. The 1850 Montgomery County, Tennessee, Census lists him as age 50, a farmer, in the household with Sally Ogburn, 44; Adeline, 18; Harriet, 16; Benjamin, 14; Dawson, 12; Hockett, 10, and Ethalinda, 6. His first wife, Sally Ogburn (1805–1856), is buried in Mount Pleasant Cemetery, Montgomery County, Tennessee. On September 3, 1860, in Montgomery County, Tennessee, Thomas Ogburn married Ethalinda Brodie Jones, widow of Thomas A. Jones.

19. Ethalinda Brodie Jones was the widow of Thomas A. Jones. The 1850 Montgomery County, Tennessee, Census lists Thomas A. Jones, 26, with E. E. Jones, 26; Joseph H. 3; and Lucy, 1. Thomas A. Jones died Sept 11, 1857, in Montgomery County, Tennessee. The 1860 Montgomery County, Tennessee, Census lists her as E. E. Ogburn, 34, in the household of Thomas Ogburn, 60; H. A. Ogburn, male, 18; Editha Ogburn, 16; Joseph Jones, 12; Lucy Jones, 16; E. M. Jones, female, 8; Susan Jones, 6; T. A. Jones, male, 3; and Robert Williams, 27.

20. Hockett Allen Ogburn died in 1861. Hockett, Benjamin, Dawson F., and Josiah H. were all children of Thomas and Sallie Ogburn. Benjamin (1832–1858) and Dawson (1839–1857) both died of consumption. Dr. Josiah H. Ogburn (1833–1858) died after a lingering illness. Benjamin, Dawson, Josiah, and Hockett are all buried in Mount Pleasant Cemetery, Montgomery County, Tennessee.

21. The 1860 Montgomery County, Tennessee, Census lists Irina Wilson, 20, in

the household of E. J. Wilson, 26, merchant, with Eunice W., 6 months; and R. A. Wilson, male, 23, family 709.

22. James Minor Quarles (1823–1901) was a Clarksville attorney, serving as attorney general for the Tennessee Tenth Judicial District in 1853. Elected to Congress as an Opposition Party candidate in 1859, he served until March 1861. The *Clarksville Jeffersonian* reported, "He spoke for two hours and fifteen minutes. The odd minutes were devoted to the advocacy of Mr. Bell, and the two hours, directly and indirectly, to the firm of Bell and Douglas." *Biographical Directory of the United States Congress, 1774 –Present,* accessed February 1, 2011, http://bioguide.congress.gov/scripts/biodisplay.pl?index=Q000002; *Clarksville Jeffersonian,* September 12, 1860. The 1860 Montgomery County, Tennessee, Census lists James Quarles, 37, lawyer, with Mary W. Quarles, 30; R. T., 10; E. T., 8; E. B., 3; L. M., 5; J. M., 1, family 204. Quarles served in the Civil War, died March 3, 1901, and is buried in Mt. Olivet Cemetery, Nashville.

23. Billy Archy was probably William A. Donaldson, son of William and Allatha Mallory Donaldson. 1850 Montgomery County, Tennessee Census, family 288.

24. A tuck is a small fold or pleat that is sewn in place.

25. Jennie Fauntleroy Smith was the sister of Kate, Eugenia, Florence, and Thomas Fauntleroy. Eugenia Fauntleroy married James Henry Smith, tobacco dealer, in Montgomery County, Tennessee, on December 6, 1859. See Chapter 1, Note 216 for more information on the Fauntleroy family.

26. A type of bobbin lace has been made at Honiton, Devonshire, England, since the seventeenth century. The lace made in the nineteenth century had strong floral motifs joined to a net background.

27. *The Talisman* (1825) and *Ivanhoe* (1820) are novels by Sir Walter Scott. Some historians have argued Scott had a major influence on Southern character and culture. In fact, in *Life on the Mississippi* (1883) Mark Twain suggested, only partly facetiously, "Sir Walter had so large a hand in making Southern character, as it existed before the war, that he is in great measure responsible for the war." Rollin G. Osterweis called the South "Walter Scottland." Osterweis, *Romanticism and Nationalism in the Old South* (New Haven: Yale Univ. Press, 1949), 26, 51. Southerners had long felt they exemplified the ideals and manners of Scott's novels; however, postwar Southerners felt a particular affinity with Scott's novels of Bonnie Prince Charlie and the "Lost Cause" of the Jacobite uprising of 1745.

28. Trice families had a number of George Trices. However, this George Trice does not appear to be one of the three closest to Serepta. May Trice, infant son of George May Trice and grandson of May and Jane Trice, lived to 1932. No records could be found of children of either George Trice, son of Bingham and Eleanor Trice, or George Washington Trice, son of Leigh and Sarah Trice, as early as 1860.

29. The 1850 Montgomery County, Tennessee, Census lists George, 16, and

Will, 14, in the household of Bingham Trice, 60, with Eleanor, 45; John, 19; Judith, 17; Frances, 14; Martha, 11; Mary, 10, and Margaret, 7, family 1333.

30. William H. Burgess was the son of J. M. and Lucy A. Burgess. The 1860 Montgomery County, Tennessee, Census, family 820, lists William H. Burgess, 20, farmer, in the household of J. M., 48, hotel keeper.

31. Miss Settle was Fannie E. Settle, 19, of Christian County, Kentucky. Frances Settle married W. H. Burgess September 20, 1860, in Christian County, Kentucky. *Marriage Records 1851–1900 Christian County, Kentucky.*

32. Emma was one of Elsey Trice's enslaved girls. It seems she was about the same age as Inez.

33. A trundle bed is a low bed on wheels that can be stored underneath a larger bed, saving floor space until the extra bed is needed.

34. Serepta was referring to menstruation; "all under my apron" referred to stomach pains associated with menstruating.

35. B. W. Boatwright and Z. H. (Zebiah) Donaldson were married September 25, 1860, in Montgomery County, Tennessee. *Montgomery County, Tennessee Compiled Marriages.* The 1860 Montgomery County, Tennessee, Census lists B. W. Boatwright, 27, in the household of L. A. Boatwright, 50 female, with J. O. Cook, 30, male.

36. The 1860 Montgomery County, Tennessee, Census lists John Godsey, 56, bootmaker, with Reggie, female, 56; John, 26, carpenter; H. A., female, 23; William, 6; John, 1; and Branch, 23, male, laborer, family 524.

37. An annual meeting of the Tennessee Conference of the Methodist Church consisted of the churches of Middle Tennessee and Northern Alabama. During the conference ministers were assigned to the various churches, new ministers were admitted to preach, older ministers were retired, and financial reports were submitted. *Minutes of the Annual Conferences of the Methodist Episcopal Church, South, for the year 1860, Part 6, Tennessee Conference* (Nashville, Tenn.: Southern Methodist Publishing House, 1861) 211–217.

38. Since the Reverend John B. Duncan served as pastor of New Providence Baptist Church, it appears Serepta had moved on from the Methodists to Baptists. Representatives of each Baptist church in the area met to discuss the business of the churches.

39. Russellville, the county seat of Logan County, Kentucky, is about thirty-five miles northeast of New Providence.

40. "I'd as live been in the penitentiary" is a variation of "I'd as soon have been in the penitentiary."

41. Bell hoops replaced layered petticoats to add volumes to the skirts, probably providing more comfort.

42. Susan W. Bone Knox was the wife of James O. Knox, who operated a livery stable. The family had recently moved to New Providence from Hopkins County, Kentucky. *Hopkins County, Kentucky, Marriages, 1851–1900* [database on-line]

(Provo, UT: The Generations Network, Inc., 2001); 1860 Montgomery County, Tennessee, Census, family 815.

43. Ann E. Ricks was the widow of Philip W. Ricks. 1850 Brunswick County, Virginia, Census, family 72. The 1860 Montgomery County, Tennessee, Census, family 744, lists her as age 35 in the household of Dr. B. N. Herring.

44. Ann Elizabeth Blakemore Helm was the wife of Presley Neville Helm, a lumber merchant. "Marriages Records Frederick County, Va.," *Virginia Marriages, 1740–1850*; 1860 Montgomery County, Tennessee, Census, family 700. See Chapter 1, Note 74 for more information on the Helm family.

45. The "strikers" were ministers advanced or worn with age. *Webster*, s.v. "Strike."

46. Russell Escue was from Shady Grove Church in Wilson County. During the conference, the delegates preached each night at all the local churches, "except the Roman." *Minutes*, 215; *Clarksville Chronicle*, October 19, 1860.

47. Philip L. Henderson was being transferred from Sumner County to the Louisiana Conference. *Minutes*, 217.

48. Bishop George Foster Pierce, D.D., of Culverton, Georgia, served as president of the Conference. *Minutes*, 211.

49. 1 Peter 1:20–21: Who verily was foreordained before the foundation of the world, but was manifest in these last time for you, Who by him do believe in God, that raised him up from the dead, and gave him glory; that your faith and hope might be God. KJV.

50. Joseph Cross had just been transferred to the Tennessee Conference and assigned to Gallatin to replace Philip Henderson. *Minutes*, 211, 215.

51. Psalm 42:4: When I remember these things, I pour out my soul in me: for I had gone with the multitude, I went with them to the house of God, with the voice of joy and praise, with a multitude that kept holy day. KJV.

52. Two Cherrys are mentioned in the minutes—Sterling M. Cherry from Alabama, assigned to Winchester, Tennessee, and William D. Cherry, a new minister just admitted "in full connection" with the church and assigned to Cumberland in the Carthage District. *Minutes*, 211, 215.

53. Ministers coming to the conference by rail traveled free of charge. *Clarksville Chronicle*, October 12, 1860.

54. The 1860 Wilson County, Tennessee, Census lists Samuel Baldwin, Methodist minister, 41, with Eliza, 30; Charles, 11; Thompson 10; Sallie, 5; Minnie, 4; Samuel, 2. Samuel Baldwin married Eliza Caroline Morman in Davidson County, Tennessee, in February 1848.

55. Carroll C. Mayhew of Nashville was currently assigned to Middleton in the Murfreesboro District. The 1860 Davidson County, Tennessee, Census lists Carroll C. Mayhew, 34, a Methodist minister, with Paula C., 26, and Jimmie R., 6, living in the household of William P. Newland, 33, brick mason, family 1027.

56. 2 Corinthians 9:8: And God is able to make all grace abound toward you;

that ye, always having all sufficiency in all things, may abound to every good work. KJV.

57. In rural areas it was common for several churches to share the same minister. The Reverend Mr. Hart's schedule of services would be a circuit and he would be called a circuit rider.

58. Dr. Pirtle was assigned to Red River in the Clarksville District. *Minutes,* 216.

59. Tom Traubue was a friend and potential suitor of Serepta's. They carried on a correspondence when he left for Memphis to join the military. The 1850 Logan County, Kentucky, Census lists Tom Trabue as the son of Dr. John E. and Elizabeth Atkinson Trabue. He was the grandson of Thomas W. Atkinson and his first wife Elizabeth Hundley Atkinson (deceased), family 395. "Ford-Young Family Tree," accessed January 14, 2019, http:www.ancestry.com.

60. In a letter to Serepta from Memphis dated May 19, 1860, Tom Trabue wrote: "I am aware some young men correspond with Ladies for pastime and improvement. I have done that thing myself but I think you do our sex great injustice when you say they correspond with the Ladies to make sport of them. I cannot admit that. Therefore cannot promise to try to work a reformation. I will promise though not to show your letters to more than ½ a dozen young men and also promise that they shall not laugh at them more than ½ a dozen times Each." *Dear Rep: Letters to Serepta Jordan Homer of New Providence, Tennessee.*

61. Mrs. John Wilson was Mary T. Jones Flemming Wilson. *Goodspeed's Histories of Tennessee,* 1119. The 1860 Montgomery County, Tennessee, Census lists M. T. Wilson, female, 62, with John Wilson, 57, farmer, and N. C. Jones, 40, female.

62. Sylus Trice was the son of May and Jane Trice and brother of Mildred and George May Trice.

63. This was the first Agricultural Fair in Montgomery County. See the introduction for more discussion. For a good overview of Southern agriculture, see Melissa Walker and James C. Cobb (eds.), *Agriculture and Industry* (Chapel Hill: Univ. of North Carolina Press, 2008) 3–29; Julie A. Avery (ed.), *Agricultural Fairs in America: Tradition, Education* (East Lansing, MI: Michigan State University Museum, 2000); Paul Hyatt, Marie Riggins, Ralph Winters and Thurston L. Lee, *One Hundred Years of County Fairs in Montgomery County, Tennessee* (Clarksville, TN: Clarksville-Montgomery County Historical Society, 1960).

64. The fairground site consisted of 43 acres and had an amphitheater which could seat 4,000 and 3,000 standing room. It had a show ring 200 feet in diameter with a judges' stand three stories high. The organizers hired Fenton's Nashville Band and had two 600-barrel cisterns to provide water. M. C. & L. Railroad established a convenient schedule and the toll turnpike reduced rates. The Omnibus Passenger Service transported people from Clarksville. Hyatt *et al., One Hundred Years of County Fairs.*

65. This phrase refers to seeing remarkable sights. Once you have seen the elephant, no other sight could be as interesting.

66. Serepta was contrasting her opinion with the excitement of those who saw the fair as an "elephant"—large and impressive. She deemed it a "monkey," a name of contempt or slight kindness. *Webster*, s.v. "monkey."

67. The 1860 Montgomery County, Tennessee, Census, family 386, lists the household of William Griffy, 46, farmer, with Mary, 25; Marcellus, 14; William G., 12; and Ella, 2.

68. *The Betrothed* (1825) is the first novel in Sir Walter Scott's *Tales of the Crusaders*. It was followed by its better known sequel, *The Talisman* (1825).

69. This phrase means everyone in the county. McAdoo Creek was on the eastern side of the county and Dover Road was on the west side.

70. The Medieval custom of jousting became popular in the South about the mid-1800s. Rings were suspended about nine feet above the ground to be speared by the "knight." National Jousting Association, *The Romantic Revival*, accessed March 30, 2008, http://www.nationaljousting.com/history/romantic.htm.

71. The 1860 Montgomery County, Tennessee, Census lists James Foster, 60, laborer, in the household of J. N. Neblett, 34; Martha, 22; Althia, 3; Dreury, 1; and W. F. Grigg, 28, clerk, family 132.

72. Jane E. Brunty, 33, is listed as the only other person in the household of James Brunty, 42, farmer, in the 1860 Montgomery County, Tennessee, Census, family 894.

73. *The Clarksville Chronicle*, on November 2, 1860, printed an article describing this contest on page 3. Mr. Gill was S. H. Gill. Hyatt *et al.*, *One Hundred Years of County Fairs*, 10. The 1860 Logan County, Kentucky, Census lists Sam H. Gill, 35, farmer, with Corinna A., 11; Mary, 9; and George S., 4; and Seth W. 1.

74. Maggie Gill of Todd County, Kentucky, was crowned Queen of Love and Beauty. Hyatt *et al.*, *One Hundred Years of County Fairs*, 10.

75. J. C. Fields, 23, carpenter, is listed in the 1860 Montgomery County, Tennessee, Census in the household of S. H. Monroe, family 740.

76. "Liked" is Southern vernacular for "lacked."

77. Missouri Madole was the daughter of John W. and Margery Madole. 1850 Census, Montgomery County, Tennessee, family 143. The 1860 Montgomery County, Tennessee, Census lists J. W. Madole, 57; M. [Margery], 41; M. M. A. [Missouri], 15; A. J. [Augusta T.], 10; B. F. [Benjamin], 23, carpenter, family 842.

78. Horace was one of Elsey Trice's enslaved men.

79. Laura Helm was the 15-year-old daughter of Presley Neville and Ann E. Helm. See Chapter 1, Note 74 for more information on the Helm family.

80. Marshal was one of Elsey Trice's enslaved men.

81. In addition to his medical practice, Dr. Walter H. Drane (1798–1865) was active in the development of the Hopkinsville Turnpike and the Memphis, Clarksville & Louisville Railroad. William P. Titus, *Picturesque Clarksville*,

Past and Present: A History of the City of the Hills (Clarksville, TN: W. P. Titus Publishing Company, 1887; repr. Ann Alley and Ursula Beach, 1973), 182. The 1850 Montgomery County, Tennessee, Census lists Walter H., 51, farmer, with Eliza McClure Drane, 40; William, 24; Walter Harding Drane Jr., 21; Louisa, 15; Hugh, 13; Jane, 10; James, 7; Marion, 5; and Edward, 2. The 1860 Montgomery County, Tennessee, Census also listed H. T., male, 9, family 791.

82. Hellen was one of Elsey Trice's enslaved women.

83. Cousin Jennie was probably Lorinah Jane Mallory, daughter of Stephen Smith and Nancy Wilson Collins Mallory. Cousin Alley was probably Alla Jane Trice Waller, daughter of Zelpha Mallory and James Pinhook Trice. Mrs. Blakeney was Zilpha Donaldson Blakeney, daughter of Allatha and William Donaldson. Cousin Alley's babe was probably Lilly Crawford Waller, born in 1860.

84. The Dudleys were Henry Minor and Lucy Elizabeth Waller Dudley. Marriage Records, Todd County, Kentucky, Book B, 57. The 1850 Montgomery County, Tennessee, Census lists Henry M. Dudley, 38, farmer, with Lucy E., 25; William A., 6; Robert D., 12. He is also listed in the 1860 and 1870 census and in the1880 census as widower with two children.

85. Mary was the daughter of Ezekiel Jones (deceased) and Rebecca Mallory Jones, and wife of John Wilson. Division of land of Ezekiel Jones, Montgomery County, Tennessee, Book F, 332; 1850 Census Montgomery County, Tennessee., family 632.

86. Nancy Jones was the sister of Mary Jones Wilson. Division of land of Ezekiel Jones, Montgomery County. The 1860 Montgomery County, Tennessee, Census lists M. T. (Mary) Wilson, 62, and N. C. (Nancy) Jones, 40, in the household with John Wilson, 57.

87. Dr. Samuel A. Neblett, 23, died unexpectedly of a congestive chill at Augusta, Georgia, on October 30, 1860. *Clarksville Weekly Chronicle*, November 7, 1860, 3.

88. In the presidential election of 1860, the Democratic Party was split. At the center of the split was slavery. Stephen Douglas was their natural candidate, but Southern Democrats disliked him, although he supported slavery, because he wanted to allow territories to decide whether to have slavery. They left the Democratic convention and nominated John C. Breckenridge to be their candidate. The Northern Democrats stuck to Douglas. The new Republican Party nominated Abraham Lincoln, who was nationally known because his earlier debates with Douglas had been published. Another new party, the Constitutional Union Party, nominated Tennessean John Bell, a wealthy slaveholder and moderate who believed that differences over slavery could be worked out peacefully. Lincoln did not appear on the ballot in Tennessee. Bell overwhelmingly won in Tennessee with 47.7 percent followed by Breckinridge with 44.6 percent.

89. Mary Ann Leigh Smith was the wife of Valentine (Tine) W. Smith and

daughter of Henry and Nancy Lucinda Trice Leigh. Their baby son born on November 9, 1860, was Mediceas A. Smith (1860–1938).

90. Will Ogburn was the son of Mary Ann Caroline Hunt Ogburn and the late John Noble Ogburn.

91. Chine is a cut of meat, probably pork, containing the backbone, or part of it, and the surrounding flesh.

92. Cousin Bet was Betty Trice Lynes, sister of Laurena Jane Crabtree and Marion Oborne. Griffey, *Riverview Cemetery*, 65–66.

93. This meeting was probably at New Providence Baptist Church, located on the Hopkinsville Pike (currently called New Providence Boulevard). See Williams, *Worship along the Warioto*, 187: "Those of 'color' were received into the fellowship of the church during these early years and the church provided pastoral services and preaching for them on the 'Sabbath day at 3:00 p.m. and on Thursday evenings.'" Dinner in the South was usually the main meal at midday.

94. The 1860 Montgomery County, Tennessee, Census lists J. H. Duncan, 38, apprentice, with Isabella, 22; Eliza, 16; Alex, 14; Tennessee, 12; A. C., 6, female; Thomas M. F., 4, along with several families living in household of W. D. Rarick, bootmaker, 32, with Mary, 22; Libbie, 2; and Gus Baker, 7, family 145.

95. Perhaps Serepta was making a bonnet in the style of the straw hats initially designed and manufactured by Thomas de la Rue in London in 1816. De la Rue is better known as a printer. In 1831, he was granted the right to print playing cards, making his the first company to do so. Today, the De La Rue Company is considered the biggest papermaker and security printer in the world.

96. The 1860 Montgomery County, Tennessee, Census lists Henry McFerrin, 33, shoemaker, with Mary, 23, and William, 6 months, family 720.

97. The 1860 Montgomery County, Tennessee, Census lists James Oldham, 35, living with W. D. Clardy, 34, farmer, family 891.

98. There was no single regional convention that decided on secession. From December 20, 1860, to June 8, 1861, individual states held conventions to vote on secession. Tennessee voted for secession on June 8, 1861. It was the last state to secede. In February 1861, the first seven states to secede sent delegates to Montgomery, Alabama. They adopted a constitution modeled on the US Constitution (almost word for word) and elected Jefferson Davis as president.

99. According to the guardian bond for the minor heirs of his father, Josiah Neblett, in 1849, Samuel Neblett had at least four brothers. *Montgomery County, Tennessee, Will Book L,* 335.

100. Ann Johnson Ogburn was the widow of James M. Ogburn. Mary Ogburn may have been Mary Hart Ogburn, wife of Edwin Ogburn.

101. Within days of Lincoln's election, Southern states began war preparation including organizing an army, raising supplies and building up armaments. Southern states began seceding, starting with South Carolina in December

1860. The first military hostilities began with the firing on Fort Sumter in April 1861.

102. There are two Mrs. Tolers shown on the 1860 Montgomery County, Tennessee, Census: Eda, 42, widow of Isaiah Toler (family 715), and F. J., 26, wife of J. T. Toler (family 751). The 1850 Montgomery County, Tennessee, Census lists Eda Toler, 38, in the household of Isiah, 38, with Elender, 12; Margaret J., 10; Mary E. 4; and Morris Council, 12, family 1428. The 1860 Montgomery County Census, lists E. Toler, 42, housekeeper, with E. F., female, 31, and T. A. female, 7, family 1428.

103. "Hickrenuts" was Screpta's fanciful spelling for hickory nuts.

104. Serepta left the name blank.

105. Mary Jane Britton was the daughter of William T. (deceased) and Susan Thompson Britton. 1850 Census Montgomery County, Tennessee, family 91. The 1860 Montgomery County, Tennessee, Census lists S. B. (Susan) Britton, farmer, 52, with M.T. Clardy, 2, female; M. J. (Mary Jane) Britton, 16; Frances Britton, 14; and Anne E. Britton, 12, family 859.

106. No record could be found of a marriage for Louisa "Cousin Lou" V. Peterson (1823–1865).

107. Eliza Barbee was the daughter of Solomon G. and Nancy Trice Barbee. *Goodspeed's Histories of Tennessee*, 1119.

108. Drucilla Kirby, 52, was the wife of James Kirby, 51, carpenter. 1860 Montgomery County, Tennessee, Census, family 684.

109. Mollie (Mary) Barbee (1847–1915) was the sister of Eliza Barbee and daughter of Solomon Gray and Nancy Trice Barbee. The 1850 Montgomery County, Census lists Solomon Barbee, 38; Nancy, 38; Mary, 14; George, 11; Eliza, 7; James, 2, family 73.

110. Mollie Trice could have been Mary Trice (ca. 1840–?), daughter of Bingham and Eleanor Trice, or she could have been Mary Trice (1843–1906), daughter of Nace and Alley Allen Trice. The daughters of Nace and Bingham Trice were first cousins and were probably Serepta's second cousins.

111. Mollie McDaniel was possibly Mary McDaniel, daughter of Dr. George (deceased) and Susan McDaniel. The 1850 Montgomery County, Tennessee, Census lists George, 49, physician; Susan, 34; Gertrude H., 21; Ellen, 12; Mary A., 9; Eunice, 8; Juliet, 7; Henry Clay, 6; Eugene, 5; George, 4; and James, 1, family 1257. The 1860 Montgomery County, Tennessee, Census, family 407, lists Susan McDaniel as head of household.

112. Serepta was referring to dresses made from tarleton fabric, a thin, stiffly starched muslin in an open weave.

113. "Tell me, ye winged winds," is the first line in a poem by Charles Mackay (1812–1889). The poem talks about finding a spot where there is no toil, pain, or sorrow and where friendship and happiness abide. It does not, of course, mention

food. Charles MacKay, "Tell Me, Ye Winged Winds," in Edmund Clarence Stedman, ed., *A Victorian Anthology, 1837–1895*, (Cambridge: Riverside Press, 1895); New York: Bartleby.com, 2001, accessed January 12, 2019.

114. Nannie Davidson was the daughter of Jesse and Elizabeth Davidson. The 1860 Census Montgomery County, Tennessee, Census lists Jesse Davidson, 76, farmer, with E, 62, female; N.E, 27, female; Amanda, 20; and J. R., 19, male, family 1121.

115. Mary Jane Holmes (1825–1907) was a bestselling and prolific American author who published thirty-nine popular novels, as well as short stories.

116. *Maggie Miller· The Story of Old Hagar's Secret* by Mary Jane Holmes was published in 1858.

117. After the election of 1860 on November 6, the uncertainty of potential war caused economic distress. For a discussion see David M. Potter, *The Impending Crisis, 1848–1861* (New York: HarperCollins Publisher, 1976; reprinted by Harper Perennial, 2011).

118. The 1860 Montgomery County, Tennessee, Census lists J. O. Knox, 34, stable keeper, with S. W., female, 26, and Thomas, 2.

119. Mr. Garrett (or Garrott) was probably Pleasant B. Garrett of Garrettsburg, Christian County, Kentucky. The 1860 Christian County, Kentucky, Census lists P. B. Garrett, male, 58, farmer; M. J., female, 57; Julia Buckner, 32; William Garrett, farmer, 25; Inez, 21; Justine, 41; Amelia, 17; William Drinkard, overseer, 27, family 1045. Pleasant Bonapart Garrett died December 12, 1876, in Christian County, Kentucky. He married Martha J. Radford in February 1827 in Christian County, Kentucky.

120. In the 1860s, roads were not usually paved and not maintained by local governments. Turnpikes were toll roads that were maintained with the revenue generated by travelers. Serepta was complaining about the lack of a good road and how rough her journey was.

121. The context indicates Serepta was referring to Inez, the Garretts' daughter, not her enslaved girl of the same name.

122. Ella Riggins was the 2-year-old granddaughter of the Garretts and the daughter of Thomas and Alice Garrett Riggins. See the entry for June 17, 1858, for an account of Ella's birth.

123. The Hopkinsville Asylum still operates today under the name Western State Hospital. It suffered a fire on November 30, 1860, caused by sparks from the chimney. The building had a wooden roof, and that day was dry and windy. The roof ignited, and the fire spread rapidly through the structure. Only one patient was lost of the 210 in the facility. He barricaded himself in his room and refused to come out. Several patients ran away during the confusion.

124. The 1860 Cheatham County, Tennessee, Census lists H. J. Shaw, male, 34, with N. W. Shaw, female, 22, family 444.

125. This Mary Trice was probably Mary Trice (1844–?), daughter of Anderson and Harriett McCorkle Trice. In her October 8, 1863, diary entry, Serepta wrote disparagingly of Mary and her mother, suggesting they had always been wealthy, with many slaves to take care of household chores. Serepta and Mary were probably second cousins.

126. The context of the word "choice" indicates Serepta meant "choosy."

127. The 1860 Christian County, Kentucky, Census, family 234, lists L. (Lewis) A. Waller, tobacco buyer, male, 35; A. (Alley) J., female, 27; W. (William) L., male, 12; F. (Frank) W., male, 10; J. F., male, 88; C. B. (Bailey), male, 6; L. C., female, 2 months; William Trice, bank teller, 33; Delila Level, mulatto, house servant, 17. Delila must have been a servant and not a slave since slaves were listed separately on the census under the slave schedule and only the gender and age were listed. Lewis Waller married Alla Jane Trice, daughter of James Pinhook Trice (1787–1852) and Zelpha Mallory Trice (1793–1860), in 1847. William Trice was probably Alley's older brother; William Lewis Trice and Steven Edward Trice were Alley's older brothers.

128. The 1860 Christian County, Kentucky, Census lists Achilles D. Sears, Baptist minister, 52; Ann B., 51; Marietta, 23, family 263. Dr. Sears came to First Baptist Church in Clarksville in 1866 and reorganized the church after the Civil War. Williams, *Worship along the Warioto,* 311–314.

129. This may be S. Y. Trimble, a Baptist minister in Cadiz, Trigg County, Kentucky. 1860 Trigg County, Kentucky, Census, family 839. Wyatt, in "History of New Providence," also wrote of a Mr. Trimble, who was a teacher in New Providence in the 1870s or 1880s: "Among other teachers I call to mind was the Reverend Mr. Trimble, a tall lanky muscular Christian of the Baptist faith, who believed in moral [*undecipherable*] to a certain extent but who was always ready to back up his rules and commands with a very long tough hickory."

130. Archy Ferguson was the son of Peter T. and Elizabeth Ogburn Ferguson of Mecklenburg County. The 1860 Mecklenburg County, Virginia, Census lists Peter Ferguson, 77, farmer; Elizabeth, 61; Mary E., 31; Archer Hansard, 25; Harriet, 20; Nancy A., 16; and Peter T., 14. Peter Ferguson married Elizabeth Ogburn on December 2, 1818, in Mecklenburg County, Virginia, family 779.

131. Mr. Osborne was probably Noble Osborne. The 1860 Montgomery County, Tennessee, Census, family 403, lists Noble Osborne, farmer, 72, in the household with Marion, 25, and J.B. (John Bryan), 8. Noble Osborne must have been Cousin Marion's father-in-law.

132. Serepta kept her letters received between 1852 and 1894. Only one letter from B. B. Homer survives and it is dated April 3, 1863. If he wrote her at this point, the letter may never have caught up with her. *Dear Rep: Letters to Serepta Jordan Homer of New Providence, Tennessee.*

133. Mary Britton was the daughter of William T. (deceased) and Susan

Thompson Britton. See Chapter 2, Note 105 for more information on the Britton family.

134. Perhaps Jo Wray was Joseph Wray, 53, farmer, listed in the 1860 Montgomery County, Tennessee, Census, family 870, with Elnor Wray, 96; M. E. Wray, 26, female; and the Mallory family: William, 35; Eliza, 30; M. E., 16, female; M. J., 12, female; Thomas, 10; Henry, 8; and Luella, 2. Joseph Wray married Leticia Jenkins in 1863 in Montgomery County. The connection of this Mallory family to others mentioned in the diary is unknown.

135. South Carolina became the first slave state to secede on December 20, 1860. People across the nation waited to see which other states would follow. Serepta was correct that the cotton states would secede: Mississippi on January 9, 1861; Florida on January 10, 1861; Alabama, January 11, 1861; Georgia, January 19, 1861; Louisiana, January 26, 1861; Texas, February 1, 1861; Arkansas, May 6, 1861; North Carolina, May 20, 1861; Virginia, May 23, 1861; Tennessee, June 8, 1861. Initially, it was unclear if the Upper South and Border States would leave the Union. Lincoln understood their vital strategic importance and is reported to have said, "I hope to have God on my side but I must have Kentucky." Kentucky stayed in the USA, but between 25,000 and 40,000 Kentuckians served in the Confederate Army, the most famous being the "Orphan Brigade," which got its name at the Battle of Stones River on January 2, 1863, after suffering heavy casualties. Its commander, Major General John C. Breckenridge, reportedly rode among the survivors, crying out repeatedly, "My poor Orphans! My poor Orphans!" The phrase alluded to Kentucky's not having joined the Confederacy.

136. Miss Mollie B was Mary "Mollie" Jane Penoply Barbee (1837–1915), daughter of Solomon and Nancy Trice Barbee.

137. Masquerading at Christmas was common with some Southerners at this time. "Christmas in Nineteenth-Century America," Christmas Celebrations and New Year's Celebrations, accessed March 5, 2011, http://christmas-celebrations.org/11-christmas-in-nineteenth-century-america.html.

138. Serepta mentioned Mr. Garriques twice and Mr. Garrigues three times in the diary entries. She was probably referring to Private Henry H. Garrigus, who enlisted in the 14th Tennessee Regiment, Company A, at Camp Duncan on May 14, 1861. Cross, *Ordeal by Fire*, 129. The 1860 Montgomery County, Tennessee Census lists a William H. Garrigus, 19, clerk in the household of R. T. Pollard, 35, merchant; N. B., female, 26; Susan, 7 months; and W. W. Hover, male, 25, family 745.

139. TT referred to Thomas E. Trabue of Memphis. See Chapter 2, Note 59 for more information on Tom Trabue's family.

140. J. G. Ward, a minister, and his wife Elizabeth had six children. The 1860 Montgomery County, Tennessee, Census lists J. G. Ward, preacher, 58; Elizabeth, 52; Virginia, 21; Susan, 18; Bascom, 12; Mary, 10; Ann Baswell, 23; Ellen, 11, family 290. By 1880 Ward and family were living in Mineral Springs, Arkansas.

141. Sylus was probably Silas Trice, son of May and Jane Frances Trice. Tandy was a 20-year-old druggist living with the Valentine. W. Smith family. 1860 Montgomery County, Tennessee, Census, family 707. See Chapter 1, Note 238 for more information on Silas Trice.

142. Jane Bridgewater was the wife of Richard F. Bridgewater, a shoemaker. The 1860 Montgomery County, Tennessee, Census lists R. C., 35; Jane, 32; A. J., 12; Augustus, 9; M. L., 6; F. L., 3, family 718.

143. President James Buchanan served out his entire term but had to watch the country come apart in the four months between the election and President Lincoln's taking office. In December 1860, President Buchanan lost three members of his cabinet to resignations: Secretary of State Lewis Cass, Secretary of the Treasury Howell Cobb, and Secretary of War John B. Floyd. Floyd was forced to resign because of suspicions that he sent cannons and other arms to places in the South so that they could be captured when those states seceded.

144. Arabella Jenkins married C. H. Dunn. Montgomery County, Tennessee. Marriage Book Volume 3, 87.

145. Mary Ann Caroline Hunt Ogburn's son Will married Z. Ann Smith, older sister of Valentine W. Smith, on December 17, 1855, in Montgomery County, Tennessee.

146. "Indispensables" was a Victorian term for a reticule, which is a fabric drawstring bag. They were the purses of the late eighteenth and early nineteenth centuries. Suzi Love, *Fashion Women 1800: History Notes, Book 12* (Amazon Digital Services LLC, 2018) Chapter 7, p. 3.

147. Dora Broadie was probably the daughter of Dr. David Broadie. The 1860 Montgomery County, Tennessee, Census lists M. M. (possibly Medora) Broadie, female, 22, in the household of David Broadie, physician, 68, with Henry, 18, and Frank, 10, family 156.

148. See Chapter 1, Note 216 for more information on the Butler Fauntleroy family.

149. Paducah, Kentucky, is the county seat of McCracken County. It is at the confluence of the Tennessee and Ohio rivers. It is halfway between St. Louis and Nashville, about ninety miles northwest of New Providence.

150. Billie Watts was the 17-year-old son of H. W. Watts, a merchant. The 1860 Montgomery County, Tennessee, Census, lists H. W. Watts, 38, merchant; S. O. Watts, female, 18; W. W., male, 17, family 734.

151. In a message to the people on December 12, 1860, President James Buchanan designated January 4, 1861, as a day for "fasting, humiliation, and prayer throughout the nation." Many places throughout the nation held special church services. Public buildings were closed along with many businesses.

152. Samuel Griswold Goodrich (1793–1860) wrote *Reflections of a Lifetime: Or Men and Things I Have Seen; In a Series of Familiar Letters to a Friend; Historical, Biographical, Anecdotal, and Descriptive* (New York: Miller, Orton, and Mulligan,

1856). The book looks at more than fifty years of American culture. "Voices from 19th Century America," accessed May 10, 2008, http://www.merrycoz.org/sgg /lifetime/lifetime.htm.

153. In late December 1860, South Carolina seized all federal property in the Charleston area except Fort Sumter. By January 7, 1861, Alabama, Georgia, and Florida had followed, seizing federal forts and arsenals in strategic areas. E.B. Long, *The Civil War Day By Day: An Almanac, 1861–1865* (Garden City, NY: Doubleday and Company, Inc., 1971) 17–22.

154. There are several Henry families listed in the 1860 Montgomery County, Tennessee, Census

155. There are several Richardson families listed in the 1860 Montgomery County, Tennessee, Census.

156. Mr. Holland was probably the Reverend Shandy Holland, pastor of New Providence Baptist Church and a farmer. See Chapter 1, Note 79 for more information on the Holland family.

157. This reference to Johnson is unclear. Perhaps she was referring to Samuel Johnson as a foremost man of letters. Johnson (1709–1784) wrote the preeminent English dictionary published in 1755. The reference says she could not find the words to sum up adequately the day's conversations in her diary entry.

158. This vague entry might indicate that Tom and Serepta talked of marriage. On January 22, she wrote of a letter from Tom that implied they were engaged. She felt uneasy about making such an inference even though on January 11, she had accepted a ring from him in pledge.

159. See Serepta's diary entry of February 19, 1858, for a detailed account of the death of Joseph H. Harris.

160. Serepta may have been referring to the run-up to the Montgomery Convention which started on February 4, 1861, in Montgomery, Alabama. As early as December 14, 1860, South Carolina called for a convention to set up a national government for the new Confederate States of America. Although this convention agreed on a provisional constitution in a very short time (four days), there were at least three plans for writing the constitution. The one that was finally approved was the Georgia Plan, which adopted the US Constitution with a few tweaks.

161. Fannie Holland was the daughter of the Reverend Shandy A. Holland, a Baptist minister, and Almeda Holland. See Chapter 1, Note 79 for more information on the Holland family.

162. Frances Ann Holland married Benjamin Downer Bradshaw (1840–1902) on January 17, 1861, in Christian County, Kentucky.

163. John Jordan Crittenden, US senator from Kentucky, opposed secession and supported the Lincoln administration. In December 1860, Senator Crittenden introduced legislation in an attempt to avert war. Known as the Crittenden Compromise, it called for six constitutional amendments that included a guarantee that slavery would continue in the slave states by re-establishing the Missouri

Compromise where the latitude and longitude 36–30 marked where slavery could exist. Northern Republicans including President Lincoln rejected the compromise.

164. *The Clarksville Weekly Chronicle*, January 18, 1861, reported on page 2 that a debate took place between unionists and secessionists and the result was the adoption of a modified version of the Louisville Resolutions, which embodied the main features of the Crittenden proposal.

165. On January 9, 1861, the *Star of the West* sailed into Charleston Harbor to resupply Fort Sumter. It was turned back by fire from Citadel cadets from a battery on the north end of Morris Island at the harbor's mouth. The first shots of the war had been fired—even though no war had been officially declared. Fort Sumter remained in Union hands for another several months. The same day, the State of Mississippi voted 84 to 15 for secession and became the second state to leave the Union.

166. Calico is a fabric made from unbleached, and often not fully processed, cotton with a small all-over floral print.

167. *The Complete Poetical Works of John Milton* was first published in 1794. A number of updated editions of the poems of Milton (1608–1674) have been published through the next two centuries to the present day.

168. Andrew Long was a 40-year-old farmer from Ohio. The 1860 Montgomery County, Tennessee, Census, lists Andrew Long with F. W., female, 33, family 251.

169. The 1860 Montgomery County, Tennessee, lists James Edlin, 28, bootmaker; Sarah, 27; J. B., male, 15; Cashus, male, 14; G. A., male, 11; Thomas, 9; M. E., female, 5; Nancy, 4; Adam Starkey, 21, shoemaker, born in Germany, family 748. Paul Wyatt notes, "Mr. Edlin was known far and wide as a fine workman and his specialty was high top boots. He was a man who had read extensively and when the spirited move was on him, he would talk entertainingly by the hour." "History of New Providence."

170. This appears to be a request by Edlin to hire Trice's enslaved woman Emma. The names of all the Trice enslaved people are unknown unless mentioned in the diary specifically.

171. The 1860 Montgomery County, Tennessee, Census lists B. T. Pollard, 33, farmer, with S. C., female, 35; J. W., male, 15; E. H., female, 10, family 468. Byard T. Pollard married Susanna C. Herndon on September 17, 1844, in Montgomery County, Tennessee.

172. While Elsey Trice's financial obligations seem to have had potentially dire consequences, Serepta never mentioned this transaction again. Perhaps, settlement occurred after she left his household or after the diary ended. Trade between New Providence and New Orleans was brisk as boats set out from landings like Trice's Landing to bring the dark-fired tobacco of Tennessee and Kentucky's Black Patch region to world markets.

173. Adoniram Judson, a Baptist missionary to Burma for almost forty years,

wrote *Records of the Life, Character and Achievements of Adonirum Judson* (New York: Edward H. Fletcher, 1854).

174. Cairo, Illinois, is the county seat of Alexander County and is the southern-most city in Illinois. Located at the confluence of the Ohio and Mississippi rivers, it was vital for strategic control during the war. It is about 125 miles northwest of New Providence.

175. Tabitha Trice smoked a pipe, which was not unusual for Southern women. First Ladies Dolly Madison, Rachel Jackson, and Margaret Taylor were pipe smokers. Women in America commonly smoked from the colonial period. They usually favored pipes or snuff. It was acceptable in America for women to smoke in public. By the 1860s, the practice had become less acceptable for women in the upper and middle classes in the North but was still socially acceptable in the South for quite a while after the war. "Coffin Nails: The Tobacco Controversy in the 19th Century," accessed May 13, 2019, https://tobacco.harpweek.com/hubpages /CommentaryPage.asp?Commentary=PipesAndSnuff.

176. March 4, 1861, was inauguration day for President Abraham Lincoln. Long, *Day by Day*, 45.

177. Ann Amelia, 19, and Laura, 16, were the daughters of Presley Neville and Ann E. Helm. See Chapter 1, Note 74 for more information on the Helm family.

178. "Quiet nature's sweet restorer, balmy sleep" is a phrase from Edmund Flagg, *The Far West, Or A Tour Beyond the Mountains* (New York: Harper & Brothers, 1838), 369.

179. This entry was a reference to the rejection of the Crittenden Compromise proposed by US Senator John Jordan Crittenden as an amendment to the Con-stitution to reestablish the old Missouri Compromise line that would permanently allow slavery below 36° 30' and permanently establish the area above as slave free. The Crittenden Compromise was rejected in March of 1861 by President Lincoln and the Republicans.

180. W. Upton Hoover does not appear on the 1860 Census of Montgomery County, but he is listed on the 1860 and 1861 tax list of Montgomery County with no land and a value of "other property" of $50 and $75 respectively. He was not identified again until 1880 when he and Nannie were enumerated in Bowling Green, Warren County, Kentucky, Census, family 177. They had one child in the household, Georgia, 19. His profession was given as traveling agent.

181. Nannie Smith was the daughter of Catherine Smith of Todd County, Kentucky. In 1860, Nannie was living in the household of William Griffy, who was married to her sister Mary. 1850 Todd County, Kentucky, District 2, Census, family 112; 1860 Montgomery County, Tennessee., Census, family 386.

182. In 1858, Dr. R. B. McMullen was serving as pastor of the First Presby-terian Church of Knoxville, Tennessee, when he was called to become president of Stewart College in Clarksville and professor of Mental and Moral Sciences. A

Renaissance man, he had also served a brief stint as Chair of Chemistry at East Tennessee University. He excelled in fundraising, which allowed the construction of the first dormitory, Robb Hall, named after Colonel Alfred Robb, local lawyer and college benefactor. During the winter of 1861–62, Confederate forces commandeered the entire campus, including the president's house, as a military hospital. McMullen used rooms at First Presbyterian Church to keep the preparatory school operating. Clarksville suffered a smallpox outbreak late in 1864. Dr. McMullen volunteered as a nurse in Robb Hall and contracted smallpox. He died in January 1865.

183. There was a valid report of a plot to assassinate Lincoln as he went through Baltimore. Allen Pinkerton, head of the private security agency, wanted Lincoln to disguise himself and slip into Washington undetected. Lincoln agreed to wear a disguise to avoid attention. He chose a soft felt hat instead of his usual stovepipe, draped an overcoat over his shoulders, and hunched down to hide his unusual height. The presidential train moved through Baltimore in the dead of night causing extreme anger the next morning when citizens arrived to greet the train only to discover it had passed hours earlier. Daniel Stashower, *The Hour of Peril: The Secret Plot To Murder Lincoln before the Civil War* (New York: Minotaur Books, 2013).

184. Since Lincoln's election, Washington was awash in rumors of plots to kill or kidnap him before he could take the reins of government. General Winfield Scott, head of the Army, actually received death threats trying to prevent him from using the military to protect Lincoln. Scott rounded up every soldier that he could get to the ceremony to protect the President elect. There was no attempt on Lincoln at the inauguration.

185. The breastpin, or brooch, made of hair was a common ornament in the middle nineteenth century. Having it "tipped" may have referred to having the woven hair bound in metal. *Godey's Ladies Book* mentioned patterns to make breastpins.

186. Mr. Keezee was probably one of the sons of John Keesee, who lived on the south side of the Cumberland River: George S., 43; John A., 38; Henry P., 30; or Robert J., 27. 1850 Census, Montgomery County, Tennessee, family 407; 1860 Census, Montgomery County, Tennessee, families 133, 134, and 112–116.

187. The "old history of Rome" could have been *The Decline and Fall of the Roman Empire* by Edmund Gibbon, six volumes, published between 1776 and 1781. Gibbon is known as the first modern historian because of his objective approach and use of primary sources. Serepta mentioned reading works of Flavius Josephus in her March 10, 1861, entry. The "old history" may have referred to his work.

188. Serepta was referring to Lincoln's First Inaugural Address on March 4, 1861. The majority of his address dealt with the Constitutional issues with dis-

union, arguing the Constitution did not allow it. He promised the duties of the government would continue to be carried out and no violence would be started by the Federal Government. He noted the Government would "hold, occupy, and possess the property and places belonging to the Government . . ." He also assured Southerners that their personal property would be protected.

189. Flavius Josephus (37 – c. 100), also called Joseph ben Matityahu, was a first-century Jewish historian, Roman consultant, and writer; he documented aspects of life during the time of Christ. His work has been translated and published multiple times. A popular English translation was by William Whiston. One version of Whiston's translation was published by Mack, Andrus, and Co., Ithaca, 1846.

190. *The Clarksville Chronicle,* March 15, 1861, reported, "The Brass Band of New Providence will give a grand concert, in that town, to-night. It is a complimentary benefit, and as the Band is highly meritorious, individually, collectively, and artistically, we hope they will have a crowded house."

191. French hens are members of the pheasant family. Both the birds and their eggs are edible. Whit Gibbons, "What Do You Do with 184 Birds at Christmas?" Accessed May 13, 2019, https://www.tuscaloosanews.com/news/20051218/whit -gibbons-what-do-you-do-with-184-birds-at-christmas.

192. Velouren is the Dutch word for velvet.

193. Mattie Carneal was the 17-year-old daughter of Josiah Carneal and his first wife, Catherine Galbreath Carneal (deceased). Gary, *Marriages, 1797–1850;* 1850 Christian County, Kentucky, Census, family 151. The 1870 Christian County, Kentucky, Census lists Mattie Carneal, 25, in the household of Josiah Carneal, farmer, and Lucy Carneal. Also listed are Eliza, 24; Robert, 22; Josiah, 19; Isaiah, 14; Victoria, 12; William, 10; Wesley, 8; Demetrius, 6; Paul, 5; and Fannie, 3.

194. Alexander Campbell (1788–1866) was a theologian who led the "Restoration Movement" stressing adherence to scripture. Several church groups have historical origins in this movement, including Churches of Christ, Christian churches and Disciples of Christ.

195. Church of Christ accepts immersion for those who accept Christ as their savior as the only form of baptism. Mr. Homer's rejection of infant baptism indicated his acceptance of the teaching of Alexander Campbell.

196. The 1860 Christian County, Kentucky, Census lists at least six Pendleton families.

197. Ann, Helen, and Donay were the wife and daughters of Armistead G. Slaughter. The 1860 Christian County, Kentucky, Census lists Armistead C. Slaughter, farmer 55; Ann R., 43; Ellen (Possibly Helen), 19; Donay C., 16; and Gabriel L., 24, family 31.

198. Although Serepta would not have known it at this point, Fort Sumter was bombarded on April 12, 1861, and surrendered the next day, April 13, 1861, after enduring thirty-four hours of shelling.

199. Mr. Lowrie was possibly a Methodist circuit rider. No Montgomery County records of a local Methodist minister named Lowrie could be found.

200. People in New Providence felt a rivalry to Clarksville, which was across the river. Serepta resented Clarksvillians she believed were looking down on New Providence residents.

201. The 1860 Christian County, Kentucky, Census lists in the household of James M. Williams, 59, farmer; Elizabeth, 42; Carolyn, 16; Sara B., 9; Alice B. Oliver, 7; and Mary R. Oliver, 5, family 368.

202. Serepta was referring to the bombardment of Fort Sumter. The commander, Major Robert Anderson, and eighty-six soldiers surrendered after thirty-four hours of shelling, and the fort was garrisoned by Confederate forces until the end of the war.

203. The April 10, 1861, *Clarksville Jeffersonian* ran an item on page one about Mexican General Pedro Ampudia organizing a force on the Rio Grande, suggesting his motive was to retake Texas. The news item also mentioned increased warlike behavior on the part of Native Americans. On April 3, 1861, the paper ran Sam Houston's farewell speech. Houston had been forced out of the governor's office because he would not take an oath of allegiance to the Confederacy. In the speech he warned that the removal of federal troops without a rapid replacement by state troops would result in an increase of attacks by Native Americans.

204. Serepta was referring to Company A of the 14th Tennessee Infantry, which was officially established in May 1861. The regiment was commanded by William Forbes, mathematics professor at Stewart College, and made up of men from Clarksville and surrounding Montgomery County.

205. During the Civil War, local ministers would enlist to serve as chaplains for local units. The advantage was that the ministers knew the men and perhaps baptized them and ministered to their families. Among the local ministers who enlisted in the 14th Tennessee Infantry were J.M. Pirtle, John E. King, and Luther H. Wilson. J. H. McNeilly served as chaplain for the 49th Tennessee Infantry.

206. On April 18, 1861, the Federal troops stationed at the arsenal at Harpers Ferry blew up the armory and arsenal. The next day, local militia occupied the arsenal. Stonewall Jackson was sent to restore order and trained and drilled the militia arriving on May 23. Three weeks later Jackson evacuated Harpers Ferry. Union troops occupied the deserted town briefly, then moved to the other side of the Potomac River.

207. Mr. Layne was probably William H. Layne, listed as age 50 in the 1860 Christian County, Kentucky, Census, family 111, with Nannie Lane, 40; James C. Layne, 5; Lizzie Layne, 1; and Duncan Galbriath, 78. Duncan Galbriath was the father of Nancy C. Galbraith Layne.

208. Tom Trabue, a friend and possible suitor, joined a Memphis unit. This entry indicates that Mr. Homer might be jealous and that Serepta had rather he not know about Tom's correspondence.

209. Women primarily made these circular badges of ribbon to show support for secession, local troops, and Southern patriotism. Different regions and states used different colors. Women wore them and would gift them to soldiers. Rosettes, also called cockades, predate modern metal political campaign buttons.

210. Jefferson Finis Davis (1808–1889) was the only President of the Confederate States from 1861–1865. A Democrat, he had represented Mississippi in the US House and later the Senate. He served as Secretary of War from 1853–1857 under Franklin Pierce. He was born in Fairview, Kentucky, about twenty miles north of New Providence before his family moved to Mississippi.

211. Serepta was right to be skeptical. This news report was incorrect. The number of men quoted is interesting since on April 15, 1861, President Lincoln called for this exact number of volunteers to fight for the federal cause.

212. Montgomery County had two militia regiments, the 91st and 92nd, which all men subject to military service were required to join. The regiments were divided into companies with each civil district of the county being allotted one company. F. S. Beaumont was the first commander of the 91st Regiment. In initial meetings, the men elected officers and NCO's. These regiments seemed never to get above company size due to the efforts to raise units to go straight into the Confederate Army. Eventually these units were absorbed into the Confederate Army or became home guard units. F. S. Beaumont is listed in the 1860 census as being 27 years old with an occupation of merchant. Listed in his household are L. E. Beaumont, female, 21; Ida H. Beaumont, female, 5; and Georgia C. Beaumont, female, 1, family 106.

213. Ross was the son of William and Allatha Mallory Donaldson. The 1860 Montgomery County, Tennessee, Census, family 389, lists him as age 21. Corporal Donaldson enlisted in the 14th Tennessee Infantry, Company L, at Camp Duncan on May 31, 1861. He was discharged for sickness in October 1862. Cross, *Ordeal by Fire*, 121.

214. Serepta was referring to Edward Hewitt. The company he commanded was Company L of the 14th Tennessee Infantry.

215. Corporal Ephraim P. Manson, 24, enlisted in the 14th Tennessee Infantry, Company L, in Clarksville on May 31, 1861. He was appointed to third sergeant in July 1861, a rank he held until he was appointed fourth corporal in September 1861. Cross, *Ordeal by Fire*, 159. The 1860 Montgomery County, Tennessee, Census lists Ephraim P. Manson, 20, son of Thomas H. Manson (?-1854) and Julia A. Walker Manson (1807–1887). Also listed in the household are A. M. Manson, 23, and John, 15.

216. This company was organized at Memphis, Tennessee, on April 21, 1861. Its captain was James Hamilton. It was accepted into the Confederate Army on August 20, 1861, at New Madrid, Missouri, and was stationed at Fort Pillow.

217. Athenian military commander, statesman, and one of the main architects of the Athenian Empire (c. 525–459), Themistocles convinced Athens to invest in ships to form a navy to oppose a Persian invasion by King Xerxes.

218. Xerxes was a Persian king (519?-465 BC) defeated by the Greeks in 480–479 BC.

219. The turmoil and uncertainty about the impending war and the threat to slavery made whites fearful of African American insurrection and violence against whites.

220. Enslaved people gathered information by listening carefully to conversations and sharing among slave networks. Diaries and letters of slaveholders and whites would note the apparent lack of interest or knowledge of enslaved people. Though they may have feigned ignorance for their own protection, slave networks provided information that was as accurate as what whites knew. For general histories of slavery and slave communities, see David Brion Davis, *Inhuman Bondage: The Rise and Fall of Slavery in the New World* (New York: Oxford Univ. Press, 2006); Ira Berlin, *Generations of Captivity: A History of African-American Slaves* (Cambridge, MA: Harvard Univ. Press, 2004); and Anthony E. Kaye, *Joining Places: Slave Neighborhoods in the Old South.* (Chapel Hill: Univ. of North Carolina Press, 2007).

221. Ann Eliza Brittain was the 12-year-old daughter of J. B. Brittain. 1860 Montgomery County, Tennessee Census, family 859.

222. Diphtheria is a bacterial infection that can result in nerve damage, paralysis, and death. Symptoms begin about five days after exposure with a sore throat, fever, and coughing. The neck may swell, making breathing difficult. Today, there is a vaccine but not in the nineteenth century.

223. Women's organizations formed in most communities to support the war effort.

224. Fort Pickens in Pensacola, Florida, was one of only four United States forts in Southern territory never occupied by Confederate forces during the Civil War. The fort was reinforced the day after Fort Sumter surrendered, preventing the Confederates from controlling Pensacola Bay and using the Pensacola Navy Yard. National Park Service, US Department of the Interior Gulf Islands National Seashore: Fort Pickens, accessed April 20, 2011, http://www.nps.gov/guis/plan yourvisit/fort-pickens.htm. At the time of publication, this information was not available on the Fort Pickens website.

225. Isham Green Harris (1818–1897) was Tennessee governor from 1857 to 1862 and US senator from 1877 to his death. He was instrumental in leading Tennessee out of the Union and into the Confederacy.

226. William A. Forbes was colonel of the 14th Tennessee Infantry. Cross, *Ordeal by Fire*, 128. He was killed in action on August 31, 1862, at the Battle of 2nd Bull Run, or 2nd Manassas, as it was called by the Confederates. Henry Garrigus was wounded in action at Cedar Run but survived the war, according to Cross, *Ordeal by Fire*, 129.

227. *The New York Times* reported in an article on April 27, 1861, that the steamer *C. E. Hillman* from St. Louis to Nashville was abandoned by its crew

near Cairo. A boarding party discovered 1000 kegs of powder and other contraband goods on the steamer.

228. Psalm 17:15: As for me, I will behold thy face in righteousness: I shall be satisfied, when I awake, with thy likeness. KJV

229. Brevet Second Lieutenant William H. (Billie) Burgess enlisted in Company A, 49th Tennessee Infantry, on November 29, 1861. Cross, *Cry Havoc*, 101.

230. Serepta was referring to her relationship with Tom Trabue.

231. The 1860 Nelson County, Virginia, Census lists Ann B. Helm, 84; John B., 48, clerk; William, 16; George, 13; Robert, 11; Martha, 9; and Mary 7, family 950. Anna Buck Helm (1775–aft 1861) was the mother of Presley Neville Helm.

232. On April 26, 1861, the *Clarksville Weekly Chronicle* reported on a public meeting which resulted in the formation of a Home Guard for Montgomery County. Thomas Ramey was elected captain.

233. The *Clarksville Chronicle* appeared as a weekly newspaper under various names as early as 1808. In 1890, the *Clarksville Daily Chronicle* merged with the *Clarksville Daily Tobacco Leaf* to form what is now *The Leaf Chronicle*, part of the Gannett newspaper chain.

234. Private Quintus C. Atkinson (1840–1894) enlisted in the 49th Tennessee Regiment, Company A, in Clarksville. He was sent home on sick furlough and discharged on December 21, 1862. Cross, *Cry Havoc*, 89. Quintus Cincinnatus Atkinson Jr. is found in the 1850 Todd County, Kentucky, Census living in the household of Betsy Watkins, 69, Joseph, 29, family 569. The 1870 Montgomery County, Tennessee, Census lists Quentus, 30, Sally E., 24; Q. C., male, 4; T.W, male, 2; and Babe, female, 6 months, family 831. Quint had proposed to Serepta, but she turned him down. See her diary entries on June 15, July 2, and July 19, 1862. He married Sally McKoin in 1865.

235. A cockade is a rosette or knot of ribbons worn on a hat as a badge of office or party, or as part of a livery.

236. Giuseppe Garibaldi was a brilliant Italian military leader who fought his entire life to free Italy from foreign occupation by the French and Austrian. He was born on July 4, 1807, in Nice, France. Garibaldi joined the Piedmontese Navy in 1833 and had to flee to France in 1834 after participating in a failed mutiny. He returned to Italy in 1848 to participate in a revolt in the French-occupied area of Italy and once again had to flee, this time to America. Garibaldi returned again in 1860 and this time conducted a successful campaign that brought Sicily and Southern Italy under his control. He declared himself dictator of the Two Sicilys. On November 7, 1860, he turned all this territory over to Victor Emmanuel, King of the Piedmont. He died June 2, 1882.

237. While this discussion appears to involve matters of war in Europe, no European conflicts beyond Italy's wars of unification and the Franco-Mexican War occurred in this period. Serepta's underlying concern must have been with

how France and England would react to the American Civil War. Both the United States of America and the Confederate States of America desperately tried to get Great Britain and France to ally with them. The Confederacy was convinced that the economic impact of cotton would tip Great Britain in its favor. The issue of slavery proved to be important as both countries had strong abolitionist movements.

238. According to the *Clarksville Chronicle* on May 10, 1861, the altercation occurred after an election of permanent officers. Anderson was elected as Provisional Orderly Sergeant. Mr. Brown made "ungenerous" remarks about Anderson after the election, leading to a fist fight. Brown stabbed Anderson twice with a pocket knife, killing him. Brown was arrested and released on $2,000 bond.

239. On May 6, 1861, the Legislature passed "Declaration of Independence and Ordnance Dissolving the Federal Relations Between the State of Tennessee and the United States of America" and set June 8 as the day for qualified voters to accept or reject the Declaration. *Public Acts of the State of Tennessee, April 1861*, Chapter 1.

240. Missouri Madole's brother Benjamin, 24, would enlist in the 14th Tennessee Infantry, Company C, on May 16, 1861, in Springfield, Tennessee. He was promoted to sergeant and was on detached service since January 1862. He was paroled at Appomattox, Virginia, on April 9, 1865. Neither the 1860 nor the 1870 Montgomery County, Tennessee, Census listed George in the Madole family household.

241. The *Clarksville Chronicle* of May 17, 1861, had a note on page 3 about an Irish volunteer company, the Montgomery Guards commanded by Captain Daily. It was mustered into service at Paducah, Kentucky.

242. This incident probably referred to what is known as the Camp Jackson Affair, which occurred in May 1861. Nathaniel Lyon was a graduate of West Point and a professional army officer who was commander of the Union arsenal in St. Louis, Missouri, in 1861. Missouri had a pro-Confederate governor and militia. Fearing an attack on the arsenal, Lyon moved to capture the pro-Confederate militia. He marched them through St. Louis to the arsenal to imprison them. This action provoked a riot. Citizens started throwing rocks at the soldiers, who then fired on the civilians. Twenty civilians were killed. The rioting continued for several days and ended when regular Federal Army troops were called in. Lyon was promoted for his actions.

243. George M. Helm was the 23-year-old son of Presley Neville and Ann E. Helm. See Chapter 1, Note 74 for more information on the Helm family.

244. Miss Poore was either Martha E., 20, or her sister Sarah E., 17, daughters of Zachariah H. Poor. 1850 Census Christian County, Kentucky, District 2, family 110; 1860 Census Montgomery County, Tennessee., family 800.

245. During the mid-nineteenth century it was unusual for women to speak in public. It was considered "promiscuous." The fact that Serepta wrote of Miss

Poore's speech approvingly gives insight to her feelings of women in the public space. She compared Miss Poore's comments favorably to John Mallory's, approving preparation and content of a woman's speech over a man's ill prepared response. Perhaps Miss Poore's talk was socially acceptable because she was in attendance with Captain Edward Hewitt.

246. Mary Trice was probably the daughter of Anderson and Harriett Trice.

247. Army worms refer to the larval stage of several species of moths. They damage and destroy a wide variety of crops because they eat any plant matter they come into contact with.

248. The 1850 Montgomery County, Tennessee, Census lists C. S. Peterson, 35, living with Mary A., 22, and Martha H., 10, family 7. The Peterson Kirkes Family Tree on ancestry.com, accessed January 13, 2018, lists Charles Stewart Peterson as Louisa Peterson's brother.

249. Fort Wright was a Confederate training camp on the Mississippi River at Randolph in Tipton County, Tennessee. It was established in April 1861 and named for Lieutenant Colonel Marcus Wright, 154th Militia Regiment at Memphis. The location was selected to fortify the Chickasaw Bluffs with artillery batteries and earthen field defenses to guard against the expected Union naval and land attack. Angela Wallace Finley, "Fort Wright," *Tennessee Encyclopedia*, 331; Letter, T. C. Trabue to S. M. Jordan, May 12, 1861, Camp Harris near Fort Wright, Randolph, Tennessee. Copy in editors' possession.

250. Kentucky remained neutral during the war although Kentucky men joined both the Union and Confederate armies. See Gary R. Matthews, *More American than Southern: Kentucky, Slavery and the War for American Ideology, 1828–1861* (Knoxville: Univ. of Tennessee Press, 2014).

251. Beriah Magoffin (1815 –1885) was the twenty-first governor of Kentucky and served during the lead-up and early part of the war. He supported states' rights and the right to secede and sympathized with the Confederates. Nevertheless, when the Kentucky General Assembly adopted a position of neutrality in the war, Magoffin ardently held to it. He refused calls for aid from both the Union and Confederate governments.

252. Ailsey Collishaw was the widow of John J. Collishaw. 1850 Montgomery County, Tennessee Census, family 1245; 1860 Census, Montgomery County, Tennessee, family 688.

253. Aunt Pollie Campbell was Mary Trice Campbell, wife of Thomas P. Campbell of Christian County, Kentucky, and sister of Bingham, Elizabeth, Leigh, Jesse James, Nace, May, Jane, Thomas Alexander, Greenberry, Elsey Trice, and Nancy Barbee. Bettie Homer was living with her great aunt since the death of her mother, Harriet Trice Homer. 1860 Census Christian County, Kentucky, family 911; will of Nace Trice, Montgomery County Wills, Book O, 583.

254. Bud Campbell was probably T. G. Campbell, son of the Pollie and Thomas P. Campbell.

255. It is unclear whether the pipe tongs were used in a smoking pipe or tongs used for cooking.

256. Serepta may have been referring to a little-known skirmish called the Battle of Sewell's Point, which occurred on May 18 and 19, 1861. Confederates started building a battery on a peninsula at the mouth of the port of Hampton Roads, Virginia. Two Union ships from Fort Monroe fired on the fledgling battery. After an initial shock, the battery fired back damaging the main attacking ship which returned to Fort Monroe. Total casualties were one Confederate wounded by a piece of shrapnel from an exploding shell.

257. Camp Duncan was at the old Montgomery County Fairgrounds on Dunbar Cave Road across the railroad tracks, east of what is now Wilma Rudolph Boulevard. Today, this site is within the Clarksville, Tennessee, city limits.

258. Mary and Fannie were the daughters of William T. (deceased) and Susan Thompson Britton.

259. Randall E. Rubel, in his introduction to the roster of the 14th Tennessee Infantry, reported that 1,251 men had been identified as having served in the regiment in the years from 1861 to 1865. Cross, *Ordeal by Fire*, 87.

260. Southerners called Lincoln a "black Republican" as a term of derision.

261. Serepta was describing the making of hardtack. The only ingredients are flour, salt, and water. These are combined, shaped into a cracker, and baked. As long as they stay dry, they have a very long shelf life. Hardtack gets very hard and is difficult to eat without soaking it in something first. There are stories of soldiers resorting to smashing hardtack with their rifle butts in order to eat it.

262. Montgomery County, Tennessee, and the cities of Clarksville and New Providence raised three infantry regiments: the 14th Tennessee, which fought in Virginia; the 49th Tennessee and the 50th Tennessee, both of which fought at Fort Donelson and were captured there. These two units were part of a prisoner exchange later in the war.

3. June 1861–December 1861

1. John H. Garrard was the 18-year-old son of Sanford and Mary J. Garrard. 1850 Montgomery County, Tennessee, Census, family 1493.

2. Jesse Ferguson was a candidate for "Floater" representing the counties of Montgomery, Robertson, Cheatham, and Davidson in the state legislature and advocate for "Southern Independence." *Clarksville Jeffersonian*, May 29, July 9, and July 17, 1861.

3. Southern Rights men were encouraged to leave the ballot unfolded so they could publicly be distinguished from the Lincolnites. *Clarksville Chronicle*, May 17, 1861.

4. Bud Jenkins was probably James Jenkins, 14, in 1850, brother of Bell Jenkins Dunn.

5. United States Colonel Robert Anderson was transferred from his command at Fort Sumter to assume command of the Department of Kentucky, later renamed the Department of the Cumberland.

6. John Letcher (1813 – 1884) was governor of Virginia during the war. He served as a representative to Congress before the war and served in the Virginia General Assembly after the war.

7. Serepta was referring to the man who caused the first death of a Union officer in the war. Colonel Elmer E. Ellsworth was a friend of Lincoln's and had worked in his law offices in Springfield. He was originally from New York and returned there to raise the 11th New York Volunteer Regiment. This regiment entered Alexandria, Virginia, on May 24, 1861. The colonel and four soldiers entered the Marshall House Inn to take down a large Confederate flag that could be seen from the White House. They took the flag down and were coming down the stairs when they encountered the innkeeper, James Jackson. Jackson shot Ellsworth at point-blank range with a shotgun. He, in turn, was shot by Corporal Francis Brownell. Brownell was awarded the Medal of Honor after the war.

8. Lincoln's reported disguise was to avoid an assassination plot in Baltimore on his way to Washington. He was to lose his usual tall hat and to slouch to try to hide his height.

9. James Minor Quarles was the brother of General William A. Quarles. Both brothers were attorneys in Clarksville. James was a member of the US House of Representatives from 1859 to 1861. William raised the 42nd Tennessee Infantry, was promoted to Brigadier General, and commanded a brigade. James served under his brother's command for the entire war.

10. On June 8, 1861, Tennessee formally left the Union. It was the last state to do so. Middle Tennessee's vote proved decisive. East Tennessee voted overwhelmingly to stay in the Union. Middle Tennessee went from 51% against disunion in an earlier vote to 88% in favor of disunion. In Montgomery County, the vote for secession was 2,742 to 3. Beach, *Along the Warioto*, 176.

11. *Woodstock; Or, The Cavalier* by Sir Walter Scott was first printed by Archibald Constable and Company in Edinburgh in 1826.

12. English bergh, Ticklenbergh, or towcloth is a type of linen cloth.

13. Hampton Springs probably referred to what was later called Camp Quarles, located at the present US 79 and Hampton Station Road.

14. Writing under the pen name Fannie Fern, Sarah Willis was one of the most successful columnists of her day. A prolific writer, she was known for her advocacy of women's rights and independence and was a strong advocate for educational reform for children. Kevin McMullen, "Fannie Fern: A Brief Biography," Fanny Fern in *The New York Ledger*, accessed May 13, 2019, https://fannyfern .org/bio.

15. John may have been John Bryan Osborne Jr. (1851-?), son of Marion Trice Osborne and the late John Bryan Osborne Sr.

16. Made up largely of men from Christian County, Kentucky, with Thomas G. Woodward as captain, the group was later designated as companies A and B, 1st Kentucky Cavalry. Charles Mayfield Meacham, *A History of Christian County Kentucky: From Oxcart to Airplane* (Nashville: Marshall & Bruce County, 1930). 3

17. Miss Rollins was one of the daughters of Thomas Rollins (spelled "Rawlings" in the *Chronicle*). The 1860 Montgomery County, Tennessee, Census lists Tom Rollins, 48, with E.C., female, 47; E.A., female, 24; Lucrecia, 22; and J.C., male, 20, family 879. *The Clarksville Chronicle*, June 21, 1861, noted on page 3, "The body of a young lady, named Rawlings, who lived at her father's, in the vicinity of Peacher's Mill in this county, was drowned in West Fork, near her home, one day last week. It is said she committed suicide on account of domestic troubles."

18. June 13, 1861, was declared as a National Fast Day by Jefferson Davis "to recognize our dependence upon God." Most churches in the South gave sermons in support of this proclamation. This was the first such day; Davis issued several of these proclamations throughout the war.

19. Dr. J. W. Castney had his dental office and home at the northwest corner of Fourth and Franklin streets in Clarksville. Williams, *Clarksville Directory, City Guide and Business Mirror*, Vol. 1 (1859–60).

20. According to Cross, *Ordeal by Fire*, 139, Edward Hewitt was captain of Co. L. He enlisted and was commissioned in Clarksville, Tennessee, on May 31, 1861. He was 29 years old. He retired when the 14th Tennessee was reorganized at Yorktown, Virginia, on April 27, 1862. No Hewitts or Hewetts are listed in Company E, which was raised in Stewart County. The unit was originally at Camp Duncan, located at the Fairgrounds (present day intersection of Dunbar Cave Road with Wilma Rudolph Boulevard). Camp Quarles was near Hampton Springs (now Hampton Station).

21. Missouri Governor Claiborne Fox Jackson tried to take Missouri out of the Union using a secession convention. Although Missouri had a large portion of the population extremely sympathetic to the South, the convention failed, and pro-Union factions set up their own legislature and governor, which were recognized by Washington, D.C. Missouri was under Union military control for the entire war.

22. The first major battle of the Civil War took place on July 21, 1861, at Manassas Junction, Virginia, about 170 miles north of Newsoms, Virginia.

23. The Confederate capital moved from Montgomery, Alabama, to Richmond, Virginia, soon after Virginia left the Union. Richmond was the second largest city in the Confederacy and was the capital city of a state with the largest manufacturing base in the new nation. The move of the capital to Virginia helped solidify Virginia's Confederate identity as well as linked the new government to the revolution. "Why Richmond?" Virginia Museum of History and Culture, accessed February 8, 2017, http://www.vahistorical.org/collections-and-resources/virginia-history-explorer/american-turning-point-civil-war-virginia-1/wh-1.

24. Mollie McDaniel was probably the daughter of Susan and the late Dr. George McDaniel. Sue McDaniel could have been Mollie's mother or her younger sister, Susan, listed as age 6 in the 1860 Montgomery County, Tennessee, Census.

25. Serepta was talking about the battle of Bethel Church, the first land battle fought in Virginia, a Confederate victory. General Benjamin Butler sent Federal troops against entrenched Confederate troops. The Confederates beat the Union troops back suffering only eight casualties. The Union suffered seventy-nine casualties. The *Clarksville Chronicle*, July 5, 1861, reported Federal losses as "between five and six hundred killed and wounded."

26. Charles Slaughter Morehead was an attorney from Hopkinsville, Kentucky, who had held various elected offices culminating with election as Governor of Kentucky in 1855. He was a Southern sympathizer who worked for a peaceful solution to avert war. He was highly critical of the Lincoln administration which got him arrested in September 1861 and charged with treason. Influential Unionist Kentuckians convinced Lincoln to release him in January 1862.

27. Although Kentucky Governor Beriah Magoffin was sympathetic to the South, when Kentucky declared itself neutral, he was successful for a time in keeping the state out of the fight. Magoffin rejected calls from both sides to supply troops but turned a blind eye to Confederate recruiters. In June 1861, Kentucky Unionists won a majority of Kentucky's congressional seats in a special election followed by winning majorities in both houses of the state legislature in an August election. On September 3, 1861, Confederate troops invaded Kentucky under Leonidas Polk, breaking the state's neutrality. This action led to the Union occupation of Kentucky until the end of the war. Magoffin resigned as governor in 1862. Robert C. Kennedy, "On this Day," *New York Times*, accessed July 13, 2017, https://www.nytimes.com/learning/general/onthisday/harp/0629.html.

28. Union forces crossed over to Ballard County, Kentucky, from Cairo, Illinois, to disperse a body of unarmed militia, assembled for training. Letter to General Benjamin Prentiss, commanding forces at Cairo, Illinois, from Dr. John M. Johnson, Paducah, Kentucky. Saturday, June 8, 1861. *New York Times*, June 15, 1861, accessed July 22, 2012, http://www.nytimes.com/1861/6/15/news /important-cairo-operations-. At the time of publication, this webpage was not available.

29. A steamer with two federal companies and a squad of artillery "broke her machinery" and drifted ashore a few miles below Columbus, Kentucky. A party went ashore and cut down a Confederate flag and trampled on it. *New Orleans Daily Delta*, June 14, 1861, 2.

30. Bergere bonnets, or hats, were usually flat brimmed, made of straw, and had a shallow crown. Usually trimmed with ribbons, they could also be highly decorated to the point of covering the whole hat with silk.

31. Serepta was referring to the Camp Jackson Affair described in the May 13, 1861, entry.

32. First Lieutenant/Captain James B. Howard, 25, son of Meredith and Minerva

Peterson Howard, enlisted in the 49th Tennessee Infantry, Company G, at
Palmyra, Tennessee, on December 3, 1861. He was captured as a prisoner of war
at Fort Donelson on February 16, 1862; sent to Camp Chase, Ohio, on March 1,
1862; transferred to Johnson's Island on March 16, 1862; exchanged at Vicksburg,
Mississippi, on September 1, 1862. He was detached from Company G and
ordered on recruiting service on October 12, 1862; rejoined his company on
December 6, 1862; promoted to the rank of captain on August 26, 1863. He was
killed in action at the Battle of Lick Skillet Road near Atlanta on July 28, 1864.
Cross, *Cry Havoc*, 140–141; 1850 Montgomery County, Tennessee, Census,
family 1469.

33. "To cut a figure" is slang for "to make an impression."

34. Mrs. Magaren was probably Affiah (or Effice) Magaren, 26, listed in the
1850 Christian County, Kentucky, Census, family 184, with Peter W. Magaren,
35; Charles, 10; and Dudley, 3. Peter Magaren was appointed postmaster of
Cottonwood, Christian County, in 1848. By 1860, the Magarens had moved to
Montgomery County. The 1860 Montgomery County, Tennessee, Census lists
Mrs. Magaren as Effice, family 804.

35. John W. Mallory was a lieutenant in Captain Edward Hewitt's company,
Company L of the 14th Tennessee Infantry. That James B. Howard would tease
Serepta about John Mallory suggests others were aware of their close friendship.

36. Serepta may have been referring to Belle Boyd, who recruited women to
steal arms and clothing from Union camps at night. She would attach the items
to their hoops and bring them across to Confederate troops. Boyd also spied for
the Confederacy and was briefly imprisoned in July 1861. See *Occupied Women:
Gender, Military Occupation, and the American Civil War*, edited by LeeAnn
Whites and Alecia P. Long (Baton Rouge: Louisiana State Univ. Press, 2009)
about how women assisted the Confederacy. Just north of Montgomery County,
Tennessee, Caroline Meriwether Goodlett, founder of the United Daughters of
the Confederacy, would mount one of her thoroughbreds and carry medicine and
supplies through the Federal lines. She grew up on Woodstock, a plantation in
Todd County, Kentucky, but after she married, her father gave her three hun-
dred acres of land in Montgomery County near Woodstock. "Meet the Founders;
Caroline Meriwether Goodlett," United Daughters of the Confederacy, accessed
July 23, 2017, www.hqudc.org/caroline-meriwether-goodlett/.

37. Sergeant William A. Donaldson was the son of William Donaldson and
Allatha Mallory Donaldson. The 1860 Montgomery County, Tennessee, Census,
family 389, lists him as age 24. He enlisted, with his brother Ross, in the 14th
Tennessee Infantry, Company L, at Camp Duncan on May 31, 1861. He was discharged for disabilities in November 1861. Cross, *Ordeal by Fire*, 121.

38. Frank Smith was the son of John K. Smith, New Providence tobacconist.
1860 Montgomery County, Tennessee, Census, family 727. Cross, *Ordeal by Fire*,
does not list a Frank Smith on the 14th Tennessee roster. He does list a Frank

Smith as a member of the 49th Tennessee in *Cry Havoc*, 194. However, that Frank Smith enlisted in Benton County, Tennessee, and so was probably not the Smith mentioned here.

39. Private Louis T. Gold, Second Lieutenant Thomas Herndon, and Private George B. Barbee enlisted in the 14th Tennessee Infantry, Company L, in 1861 in Clarksville, Tennessee. Gold was absent, sick in Tennessee, at the reorganization of the regiment April 27, 1862, and joined the 49th Tennessee Regiment. Barbee was discharged July 22, 1861, with a disability. Herndon went on to be elected second lieutenant in the April 1862 reorganization. He was wounded at Manassas; missing in action at Gettysburg; prisoner of war and sent to Fort McHenry, Fort Delaware, and Sandusky (Ohio); paroled at Johnson's Island, Ohio; and forwarded to Point Lookout, Maryland, for exchange on March 14, 1865. Cross, *Ordeal by Fire*, 94, 131, 138.

40. In fact, John Mallory was concerned about the health of soldiers in the 14th Tennessee. He expressed his concerns in a series of letters to Serepta written from July 1861 to January 1862, reporting, "The sickness in our Regt. has been increasing. Typhoid fever and chills are getting to be common." Quoted in Cross, *Ordeal by Fire*, 19.

41. During the Civil War, units elected their commanders.

42. Emma Staton Jackson was the 22-year-old daughter of Jo and Clarissa Staton.

43. Serepta's Aunt Tabitha seems to have suffered a cerebral hemorrhage or stroke.

44. The physician was probably J. D. Martin, 24-year-old assistant surgeon, Forbes regiment. *Clarksville Chronicle*, July 5, 1861; Cross, *Ordeal by Fire*, 160.

45. Mr. Hampton was G. W. Hampton, *Clarksville Chronicle*, July 5, 1861.

46. Proverbs 27:1 (KJV).

47. Several letters from Tom Trabue to Serepta from the time he was stationed in Memphis survive. Serepta may have been referencing Fort Pillow, where Trabue may have been serving. Built in 1861 by Confederates as part of the Mississippi River defense, Fort Pillow is approximately 40 miles north of Memphis and named for General Gideon Pillow. Union troops gained control of Memphis in June 1862 and Confederates abandoned Fort Pillow. Fort Pillow is best known for the attack on it April 12, 1864, by Confederate General Nathan Bedford Forrest. His forces greatly outnumbered the Union Garrison. Approximately 300 Union troops were killed after they surrendered according to Union survivors. The majority killed were soldiers serving in the US Colored Troops.

48. Serepta was possibly referring to the Battle of Hoke's Run fought on July 2, 1861. It was part of the Manassas Campaign. Union General Robert Patterson's division crossed the Potomac River near Williamsport and encountered Stonewall Jackson's troops near Hoke's Run. Jackson's orders were just to delay the Union advance, which he did and then withdrew.

49. Elsey was probably Elsey Dycus, daughter of Susannah Trice Dycus and Greenberry Dycus. She was Serepta's first cousin and would have been visiting in Montgomery County.

50. Winnie was one of her Uncle Trice's enslaved women. A series of diary entries from May 1862 through February 1864 described the back-and-forth efforts of Winnie to escape to freedom and to rescue her baby, Ida, from Uncle Trice. The last entry on Winnie on February 12, 1864, reported that she was "back at camp" and wondered what the Trices would do, commenting that African Americans were leaving Christian County, Kentucky, "by the hundred."

51. W. J. McCormac operated a photographic gallery visited by local citizens and Union soldiers. By the time of the Civil War, collecting photographs of friends and famous people in albums had become popular. "Photographic Artist," Williams, *City Directory*.

52. Mr. Forbes may have been Elsey Dycus's husband. Her sister, Cassus, married J. Hoodless and they were living close to her father and stepmother, Greenberry and Mary E. Reed Aiken Dycus in Milton, Santa Rosa County, Florida, sometime around 1861. No record could be found for Elsey, but a number of Forbes families are listed in Milton, Florida, censuses.

53. Serepta was referring to the Battle of Carthage where a Union force under Colonel Franz Siegl caught up with the Missouri Militia under Governor Claiborne Jackson. Seeing the militia was a much larger force, Siegl withdrew.

54. Serepta might have been talking about the battles of Sewell's Point and Aquia Creek. These were both Navy engagements involving Union gunboats firing on Confederate land batteries. Both engagements were brought on by the Union blockade of the Southern coast. There were two land battles in Virginia during this time: Bethel Church and Blackburn's Ford in July 1861, but these were Confederate victories.

55. Serepta was referring to the First Battle of Bull Run, or First Manassas, which was a Confederate victory. The Union suffered 460 killed and 1,124 wounded. Ellsworth's Zouaves were a New York Militia unit (called the Fire Zouaves because they were volunteers raised from the city's fire department), formed by Colonel Elmer Ellsworth, who was killed in May 1861 when he removed a Confederate flag from an inn in Alexandria, Virginia. He was the first Union officer killed in the Civil War. Brigadier General Pierre Gustave Toutant Beauregard was commander of Confederate forces at Bull Run and was also the general who ordered the first shots fired at Fort Sumter.

56. The First Battle of Manassas, fought on July 21, 1861, was a Confederate victory. Thirty-five thousand Union troops clashed with 20,000 Confederate troops at a place near Manassas Junction, Virginia. The Union name for the battle, Bull Run, comes from a small river that ran through the battlefield. The Union troops broke and ran for Washington after the Confederates broke the

Union right flank. Many civilians from Washington came out to watch the fight and made the retreat even more chaotic by clogging the roads with their carriages.

57. Jefferson Davis was not at the First Battle of Bull Run, or Manassas. Brigadier General P. G. T. Beauregard was overall Confederate commander. The day was saved when General Joe Johnston's troops arrived from the Shenandoah Valley. This is the battle where Thomas Jackson earned the nickname "Stonewall" and where the rebel yell was first heard. The troops were following Stonewall's order, "And when you charge, yell like furies!"

58. Brigadier General Irvin McDowell was the Commander of the Union Army at Manassas. After the defeat, he was replaced by General George McClellan Major General Robert Patterson failed to stop Confederate General Joseph Johnston from joining Brigadier General P.G.T. Beauregard at First Manassas. Union General Winfield Scott was 75 years old and 300 pounds at the time of this battle. He had to be carried from place to place so was not physically at the battle.

59. On July 12, 1861, the 14th Tennessee Infantry left Clarksville, Tennessee, by train for Virginia. Cross, *Ordeal by Fire*, 12.

60. Fort Pillow is in western Tennessee about 40 miles north of Memphis. It sits on bluffs overlooking the Mississippi River. Tom Trabue was stationed there.

61. On July 19, 1861, the United States House of Representatives approved a tariff that increased the price of such items as coffee, tea, and sugar. The Direct Tax Law that Serepta mentioned had a much tougher time passing as it included a tax on property. It was rewritten to include an income tax of 3% on all incomes between $600 and $10,000 and 5% on those above $10,000. Lincoln signed this bill into law in 1862. It was the first income tax bill for the United States. The Confederacy authorized its first national income tax measure in 1863. "Financing the Civil War," accessed March 29, 2017, https://www.gpo.gov/fdsys/pkg/GPO -CDOC-100hdoc244/pdf/GPO-CDOC-100hdoc244–13.pdf. "The First Income Tax," American Battlefield Trust, accessed January 13, 2019, https://www.battle fields.org/learn/articles/first-income-tax.

62. The regiment she was speaking of was the 14th Tennessee Infantry, which was commanded by Colonel W. A. Forbes. The regiment did suffer heavy fatalities over the course of the war. Wallace Cross commented, "The regiment went out a thousand strong in 1861; it returned a mere shadow in 1865." *Ordeal by Fire*, 11.

63. Camp Trousdale was located in Sumner County, Tennessee.

64. According to the Centers for Disease Control, about one in ten children with measles suffer from ear infections that can result in permanent hearing loss. This complication is more likely to affect children younger than 5 or adults older than 20. "Measles," Center for Disease Control and Prevention, accessed July 23, 2017, https://www.cdc.gov/measles/about/complications.html.

65. Mr. Hirst was A. C. Hurst, 22, a teacher living in the household of Dr.

R. B. McMullen, professor. 1860 Montgomery County, Tennessee, Census, family 1165.

66. To give someone "gup" or "gop" is akin to giving the person "a hard time," to complain about the person's behavior.

67. Serepta may have been referring to the Battle of Cedar Mountain fought on August 4, 1861. This battle occurred about seven miles south of Culpeper, Virginia, between Confederate Generals Stonewall Jackson and A. P. Hill and Union General John Pope. This battle was a Confederate victory. "Our regiment" was the 14th Tennessee, part of Archer's Brigade, which was sent to Stonewall Jackson to help during the battle. According to Cross, in *Ordeal by Fire*, 37, the regiment lost 19 killed and 116 wounded.

68. According to *Martine's Hand-Book of Etiquette* (New York: Dick & Fitzgerald, 1866), 116, "Such visits are necessary, in order to maintain good feelings between the members of society; they are required by the custom of the age in which we live, and must be carefully attended to." The book goes on to say that half an hour is an acceptable amount of time to be spent on a visit and advises women to keep track of their visits and how soon the calls are returned. Failure to return visits was considered a "grievous slight," accessed January 16, 2018, https://archive.org/details/martineshandbookoomartrich.

69. Union General Nathaniel Lyon (1818–1861) was killed August 10, 1861, at Wilson's Creek, Missouri, becoming the North's first military hero. This battle was the first major engagement west of the Mississippi River. Lyon's forces attacked Confederate forces commanded by General Sterling Price (1809–1867) and General Benjamin McCulloch (1811–1862). The Confederates were forced to retreat, but the Union Army was disorganized, low on ammunition, and soon retreated to Springfield, Missouri. Losses were heavy on both sides: 1,200 Union casualties and 1,100 Confederate. "Confederate Casualties," History, accessed May 13, 2019, https://www.history.com/topics/american-civil-war/battle-of-wilsons-creek.

70. Throughout August 1861, groups of Democrats unhappy with Lincoln were holding meetings and rallies for peace. Instead of raising the Liberty Flag, they signified the meeting by flying a white flag. Many newspapers joined these peace meetings. They eventually ended with the Confiscation Act, which gave the federal government the right to seize any property of anyone supporting the rebellion. Many Democratic newspapers found themselves the targets of angry mobs who would ransack and destroy their offices and printing presses.

71. The 1880 Montgomery County, Tennessee, Census lists J. W. Cabaniss, 51, living in New Providence, Tennessee, with the occupation of dentist.

72. Private Albert Newell enlisted in Company A, 14th Tennessee Infantry, on May 14, 1861. Cross, *Ordeal by Fire*, 170.

73. Tommie Grinstead was the son of Richard and Sarah Pettus Grinstead of Todd County. William T. Grinstead enlisted in the 14th Tennessee Infantry,

Company A, on May 14, 1861. He was discharged in September 1862. 1850 Todd
County, Kentucky Census, family 464; Cross, *Ordeal by Fire*, 133. Serepta men-
tioned in her October 25, 1862, entry that he had recently reentered service under
Thomas Woodward. Woodward raised his third command, the 2nd Kentucky
Cavalry, on December 9, 1862. Co. B had some earlier formation as of September
1862, including two Clarksville men, according to Greg Biggs, "Woodward's 2nd
Ky. Cavalry, CSA," The Kentucky in the Civil War Message Board, accessed
May 11, 2019, http://www.history-sites.com/cgi-bin/bbs62x/kycwmb/webbbs
_config.pl?md=read;id=5849

74. Joseph E. Hatcher, son of Samuel Hatcher, was living with the Richard
Grinstead family in 1860. He enlisted as a private at age 23 in the 14th Tennessee
Infantry, Company A, on May 14, 1861. He was discharged in October 1861.
Cross, *Ordeal*, 137; 1850 Census Todd County, Kentucky, family 472; 1860 Census
Todd County, Kentucky, family 624.

75. Emma Staton Jackson was the widowed daughter of Joseph and Clarissa
Staton.

76. Serepta, called Rep by her friends, had an occasional habit of having other
people write entries. Emma Jackson spent the night and so this entry was probably
written by her. This observation gives insight into the dynamic of Mr. Homer's
relationship to Serepta.

77. The Reverend Thomas Delancey Wardlaw, born 1826 in the fishing village
of Warrenpoint, County Down, Ulster (now Northern Ireland), immigrated to
Canada in June 1845 after graduating from Belfast College in 1844. Wardlaw immigrated to the United States in 1845 and continued his education at Princeton
Theological Seminary, receiving his degree in 1849. He was ordained in 1850 and
served the Presbyterian Church for two years in the coal fields of Port Carbon,
Pennsylvania. Immediately after his marriage in 1850, Wardlaw answered the
call from the church in Paris, Kentucky, where he preached for six years before
taking the pastoral position in the First Presbyterian Church in Clarksville in
March 1859.

78. William Starke Rosecrans (1819–1898) was a West Point graduate whose
career before the Civil War was fairly routine. He resigned from the Army in 1854
due to poor health. He wore a beard to cover scars caused by an exploded oil lamp.
Rosecrans rejoined the Union Army right after Fort Sumter was surrendered and
was assigned to General George B. McClellan's staff. In 1861, he was promoted to
brigadier general and served under McClellan during the western Virginia Union
campaign that led to the formation of the State of West Virginia. This campaign
in western Virginia is the one Serepta was chronicling.

79. A quire of paper is a quantity consisting of twenty-four or twenty-five
sheets of paper, which is one twentieth of a ream.

80. Uncle (or Aunt) was an honorific sometimes given to African Americans. It
did not indicate actual kin.

81. Serepta was disagreeing with William Shakespeare, who wrote, "Frailty, thy name is woman," *Hamlet*, Act I, Scene 2.

82. In 1861, the Confederate States issued a five-cent green postage stamp depicting Jefferson Davis. In 1861, the post office issued a ten-cent blue stamp featuring Thomas Jefferson.

83. Confederate General Gideon Pillow occupied Columbus, Kentucky, on September 3, 1861. In answer to this action, Union General Ulysses Grant occupied Paducah on September 6, 1861.

84. Pontius Pilate was the prefect, or governor, of Judea between 26 and 36 AD. He tried and convicted Jesus of treason.

85. On July 27, 1861, Confederate General Gideon Pillow marched his troops from Fort Randolph in Tennessee into Missouri occupying the town of New Madrid. The ultimate idea of the expedition was to capture St. Louis. The area commander was General Leonidas Polk, who was extremely cautious and unsure. Confederate plans changed back and forth so many times amid much bickering between the generals that nothing was accomplished. On September 4, Pillow brought his forces to Columbus, Kentucky, which was the beginning of the end of Kentucky neutrality.

86. Smithland, Kentucky, is a small town about twenty miles northeast of Paducah, near the confluence of the Ohio and Cumberland rivers.

87. Jeremiah 29:12–13: Then shall ye call upon me, and ye shall go and pray unto me, and I will hearken unto you. And ye shall seek me, and find me, when ye shall search for me with all your heart. KJV.

88. Serepta may have been enjoying a pun with this sentence. "Union sentiments" probably referred more to marital union than to the Union government.

89. Mr. Osborne was Noble Osborne, 72 in 1860, father of Marion Trice Osborne's deceased husband, John Bryan Osborne Sr. Marion and her son John were living with Noble Osborne.

90. Dr. Johnson was probably James F. Johnson, partner of Dr. Edward Branch Haskins. Apparently, Dr. Johnson came to deliver a baby of one of the slaves. He left at 9 p.m., but the horn blew to alert him that he was needed around 1 a.m. and he arrived back by 2 a.m. The baby girl must have been born around 3 a.m.

91. Mr. Whitfield was perhaps L.S. Whitefield, who married Eliza J. Trice on December 3, 1857, in Montgomery County, Tennessee, *Tennessee Compiled Marriages* 1851–1900. Legrand Stanley Whitefield was born November 24, 1824, died February 22, 1906, and is buried in Trice-Whitefield Cemetery in Clarksville, Tennessee.

92. Elsey Trice must have been visiting Fannie Pettus, whom he would marry on April 8, 1862. See Chapter 1, Note 266 for more information on the Pettus family.

93. Serepta was referring to Hamlet's mother, Gertrude, queen of Denmark.

While interpretations of her character vary, some critics surmise that she was involved with Hamlet's uncle, Claudius, even before the death of her husband.

94. Merino is wool made from the fleece of Merino sheep.

95. Martha A. Harrelson was the daughter of John B. and Catherine Galbreath Harrelson (deceased). The 1850 Christian County, Kentucky, Census, family 152, lists Martha A., 15, in the household of John, B, 49, with Daniel G., 18; Elizabeth C., 10; and William H., 8.

96. Captain James Hamilton died on September 15, 1861, at Columbus, Kentucky, after a brief illness and was buried in Memphis. *The Southern Monthly Volume 1* (Memphis: Hutton and Freligh, 1861), accessed March 29, 2017, available at https://books.google.com/books under "The Southern Monthly volume 1."

97. On September 7, 1861, the Kentucky state legislature, angered by Confederate General Simon Bolivar Buckner's move to invade Bowling Green, Kentucky, declared its allegiance with the Union. The legislature also passed the "Non-Partisan Act," which said "any person or any person's family that joins or aids the so-called Confederate Army was no longer a citizen of the Commonwealth." The legislature denied any member of the Confederacy the right to land, titles or money held in Kentucky or the right to legal redress for action taken against them. Kentucky's "neutrality" was officially over. Damian Beach, *Civil War Battles, Skirmishes, and Events in Kentucky* (Louisville: Different Drummer Books, 1995), 20.

98. A sweet potato pie is sweetened by sugar, cinnamon, and nutmeg.

99. Long View is a community just north of Oak Grove, Kentucky, along the Clarksville-Hopkinsville Turnpike.

100. Residents of Louisville were divided in their loyalties to the Union or the Confederacy. The *Louisville Courier* was very much pro-Confederate, while the *Louisville Journal* was pro-Union.

101. Confederate General Sterling Price, fresh from his victory at Wilson's Creek, Missouri, turned his attention to the Union garrison at Lexington, Missouri. On September 12, 1861, hostilities started with a skirmish, but Price waited for the rest of his unit. They arrived on September 17 and encircled the town. On September 20, Price attacked the 2,500 Union soldiers. Union Colonel James Mulligan surrendered the town after a short battle.

102. The "Hopkinsville battle" was a skirmish fought on September 29, 1861, between Confederate General Simon Buckner and the Hopkinsville Home Guard (Union). Buckner occupied Hopkinsville and established a garrison there at Camp Alcorn. Sadly, this garrison suffered massively from disease and a measles epidemic that left barely enough men to guard the town.

103. Serepta was paraphrasing a comment attributed to Julius Caesar, "Veni, vidi, vici" (I came, I saw, I conquered) to describe his swift victory in the Battle of Zela in 47 BCE in present-day Turkey.

104. Albert Sidney Johnston (1803–1862) was born in Kentucky and was a West

Point graduate. He gained his military experience in the Black Hawk War in 1832. In 1834, he resigned from the US Army and fought in the Texas Army during the Texas Revolution. He also fought during the Mexican-American war. He rejoined the US Army in 1849. He resigned again in May 1861 when his adopted state of Texas seceded. He was a personal friend of Confederate President Jefferson Davis and was given the rank of full general in the Confederate Army. He was placed in command of the Western Theater but was not given the troops or equipment to effectively defend such a large area.

105. *Life of General Lafayette* is a book by William Cutter, (New York: Derby & Jackson, 1859).

106. Mrs. Smith was possibly Mary Ann Leigh Smith, wife of Valentine (Tine) W. Smith and daughter of Henry and Nancy Lucinda Trice Leigh. Serepta mentioned the birth of her son in her November 10, 1860, entry, and the 1870 Montgomery County, Tennessee, Census lists her children Mediceas, 9, and Blanch, 8. Blanch could have been born less than a year after Mediceas.

107. The 1st Regiment 1st Brigade Army of the Mississippi was organized in August 1861 and sent to Kentucky to reinforce Confederate General Albert Sidney Johnston. They went into winter camp in Hopkinsville, Kentucky, on October 17, 1861. Eleven members of the regiment are buried in Hopkinsville. The regiment moved to Fort Donelson in February 1862.

108. Psalm 42:11: Why art thou cast down, O my soul? and why art thou disquieted within me? hope thou in God: for I shall yet praise him, who is the health of my countenance, and my God. KJV.

109. Privates James M. Drane and Hugh McClure Drane enlisted in Company A of the 14th Tennessee Infantry on May 20, 1861. Their father, Dr. W. A. Drane, followed the 14th Infantry as surgeon. James was killed in action at Cheat Mountain, West Virginia. Military records show a letter written to General Leonidas Polk on Hugh's behalf for promotion to lieutenant and transfer to a light artillery unit. No further military record was found. Hugh did survive this illness and is listed in the 1870 Montgomery County, Tennessee, Census in a household with Bettie W. Drane, 24. Hugh died at age 40 in 1878. Both brothers are buried in Greenwood Cemetery in Clarksville, Tennessee. Cross, *Ordeal by Fire*, 122.

110. Willie Mills was the 4-year-old son of Nathaniel Jackson and Mary Elizabeth Mallory Mills. 1860 Census Montgomery County, Tennessee, family 868.

111. Jennie Howard was probably Jane Howard, daughter of Meredith and Minerva Peterson Howard.

112. The 1870 Montgomery County, Tennessee, Census lists Brown Cherry, 19, in the household of Mann Riggons, 44; Francis Riggons, 35; Walter Riggons, 15; Norman Riggons, 11; and W. Cherry, 27.

113. Inez Davis was the daughter of Henry J. and Ann Herring Davis. "Davis Family Tree," accessed September 6, 2012, http://www.ancestry.com.

114. Elmore may have been H. E. Herring, listed as male, age 11, in the 1860 Montgomery County, Tennessee, Census in the household of Dr. B. N. Herring.

115. Hydrophobia, fear of water, is the historic name for rabies. The name derives from symptoms that occur in the later stages of the disease: difficulty swallowing, panic when offered liquids to drink, unquenchable thirst.

116. Lieutenant Robinson Brown enlisted in the 14th Tennessee Volunteer Infantry, Company L, on May 31, 1861. He was wounded in action at Second Manassas on August 30 and died September 2, 1862. Cross, *Ordeal by Fire*, 104.

117. 1 John 3:1–2: Behold, what manner of love the Father hath bestowed upon us, that we should be called the sons of God: therefore the world knoweth us not, because it knew him not. Beloved, now are we the sons of God, and it doth not yet appear what we shall be: but we know that, when he shall appear, we shall be like him; for we shall see him as he is. KJV.

118. A press is a piece of furniture used for storage, sometimes called a linen press. The same applies to a safe, sometimes called a pie safe.

119. Food storage required a dry place away from vermin. The jar of eggs probably contained pickled eggs.

120. Serepta was referring to the 7th Texas Infantry. Richard P. Gildrie, Phillip Kemmerly, Thomas H. Winn, "Clarksville, Tennessee, In the Civil War: A Chronology," Unpublished paper, Clarksville, Tennessee, 1984, 2; copy in editors' possession; *US War Department, The War of the Rebellion: A Compilation of the Official Records of the Union and Confederate Armies*, 128 vols. (Washington, DC, 1880– 1901), Series 1, Vol. 4, 495. Hereinafter referred to as *OR*, followed by series, volume number, and page number.

121. Lloyd Tilghman (1818–1863) was born in Maryland and was a West Point graduate. In 1838, he resigned from the Army and went to work as a civil engineer for the railroad system. He rejoined the Army in 1846 to fight in the Mexican-American War. He moved to Paducah, Kentucky, in 1852 where he worked for the railroad. In October 1861, he became the colonel of the Confederacy's 3rd Kentucky Infantry and was promoted to brigadier general at Fort Henry just before its surrender in February 1862.

122. Mathew 25:40. (KJV).

123. Known as the Battle of Belmont, the action was actually only a large raid or a reconnaissance. Even though the casualties were heavy, nothing of strategic value to either side was attained. Long, *Day by Day*, 136.

124. The grave had probably settled, leaving a slight indentation. A paling fence is a short fence, usually of wrought iron, around a single grave or a family plot.

125. On the same day as the action at Belmont (November 7, 1861), Union naval forces steamed into Port Royal Sound, South Carolina, and attacked Fort Walker on Hilton Head Island and Fort Beauregard to the north. The Confederates were forced to withdraw allowing Union Brigadier General Thomas W. Sherman's troops to begin the occupation of the Hilton Head-Port Royal area.

126. Nero (37–68 A.D.) was a Roman Emperor known for ruthlessness, tyranny, and extravagance. One of his more infamous executions included his mother.

127. Demetrius (37–71 A.D.) was a philosopher from Corinth. He lived in Rome during the reigns of Caligula, Nero, and Vespasian.

128. The *Union and American* was a Nashville, Tennessee, newspaper.

129. Mollie Smith may have been Mary Ann Leigh Smith, wife of Valentine (Tine) W. Smith and daughter of Henry and Nancy Lucinda Trice Leigh.

130. Serepta was referring to Catherine, Georgina, William H., and Leonard H. Smith. 1850 Todd County, Kentucky, Census, family112.

131. Tennessee "Tennie" Haskins (1822–1903) was married to physician Edward Haskins (1813–1868). The Haskinses were a prominent and well-connected Clarksville family. This entry reveals Serepta's resentment toward Clarksvillians, who lived across the river in the big, sophisticated city. Clarksvillians may very well have had the same attitude toward Nashvillians. Tennie's daughter, Nannie, kept a diary, *The Diary of Nannie Haskins Williams: A Southern Woman's Story of Rebellion and Reconstruction, 1863–1890*, (Knoxville: Univ. of Tennessee Press, 2014).

132. Mrs. Henry was Marion Henry, wife of Clarksville attorney Gustavus Adolphus Henry, Sr., who served as a senator in the Confederate Congress.

133. Serepta was speaking metaphorically, believing that the Clarksville women thought so little of the New Providence women that for all the Clarksville women cared, once the New Providence women provided blankets they could disappear to Africa. Guinea is on the west coast of Africa and thousands of Africans were captured and exported to the Americas for enslavement.

134. Serepta was talking about Fort Clark, built just south of where the Red River flows into the Cumberland River at Clarksville, Tennessee. This area is in the flood plain of the Cumberland. Today, Fort Clark is buried under 30 to 50 feet of fill designed to help control flooding.

135. Ninety-six-year-old Elnor Wray was the grandmother of Joseph Wray. 1850 Montgomery County, Tennessee, Census, family 89.

136. Uncle Trice began seeing Fannie Pettus about four months after Aunt Tabitha's death. They would not marry for almost another five months, on April 8, 1862, about nine months after Aunt Tabitha's death. Victorian mourning rules requiring a year of grieving for widows apparently did not apply to widowers. See Chapter 1, Note 266 for more information on the Pettus family.

137. Whitleather refers to a leather that has been treated with alum and/or salt. It is usually a leather that is pale or white and is strong but supple. This reference suggests the meat Serepta could buy was as tough as whitleather.

138. Rollin may have been the French historian, Charles Rollin (1661–1741), who authored a six-volume *Ancient History of the Egyptians, Carthaginians, Assyrians, Babylonians, Medes and Persians, Macedonians and Grecians*. It was translated into English and multiple editions were printed in England.

139. Serepta was referring to bone marrow pie, for which you can still find recipes.

140. Babe Trahern may have been Althea A. Trahern, 20, in 1860. She was the sister of Ethalinda Trahern, who married Joel Rice Oldham in 1856. 1850 Christian County, Kentucky, Census, family 261; Kentucky, County Marriages, 1783–1965.

141. Alice R. was Alice Garrett Riggins, daughter of Pleasant B. and Martha Radford Garrett.

142. In June 1861, William Durham Lyles was commissioned as surgeon in the Provincial Army of the Confederate States. After serving the Army of the Potomac, he was transferred by the Secretary of War to Kentucky and on December 1, 1861, to Hopkinsville. "Elizabeth Ann Lyle Antecedents and Descendants," Rootsweb, accessed September 19, 2012, http://wc.rootsweb.ancestry.com/cgi-bin/igm.cgi?op =GET&db=Robert. At the time of publication, this webpage was not available.

143. General Robert E. Lee had planned a simultaneous attack on the Cheat and Elkwater fortifications in West Virginia. Defeated by the rough terrain, rainy weather, and Colonel Albert Rust's failure to attack as planned, the mission failed, and Lee withdrew his forces. With his reputation as a general severely damaged, Lee was given the name "Granny Lee." Rich Mountain Battlefield Foundation, "Lee's Cheat Mountain Campaign," *Northwestern Virginia in 1861: The First Campaign*, accessed September 20, 2012, http://www/richmountain.org/history /wv1861.html.

144. Three forts were eventually built in Clarksville: Fort Clark, which was then just outside of Clarksville in the flood plain of the Cumberland River where the Red River joins it; Fort Sevier, which was on the bluff on the opposite side of the Red River from Fort Clark; and Fort Terry which was further up the Red River. The name Fort Sevier appears in the reports that the local engineer, Edward Sayers, made on its progress, but that is not the name commonly used today. Flag Officer Andrew Hull Foote referred to the fort, perhaps facetiously since it was undefended and flying a white flag when he arrived, as Fort Defiance in his report on Clarksville's capture, and it had a final name change to Fort Bruce after Union troops established a permanent garrison at Clarksville. It is probable that from this point in the diary when Serepta refers to "the fort," it is to the fort on the bluff in her neighborhood. The name Fort Defiance is the name applied to that fort today.

145. William Henry Leigh was the son of Henry Leigh and Nancy Lucinda Trice Leigh. 1850 Montgomery County, Tennessee, Census, family 1455; Williams, *Cabins to Castles,* 163.

146. James E. Bailey enlisted as a captain on November 29, 1861. He raised Company A of the 49th Tennessee Infantry. This unit fought at the Fort Donelson in Dover, Tennessee. Cross, *Cry Havoc,* 90–91.

147. George Barbee was probably the son of Solomon and Nancy Trice Barbee. He was 11 in 1850.

148. According to Cross, *Ordeal by Fire*, J. M. Pirtle was chaplain to Company F of the 14th Tennessee Infantry and resigned in February 1862.

149. Dr. Pirtle was probably speaking of John Mallory.

150. "E" was Ed Pettus, 12-year-old son of Thomas F. Pettus. See Chapter 1, Note 174 for more information on the Thomas F. Pettus family. Serepta's age guess for Fannie Pettus was off as well; she was 35 instead of 40.

151. On December 3, 1861, 23-year-old Medora (Dora) Brodie married 53-year-old Archibald Fletcher of Christian County, Kentucky. Montgomery County, *Tennessee, Marriage Book 3,* 116; 1860 Christian County, Kentucky, Census, Archibald D. Fletcher, 52, farmer, real estate $60,000, family 120.

152. John Garrard enlisted in the 49th Tennessee Infantry in October 1862 and was assigned to Company G. Cross, *Cry Havoc,* 125.

153. Joshua M. Rice and Wm. S. Moore, Staple and Fancy Dry Goods, was located on the south side Franklin Street. Williams, *Clarksville Directory,* 1859, reprint 1976.

154. G. E. Cooke, Watches, Jewelry, Silverware, &c, stood on the east side of Public Square. Williams, *Clarksville Directory,* 1859, reprint 1976.

155. W. M. Bailey & Benj. F. Coulter, Staple and Fancy Dry Goods, was located on northeast corner Public Square and Franklin Street. Williams, *Clarksville Directory,* 1859, reprint 1976.

156. Billie Steven was probably First Sergeant/First Lieutenant W. S. (William Stephen) Mallory, who enlisted in Company H of the 49th Tennessee Infantry on December 3, 1861, in Palmyra, Tennessee. He was captured at Fort Donelson; sent to Camp Douglas, Illinois; exchanged at Vicksburg, Mississippi; captured at Port Hudson, Louisiana; sent to Point Lookout, Maryland; and released on March 21, 1865. Cross, *Cry Havoc,* 157. William Stephen Mallory (1833–1898) was the son of Stephen Smith Mallory and his first wife, Nancy Wilson Collins Mallory.

157. Jennie was probably Lorinah Jane "Jennie" Mallory (1835–1886), sister of William Stephen Mallory.

158. John Collins was the 18-year-old son of Daniel and Henrietta Mallory Collins and youngest brother of Henrietta Jane, Lucinda Ann, William, Stephen, Alexander, and Sarah Frances (Fannie) Collins. 1850 Montgomery County, Tennessee, Census, family 306.

159. Joseph C. Gold enlisted as a first lieutenant in Company H of the 49th Tennessee Infantry on December 3, 1861. Cross, *Cry Havoc,* 127.

160. "Oh War, what horrors . . ." is a quote from Dr. John Lofland, the Milford Bard, "Thoughts," *The Poetical and Prose Writings of Dr. John Lofland, the Milford Bard* (Baltimore: John Murphy & County, 1853).

161. Ike may have been Isaac P. Howard (1840–1923), son of Meredith and Minerva Peterson Howard. He was a first lieutenant in Company G of the 14th

Tennessee Infantry. A sworn statement of the Justice of the Peace in Davidson County, Tennessee, states the resignation was accepted on November 19, 1861. Cross, *Ordeal by Fire*, 144.

162. William A. Quarles, a Clarksville lawyer, organized the 42nd Tennessee Infantry, which fought at Fort Donelson in Dover, Tennessee.

163. At the end of a church Sunday school term, children would be rewarded with a religious pamphlet, book, or perhaps a trinket or toy. It was viewed as reward and a bridge to the next level of religious training. In the fourth chapter of *Tom Sawyer*, Mark Twain writes of the children getting church tickets for rewards of memorizing Bible verses.

164. Oranges were a treat that Southerners enjoyed at Christmas.

4. January 1862–August 1862

1. George Trice, son of Bingham and Eleanor Kenner Trice, married Molly E. Ward. *Montgomery County, Tennessee Marriage Book 3*, 116.

2. Elizabeth Atkinson Trabue, mother of Tom Trabue and aunt of Quint Atkinson Jr., was the sister of Quintus Cincinnatus Atkinson, Sr.

3. Confederate Brigadier General Samuel R. Anderson commanded a brigade assigned to General William W. Loring's Division. In December 1861, Loring's Division was assigned to Stonewall Jackson and moved to Winchester, Virginia.

4. "Shinplaster" was a term for low denomination paper money. The implication was the paper could be used to plaster shins. Before regulations, banks, associations, and merchants could print paper money.

5. Emma Staton had married Thomas H. Jackson in 1855. *Tennessee Marriage Book*, 4. The 1860 Montgomery County, Tennessee, Census lists her at age 22 with her daughter, Lenora Jackson, 4, in the household of her parents, Jo and Clarissa Staton.

6. This rumor was untrue but was probably prompted by the numerous times Federal gunboats made scouting runs past Fort Henry trying to discover its strength.

7. Beulah is a Hebrew name used in the Book of Isaiah as an attribute of Israel. William Blake used the Beulah as the name of a mystical place, somewhere between earth and heaven, a dreamy paradise.

8. This report was false. The Battle for Fort Henry did not occur until February 6, 1862.

9. Billie Donelson is probably William A. Donaldson, son of William and Allatha Mallory Donaldson. Why Serepta changed the spelling of his last name is unclear. She referred to members of the Donaldson family as "Donaldson" twenty-four times before February 1862; however, after the fall of Fort Donelson, she referred to family members four times as "Donelson." Census records do not

help unravel this mystery: the 1850 Census lists the family as Dollanson and the 1860 Census names the family Donelson. Cross, *Ordeal by Fire*, 121, lists William (Billie) and his brother Rueben Ross as Donaldson.

10. Sallie Rochester Ford wrote *Grace Truman, or Love and Principle* (New York: Sheldon and County, 1860).

11. During the early part of the Battle of Mill Springs, Kentucky, bad weather made visibility poor. Confederate Brigadier General Felix Zollicoffer became convinced that his troops were firing on another Confederate unit. He rode out to reconnoiter. The unit they were firing on was actually a Union unit whose officer also rode out to reconnoiter. Zollicoffer and the Union officer met on the road and due to the rain, poor visibility, and Zollicoffer being nearsighted and wearing a raincoat, neither of them realized they were talking to the enemy until Captain Henry Fogg of Zollicoffer's staff rode out of the woods to warn him and fired on the Union officer. The Union line opened fire killing Zollicoffer.

12. Serepta was documenting the start of the building of a fort that is today called Fort Defiance. At the time the fort was being built, it was called Fort Sevier by the engineer directing its construction. The name Fort Sevier, for Tennessee's first governor John Sevier, matches names for other forts along the Tennessee and Cumberland rivers: Fort Henry, named for Confederate Senator Gustavus Adolphus Henry, and Fort Donelson named for Daniel S. Donelson, Tennessee's adjutant-general.

13. This line is from a poem titled "Thoughts," by Dr. John Lofland, published in *The Poetical and Prose Writings of Dr. John Lofland, The Milford Bard* (London: John Murphy and Company, 1853).

14. Blondel was an elite minstrel of the twelfth century, who according to legend, rescued King Richard the Lionheart from imprisonment by Duke Leopold of Austria. "Blondel the Minstrel," accessed May 9, 2012, http://www.middle-ages .org.uk/blondel-the-minstrel.htm.

15. Old Mr. Howard was Meredith Howard, husband of Minerva Peterson, and brother-in-law of Cousin Lou Peterson.

16. Old Mr. Atkinson was Thomas Walton Atkinson (1778–1862), grandfather of Tom Trabue and Quint Atkinson Jr.

17. When Serepta talked about the Battle of Fishing Creek, she was talking about the Battle of Mill Springs. Fishing Creek was a body of water in the area of Mill Springs and had to be crossed by the Union to get to the battle area. Many Civil War battles have more than one name. Only Zollicoffer and Captain Fogg were killed in the encounter with the Union officer. First Lieutenant Baily Peyton was killed leading Company A, known as the Hickory Guards, in a charge on the Union line.

18. Perhaps Confederacy lace was lace, sometimes gold, that would adorn a Confederate uniform.

19. The *Nashville Daily Union* was a Unionist newspaper, endorsed by Governor Andrew Johnson and published from 1862 to 1866. The *Chronicle* was the weekly *Clarksville Chronicle*. Serepta mentioned reading the *Courier* in several entries. It may have been the *Louisville Courier*, which combined with the *Journal* in 1868 to form the current *Louisville Courier-Journal*. The *Louisville Courier* was a pro-Confederacy newspaper.

20. Serepta must have been referring to the Battle for Fort Henry. This battle occurred, however, on February 6, 1862. The Battle for Fort Donelson did not start until February 12. Federal ironclad ships began a bombardment of Fort Henry at about 11:45 a.m. The fort surrendered at about 2 p.m. Confederates had built a series of forts on the Tennessee and Cumberland rivers to defend middle Tennessee, an important region for provisions for soldiers in the Western Theatre—Fort Henry, Fort Donelson, Fort Sevier. Fort Henry was constructed in the flood plain of the Tennessee River and it was nearly inundated by heavy rains when Flag Officer Andrew Foote's gunboats attacked.

21. Confederate General Charles Clark was sent by Mississippi Governor John J. Pettus to Hopkinsville in October to reinforce General Albert Sidney Johnston. Clark himself was inaugurated governor of Mississippi in November 1863 and served until he was forcibly removed from office by Federal troops in 1865.

22. The brigade commanded by General Charles Clark, containing the 1st and 3rd Mississippi, moved to Fort Donelson before the battle there.

23. Mr. Gold was probably Daniel Gold. He enlisted in the 49th Tennessee Infantry as a private and was appointed assistant quartermaster of Company A on December 24, 1861. He did not reenlist on September 27, 1862, when prisoners of war from the 49th were released on parole at Vicksburg, Mississippi. Cross, *Cry Havoc*, 27, 127.

24. Sy Crabtree was probably Cousin Jane Crabtree's brother-in-law. On January 27, 1864, Serepta wrote that Sy Crabtree sent word to Jane that he was at Fort Donelson, wounded, and thought he might be dying. Jane went to take care of him. Sy Crabtree may be Cyrus Weir Crabtree. Details are few, but we know he grew up in Christian County, Kentucky, had a brother named James (Jane's husband's initials were J.M.) and he did not marry until 1867, and so he might have depended on his sister-in-law for nursing. Cyrus Weir Crabtree served in Company K of the 1st Kentucky Cavalry and could well have been at the Battle of Fort Donelson. "Lopez-Edwards Family Tree," accessed January 14, 2019, http://www.ancestry.com; Confederate Kentucky Volunteers War 1861–65.

25. Serepta was referring to Tuscumbia, Alabama.

26. At dances ladies were given a card to record the names of the gentlemen to whom they had promised each dance. The card and the pencil were attached either to their gowns or their wrists for easy access.

27. On both February 12 and February 13, 1862, the ironclad *Carondelet* fired shells into Fort Donelson to try to determine the strength of its defenses.

28. Confederate Generals John B. Floyd and Gideon Pillow were instructed by General Sidney Johnston to hold Fort Donelson until the Confederate Army left Bowling Green and reached Nashville. They were then to break out of Fort Donelson and bring their army to Nashville to join the Confederate forces there. Pillow began the breakout from Fort Donelson on February 15, 1862. The whole Union army had not yet arrived at Fort Donelson, so this breakout attempt was not only successful, but rolled up the Union right flank. This action seems to have convinced Pillow that he could defend Fort Donelson, so rather than proceed to Nashville, he sent his troops back into the fort and sent off a victorious dispatch.

29. Jack was the nickname for Mary Jackson Oldham Gold. *Tennessee, Compiled Marriages, 1851–1900* shows Mary Jackson Oldham married Benjamin Knox Gold on September 18, 1860, in Montgomery County, Tennessee. Benjamin Gold was a prominent tobacconist in New Providence and Clarksville, according to *Goodspeed's Histories of Tennessee*. Mary Jackson was the daughter of Moses Oldham. The 1850 Montgomery County, Tennessee, Census lists Mary Jane, 10, in the household of Moses Oldham, farmer, 50, with Richard, 2; Rebecca, 17; Helen A., 13.

30. Serepta had gone to the home of Nathaniel Jackson and Mary Elizabeth "Cousin Mollie" Mallory Mills for safety.

31. Wearied by exposure to snow and sleet without shelter, the Confederate generals met in council the night of February 15, 1862, and discussed the possibility of fighting their way out. This plan was rejected, considering the high cost of lives. The Union was being reinforced by fresh troops. The alternate decision was made to surrender the position. Considering the possibility of either death or becoming a prisoner of war, General John B. Floyd turned command of the fort over to General Gideon Pillow and escaped down river with 1500 of his Virginia troops. Pillow, fearing the same, passed command over to General Simon Buckner and escaped with his staff across the Tennessee River in a skiff. Buckner, before surrendering, allowed Forrest to escape with 700 of his men by crossing an icy stream too deep for infantry to ford. James M. McPherson, *Battle Cry of Freedom: The Civil War Era* (New York: Oxford University Press, 1988) 401–402; Edward A. Pollard, *The First Year of the War* (Richmond, VA: West & Johnston, 1862; reprinted: London: Forgotten Books, 2015), 244–245.

32. Esq. Collins may have been William B. Collins, brother-in-law of William Mallory's brother Stephen.

33. Assistant Quartermaster Daniel Gold enlisted in the 49th Tennessee Infantry, Company A, on November 29, 1861, in Clarksville, Tennessee. He did not reenlist on September 27, 1862. Paul Wyatt, in "History of New Providence" mentioned "the genial and big hearted Dan Gold," noting that he was a tobacco auctioneer after the war. Dan Gold married Sarah A. Davie in 1856 and the couple

had a one-year-old daughter listed in the 1860 Montgomery County, Tennessee, Census, family 716.

34. Cousin Mollie F was Mary Frances Donaldson Mallory, wife of William S. Mallory (Cousin Billie), who was indeed captured as a prisoner of war when Fort Donelson was surrendered. He was sent to Camp Douglas, Illinois, and was exchanged with other members of the 49th Tennessee at Vicksburg in September 1862. Cross, *Cry Havoc*, 157. For a detailed account of life as a prisoner of war in Camp Douglas, see George Levy, *To Die in Chicago: Confederate Prisoners at Camp Douglas* (New Orleans: Pelican Publishing Company, Inc., 1999).

35. Forest Cottage appears to have been the name of Stephen Mallory's home based on the previous entry about fleeing to Uncle Steven's. Stephen Mallory was the uncle of Mary Elizabeth "Cousin Mollie" Mallory Mills.

36. Admiral Andrew Hull Foote (1806–1863) was born in Connecticut and attended West Point for a short time before leaving to join the Navy as a midshipman. Foote was highly religious and was the driving force that resulted in the Navy's stopping the issuance of rations of alcoholic beverages to sailors (spirit ration). When the war began in 1861, Foote commanded the Brooklyn Navy Yard. He was reassigned to the Western Theater to command the Brown Water Fleet. He commanded the naval attacks at both Fort Henry and Fort Donelson. He accepted the surrender of Clarksville, one of the few inland towns to surrender to the Navy.

37. The Confederate Army would continue retreating until it got to Corinth, Mississippi. This retreat left Middle and Western Tennessee open to Union occupation.

38. Cousin Nat may have been Nathaniel Jackson Mills, husband of Cousin Mollie Mallory Mills.

39. Serepta was probably referring to two men enslaved to Nathaniel and Mollie Mills.

40. The 1860 Montgomery County, Tennessee, Census lists Mary Collins, 21, and S.G. (Sarah Gold), 16, in the household of W. B. Collins, 62, real estate valued at $7,890 and personal $13,000, family 865. William B. Collins was the brother-in-law of Stephen Smith Mallory.

41. Pierre Gustave Toutant Beauregard (1818–1893) was a native of Louisiana and a graduate of West Point. He was the Confederate general who ordered the bombardment on Fort Sumter that started the Civil War. Beauregard was the commanding general at the First Battle of Bull Run. Beauregard had a strained relationship with Confederate President Jefferson Davis due to his criticism of Davis and other politicians for interfering in military decisions.

42. Sterling Price (1809–1867) was a politician from Missouri when the Civil War started. He resigned from Congress at the start of the Mexican American War and served as the colonel of the Second Missouri. He became the military governor of New Mexico and put down the Taos Revolt. After the Mexican

American War was over, he was elected governor of Missouri. When the Civil War started, he tried unsuccessfully to lead Missouri out of the Union. He assumed command of the Missouri State Guard and led them to fight for the Confederacy. By 1862, he had won the Battle of Wilson's Creek, the First Battle of Lexington, and the Battle of Pea Ridge.

43. Don Carlos Buell (1818–1898) was a native of Ohio and a West Point graduate. He fought in the Second Seminole War in Florida and in the Mexican-American War. When the Civil War started, Buell was promoted to brigadier general and helped General George McClellan train the Army of the Potomac. In November 1861, Buell was transferred to Kentucky and given command of the Army of the Ohio. He occupied Nashville in February 1862.

44. "Dutch," a variation of "Deutsch," probably referred to Americans of German descent.

45. Although he opposed the spread of slavery to new states, Lincoln, in his inaugural address, again assured the people of the South that where slavery existed, he had no power or intention of interfering with their right to own slaves. He reinforced the right of each state to control its domestic institutions. "First Inaugural Address of Abraham Lincoln," *A Compilation of the Messages and Papers of the Presidents*, vol. IV, (New York: Bureau of National Literature, Inc., 1897), 3206–3213.

46. Roaring Spring is a community northwest of Hopkinsville in Trigg County, Kentucky.

47. J. M. Pirtle resigned from the 14th Tennessee Infantry in February 1862.

48. Andrew Johnson (1808–1875) was born in North Carolina and grew up poor. He never attended school but became a successful tailor. He moved to Tennessee in 1826 and eventually became prosperous enough to acquire property and buy several slaves. Johnson was a very good public speaker and was elected to the Tennessee State Legislature in 1835 and the US House of Representatives in 1843 where he introduced the Homestead Act. Johnson was a strong Unionist and was the only Southern senator to remain loyal to the Union after his state seceded. In 1862, Lincoln appointed Johnson Tennessee's military governor. Serepta compared him to the famous Revolutionary War traitor Benedict Arnold.

49. On March 6, 1862, President Lincoln sent a message to Congress asking them to consider a plan of gradual, compensated emancipation of slaves. He wanted a joint resolution that would assure Southern states of Federal help to pay slave owners the compensation. He envisioned that the compensation would not be a reward but an aid in allowing slave owners to be able to afford to hire their former enslaved people. This plan was aimed at the boarder slave states that were still in the Union, and it was soundly rejected by them.

50. J. W. Lackey was the son-in-law of T. W. and Elizabeth Carlilse Atkinson

and brother-in-law of Elizabeth Atkinson Trabue and Quintus Cincinnatus Atkinson, Sr.

51. Brigadier General John Hunt Morgan (1825–1864) was born in Huntsville, Alabama, and moved to Kentucky at a young age. He fought in the Mexican War and liked it so much that he tried to join the Regular Army. However, the Army would not accept him, so he went into business in Lexington, Kentucky, and started a militia company called the Lexington Rifles. When the Civil War started, the Lexington Rifles stole the rifles from the Kentucky State Arsenal and slipped into Tennessee where they formed the 2nd Kentucky Cavalry. Morgan earned his nickname as "Thunderbolt of the Confederacy" by leading successful raids against Union forces in Kentucky and Tennessee.

52. Serepta was describing Morgan's attack on Gallatin, Tennessee. Gallatin was a target because the Union was using it as a supply point and attacking it would help disrupt Buell's Tennessee campaign. Morgan claimed in his report of the attack that he was motivated by the fact that 300 Union infantry soldiers were arresting citizens that had helped Morgan's troops. Morgan captured the Union infantry, burned the train station, and destroyed a railroad tunnel near the town by running a burning train into the tunnel.

53. Blanche Howard was the 15-year-old-daughter of Minerva and Meredith Howard. 1860 Montgomery County, Tennessee, Census, family 150.

54. The Battle of New Madrid, or Island Number 10, occurred between February 28 and April 8, 1862. The island in the Mississippi River about sixty miles below Columbus, Kentucky, was fortified by Confederate General P. G. T. Beauregard after the loss of Fort Henry and Fort Donelson and the evacuation of Columbus, Kentucky, as a defense of the Mississippi River. The Island is close to the city of New Madrid, Missouri, which was attacked by Union Brigadier General John Pope on March 3, 1862. The Confederate Army withdrew from New Madrid to Island Number 10 on March 13. The Union sent a flotilla of gunboats to the area under Flag Officer Andrew Foote. They provided the cover for General Pope's army to cross the river, cutting off the Confederate escape. Island Number 10 surrendered on April 8, 1862.

55. Colonel Moses M. Bane was with the 50th Illinois Infantry Volunteers. "Adjutant General's Report," 50th Illinois Infantry Regiment History, transcribed by Linda Lee, accessed May 11, 2019, https://civilwar.illinoisgenweb.org/history/o50.html.

56. Colonel Crafts J. Wright, commander of the 13th Missouri Infantry at Clarksville, "carried off two young African Americans" from the city. This caused quite a stir in town since the slaves had done no war work and were the sole support of their owner, Mrs. R. W. Thomas. Benjamin F. Cooling, *Fort Donelson's Legacy: War and Society in Kentucky and Tennessee, 1861–1863* (Knoxville: Univ. of Tennessee Press, 1997), 18–19.

57. Early in the Civil War, Federal authorities pursued a policy which was known as the "velvet glove" policy. They believed that a lenient policy would cause secessionist citizens to return their loyalty to the Union. This plan caused uneven treatment of slaves and requisitioned goods. If the Union commander was anti-slavery, slaves would not be returned to owners. Other commanders would return all slaves trying to enter their camp. Policy at first called for owners to be given receipts for all goods requisitioned. As the war progressed and Southern citizens still proved hostile, this policy was used by some commanders as a means to punish pro-Confederate citizens. In time, the policy changed so that receipts were only given to loyal Unionists. Receipts could only be collected on at the end of the war.

58. Washing butter is the step in butter production that removes excess liquid; butter is kneaded until the liquid drains out and then the butter is rinsed with water until the water runs clear.

59. As military governor, Andrew Johnson established policies to eliminate rebel influence, demanded loyalty oaths from public officials, and shut down all newspapers owned by Confederate sympathizers. He later served as Lincoln's vice president and became president during Reconstruction after Lincoln's assassination.

60. Isaac Garrett is listed as age 68 in the 1860 Christian County, Kentucky, Census, family 480, with Mary, 36, and Edmund, 22.

61. Serepta was referring to the First Battle of Kernstown, Virginia, which was the first battle in the Shenandoah Campaign. To prevent Union General Nathaniel Banks from sending troops to General George McClellan for an attack on Richmond, Virginia, Stonewall Jackson attacked on March 23. March 23 was a Sunday, and Jackson tried to avoid fighting on the Sabbath. He was forced to do so because the Union could see his troop deployment. He thought Banks only had 3,000 troops and did not realize that General James Shields was also in the area bringing the Union total to 9,000 troops to Jackson's 4,000. This battle was one of Jackson's few defeats.

62. Following the fall of Fort Donelson in February 1862, publication of the *Clarksville Chronicle* was suspended and did not resume until July 1865. The *Clarksville Jeffersonian* also had its publication stopped about the same time. Both papers did put out an occasional extra edition as evidenced by Serepta's mention of a *Jeffersonian* extra in her September 22, 1862, entry.

63. This information was incorrect. General Sidney Johnston's Confederate troops were at Corinth, Mississippi, and moved out on April 3, 1862, to attack Union troops at Shiloh, Tennessee. They would engage the Union on April 6, 1862.

64. Clarksville attorney James O. Shackleford was in partnership with Gustavus Adolphus Henry, Sr. His son Robert was in Company A, 14th Tennessee Infantry.

Robert was killed in action July 2, 1863, at Gettysburg, Pennsylvania. Cross, *Ordeal by Fire*, 186.

65. Elsey Trice married Fannie Pettus on April 8, 1862, *Montgomery County Marriage Book 3*, 118. Frances Pettus was the daughter of Mary M. Watson Pettus and Stephen Pettus (deceased).

66. On April 6, 1862, Confederate General Albert Sidney Johnston was worried about the performance of some of his inexperienced units and elected to lead them in battle himself. During a charge on Union lines, he was struck in the back of his knee by a bullet. It hit the popliteal artery, which is a branch of the femoral artery. Damage to this artery meant that he would bleed to death in a very short time. His doctor was attending to wounded soldiers and returned too late to save Johnston. Scholars today believe that possible nerve damage from an old dueling wound prevented Johnston from realizing he was wounded.

67. The Battle of Pittsburg Landing, or Shiloh, was fought on April 6 and 7, 1862. Confederate troops under Albert Sidney Johnston left Corinth, Mississippi, on April 3, arriving at Pittsburg Landing on April 6. Confederate forces were spotted by a Union patrol at dawn. Johnston attacked, surprising the main body of Union troops who were either sleeping or just eating breakfast. Many Union units had no previous experience and broke and ran. The Union Army was driven back two miles but managed to hold until reinforced by the troops of Union General Don Carlos Buell. The Confederates, who were exhausted from the previous day's battle, were forced to retire to Corinth. Union casualties were 13,000 out of a strength of 62,000. Confederates lost 10,000 casualties out of a troop strength of 23,000. Shiloh shocked the nation because of the high number of casualties.

68. Mr. Blakemore may have been W. T. Blakemore. 1860 Shelby County, Tennessee Census, family 596.

69. Fort Pillow was a Confederate-constructed fortification 40 miles north of Memphis. After Island Number 10 fell, Fort Pillow was the last obstacle to the Union capture of Memphis. On April 14, 1862, Fort Pillow was bombarded by the Western Flotilla made up of a number of gunboats and ironclads under Flag Officer Charles H. Davis. It would take over a month before the Confederates abandoned Fort Pillow to the Union.

70. A hogshead of sugar standard was 1000 pounds; however, the amount could vary from 800 to 1,200. Kenneth Follett, "Documenting Louisiana Sugar 1845–1917," accessed April 28, 2017, http://www.sussex.ac.uk/louisianasugar/sources/champomier.

71. Ike Howard was the son of Meredith and Minerva Howard. 1850 Montgomery County, Tennessee, Census, family 1469.

72. First Lieutenant James B. Howard, son of Meredith and Minerva Peterson Howard, was indeed a prisoner of war, having been captured at the fall of Fort Donelson in February 1862. Records show he was sent to Johnson's Island, Ohio,

on March 16, 1862, and exchanged at Vicksburg, Mississippi, on September 1, 1862. So, what he was doing in Saint Louis in April 1862 is a bit of a mystery. Cross, *Cry Havoc*, 140–141; 1850 Montgomery County, Tennessee, Census, family 1469.

73. Missouri was a Border State during the Civil War, and like all Border States, the population was divided in its loyalties. The former governor, Sterling Price, was a hardline pro-Southerner who led militia forces in the field against Union troops. St. Louis was a Mississippi River port of great strategic importance. The largest pro-Southern group in the city were Irish immigrants who distrusted and feared a strong central government. When Union forces under General Nathaniel Lyon captured the pro-Southern forces at Camp Jackson, they marched their prisoners through the streets of St. Louis. Taunting by the crowd and the throwing of dirt and stones led the Union Home Guard to fire into the crowd. Twenty-eight people were killed or wounded. This action led to a rise in pro-Southern sympathies. Ultimately, Union forces prevailed in keeping Missouri and St. Louis in the Union.

74. Serepta seems to have been describing the first day of battle at Shiloh/ Pittsburgh Landing. In late April, Confederate forces were at Corinth, Mississippi, recovering from the bloody Battle of Shiloh. There were no battles at this time. Union General Henry Halleck had come to Pittsburg Landing and taken command from General Ulysses S. Grant. Halleck reorganized Grant's army and with reinforcements that raised the number of Union troops to 100,000 men, started marching toward Corinth at the end of April. Because Halleck insisted that the army entrench every night when they stopped, it took him a month to bring the army the 22 miles between Pittsburg Landing and Corinth.

75. The Battle of Shiloh got its name from a one-room log Methodist meeting house. Union General William T. Sherman's division camped on the grounds of the church and formed his first battle line there on April 6, 1862, when the Confederates attacked. He fought for two hours before he withdrew. The Confederates established a headquarters at the church after the Union withdrew.

76. Union Brigadier General Benjamin Mayberry Prentiss (1819 – 1901) was born in Belleville, Virginia, but moved to Missouri at a young age. He raised a company of volunteers to fight in the Mexican American War. He remained active in the state militia and when the Civil War broke out, he was placed in charge of Cairo, Illinois. In August 1861, he was promoted to brigadier general and was placed in charge of a division in General U. S. Grant's Army of the Tennessee. He fought at the Battle of Shiloh, Tennessee, where he found himself in command of the troops fighting in the Hornet's Nest when General W. H. L. Wallace was mortally wounded. His troops held out for another half-hour against Confederate troops, who had surrounded the position and had the Union troops in a murderous cross fire. At 5:30 p.m. he surrendered 2,250 Union soldiers to the encircling Confederates.

77. Barker's Mill is located in the southeast corner of Christian County, Kentucky,

near the Tennessee line. It consisted primarily of land owned by Chiles T. Barker (1816–1898) and Josiah Carneal (1810–1896). The Mill is on the West Fork Creek. Later, Barkers Mill community had a store, post office, blacksmith shop, cooperage, two schools (one for whites and one for African-Americans), a church, and a cemetery.

78. The surrender of New Orleans was a Brown Water Navy victory. The Confederates counted on eight ironclads to block Union movement down the Mississippi River and had 3,000 militia troops to defend the city from land attack. Union Admiral David Farragut ran 24 gunboats, 19 mortar boats, and 15,000 soldiers past two defensive forts to capture the city. Confederate General Mansfield Lovell surrendered New Orleans on April 29, 1862.

79. On May 7, 1862, Union General John Pope sent a small force forward of the Union position to see if rumors were true that the Confederates were retreating from Corinth, Mississippi. At the same time, the Confederates launched a feeble, unsuccessful attack on the Union line. They retreated back to their fortified line in Corinth. On May 5, 1862, Union Calvary surprised John Hunt Morgan at dawn. In the ensuing skirmish, Morgan and most of his men escaped. This skirmish marked the Federal Calvary coming into its own as a fighting force.

80. On May 11, 1862, Morgan with 150 men captured the train station and the telegraph office in the little railroad town of Cave City, Kentucky. In the train station was a train that the raiders set fire to and sent it running south down the tracks with no one on board. While the raiders were in Cave City, another train came into the station headed south. Morgan captured this train that contained Union soldiers, women, and $6000 in cash. Morgan paroled the soldiers, kept the cash, and allowed the women to return to Louisville on the train.

81. The Battle of Yorktown, or Siege of Yorktown, lasted from April 5 to May 4, 1862, and the Battle of Williamsburg took place on May 5, 1862. On April 5, Union Major General George B. McClellan's Army of the Potomac encountered Major General John B. Magruder's small Confederate force at Yorktown, Virginia. McClellan suspended his march up the Peninsula toward Richmond and settled in for a siege of Magruder's fortifications. McClellan planned a massive bombardment for dawn on May 5, but the Confederate army slipped away during the night of May 3 toward Williamsburg. On May 5, Union General Joseph Hooker caught up with the Confederate rear guard. He led an unsuccessful assault on a Confederate-occupied earthen-walled fort on the Williamsburg Road. Confederates under James Longstreet counterattacked and nearly broke the Union left flank. The timely arrival of Union reinforcements stabilized the Union line. The Confederate forces continued their retreat during the night. The Battle of Williamsburg is considered the first pitched battle of Union General McClellan's Peninsula Campaign. Serepta reported in her May 31, 1862, entry that the 14th Tennessee was involved in this battle.

82. On May 11, 1862, the Confederate Navy blew up the *CSS Virginia*, the

famous ironclad that had fought in the Battle of Hampton Roads earlier in the year. The Union had occupied Norfolk, Virginia, and the *CSS Virginia* was not seaworthy and could not go up the James River because she had too deep a draft for the river's water level. Serepta referred to the *Virginia* as the *Merrimack* because the *CSS Virginia* was built from the remains of the steam frigate *USS Merrimack,* which was scuttled when Virginia left the Union.

83. George Brinton McClellan (1826–1885) graduated second in his class at West Point and served during the Mexican War. Following the war, he returned to West Point as an instructor. At the start of the Civil War, he was appointed Major General of Volunteers by the governor of Ohio. He was named General-in-Chief of the Union Army in November of 1861 when Winfield Scott retired from that position. He reorganized and retrained the Army, winning the nickname "Little Mac" from the soldiers. Though brilliant at organization, McClellan was cautious and slow moving as a commander in the field. He constantly complained of being outnumbered by the enemy although he rarely was.

84. Unless Serepta was talking about the first day of the Battle of Shiloh, this was an incorrect report. On May 7, 1862, there was a skirmish when a Union reconnaissance force investigating reports that the Confederates were evacuating Corinth was attacked by the Confederates. The Union withdrew back into their lines.

85. Mr. Peterson was probably Isaac Peterson, 42, farmer, listed in the 1860 Montgomery County, Tennessee, Census, with M. A. (Mary Ann Long Peterson), 29, female, and James Howard, 21. James Howard was the son of Meredith and Minerva Peterson Howard. Isaac Rowland Peterson III was the brother of Charles and Louisa Peterson and Minerva Peterson Howard.

86. C. Wallace Cross Jr., in *Ordeal by Fire,* reported that while the 14th Tennessee Infantry was encamped at Yorktown, Virginia, they underwent a reorganization because the men had enlisted for only twelve months. Captain Edward Hewitt of Company L retired at the reorganization on April 27, 1862. He was replaced by John Mallory.

87. Uncle Tom Campbell of Christian County, Kentucky, was married to Mary "Pollie" Trice. Mollie and Pollie were common nicknames for Mary. Pollie Campbell was the sister of Bingham, Elizabeth, Leigh, Jesse James, Nace, May, Jane, Thomas Alexander, Greenberry, Elsey, and Nancy Barbee.

88. Marion was probably Jane Crabtree's daughter rather than her sister.

89. George T. Barbee was the 13-year-old son of William P. and Susanna Trice Barbee. 1860 Montgomery County, Tennessee, Census, family 702.

90. Lafayette is a community located northwest of New Providence in Christian County, Kentucky.

91. Dr. Bacon was probably 24-year-old Charles P. Bacon, listed in the 1860 Trigg County, Kentucky, Census (penned), family 1107.

92. The Confederacy had a real problem with currency. There were only twenty

paper mills in the Confederate States. The CSA also had a problem making coinage since almost all of their metal was being used in the war effort. At first, the Confederate national government did not tax heavily and left the money shortage problems up to the states to solve. When the individual states issued their own bonds and paper money, it led to inflation.

93. Flux is an old term for dysentery. It also was a term for menstruation.

94. A newspaper named the *Louisville Daily Express* was published for the year of 1869 only. This paper may have been a short-lived forerunner of the later newspaper.

95. On May 23, 1862, Confederate General Stonewall Jackson was determined to drive Union General Nathaniel Banks out of the Shenandoah Valley. He hit Banks's eastern flank at Front Royal. Jackson had about 3,000 men to the Union's 1,000. The Union forces held on for two hours before they had to retreat across two forks of the Shenandoah River. The Union forces attempted to burn the bridges across these two forks to slow down the pursuit but were unsuccessful. Confederate cavalry caught the Union forces and decimated them. The Union suffered 900 casualties to 56 Confederate casualties.

96. A shoat is a piglet that has been weaned.

97. On May 5, 1862, units of General George McClellan's army under Major Generals Joseph Hooker and Philip Kearny clashed with rearguard divisions of Lieutenant Generals James Longstreet and D. H. Hill. Long, *Day by Day*.

98. Judges 10:13–14: Yet ye have forsaken me, and served other gods: wherefore I will deliver you no more. Go and cry unto the gods which ye have chosen; let them deliver you in the time of your tribulation. KJV.

99. Campbellites were followers of Alexander Campbell (1788–1866), a religious leader of the Restoration Movement, which stressed reliance on scripture. The Disciples of Christ, Christian and Churches of Christ developed from his teaching.

100. Almeda Pettus was the daughter of Stephen (deceased) and Mary Watson Pettus and sister of Fannie Pettus, Thomas Pettus, and Sallie Pettus Grinstead. Obituary Mary (Watson) Pettus, *Clarksville Weekly Chronicle*, July 21, 1877, 3; Obituary Thomas F. Pettus, *Clarksville Weekly Chronicle*, July 10, 1875, 3.

101. On May 30, 1862, the Union army entered Corinth, Mississippi, to find the Confederate army gone. Brigadier General P. G. T. Beauregard had kept campfires burning and mounted fake artillery manned by mannequins to buy time to get his army out. The Union brought 100,000 troops to the siege of a Confederate army numbering about 65,000.

102. Union General George B. McClellan had followed the Confederate Army up the James Peninsula with the Confederates under General Joseph Johnston retiring until gaining the Richmond, Virginia, perimeter. On May 31, 1862, a storm hit the area that made the ground held by McClellan hard to move in. The Chickahominy River had risen and was flowing fast. This threatened to split the

two wings of the Union Army. With these favorable conditions, Johnston attacked. Unfortunately, confusion caused a delay in the attack, and McClellan was able to bring up reinforcements, avoiding defeat. The big result of this battle was that Johnston was wounded, causing the appointment of Robert E. Lee to replace him as the head of the Confederate Army.

103. While women had worked as private tutors for families, teaching was primarily a male occupation. This is the beginning of women becoming teachers. By the next generation, female teachers were common, in part because women could be paid less than men.

104. On June 6, 1862, the Union sent five ironclads and two rams under Flag Officer Charles H. Davis and Colonel Charles Ellet against eight Confederate rams under Captain James E. Montgomery and General M. Jeff Thompson. The battle lasted for about ninety minutes and was a Union victory. Only one Confederate ship got away. The city of Memphis was surrendered to Davis soon after the battle.

105. Vicksburg was a fortified city on the Mississippi halfway between New Orleans, Louisiana and Memphis and was the only obstacle to total Union control of the Mississippi River. The attempt to capture Vicksburg began on May 18, 1862, and then settled into a siege that would last for more than a year.

106. The First Battle of Fair Oaks, or Seven Pines, was part of Union General George McClellan's Peninsula campaign in Virginia. On May 31, 1862, Confederate General Joseph Johnston attacked McClellan, whose army was on swampy ground along the Chickahominy River. Due to inexperience, the Confederate attack was delayed long enough for McClellan to bring up reinforcements and the Confederates were driven back. The Union Army suffered 5,000 casualties and the Confederate Army 6,000. This battle made McClellan more cautious and timid in battle.

107. The 1860 Montgomery County, Tennessee, Census lists Jane T. Crabtree, 32, housekeeper, with Florence, 11; Robert, 8; and Mary, 5. However, the entries on her dress and singing suggest that Cousin Jane's younger daughter may have been named Marion rather than Mary.

108. "Her Bright Smile Haunts Me" was a popular song with Confederates. It was composed by W. T. Wrighton, with lyrics by J. E. Carpenter, published by John C. Schreiner & Son, Macon. "Image of 'Her bright smile haunts me still,'" Library of Congress, accessed July 21, 2017, https://www.loc.gov/resource/ihas .200002476.0/?sp=2.

109. Serepta was referring to the Battle of Seven Pines. Confederate General Joseph Johnston had settled into a strong defensive position around Richmond, Virginia. Union General George McClellan's position had his army straddling the Chickahominy River. This position enabled McClellan to bring up supplies and heavy siege guns. The battle started on May 31, 1862, when Johnston attacked Union forces south of the Chickahominy River and drove the Union troops back.

The Confederates on the battle line received reinforcements and attacked the Union second line of defense, which was driven back further. During the night both sides received further reinforcements. The Confederates resumed the attack the next day but were unsuccessful in breaking the Union line. They withdrew to earthworks west of Seven Pines and the battle ended. The two big results of this battle were McClellan's drive to take Richmond ended, and Joseph Johnston was wounded prompting his replacement by Robert E. Lee.

110. John D. Martin, son of William R. and Louisa Burney Martin, was the assistant surgeon for the 14th Tennessee Infantry. The 1860 Montgomery County, Tennessee, Census, family 352, lists his occupation as farmer and his older brother, David B. as physician. 1850 Census Montgomery County Tennessee, family 1400; Cross, *Ordeal by Fire*, 160; *Appendix I, Field and Staff Officers;* "William R. Martin, Overview," Ancestry.com, accessed May 3, 2013, http://trees.ancestry .com/tree/12825626/person/12175433182?ssrc=.

111. Thomas "Stonewall" Jackson (1824–1863) was a West Point graduate (17th out of a class of 59), who at the start of the Civil War was an artillery instructor at the Virginia Military Institute. He served in the Mexican War gaining the rank of brevet major and a public congratulation from General Winfield Scott for his outstanding performance. He resigned from the Army to become a professor at VMI in 1852. He was given the rank of brigadier general in June 1861 by the Confederate government. He earned his nickname, Stonewall, at the First Battle of Bull Run when an officer trying to rally his troops to attack told them, "There is Jackson, standing like a stone wall." Serepta was referring here to Jackson's Shenandoah Valley Campaign.

112. Muslin was a lighter weight fabric than others available during the mid-nineteenth century. This reference indicates that the weather was warm.

113. This comment seems clearly to indicate that the Jeff Davis bonnets had become the accepted fashion of the Confederacy. Since Hopkinsville was in Kentucky and still part of the Union, this regular style bonnet, "Yankee looking" would still be appropriate.

114. The stereoscope became popular in Europe in 1851 when Queen Victoria was enchanted with it at the Crystal Palace Exhibition in London. A stereoscope presents two slightly different images of the same thing to the two eyes resulting in a 3-D image. Stereoscopes held widespread appeal in the United States in 1860.

115. Dunstable straw was a fabric of woven or plaited straw, originally made in Dunstable, England. *Century Dictionary and Cyclopedia*, s.v. "Dunstable," accessed May 3, 2013, http://www.wordnik.com/words/dunstable.

116. Lasting is the process of attaching the sole of the shoe to the upper part of the shoe. This process was done by hand until 1883 when Jan Matzeliger, a black cobbler, invented a machine that could do this. By hand, an experienced laster could complete fifty pairs of shoes in a ten-hour day. Matzeliger's machine could complete seven hundred in a day, making shoes much more affordable. Gaiters,

today, are coverings separate from the shoe and fastened around the ankle and calf to protect the leg while hiking. It seems here that Serepta was talking about a pair of shoes that covered the leg higher than the ankle.

117. Serepta's reference to the warm evening being an excuse to wear the new Swiss suggests she may have been referring to the fabric of her dress, Dotted Swiss, a sheer cotton fabric embellished with small dots. Dotted Swiss is said to date back to around 1750 in the textile center of St. Gallen, Switzerland.

118. Serepta was again referring to the Battle of Seven Pines. Confederate casualties in this battle were estimated at 13,736 out of a force totaling 39,000.

119. A Jeff Davis bonnet was made of calico and gingham and supposedly designed by Varina Davis, the First Lady of the Confederacy. These bonnets were popular in parts of the South controlled by the Union because they were inexpensive and hid the face so that Union soldiers could not see it. "Short Rounds: Generals' Threads," Strategy Page, accessed May 11, 2017, www.strategypage.com /cic/docs/cic236b.asp.

120. Eugene was probably one of Elsey Trice's slaves.

121. Old Mrs. Evans was probably 56-year-old Maria H. Evans. 1860 Census Christian County, Kentucky, (penned), family 110.

122. Tomy G. was the 21-year-old son of Richard and Sarah Pettus Grinstead. 1850 Census Todd County Kentucky, family 464. Sarah Pettus Grinstead was the sister of Fannie Pettus Trice.

123. Serepta was describing the Battle of Glendale, also known as the Battle of Frayser's Farm, which took place on June 30, 1862. It was the fifth of what are known as the Seven Days' Battles. The Union Army was in retreat after the Battle of Savage's Station, and the Confederate Army caught up with them near Glendale. Their attack routed a Union division and the division's commander, General George A. McCall, was captured. A counterattack by the Union sealed the break in the Union line. Another Confederate attack on the Union left flank was driven off by Union gunboats. The fight was inconclusive. Confederate casualties were 3,673 and Union casualties were 3,797.

124. This entry indicates that the Union occupied not only Fort Defiance on the bluff in New Providence but also used Fort Clark, which was nearer Clarksville proper (behind what is now Two Rivers Mall). If the firing had been from Fort Defiance, it would have been almost in Serepta's backyard.

125. At the start of the war, the Union had forty-two warships in its navy and many established ship yards. The Confederate Navy had no ships and one established ship yard in Norfolk, Virginia, which the Union failed to destroy before they abandoned it. Confederate capacity for manufacturing steam engines and iron plate for the ships was limited by lack of skilled workers and scarce supplies of iron. They did attempt to have ironclad ships built in Europe but aside from acquiring two rams, this effort failed mainly due to lack of funds. The Confederacy completed at

least eight ironclads: *CSS Tennessee, Atlanta, Chicora, North Carolina, Palmetto State, Raleigh, Mississippi,* and, of course, the *CSS Virginia.* Confederates destroyed their own ironclads to prevent capture; some were not completed before destruction.

126. Reny Ogburn may have been Irene Ogburn (1844–1930), daughter of Mary Ann Caroline Hunt Ogburn and the late John Noble Ogburn.

127. The 1860 Montgomery County, Tennessee, Census lists William B. Collins's daughters in the household as Mary, 21; V. J. (Virginia Jane), 18; S. G. (Sarah Gold), 16; and S. M. A. (Susan Martha Ann), 13.

128. Miss Cowherd was 62-year-old Anna Coward (Cowherd). 1860 Montgomery County, Tennessee Census, family 871.

129. Joseph Hatcher had been discharged from the 14th Tennessee Infantry in October 1861. Cross, *Ordeal by Fire,* 137.

130. Serepta was referring to the last of the Battles of Seven Days, the Battle of Malvern Hill. Also known as the Seven Days' Campaign, the fighting occurred from June 25 to July 1, 1862, and encompassed seven battles. General George McClellan had a strong defensive position on Malvern Hill just north of the James River. General Robert E. Lee's Confederate Army repeatedly, unsuccessfully attacked the position.

131. McClellan's Union Army was approximately 100,000 men strong. The Confederates had approximately 92,000 troops.

132. Serepta was talking about the fifth battle of the Seven Days' Campaign called the Battle of Glendale. On June 25, 1862, a Confederate attempt to turn the Union left flank was halted by fire from Federal gunboats in the James River.

133. Young Trice was probably Private James E. Trice. On May 19, 1862, he appeared on a Register of Chimborazo Hospital No. 5, in Richmond. His Certificate of Disability for Discharge issued June 24, 1862, states "Injury to the hip joint and knee. . . is in all probably permanently disabled from marching." *Fold 3,* Civil War Service Records-Confederate, accessed May 8, 2013, www.fold3.com/image /#71033018.

134. The 14th Tennessee Infantry fought at the Battle of Gaines' Mill, Battle of Glendale, and the Battle of Malvern Hill. The 14th lost approximately 28 killed in the Seven Days' Campaign.

135. John Hunt Morgan raided Cave City, Kentucky, on May 11, 1862, and spent only one day there. In July 1862, Morgan began his First Kentucky Raid from Knoxville, Tennessee. He first raided Tompkinsville, then Glasgow, and Horse Cave, Kentucky. By July 11, 1862, Morgan and his Raiders were in Saloma, Kentucky. Later that evening, Morgan was involved in a skirmish at New Market, Kentucky. He arrived in Lebanon, Kentucky, on July 12, 1862.

136. On July 13, 1862, Nathan Bedford Forrest arrived in Murfreesboro at about 4:30 a.m. He intended to free local men held in the jail on charges of aiding

the Confederates. The Union troops were caught sleeping. Forrest's men quickly captured the 7th Pennsylvania Cavalry but encountered stiff resistance from the 9th Michigan. While the fight was going on, someone set the jail on fire. Forrest and a battalion of men managed to rescue the prisoners from the burning jail. Union Brigadier General T. T. Crittenden was captured when Forrest's troops set fire to the courthouse to flush out Union officers who had taken up position there. Although a report was turned in stating that two brigadier generals were captured, Forrest only captured one. He did capture four colonels and three units.

137. On July 17, 1862, John Hunt Morgan encountered Union resistance as he was crossing Licking River Bridge. After a sharp fight, Morgan captured the Union defenders and 300 horses. He destroyed the Cynthiana railroad depot, railroad tracks, and the Union camp. Cynthiana is 29 miles north of Lexington, Kentucky.

138. John 1:1: That which was from the beginning, which we have heard, which we have seen with our eyes, which we have looked upon, and our hands have handled, of the Word of life. KJV.

139. The 1860 Montgomery County, Tennessee, Census lists Mary Cook, 13, in the household of Samuel R. Cook, 52, brick mason, and N. J., 42, with Samuel, 18; Martha, 15; Louisa, 10; Mary Barksdale, 70; and M. J. Davidson, female, 22, family 856.

140. Nannie Grinstead was probably one of Sallie Pettus Grinstead's daughters. She and Mary Cook may have been going to visit Nannie's grandmother, Mary Watson Pettus, or her aunt, Martha A. Cowherd Pettus.

141. Southerners found creative ways to circumvent the US Postal system when trying to send mail to people in the North.

142. Thomas Woodward organized the Oak Grove Rangers in April 1861. They were accepted into the Confederate Army as two companies in the 1st Kentucky Cavalry on one-year enlistments. They were mustered out and disbanded on June 25, 1862, upon the completion of their enlistment. Many of the men enlisted in other units. Woodward went on to raise another unit, the 2nd Kentucky Cavalry, which was later renumbered to the 15th Kentucky Cavalry.

143. The main Confederate Army was occupying Chattanooga from July 23 through August 8, 1862, so the "Rebels" Serepta reported were probably Partisan Ranger Groups. John Hunt Morgan was on his Kentucky Raid during this time. Nathan Bedford Forrest was definitely in Tennessee at this time.

144. It is unclear where this information came from. At this time, Colonel Rodney Mason of the 71st Ohio was the Union commander of Clarksville. His troops were quartered at Stewart College (where Austin Peay State University is located today). He had 300 soldiers at Clarksville at the time and would surrender the garrison without a shot in August 1862 to Confederate partisan groups under Colonel Adam Rankin "Stovepipe" Johnson and Colonel Thomas Woodward.

5. August 1862–June 1863

1. That date would be July 29, 1862.

2. Serepta was visiting Alley Trice Waller, her husband Lewis, and children Frank, Bailey and Lilly. Alley was the daughter of James Pinhook and Zelpha Mallory Trice.

3. Steven Edward Trice and William Lewis Trice were Alley Trice Waller's brothers.

4. Colonel Adam Rankin "Stovepipe" Johnson received the name "Stovepipe" on July 18, 1862, when he raided Newburgh, Indiana, seizing a store of weapons at a riverside warehouse and capturing eighty Union soldiers by positioning two cannons across the river pointing at the town. The cannons were actually dummies made of blackened logs and stovepipes. The same ruse was used at Clarksville on August 18, 1862, when Colonel Thomas Woodward's Oak Grove Rangers and Johnson's partisans liberated the town, capturing Colonel Rodney Mason and the 71st Ohio soldiers stationed there. George W. Geib, *Adam Johnson's Raid on Newburgh*, accessed May 13, 2019, https://www.in.gov/history/3992.htm; *Recapture of Clarksville*, accessed May 13, 2019, https://www.historicalmarker project.com/markers/HM1ASS_recapture-of-clarksville_Clarksville-TN.html.

5. This would be the week of August 10–16, 1862. Colonel Adam Rankin "Stovepipe" Johnson issued a proclamation on August 11, 1862, while he was headquartered in Union County, Kentucky. He raided Hopkinsville, Kentucky, because he needed more rifles for the men he recruited while in Union County. According to his account, he took Hopkinsville from the Home Guard. He needed more ammunition so he left for Clarksville, Tennessee, on the evening of August 17, 1862, arriving in Clarksville at dawn the next day. Adam Rankin Johnson, *The Partisan Rangers of the Confederate States Army*, William J. Davis, ed., (Louisville, KY: G.G. Fetter Company, 1904), accessed February 3, 2019, https://archive.org /details/partisanrangersooojohn; OR Vol. 16, Serial No. 22, 225, Report of Colonel Adam Rankin Johnson, Kentucky Partisan Rangers, C. S. Army, of operations from June 11–September 1862.

6. Colonel Rodney Mason of the 71st Ohio was commander of Clarksville and had 300 men quartered at Stewart College. He was bluffed into believing the Confederate strength was larger than it was. Adam Rankin Johnson and Thomas Woodward together had about 300 men. The Clarksville garrison was surrendered without firing a shot.

7. On August 19, 1862, Miss Tennie Moore presented Colonel Adam Rankin Johnson with a silk banner that she claimed the Union soldiers had been looking actively for. It was made for the 14th Tennessee Infantry but they had been unable to get it to this regiment. It was hidden by an enslaved woman. The flag presented was undoubtedly the First National Flag of the Confederate States of America,

which was the official national flag until May 1863. Johnson, *The Partisan Rangers*, 355.

8. Mr. Homer may have been referring to the contentious presidential election of 1844. Tennessean Democrat James K. Polk defeated Whig Henry Clay. Clarksvillians Cave Johnson and Gustavus Henry debated, Johnson spoke for Clay and Henry spoke for Polk on July 1, 1844. A main issue was annexation of Texas and the expansion of slavery. The *Clarksville Weekly Chronicle,* July 2, described the debate and a massive American flag by the Whig Ladies of Clarksville. The *Chronicle* said Henry won and The *Jeffersonian* said that Johnson won.

9. The paroled prisoners were part of the 71st Ohio, which was at Fort Donelson at this time. The soldiers did not head home but went to Dover and rejoined the Regiment. Colonel Rodney Mason was later cashiered out of the Army for surrendering Clarksville.

10. On August 25, 1862, Thomas Woodward tried to bluff the garrison at Fort Donelson into surrender. The commander had already heard the details of the surrender of Clarksville from the paroled soldiers that had returned to the Regiment. He requested help from the garrison at Fort Henry which brought Colonel William Lowe and his Iowa Cavalry to his aid. After a 30-minute battle, Woodward determined that he could not take Fort Donelson and retreated toward Clarksville with Colonel Lowe and the Iowa Cavalry hot on his trail. Adam Rankin Johnson did not participate due to a warning that a Federal unit was headed toward Munfordville, Kentucky, where he had left a large stash of supplies. He and his men left Clarksville to protect these supplies.

11. Cousins Lourane and Jennie M were probably Laurana Donaldson (1825–1885), daughter of Allatha and William Donaldson, and Lorinah Jane "Jennie" Mallory, daughter of Stephen Smith and Nancy Wilson Collins Mallory. A number of Mallory/Trice/Collins/Donaldson cousins were named Laurana, Lourana, Lorinah, Loraniah, Lorana after their grandmother, Lorainah Sims Mallory (1772–1846).

12. Cousin M could have been Cousin Mary, Mary Elizabeth Mallory Morris (1831–1913), daughter of Stephen Smith and Nancy Wilson Collins Mallory, or she could have been Cousin Mollie, Mary Elizabeth Mallory Mills, daughter of William and Lucinda Draper Mallory.

13. This phrase is a variation of John Bunyon's quote in *Pilgrims Progress,* "Every fat (vat) must upstand on his bottom."

14. There are two Sulphur Springs, both northwest of New Providence. One is near Fletchers Fork and one near Dry Fork Branch.

15. Colonel Dortch was probably Captain John B. Dortch. He was the grandson of Governor Willie Blount and nephew of Cave Johnson, Postmaster General during President James K. Polk's administration. He had enlisted November 1861 in the 50th Tennessee Infantry and fought at Fort Donelson. Following the surrender he escaped with some of his men. In April Governor Isham Harris authorized

him to raise a company of Partisan Rangers, which he took to Kentucky, and in August he was assigned to Company G, 7th Kentucky Cavalry, part of John Hunt Morgan's division.

16. Serepta was actually talking about a series of battles, or skirmishes, known as Rappahannock Station that occurred between August 22 and 25, 1862. The two armies fought a series of inconclusive minor battles along the Rappahannock River at Waterloo Bridge, Lee Springs, Freeman's Ford, and Sulphur Springs, which culminated with Stonewall Jackson capturing Bristoe Station and destroying federal supplies near Manassas Junction. Estimated casualties from these engagements were 225 in total.

17. Serepta was talking about the Second Battle of Bull Run, or Manassas, not the Battle of Culpeper Court House, which occurred on September 13, 1862. Union General John Pope was caught between Confederate General Stonewall Jackson's cavalry and Confederate General James Longstreet's force at Manassas Junction (the site of an earlier battle), forcing Pope to retire toward Washington, D.C.

18. On August 27, 1862, Stonewall Jackson captured and destroyed a large Union supply depot at Manassas Junction. On August 29, 1862, in the Second Battle of Manassas, federal troops fought with Jackson's troops, who had taken positions in the woods. General Robert E. Lee arrived with reinforcements allowing Jackson to counterattack. This action forced Pope to withdraw from his defensive line along the Rappahannock River.

19. Captain George A. Harrell was killed August 15, 1862, at Cedar Run, Virginia. Cross, *Ordeal by Fire*, 136.

20. Union Colonel William Lowe and his 5th Iowa Cavalry pursued Colonel Thomas Woodward and his men from Dover.

21. William Marr had joined A. R. "Stovepipe" Johnson's 10th Kentucky Partisan Rangers, which fought with the Confederacy on August 15, 1862, in Clarksville.

22. Serepta was describing the Battle of Riggins Hill. Colonel William Lowe, 5th Iowa Cavalry, reported that according to Confederate Colonel Thomas G. Woodward, there were seventeen killed and from forty to fifty wounded. Some of Woodward's men were buried on the field and others taken to New Providence and Clarksville. *Report of W. W. Lowe, OR*, Chap. XXVIII, 955–956.

23. Jo Jones may have been Brevet Second Lieutenant J. M. Jones, an officer in the Oak Grove Rangers mustered into service June 25, 1861, near Camp Boone, Montgomery County, Tennessee, under the captainship of Thomas G. Woodward. William Henry Perrin, ed., *County of Christian, Kentucky: Historical and Biographical* (Louisville: F. A. Battey Publishing Company, 1884), accessed December 29, 2017, www.westernkyhistory.org/christian/perrin/index.html.

24. G. Marr was possibly, G. L. Marr, 26, male, listed in the 1860 Montgomery County, Tennessee, Census in the household of E. S. Marr, 63, female. George L. Marr served as a private in the 10th Kentucky Cavalry, Company B.

25. Denison and his family were James Denison, a shoemaker from New York, his wife and 3-year-old son. The other Lincolnites may have been John McHaber, a carpenter also from New York, his wife, and three children ages 12, 7, and 5. 1860 Census Montgomery County, Tennessee, family 663.

26. Union soldiers appropriated horses and livestock from locals.

27. All of these rumors were false. Union General Don Carlos Buell was in Kentucky trying to stop an invasion by Confederate General Braxton Bragg. General Nathan Bedford Forrest was in Mississippi. General John Hunt Morgan had just finished his first Kentucky Raid but was not in the area.

28. Mr. Ware was probably William Ware, listed as waggoner, age 50, in the 1860 Census Montgomery County, Tennessee, Census, family 59.

29. Confederate Lieutenant General Edmund Kirby Smith (1824–1893) was a graduate of West Point and fought in the Mexican-American War. He was a professor of mathematics for a time at West Point and then was sent west and participated in the campaigns against the Native Americans. After the war started, he was quickly promoted to brigadier general in the Confederate Army and fought at the First Battle of Manassas, or Bull Run. At the time of this entry, he was supporting General Braxton Bragg's invasion of Kentucky. Kirby Smith entered Lexington, Kentucky, on September 1, 1862. He was supposed to meet Bragg at Bardstown, Kentucky, on September 23, 1862, to mount an attack on Louisville but sent word to Bragg that he would be staying in Lexington. The attack never materialized.

30. Serepta was talking about the Battle of South Mountain in Maryland fought on September 14, 1862. The battle lasted all day and was not confined to a particular area since they were fighting over mountain passes. At the end of the day, Union General George McClellan had his first victory over Confederate General Robert E. Lee. Total casualties from both sides were about 5,000 men.

31. Serepta was talking about the Second Battle of Bull Run (Manassas) which was fought on August 29 and 30, 1862. Confederate General Stonewall Jackson led his men against the Union supply depot at Manassas, Virginia, seizing supplies and then burning the depot. Alerted that a Union army was coming, Jackson's men hid in the woods. On August 29, Union General John Pope's army clashed with Jackson's forces resulting in heavy casualties on both sides. Jackson's men held their ground and the battle became a Confederate victory when the rest of Confederate General Robert E. Lee's army arrived. This was a high-cost victory since Confederate casualties numbered 9,000. McClellan was not killed. Perhaps this rumor occurred because he was relieved as Commander-in-Chief of Union forces and retained just the command of the Army of the Potomac in March of 1862. McClellan died in 1885.

32. Serepta probably referred to crewel, a thin, loosely twisted worsted yarn used for embroidery or tapestry.

33. Silas Wright Trice (1838–1871), son of May and Jane Frances Trice, married

Mary Trice (1843–1906), daughter of Nace Trice and his second wife, Alley Alice Allen Trice.

34. Sap of a sweetgum, known as storax, has been used for centuries to treat common ailments such as skin problems, coughs, and ulcers.

35. A rockaway is a light, low, four-wheeled carriage with the driver's seat built into the body to protect the driver in bad weather. *Encyclopaedia Britannica*, s.v. "Rockaway," accessed March 27, 2013, http://www.britannica.com/print/topic /506229.

36. John Mallory and Stephen L. Mallory were trustees of Little West Fork Baptist Church, organized by Elder Reuben Ross Williams, *Worship along the Warioto*, 144. Neither of these men is listed in the family of William, Zelpha, Elizabeth, Stephen Smith and Allatha Mallory although they were contemporaries of this generation of Mallorys. Perhaps they were cousins.

37. Campbellism was a Christian doctrine of Restoration Movement espoused by Church of Christ. It is the belief that modern Christians should emulate early Christians of the first century to return to the purity of Christ's teachings.

38. Lilly Crawford Waller (1860–1949) was the daughter of Lewis and Alley Trice Waller.

39. William Archibald Forbes was a graduate of the Virginia Military Institute. Prior to the war, he was a teacher and then President of the Faculty of Stewart College in Clarksville, Tennessee. He died of wounds received at the Battle of Second Manassas on September 2, 1862.

40. First Lieutenant and Adjutant George Boyd Hutcheson may have been wounded at Second Manassas but not severely enough to be discharged. He was, however, severely wounded at the Battle of Chancellorsville on May 3, 1863, and died several weeks later. Cross, *Ordeal by Fire*, 145.

41. Cross, *Ordeal by Fire*, 151, lists five soldiers in the 14th Tennessee Infantry with the last name of King. None was a major; four were privates and John W, King was a junior second lieutenant. He was wounded at Bull Run or Manassas on August 30, 1862, and mortally wounded at the Battle of Fredericksburg, Virginia, in December 1862.

42. Lt. Robinson Brown of Company L, 14th Tennessee Infantry Regiment, enlisted on May 31, 1861, in Clarksville. He was wounded at Second Manassas on August 30 and died on September 1, 1862. Cross, *Ordeal by Fire*, 104. The 1850 Montgomery County, Tennessee, Census lists Robinson Brown, 9, in the household of A. G., 38; Elizabeth A., 35; James A., 18; Mary A., 16; Elizabeth J., 13; Fredonia, 11; Eugenia, 3; and Edney, 1, female, family 1468.

43. Serepta was referring to the Battle of Antietam, which occurred in Maryland on September 17, 1862. It is considered the bloodiest day in American history with a total casualty count of 22,700. In August of 1862, Confederate General Robert E. Lee led the Confederate Army on its first invasion of the North. A copy of Lee's plan was found by Union soldiers wrapped around some

cigars in a field. General George McClellan allowed seventeen hours to pass before he acted on the intelligence, giving the Confederates time to get into a good position near the town of Sharpsburg. By the time he attacked, all of Lee's forces had arrived. The fighting was fierce and bloody. It is considered a Union victory only because McClellan retained the battlefield and Lee retreated with little to show for his invasion. Lincoln fired McClellan for the second and last time after this battle because McClellan refused to follow Lee and destroy the Confederate Army. Lincoln used this victory as a good time to publish a preliminary Emancipation Proclamation. The final version was issued on January 1, 1863.

44. On September 17, 1862, the Union garrison protecting the railroad bridge across the Green River at Munfordville, Kentucky, surrendered to Braxton Bragg's Confederate forces after a siege lasting two days. Four thousand Union soldiers surrendered, and five thousand rifles and a large cache of ammunition were captured.

45. Blanche was probably Blanche Howard, daughter of Meredith and Minerva Peterson Howard and niece of Lou Peterson.

46. Frank Washington Waller was the brother-in-law of Alley Trice "Cousin Alley" Waller.

47. Dunbar Cave in Montgomery County, Tennessee, goes 8.067 miles inward. The cave is located in an area of karst topography, including sinkholes, springs, and limestone bedrock. The cave offered shelter to pre-historic Native Americans. During Serepta's time, it was a venue of picnics and social gatherings. In the mid-twentieth century, country music artist Roy Acuff owned the cave, which was a popular place for dances and concerts. Today, Dunbar Cave is a state natural area.

48. Alley Trice "Cousin Alley" Waller's sister-in-law, Lucy Elizabeth Waller, married Henry Minor Dudley in 1849.

49. Stewart County, Tennessee, is adjacent and west of Montgomery County. Dover is the county seat and Fort Donelson is located in Stewart County.

50. Union occupying forces regulated church services to ensure ministers were loyal to the United States. Ministers were often arrested and forced to take an oath of allegiance. See Stephen V. Ash, "A Community at War: Montgomery County, 1861–65," *Tennessee Historical Quarterly* 36 no. 1, 30–43, and Ash, *Middle Tennessee Society Transformed, 1860–1870: War and Peace in the Upper South* (Knoxville: Univ. of Tennessee Press, 2006).

51. 2 Corinthians 5:8: We are confident, I say, and willing rather to be absent from the body, and to be present with the Lord. KJV.

52. Outlaw's Spring is southwest of New Providence in the Dotsonville community. It was probably named after Dr. J. F. Outlaw, whose residence was nearby.

53. It is interesting that Serepta referred to being an American. Apparently, citizens of the United States of America and of the Confederate States of America both thought of themselves as Americans. She seemed to expect to continue to

have the same white supremacy over African-Americans that she benefited from under slavery. Losing mastery was hard for slave owners.

54. Serepta was probably referring to a bodice made of black fabric.

55. On October 3, 1862, Confederate Generals Earl Van Dorn and Sterling Price attempted to retake Corinth, Mississippi, from Union General William Rosecrans. The Union forces were protected by concentric rings of trenches that had been built around the city. Van Dorn managed to capture the outer ring but suffered heavy losses when he attacked the inner ring of trenches. The Confederates were driven off with losses of 1,423 dead and 5,692 wounded to the Union losses of 315 dead and 1,812 wounded. The Union took 2,268 prisoners.

56. Sterling Price was governor of Missouri from 1853 to 1857. When the Civil War broke out, he sided with the Confederacy and led the Missouri Militia against Union forces. In March 1862, he and his troops officially joined the Confederate Army.

57. Earl Van Dorn was a West Point graduate who fought in the Mexican American War and held the rank of major at the end of the war. He was then stationed in the West where he fought the Comanche Indians. He resigned from the Army at the start of the Civil War and received the rank of brigadier general in the regular Confederate Army on June 5, 1861.

58. In August 1862, Confederate Generals Kirby Smith and Braxton Bragg invaded Kentucky trying to draw Union General Don Carlos Buell away from Chattanooga, Tennessee. They had early success by taking the Cumberland Gap and Richmond and Lexington, Kentucky. On October 8, 1862, Buell's Union army, 22,000 men strong, met Bragg's Confederate army of 16,000 men outside of the small Kentucky town of Perryville. The Confederate army won a tactical victory after five hours of fighting but withdrew due to being outnumbered by 40,000 fresh Union troops in the area. The Confederate army withdrew to Tennessee, ending the invasion of Kentucky.

59. Serepta was probably talking about Union Brigadier General James S. Jackson (1823–1862). The *New York Times* described him as "brusque and overbearing" and referred to a rumor that he killed a man in a fight in Hopkinsville, Kentucky. He was killed at Open Knob, an elevated position where his unit was defending an artillery battery in the Battle of Perryville, Kentucky.

60. Mr. Kellogg may have been John Kellow, a private in Company F of the 14th Tennessee Infantry. John Mallory's company was L, not F. Cross, *Ordeal by Fire*, 150.

61. Romney, Virginia, (now West Virginia) was a small, Southern-sympathizing town of 450 people during the Civil War. It ranks second behind Winchester, Virginia, in the number of times the town changed hands during the war. What made Romney so desirable was that it was the center of a number of good roads and it was on the route of the B&O Railroad, the Union's main supply line to troops in Ohio.

62. Robert W. Pritchett served as a private in the 14th Tennessee Infantry, Company H. Cross, *Ordeal by Fire*, 178.

63. Serepta was referring to Warrenton, Virginia, which changed hands quite a number of times. It was in close proximity to the following battles: Rappahannock Station, Thoroughfare Gap, Kelly's Ford, and First and Second battles of Manassas. In April 1862, Union troops occupied the town.

64. Confederate Colonel Thomas Woodward was not killed or imprisoned in the fall of 1862. In fact, by December 1862, he was busy raising his third command, the 2nd Kentucky Cavalry, at Williamsport, Tennessee. Members of his first two units had signed up for one-year-only terms.

65. Bobbie was probably Robert Crabtree (1852–?), son of Jane Trice Crabtree.

66. Serepta was talking once again about the Battle of Perryville, Kentucky. Union casualties were 845 killed, 2,635 wounded, and 515 missing and captured. The Confederates suffered 510 killed, 2,641 wounded, and 251 captured.

67. The enlisted men of the 49th Tennessee Infantry were held at Camp Douglas near Chicago. When the soldiers were exchanged, they made the trip from Camp Douglas to Vicksburg, Mississippi, on one steamer crammed in with 600 other soldiers captured at Fort Donelson. They started their trip on September 3, 1862, and arrived in Vicksburg on September 17, 1862. They were officially released on parole on September 26, 1862, and reorganized in Clinton, Mississippi, on September 27, 1862. Cross, *Cry Havoc*, 27.

68. Serepta has several cousins named Will. This Will was probably William N. Trice (1822–1873), son of Leigh and Sarah Brumfield (Broomfield) Trice. He was discharged from the 49th Tennessee Infantry because of disabilities on October 13, 1862. Cross, Cry Havoc, 207.

69. Approximately 14,000 soldiers died from consumption, the nineteenth century term for tuberculosis, during the Civil War and countless more had latent forms of the disease. "Diseases," Civil War Medicine, accessed January 19, 2018, https://civilwarmedicalhistory.weebly.com/diseases.html.

70. Serepta was mistaken. John Hunt Morgan never came to Hopkinsville. Morgan was in the Ohio Penitentiary from July 26 through November 27, 1862, when he and six of his officers escaped.

71. At the end of August 1862, two divisions of Union troops were in Bowling Green, Kentucky: Major General A. McCook's division and General Thomas Leonidas Crittenden's division. These divisions stayed in the Bowling Green area for about five days. They then marched to Louisville, Kentucky.

72. Garrettsburg, Kentucky, is just west of Oak Grove, Kentucky, on Palmyra Road. It was about ten miles from New Providence. It still exists today but is an extremely small community.

73. Netting was the practice of putting nets about where birds roosted. The nets would catch them as they flew away.

74. Romans 8:1: There is therefore now no condemnation to them which are in Christ Jesus, who walk not after the flesh, but after the Spirit. KJV.

75. Archer Furgusan enlisted in Company G of the 14th Tennessee Infantry Regiment on May 18, 1861, at Clarksville, Tennessee, and was discharged in November 1861. Cross, *Ordeal by Fire*, 129. This entry indicates that he had enlisted in another unit and been promoted to lieutenant.

76. Dr. Walter H. Drane was born in Maryland in 1788. He grew up in Logan County, Kentucky, and graduated from Transylvania University in Lexington, Kentucky. He moved to Clarksville, Tennessee, and began to practice medicine, becoming a distinguished surgeon. He married Eliza J. McClure, daughter of one of Clarksville's wealthiest citizens in 1825. In 1843, Dr. Drane devoted himself to the cultivation and manufacture of tobacco. He was one of the wealthiest and most prominent of Clarksville's citizens until his death in 1865. William P. Titus, *Picturesque Clarksville, Past and Present: A History of the City of the Hills* (Clarksville, TN: W. P. Titus Publishing Company, 1887. Reprinted by Ann Alley and Ursula Beach, 1973).

77. Across time and place, left-handedness has been seen as a sign of evil or ill-luck or weakness. The English word "sinister" derives from the Latin "sinister," which translates for "left," "on the left hand," "unfavorable," or "unlucky." Judeo-Christian traditions associate left with weakness or even immorality: Matthew's parable of the sheep and the goats casts the evil-doers on the left. In the military and with flags, the honored position is on the right; it stands to reason anything from the left is an insult.

78. Z. M. Taylor was a Methodist minister. He donated property for the first historically African-American Baptist church in Clarksville, St. John Missionary Baptist Church. 1860 Montgomery County, Tennessee, Census, family 213; Williams, *Worship along the Warioto*, 131.

79. Psalm 34:8: O taste and see that the LORD is good: blessed is the man that trusteth in him. KJV.

80. The British pattern 1853 Enfield rifle musket was the second most widely used infantry weapon of the Civil War. Both Federal and Confederate troops used the rifle throughout the war and almost one million were shipped to combatants from several British manufacturers.

81. The 1860 Montgomery County, Tennessee, Census, family 161, lists M. F. Couts, female, 26, in the household of J. F. Couts, 41, merchant, with Poston, clerk, 16; E. Withers, city marshal, 26; Rachel Withers, 19. John F. Couts married Adeline Nelson Poston in 1842; she died in 1847. Martha Fletcher McNelley Couts was his third wife. Couts was a Clarksville undertaker and furniture dealer. Born in Robertson County, Tennessee, in 1818, he was the son of William Couts and Nancy Johnson Couts, sister of Cave Johnson, Postmaster General under President James K. Polk. Titus, *Picturesque Clarksville*, 283.

82. Camp Chase was a US Army staging and training camp in Columbus, Ohio, established in May 1861. It was also a prison of war camp for Confederates. Up to 150,000 Union soldiers and 25,000 Confederate prisoners were housed there from 1861–1865. By February 1865, more than 9,400 men were held at the prison. About 2,600 Confederates are buried in the Camp Chase Confederate Cemetery.

83. Ross Donaldson was discharged from the 14th Tennessee Infantry in October 1862 on account of sickness. Cross, *Ordeal by Fire*, 121.

84. Mary Pollard Boston, 30, was the wife of George P. Boston, 44, farmer. 1860 Montgomery County, Tennessee, Census, family 270.

85. Colonel Sanders Bruce was born in Lexington, Kentucky, and was the brother-in-law of Confederate General John Hunt Morgan. Bruce helped raise the Union 20th Kentucky Infantry and commanded the 22nd Brigade at the Battle of Shiloh. After Shiloh, Bruce commanded the 1st Brigade and at the time of this entry was commanding at Russellville, Kentucky.

86. W. J. Barbee married Bettie Ann Fields on December 4, 1862. He had married Ally J. Fields on December 28, 1856, Frances M. Trice on December 20, 1854, and an earlier bride, unknown, not listed on record, on January 2, 1849. *Tennessee Compiled Marriages, 1851–1900.*

87. Jimmie Donaldson may have been James W. Donaldson, 4th Regiment Kentucky Mounted Infantry. Parts of this unit were raised in Trigg County, Kentucky. Civil War Soldiers and Sailors data base.

88. The Reverend Frances Marion Dimmick wrote *Anna Clayton; or The Mother's Trial.* (Boston: James French and Company, 1855).

89. Grace Greenwood was the pen name for Sara Jane Clarke, nineteenth century poet, journalist, and activist. A staunch abolitionist and women's rights champion, she was the first female writer for the *New York Times.* President Abraham Lincoln praised her activities in support of the Union Army. *Greenwood Leaves: A Collection of Sketches and Letters* (Boston: Ticknor, Reed and Fields, 1850) was one of her many books.

90. Mrs. Gregg Baynham was Mary Baynham, listed as age 17 in the 1860 Christian County, Kentucky, Census in the household with G E Baynham, 23; Rebecca, 43: Ed, 21; Elizabeth, 17; and Hillary, 14, family 825.

91. The 1860 Montgomery County, Tennessee, Census lists the household of T. F. Pettus, 42, farmer; M.A., 39, female; J.H., 17, male; Stephen, 15, male; E.H., 11, male; Nannie, 8, female; Sallie, 6, female; T.F., 4, male. Wyatt, in "History of New Providence," called Thomas F. Pettus, "one of the most progressive and broad-minded citizens the town ever had, and its first mayor." John L. Mitchell's *Tennessee State Gazeteer and Business Directory for 1860–61* lists T. F. Pettus as mayor of New Providence, accessed July 14, 2017, www.tngenweb.org /Montgomery/1860towns.pdf. Martha A. Cowherd Pettus lived through this bout with pneumonia and died in 1870. See Chapter 1, Note 174 for more information on Thomas F. Pettus.

92. The Oak Grove Rangers under Confederate Colonel Thomas Woodward had signed on for only one year's service and so were disbanded in June 1862. Woodward then raised another unit which also signed on for only one year. This unit was involved in the retaking of Clarksville and the attack on Dover in September 1862. About the time of this entry, this unit's service was offered to the Confederate government, which refused them because it was no longer accepting units with less than three-year commitments. On December 9, 1862, Woodward raised his third command, the 2nd Kentucky Cavalry, renumbered to the 15th Kentucky when the paperwork was submitted to the War Department.

93 After Confederate General Braxton Bragg withdrew from Kentucky, John Hunt Morgan was recalled to Tennessee and ordered to harass the Union around Nashville. Morgan received permission to attack the Union garrison at Hartsville, Tennessee, which was situated at a ford on the Cumberland River and did so on December 7, 1862. The battle lasted an hour and fifteen minutes against green Union troops. Morgan was successful and captured approximately 1,800 to 2,000 Union troops plus sixteen wagons full of clothes and stores. Morgan lost 149 men in the engagement. Union Colonel Absalom Moore resigned in disgrace after the battle. John Hunt Morgan was promoted to brigadier general.

94. Christian County, Kentucky, is on the Kentucky/Tennessee line north of Montgomery County, Tennessee. Hopkinsville is the county seat.

95. J. B. Helm married R. Buck on December 16, 1862, in Montgomery County, Tennessee. *Tennessee Compiled Marriages, 1851–1900.*

96. The Battle of Fredericksburg, Virginia, occurred on December 13, 1862, and involved approximately 200,000 soldiers. This was the first major battle with Union General Ambrose Burnside in command of the Union Army. Eighty thousand Confederates occupied Fredericksburg when Burnside sought to send 120,000 Union troops across the Rappahannock River. Burnside was delayed in attacking because he had to wait for pontoon bridges to arrive so his troops could cross the river. This delay allowed Confederate troops time to dig in on high ground. The Union lost 1,284 killed, 9,600 wounded, and 1,769 missing compared to 595 killed, 4,061 wounded, and 653 missing for the Confederates. Most of the Union casualties occurred in attacking Marye's Heights commanded by Stonewall Jackson.

97. Butternut was a slang term used for a Confederate soldier. Many soldiers' uniforms were sewn from a homespun yellow-brown cloth died with husks, leaves, bark, branches, and/or roots of butternut and walnut trees.

98. This incident must have been widely circulated in Clarksville. Nannie Haskins wrote of it in her first diary entry which summarized the first year of war activity, *The Diary of Nannie Haskins Williams*, 3–4.

99. Len. H. Johnson, Sr., a 64-year-old farmer born in Virginia, is listed in the 1860 Montgomery County, Tennessee, Census as living near Palmyra with Elizabeth, 28, and Jane, 24, family 269. In 1860, Len H. Johnson Jr., 38, was living

in a separate household with his wife, Martha, 28, and children, Mary, 6; Hart, 3; and William, 8 months.

100. Jane was the daughter of Len Johnson, Sr. 1860 Census Montgomery County, Tennessee, family 269. See Chapter 5, Note 99, for a full listing of the family.

101. Marion Harland was the pen name of Mary Virginia Terhune (1830–1922). She was a prolific writer, publishing twenty-five novels, twenty-five homemaking books, three volumes of short stories, and more than a dozen books on travel, colonial history, and biography as well as numerous essays, short stories, and articles for magazines and newspapers.

102. George D. Prentice (1802–1870) was founder and editor of the Unionist *Louisville Journal*. His editorials, noted for their wit and bite, were often copied by other newspapers. Thomas D. Clark, "George D. Prentice," *Encyclopedia of Louisville*, John E. Kleber, ed., (Lexington: University of Kentucky, 2001) 722.

103. Serepta was referring to the Emancipation Proclamation, which took effect on January 1, 1863. Exempted from the proclamation were the Border States and the parts of three Confederate states controlled by the Union because they were not in rebellion. The proclamation also paved the way for black soldiers serving in the Union Army. Because of Andrew Johnson's lobbying of Lincoln, Tennessee was exempted from the Emancipation Proclamation.

104. Serepta was referring to the Battle of Stones River, which started on December 31, 1862, and ended on January 2, 1863. Thirty-five thousand troops under Confederate General Braxton Bragg attacked Union General William Rosecrans's 42,000 at their position just outside of Murfreesboro, Tennessee, along the Stones River. The Union position withstood the initial attack on December 31 and then withdrew to defensive positions that enabled them to beat back two more assaults. The last assault was met with artillery fire that convinced Bragg to order a general retreat at the end of the battle. Stones River ranks high in the pantheon of deadly battles with a total casualty tally of 24,000.

105. In preparation for his attack on Union General William Rosecrans at Stones River, General Braxton Bragg ordered John Hunt Morgan to disrupt Rosecrans's supply line which Bragg thought extended all the way back to Louisville, Kentucky. On December 26, 1862, Morgan's Raiders burned two L&N Bridges over Bacon Creek and Nolan Creek north of Munfordville, Kentucky. On December 27, 1862, Morgan successfully attacked Elizabethtown, Kentucky. On December 28, 1862, Morgan's men burned two railroad trestles on Muldraugh's Hill, one at the Sulphur Fork and the other at Broad Run, both tributaries of Clear Creek. They also tore up railroad tracks in Nelson County, Kentucky. Morgan returned to Tennessee by January 3, 1863, with his mission accomplished. It would be five weeks before the destruction along the L&N Railroad lines was repaired.

106. Major General Lovell Rousseau (1818–1869) was born in Kentucky, and

prior to the war, was a lawyer, Indiana state representative, state senator in both Indiana and Kentucky, and Mexican-American war veteran. As the colonel of the 5th Kentucky Infantry, USA, he helped save Louisville from the Confederates in 1861. He fought in the battles of Shiloh, Stones River, and Perryville, and took part of the Tullahoma Campaign. During the time of this entry, Rousseau was in command of the defense of Nashville. Serepta was right in that it would have been a career setback for Rousseau to be assigned the command at Clarksville. This rumor was false.

107. Union Brigadier General Joshua W. Sill was a friend of General Philip Sheridan from their time at West Point. Both were members of the class of 1853. Sill commanded one of Sheridan's brigades at the battle of Stones River. He was killed leading a charge on the retreating Confederates on the first day of fighting. Sheridan ensured that Fort Sill, Oklahoma, was named after his friend.

108. Sarah Jackson was the 3-year-old daughter of Martha and Andrew Jackson, a grocer. 1860 Census Montgomery County, Tennessee, family 290.

109. Union Colonel James M. Shackelford originally commanded the 25th Kentucky Infantry during the Battle of Fort Donelson. He resigned in March 1862 due to poor health. As he was recovering, he raised the 8th Kentucky Cavalry and was elected its colonel. They were assigned to the brigade that Colonel Sanders Bruce brought to Clarksville in December 1862.

110. On January 13, 1863, Confederate General Joseph Wheeler and his cavalry captured the Federal transports: *Hasting*, *Trio*, and *Parthenia* and the gunboat *Major Siddell*. The Harpeth's Shoals are a five-mile stretch of the Cumberland River near Charlotte, Tennessee, where the water is rough and navigation is difficult.

111. Serepta was writing of the fort that is today known as Fort Defiance in Clarksville, Tennessee. Started in early 1862 by the Confederates as a part of a series of forts designed to control the Cumberland and Tennessee rivers, the fort was called Fort Sevier when construction started at the confluence of the Cumberland and Red rivers. When Clarksville was captured, Flag Officer Andrew H. Foote sent a report of the capture referring to it as Fort Defiance. His report was probably a bit of sarcasm since the fort was flying a white flag when he sailed up. Around the time of this entry, the fort was renamed Fort Bruce by the Union troops after the commander in Clarksville, Colonel Sanders D. Bruce. For unknown reasons, the name that stuck was Fort Defiance despite the fact that there was no fighting at that site. Few mentions of the Confederate name of the fort appeared in contemporary diaries or letters. Nannie Haskins called it "Fort Severe" in her October 15, 1864, entry. *Diary of Nannie Haskins Williams.*

112. Grain was used to bait a trap used to catch birds such as quail, dove, woodcock, crow or robin.

113. Lenora Jackson was the daughter of Emma Staton Jackson and the late Thomas H. Jackson. The 1860 Montgomery County, Tennessee, Census lists

Emma as age 22 with her daughter, Lenora, 4, in the household of her parents, Jo and Clarissa Staton.

114. Ada Kelly was the daughter of Edwin F. and Emily Kelly. She was married to J. H. Hirch by the Reverend R. B. McMullen. 1860 Christian County Kentucky, Census, family 114; *Tennessee State Marriages, 1780–2002.*

115. Paul Wyatt (1865–1927) remembered of his childhood in New Providence: "In winter a great many of the old residents put ice in their underground ice houses, and it was no infrequent thing to hear the ice wagons begin to rattle over the frozen ground at 2 o'clock in the morning when the ice was considered thick enough to put up. At such times the negroes, under a foreman, would build a big bon-fire on the bank for both light and warmth, and well wrapped, and with the inevitable jug of whiskey with which they were kept supplied, it soon turned out to be a race between the haulers and the cutters, and a frolic was made of a hard job." "History of New Providence."

116. Seigneur in French is a lord, especially a feudal lord. *Dictonary.com*, s.v. "Seigneur," accessed April 18, 2014, http://dictionary.reference.com/browse /seigneur.

117. Serepta was referring to the Battle of Dover. Confederate Cavalry General Joseph Wheeler was ordered to take a force and shut down Union traffic on the Cumberland River. Unfortunately for Wheeler, the Union had already ordered a cessation of traffic on that river. Deprived of a fight, Wheeler decided to attack the Union forces at Fort Donelson in Dover, Tennessee. General Nathan Bedford Forrest, who was part of the force, objected. Most of Wheeler's men were short of ammunition and the Confederate force was too small to take and hold Fort Donelson. Wheeler refused to listen. The Union garrison at Dover held on and were reinforced by units from Fort Henry. Wheeler's forces were forced to retreat. This ill-advised expedition prompted Forrest to tell Wheeler, "I'll be in my coffin before I'll fight again under your command." Quoted in Richard Tillinghast, "Nathan Bedford Forrest: Born to Fight." *Sewanee Review*, vol. 123 no. 4, 2015, 60, Project MUSE, accessed January 15, 2019, doi:10.1353/sew.2015.0108.

118. Balmoral is another name for Oxfords, plain formal shoes made of leather. Balmorals first appeared in Scotland and Ireland and showed up in America in the 1800s.

119. Joseph Staton was a second lieutenant in Woodward's 2nd Kentucky Cavalry. Woodward's 2nd Kentucky was at the Battle of Stones River December 31, 1862 – January 1, 1863, and in a skirmish near Woodbury, Tennessee, on January 24, 1863. Staton may have died from wounds sustained in one of these actions.

120. Mary Virginia Hawes Terhune (1830–1922), using the pseudonym Marion Harland, wrote the antebellum plantation romance, *Moss-Side*, in 1857.

121. Mr. Newell was perhaps Albert Newell, who had been in the 14th

Tennessee Volunteer Infantry Regiment and discharged July 20, 1862, Cross, *Ordeal by Fire*, 170.

122. Darwin Bell (1828–1913) was a captain in Woodward's 2nd Kentucky Cavalry. A lifelong resident of Christian County, Kentucky, he was married to Mary Walker Meriwether Bell and the couple had four children.

123. Russellville, Kentucky, is a town about halfway between Clarksville, Tennessee, and Bowling Green, Kentucky.

124. *Nellie Bracken: A Tale of Forty Years Ago* (Philadelphia: Lippencott, Grambo and Company, 1855) was written by Memphis resident Annie Chambers Ketchum. Ketchum's husband joined the Confederate Army and died in 1863 from a wound he had received in the Battle of Shiloh. She was arrested by Federal authorities for writing new verses to a favorite Confederate song, *The Bonnie Blue Flag*. When she refused to take the Oath of Allegiance, she and her children were banished from Memphis. She returned to her native Georgetown, Kentucky.

125. Nannie Haskins recorded this same experience in the February 22, 1863, entry: "This morning we were all awakened by the ringing of the church bells and the firing of the cannon. At first we could not conjecture what it was. Pa thought it was a fire. I was sure Morgan had come, but Ma suggested that it was Washington's birthday, and she was right. It is the twenty- second of February. This day one hundred and thirty-one years ago George Washington was born the Father of this country and the Prince of rebels. He was the great leader of our forefathers who were his followers when they rebelled against the tyrannical government of our mother country." *The Diary of Nannie Haskins Williams*.

126. This report was false. Confederate General John B. Floyd was in poor health and was raising partisan ranger units in Virginia. General James Longstreet was in charge of the Department of Virginia and North Carolina. In February 1863, he was starting his Tidewater campaign. Serepta's reference to "Marshall" may have been to Brigadier General Humphrey Marshall, who had participated in General Braxton Bragg's Kentucky operations that fall; however, Marshall saw little activity during the war and resigned twice from the Confederate Army, the final time in June 1863.

127. *Queen of the West* started her life as a 406-ton side-wheel towboat built in 1854. She was converted into a ram in 1862 and served in the Battle of Memphis on June 6, 1862. In February 1863, she was operating on the Mississippi in the Vicksburg area where she captured four Confederate steamers. She ran aground on the Black River near a Confederate shore battery and was captured. She was repaired by the Confederates and commissioned as the Confederate warship *Queen of the West*.

128. *Mabel Vaughan* was the second novel by Maria Susanna Cummings. (Leipzig, Germany: B. Tauchnitz, 1857).

129. Serepta was referring to the Battle of Thompson's Station. Union Colonel

John Coburn took a reinforced infantry brigade from Franklin, Tennessee, to reconnoiter south. Four miles from Spring Hill, he encountered two Confederate regiments and attacked them. He was repulsed and took a position on a nearby hilltop. Confederate Major General Earl Van Dorn made a frontal attack while Brigadier General Nathan Bedford Forrest's Cavalry Division swept around the Union flank cutting off their retreat. The Union troops repulsed three attempts to take the position, but after running out of ammunition and perceiving they were surrounded, Coburn surrendered.

130. Serepta was referring to General Order No. 38, dated April 13, 1863. It stated that carriers of secret mails, writers of letters sent by secret mails, secret recruiting officers within the lines, people who pass through the lines for the purpose of joining the enemy, persons concealed within the lines belonging to the service of the enemy, persons within the lines who harbor, conceal, feed, or clothe the enemy, or declare sympathy with the enemy would be tried as spies or traitors and if convicted, would suffer death.

131. The 1860 Todd County, Kentucky, Census lists J. S. Downer, a nurseryman, family 308.

132. Heliotrope is a purple-pink flower. Lemontrifolia may be lemonchina (Triphasia trifolia, Limeberry), a tropical shrub bearing sweet berries that have not only been used as food, but also for medicine. Both of these plants would probably have been grown as annuals in Tennessee.

133. Butternut jewelry was carved from butternuts (the same nut used to dye uniforms). This type of jewelry was favored by Copperheads (former Southerners living in the North who wanted to end the war but keep slavery). This type of jewelry would declare their Southern loyalties.

134. Donay C. Slaughter, 16 in 1860, was the daughter of Amistead C. and Ann R. Slaughter.

135. W. E. Webb was rector of Grace Episcopal Church in Hopkinsville, Kentucky, from 1861 to 1864, according to the Grace Episcopal Church entry on the Western Kentucky History and Genealogy website, Christian County, accessed March 3, 2013, http://www.westernkyhistory.org/christian/church/chindexG.html#Grace.

136. General James M. Shackelford's 8th Kentucky was part of the brigade that Colonel Sanders Bruce brought with him to Clarksville, Tennessee. Shackelford was not promoted to brigadier general until April 23, 1863.

137. An historical landmark located on the county line between Christian and Todd counties, Pilot Rock is the highest point in both counties, rising 966 feet above sea level. *Western Kentucky Hiking: Pilot Rock—USDA. Saturday 1, 2012,* accessed May 23, 2019, kyhiker.blogspot.com/2012/09/pilot-rock.html.

138. Mr. Goodall was A. C. Goodall, a nurseryman. 1860 Christian County, Kentucky, Census, family 378.

139. Mrs. Callis was Susan M. Callis. 1850 Christian County, Kentucky, Census, family 317.

140. Union General Joseph Hooker was born in Massachusetts and was a graduate of West Point. He fought in the Second Seminole War in Florida and in the Mexican War, proving himself to be a brave and capable soldier. He resigned in 1853 and settled in California. He had failed careers as a farmer and timber merchant. In August 1861, he rejoined the Army as a brigadier general. He distinguished himself during the Seven Days' Battles and was promoted to major general of volunteers. After the disaster that was Fredericksburg, Burnside was relieved of duty and in January 1863, Hooker was selected to command the Army of the Potomac.

141. The Battle of Chancellorsville was fought from April 30 to May 6, 1863. Union General Joseph Hooker's force greatly outnumbered the Confederate force under General Robert E. Lee and General Stonewall Jackson. In a move that went against all military tactical training at the time, Lee split his force into two sections. Lee sent Jackson with one section of the army around Hooker's right flank. This attack destroyed half of Hooker's line. On May 3, Lee attacked Hooker and, at the same time, defeated an attack in his rear. Hooker crossed the Rappahannock River on May 6, leaving Lee in possession of the battlefield. Union losses were 17,278 to Confederate losses of 12,826.

142. On May 2, 1863, Confederate General Stonewall Jackson was shot by his own pickets while reentering his lines after dark from scouting the area between the two armies. He was severely wounded in the left arm, which was amputated. He was recovering from the amputation when he contracted pneumonia. Jackson died on May 10, 1863.

143. The celebration by the soldiers was premature. Vicksburg did not fall until July 4, 1863. Vicksburg was under siege from the spring of 1862 until its surrender. Efforts to raise the siege were unsuccessful. Residents moved to caves and tunnels dug in the hillside trying to escape the constant artillery bombardments. Vicksburg did not celebrate the Fourth of July for the next eighty-one years.

144. Mull is a soft, plain muslin.

145. In 1803, John Dalton gave an oral presentation where he proposed that each chemical element consists of a single type of atom which cannot be destroyed by any chemical means. He published his atomic theory in 1805.

146. O. M. Blackman was a merchant from Ohio. 1860 Montgomery County, Tennessee, Census, family 357.

147. Major Henry was probably a reference to Gustavus Aldolphus Henry, Sr., whose home, Emerald Hill, now houses the Pace Alumni Center of Austin Peay State University. Titus, *Picturesque Clarksville*, called G.A. Henry, Sr., "Major Henry" in several references. It is less likely that she was referring to his son, Major Gustavus Adolphus Henry Jr., a West Point graduate who served on the

staff of Brigadier General Gideon J. Pillow. In his Report #51 of February 12–16, 1862, "Siege and Capture of Fort Donelson, Tennessee," Pillow acknowledged his "obligations to Capt. Gus. A. Henry Jr., my assistant adjutant-general." *OR*, series 1, vol. 7, chapt. 17, 278–85.

148. Mrs. Fielding Williams operated a school on Mill Road in northern Montgomery County, Tennessee, known as White Hall. Beach, *Along the Warioto*, 155.

149. Serepta was talking about the 5th Iowa Cavalry, which was stationed at Fort Donelson from February to June of 1863. They moved from Fort Donelson to Nashville and Murfreesboro June 5–11, 1863.

150. Serepta was correct when she stated that the 5th Iowa Calvary was moving to reinforce Union General William Starke Rosecrans but was wrong about a fight commencing. At this time, Confederate General Braxton Bragg had formed a defensive line along the Duck River stretching from Shelbyville to Wartrace, Tennessee. The Union high command was afraid Bragg would send units out to attack Union units involved in the Siege of Vicksburg. They urged Rosecrans to attack Bragg to prevent this. Rosecrans did not move to attack this line until June 23, 1863.

151. When he died, Tom Trabue was probably serving in garrison duty at Fort Tyler, West Point, Georgia, under the command of General Robert C. Tyler. Trabue's militia unit is not readily traceable in published Confederate records, which might indicate it may not have been accepted into the regular Confederate Army.

152. Lewis Meacham is listed in the 1860 Montgomery County, Tennessee, Census, family 277, as age 6 in the household of J.H. Meacham, 27, farmer; Eliza, 29; William, 4; John, 2; and Etha, 1.

153. The Wisconsin regiment was probably part of the 13th Wisconsin Infantry, which was on garrison duty at Fort Donelson in the summer of 1863.

154. The horses that Serepta was referring to may have been worn-out horses from the garrison troops. Horses that broke down or wore out in the combat units were generally shot, but with the shortage of civilian horses due to confiscation, the worn-out horses may have been sold, not shot. Mark Wilson in *The Business of Civil War* describes how the Union developed procurement policies to purchase the massive numbers of horses and mules necessary to conduct war. Wilson, *The Business of Civil War* (Baltimore: Johns Hopkins University Press, 2006). For more information on the historical importance in horses in wartime, see Ann Norton Green, *Horses at War: Harnessing Power in Industrial America* (Cambridge: Harvard Press, 2008).

155. Both armies had legal power to appropriate livestock they deemed necessary. Owners were fortunate to have their property confiscated by military regulation because they would be reimbursed. With the rule of law broken in some areas, unsanctioned stealing occurred. Property owners were out of luck in these cases.

156. After the victory at Chancellorsville, Virginia, Confederate General

Robert E. Lee decided to bring the war to the North. Lee started his invasion of Pennsylvania on June 3, 1863, with 75,000 troops.

157. In early May 1863, Confederate Lieutenant General Edmund Kirby Smith was placed in charge of the Trans-Mississippi Department. In 1863, there were battles fought around trying to relieve the siege of Vicksburg and Port Hudson garrisons. All of the major battles around this effort were Union victories.

6. July 1863–June 1864

1. Colonel Sanders Bruce, commander in Clarksville, was from Lexington, Kentucky, and believed in the velvet glove approach to citizens of occupied areas. He tried to reduce hostilities between soldiers and citizens, and this barbecue was part of that effort.

2. The speech was given by Colonel William Given, 102nd Ohio Infantry. Larry Stevens, *102nd Ohio Infantry*, 1995, accessed June 5, 2014, http://www.ohiocivil war.com/cw102.html. At the time of publication, this webpage was not available.

3. George Meade entered the Civil War as a brigadier general and was known for being a cautious commander. He was wounded during the Seven Days' Battles and conducted himself well at Antietam and Fredericksburg. He was appointed Commander of the Army of the Potomac in June of 1863.

4. Serepta was referring to the Battle of Gettysburg, which occurred July 1–3, 1863. Confederate General Robert E. Lee invaded the North in June 1863 after the Confederate victory at Chancellorsville, Virginia. On July 1, Confederate troops, looking for supplies, clashed with Union troops just outside of Gettysburg, Pennsylvania, and drove the Union troops back through the town to a ridge on the other side. The Confederates failed to pursue the attack, and by dusk, Union reinforcements arrived. By the following morning, the Union line was strongly established along Cemetery Ridge with one end of the line anchored on Culp's Hill and the other on a hill called Little Round Top. On July 2, Lee ordered attacks on both hills, but both were unsuccessful. On July 3, Lee ordered a frontal attack on the center of the line (famously known as Pickett's Charge). This attack failed disastrously. On the evening of July 4, during a heavy rainstorm, Lee withdrew his army. Union losses were 23,000 men. The Confederates lost 28,000 (about a third of Lee's army). Lee offered his resignation to Confederate President Jefferson Davis, but his offer was refused.

5. Confederate Brigadier General John Hunt Morgan led his cavalry on a highly publicized invasion of Northern states from June 11 to July 26, 1863, in what became known as Morgan's Raid. He was attempting to draw Union troops away from Vicksburg and Gettysburg and to push civilians into demanding a recall of their troops to defend their homes. The maneuver was initially successful; however, his cavalry ultimately met the same fate as the Confederate armies at Vicksburg and Gettysburg. After being defeated at Tebbs Bend, Kentucky, on

July 4, 1863, Morgan moved into Lebanon, Kentucky, on July 5. He encountered
a determined 400-man garrison there under the command of Union Colonel
Charles S. Hanson. The Union troops established a defensive position in the
railroad depot and held off Morgan for five hours. Morgan brought the battle to an
end by setting fire to the depot, causing the Union troops to surrender. Morgan's
brother Thomas was killed in the fight. The Union troops were from the 20th
Kentucky Infantry, which Sanders Bruce helped to raise. He served as colonel of
the unit until he was given a brigade command.

6. Ann Amelia Helm was the daughter of Presley Neville and Ann E. Helm.
The 1860 Montgomery County, Tennessee, Census lists her as age 18.

7. Despite being from opposing sides of the war, young men and women sometimes found themselves attracted and formed attachments even though family and
friends did not approve. Clarksville diarist Nannie Haskins Williams also wrote
disparagingly of Rebel/Yankee relationships, which seem to have been common
despite societal disapproval. *Nannie Haskins Williams Diary*, 39, 116.

8. Vicksburg, Mississippi, and Port Hudson, Louisiana, were both besieged. By
May 1863, both were encircled and cut off by the Union Army with the purpose
of controlling the entire Mississippi River. Vicksburg surrendered on July 4, 1863.
Once Vicksburg surrendered, Port Hudson followed suit on July 9. With the fall
of these positions, the Union finally controlled the Mississippi River, splitting the
eastern Confederacy from the western Confederacy.

9. Serepta accepted Mr. Homer's proposal just six weeks after learning of Tom
Trabue's death. She had firmly turned down Quint Atkinson's proposal. She
had not heard from John Mallory since reading a letter he wrote to his family in
January. He was in Virginia with a broken leg and in his letter extolled the virtues
of Virginia women. She must have felt desperate to get away from Fannie and
Elsey Trice's resentment. Serepta and Bladen Beverly Homer were married on
July 22, 1863.

10. The 1860 Montgomery County, Tennessee, Census lists J. Rice Oldham, 30;
Etha, 23; Ada, 3; George, 1; J. W. Trahern, laborer, 25. Joel Rice Oldham married
Ethalinda Trahern on December 18, 1856, in Christian County, Kentucky. He
served in Company E, Tennessee 4th Cavalry Regiment. Rice J. Oldham is also
listed as serving in Woodward's 2nd Kentucky Cavalry. The relationship between
Joel Rice Oldham and Mary Jackson "Jack" Oldham Gold is unclear; they may
have been first cousins: her father, Moses Oldham, the brother of his father, Elisha
Oldham. Or they may have been siblings, both children of Moses Oldham.

11. Quincy Adams Gillmore graduated first in his class from West Point in
1849. He joined the Corps of Engineers and taught for a time at West Point. At
the start of the Civil War, Gillmore joined the staff of Union General Thomas W.
Sherman. He took part in the successful Siege of Fort Pulaski, Georgia, and was
promoted to brigadier general on April 28, 1862. On July 10, 1863, he was promoted to major general and placed in command of the Department of the South

and 10th Corps. What Serepta was talking about here was the campaign to recapture Fort Sumter, South Carolina. Gillmore accomplished the capture of Batteries Wagner and Gregg, near Charleston Harbor, using United States Colored Troops.

12. Charles W. Staton served in Woodward's 2nd Kentucky Cavalry, Company A.

13. Serepta may have been referring to the Second Battle of Winchester, Virginia, which occurred on June 14, 1863. Winchester has the distinction of having changed hands throughout the war more than any other town. At this time, it was held by a small Union garrison who were taken by surprise. An evacuation order had been sent to them, but they did not receive it because the Confederates had cut the telegraph wires. Four thousand of the outnumbered Union soldiers were captured in this short battle. It is doubtful, however, that Woodward's regiment took part in this battle since his unit was in a skirmish at Greasy Creek, Kentucky, on May 10, 1863, and in Woodbury, Tennessee, on June 24, 1863. No record of a cavalry fight near Winchester, Tennessee, or Winchester, Kentucky, in this time-period could be found.

14. John Hunt Morgan was captured near New Lisbon, Ohio, on July 26, 1863. He escaped but was restricted to minor operations after his unauthorized and unsuccessful Northern raid. Mark M. Boatner, III. *The Civil War Dictionary* (New York: Vintage Books, 1991).

15. On July 26, 1863, Confederate General John Hunt Morgan and 360 of his men were captured at Salineville, Ohio, bringing Morgan's brilliant raid into the North to an end. This raid began from Knoxville, Tennessee, with 2,400 men. For two and one-half weeks, Morgan and his men spread terror and destruction through Ohio and Indiana all the while being chased by Union cavalry. At Pomeroy, Ohio, Morgan lost a large number of his men to Union capture. Morgan and his officers were sent to the Ohio State Penitentiary. On November 27, 1863, Morgan and some of his officers succeeded in tunneling out and escaping.

16. Annie Trice (1851–1944) was probably the daughter of Steven Edward and Martha Virginia Buckner Trice.

17. French confectioner and brewer Nicolas Appert (1749–1841) discovered that food cooked inside a jar did not spoil if sealed. Decades before Louis Pasteur demonstrated that microbes caused food to spoil, Appert published a book describing his process for the public. Canning spread to other European countries and the United States.

18. Serepta may have been referring to Virginian John Brown Baldwin (1820–1873), who served in both the First and Second Confederate Congresses. He was a vocal critic of Jefferson Davis. John R. Hildebrand, *The Life and Times of John Brown Baldwin, 1820–1873: A Chronicle of Virginia's Struggle with Slavery, Secession, Civil War, and Reconstruction*, published for The Augusta County Historical Society (Staunton, Virginia: Lot's Wife Publishing, 2008) 300.

19. John Fletcher was the son of R. B. Fletcher. Fletcher was a private in the 49th Tennessee Infantry. He was captured at Fort Donelson; sent to Camp

Douglas, Illinois, as a prisoner of war; and exchanged at Vicksburg in September 1862. Hospitalized for an illness in Clinton, Mississippi, he deserted near Canton, Mississippi, on June 30, 1863. 1860 Montgomery County, Tennessee Census, family 121; Cross, *Cry Havoc*, 122.

20. A tucking comb is a small, ornamental comb used to tuck up and hold a woman's hair in a topknot.

21. Private William T. Hargrave enlisted in the 49th Tennessee Infantry, Company A, in 1861 in Clarksville. He was taken prisoner of war at Fort Donelson in February 1862; sent to Camp Douglas, Illinois; exchanged at Vicksburg, Mississippi, in September 1862; captured at the Battle of Port Hudson, Louisiana; paroled and went home on July 10, 1863. Cross, *Cry Havoc*, 132.

22. Mildred Goodall was the wife of nurseryman A. C. Goodall. 1860 Christian County, Kentucky Census, family 378.

23. Today, we think of catsup as a tomato-based condiment. In the nineteenth century, cucumber catsup was common and was more like what we think of as a type of relish.

24. Serepta used both spellings of catsup and ketchup. Perhaps she was using the different terms for different kinds of condiments. Ke-tchup came from the Fujian Province, China, where it was a pickled fish brine or sauce. Ke-tchup made its way to Europe in the 1600s. In English, the name was ketchup or catsup, with the latter spelling first appearing in print in 1699. By the 1740s, it was part of English cuisine and meant any type of spiced sauce. By the 1800s, there were numerous recipes for ketchup, and many flavors of it were popular, including lemon, oyster, mushroom, walnut, and elderberry. The first known tomato ketchup recipe was published in 1812 and was an American variation. Tomato ketchup won as the standard sauce after the Civil War with the Heinz Company marketing the product. The ketchup spelling became the accepted spelling in America during the 1800s.

25. The papers were mistaken. No foreign power ever recognized the Confederacy. The Federal government made it clear that countries that recognized the CSA risked war. No country chose to take the risk partially because of the Confederacy's inability consistently to win consecutive victories.

26. Batter cakes are made using hominy or corn meal instead of flour.

27. Aunt Lucy was enslaved to B. B. Homer. She may have been married to Uncle Donel.

28. Nettle rash (also known as urticaria or hives) is composed of reddish itchy swellings on the skin similar to those resulting from contact with stinging nettle. The rash can vary in shape and size and may occur repeatedly or as a single episode.

29. The 28th Kentucky Infantry was organized at Louisville and New Haven, Kentucky, in October 1861 and became part of the Army of the Ohio. The unit came to Clarksville as part of Sanders Bruce's brigade in December 1862. The

regiment was mounted while in Clarksville and engaged in scouting, which resulted in numerous skirmishes with Confederate partisan rangers. They left Clarksville and were assigned to Columbia, Tennessee, in August 1863.

30. The 102nd Ohio Infantry was organized at Mansfield, Ohio, in August 1862 under the command of Colonel William Given and was assigned to the Army of the Ohio. They arrived in Clarksville in December 1862 as part of Sanders Bruce's brigade. While in Clarksville they built bridges and forwarded supplies. They probably were responsible for getting supplies, which may be the source of the villainy Serepta accused them of. They moved to Dover and then to Nashville in September 1863

31. Haversacks were vital to Civil War soldiers to store food and hold their personal possessions. They were usually made of cloth.

32. Slave owners went to extraordinary lengths to keep their enslaved people. Newly freed people went to extraordinary lengths to maintain control of their children. Winnie enlisted the authority of Union troops to help secure her child from Elsey Trice.

33. Davis (possibly Davie) Spring is northwest of New Providence.

34. After the Battle of Stones River, Union General William Starke Rosecrans pursued Braxton Bragg to Chattanooga. When his supply lines were threatened, Bragg abandoned Chattanooga and withdrew into the mountains across the line in Georgia. In this campaign, Rosecrans lost just six men, four of them in accidents.

35. Anna (Bowie) Sears was the wife of the Reverend A. D. Sears. Their daughter Marietta married John Newton Major. Titus, *Picturesque Clarksville*, 59; Gary, *Marriages, 1851–1900*, Vol. II.

36. Roberta Virginia Killebrew is mistakenly listed in the 1850 Montgomery County, Tennessee, Census as Robert V. Killebrew, male, 7, in the household of Whitfield, 58; Frances, 50; Sarah W. 22; Martha P., 18; Eliza, 16, family 312. She married Malcolm Hart Branaugh on December 17, 1867, in Montgomery County. She died November 28, 1900, in Hopkinsville, Kentucky.

37. Emma Robb was the daughter of Colonel Alfred Robb, who was killed in the Battle of Fort Donelson. Emma married Polk Grundy Johnson, son of Cave Johnson, in 1868 and the couple had twin daughters. Emma Robb Johnson died in 1872. 1860 Montgomery County, Tennessee Census, family 30.

38. Juliet McDaniel was the daughter of Dr. George (deceased) and Susan McDaniel. 1860 Montgomery County, Tennessee Census, family 407; 1850 Montgomery County, Tennessee Census, family 1287.

39. Under Union occupation, Clarksvillians' travel was restricted, and citizens would have to obtain a travel pass to leave the city.

40. The term "Jayhawker" originated in "Bleeding Kansas," a small civil war fought between pro- and anti-slavery forces from 1854 to 1859 over whether to admit Kansas to the Union as a slave or free state. Jayhawker eventually became the generic term for armies plundering and looting from the civilian population.

41. The unit referred to here is the 83rd Illinois Infantry, which was organized and mustered into the US Army in August 1862. They were assigned garrison duty at Forts Henry and Donelson under Colonel William Lowe. On September 20, 1863, the right wing of the unit was moved to Clarksville for garrison duty and anti-guerrilla duty. The part of the regiment which remained at Fort Donelson took part in repulsing Wheeler and Forrest's attack on Fort Donelson in February 1863.

42. Jack Oldham may have been Mary Jackson Oldham Gold, wife of Benjamin Gold. Although Serepta called her Jack Gold in most of her references, she may have used her maiden name in this reference.

43. Mary, age 21 in 1860, and Gold, age 16 in 1860, Collins were the daughters of W. B. and Frances Collins. 1860 Montgomery County, Tennessee Census, family 865.

44. Mete Sypert was possibly Demetrius Sypert, the 1860 Christian County, Kentucky, Census lists Demetrius P. Sypert, 20, clerk, with H. S. Sypert, 58, merchant, and Ann C. Sypert, 58; Henretta, 24; and Theresa, 17, family 822.

45. Fannie Britton stayed with the E.B. Haskins family while she attended school in Clarksville.

46. The Battle of Chickamauga occurred on September 19 and 20, 1863, and was a Union defeat. This battle was in response to Union General William Starke Rosecrans's earlier victory in pushing the forces of Confederate General Braxton Bragg out of Chattanooga. Bragg counterattacked at Chickamauga Creek and, after two days of fierce fighting, forced Rosecrans to retreat. Bragg did not pursue Rosecrans and allowed the Union general to return safely to Chattanooga where he was reinforced by Union General Ulysses S. Grant.

47. After his defeat at Chickamauga in September, Union General William Starke Rosecrans withdrew to Chattanooga. Confederate General Braxton Bragg then laid siege to the city. The Confederate Army held the ridges that ringed the city. On September 29, Lincoln ordered General U. S. Grant to go to Chattanooga and break the siege. Grant removed Rosecrans and replaced him with General George Thomas. Grant then moved to reopen the Tennessee River supply line to Chattanooga. This move was what was behind the rumors Serepta heard.

48. The cars were railroad cars, which apparently had been pressed into military service.

49. We know from the Civil War Correspondence of the Wadsworth Brothers in the Tennessee State Library and Archives that a recruiting station for the 16th USCT was established near what is known today as Fort Defiance. This recruiting station existed from November 1863 through April 1864. Also in this same area was a Contraband Camp, which was a prime recruiting spot for the Union Army. Elihu, and Orry Wadsworth, *"Brother Charles": Letters Home to Michigan*, Civil War Correspondence of the Wadsworth Brothers, 1861–1865, Tennessee

State Library and Archives, Nashville, Tennessee. The best estimate is that three thousand ex-slaves from as far away as Louisville, Kentucky, were recruited at Clarksville from 1863 to 1865 for service in the Union army. These men played significant roles in constructing railroads and fortifications, defending essential posts, and fighting battles at Nashville and Chattanooga. Richard P. Gildrie, "Black Regiments, 1863–1865," Mount Olive Cemetery Historical Preservation Society webpage, accessed January 16, 2013, http://mtolivecemetery.sharepoint .com/Pages/MilitaryHistory.aspx. At the time of publication, this information was not available on the Mount Olive website.

50. Old Mrs. Trice was probably Mary Carlisle Trice (1792–1865). Mary "Polly" Carlisle married Thomas Alexander Trice (1802–June 15, 1860), son of James and Susannah Leigh Trice, and brother of Bingham, Elizabeth, Leigh, Jesse James, Nace, May, Jane, Greenberry, Mary "Pollie" Campbell, Elsey, and Nancy Barbee. The couple had three daughters, Sarah "Sallie" Cates Trice Tandy (1826–1884), Mary A. Trice Trice (1828–?), and Elizabeth Jane Trice Whitefield (1833–1903). Various family trees mention the possibility of two sons, Edward and Thomas H. (or A.). The T. A. Trices lived in Montgomery County. The 1840 Montgomery County, Tennessee, Census, lists twenty-eight people in their household: six free white persons, five free colored persons, and seventeen slaves. The 1850 Montgomery County, Tennessee, Census lists Mary, 62, and T.A., 48, with Green Chastain, 24, and Eliza M., 16. By the 1860 census, Mary, 69, farmer, was listed as living alone. Despite the inconsistency in Mary Trice's age from the 1850 census to the 1860, these are the ages recorded in each census.

51. Jane and Paralee were probably the two enslaved women who left "old Mrs. Trice." Apparently, they came back for their mother and Jane's two children. Even then, Mrs. Trice seems to have had Tom for labor. This incident is an example of the uneven breakdown of slavery.

52. Serepta was mistaken. Confederate General Nathan Bedford Forrest was part of General Braxton Bragg's army and, along with Wheeler, was disrupting the Union supply lines into Chattanooga. Forrest disliked Bragg and requested a separate command, which President Jefferson Davis granted him on October 29, 1863.

53. On September 30, 1863, Confederate Cavalry General Joseph Wheeler crossed the Tennessee River with the goal of severing the only supply route that Union forces in Chattanooga had. On October 3, Wheeler attacked a Union supply convoy of 32 wagons and captured the wagons with all the supplies. An hour later, the Confederates encountered an even larger supply convoy and attacked it. The Confederates captured 1,200 Union officers and men, 800 wagons loaded with supplies, and 4,000 mules. They destroyed any supplies they could not take. On October 4, 1863, the Confederates convinced the garrison of the Union supply depot at McMinnville, Tennessee, to surrender. The captured supplies were sent south.

54. Pea Ridge is a community northeast of New Providence.

55. John A. Murrell (1806–1844) was a notorious outlaw convicted for horse and slave stealing. He was imprisoned at Tennessee State Penitentiary in Nashville.

56. Serepta was talking about the Bristoe Campaign, a series of five battles fought in Virginia between Union General George Meade and Confederate General Robert E. Lee. Only one of the battles was a defeat for the Union, a cavalry battle known as Buckland Races. This is probably the specific battle Serepta was referring to. Union cavalry were lured into an ambush near Chestnut Hill and were scattered. The Confederate cavalry chased them for five miles. At the end, Meade wound up in a good position, sitting in the Union supply base near Manassas Junction. Lee returned to his old position behind the Rappahannock River.

57. In May 1863, the Bureau of US Colored Troops was established and recruitment of black men into the Army began in earnest. At first, these troops were used for "fatigue duty" which included guard duty, building fortifications, and building railroads. The army doubted that black men would fight. By late 1863 and early 1864, this attitude changed for two reasons. First, it became harder to recruit white men and the Army started having a manpower problem. Second, black men had proved by this time that they would fight — and fight well.

58. Pone is a baked or fried bread usually made of cornmeal and cooked in a cast iron skillet.

59. The 1860 Montgomery County, Tennessee, Census lists the family of J.M. Burgess, 48, male, hotel keeper; L.A. (Lucy), 43; W.H. (William), 20; Frances, 20; and Geo, 18.

60. William H. Burgess enlisted as a brevet second lieutenant in the 49th Tennessee Infantry in November 1861. He was captured at Fort Donelson; sent to Camp Chase, Maryland, as a prisoner of war; transferred to Johnson's Island, Ohio; exchanged at Vicksburg in September 1862. He was captured at Charlotte, Tennessee, in December 1862 and exchanged at City Point, Virginia, in April 1863. He resigned his commission and reported to Woodward's 2nd Kentucky Cavalry as a private in August 1863.

61. A George E. Burgess enlisted as a private in the 14th Tennessee Infantry in May 1861. According to Cross, *Ordeal by Fire*, 105, he "Furnished substitute who was not received" and Cross could find no further record. In her December 10, 1861, entry, Serepta reported that Silas Trice went to Western Virginia "to take George Burgess's place." A George E. Burgess also enlisted as a private in the 49th Tennessee Infantry in November 1861. He was reported Absent Without Official Leave from Fort Donelson on February 16, 1862, and Cross, *Cry Havoc*, 101, lists him "deserted." This entry suggests he may have joined another regiment that was sent to South Carolina although Serepta seemed skeptical of some of his stories.

62. The *Democrat* was a Louisville, Kentucky, newspaper.

63. New York Governor Horatio Seymour, a Democrat, believed the

government was in error by confiscating property and freeing the slaves of the South. Harold Holzer and Craig L. Symonds, eds., *The New York Times Complete Civil War, 1861–1865* (New York: Black Dog and Leventhal Publishers, 2010), 191–192.

64. On this same date, Sarah Kennedy wrote her husband about this same fire which occurred on Saturday, November 7, with the last fire occurring in the dawn hours of Sunday, November 8. In all, seven structures were burned, Frank Beaumont, Mrs. Winston, Mr. Landrum, and William Shackelford all lost houses. The Masonic Hall stable was burned, and the fire spread to the Masonic Hall, which also burned down. In the early hours of November 8, the Reverend D. T. Wardlow's stable was burned down. Sarah Kennedy, Letter dated November 9, 1863, *Civil War Collection: Confederate and Federal 1861–1865*, Confederate Collection, Box 10, Tennessee State Library and Archives.

65. This report of a Col. or Gen. Stones coming to Clarksville to recruit African Americans was false. There was a Brigadier General Charles Pomeroy Stone (1824–1887), but he was never stationed in Tennessee. He got into trouble with two powerful Massachusetts politicians, who were instrumental in his arrest after the Battle of Balls Bluff in October 1861. He was held in solitary confinement for six months and never brought to trial. He was later cleared of charges. In May 1862, he was assigned to General Nathaniel Banks as his chief of staff. On April 4, 1864, Secretary of War Edwin Stanton ordered Stone mustered out, causing him to revert to his regular rank of colonel.

66. Prosy, showing no imagination, commonplace or dull, comes from the same stem as prosaic. Mending shirts and darning socks certainly are prosaic tasks.

67. Serepta was referring to the Second Battle of Rappahannock Station, which occurred on November 7, 1863. It was the last of the five battles of the Bristoe Campaign. Union General George Meade moved to attack General Robert E. Lee, who was in position on the other side of the Rappahannock River. Meade divided his forces, with one attacking Rappahannock Station, where the only bridge between the two forces was located, and the other attacking Kelly's Ford further downstream. Both forces were successful. A nighttime bayonet attack at the bridge resulted in Meade capturing 1,600 prisoners. Lee retreated into Orange County, south of the Rapidan River.

68. Allen family tradition holds that Bailey F. Allen Sr. (1816–1880) had just come back after selling his tobacco crop and was counting the money from the trip when the robbers knocked on the door. When he heard a commotion at the back door, as a precaution, instead of putting the money in the money box, he threw the bag behind the couch. Masked men burst through the door and demanded his money. Bailey Allen was crippled and was having a hard time with the robbers when his sister Betsy came down the stairs with a horse pistol. She walked up to one of the robbers and said, "I know who you are" and yanked off his mask. At that point, the robbers ran. Bailey Allen lived with his sisters, Nancy (Nannie)

Allen (1810–1880) and Elizabeth (Betsy) Allen (1814–1900). The 1860 Montgomery County, Tennessee, Census lists Bailey Allen, 42, with his sisters and his wife, M. J., 34, and children E. M., 12, female; F. P., 11, male; H. A., 5, male; and Noble, 2, family 886.

69. The 1860 Montgomery County, Tennessee, Census lists E.B. Fairfax, 22, grocer, estate worth $800, in the household of J. B. Fairfax, merchant, 55, real estate $3,500, personal $4,200, with Tennyson Fairfax, 44, family 712.

70. *Kentucky County Marriages*, 1783–1965, records show E. B. Fairfax, 26, married M. M. Trice on November 16, 1863, in Trigg County, Kentucky. The 1880 Montgomery County, Tennessee, Census lists the household of Ephraim, 43, and Mollie, 38, with children John, 14; Mattie, 10; Henry, 9; George, 3; and Annie, 4 months. Paul Wyatt recalls, ". . . Uncle Johnny Fairfax and his son, Eph, who was a never ending source of entertainment and amusement to the boys. For many years Eph carried the mail between New Providence and Clarksville, and with "Kate" and the cart served Uncle Sam faithfully as any mail carrier he could boast about. Eph was the efficient sexton of the Methodist Church long as he lived in New Providence and it was his greatest delight to ring the bell which he would do long and loud on every occasion. Many and varied were the tricks the boys would pay on Eph, but woe unto the unlucky one who made him mad and then came within the reach of his ever ready crooked walking stick." "History of New Providence."

71. In December 1863, the 16th US Colored Troop Infantry set up a recruiting station very near what is now called Fort Defiance. They recruited troops in Clarksville, New Providence, and Dover, Tennessee. Clarksville was a fertile recruitment area for the US Colored Troops. Elihu Wadsworth wrote the following in a letter to his brother Charles: "Recruiting goes on slowly at present at Donelson and Clarksville for the reason that just without our lines the rebels keep up a line of patrols to keep the Negroes from coming in. A party of sixty started and only one got through. Although they are watching so diligently about ten per day get through the lines and enlist immediately. When we get two companies armed we will break the blockade and the men will come in in swarms. It would do you good to see those ragged men come in and put on a suit of US clothes. When they learn they are freemen they stand up their full height, men." *"Brother Charles": Letters Home to Michigan*, Civil War Correspondence of the Wadsworth Brothers 1861–1865, Tennessee State Library and Archives.

72. After complaining about General Braxton Bragg to President Jefferson Davis, Confederate General James Longstreet was dispatched to attack Union forces at Knoxville, Tennessee. Union General Ambrose Burnside was also headed for Knoxville. The two armies literally raced each other to get to Campbell's Station, where two major roads intersected. If Longstreet got there first, he could prevent Burnside from getting to Knoxville. Burnside got there fifteen minutes before Longstreet. Longstreet attacked both flanks of the Union

line at once, but the Union forces held. Burnside was able to move into Knoxville. Longstreet tried to encircle the city but could not totally cut off supplies to it. Longstreet ended the siege on December 6, 1863, when Union General William T. Sherman arrived with reinforcements.

73. Carbonic acid gas is an archaic term for carbon dioxide.

74. This was a reference to the Battle of Chattanooga, which took place between November 23 and 25, 1863. The Battle of Chattanooga comprised two battles, the Battle of Lookout Mountain and the Battle of Missionary Ridge. After losing the Battle of Chickamauga, the Union Army retreated to Chattanooga, and Confederate General Braxton Bragg laid siege to the city, cutting off the Union supply lines. General U. S. Grant quickly reopened the supply lines and refortified the city. On November 23, 1863, Union General George H. Thomas, known as the Rock of Chickamauga, attacked the center of the Confederate lines and drove them up to the top of Missionary Ridge.

75. During the attack on the Confederate center in the Battle of Chattanooga, a miscommunication about whether they were to take just the rifle pits at the base of the ridge or advance to the top of the ridge led the Union troops to continue the attack to the top of Missionary Ridge where they broke the Confederate center. The Confederates retreated on November 26, 1863, into Georgia.

76. Confederate General John Hunt Morgan was captured on July 26, 1863, and sent to the Ohio State Penitentiary with his top officers. Morgan and his officers cut a hole in their prison cell into a ventilation crawl space. They tunneled from the crawl space to the outside and escaped to the South.

77. Through the 1800s, American cooks made hominy grits by soaking dried corn kernels in a lye solution and then pounding the kernels with a large mortar and pestle. Hominy grits remain popular today as a Southern breakfast staple.

78. Uncle Donel was one of the men B. B. Homer held as a slave.

79. Union Colonel Arthur A. Smith commanded the 83rd Illinois Infantry Regiment. The main unit was garrisoned at Fort Donelson, but the right wing of the unit moved on September 20, 1863, to Clarksville where they patrolled a large area and had daily skirmishes with guerillas.

80. Union interference with church worship occurred throughout occupation. The Union wanted to ensure the loyalty of ministers to the United States, and ministers had to sign a loyalty oath to continue their ministry. The Episcopal minister traveled with troops; the Presbyterian minister left for a while for Canada and Philadelphia. All the churches held services, though intermittently. Williams, *Worship along the Warioto*, 220.

81. This rumor was true. Occupying forces did appropriate household items to be used by US Colored Troops or in contraband camps. White Southerners filed claims for reimbursement with the Southern Claims Commission.

82. Several reasons could have contributed to Cousin Jane's bad mood. With the Homers removing to the Golds' house, she was losing the protection of a male

household member in times of increased lawlessness. She was probably also losing rental income. With these concerns, Uncle Trice's complaints may have influenced her to see the Homers as self-serving.

83. Fannie appears to have been a slave that the Golds left living in a cabin behind their house.

84. Tine Smith was Valentine or V. W. Smith. See Chapter 1, Note 125 for more information on Valentine Smith.

85. Lard is pork fat which is rendered or boiled down. To dry it, you subject it to hot air that drives all the water out of the rendered lard. Lard was used in baking and cooking, very much as we use butter or margarine today.

86. Animal brains have been eaten by many cultures and were most popular during the time when farmers slaughtered their own animals. Slaughtering occurred during cool weather so that the meat would not spoil. While most other meat on the animal could be preserved, organs had to be eaten quickly because they could not be preserved. Scrambled eggs and brains was a dish associated with the American South. Brains became a less popular dish after the 1990s when mad cow disease caught the public notice. The fear that eating infected animal brains could lead to Creutzfeldt-Jakob disease became widespread. "Scrambled Eggs Are Coming back from the Dead," Extra Crispy, accessed January 23, 2018, http://www.extracrispy.com/food/534/scrambled-eggs-and-brains-are-coming-back-from-the-dead.

87. Aunt was a term given to older enslaved women. Delony or Demuslin was probably an African American slave rented or borrowed from someone Serepta knew, or she could have been an African American she hired for temporary labor from a contraband camp. If this woman were truly her aunt, she would have known her name and not written "whatever she is."

88. Laundry in the nineteenth-century was one of the most arduous housekeeping tasks a woman faced. Washing would have taken a full day, from hauling and heating water in tubs, scrubbing by hand, bleaching and treating stains, rinsing and starching, wringing out by hand or cranking clothes through a wringer, and hanging to dry. Then came the ironing. While clothes were sprinkled and rolled up to dampen, several flat irons were commonly heated on the stove for the bulk of the ironing. Most households also had specialty irons; tally or Italian irons were used for smoothing out bows and bonnet strings, French or mushroom irons for puffy sleeves, and fluting irons for making flutes or pleats. Since Serepta did not mention laundry as one of her chores, one assumes a slave took on these tasks for her.

89. In December 1863, the 16th United States Colored Troops established a recruiting station "one mile west of Clarksville on a hill about one hundred and fifty feet above the waters of the Red and Cumberland rivers." Elihu Wadsworth, *"Brother Charles": Letters Home to Michigan*, Civil War Correspondence of the Wadsworth Brothers 1861–1865, January 14, 1864, Tennessee State Library and Archives.

90. A gold and silver cake has silver layers made with egg whites and gold layers made with egg yolks. The layers are alternated.

91. A bedstead is the frame on which the mattress is placed.

92. Serepta was making something called hogshead cheese. The brains and eyes of the hog are removed and the head is boiled with herbs and seasoning for about six hours. When it is done, the meat is easily removed from the head. When chilled, gelatin that comes out when the head is boiled will hold the meat together. Recipes are easily found on the internet to make this dish.

93. On the brink of bankruptcy and pressed to finance the Civil War, Congress for the first time authorized the US Treasury to issue paper money in the form of non-interest-bearing treasury notes, commonly called "greenbacks" because of their ink color. The bill authorized Treasury Secretary Salmon P. Chase to issue $150 million in paper notes as "lawful money and a legal tender in payment of all debts, public and private, within the United States." Because greenbacks were not backed by gold or silver, the standard basis for economic transactions, the bill, signed into law by Abraham Lincoln on February 25, 1862, was challenged in court. The suit went to the US Supreme Court, which ruled it constitutional on December 18, 1863, just three days after hearing arguments. Dawinder S. Sidhu, "Opinionator: The Birth of the Greenback," *New York Times*, December 31, 2013, accessed August 14, 2017, https://opinionator.blogs.nytimes.com/2013/12/31/the -birth-of-the-greenback/.

94. A mid-nineteen century definition of jumper probably referred to a 'short coat,' perhaps from Scots jupe 'a man's loose jacket or tunic.

95. Elihu Wadsworth wrote to his brother Charles on January 14, 1864, "The men are learning the drill very rapidly and are going to make the best of soldiers. I maybe partial but I think our company the best drilled of any in camp." *"Brother Charles": Letters Home to Michigan*, Civil War Correspondence of the Wadsworth Brothers 1861–1865, Tennessee State Library and Archives.

96. Serepta's Adjutant Perkins was Lieutenant Bishop W. Perkins, adjutant of the 16th United States Colored Troops. He originally joined Company D of the 83rd Illinois in August 1862 and was stationed at Fort Donelson. He held the rank of sergeant with this unit until he transferred to the 16th USCT, where he was promoted to lieutenant. He went on to become the captain of Company C, 16th USCT. Officers in the USCT were white.

97. These spoons have passed down through Serepta's descendants along with the story of why she had her nickname engraved on them. See the photograph of the spoon on page 152.

98. Serepta was probably referring to a chamber pot, which people used during the night before indoor plumbing was installed.

99. It is unclear what C. O. stood for. Commanding Officer was not used at that point. Perhaps it was the initials of the person who wrote the pass.

100. Nainsook is a fine, soft cotton fabric, originally from South Asia.

101. Referred to as the "Damnesty Oath," Johnson's new oath was much stricter than the one Lincoln wrote for reconstruction. It required the oath taker not only to support the laws and Constitution but also to aid and assist in the suppression of the current rebellion.

102. Serepta was talking about turning green, unroasted coffee beans into brown, roasted beans suitable for grinding.

103. A candy stew, or candy pull, was a popular party in the nineteenth century. The Dictionary of Slang (1897) described a typical party as "a party of both sexes at which molasses or sugar is boiled and pulled by two persons (whose hands are buttered) to give it proper consistency, and then mixed and pulled again, till it becomes true candy." Patricia Bixler Reber, Culinary History Online, "Candy pull, Candy stew and other pull parties," accessed July 16, 2017, www.angelfire.com /md3/openhearthcooking/aaCandypull2.html.

104. Mrs. Parker may have been E. J. B. Parker, 39, wife of M. E. Parker, 43, millwright. 1860 Montgomery County, Tennessee, Census, family 650.

105. In 1863, the Freedman's Committee of the Indiana Yearly Meeting of Friends sent Walter Totten Carpenter to Tennessee and Alabama to inspect Contraband Camps and Hospitals and report back on the help they would need. He visited Clarksville on January 23, 1864, and wrote in his diary, "the colored people here, both residents and contrabands, are to all appearances as well dressed and clothed as they are at the north and if anything is done for them here it should be in the way of instruction." Carpenter noted in his diary when conditions were dirty or unhealthy. No such note appears in his Clarksville entry. *The Diary of Walter Trotter Carpenter*, Archives and Manuscript Division, Ohio Historical Society, Columbus, Ohio.

106. Charlie Jackson was the 24-year-old son of N. A. Jackson (female). 1860 Census Montgomery County, Tennessee, family 205.

107. James S. Meacham was the 22-year-old son of John S. and Mary Meacham. 1850 Census Montgomery County Tennessee, family 1443; 1860 Census Montgomery County, Tennessee, family 280.

108. Serepta was referring to the Battle of Olustee, the largest battle fought in Florida during the Civil War. This battle marked the high point of the Union invasion of Florida. Union General Truman Seymour had taken the town of Jacksonville on February 7, 1864, and was now intent on taking Lake City, which had a railroad bridge the Union wanted to destroy. Confederate General Joseph Finegan attacked on February 20 near the Olustee railroad station. The fight lasted all day with the Confederates driving the Union from the field. Union casualties were 1,800 while the Confederates suffered 900 casualties. Florida remained under Confederate control until the end of the war.

109. Ulysses S. Grant was promoted to Lieutenant General of the Army on March 1, 1864. The only other officer to hold that rank before Grant was George

Washington. With this promotion, Grant replaced Henry Halleck as the commander of all Union armies.

110. In March 1864, Confederate General Nathan Bedford Forrest left Columbus, Mississippi, on an expedition into Western Tennessee and Kentucky designed to disrupt the Union rear area, recruit new troops, and re-outfit using captured Union supplies. He arrived in Paducah, Kentucky, on March 25 and forced the 650-man Union garrison to retreat into Fort Anderson where they repulsed all attacks. Forrest took all the supplies he wanted and destroyed the rest. He also took a large number of horses and mules when he left.

111. The Jordan Homer Family Tree public family history in Ancestry.com lists the children of Serepta Mildred Jordan Homer and Bladen Beverly Homer as Tabitha Homer (1865–1926), Evaline "Eva" Homer (1867–1934), Bailey Homer (1869–1871), and Janie Homer (1870–1937). This entry indicates Tabitha was born April 10, 1864, not in 1865. The 1870 Montgomery County, Tennessee, Census lists their household as Bladen Homer, 51, justice of the peace; S. Homer, 31; Liby (sic), 6; Eva, 3; and Baily, 2 months, family 207.

112. Fighting in Chattanooga ended in November 1863. At the time Serepta was writing, Chattanooga was becoming the supply base for Union General William T. Sherman's Atlanta campaign.

113. Serepta was referring to the Battle of Sabine Crossroads in Louisiana. Union Major General Nathaniel P. Banks and 3,000 troops had been working their way across Louisiana toward Texas thinking that another Union army coming to join them from Arkansas would draw off any Confederate troops in the area. On April 8, 1864, they were attacked by Confederate cavalry made up of Texans and three infantry brigades at a crossroads near Mansfield, Louisiana, only 40 miles from the Texas state line. The Confederates outflanked the Union line forcing them to retreat. As a result, Banks ordered a general retreat and abandoned the campaign into Texas. In the fight, Confederate losses were 1,621 to 1,369 Union losses.

114. On May 5, 1864, General Robert E. Lee attacked General U. S. Grant's army in the Battle of the Wilderness. This was the second battle fought on this ground and was a good choice by Lee. The dense vegetation made maneuvering a large army extremely difficult and cancelled Grant's numerical superiority. The battle was halted by darkness but resumed the next day. By the morning of May 7, both armies were back to where they had started. Grant refused to retreat and instead moved the army to Spotsylvania Courthouse. The battle was not a victory for either side, costing the Union 17,500 men and the Confederates 10,500.

115. Confederate General James Longstreet was wounded on May 6, 1864, by his own men, but recovered. Almost a year previous, Jackson had been killed under similar circumstances only a few miles away.

116. Union Major General John Sedgwick was killed on May 9, 1864, by a

sharpshooter at Spotsylvania while making a reconnaissance and directing the placement of artillery. Sedgwick and Major General John F. Reynolds (July 1, 1863, Gettysburg) were the highest-ranking United States soldiers to be killed in the war.

117. Serepta was referring to the Battle of Spotsylvania Court House. The fighting around this area lasted twelve days and included ferocious battles that did not seem to advance either side. When this stalemate became clear, General U. S. Grant disengaged and moved southeast in a flanking movement toward Richmond, Virginia. The Union lost 18,000 men to the Confederates' 12,000 men. However, the Confederacy could not afford to lose these casualties because they could not replace them while the Union could.

118. Letter in family's possession.

BIBLIOGRAPHY

Primary Sources

CENSUS AND MARRIAGE RECORDS

Ballard County, Kentucky, Census, Lovelaceville District (1870).

Bowling Green, Warren County, Kentucky, Census (1880).

Brunswick County, Virginia, Census (1850).

Caldwell County, Kentucky. County Marriages, Kentucky, 1783–1965.

Caldwell County, Kentucky, Census (1860).

Caldwell County, Kentucky, Census (1850).

Cheatham County, Tennessee, Census (1860).

Christian County, Kentucky, Census (1850, 1860, 1870).

Christian County, Marriage Records 1851–1900, Kentucky.

Concord Township, Clinton County, Missouri. Census (1860).

Davidson County, Tennessee, Census (1850, 1860).

Edmonson County, Kentucky, Census (1860).

Federal Census Mortality Schedule, Montgomery County (1860).

Gary, Cordelia C. *Christian County, Ky., Marriage Records 1797–1850.*
Hopkinsville, KY: Christian County Genealogical Society, 1997.

Hopkins County, Kentucky Marriages, 1851–1900 [database on-line].
Provo, UT: The Generations Network, Inc., 2001.

Kentucky, County Marriages, 1783–1965.

Livingston County, Kentucky, Census (1870).

Logan County, Kentucky, Census (1850).

McCracken County, Kentucky, Census (1850).

McCracken County, Kentucky, District 2, Census (1860)

Mecklenburg County, Virginia, Census (1850, 1860)

Montgomery County, Tennessee, Census (1850, 1860, 1870, 1880).

Montgomery County, Tennessee, Marriages, Books 1, 2, and 3.

Montgomery County, Tennessee, Census Slave Schedule (1860).

Nelson County, Virginia, Census (1860).

Sixth Ward Memphis, Shelby County, Tennessee, Census (1860).

Sumner County, Tennessee, Census (1850).

Stewart County, Tennessee, Census (1860).

Tennessee, Compiled Marriages, 1851–1900.
Todd County, Kentucky, Census (1850, 1860).
Todd County, Marriage Records, Kentucky, Book B.
Trigg County, Kentucky, Census (1860).
Virginia Marriages, 1740–1850, Frederick County.
Wilson County, Tennessee, Census (1860).

WILLS, DEEDS, SERVICE RECORDS, AND GENEALOGICAL SOURCES

Abstracts of Wills and Settlements, Logan County, Kentucky 1856–1874. Logan County Genealogical Society; Russellville, KY, 1989.
"Adjutant General's Report." 50th Illinois Infantry Regiment History. Transcribed by Linda Lee. Accessed May 11, 2019. https://civilwar.illinois genweb.org/history/050.html.
Blackman Family Tree. Accessed January 20, 2019. Ancestry.com.
Bordewick Master 2012 Family Tree. Accessed January 10, 2019. Ancestry.com.
Bennett Family Tree. Accessed January 10, 2019. Ancestry.com.
Buchanan Family Tree. Accessed January 18, 2019. Ancestry.com.
Choate Family Tree. Ancestry.com. Accessed January 18, 2019.
Civil War Service Records—Confederate. *Fold 3.* Accessed May 8, 2013. www .fold3.com/image/#71033018.
Confederate Kentucky Volunteers War 1861–65.
Davis Family Tree. Accessed September 6, 2012. Ancestry.com.
"Elizabeth Ann Lyle Antecedents and Descendants." Rootsweb. Accessed September 19, 2012. http://wc.rootsweb.ancestry.com/cgi-bin/igm.cgi?op =GET&db=Robert. At the time of publication, this webpage was not available.
Field and Staff Officers, Appendix I.
Ford-Young Family Tree. Accessed January 14, 2019. Ancestry.com.
Futrell Family Tree. Accessed January 14, 2019. Ancestry.com.
Garner Family Tree. Accessed February 11, 2019. Ancestry.com.
Higgins, Gladies. "Some Descendants of George Sims and John Mallory, Caswell County, N.C." *The Montgomery County [Tennessee] Genealogical Journal 9,* (June 1980).
Hille Family Tree. Accessed January 14, 2019. Ancestry.com.
Hunter-Worley Family Tree. Accessed January 20, 2019. Ancestry.com.
Jordan-Homer Family Tree. Ancestry.com. Accessed January 10, 2019.
K-Kingins Family Tree. Accessed January 10, 2019. Ancestry.com.
Kentucky Will and Probate, Volume 1–4, 1831–1979.
Logan County Genealogical Society, *Logan County, Kentucky Marriages, 1790–1865.* Logan County Genealogical Society: Russellville, KY, 1981; Additions and Corrections, 1985.
Lopez-Edwards Family Tree. Accessed January 14, 2019. Ancestry.com.

Martin, William R., Overview. Accessed May 3, 2013. Ancestry.com.

Minutes of the Annual Conferences of the Methodist Episcopal Church, South, for the Year 1860, Part 6, Tennessee Conference. Nashville, TN: Southern Methodist Publishing House, 1861.

Mitchell, John L. *Tennessee State Gazeteer and Business Directory for 1860–61.* Accessed July 14, 2017. www.tngenweb.org/Montgomery/1860towns.pdf.

Montgomery County, Tennessee, Deeds, Book 3.

Montgomery County, Tennessee, Records, Books F and H.

Montgomery County, Tennessee, Wills, Books L, M, O.

Overby-Mitchell Family Tree. Accessed January 13, 2019. Ancestry.com.

Peterson Kirkes Family Tree. Accessed January 13, 2018. Ancestry.com.

Public Acts of the State of Tennessee, April 1861, Chapter 1.

Robertson County Probates: Will Book 9.

Stevens, Larry. *102nd Ohio Infantry,* 1995. Accessed June 5, 2014. http://www.ohiocivilwar.com/cw 102.html. At the time of publication, this webpage was not available.

Thetford-Meyer Family Tree. Accessed January 10, 2019. Ancestry.com.

US Find A Grave Index, 1600s-Current.

US War Department. *The War of the Rebellion: A Compilation of the Official Records of the Union and Confederate Armies.* 128 vols. Washington, D.C., 1880–1901.

Wyatt, Paul. "History of New Providence" Unpublished paper, Clarksville-Montgomery County Public Library Genealogy Room, Clarksville, Tennessee, 1923.

UNPUBLISHED LETTERS, MEMOIRS, AND FAMILY RECORDS

Carpenter, Walter Trotter. *The Diary of Walter Trotter Carpenter.* Archives and Manuscript Division. Ohio Historical Society. Columbus, Ohio.

Drane Family Papers, Microfilm Accession Number 1143a. Tennessee State Library and Archives, Nashville, TN.

Homer, Serepta Jordan. Civil War diary, 1857–1864. Customs House Museum and Cultural Center. Clarksville, Tennessee.

"Image of 'Her bright smile haunts me still.'" Library of Congress. Accessed July 21, 2017. https://www.loc.gov/resource/ihas.200002476.0/?sp=2.

Johnson, John M. "Letter to General Prentiss, commanding forces at Cairo, Illinois, from Dr. John M. Johnson, Paducah, Kentucky, Saturday, June 8, 1861." *New York Times,* June 15, 1861. Accessed July 22, 2012. http://www.nytimes.com/1861/6/15/news/important-cairo-operations-. At the time of publication, this webpage was not available.

Kennedy, Sarah. Letter from Civil War Collection: Confederate and Federal 1861–1865, Confederate Collection. Tennessee State Library and Archives.

Trabue, T.C. "Letter to S. M. Jordan, May 12, 1861, Camp Harris near Fort
   Wright, Randolph, Tennessee." Copy in editors' possession.
Wadsworth, Elihu, and Orry Wadsworth. *"Brother Charles": Letters Home to
   Michigan.* Civil War Correspondence of the Wadsworth Brothers, 1861–1865.
   Tennessee State Library and Archives. Nashville, Tennessee.

Newspapers

Clarksville Chronicle
Clarksville Jeffersonian
Clarksville Leaf Chronicle
Clarksville Weekly Chronicle
New Orleans Daily Delta
New York Times

Secondary Sources

Ash, Stephen V. "A Community at War: Montgomery County, 1861–65,"
   Tennessee Historical Quarterly 36 no. 1, 30–43.
———. *Middle Tennessee Society Transformed, 1860–1870: War and Peace in the
   Upper South.* Knoxville: Univ. of Tennessee Press, 2006.
Avery, Julie A., ed. *Agricultural Fairs in America: Tradition, Education.* East
   Lansing, MI: Michigan State University Museum, 2000.
Baird, Nancy Dasher, ed. *Josie Underwood Civil War Diary.* Lexington:
   University of Kentucky Press, 2009.
Bazar, Jennifer L., and Jeremy T. Burman. "Asylum Tourism." *Monitor on
   Psychology*, 45, no. 2 (February 2014), Accessed May 10, 2017. Print version;
   http://www.apa.org/monitor/2014/02/asylum-tourism.aspx.
Beach, Damian. *Civil War Battles, Skirmishes, and Events in Kentucky.* Louisville:
   Different Drummer Books, 1995.
Beach, Ursula Smith. *Along the Warioto.* Nashville: McQuiddy Press, 1964.
Berlin, Ira. *Generations of Captivity: A History of African-American Slaves.*
   Cambridge, MA: Harvard Univ. Press, 2004.
Biggs, Greg. "Woodward's 2nd Ky. Cavalry, CSA." The Kentucky in the Civil
   War Message Board. Accessed May 11, 2019. http://www.history-sites.com
   /cgi-bin/bbs62x/kycwmb/webbbs_config.pl?md=read;id=5849
Biographical Directory of the United States Congress, 1774 –Present. Accessed
   February 1, 2011. http://bioguide.congress.gov/scripts/biodisplay.pl?index
   =Q000002.
"Blondel the Minstrel." Accessed May 9, 2012. http://www.middle-ages.org.uk
   /blondel-the-minstrel.htm.

Boatner, Mark M., III. *The Civil War Dictionary*. New York: Vintage Books, 1991.

"Caroline Meriwether Goodlett—Founder." United Daughters of the Confederacy. Accessed July 23, 2017. www.hqudc.org/caroline-meriwether-goodlett/.

Centers for Disease Control. "Measles." Accessed July 23, 2017. https://www.cdc.gov/measles/about/complications.html.

Century Dictionary and Cyclopedia. Accessed May 3, 2013. http://www.wordnik.com/words/dunstable.

Chesnut, Mary. *Mary Boykin Chestnut*. Edited by C. Vann Woodward. New Haven: Yale University Press, 1981.

"Christmas in Nineteenth-Century America." Accessed March 5, 2011. http://christmas-celebrations.org/11-christmas-in-nineteenth-century-america.html.

"Civil War Medicine." Accessed January 19, 2018. https://civilwarmedicalhistory.weebly.com/diseases.html.

Clark, Thomas D. "George D. Prentice." *Encyclopedia of Louisville*. Edited by John E. Kleber. Lexington: University of Kentucky, 2001.

Clinton, Catherine. *Step-Daughters of History*. Baton Rouge: LSU Press, 2016.

"Coffin Nails: The Tobacco Controversy in the 19th Century." Accessed May 13, 2019. https://tobacco.harpweek.com/hubpages/CommentaryPage.asp?Commentary=PipesAndSnuff.

Cooling, Benjamin F. *Fort Donelson's Legacy: War and Society in Kentucky and Tennessee, 1861–1863*. Knoxville: Univ. of Tennessee Press, 1997.

"Confederate Casualties." History. Accessed May 13, 2019. https://www.history.com/topics/american-civil-war/battle-of-wilsons-creek.

Cross, Wallace C. *Cry Havoc: A History of the 49th Tennessee Volunteer Infantry Regiment, 1861–1865*. Franklin, TN: Hillsboro Press, 2004.

———. *Ordeal by Fire: A History of the Fourteenth Tennessee Volunteer Infantry Regiment, CSA*. Clarksville, TN: Clarksville-Montgomery County Museum, 1990.

Davis, David Brion, *Inhuman Bondage: The Rise and Fall of Slavery in the New World*. New York: Oxford Univ. Press, 2006.

Dear Rep: Letters to Serepta Jordan Homer of New Providence, Tennessee. Privately published book, Genealogy Room, Clarksville-Montgomery Public Library, Clarksville, Tennessee, N.D.

"Dental Health and Diseases in the Past." Accessed July 21, 2017. http://www.digitiseddiseases.org/dental_health_and_disease_in_the_past.php.

Dew, Charles P. "Black Ironworkers and the Slave Insurrection Panic of 1856," *The Journal of Southern History*, Vol. 41, No. 3 (Aug., 1975), 321–338.

Dvorsky, George. "How We Died 200 Years Ago, Compared to How We Die Today," *The New England Journal of Medicine*, 2012. Accessed July 21, 2017. http://io9.gizmodo.com/5920871/how-we-died-200-years-ago-compared-to-how-we-die-today.

Emmett, Lucas S. *Marriage Record Book 1, January 2, 1789–December 13, 1837, Davidson County, Tennessee.* Easley, SC: Southern Historical Press, 1979.

"Financing the Civil War." Accessed March 29, 2017. https://www.gpo.gov/fdsys /pkg/GPO-CDOC-100hdoc244/pdf/GPO-CDOC-100hdoc244-13.pdf.

"First Income Tax," American Battlefield Trust. Accessed January 13, 2019. https://www.battlefields.org/learn/articles/first-income-tax.

Follett, Kenneth. "Documenting Louisiana Sugar 1845–1917." Accessed April 28, 2017. http://www.sussex.ac.uk/louisianasugar/sources/champomier.

Freeman, Edward Augustus. *The History of the Norman Conquest of England,* Vol. IV. Oxford: Clarendon Press, 1871.

Geib, George W. *Adam Johnson's Raid on Newburgh.* Accessed May 17, 2019. https://www.in.gov/history/3992.htm

Gibbons, Whit. "What Do You Do with 184 Birds at Christmas?" Accessed May 13, 2019. https://www.tuscaloosanews.com/news/20051218/whit-gibbons -what-do-you-do-with-184-birds-at-christmas.

Gildrie, Richard P. "Black Regiments, 1863–1865." Mount Olive Cemetery Historical Preservation Society. Accessed January 16, 2013. http://mtolive cemetery.sharepoint.com/Pages/MilitaryHistory.aspx. At the time of publication, this information was not available on the Mount Olive website.

———. "Dilemma and Opportunities, 1860–1900." Edited by Charles M. Waters. *Historic Clarksville, The Bicentennial Story, 1784–1984,* Clarksville: Jostens Publications, 1983.

Gildrie, Richard P., Phillip Kemmerly, and Thomas H. Winn. "Clarksville, Tennessee, in the Civil War: A Chronology." Unpublished paper. Clarksville, Tennessee, 1984; copy in editors' possession.

Goodspeed's Histories of Montgomery, Robertson, Humphreys, Stewart, Dickson, Cheatham, and Houston Counties of Tennessee. Chicago and Nashville: Goodspeed, 1886. Reprinted Columbia, TN: Woodward and Stinson Printing Company, 1972.

"Grace Episcopal Church." Western Kentucky History and Genealogy, Christian County. Accessed March 3, 2013. http://www.westernkyhistory.org/christian /church/chindexG.html#Grace.

Greene, Ann Norton. *Horses at War: Harnessing Power in Industrial America.* Cambridge: Harvard Press, 2008.

Griffey, Irene. *Riverview Cemetery; Looking Back to Those Who've Gone Before.* Clarksville, TN: Montgomery County Historical Society, 2002.

Hildebrand, John R. *The Life and Times of John Brown Baldwin, 1820–1873: A Chronicle of Virginia's Struggle with Slavery, Secession, Civil War, and Reconstruction.* Staunton, VA: Lot's Wife Publishing, 2008.

"Historic Nashville." Accessed May 25, 2017. https://historicnashville.wordpress .com/2009/03/05/tennesse-school-for-the-blind/.

Holzer, Harold, and Craig L. Symonds, eds. *The New York Times Complete Civil War, 1861–1865.* New York: Black Dog and Leventhal Publishers, 2010.

Hyatt, Paul, Marie Riggins, Ralph Winters and Thurston L. Lee. *One Hundred Years of County Fairs in Montgomery County, Tennessee.* Clarksville: TN: Clarksville-Montgomery County Historical Society, 1960.

Johnson, Adam Rankin. *The Partisan Rangers of the Confederate States Army.* Edited by William J. Davis. Louisville, KY: G. G. Fetter Company, 1904. Accessed February 3, 2019. https://archive.org/details/partisanrangers000john.

Joyner, William S. "Infectious Diseases, 2006," disease. Accessed July 21, 2017. http://www.ncpedia.org/infectious-diseases.

Kaye, Anthony E. *Joining Places: Slave Neighborhoods in the Old South.* Chapel Hill: Univ. of North Carolina Press, 2007.

Kennedy, Robert C. "On this Day," Accessed July 13, 2017. https://www.nytimes .com/learning/general/onthisday/harp/0629.html.

"Lee's Cheat Mountain Campaign." *Northwestern Virginia in 1861: The First Campaign.* Rich Mountain Battlefield Foundation. Accessed September 20, 2012. http://www.richmountain.org/history/wv1861.html.

Levy, George. *To Die in Chicago: Confederate Prisoners at Camp Douglas.* New Orleans: Pelican Publishing Company, Inc., 1999.

Lincoln, Abraham. First Inaugural Address of Abraham Lincoln. *A Compilation of the Messages and Papers of the Presidents, vol. IV.* New York: Bureau of National Literature, Inc., 1897.

Long, E. B. *The Civil War Day by Day: An Almanac, 1861–1865.* Garden City, NY: Doubleday and Company, Inc., 1971.

Love, Suzi. *Fashion Women 1800: History Notes, Book 12.* (Amazon Digital Services LLC, 2018)

Martine, Arthur. *Martine's Hand-Book of Etiquette.* New York: Dick & Fitzgerald, 1866. Accessed January 16, 2018. https://archive.org/details/martineshand bookoomartrich.

Matthews, Gary R. *More American than Southern: Kentucky, Slavery and the War for American Ideology, 1828–1861.* Knoxville: Univ. of Tennessee Press, 2014.

McMullen, Kevin. "Fannie Fern: A Brief Biography." Fanny Fern in *The New York Ledger.* Accessed May 13, 2019. https://fannyfern.org/bio.

McPherson, James M. *Battle Cry of Freedom: The Civil War Era.* New York: Oxford University Press, 1988.

Meacham, Charles Mayfield. *A History of Christian County Kentucky: From Oxcart to Airplane.* Nashville: Marshall & Bruce County, 1930.

Mitchell, John L. *Tennessee State Gazeteer and Business Directory for 1860–61.* Accessed July 14, 2017. www.tngenweb.org/Montgomery/1860towns.pdf.

National Jousting Association. *The Romantic Revival.* Accessed March 30, 2008. http://www.nationaljousting.com/history/romantic.htm.

National Park Service, U. S. Department of the Interior Gulf Islands National
   Seashore. "Fort Pickens." Accessed April 20, 2011. http://www.nps.gov/guis
   /planyourvisit/fort-pickens.htm. At the time of publication, this information
   was not available on the Fort Pickens website.
Osterweis, Rollin G. *Romanticism and Nationalism in the Old South.* New Haven:
   Yale Univ. Press, 1949.
Perrin, William Henry, ed. *County of Christian, Kentucky: Historical and
   Biographical.* Louisville: F. A. Battey Publishing Company, 1884. Accessed
   December 29, 2017. www.westernkyhistory.org/christian/perrin/index.html.
"Phrenology." Accessed January 14, 2018. http://www.historyofphrenology.org
   .uk/temperament.htm.
Pollard, Edward A. *The First Year of the War.* Richmond, VA: West & Johnston,
   1862; reprinted: London: Forgotten Books, 2015.
Potter, David M. *The Impending Crisis 1848–1861.* New York: HarperCollins
   Publishers, 1976. Reprinted by Harper Perennial, 2011.
Reber, Patricia Bixler. Culinary History Online. "Candy pull, Candy stew and
   other pull parties." Accessed July 16, 2017. www.angelfire.com/md3/openhearth
   cooking/aaCandypull2.html.
Recapture of Clarksville. Accessed May 13, 2019. https://www.historicalmarker
   project.com/markers/HM1ASS_recapture-of-clarksville_Clarksville-TN.html.
"Rockaway." *Encyclopaedia Britannica.* Accessed March 27, 2013. http://www
   .britannica.com/print/topic/506229.
Rothman, Shelia M. *Living in the Shadow of Death: Tuberculosis and the Social
   Experience of Illness in American History,* New York: Basic Books, 1994.
"Scrambled Eggs Are Coming Back from the Dead." Extra Crispy. Accessed
   January 23, 2018. http://www.extracrispy.com/food/534/scrambled-eggs-and
   -brains-are-coming-back-from-the-dead.
"Seigneur." Accessed April 18, 2014. http://dictionary.reference.com/browse
   /seigneur.
"Short Rounds: Generals' Threads." Strategy Page. Accessed May 11, 2017.
   www.strategypage.com/cic/docs/cic236b.asp.
Sidhu, Dawinder S. "Opinionator: The Birth of the Greenback." *New York
   Times.* December 31, 2013. Accessed August 14, 2017. https://opinionator.blogs
   .nytimes.com/2013/12/31/the-birth-of-the-greenback/.
The Southern Monthly Volume 1. Memphis: Hutton and Freligh, 1861. Accessed
   March 29, 2017. Available at https://books.google.com/books under "The
   Southern Monthly volume 1."
Stashower, Daniel. *The Hour of Peril: The Secret Plot to Murder Lincoln before the
   Civil War.* New York: Minotaur Books, 2013.
Stedman, Edmund Clarence, ed. *A Victorian Anthology, 1837–1895.* Cambridge:
   Riverside Press, 1895; New York: Bartleby.com, 2001. Accessed January 12,
   2019.

Stern, A. M., and H. Markel (2005), "The history of vaccines and immunization: familiar patterns, new challenges," *Health Affairs* 24 (3): 611–21.

Sutherland, Daniel E., ed. *A Very Violent Rebel: The Civil War Diary of Ellen Renshaw House* Knoxville: University of Tennessee Press, 1996.

Tillinghast, Richard. "Nathan Bedford Forrest: Born to Fight." *Sewanee Review*, vol. 123 no. 4, 2015, 599–612. Accessed January 15, 2019. Project MUSE, doi:10 .1353/sew.2015.0108.

Titus, William P. *Picturesque Clarksville, Past and Present: A History of the City of the Hills.* Clarksville, TN: W. P. Titus Publishing Company, 1887. Reprinted by Ann Alley and Ursula Beach, 1973.

Uffelman, Minoa, Ellen Kanervo, Phyllis Smith and Eleanor Williams, eds. *The Diary of Nannie Haskins Williams: A Southern Woman's Story of Rebellion and Reconstruction, 1863–1890.* Knoxville: Univ. of Tennessee Press, 2013.

"Voices from 19th Century America." Accessed May 10, 2008. http://www .merrycoz.org/sgg/lifetime/lifetime.htm.

Walker, Melissa, and James C. Cobb, eds. *Agriculture and Industry.* Chapel Hill: Univ. of North Carolina Press, 2008.

Way Jr., Frederick. *Way's Packet Directory, 1848–1994.* Athens, Ohio: Ohio Univ. Press, 1994.

West, Carroll Van, ed. *Tennessee Encyclopedia of History and Culture.* Nashville: Rutledge Hill Press, 1998.

Western Kentucky Hiking: Pilot Rock—USDA. Saturday 1, 2012. Accessed May 23, 2019. kyhiker.blogspot.com/2012/09/pilot-rock.html.

Whites, LeAnn, and Alecia P. Long, eds. *Occupied Women: Gender, Military Occupation and the American Civil War.* Baton Rouge: Louisiana State Univ. Press, 2009.

"Why Richmond?" Virginia Museum of History and Culture. Accessed February 8, 2017. http://www.vahistorical.org/collections-and-resources /virginia-history-explorer/american-turning-point-civil-war-virginia-1/wh-1.

Williams, Eleanor S. *Cabins to Castles, Historic Clarksville.* Oxford, MS: Guild Bindery Press, 1994.

Williams' Clarksville Directory, City Guide and Business Mirror, Vol. 1, 1859–60. Clarksville, TN: C.O. Faxon, 1859. Reprinted by Ursula Beach, 1976.

Wilson, Mark. *The Business of Civil War.* Baltimore: Johns Hopkins University Press, 2006.

———. *Worship along the Warioto: Montgomery County, Tennessee.* Clarksville, TN: First Federal Savings Bank, 1995.

INDEX

Page numbers in **boldface** refer to illustrations.

soldiers, USA. *See* US Colored Troops; Yankees

Soldiers Aid Society, 133, 140. *See also* Volunteer's Friend Society

soups, 312

South Carolina, secession of, 66, 69, 367n135, 369n153

South Mountain, Battle of (MD) (1862), 216, 418n30

spare ribs, 62, 64, 137, 298

Speaker, Miss, 7

speculation, on merchandise, 164

speeches, 89, 378–79n245

Spence, Brent, 36, 349n211

Spence, Joseph, 18, 44, 342n135, 349n211

Spence, Mr. (Joseph's father), 21

Spence, Mr. (of Paris), 129

Spence, Mr. (with Dick Ogburn), 142

Spence, Sarah Ann Ogburn (Mrs. Joseph), 18, 21, 26, 36–37, 44, 342n135, 349nn211 and 221

Spiritualism, 46

spoons, silver, xxxi, 152, 189, 304, 307–8, 311, 314, 445n97

Spotsylvania Court House, Battle of (VA) (1864), 319, 448n117

Spring Creek Baptist Church (Clarksville, TN), 6, 329n26

Spring Hill, Battle of. *See* Thompson's Station, Battle of

Springfield, TN, 6, 329n30

squirrels, 80, 264, 281, 316

St. Louis, MO, 88, 188, 378n242, 406n73

Star of the West (ship), 370n165

stationery, 30

Staton, A. E. (Ervy) (male), death of, 45, 352n255

Staton, Ann Mary, 267

Staton, Anna, 294

Staton, Anne, 101, 215, 311

Staton, Charles W. (Charlie), 207, 270, 435n12

Staton, Clarissa (Mrs. Joseph T.), 12, 17, 19, 28, 32, 35, 51, 69, 78, 88, 104, 122, 133, 186, 215, 243, 247, 255, 257, 270, 336–37n87

Staton, Joseph T. (father), 29, 38, 191, 215, 247, 336–37n87

Staton, Joseph W. (Jo) (son), 3, 30, 32, 46, 51, 56, 67, 207, 336–37n87; death of, 247, 428n119

Steeger, Mr., 131

Stepdaughters of History (Clinton), xix

stepmothers, 136

stereoscopes, 201, 286, 411n114

Stevens, Mrs., 18

Stewart College (Clarksville, TN), xxvi, xxviii, 371–72n182; used as hospital, 130

Stewart County, TN, 219, 420n49

stockings, 24, 175, 282; mending, 220, 291

Stone, Charles Pomeroy, 291, 441n65

Stones River, Battle of (Murfreesboro) (TN) (1862–63), 209, 240–41, 426n104

Story, Amy Cullom (Mrs. William H.), 9, 334–35n68

Story, Sarah Cartwright (Mrs. Jesse), 9, 334–35n68

strawberries, 88, 90–91, 194, 196–97, 252

stroke, 105, 385n43

sugar, 110, 188, 247, 297, 300, 405n70

sulphur spring, 211, 257, 416n14

sunburn, 87

Sunday school, 24, 33–34, 43, 53, 61–62, 66, 71, 77, 79, 81, 102, 109, 121, 124, 127–28, 130, 156, 163, 166, 190, 197, 200, 204, 207, 217, 226, 228–29,